'Talking Proper'

The Rise of Accent as Social Symbol

'Talking Proper'

The Rise of Accent as Social Symbol

LYNDA MUGGLESTONE

OXFORD

UNIVERSITY PRESS

OXFORD

UNIVERSITY PRESS

Great Clarendon Street, Oxford OX2 6DP

Oxford University Press is a department of the University of Oxford.
It furthers the University's objective of excellence in research, scholarship,
and education by publishing worldwide in

Oxford New York

Auckland Cape Town Dar es Salaam Hong Kong Karachi
Kuala Lumpur Madrid Melbourne Mexico City Nairobi
New Delhi Shanghai Taipei Toronto

With offices in

Argentina Austria Brazil Chile Czech Republic France Greece
Guatemala Hungary Italy Japan Poland Portugal Singapore
South Korea Switzerland Thailand Turkey Ukraine Vietnam

Oxford is a registered trade mark of Oxford University Press
in the UK and in certain other countries

Published in the United States
by Oxford University Press Inc., New York

First edition published 1995 (paperback 1997)
Updated second edition first published 2003
First published in paperback 2007

The moral rights of the author have been asserted
Database right Oxford University Press (maker)

British Library Cataloguing in Publication Data

Data available

Library of Congress Cataloging in Publication Data
Mugglestone, Lynda.
Talking proper: the rise of accent as social symbol / Lynda Mugglestone.
p. cm.
Includes bibliographical references and index.
1. English language–Great Britain–Standardization. 2. English language–Spoken
English–Great Britain. 3. English language–Social aspects–Great Britain. 4. English
language–Variation–Great Britain. 5. English language–Accents and accentuation.
6. Speech and social status–Great Britain. 7. Great Britain–Social life and customs.
8. Social classes–Great Britain. I. Title.
PE1074.7 .M84 2002   306.44'0941–dc21   2002032652

Typeset by Newgen Imaging Systems (P) Ltd., Chennai, India
Printed in Great Britain
on acid-free paper by
Biddles Ltd., King's Lynn, Norfolk

ISBN 978–0–19–925061–5 (Hbk.)   978–0–19–925062–2 (Pbk.)

3 5 7 9 10 8 6 4 2

CONTENTS

LIST OF ILLUSTRATIONS

PREFACE TO THE SECOND EDITION

Within a few years of the first appearance of '*Talking Proper*' in 1995, it became clear that a new edition would be necessary, not least to take into account the shifting nature of those debates which had come to surround the issue of accent and pronunciation during the closing years of the twentieth century as well as the first few years of the twenty-first. 'Estuary English', in particular had emerged as a prominent area of comment in the press and media, as well as in a variety of academic theses; similarly, controversies about the 'Queen's English', and on-going changes within this, revealed the nature of other issues which had come to be at stake. These and other areas of discussion occupy the new Chapter 8 which has been able to place greater emphasis on post-1900 changes in language attitudes and images of accent than was possible in the previous edition. Throughout the volume, however, chapters have been rewritten and revised, incorporating new material where necessary, especially with reference to what individuals of the relevant periods thought and said about the nuances of speech. This biographical component (from a wide range of sources) documents the changing image of accent in ways which productively extend the frame of reference of the first edition, mapping though the eyes (and ears) of ordinary speakers the shifting contemporary consciousness of accent and its variously assumed proprieties. For this paperback edition, an expanded section on language and the early BBC has also been added into the final chapter.

ACKNOWLEDGEMENTS

My thanks are due to Cambridge University Press for allowing me to use data from Peter Trudgill, *The Social Stratification of English in Norwich* (CUP, 1974) and material by David Rosewarne from *English Today*. Thanks are also due to the BBC for permission to quote from a number of unpublished documents in the BBC Written Archives Centre, Caversham, Reading, and to the Bodleian Library Oxford, for permission to reproduce the Advertisements for Thomas Sheridan's lectures on elocution in May 1759 (Folio 66 items 67(a) and 67(b) entitled 'Oxford, May 25, 1759. Mr Sheridan'. Shelfmark = *Don. b. 12*). Permission from *Punch* to use two cartoons, 'Evil Communications' and 'Popular Misconceptions – A London Announcer' is gratefully acknowledged. I am grateful also to the readers of Oxford University Press for their many helpful comments, and to Professor Eric Stanley in particular for his time and energy in discussing the various drafts of this book.

Introduction: 'A National Obsession'

'ACCENT and Pronunciation must be diligently studied by the conversation-alist. A person who uses vulgarisms will make but little way in good circles... A proper accent gives importance to what you say, engages the respectful attention of your hearer, and is your passport to new circles of acquaint-ance'. So wrote the anonymous author of *Talking and Debating* (1856),[1] a manual of linguistic etiquette which, like many others published during the late eighteenth and nineteenth centuries, sought to teach the social propri-eties of linguistic usage to those who felt themselves disadvantaged in this respect. Pronouncing dictionaries, works on elocution, tracts on speech and articulation, and handbooks of social advice were regularly to unite over this time in stressing the social import to be conveyed within the nuances of speech. As *Talking and Debating* indicates, accent was itself to be regarded as a marker of social acceptability, facilitating or impeding social advance; it could secure deference or disrespect, acting as an image of 'worth' in a cul-ture which, as many writers were to stress, was increasingly attuned to the significance of phonetic propriety. 'No saying was ever truer than that good breeding and good education are sooner discovered from the style of speak-ing... than from any other means', the Reverend David Williams affirmed,[2] similarly endorsing the importance of assimilation to the notionally 'correct' forms of speech. Social and linguistic prescription commonly fused in these contexts, their implications readily absorbed by writers such as George Gissing or Thomas Hardy, not only in their novels but in their own linguis-tic practices too. Gissing, for example, read Thomas Kington-Oliphant's *The Sources of Standard English*, as well as George Craik's *Manual of English Language and Literature*, eagerly absorbing their dictates on the shibboleths and social markers to be found in the spoken English of the late nineteenth century. George Bernard Shaw, 'a social downstart' as he termed himself, devoted his attention to works on elocution in the British Museum, as well as to books such as *The Manners and Tone of Good Society* with its subtitle 'Solecisms to be Avoided' and its advice that 'the mispronunciation of certain surnames falls unpleasantly upon the educated ear, and argues unfavourably as to the social position of the offender'.[3] Thomas Hardy pur-chased a copy of Nuttall's *Standard Pronouncing Dictionary*,[4] along with *Mixing in Society: A Complete Manual of Manners* which carefully informed its readers that 'the best accent is undoubtedly that taught at Eton and Oxford. One may be as awkward with the mouth as with the arms or legs'.[5] Hardy's application in this context was, however, apparently to leave some-thing to be desired, at least in terms of George Gissing's high standards in these matters. As Gissing commented in his diary on 13 July 1895, 'With Hardy I talked a little, and he asked me to write to him...I caught a few notes of the thick western utterance'.[6]

Gissing's own hypersensitivities to the social symbolism contained within contemporary notions of 'talking proper' exemplify in many ways the pre-occupations, and prejudices, about speech which came to form a hallmark of the late eighteenth and nineteenth centuries. The interrelationships of language and identity form recurrent images in his novels, iterated again and again in terms of articulation and the spoken word; 'His utterance fell short of perfect refinement, but seemed that of an educated man', we are, for example, told of the erstwhile clerk, Edmund Widdowson in *The Odd Women*.[7] 'Her intonation was not flagrantly vulgar, but the accent of the London poor, which brands as with hereditary baseness, still clung to her words, rendering futile such propriety of phrase as she owed to years of association with educated people', runs the description of Mrs Yule in *New Grub Street*.[8] Accent assumes a role as prime social signifier for Gissing's characters, their ears ever alert for the dropped [h], a shibboleth which was itself encoded over the course of the eighteenth and nineteenth centuries,[9] or for the imperfectly articulated vowel sounds which might label them as members of the working class: ' "How I like your way of speaking...your voice—accent" ', says the Newcastle-born Mrs Wade to Lilian in *Denzil Quarrier*; ' "As a child I had a strong northern accent; you don't notice anything of it now?" ', she adds, seeking reassurance that her voice conforms to the articulatory models located in 'good' southern speech.[10] As Gissing recognized all too well, and as William Phyfe cautioned his audience in *How Should I Pronounce?* (1885), by the late nineteenth century popular attitudes towards acceptability all too willingly endorsed assumptions that it was accent, together with appearance, which made the strongest impression on any new acquaintance. 'The first impression made upon a person's mind by the presence of a stranger is gathered from his personal appearance; the second, from his speech', Phyfe duly averred, further specifying that 'in spoken language the most conspicuous element is pronunciation, and we naturally estimate one's condition, both mental and social, by his practice in this regard'.[11]

Subject to a veritable barrage of information on this head, it was, it appeared, difficult to remain completely unaware of the repercussions which speaking with the 'right' or indeed the 'wrong' accent might have. Popular penny journals such as *The Family Herald* or the *London Journal*, with combined circulations of *circa* 750,000 by the 1850s, urged their readers, largely located among the upper working and lower middle sections of society, to improve their modes of speech and in turn improve their station in life (or, at least, perceptions of it). Readers responded by writing in, asking for precise instructions on articulation, the 'proper' ways to speak. As Mitchell notes of this process:

The readers of the *London Journal* and the *Family Herald* actively sought information about the values, standards, and mechanical details of living in a milieu that was new to them. Their letters to the correspondence column reveal their conscious mobility. They want to eradicate the traces of their origin that linger in their grammar and pronunciation. They ask the kinds of questions about etiquette and general knowledge that would be impossible for anyone with a polite background and more than a rudimentary education. The advertisers urge them to buy textbooks, life assurance, and fashion magazines, to learn elocution, French, Italian, and music.[12]

Sixpenny manuals, such as *P's and Q's. Grammatical Hints for the Million* (the opening page of which admonishes that 'A knowledge and practice of the rules of the English language are absolutely essential to respectability and a comfortable passage through decent life'),[13] or *Poor Letter H. Its Use and Abuse* by the anthropomorphized 'Hon. Henry H.' (also the author of *P's and Q's*), were correspondingly sold in their thousands. As the Honourable Henry H. was made to opine in the Preface to the fortieth edition of *Poor Letter H*, in this context the public displayed a seemingly voracious appetite for instruction in the proprieties of speech ('the circulation of forty thousand have been but as drops poured into the mighty tide of human life, whereon float hundreds and thousands who don't know an H from an A').[14] That such evident popularity should be the case was not, however, entirely surprising given a cultural climate in which /h/ in particular had assumed a role which was, it seemed, critically imbued with social meaning. 'Social suicide' was committed by its omission in words such as *house* and *heart*, as the philologist Alexander Ellis, one of the more objective observers of the language, recorded in 1869.[15]

The new popularity of elocution, as a private as well as public pursuit, likewise stressed the import of 'talking proper'. Five times as many works on elocution appeared between the years 1760 and 1800 than had done so in the years before 1760,[16] and this tendency did not abate with the coming of the nineteenth century. Works on the arts of speech were published and republished in a way which clearly attests contemporary interest in the issues of articulation, especially given the growing conviction that accent could provide a way of articulating social identity as much as words in themselves. Whether in terms of the prolific (and highly influential) Thomas Sheridan's early *Lectures on the Art of Elocution* (1762), or George Vandenhoff's *Art of Elocution* of 1855, the central tenets were clear. 'Pronunciation... is a sort of proof that a person has kept good company, and on that account is sought after by all, who wish to be considered as fashionable people, or members of the beau monde,' as Sheridan categorically stated.[17] Or as Vandenhoff later

wrote in his own endeavours to inculcate a due sense of phonemic propriety
(as well as social polish) in his readers, it was 'pronunciation' which, first and
foremost, 'distinguishes the educated gentleman from the vulgar and unpolished man'.[18]

It is this shift in sensibilities surrounding accent and the role it was to
play in assumptions about social definition and notions of social standing
which is to occupy this and the following chapters. Language rarely exists in a
vacuum and its interactions with prescriptive ideologies and associated attempts
to standardize one accent for all, its links with developments in educational
provision, and its reflection in contemporary literature (which also regularly
served to encode common preconceptions about the social alliances of speech
and speakers) will all be considered as part of a large-scale shift in language
attitudes and images of social response in terms of pronunciation over the late
eighteenth and nineteenth centuries (as well as afterwards). When Thomas
Sheridan began his elocutionary career in the late 1750s, even if the metropolitan accent of the court possessed evident (and higher) prestige, it had
been seen as no disadvantage for either upper or under class to speak in a way
influenced by their regional location. 'Even the gentry thought it no disgrace
to speak with a provincial accent', as the historian Dorothy Marshall has
noted of this time.[19] Yet by the end of the nineteenth century such attitudes
had changed. Notions of an accent free from regional markers (and assimilation to this) had come to act as a dominant social symbol throughout the
nation, forming the salient element in what the phonetician Henry Sweet was
to define as 'a class-dialect more than a local dialect...the language of the
educated all over Great Britain'. As he added, 'the best speakers of Standard
English are those whose pronunciation, and language generally, least betray
their locality'.[20] As many writers stressed for the ostensible benefit of their
readers, a 'provincial' accent was to be seen as incompatible with any ambitions for social acceptability, as well as with any pretensions to either 'culture'
or 'cultivation'. Framed by language attitudes of this order (with all the attendant fallacies and fictions which their proponents espoused), it is this creation
of a set of non-localized and supra-regional norms, or of what can perhaps
best be seen as a set of 'standard pronunciation features' which provides a
major focus of this period, widely infusing how people talked about, wrote
about, and chose to represent the nuances of the spoken voice.

Culminating in notions of 'received pronunciation' or RP—the non-localized
accent which was and is 'widely regarded as a model for correct pronunciation'[21]—the period from the late eighteenth century onwards was to see the
creation, and consolidation, of a number of national stereotypes in terms of
speech: the 'educated accent', the 'Public School' accent, the 'Oxford' accent,
'talking without an accent', 'talking proper', and eventually 'BBC English' too.
'Estuary English' has, in the late twentieth century and afterwards, come to
share in the continuing pattern of sensibilities which surround the act of

speech, though in this instance it is images of 'classlessness' rather than 'class' which have often come to the fore. Over two centuries of comment on the images of accent and its associated properties bear witness to the rise of a whole range of socially sensitive variables for the spoken word in which notions of the 'dropped letter', such as the 'h' in *house*, or the 'g' in words such as *walking*, can still, of course, remain prominent. Revealing the strategic integration of pronunciation within the concerns of prescriptivism and its attendant ideologies, the late eighteenth century (and afterwards) emerges as a period in which issues of correctness and purism relating specifically to matters of accent attained hitherto unprecedented levels of detail and attention. Articulated in treatises on education and on elocution, in manuals of etiquette and handbooks of social advice, in the grammars and pronouncing dictionaries intended for private as well as for educational use, and in the many works explicitly devoted to creating the 'right' accent which were published over this time, notions of 'talking proper' were gradually subject to a large-scale shift in terms of both perception and attitude. The widespread existence of a specifically linguistic form of conduct literature, concentrating above all on the phonetic markers which popularly made up 'talking proper', is in itself eloquent testimony to the anxieties and insecurities which were generated in the wake of such newly articulated preoccupations. Though language is, and was, innately variable, speakers locating themselves on continua of formality (and 'proper' language) depending on their immediate audience and varying the way they choose to speak accordingly, this fact was commonly ignored. Writers, whether in works of fiction or fact, instead attempted to affirm the hegemony of one way of speaking whilst they attempted to exert its persuasions upon their readers, pointing out selected details of 'deviation' and 'vulgarity' in ways which are unparalleled in previous writings on the spoken language. Like class itself, accent was, in effect, to become a major national obsession over this time. 'Classes are getting mixed, confused...we are so conscious of the process that we talk of class distinctions more than anything else,—talk and think of them incessantly,' as George Gissing stressed in *Born in Exile*.[22] Since it was accent which popularly came to be conceived as a prime marker of such class distinction, this habit was, in many ways, thus almost guaranteed to ensure its prominence in the public mind.

I

The Rise of a Standard

IN a number of ways, how one speaks has of course almost always been bound up with conceptions of social identity. In the fourteenth century, for instance, those seeking to stress their superiority sought to speak French, the language of the court, rather than an English which was, as Caxton later declared, fundamentally 'rude and barbarous'. Then, as now, language varieties seemed emblematic of the social order. 'Gentilmens children ben lerned & taught from their yongth to speke frenssh', the Benedictine monk Ranulph Higden noted in his *Polycronicon*,[1] revealing the shared forces of social and linguistic emulation in his comment that 'vplondissh men wyll counterfete & likene hem selfe to gentilmen/ & arn besy to speke frenssh for to be more sette by'. The ambition 'to be more sette by' (or, in other words, to be regarded more highly), and the linguistic ways in which this might be achieved, are clearly of long standing in England, their fourteenth-century resonances encapsulated by Higden in the proverb he provides: 'Jack wold be a gentilman if he coude speke frenssh'.

Seeking to establish status by the habits of speech one adopted was nevertheless signally different at this time. It relied, for example, upon choice (and the ability to choose) between two different languages rather than, as in the nineteenth century, between different ways of pronouncing the same word, articulating the same thing. The notion that 'a provincial dialect should always receive a check, since however good a speaker's argument may be, it becomes ridiculous by the manner in which it is conveyed', a precept encoded by the grammarian Thomas Smetham in 1774,[2] is meaningless at a time when all native varieties of the language were fundamentally perceived as 'dialects'. In the absence of a non-localized and national 'standard' in the sense later to emerge, all dialects in Middle English assumed an equality they were never after to attain. As a result, though Chaucer in his *Reeve's Tale* does indeed pick out dialect difference in the Northern markers (such as *falles* instead of *falleth*) which are allotted to the two Cambridge men, Aleyn and John, both of whom originally come 'from fer in the north', it is worth remembering that in this tale it is they who are the 'educated' and 'superior' characters. In spite of his London forms, it is the miller who takes on the implications of lower status, and of loser too. Medieval assumptions about mispronunciation are similarly most overt in, for example, the mangled articulations of the drunkard who 'meaðeleð his wordes' ('pronounces his words awry') in the thirteenth-century *Ancrene Wisse*, rather than being centred on the differences

which arise in different nineteenth-century accents as a result of, say, the
presence or absence of /ʌ/ (the central vowel in *cut* which typifies modern south-
eastern forms of speech, particularly those used as a basis for a non-localized
norm). Still less did they trade on notions—often explicitly endorsed in educational works of the nineteenth century—that the absence of such a sound
was a signifier in itself of lack of intelligence as well as compelling proof of
uneducatedness per se.[3] Assumptions that southern or London speech
already contained—and conveyed—associations of authority can already
come to the fore in Middle English. One often cited example is, for instance,
found in the *Second Shepherd's Play* of the Townley cycle, in the appropriation
of southern tones and authoritative diction by Mak, the Yorkshire shepherd
and sheep stealer. Such convergence is rapidly abandoned, constructed as a
source of comedy as well as inappropriateness. 'Goyth hence/ Oute of my
presence/ I must have reverence', states Mak, assuming a social and linguistic guise as 'yoman' of the king. 'Take outt that sothren tothe', his fellow shep-
herds conversely urge, rejecting such alien forms in preference to their own
familiar northern discourse. From a wider perspective, however, the influence
of the court was already beginning to have an effect. It was the 'men. . . of
myddell Englond' who had the advantage in national communication, notes
Higden, placing perceptions of the greater comprehensibility of this form of
speech against the 'grisbyting' of Yorkshire and the North.[4]

It is the presence or absence of standardization, both as a process and, perhaps more significantly, as an *ideology* (the particular set of beliefs which
comes to surround one variety as against other co-existing forms) which
nevertheless serves to provide the major difference between these fourteenth-
and nineteenth-century conceptions of language, linguistic choice, and
language variety. Though the emergence of 'incipient standards' can, for
example, be detected in the Wycliffite writings of the late fourteenth century
and, in the early decades of the next century, in the development of what has
been termed 'Chancery Standard' (the widely disseminated and regularized
form of written English used by the scribes of the Chancery in official
documents),[5] even these are somewhat different to the notions of a 'standard' which were later to develop. As David Burnley points out:

In modern times, ['Standard English'] denotes a form of language—that is of its
phonology, morphology, syntax, and lexis—which is superordinate to geographically
variant forms, and which is realised in both spoken and written modes, and in the latter by a consistent orthography. Middle English standards, however, differ sharply
from this modern conception, firstly in that they exist. . . *only* in the written mode,
for standardisation in spoken English belongs to a much later period. . . Secondly,
they are distinct in that the consistency of their orthography does not approach that
of Modern Standard English.[6]

In the fourteenth century, the absence of a dominant, non-localized, or
superordinate standard variety meant, for example, that all regional varieties of

language had not only spoken but also written forms. The poet of *Sir Gawain and the Green Knight* hence wrote in the dialect of the north-west Midlands, Michael of Northgate wrote *Ayenbite of Inwyt* ('the remorse of conscience') in his native Kentish, Trevisa translated Higden's *Polycronicon* from Latin into the dialect of the south-west of England, reflecting his own location near Gloucester rather than any perception of a national standard, or the sense that any one variety was more—or less—appropriate for the transmission of discourses of this kind. While Chaucer selected London English in which to write poems such as the *Canterbury Tales* and *Troilus and Criseyde*, this was largely because, just as in Trevisa's selection of the idioms of the south-west, it was the form of language current in the area where he lived. That it was also the variety used by educated Londoners of the day in Westminster and at court was presumably also not immaterial. Once a standard variety does emerge, however, discernible at least in part in the written language with the rise of fifteenth-century Chancery English as a non-localized written norm (a transition which becomes especially marked after the emergence of printing in the 1470s), perceptions of dialect, status, and appropriate usage tend to change accordingly.

'After a speach is fully fashioned to the common vnderstanding, & accepted by consent of a whole countrey & nation, it is called a language', stated the writer George Puttenham in 1589.[7] This is, in effect, what happens over the course of the fifteenth and sixteenth centuries as one variety of London English, originally perceived as a 'dialect',—a geographical and regional variety—shifts status to function as a non-localized, and superordinate, written 'language'. The sense that other, still regional, dialects are subordinate to this emergent standard is in turn reflected in their displacement from the written, and statusful, channels of communication to which they previously had access. It was, for instance, into this one variety that literature, itself a statusful domain of usage, was henceforth also to be largely confined, and into which the Bible too was translated. Though private documents such as letters could, and did, continue to betray the influence of regional variation, public documents make this development particularly clear. One variety of written English, and one alone, was disseminated all over England in the form of print.

These processes of standardization are not, of course, limited simply to the means by which one variety of language is endowed with a national and written mode of communication. An ideal standard language can, for instance, additionally be defined in terms of a formula which combines 'maximum variation of function' with 'minimal variation of form'. With reference to the former therefore, a standard must be omnifunctional or, in other words, it must be able to fulfil a range of prestigious and official roles within the nation rather than merely being the coin of common exchange. In the use of English (rather than French) in the domains of government and law after the mid-fourteenth century, one can see moves towards precisely that elaboration of function deemed significant in such definitions, a movement further aided by the later Biblical translations into the vernacular (and more particularly, into one specific variety of it). This development alone was notably to assist the claims of English to be considered a language just as worthy as Latin for the writing of important texts. Over the course of the seventeenth century, English continued to consolidate its hold in the transmission of intellectual discourse. Though Latin, the traditional language of international scholarship and cultured erudition, remained the vehicle for Thomas More's *Utopia* (1516) and Isaac Newton's *Principia* of 1689, nationalism, and the role of language within it, nevertheless came to ensure that the emergent standard variety of English was ultimately to encompass these functions as well. As Richard Mulcaster, headmaster of Merchant Taylors' School and author of *The First Part of the Elementarie* (1582), had demanded, 'why not all in English?' By the end of the seventeenth century, his question would have been largely rhetorical. The texts written in Latin after this date, such as Newton's *Opticks* of 1704, appeared significantly out of tune with the prevailing climate of linguistic (and cultural) thought in which the standard variety of English was regularly praised for its copious vocabulary, its qualities of elegance, its capacities for rhetoric, and its potential for stylistic and intellectual polish.

By the late seventeenth century, a sense of a 'standard' of English was, at least in terms of the written language, thus clearly in existence though in popular opinion even this was seen as deficient in the rules by which a standard should 'properly' be used (and with which Latin was of course abundantly supplied). It is this perception, articulated by writers such as Jonathan Swift in his 1712 proposal for an official academy which might regulate such matters, or in Addison's plea one year earlier for 'Superintendents' to curtail aspects of change deemed 'incorrect', which hallmarks the era of codification, an important stage in notions of standardization. In simple terms, this can be seen as the inception of issues of linguistic control which are to be applied to language in the attempt to impose 'ordered' patterns of corrected usage. Though usage is the basis and reality of language per se, its forms were, from viewpoints such as these, regularly seen as fallible. Newly perceived norms of correctness were instead encoded in the spate of prescriptive grammars and dictionaries which were produced over the eighteenth and nineteenth centuries. Beginning in the seventeenth century, it was by such means (at least within the tenets of popular prescriptivism) that the 'minimal variation of form' deemed essential to a standard, and standardized, language, might itself be achieved. After all, as the influential grammarian Robert Lowth argued, why should both *less* and *lesser* be tolerated when a single norm would surely—and rationally— be better? The inherent variabilities of language were in such ways seen as indicative of weakness and neglect, while Addison's fallibility in deploying *lesser* ('Attend to what a lesser Muse indites') was duly censured.[8] The poet and critic John Dryden thus made plain a central axiom in this context when he asserted that 'the foundation of the rules is reason'.

Dryden's words foregrounded the prime import of the ostensibly 'rational' in such matters. Appeals to logic, analogy, and affinities with mathematical thinking were indeed often to appear as dominant criteria in a number of contemporary approaches to language over the course of the eighteenth century, many writers duly attempting to formulate rules by which 'proper' English might be regulated and the 'best' speakers in turn recognized. Dryden himself, for instance, early set forth the 'incorrectness' of using prepositions in final position as in 'Where are you going to?' for, although such constructions were long legitimized by standards of usage in English, they were absent from Latin, the language deemed paradigmatic of grammatical perfection. Both etymology and prescriptive logic combined to suggest that preposition (deriving from Latin *præpositiōn-em*, literally 'a putting before') necessarily implied that the word in question should come before the verb, a view which has contributed to one of the still enduring myths of English normative grammar. Matching practice with his own newly articulated principle, it was on such grounds that Dryden painstakingly changed all relevant constructions in the 1668 edition of his *Essay on Dramatic Poesy*. Dryden was moreover by no means alone in such preoccupations, and self-appointed regulators of the English language flourished. Lowth, Archdeacon of Winchester and later Bishop of London, assumed seemingly divine rights on linguistic legislation too in his *Short Introduction to English Grammar* (1762). Asserting that 'in many instances [English] offends against every part of grammar', he castigated a range of constructions then in normal use such as *you was* ('an enormous Solecism'), the 'improper' use of *who* and *whom* (so that Dryden's own 'Tell who loves who' comes in for condemnatory comment), as well as the use of the flat adverb as in *extreme unwilling* ('Adjectives are sometimes employed as adverbs; improperly, and not agreeably to the Genius of the English Language'), and the 'improper' deployment of *shall* and *will*.[9] In other words, grammarians such as Lowth formulated and endorsed many of the rules by which 'correct' language is now popularly thought to be ascertained, regularly disregarding the realities of linguistic usage in favour of somewhat more theoretical (and tenuous) notions of correctness. 'It is not the Language but the Practice which is in fault', Lowth informed his readers, thereby urging the necessity of remedial reform upon the stated errors of ordinary English. In consequence, as the linguist Dick Leith has pertinently observed with reference to such grammatical thinking in his own social history of the English language, 'to a large extent, our whole perception of grammar has been distorted by their work'.[10]

'The principal design of a grammar is to teach us to express ourselves with propriety; and to enable us to judge of every phrase and form of construction whether it be right or not', Lowth firmly declared, expressing a belief in the binary oppositions of 'right' and 'wrong' which prescriptivism was often to endorse above the heterogeneities of actual usage. It is in these terms that

codification, and its accompanying traditions of proscription, comes to operate as an ideology, a set of assumptions about language behaviour which can,
in real terms, sometimes exert more influence on speakers' attitudes than
does direct observation of the language itself. It is this dichotomy, for
instance, which lies behind modern attitudes to *hopefully* as a sentence
adverb (as in constructions such as 'Hopefully it won't be raining later')
where its use can attract widespread censure—in spite of its undoubted
currency in all domains of usage. Attitudes and actuality divide, and notions
of correctness can dominate in popular beliefs about what individual users
do and, perhaps more importantly, *should* do in their choice of words.[11]
Standardization too can productively be seen in similar terms, consisting not
only of the historical and linguistic processes by which one variety of the language has come to assume superordinate and non-localized roles within the
nation, but equally being formed of a complex of beliefs and attitudes which
evolve around the 'standard' which results. Like the processes of standardization in themselves, such notions undergo a slow and gradual development,
underpinning a history of the language which is, in reality, far from unilinear
(though paradoxically, images of unilinearity are often fostered as a salient
part of popular images of 'standardness' in itself). While Renaissance debates
about the status of English as a language for intellectual expression exemplify,
for instance, the increasing consolidation of one variety alone in the
functional roles by which a standard may be determined, they also, and more
pertinently, reveal advances in accompanying ideologies whereby this one
variety of the language comes to be reified as the language in itself, and
as exemplifying its 'best' qualities. Joseph Priestley, scientist, theologian,
and grammarian, reveals the operation of exactly these ideas in his eighteenth-century conviction that the standard variety emerges not as a result of
arbitrary and external circumstance (the prominence of London as capital,
the role of the Chancery, William Caxton's decision to set up his printing
press outside Westminster) but rather as the consequence of some superior
merit and inherent value which is located within this one variety. As he
stressed, 'the best forms of speech, the most commodious for use, and
the most agreeable to the analogy of the language, will at length establish
themselves and become universal, by their superior excellence'.[12]

   Attempted codification of this variety tended to take all these conceptions
one step further. Often choosing to set forth for the erudition of users of the
language recommended constructions in which what 'ought' to be predom-
inates over what is, the grammars, dictionaries, and manuals of linguistic
usage of the eighteenth and nineteenth centuries gradually moreover began
to take on important implications for pronunciation too—and for those
issues of 'propriety', and 'impropriety', 'correctness' and 'mistake', which
also began to infuse attitudes towards spoken English at this time. In that
search for a standard of spoken language which was to preoccupy many

writers of the late eighteenth century and afterwards, it was in many ways this ideology of standardization, and the myth of a language which prescription might perfect, which was to be of greatest significance.

In terms of pronunciation, it was the era of codification, with its transparently reforming zeal, which was therefore to enact significant change in attitudes towards acceptability and its converse, readily specifying notions of 'norm' and corresponding 'deviation' on the model adopted by Bishop Lowth with reference to English grammar. Of course, in other respects, the subject of pronunciation had not been entirely neglected before this time. Phoneticians such as John Hart, William Bullokar, and Christopher Cooper had, for example, written extensive and detailed works on the articulatory mechanisms of English in the sixteenth and seventeenth centuries, classifying sounds and endeavouring to determine the phonetic characteristics which made up the language. They had, however, largely done so without engaging in specifications of a supra-regional 'standard' for all and, more particularly, without the associated social and cultural prescriptions for patterns of convergent behaviour which later came to be so prominent. Instead their prime concern had been to document the phonemic structures which then existed in English, demarcating the distances between grapheme and phoneme in a language which, as William Bullokar urged in 1580, merited a new orthography on these grounds alone ('fower and twentie letters, are not sufficient to picture Inglish spéech: For in Inglish spéech, are mo distinctions and divisions in voice, than these fower and twentie letters can seuerally signifie, and giue right sound vnto').[13] Writers such as George Puttenham with his clear depiction in 1589 of an emergent standard of speech based in 'the vsuall speach of the Court and that of London and the shires lying about London within lx. myles' nevertheless already evince the marked awareness that the speech of London was, in a number of ways, regarded as 'better' than that of the provinces.[14] Similarly, John Hart's principles of reformed spelling are set down in his *Orthographie* of 1569 with the intent that, by their use, 'the rude countrie Englishman' will be able to pronounce English 'as the best sort use to speak it'.

London, as political, legal, administrative, commercial, and cultural centre of the country, naturally assumes prominence in such comments, as does the language of the learned above that of the majority of the populace. Alexander Gil, High Master of St Paul's and author of the *Logonomia Anglicana* (1619), hence expresses his notion of standard speech in the precept that spelling is not to be accommodated to the sounds used by ploughmen, maidservants, and porters but by learned or elegantly refined men in speaking and reading. As the poet and essayist James Beattie was later to write, it is natural to 'approve as elegant what is customary among our superiors',[15] and the superiority vested in knowledge of the written word, and in familiarity with the metropolitan above the provincial, readily served as major determining factors in these

early perceptions of linguistic 'elegance' with regard to speech. Over the course
of the sixteenth and seventeenth centuries, a clear sense of an emergent (if
highly variable) standard of spoken as well as written English does therefore
start to become perceptible. The schoolmaster and writer on language Owen
Price notes in *The Vocal Organ* that his work 'has not been guided by our vulgar pronunciation, but that of *London* and our *Universities*, where the language
is purely spoken'.[16] Elisha Coles in *The Compleat English Schoolmaster* (1674)
specifies on the title page that the basis of his work is 'the present proper pronunciation of the Language in OXFORD and LONDON'.

Nevertheless, it should not be assumed that such statements indicate the
existence of a 'standard' of speech, in terms of either process or ideology,
which is akin to that described or, perhaps more accurately, prescribed for
general use over the late eighteenth and nineteenth centuries. Coles, for
example, in the late seventeenth century evidently feels constrained to
defend the one variety of 'proper' pronunciation which he had chosen to
document, a situation which would have been entirely inconceivable a century later. As he states:

because men usually espouse that pronunciation as properest which they have been
accustomed to, therefore they will be quarrelling at some particulars.
    Let them know, that in these things I have been jealous of, and have oftentimes
divorc'd my self, and have followed that pronunciation which I have for many years
observ'd to be most in use among the generality of Schollars.[17]

'I have had opportunity of making observations', he admonishes in further
justification of these stated preferences for London speech. Likewise, John
Hart's 1569 specifications of the 'flower' of speech located in London does
not, at that date, exclude all other varieties from consideration. His tolerance,
and moreover, acceptance of the validity of pronunciations used in other
parts of the country provides a striking contrast to later comments in which
such varieties are, in the words of Thomas Sheridan, lexicographer, elocutionist, and one of the foremost writers on pronunciation in the late
eighteenth century, necessarily to be conceived as a sign of 'disgrace'. As
Sheridan was to assert in 1762, 'all other dialects are sure marks, either of a
provincial, rustic, pedantic, or mechanic education, and therefore have some
degree of disgrace attached to them'.[18] Hart, two centuries earlier, instead
proffered his conviction that speakers of dialects outside the standard variety have a right to spell as they pronounce, and their way of doing so should
give no more offence than should the fact of their difference in accent.
Notions of 'disgrace' seem far removed from the liberal attitude his words
express:

if any one were minded at Newcastell upon Tine, or Bodman in Cornewale, to write
or print his minde there, who could iustly blame him for his Orthographie, to serue
hys neyghbours according to their mother speach, yea, though he wrate so to

London, to whomsoever it were, he could be no more offended to see his writing so, than if he were present to heare him speake.[19]

Christopher Cooper, a phonetician as well as headmaster of the Grammar School in Bishop Stortford, conveys a similar set of beliefs in his *English Teacher* of 1687. Though he chooses to describe 'the best dialect' of London speech since this, in his opinion, was the 'most pure and correct',[20] Cooper's attitude to variation, and variant articulations of words, is nevertheless again strikingly liberal. 'Everyone pronounceth them as himself pleases', he notes on p. 105. As the philologist Eric Dobson has commented on this position, Cooper 'admits that there are variants, and that some men use dialectal pronunciations; he is quite content that they should, but he himself will describe a defined pronunciation, that of the South'.[21] The absence of prescriptive rigour, and proscriptive rhetoric, is marked. It is the impression of overwhelming variability in terms of the potential realization of sounds which instead emerges from a comparison of contemporaneous accounts of pronunciation from this period. If an emerging (and still largely localized) norm can be detected, then 'norm' must, as a result, be understood in its loosest sense, one marked by its flux and conspicuous levels of dissent among those who strove to describe the flexible realities of spoken usage of the day.

Though sixteenth- and seventeenth-century observations about language thus do in one sense make plain notions of an emerging standard of speech centred on and around London, they evidently do not share that highly normative, restrictive, and codifying zeal which characterizes their later counterparts. Cooper, for example, simply aims to describe his 'best dialect' in all its variability; Thomas Sheridan, a century later, aims instead to disseminate— and refine—its eighteenth-century equivalent and hence to displace all other 'inferior' forms of speech from the nation as a whole. The pronouncing dictionaries which flourished as a new genre at the end of the eighteenth century and throughout the nineteenth are, in Sheridan's terms, to act as a means by which 'the pronunciation of each word' can be reduced to a 'certainty by fixed and visible marks; the only way in which uniformity of sound could be propagated to any distance'.[22] The change lies in both the process and the ideology of standardization. Whereas Cooper wrote in an era more concerned with the status of English as a language in itself, Sheridan wrote in one inspired by its codification, its reduction to rule. Whereas Hart and Puttenham described, and were moreover content to describe, a still largely localized form of spoken English, Sheridan and other writers of the late eighteenth century (and afterwards) sought instead to codify a non-localized, supra-regional 'standard', and thus explicitly to displace the linguistic diversities of accent which currently pertained throughout the nation. As Sheridan noted with evident disfavour of regional markers of speech, 'the pronunciation of all natives of these Countries, is entirely formed, from the Custom which prevails in the places of their respective birth and education'.[23]

The precise nature of this transition within attitudes to pronunciation and its framing ideologies is perhaps made most clear within a more detailed examination of notions of a standard and its social role in the work of George Puttenham in the sixteenth century and that of Thomas Sheridan in the eighteenth. Puttenham's *Arte of English Poesie* (1589) is often, and rightly, cited for the valuable information which it provides about the rise of perceptions of a standard in English usage. As we have seen, he locates this in the usage of London and the court, in 'southerne' speech ('the vsuall speach of the Court, and that of London and the shires lying about London within lx. myles and not much aboue'). He goes on moreover to develop its social affiliations, placing his linguistic model in 'the better brought vp sort . . . men ciuill and graciously behauoured and bred' rather than in 'the speach of a craftes man or carter, or other of the inferiour sort, though he be inhabitant or bred in the best towne and Citie in this Realme'.[24] As he adds in explanation, 'such persons doe abuse good speaches by strange accents or ill-shapen sounds and false ortographie'. Puttenham's standard is self-evidently a sociolect—at least in part—and one which is to be sought in the 'Courtly' and 'currant' use of the southern counties around London. More specifically still, it is located in those of breeding and education who inhabit these regions. It is the conjunction of these two factors which gives the 'standard' he describes. For those born beyond the Trent, as he says, 'whether they be noble men or gentlemen or of their best clarkes all is a matter'.

This conception of a standard has, in a number of ways, marked affinities with that later discussed by Thomas Sheridan in his own work. As Sheridan states in 1761, 'the standard of pronunciation is affixed to the custom which prevails amongst people of education at the Court, so that none but such as are born and bred amongst them, or have constant opportunities of conversing with them . . . can be said to be masters of it'.[25] Both Sheridan and Puttenham thus apparently describe what is a largely localized standard of speech, based primarily in the capital and used by those with access to this 'best' London society. Just as Puttenham notes that those living beyond the Trent, irrespective of their social rank, are not to be adopted as linguistic models, so too does Sheridan comment on the linguistic infelicities which can mark the elite outside London: 'there are few gentlemen of England who have received their education at country schools, that are not infected with a false pronunciation of certain words, peculiar to each county'.[26] As he remarks in further corroboration of a shift in attitudes, however, 'Surely every gentleman will think it worth while, to take some pains, to get rid of such evident marks of rusticity'. Though both describe speech in terms of social markers, both therefore also make it plain that elevated status in itself is no guarantee of linguistic propriety. Similarly, though both indicate that there may indeed be in existence a non-localized and supra-regional norm for the written language, they also make clear that there is, on the whole, still no corresponding one for speech. As a result, when Puttenham asserts that 'I say not this but that in euery shyre of England there be gentlemen and others that speake but specially write, as good Southerne as we of Middlesex and Surrey do, but not the common people of euery shire',[27] he merely confirms the fact of a shared and written standard which has assumed a supra-localized role for those of good standing and education against a spoken one which, influenced by social and regional factors, still remains localized to a larger degree. The fact that the whole sentence is in the subjunctive (following the negative) makes this still more plain. Puttenham does not deny that, outside the confines of the capital and the southern counties which surround it, there *may* be those of superior status who approximate to the emergent standard of speech based in London. He simultaneously reveals, however, that it is much more likely that such assimilation has been achieved in terms of the written rather than the spoken forms which they employ.

The real difference between Sheridan and Puttenham lies in the attitudes they express towards the language varieties they describe, and in the framing ideologies of a standard to which they adhere. For Puttenham, the fact that spoken language varies throughout the country, even among the 'better brought vp sort' is, for example, of far less import than is the ability to handle the 'currant termes' of the 'Courtly' and 'southerne' language variety. His text is, after all, addressed to the 'maker or Poet' and, as he states in this context: 'common desiphers of good vtterance . . . resteth altogether in figuratiue speaches'.[28] Sheridan instead devotes his work to the spoken language and, as already indicated, more specifically to the perceived need to create a uniform, and non-localized, variety of pronunciation which should, to his mind, be used throughout the entire country. As he proclaims upon the title page of his *General Dictionary* of 1780, this had expressly been written to define (and disseminate) 'a plain and permanent STANDARD of PRONUNCIATION'. Standardization itself is his major motive for, as Sheridan adds, 'in order to spread abroad the English language as a living tongue, and to facilitate the attainment of its speech, it is necessary in the first place that a standard of pronunciation should be established, and a method of acquiring a just one should be laid open'.[29] As a result, whereas for Puttenham it had been possible, and indeed acceptable, for a gentleman to speak in ways manifestly influenced by the area where he lived (even if in his written discourse he ought to approach and adopt court standards), for Sheridan the retention of such markers in speech was to be explicitly connotative of 'disgrace' as well as capable of contravening the status of 'gentleman' in itself. The right accent is, for him, a social testimony, 'a sort of proof that a person has kept good company', and it is presented in terms far more rigid, and socially aware, than those preferred by Puttenham. Sheridan, for example, formalizes the socio-symbolic affiliations of accent in ways which were carefully designed to appeal to a society in which, as contemporary commentators regularly observed, emulation and social ambition seemed to operate as a dominant social force.[30]

Sheridan's prescriptive crusade is, in consequence, deliberately constructed in terms of furthering the framing ideologies of a standard for pronunciation, and heightening awareness of its import. As he lectured his audience at the Sheldonian Theatre in Oxford in 1759 (see Figure 1.1), his aim was, in effect, to raise the linguistic consciousness not only as it applied to language in general but specifically as it applied to contemporary attitudes

---

OXFORD, *May* 16, 1759.

M R. SHERIDAN's General Courſe of Lectures on ELOCUTION, and the ENGLISH LANGUAGE (ſo far only as relates to Elocution), will commence on *Wedneſday* next the 23d Inſtant ; will be continued on the ſucceeding *Friday* and *Wedneſday*, and conclude on *Friday* the firſt Day of *June :* To begin each Morning preciſely at the Hour of Ten. Price to each Subſcriber one Guinea. Such Gentlemen as purpoſe to attend this Courſe, are requeſted to ſend their Names to Mr. *Fletcher*, Bookſeller in the *Turl*.

N. B. As Mr. SHERIDAN's Illneſs when he was laſt at *Oxford*, prevented his going through the Courſe in the Time propoſed, by which Means many of the Subſcribers were abſent during Part of the Courſe, and Others heard it in ſuch an interrupted Manner as could not be ſatisfactory, Notice is hereby given, That all Subſcribers to the former, ſhall be entitled to their Admiſſion, during this Courſe, by Virtue of their firſt Subſcription.

The Lectures will be delivered at the Muſic Room *as before.*

FIG. 1.1 Advertisements for Thomas Sheridan's Lectures in Oxford, 1759

to accent. 'No man can amend a fault of which he is not conscious; and consciousness cannot exert itself, when barred up by habit or vanity', he expounded,[31] setting forth familiar prescriptive paradigms in which 'habit', as for the split infinitive or the preposition in final position, was to be no safeguard against newly perceived 'incorrectness'. Sheridan hence urges an education into a proper consciousness of pronunciation so that its 'faults' may be recognized and its analogies restored. As for the written language, pronunciation too was, at least intentionally, thereby to be endowed with the sense of a norm and one which was configured with far more rigidity than had hitherto been the case. Prevailing imbalances in eighteenth-century

O X F O R D, May 25, 1759.

MR. SHERIDAN

TAKES this Method of acquainting such Gentlemen as are defirous of improving themfelves in the manner of reading the Liturgy, that he will be ready to give his Affiftance in that Way, by entering into a Practical Courfe for the Purpofe, as foon a fufficient Number fhall offer themfelves.------All who want farther Information on this Head, may know in what Way, and upon what Terms the Defign is to be executed, by applying to Mr. SHERIDAN at Mr. *Kemp's* in the *High-Street*, any Time before *Thurfday* the 31ft Inftant.

Such as fhould chufe private and feperate Inftruction, may alfo know upon what Terms it is to be obtained.

And as Mr. SHERIDAN has heard that many young Gentlemen are inclined to form themfelves into fmall Claffes, in order to practife together the Art of reading aloud and reciting under his Infpection, He likewife gives Notice, that upon Application to him, he will inform fuch Gentlemen how far, and in what Way he can be of Service to them during his prefent Stay at *Oxford.*

attitudes towards acceptability were duly pointed out. 'It is reckoned a great disgrace for a gentleman to spell ill, though not to speak or read ill', Sheridan stressed,[32] berating that long-established leniency in terms of divergent pronunciation and difference of accent. If the publication of Samuel Johnson's celebrated *Dictionary* in 1755 (and especially perhaps in its serial publication in the following year) had brought many to the sense that a reference model for spelling not only existed but also should be used throughout the nation, no parallel process had so far existed for the spoken word. 'Many provincials have grown old in the capital, without making any change in their original dialect', Sheridan thus noted with evident censure.[33] As he stated with similar disapprobation in 1781, 'In general. . . speakers content themselves with the thought, that they are not worse than their neighbours'.[34] This habitual exclusion of pronunciation from the normative paradigms of prescriptivism was no longer to be tenable. Since, as Sheridan additionally affirmed, it is impossible for 'consciousness' to 'be awoken without information', it was this which he, together with a host of other writers over the ensuing decades, would henceforth provide in abundance.

If one examines contemporary attitudes to language when Sheridan was writing, it is, for example, clear that though the 'consciousness' which he advocates had indeed proceeded apace with reference to grammar, and to spelling too, attitudes to accent in a number of ways did seem to lag behind, even within the eighteenth century and its habitual prescriptive zeal. Provided with the 'information' to inspire the requisite sensitization, Lord Chesterfield, the original patron of Johnson's *Dictionary*, could, for instance, advise his son in 1750 on the particular importance of good spelling: 'orthography, in the true sense of the word, is so absolutely necessary for a man of letters, or a gentleman, that one false spelling may fix a ridicule upon him for the rest of his life'.[35] Joseph Priestley in 1762 similarly stresses that the ability to use grammar with accuracy and precision functions as a major signifier of the educated and urbane. In marked contrast, pronunciation and accent were, Priestley commented, to be adjudged 'a matter of ornament only'.[36] It was the use of the double negative or the double comparative rather than the dropped [h] which, in then dominant conceptions of linguistic propriety, served to reveal the provincial rather than the polite and which were, in turn, seen as allied with the stratified patterns of an ordered society. In Fielding's *The History of Tom Jones* (1749), for instance, the 'illogical' double superlative consistently characterizes the speech of servants while its use is absent from the discourse of those higher in the social sphere: ' "That he is, the most handsomest Man I ever saw in my Life. . . his Skin be so white, and to be sure, it is the most whitest that ever was seen," ' Mrs Honour, the maid, declares.[37]

Writers on the language in the earlier part of the eighteenth century make these disparities in terms of prevailing language attitudes even clearer. The grammarian and schoolmaster James Greenwood, for example, simultaneously reveals the ways in which the legacies of prescriptivism are beginning to be felt in the context of pronunciation, as well as his impotence to do anything about them. As he states in this context in his own highly popular grammar of 1711: 'I cannot dissemble my unwillingness to say anything at all on this head [Orthoepy]; first, because of the irregular and wrong Pronounciation of the *Letters* and *Words*, which if one should go about to mend, would be a business of great Labour and Trouble, as well as Fruitless and Unsuccessful'.[38] Ten years later, the hymn-writer and educator Isaac Watts, in a text explicitly intended to delineate 'the Chief Principles and Rules of *Pronouncing* our *Mother-Tongue*', in effect entirely abdicates that authority which Sheridan (and others) are later so willing to wield. Making merely a token gesture in terms of pronunciation towards the prescriptive sensibilities which were then beginning to dominate comment on grammar, he appears content simply to describe the fluctuations in spoken usage which were currently observable. Giving a list of words illustrating variant pronunciations 'according to the Custome of the Speaker', Watts's tolerance is marked: 'I do not suppose both these Ways of Pronunciation to be equally proper; but both are used, and that among Persons of Education and Learning in different Parts of the Nation; ... Custom is the great Rule of Pronouncing as well as of Spelling, so that everyone should usually speak according to Custom'.[39]

A similar pattern can be discerned in John Owen's *The Youth's Instructor* of 1732 where, although one of the stated aims was to aid in the acquisition of a 'right pronunciation', Owen was nevertheless forced to admit that ''tis difficult (and therefore I do not pretend absolutely) to determine in so nice a Point, wherein the learned themselves are not agreed'.[40] Likewise, though Samuel Johnson had originally aimed to include the 'ascertainment' or 'fixing' of pronunciation in his *Dictionary* (his 'idea of an English dictionary' in 1747 is specified as a work 'by which the pronunciation of our language may be fixed, and its attainment facilitated'),[41] a later linguistic realism, induced by the subsequent years of lexicographical toil, served to redress such ambitions. As he concluded in 1755, 'sounds are too volatile and subtile for legal restraints; to enchain syllables, and to lash the wind, are equally the undertakings of pride, unwilling to measure its desires by its strength'.[42]

It is perceptions such as these which change so radically over the next few decades as the myth of a perfectible and invariant standard of spoken English, one prescribed for all speakers without exception, firmly took hold of the popular consciousness. In the hands of writers such as Thomas Sheridan, John Walker, Benjamin Smart, and many others, a wide-ranging belief in notions of a spoken standard, and notably in a minimal variation of form which might extend to sounds as well as spelling, did in fact lead to a general attempt to 'enchain syllables', regardless of Johnson's own belief in the futility of such endeavour. 'No evil so great can befal any language, as a perpetual fluctuation both in point of spelling and pronouncing',[43] Sheridan asserts, decrying

the changes which prevented the stability he sought to impose. In line with
this maxim (and in true prescriptive style), the inherent variabilities of usage
were, at least ideally, to be reformed by the authoritative imposition of norms.
John Walker (another prominent writer on pronunciation whose *Critical
Pronouncing Dictionary* was widely acclaimed as 'the statute-book of English
orthoepy'),[44] shared these sympathies. 'Custom' (ordinary usage) was, he
noted, to be corrected wherever it was 'silent or dubious', a formula which, as
Walker's own work confirms, could at times permit a particularly wide latitude
of operation. 'As the venerable garb of custom is often borrowed to cover the
wantonness or ignorance of innovators, it will be highly necessary to view this
legislator in language as closely as possible, that we may not mistake him for
novelty or caprice',[45] Walker further admonished in this context.

  Walker's *General Idea of a Pronouncing Dictionary*, published in 1774, was
in a number of ways thus overtly inspired by the possibilities which prescriptivism might offer for constraint. Though forced to acknowledge
the realities of usage ('custom is not only the law of language, but strictly
speaking it is language itself'), Walker nevertheless adheres to the prescriptive impulse behind his projected dictionary of pronunciation, emphasizing
the need for rational guidance in all matters where 'custom' might err. 'The
most disgraceful irregularities are daily screened under the specious authority of custom', he adds in further condemnation of the flaws which, to his
mind, ordinary usage self-evidently revealed. In terms of the prescriptive
theories thereby advanced, variation was intentionally to be resisted wherever possible for, while Walker admits that it is in fact intrinsic to language
('indeed, a degree of versatility seems involved in the very nature of language'),[46] this fact was, it seemed, paradoxically to encourage rather than
inhibit the operation of future prescriptive sanction. 'Indeed', Walker continued, variation 'is one of those very evils left by Providence for man to correct:
a love of order, and the utility of regularity, will always incline him to confine
this versatility within as narrow bounds as possible'. The tolerance which, in
earlier writers, had been widely evident in attitudes to accent variability was
also to shift. Samuel Johnson, for example, can be seen to epitomize earlier
attitudes to acceptability in this context in his conviction that provincial markers were not necessarily at odds with the polite. 'Little aberrations' in this
respect were to be seen as 'of no disadvantage', he stated. His reactions to
variation in accent were positive.[47] 'A small intermixture of provincial peculiarities may, perhaps, have an agreeable effect, as the notes of different birds
concur in the harmony of the grove, and please more than if they were all
exactly alike', he declared, similarly pointing out that people who listened to
him carefully would readily discern his own geographical origins: 'When
people watch me narrowly. . . they will find me out to be of a particular
county', just as John Dunning, the first Baron Ashburton, 'may be found out
to be a Devonshire man'.[48] By the time John Walker produces the first edition

of his own *Critical Pronouncing Dictionary* in 1791, such variability in pronunciation is—at least within the prescriptive paradigms adopted—instead
deliberately presented as 'ridiculous and embarrassing', a pattern of usage to
be avoided by all 'elegant speakers' and the truly genteel.[49]

The relevant paradigm was, it seemed, that of 'neglect', a term also
selected by Walker in this context. Its effects were rendered even more conspicuous by the apparently contrastive achievements of grapheme and
phoneme in this respect in a post-Johnson age. 'Wherever English is taught',
as Sheridan pointed out, 'all may attain a uniformity in spelling; but, with
respect to pronunciation it is left entirely to chance'.[50] The discrepancy was
highlighted further by Walker in his comment that, while 'written language,
without any considerable variation, extends to the remotest distances, . . .
speaking not only differs widely in different places at different times, but in
the same place, and at the same time'.[51] In these terms, the non-localized
norms which were formally set out in the grammars and dictionaries of the
eighteenth century with reference to acceptable constructions of syntax and
spelling did indeed seem to stand in marked contrast to the continued fluctuations of speech. Published texts, for example, tended to reproduce on a
national scale the grammatical and orthographical proprieties endorsed by
the prescriptive tradition, thus also of course achieving a nationwide exposure for their use within the authoritative registers of print. Double negatives
and double comparatives were, in turn, gradually eliminated from these particular public discourses over the whole country, though their use could and
did continue in the localized norms of speech and in private and informal
usage. In a similar way, printing as well as the popularity of the dictionary as
reference book encoded national norms of spelling which increasingly tended
towards that invariability deemed both necessary and correct.[52] In comparison, pronunciation continued to vary widely, not only in realizations of individual words in London as Walker pointed out ('the same words are often
differently pronounced by different speakers, and those perhaps, of equal
numbers and reputation'),[53] but also in the way in which, all over England, it
was localized norms rather than national standards which seemed to prevail,
a situation from which, as we have seen, not even the gentry were exempt. As
Walker stressed in the introduction to his pronouncing dictionary:

> the grand difference between the metropolis and the provinces is, that people of edu-
> cation in London are free from all the vices of the vulgar; but the best educated peo-
> ple in the provinces, if constantly resident there, are sure to be strongly tinctured with
> the dialect of the country in which they live.[54]

In terms of the standardizing impulse which, with reference to pronunciation, becomes increasingly perceptible in the writings of Walker and others,
the desired standard of speech was therefore one which was to be identical
in enunciation all over the country, regular rather than irregular, and

endowed with rules of usage whereby 'good' and 'bad', as in grammar, could be determined and duly promulgated or proscribed. In such conceptions, the 'best' accent was, in other words, not only to be 'correct' but also to be both invariant and non-localized. In the language of the time, as a range of writers argued, 'nature' was to be reformed by reason and by art. 'As nature leaves us in a rude and uncultivated form, it is our business to polish and refine ourselves. Nature gives us the organs, it is ours to acquire the skilful performance upon them', the grammarian Alexander Bicknell averred.[55] Polishing and refining the language, in its broader ideological implications, was, however, to become a matter of public as well as private responsibility and, significantly, one which was often depicted in terms of national as well as social honour.

The engagement of national sensibilities in matters of linguistic 'refinement' was, of course, of long standing by this date, being closely linked, for instance, to the rise of foreign language academies such as the Académie Française in 1635 and the Accademia della Crusca in 1584. In the continuing absence of a corresponding academy for England, the periodic decrees of these institutions were often seen as evincing a superior concern with the precision and purity which language, and specifically a national 'standard' language, ought to manifest. Already in 1640, for example, the orthoepist Simon Daines had opened his introductory address to his readers:

grieving at the strange neglect of our English Nation, that suffer our selves to be outstripped by almost all Forreigne Countries, in their daily endevours for the perfection of their Tongue … when we, as it were, lulled asleep with a kind of stupid remissenesse, forget the necessity of Precept.[56]

It was, as this and similar appeals imply, the responsibility of a good nation to refine its language; achievements in this sphere were in turn felt to redound upon conceptions of the nation's own prestige.

Though pleas for an equivalent foundation to reform English were ultimately to fail, notions that attention to language could be a matter of national honour did nevertheless remain prominent, regularly being integrated into the set of beliefs which came to surround notions of a 'correct' and perfected 'standard'. It was in these terms therefore that the publication of Johnson's dictionary was lauded as a national as well as a linguistic triumph—or as Garrick declaimed in his celebratory poem 'On Johnson's Dictionary':

> Talk of war with a Briton, he'll boldly advance
> That one English soldier will beat ten of France;
> Would we alter the boast from the sword to the pen,
> Our odds are still greater, still greater our men:
> … Johnson, well arm'd like a hero of yore,
> Has beat forty French, and will beat forty more ![57]

Moreover, since the state of the language was regularly interpreted as a mirror of the state of the nation, precepts of this order gave additional force to the rhetoric of nationalism which many writers also chose to employ in the context of language and correctness. Thomas Wilson asserted in *The Many Advantages of a Good Language to any Nation* (1724): 'an uncouth, ambiguous, imperfect Language, is a sure Sign of a slothful or low Genius in the People'.[58] The converse of this is made equally plain: 'a Language that is copious and clear ... shews a good Understanding and Capacity'. Even though the proclamations of academies abroad tended to reveal, at least to an objective observer, the dichotomies which must exist between principle and practice (or ideology and process) in matters of linguistic control—as Johnson noted in 1755, 'academies have been instituted, to guard the avenues of their languages, to retain fugitives, and repulse intruders; . . . their vigilance and activity have hitherto been in vain'[59]—this did not diminish the wider impact of their reforming zeal. They exemplified above all the ideology of standardization, and its power, and it was this that they disseminated so effectively through their respective nations and, indirectly, through England too.

Writers on pronunciation were likewise subject to the legacy of these ideas and it was in terms of national honour, and national shame, that Sheridan, for one, also sought to bring out the deficiencies of the English with regard to their spoken language. While his mentor Jonathan Swift had unsuccessfully campaigned for the creation of a regulatory body for English in the early eighteenth century,[60] it was Sheridan who therefore took up the crusade in its closing decades. 'The Italians, French, and Spaniards, in proportion to their progress in civilisation and politeness, have for more than a century been employed, with the utmost industry, in cultivating and regulating their speech', he stressed in 1780,[61] effectively pointing the contrast between 'civilisation' and its antonyms in his subsequent description of England and English: 'we still remain in the state of all barbarous countries in this respect, having left ours wholly to chance'. It was neglect of this order which, from a European perspective, formed the true hallmark of the nation: 'the English are still classed by the people of these countries, amongst the more rude and scarcely civilized countries of the North. They affix the term of barbarism to this country, in the same manner as the Greeks did to the rest of the world; and on the same principle, on account of the neglect in polishing our speech'.[62] While Swift had directed his censure at what he regarded as the general slovenliness of the language, especially in terms of certain observable lexical trends, Sheridan's attention was, however, to be fixed firmly upon the subject of pronunciation.

Albeit 'the last refuge of a scoundrel' according to Johnson's *Dictionary*, it was patriotism which was thus readily to be employed in order to heighten the necessary consciousness of 'correctness' in terms of speech, the absence of national standards of use hence lending additional force to the often stated impulses to standardize one accent for all speakers of English. Since differences of accent manifestly divided the country, revealing place of origin for virtually every speaker, the intention, at least within the tenets of prescriptive

ideology, was therefore to dispel these distinctions by formalizing one pronunciation, wherever possible, for each word just as each word had, on the
whole, received one spelling. With a certain naivety (and no little irony in
view of the consequences it was ultimately to have), early conceptions of a
non-localized accent hence stress the role it would play in creating a new
equality in speech, and indeed in uniting a nation which had hitherto been
characterized by difference and diversity in terms of the spoken word. In
Sheridan's words, since the inception of a 'proper' standard would mean that
all people would speak in the same way, the 'odious distinctions' which had
previously prevailed in Britain would by these means necessarily be eliminated. As he eloquently reasoned in this context: 'Would it not greatly contribute to put an end to the odious distinctions kept up between subjects of
the same king, if a way were opened by which the attainment of the English
Tongue in its purity, both in point of phraseology and pronunciation, might
to rendered easy to all inhabitants of his Majesty's dominions?'[63]

Both altruism and egalitarianism are thus made to predominate in the texts
of Sheridan and other writers on this subject, the former's aims to disseminate a set of supra-regional norms of accent over the whole country being
phrased not only in the familiar terms of national honour but equally in terms
of the need to increase access to a 'standard' already seen as bound up with
social and linguistic advantage. Since, as Sheridan justifiably contended, 'the
standard of pronunciation is affixed to the custom which prevails among
people of education at the Court', it was, in consequence, largely confined in
the eighteenth century to the habits of a social elite to which relatively few
could have access. Social (as well as geographical) barriers impeded the
spread of the 'proper' norms of speech which, in Sheridan's opinion, all
should rightly use. As he added in further elaboration, 'none but such as are
born and bred amongst them, or have constant opportunities of conversing
with them . . . can be said to be masters of it'.[64] Since this inequality of opportunity could moreover extend even to those of polite and educated rank who
happened to be located outside the capital, the role of accent as social symbol as it then existed was, in conceptions such as these, presented as fundamentally divisive, promoting an unnecessary exclusion (and exclusivity)
instead of creating a uniform standard for the nation. In contrast to the deft
manipulations of social nuance which predominate in later accounts of
accent, such as those expressed in 1860 in *How to Shine in Society* ('Purity of
accent is the grand distinctive feature of an educated gentleman. It belongs to
no city or district, and is acknowledged and accepted as current coin with all
grades of society'),[65] the prime motivation behind the desire to establish a
single accent for all in earlier texts on language is often not the fostering of
emulative paradigms for their own sake. Instead, adopting ostensibly different ideological strategies, it is one commonly presented in images of a greater
good, advocating social utility in the advance of standardization as a social as

well as an entirely beneficial linguistic process. The resulting myths of an egalitarian standard were both potent and persuasive.

'Talking proper', in such socially motivated rhetoric, was thereby made into a social right, utilizing conceptions of a standard which acts, as the linguist William Downes confirms, as 'part of the abstract, unifying identity of a large and internally differentiated society'.[66] If few had direct access to the fashionable (and 'correct') modes of speech in London, especially when 'compared to the millions who speak the same tongue, and cannot have such opportunity',[67] then it was this 'opportunity' which Sheridan, and many other writers, were therefore to attempt to change and to extend. A spoken standard was, at least in theory, to manifest a new equality 'throughout Scotland, Wales, and Ireland, as well as through the several counties of England', removing by means of its convergent specifications—and access to these—the 'disgrace' of dialect and the 'inequalities' of regional markers from rustic aristocracy, northern gentry, and commoner alike, features which are, as Sheridan affirms, 'chiefly kept alive by differences of pronunciation and dialect'.[68]

In idealistic visions of this order, social harmony rather than social hegemony emerges as a consequence of prescriptive endeavour, the 'ill consequences' of accent difference being removed by the adoption of an ostensibly neutral standard for all. Language and nation are again linked and not only, of course, by Sheridan. Two years after Sheridan had published his *Course of Lectures*, William Johnston offers his own pronouncing dictionary as a means 'by which, Both his Majesty's Subjects, and Foreigners, may correct an *Improper*, or acquire a *Right* Pronunciation of the English Language'.[69] John Murdoch, in his 1809 edition of Walker's *Critical Pronouncing Dictionary*, in turn commends as 'a real service to society' those who aid in 'an acquirement so desirable and important'.[70] John Walker himself depicts his own prescriptive zeal as inspired by his recognition of 'duty to the nation', stressing the fact that though 'Accent and Quantity, the great efficients of pronunciation, are seldom mistaken by people of education in the Capital . . . the great bulk of the Nation, and those who form the most important part of it, are without these advantages, and therefore want such a guide to direct them as is here offered'.[71] Samuel Oliver, writing slightly later in the nineteenth century, is, in a similar vein, driven to express his own 'due reverence for the enlightened, and patriotical spirit which has produced in Ingland so large a number of grammatik works'.[72] The central tenet of such positions is, however, perhaps best later summed up in 1864 by Henry Alford, Dean of Canterbury and a popular writer on language and 'proper' usage. 'The national mind is reflected in the national speech', he proclaimed in yet another call to individual and national responsibility in matters of linguistic correctness.[73] A reformed and, more importantly, a refined accent could in these terms only operate for the greater social good of the nation.

Prescriptive texts, as this indicates, operate very effectively as ideological discourses. In such formulations therefore, duty to the nation was regularly to reside not only in the specification of the 'proper' convergent patterns of usage but also, of course, in the censure, and proposed elimination, of divergent (and 'improper') ones. Since, in popular prescriptive thinking, it was above all regional accents which were deemed to be a primary cause of these 'odious distinctions' among the population, their 'refinement' in the direction of London norms could only be advantageous. Clearly regarded as 'other' within the rhetoric so often employed, such enunciations were necessarily presented as 'deviant' and in need of due correction, a notion which in itself rapidly exposes the ideological flaws within the egalitarian ideals which were otherwise overtly endorsed. In the stated terms of Sheridan's own attempted rhetorical persuasions in this context for example, 'ill consequences', whether social or linguistic, could be mitigated by such prescriptive means whilst differential value, long embedded in the differences which existed between modes of metropolitan against provincial speech, might thus be brought to disappear. In such ways, the intolerance of optional variability which is a staple of the standardizing impulse was made to fuse both social and linguistic ideologies, a circumstance which had seemingly obvious appeal in a society in which notions of mobility, self-help, and, as the writer (and first Baron Lytton) Edward Bulwer Lytton termed it, 'the aristocratic contagion'[74] were all deemed to operate as significant social stimuli.

The framing ideologies of a standard might in such ways be brought to shift ground on the subject of pronunciation, fostering a new sensitization to its norms as well as a sense of its social values in ways which, at least ostensibly, were more philanthropic than those which were later to pertain. Nevertheless, as Sheridan admitted, there still remained no 'method', and no easy way, in which knowledge of this intentionally non-localized and neutral accent was to be either acquired or disseminated. This had indeed initially been the factor inhibiting any earlier application of prescriptive sensibilities to the realms of speech. Jonathan Swift, whose *Proposal* for correcting the language in the eighteenth century had earlier been so influential, made it plain that, while grammar and lexis were properly to be subject to linguistic legislation, it seemed impossible to apply this to the domains of spoken English, and to accent in particular. He therefore describes with complete acceptance 'a country squire having only the provincial accent upon his tongue, which is neither a fault, nor in his power to remedy'. By the end of the eighteenth century, however, such 'remedy' was perhaps to seem within reach. Pronunciation too, as we have seen, was to become part of the taught language, its principles described, prescribed, and, perhaps most importantly, transcribed in the flood of works devoted to pronunciation, and its attendant ideologies, which appeared from the mid-eighteenth century onwards.

As Sheridan had realized already in 1761, 'if a method of acquiring a just pronunciation by books, as well as conversation, were established, [its] acquisition would not be circumscribed within such narrow bounds, but would be open to all British subjects wherever born'.[75] It was this 'method' on which he and others were to concentrate their energies, not least in terms of the dictionary and the systematic details of pronunciation which it could perhaps be made to provide for all users of the language. Almost twenty years before his *General Dictionary of the English Language* of 1780, Sheridan had set out his general aims:

The object. . .is, to fix such a standard of pronunciation, by means of visible marks, that it may be in the power of every one, to acquire an accurate manner of uttering every word in the English tongue, by applying to that standard. In order to do this, the author of this scheme proposes to publish a Dictionary, in which the true pronunciation, of all the words in our tongue, shall be pointed out by visible and accurate marks.[76]

The power of the press was to act as prime agency in the dissemination of this intended phonemic 'remedy'. 'This would be making a noble use of the invention of printing',[77] Sheridan averred, not least since to reduce 'the pronunciation of each word to a certainty by fixed and visible marks' was 'the only way in which uniformity of sound could be propagated to any distance'.[78] This was of course the aim, phonetic notation serving, in the ideal world, as a means by which a non-localized accent might be defined and in turn diffused. Many other writers were naturally to think along the same lines and, guaranteed a national distribution, it was print—in the form of books, manuals, pamphlets, and dictionaries—which was envisaged as being able to provide the non-localized access to non-localized norms which, as we have seen, was widely propagated as essential. Though later condemned as 'the greatest of all absurdities' by the philologist (and founding father of the *OED*), Richard Chenevix Trench,[79] it was the development of the pronouncing dictionary which was nevertheless to be of notable importance in these deliberate attempts to standardize one accent for the nation as a whole.

In keeping with the previous absence of sensitization towards the proprieties of accent (and its needful correction), earlier dictionaries had in fact rarely given any indication of pronunciation. Nathaniel Bailey in the second edition of his *Universal Etymological Dictionary* (1731), for example, merely marks the position of main stress (*ABA'NDON, A'NTICHAMBER*), though even this represents an advance in lexicographical practice from the neglect with which pronunciation had previously been treated. Samuel Johnson too adheres to this method in accordance with his belief in the impossibility of enchaining syllables by prescriptive means. As he notes: 'In settling the orthography, I have not wholly neglected the pronunciation, which I have directed, by printing an accent upon the acute or elevated syllable'.[80] Later dictionaries, however, began in addition to include the marking of vowel length so that, two years after the first edition of Johnson's own dictionary, James Buchanan in *A New English Dictionary* is already deploying a macron (-) for a long vowel, and a contrastive breve (˘) to indicate a short one.[81] Reflecting the gradual shifts in thinking about accent which were then taking place, even this was later considered inadequate, especially given the growing convictions about the utility of the written language for the intended reform of the spoken. William Kenrick in his *A New English Dictionary of the English Language* of 1773 is, as a result, the first to utilize the possibilities of a series of small numerals appended above individual letters in order to signify still finer details of enunciation. Sheridan himself is the first writer to combine this, in his *General Dictionary of the English Language* (1780), with the systematic respelling of the entry word, hence *echo*]ĕk'kõ[, *eavesdropper*]ē'vz-drŏp-pŭr[, thus introducing the method which, with individual modifications of notation, was to be adopted by John Walker, Benjamin Smart, and many others over the later eighteenth and nineteenth centuries (see Figure 1.2).

   The pronouncing dictionary was, in a number of ways, to be of marked significance in furthering these notions of 'proper' speech. It traded above all on the popularity of the dictionary in a post-Johnson age and on a public increasingly habituated to consult, and defer to, its authority on all matters of doubt. Writers such as William Kenrick, William Johnston, John Walker, Thomas Browne, John Longmuir, and Peter Nuttall, amid many others, all yoked Johnson's definitions to increasingly complex systems of transcription, fusing an analysis of semantic nuance with a firm indication of prescriptive propriety (or otherwise) in terms of pronunciation. Their work often met an audience which seemed to subscribe all too readily to the ideologies of a standard manipulated within the prescriptive tradition. The writer and politician William Cobbett, for example, became word perfect on the various dictates offered by Lowth's *Grammar* ('I wrote the whole grammar out two or three times; I got it by heart; I repeated it every morning and every evening, and . . . I imposed on myself the task of saying it all over once every time I was posted sentinel').[82] Similarly, as the economist Adam Smith's review of Johnson's own dictionary reveals, it was common for stringent guidance to be demanded on this vexed subject of linguistic correctness. Not content with Johnson's liberal application of status labels such as 'cant' and 'barbarous' for various words and meanings which he regarded with disfavour, Smith evidently desired still greater proscriptive rigour: 'we cannot help wishing, that the author had trusted less to the judgement of those who may consult him, and had oftener passed his own censure upon those words which are not of approved use, tho' sometimes to be met with in authors of no mean name'.[83] The culture of correctness was widespread, prominent, for example, in the way in which Mary Wollstonecraft berated Thomas Paine for his transgressions 'against the subjunctive'[84] and similarly conspicuous in the negative appraisal which the *Monthly Review* chose to give Fanny Burney's

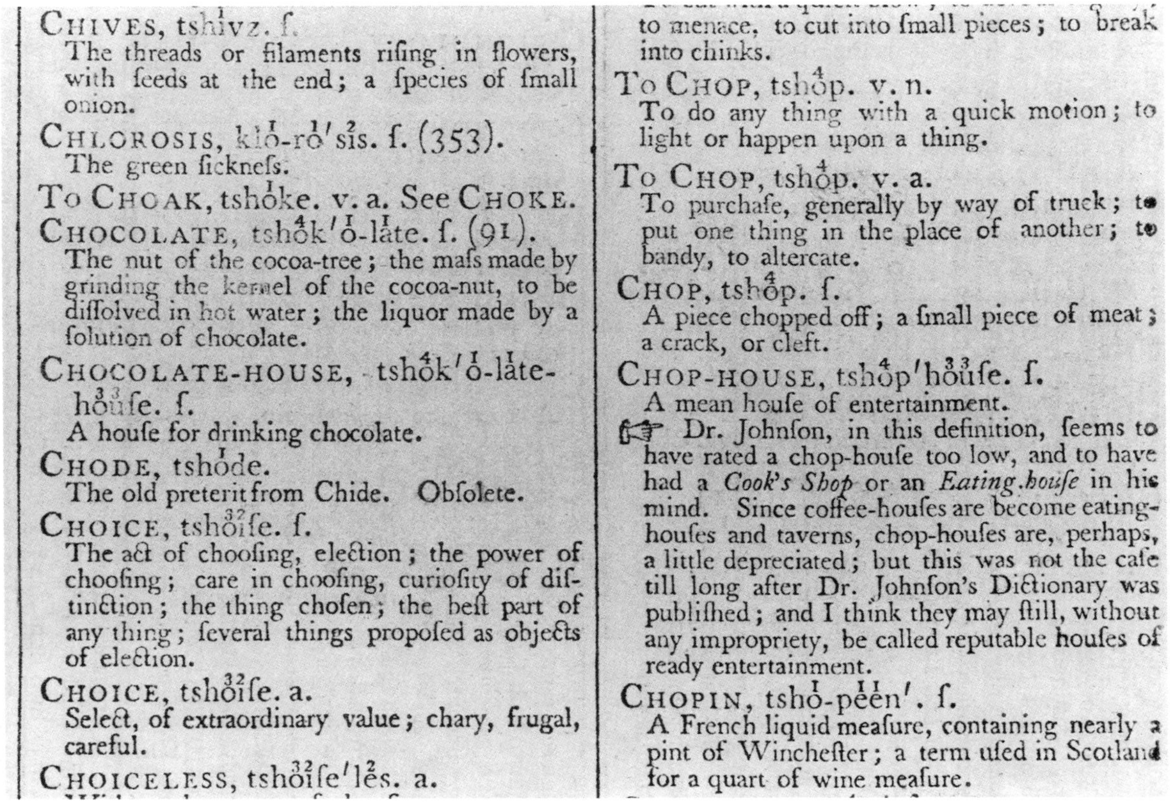

CHIVES, tſhivz. ſ.
The threads or filaments rifing in flowers, with feeds at the end; a fpecies of fmall onion.

CHLOROSIS, klo-rō'sis. ſ. (353).
The green ficknefs.

To CHOAK, tſhōke. v. a. See CHOKE.

CHOCOLATE, tſhōk'ō-lāte. ſ. (91).
The nut of the cocoa-tree;—the mafs made by grinding the kernel of the cocoa-nut, to be diffolved in hot water; the liquor made by a folution of chocolate.

CHOCOLATE-HOUSE, tſhōk'ō-lāte-hōuſe. ſ.
A houfe for drinking chocolate.

CHODE, tſhōde.
The old preterit from Chide. Obfolete.

CHOICE, tſhōiſe. ſ.
The act of choofing; election; the power of choofing; care in choofing, curiofity of diftinction; the thing chofen; the beft part of any thing; feveral things propofed as objects of election.

CHOICE, tſhōiſe. a.
Select, of extraordinary value; chary, frugal, careful.

CHOICELESS, tſhōiſe'lēs. a.

...to menace, to cut into fmall pieces; to break into chinks.

To CHOP, tſhōp. v. n.
To do any thing with a quick motion; to light or happen upon a thing.

To CHOP, tſhōp. v. a.
To purchafe, generally by way of truck; to put one thing in the place of another; to bandy, to altercate.

CHOP, tſhōp. ſ.
A piece chopped off; a fmall piece of meat; a crack, or cleft.

CHOP-HOUSE, tſhōp'hōuſe. ſ.
A mean houfe of entertainment.
☞ Dr. Johnfon, in this definition, feems to have rated a chop-houfe too low, and to have had a *Cook's Shop* or an *Eating-houfe* in his mind. Since coffee-houfes are become eating-houfes and taverns, chop-houfes are, perhaps, a little depreciated; but this was not the cafe till long after Dr. Johnfon's Dictionary was publifhed; and I think they may fill, without any impropriety, be called reputable houfes of ready entertainment.

CHOPIN, tſhō-pēen'. ſ.
A French liquid meafure, containing nearly a pint of Winchefter; a term ufed in Scotland for a quart of wine meafure.

FIG. 1.2. Extract from John Walker's *Critical Pronouncing Dictionary* (1791)

'faulty grammar' in her novel *Camilla*. It was a natural extension within popular thinking for speech too to be placed—and perceived—within the same
parameters.

Certainly once the pronouncing dictionary had been instituted, demand for
the instruction it claimed to offer was high and, together with attendant texts
on the same subject, it too was seemingly assimilated within the consequences
of that 'consumer revolution' which has been illuminatingly documented by
the historians Neil McKendrick *et al.*[85] John Walker's *Critical Pronouncing
Dictionary*, for instance, went through well over a hundred editions, appearing
in a wide variety of formats over the late eighteenth and nineteenth centuries.
As Walker noted already in 1802, it had acquired a popularity which was difficult to satisfy: 'The rapid sale of the Second Edition of this Dictionary called
upon me for a Third, at a time of life, and in a state of health, little compatible with the drudgery and attention necessary for the execution of it'.[86] In this,
as in any other area, supply and demand were to be closely linked, and a public whose attitudes to language were often constructed in terms of prevailing
prescriptive (and fashionable) thinking, was likewise, according to contemporary accounts, also increasingly attuned to the validity and virtues of linguistic
correction which such works explicitly promoted. As William Johnston
affirmed as early as 1764, again encoding these stated affiliations of altruism
and prescriptive censure, 'many who labour under the disadvantages of a
wrong pronunciation, are so sensible of these things, as to have earnest desires
to acquire a right one: and for that end, may have kindly endeavoured to fur-
nish them with some suitable assistance'.[87]

Even individuals whose incomes precluded their purchase of these dictionaries in entirety (Walker's, for example, cost over a pound at a time when, as
Richard Altick confirms, the average salary of, say, an usher in a school was
only between four and eight shillings a week)[88] were to be made so aware of
their own inadequacies in this respect that they issued public demands for
more economical formats, or for separate and thereby cheaper publication of
the extensive descriptions of 'good' speech which tended to preface these
works. William Russel in 1801, for instance, earnestly importuned Walker in
precisely these terms, desiring a format for the *Critical Pronouncing
Dictionary* which would 'be portable with convenience' and priced so that it
did not prohibit access to those 'who cannot, without inconvenience, spare a
guinea'.[89] William Kenrick, among others, acceded to similar requests, publishing the original introduction to his *New Dictionary of the English Language*
(with the detailed instructions on 'proper' speech which this contained) as a
work in its own right in 1784 on the grounds that 'the expence of that work
[the original dictionary] must have for ever precluded its merits from being
generally known to those who stood most in need of it'.[90]

Of course, not all responses to the pronouncing dictionary as a social and
linguistic institution were unreservedly favourable. Dr Johnson for one had

serious misgivings about its potential utility as a means of standardization, at least in practical terms. As he pointed out, a pronouncing dictionary 'may do very well; but you cannot always carry it about with you: and, when you want the word, you have not the Dictionary'. Potential problems are further illuminated by a typically Johnsonian simile. 'It is', he adds, 'like a man who has a sword that will not draw. It is an admirable sword, to be sure: but while your enemy is cutting your throat, you are unable to use it'.[91] Though Russel, as we have seen, did campaign for a smaller version of Walker's dictionary 'so as to be portable with ease', thereby envisaging one solution to those more practical difficulties foreseen by Johnson, other writers made it clear that the proper use of works on pronunciation of this kind was not by any means to require their constant presence about the person. As they stress in their own claims for the processes of standardization which might be enacted on the spoken word, it was to be conscientious application rather than occasional reference which would ensure command of the 'proper' and non-localized accents which such dictionaries so eloquently offered their readers.

This is perhaps expressed with greatest clarity by the lexicographer and clergyman William Johnston in 1764 for, although not dismissing the use of his *Pronouncing and Spelling Dictionary* as a reference book to be consulted in moments of phonetic indecision, he makes it plain that a somewhat more regular engagement with the text is advised if the full benefits it offered were to be gained. Like Sheridan, he places due emphasis upon the agency of the dictionary, and the 'fixed and visible marks' of transcription, in facilitating the acquisition of a 'standard' accent:

I herein offer a help to the right Pronunciation of the english Language, whereby those who generally speak well, may with great facility, rectify their peculiar Improprieties, and by which, I sincerely think, the youth of Cornwall and Cumberland, of Scotland and Ireland ... may learn by themselves to pronounce english tolerably well; and by which, were they, after this, to reside for some time in London, their pronunciation might soon, become hardly distinguishable from that of the inhabitants.[92]

This rectification of regional 'error' is clearly not to be arrived at by mere consultation of the dictionary in moments of uncertainty. Instead, both text and dictionary proper were (at least ideally) to be worked through systematically, each and every word being articulated in accordance with the notation supplied until true propriety is, Johnston dictates, not only achieved but, in addition, fully assimilated. The recommended method is intensive but it will, the reader is assured, bring its own rewards:

Three quarters of an hour, employed in pronouncing words in this distinct manner, in the order in which they occur, would be a sufficient exercise at a time; for both the attention, and capacity for pronouncing well, will by that time generally flag: But in the interval of an hour or two, they will be revived again. And this exercise repeated two or three times in a day, as affairs will permit, for a month together, will carry you several times through the book, and give you a general knowledge and practice of a right pronunciation.[93]

Johnston is not alone in such specifications. *Live and Learn: A Guide for All Who Wish to Speak and Write Correctly*, a later text which went through twenty-eight editions in seventeen years, proffers similar counsel, recommending both patience and industry in its 'general advice to those who find themselves deficient in the art of pronunciation':

> Take, every morning, some passage from a good writer, poetry or prose; mark every letter and syllable with respect to which mistake is likely to occur, using a good dictionary in every case of the slightest uncertainty; pronounce each word several times by itself, and then go through the whole passage until you can read it correctly, in a graceful and natural manner, and with ease to yourself.
> N.B.—A great deal of care, as well as humility, is required for the discovery of one's own faults.[94]

Sheridan too envisaged application of similar thoroughness on the part of his readers. As he notes with reference to [h]-dropping, a shibboleth which he is—appropriately—the first writer to record in terms which reveal negative sensitization to its use: 'The best method of curing this will be to read over frequently all the words beginning with the letter *H* and those beginning with *Wh* in the dictionary, and push them out with the full force of the breath, 'till an habit is obtained of aspirating strongly'.[95] It was modes of usage on these lines, stressing methodical, dedicated, and practical deployment rather than incidental checking, which had of course initially led to Sheridan's belief in the value of the pronouncing dictionary as an agent of standardization for the spoken word. By individual industry, users of the dictionary would, he stressed, be able to eliminate those features—and their connotative values—which 'in a manner proclaim the place of a man's birth, which otherwise could not be known by other means in mixed societies'.[96]

'A Pronouncing Dictionary is almost a necessary appendage to every library',[97] declared the grammarian David Booth in 1837, and successive editions of such works were in fact brought out, the introductory principles of pronunciation which they contained being reduced, expanded, printed in miniature, printed in paper or hard covers, or condensed to their utmost essentials so that they might come within the means of every pocket. Moreover, in terms of the real import of this particular publishing phenomenon (and its linguistic consequences), it is important to recognize that private individuals were by no means to provide the only readership for such works. On the contrary, and further confounding Johnson's original scepticism on this matter, pronouncing dictionaries were often to become essential tools in educational institutions as elementary pupils were drilled in the requisite proprieties of speech whilst they learnt to read. The parsing of sounds in line with the principles used by Walker became, for example, a commonplace mode of instruction,[98] while familiarity with Walker's *Critical Pronouncing Dictionary* was often recommended by nineteenth-century government inspectors for teacher and pupil alike. 'The master should have at hand a good English dictionary (Walker's may be purchased for 4*s* 6*d*.) and not be afraid to make use of it in the presence of his pupils', as one such inspector advised.[99] Though this integration of pronunciation into educational methodology will be discussed in more detail in Chapter 7, the fact that the emergent national educational system was also to embrace these paradigms of norm and deviation with reference to accent difference is clearly not irrelevant at this stage. 'Talking proper', as we will see, was to be an educational desideratum too and the pronouncing dictionary by no means immaterial to its encouragement.

As the sociolinguist Ralph Fasold has stressed, authors of grammars and usage books naturally have an impact on language use only 'to the extent their work is consulted'.[100] Nevertheless, the extensive evidence over the nineteenth century of the deployment of such works on pronunciation, in both public and private forms, does, in a variety of ways, combine to suggest that their influence was potentially far from minimal, at least in terms of inculcating an awareness of these issues of correctness even if not (in real terms) in achieving the national accent for all to which many writers, as we have seen, had aspired. The prominence of such works—and the agendas they raised—was unquestioned. By the end of the nineteenth century, John Walker had, for example, become a household name so that manuals of etiquette could refer to those obsessed with linguistic propriety as trying to 'out-Walker Walker'.[101] Even Dickens could allude to Walker's dictionary (without further elaboration being necessary) in *Dombey and Son*, specifying this as part of the preferred reading of the highly erudite Miss Blimber (' "If my recollection serves me," said Miss Blimber, breaking off, "the word analysis, as opposed to synthesis, is thus defined by Walker . . . *Now* you know what analysis is, Dombey" ').[102] Like Johnson, Walker had in effect become one of the icons of the age, commonly referred to as 'Elocution Walker' just as Johnson had come to be labelled 'Dictionary Johnson' in the public mind. Contemporary references to Walker's influence are thus frequent, spanning a range from the relatively objective to the downright eulogistic. For Russel in 1801, the *Critical Pronouncing Dictionary* which constituted the most important of Walker's publications was no less than 'a glorious monument of human genius, manifesting, to his contemporaries and to posterity, a happy combination of persevering industry with extensive erudition'. It would, he averred with little apparent sense of his own hyperbole, 'perpetuate his name with more erudition, and more venerable regard, than if he had amassed stones and mortar to a greater degree of elevation and circumference equal to the pyramids of Egypt'.[103] Long after Walker's death in 1807, the same commendations continued. As another prolific lexicographer, Peter Nuttall, for instance, declared in 1873, 'the name of *WALKER*, as one of our earliest orthoepists, is known and duly appreciated wherever the English language is spoken'.[104] Such praise testifies to the enthusiasm generated towards issues of linguistic control with little room for doubt. Even if the phonetician Alexander Ellis, writing from a vantage point firmly within the new (and more objective) descriptivism of the later nineteenth century, censured the fallible assumptions of authority which Walker (and other writers) had so frequently assumed in this respect, he equally felt compelled to commend and acknowledge Walker's activities and influence. As a result, while Ellis's own inclinations as a linguist were antithetical to those of writers in the prescriptive tradition (not least in his attention to the actualities of usage and their linguistic import),[105] Walker was still given his due: 'Walker has done good and hard work; he has laid down rules, and hence given definite assertions to be considered, and he has undoubtedly materially influenced thousands of people who looked upon him as an authority'.[106]

From his own standpoint in America, the lexicographer Noah Webster was, even in the late eighteenth century, amazed at the veneration (and obeisance) which could popularly be exhibited towards these self-appointed arbiters of linguistic authority. Describing the rise of 'individuals, who dictate to a nation the rules of speaking, with the same imperiousness as a tyrant gives orders to his vassals', he marvelled at the servility which could result: 'strange as it may appear, even well-bred people and scholars, often surrender their right of private judgement to these literary governors. The *ipse dixit* of a Johnson, a Garrick, or a Sheridan, has the force of law, and to contradict it is rebellion'.[107] Notions of independence could, it seemed, indeed swiftly be surrendered in these terms, the raised linguistic consciousness advocated by Sheridan bringing in its wake corresponding insecurities and anxieties which various individuals earnestly sought to resolve. In spite of Johnson's reassurances that his accent was 'not offensive', James Boswell, for instance, nevertheless abdicated his own 'right of private judgement' in precisely this way to Sheridan himself (as well as to another elocutionist, Mr Love of Drury Lane). As a result, just as Sheridan's course of lectures had expounded the ways in which 'the attainment [of the London standard] is ardently desired by an infinite number of individuals',[108] so did Boswell take personal lessons from Sheridan in a stated attempt to 'improve' his own native tones.[109] The evidence of other individuals reveals the operation of similar processes of sensitization, duly corroborating the ways in which, as the writer and teacher William Cockin had perceptively observed in 1775, 'it appears ... that works of this nature may at least be as much service in teaching us to perceive as to execute'.[110] Sir Christopher Sykes in 1778, for example, thus earnestly sought a tutor for his offspring who would be qualified to eradicate their regional accent, a mode of speech which he evidently regarded as incompatible with any pretensions to status. Sykes too desired 'improvement' in these respects. As he wrote to the Reverend Cleaver: 'the person who has hitherto had the instruction of my children is going into another line of life, indeed he is no loss as he has done them all the good he is capable of, which was to teach them to read English though but ill'. His quest was instead for 'any young man you think fit to succeed him', the one specification being that such a tutor would be able to 'correct their Yorkshire tone'.[111]

The letters of the writer Maria Edgeworth similarly expose her own increasing awareness of features which, for earlier writers such as Swift, had not been interpreted in terms of either 'error' or unacceptability. Edgeworth, in contrast, comments on the linguistic 'problems' she faced in her visit to Liverpool, the old connotative dichotomies between capital and the rest of the country evidently having been enhanced in line with the newly normative views on that 'disgrace' which the use of regional markers of speech could bring in their wake. As she concluded after meeting with Mr Roscoe of Allerton Hall, 'a strong provincial accent. . .destroys all idea of elegance'.[112] 'Ridicule' must surely attend the use of 'broad Yorkshire or Somersetshire in the drawing room',[113] averred Mrs Elizabeth Montagu in a similar vein, betraying the parallel efficacy of language attitudes in her conviction that this conjunction was clearly incompatible.

Certainly thousands of people each year flocked to the lectures of Walker and Sheridan as they individually toured the country, expounding their theories on the new elegancies of speech. Mrs Sheridan in 1762, for example, affirmed the popularity of her husband's lectures with pride:

The Course of Lectures which Mr. Sheridan is now reading in the city is attended in a manner which shows the people more warm and earnest on the subject than can well be conceived; his auditory seldom consisting of less than five hundred people, and this is the utmost the hall will contain; many have been disappointed for want of room, and he is strenuously solicited to repeat the Course again immediately in the same place. This I believe he will comply with, though he is to give another Course next month at Spring Gardens.[114]

Lest this be interpreted as being merely the evidence of wifely partiality, the writer John Watkins in 1817 provided additional confirmation of such success: 'Incredible as it may seem, the fact is certain, that he had upwards of sixteen hundred subscribers, at a guinea each, besides occasional visitors, which, with the advantage arising from the publication of the course, at half-a-guinea in boards, must have rendered his emoluments very considerable'.[115]

Walker too received considerable commendation for his lectures, even being invited to give private seminars on elocution to the Heads of Houses and assorted Fellows in the University of Oxford following his more general lectures in the Sheldonian Theatre.[116] Even Oxford dons, it seemed, could suffer anxieties on this score.

Journals of the day also served to reinforce corresponding emphases for their own readers, devoting considerable space and attention to debating the rival claims of different modes of pronunciation as well as the rival merits of different pronouncing dictionaries. The *Critical Review* in 1796, for instance, commended the potential efficacy of William Smith's pronouncing diction-ary of 1795 in terms which effortlessly reinforced the propagated links between 'talking proper' and the social mobility that might result:

we have seen an eminent lawyer getting rid almost entirely of his Northern accents, and thus making his way to the highest post in his profession: and we can take upon our-selves to say, that, with equal care, the rest of his countrymen, and the inhabitants of Ireland, might be brought nearly upon a level with the best speakers in the metropolis.

As this review moreover indicates, such issues of 'standard' speech (based on London norms) were popularly also to be deemed relevant for Scotland. As the sub-text makes plain, a 'Northern accent' in these terms too could impede social progress and professional advance, evidently being con-structed as a localized marker unacceptable within these emergent ideologies of phonetic propriety. Walker's own perceptions of deficiency in this respect lead to similar endorsements of norm and deviation; the various editions of his *Critical Pronouncing Dictionary* all helpfully contained a separate section in order to aid 'the Natives of SCOTLAND' in 'attaining a just Pronunciation of English' (the following section proffered similar assistance to the 'Natives of IRELAND'). As Sylvester Douglas (Lord Glenbervie), another Scot, reveals in his own *Treatise on the Provincial Dialect of Scotland*, this was not, however, mere rhetoric. Instead, in a number of ways (and precisely as Sheridan had originally hoped), language attitudes and attendant ideologies of a standard did indeed often seem to exert equal influence over Britain as a whole. Douglas's subtitle ('being an attempt to assist persons of that country in dis-covering and correcting the defects of their pronunciation and expression') effectively confirmed the normative frameworks often applied. As he explained: 'By a provincial dialect is understood, not strictly the dialect pecu-liar to any particular province or district, but rather that of a whole country or district where the common language is spoken with a barbarous and clas-sical impurity'. Therefore, he argued, 'it matters not whether there subsists any political connection between such district and that in which the classical idiom prevails'.[117] In such terms 'the idiom peculiar to Scotland' was to be constructed as 'a provincial and vicious dialect of English', hence being par-ticularly open to the issues of correction and the hegemonies of England in linguistic as well as political ways.[118] 'There are I believe few natives of North-Britain, who have had occasion either to visit or reside in this coun-try [i.e. England], that have not learned by experience the disadvantages which accompany their idiom and pronunciation', as Douglas continues. Notions of norm and deviation are prominent, concisely revealed by the metalanguage deployed with reference to Scottish against English; if the latter is 'classical' and 'pure', the former is surrounded by perceptions of a style of speech which is both 'vicious' and 'barbarous'—and thus markedly negative in the connotations it conveys. The prevalence of conceptions of this kind (further reinforced by the fact that many popular writers on 'proper' pronunciation such as Johnston, Kenrick, Smith, Buchanan, and Elphinston were themselves Scots) would undoubtedly have lent additional impetus to Boswell's own desire for 'improvement' in the accents which he himself, as a native of Ayrshire, had originally employed. This, for example, was the main motive in the private lessons which Alexander Wedderburn, later Lord Loughborough, also requested from Sheridan, his main concern being 'to lose [his] Scots accents'.[119]

In real terms it was, of course, precisely this education in 'perception' and language attitudes which was to be of greatest significance, precisely in line with Sheridan's own arguments on the necessary raising of the linguistic consciousness in terms of speech. In this sense it is clear that ideologies of a 'standard' (and concomitant beliefs in the extra-linguistic values which this 'best' language might suggest) did indeed gradually come to affect people's views on 'talking proper' on a scale which, at least in terms of language attitudes, almost matched the images of linguistic convergence which were so persuasively urged by writers within the prescriptive tradition. It is this, for example, which evidently lies behind the patterns of sensitization so ably illustrated by Boswell or Sir Christopher Sykes, or by the many individuals such as George Grenville (the future Marquis of Buckingham) who likewise sought private tuition from Sheridan in the closing decades of the eighteenth century. It is equally this which later motivates the undoubted popularity of sixpenny manuals such as *Hard Words Made Easy* (1855), C.W. Smith's *Mind Your H's and Take Care of Your R's* (1866), or *How to Shine in Society* (1860), which were published in such abundance throughout the nineteenth century (texts which moreover explicitly addressed such messages to those in the middle and lower sections of society too). Supply in such instances is not only generated by demand but acts equally as an index to the changing sensibilities of the age, and to the dissemination of the ideology of standardization—the belief in the need to conform—even if not, in actual fact, being able to attest the degree of conformity in itself. It is in such terms that the diffusion of these ideas exhibits the most far-reaching effects.

Ideas of a spoken and non-localized 'standard' in this sense were to prove remarkably powerful. Over the course of the nineteenth century, images of a national harmony dependent upon, and generated by, a shared and uniform accent for all remained evocative, a means by which those speakers in possession of regionalized markers might be liberated from the 'defects' which, as a variety of writers combined to suggest, would otherwise hamper their progress through life. The writer Francis Newman in 1869 still, for example,

chooses to depict England in terms of an alliance of national honour and linguistic reform which is markedly familiar from texts of a century before.
England, he declares, is 'a nation which desires to eliminate vulgar provincial
pronunciation, to educate and refine its people'. By doing so, it will 'get rid
of plebeianism, and fuse the orders of society into harmony'.[120] Precisely as
in Sheridan's own aspirations for standardization and its social consequences, a non-localized accent is, in Newman's work, portrayed in terms
which still superficially adhere to egalitarian principles of 'improvement'
with reference to these specifically social sensibilities towards speech, even if
the chosen metalanguage is anything but egalitarian in its implications.
'Provincial' pronunciation is, in such terms, inherently 'vulgar' and hence an
unaccountable marker of the 'plebeian', a marker of negative status which
must be eradicated for the good of all. The processes of accent levelling can,
it seems, beneficially operate in one direction alone.

  Even if this was an agenda which was also frequently endorsed by
nineteenth-century educational policy as we shall see in Chapter 7, such
naive beliefs in the benefits of linguistic paternalism were in reality, however,
on the whole to prove misguided. Instead, as one system of 'odious distinctions', in Sheridan's words, was changed, another was of course gradually to
arise in its place, a shift which is already marked in the language adopted by
Edgeworth and Sykes, or by Boswell and Mrs Montagu, as well as by
Newman himself, in the sensitivities which they variously display towards
the spoken word. Perceptions of a 'standard' bring not only a sense of a dia-
metrically opposed 'non-standard' but also notions of a 'sub-standard' too,
one regularly constructed in terms of lack of 'elegance', or imputations of
'ridicule' and their own associated images of disadvantage. As this suggests,
the non-localized (and intentionally 'superior') accent which Sheridan and
others had advocated as an instrument of egalitarianism was not to become
a marker of the 'harmony' which had initially been desired. In contrast, as
later linguistic history would confirm time and time again, it was instead to
lead to the consolidation of one of the most potent social symbols in existence. As a result, while non-localized norms of speech did indeed succeed in
transcending indications of 'the place of a man's birth', just as Sheridan had
originally wished, they did so by placing prominence in terms of social
meaning on the possession of an accent without regional markings as a signifier of social level. In another enduring image of popular linguistic mythology, such speakers were 'accentless', speaking 'without an accent'—or at
least without one which proclaimed their regional origin. Images such as
these were themselves products of the nineteenth century, the normative
frameworks integral to such ideas transparent even in the first edition of the
OED where the definition of *accent* (provided by Alexander Ellis) equates it
with regionality and the 'mispronunciation of vowels and consonants' as well
as the 'misplacing of stress'. Regionalized speakers were, in consequence,

to be doubly proscribed—first by the fact of their localized forms of speech, and second by the widespread notion that such markers were incompatible with any sign of status at all.

It was to take Noah Webster, outside England, to state most clearly the potentially disadvantageous social side-effects which these notions of a spoken standard, as well as differential access to its norms, might indeed have. Resistant, as already indicated, to the mantle of authority which so many writers on the language willingly assumed, Webster exposed with ease the ostensible altruism, and misplaced egalitarianism, of prescriptive ideology in this context. Like Sheridan, he acknowledges that, at least in the ideal world, 'a sameness of pronunciation is of considerable consequence in a political view'.[121] In the real one, however, as he also contends, the outcome of such ideas is likely to be somewhat different. The inception of standards of 'good' speech, especially when described by means of differential social values ('provincial', 'vulgar', 'elegant', 'refined'), was, he rightly recognized, far more likely to foster than dispel the existing asymmetries of society. It would in effect provide new sets of inequalities rather than that harmony which Sheridan (and others) had initially proclaimed. As Webster duly pointed out:

While all men are on a footing and no singularities are accounted vulgar and ridiculous, every man enjoys perfect liberty. But when a particular set of men, in exalted stations, undertake to say 'we are the standards of propriety and elegance, and if all men do not conform to our practice, they shall be accounted vulgar and ignorant', they take a very great liberty with the rules of the language and the rights of civility.[122]

Webster here tellingly exposes the dangers evident within the values and value judgements which, in Britain, were so often to surround the pressures for conformity in terms of speech. Even Sheridan's professed altruism is, as we have seen, phrased in language which equates only one variety of English with 'good' speakers and the others with 'disgrace', 'vulgarity', or aesthetic demerit: 'Would it not contribute much to the ease and pleasure of society ... if all gentlemen in public meetings, or private company, should be able to express their thoughts ... with an utterance so regulated, as not to give pain to the understanding, or offence to the ears of their auditors', as he demanded in defence of a national accent in 1781.[123] The sub-text of norm and deviation, fundamental to prescriptive ideology, is all too clear in such claims, and Edgeworth and Mrs Montagu, as well as Boswell and Alexander Wedderburn, as we have seen, reveal all too well the individual consequences of these ideas. As Webster realized, articulating preconceptions of this order in the authority of printed texts was much more likely to strengthen than diminish any system of subjective inequality already in existence. 'An attempt to fix a standard on the practice of any particular class of people is highly absurd' as well as 'unjust', he adds in further condemnation from his own, more objective, vantage point in America.[124]

The 'perfect liberty' analysed by Webster, and employed as a prime linguistic ideal by Sheridan and others, could in reality rest only in the descriptive acknowledgement that all varieties of the language are equal, and that the same equality extends to their speakers and the linguistic variations which they deploy. Though this fact has become a staple of modern descriptive comment on language and linguistic variation, perceptions of this order were, however, rarely forthcoming in the late eighteenth century (and indeed over much of the nineteenth too). In contrast, formalizing one accent as 'better', and all others as indicative of 'disgrace', was inevitably to be inimical to equality of any kind. Prescriptive ideology in these terms, in spite of its professed egalitarianism, instead merely reinforces notions of the cultural hegemony of one social group above others, offering, as in the sociolinguist James Milroy's critique of notions of prestige in accounts of linguistic change, 'a conceptualization of sociolinguistic space that is unidimensional—a space in which the elite groups set the tone in language, dress and other cultural matters, and in which lower groups strive to imitate their lead'.[125] It was paradigms of this order which were, in reality, to be fundamental to much prescriptive writing, evident in the frequent exhortations for readers to emulate their 'betters' in linguistic terms and similarly to divorce their accents (and accompanying sociolinguistic identities) from the 'vulgar' and, by extension, from the localized too. One way of speaking is, in consequence, invariably privileged above all others with the result that the fictions of 'empowerment' which were proffered by Sheridan and others in this context are made to rest only in assimilation to this one variety—and not in the liberal recognition of the validity of other co-existing modes of speech. Entirely in keeping with ideologies of a standard, the aim was, of course, to displace heteroglossia with monoglossia, and to dispel existing variation by an intentionally invariant 'norm', an entity which was, as we have seen, frequently phrased in social terms which in themselves rely on complex images of language and disadvantage far removed from the issues of equality which are otherwise so enthusiastically proclaimed. Webster in 1789 thus exposes with particular clarity the weaknesses within the notions of linguistic 'liberty' which were regularly, and at times paradoxically, advanced in the drive to disseminate a non-localized norm of speech for all. Outside utopian visions in which the workings of prescriptive ideology in the form of a non-localized accent would serve to unify rather than divide the nation, reality was instead to intrude with a vengeance. Though a non-localized accent did indeed gradually appear, it was to remain the property of a minority of 'best' speakers. In such terms, it merely acted as a further marker of social distinction for those who succeeded in assimilating to its norms.

As this indicates, norms of correctness, regardless of how widely they are propagated (and indeed recognized), will rarely tell the whole story. That this is so should not, in itself, be surprising. Taking a simple pragmatic approach, for example, it is clear that even if writers in the prescriptive tradition had been in the fortunate position of being directly able to impose upon the language of their readers the non-localized norms which they prescribed, there would necessarily still have remained vast sections of the population who, by virtue of their illiteracy, would necessarily have been immune to their dictates. Pronouncing dictionaries and the mass of other publications devoted to the norms of speech were open books only to those who could read and, though estimations of literacy over the nineteenth century vary considerably, it seems reasonable to assume, with Altick, that it could not by any means have exceeded half the population by the early 1800s. As Altick adds moreover, even generalized estimations of this kind tell us nothing of the *quality* of literacy which such figures represent.[126] The ability to read a simple chapbook would scarcely guarantee enough facility to combat the elevated prose of a Sheridan or a Walker in their declarations of the need for national norms of speech. Though increased access to education over the nineteenth century meant that levels of literacy gradually rose, Sheridan's projected solution to the localized divisions of accent nevertheless continues to manifest a certain naivety in the face of social reality in the late eighteenth and nineteenth centuries. 'If a method of acquiring a just pronunciation by books, as well as conversation, were established, the acquisition would not be circumscribed within such narrow bounds, but would lie open to all British subjects wherever born',[127] as he had, somewhat optimistically, declared.

Moreover, even if problems of equal access to this information were somehow to be resolved, it is still clear that this would not necessarily encourage the uniform adoption of that 'best' accent advocated by Sheridan, Walker, Smart, and their many followers. Accent functions in reality as a social symbol which is, in a number of ways, far more complex than the favoured binary accounts of 'good' and 'bad' language over the eighteenth and nineteenth centuries tend to suggest. Instead its differences indicate far more than social status (or otherwise). It functions, for example, as a marker of group membership and as a signal of solidarity, being able to operate across the range of social groupings in society, signalling patterns of inclusion and exclusion, of 'belonging' and 'outsiders', which by no means operate solely with reference to speakers of the so-called 'best' English. In such terms, the 'talking proper' of one speaker may well be another speaker's 'talking posh' and hence a marker of affectation and pretension. As George Bernard Shaw would later explore in *Pygmalion*, while Eliza Doolittle unreservedly aspired to contemporary ideals of 'talking proper', fully aware of the social disadvantages which her native Cockney presented ('I want to be a lady in a flower shop . . . But they won't take me unless I can talk more genteel'), her father Alfred has other ideas. Translated from dustman to the status of 'gentleman' as a result of Henry Higgin's recommendation (to the American Ezra D. Wannafeller) that Alfred Doolittle is 'the most original moralist . . . in

England', his indignation at the expected linguistic consequences is clear. 'Now I'll have to learn middle class language from you instead of speaking proper English', he informs Higgins.[128] Images of 'talking proper' radically fail to coincide. As Alfred Doolittle is made to confirm, not everyone has the same values, and not everyone will by any means desire to assimilate to the norms specified as 'best', irrespective of the number of social and intellectual virtues with which such variants may theoretically be imbued. Society is not unidimensional even if prescriptive texts tended to assume—and suggest—that it was. Forms indicative of regional location, and of lower-status groups too, as modern sociolinguistic studies have often pointed out, instead have their own prestige and their own role within the functioning of group relationships and social networks. Similarly, as the continued absence of a non-localized accent for all of course reveals, accent loyalty of various kinds can and will impede uniform change in the direction of those norms which are theoretically proffered as the most prestigious.

The sociolinguist William Labov's late twentieth-century researches on the island of Martha's Vineyard, Massachusetts, aptly illustrate the ways in which speakers may, for instance, intentionally diverge from the variants deployed by those who are (at least overtly) the most statusful groups in society. Documenting a specific linguistic change by which, in this area, the use of centralized (and 'non-standard') enunciations of the diphthongs in words such as *rise, house* (i.e. [əɪ] and [əʊ] rather than [aɪ] and [aʊ]) seemed to be increasing, Labov's work serves to confirm the more emblematic roles which accent (and individual variables) can play within a speech community. Such centralized sounds were, he found, closely associated with the rural Chilmark fishermen of the island (the descendants of the original Yankee settlers); linguistic accommodation in these contexts, as Labov contends, hence tends to take on the social meanings of indigenousness and of 'belonging'. In the sound changes which he thus observed in progress on the island, it was these connotative values which were apparently (and increasingly) being privileged by certain speakers in their adoption of centralized forms. In this particular context, the non-centralized (and overtly more 'statusful') variants took on other—and more negative—values as a result of their strong association with the tourists from the mainland who, each summer, invade the island, outnumbering the residents themselves. In these terms, the use of centralized variants was evidently aligned with a positive view of island identity—and a rejection of the overtly statusful forms of those who, regardless of their formal tokens of prestige, are categorically viewed as 'outsiders' and as aliens in the real life of Martha's Vineyard. As Labov states, 'When a man says [rəɪt] or [həʊs], he is unconsciously establishing the fact that he belongs to the island; that he is one of the natives to whom the island really belongs'.[129] That this sound change in progress is away from overtly recognized norms is of course additionally significant; it acts in response to social pressures which operate on a local rather than a national level—a process which clearly indicates that the direction of linguistic change can and does run counter to the forms used by elite groups in society. Change in progress in Martha's Vineyard therefore neatly serves to expose another fiction (or fallacy) of the prescriptive tradition of the late eighteenth and nineteenth centuries whereby one accent (and one notion of prestige) tended to dominate the propagated images of convergence for all speakers alike.

As this suggests, in real terms it is heterogeneity rather than homogeneity, pluralism rather than the monolithic, which marks linguistic usage in a multidimensional society. This, rather than uniformity, is the normal state of language and, as language history reveals, all the prescription in the world will not necessarily change this fact, nor will it bring that national uniformity of usage for which its advocates in the late eighteenth and nineteenth centuries had hoped. Language, especially in its spoken forms, instead varies regionally, socially, and contextually as speakers modify aspects of their linguistic behaviour in keeping with the demands of register or style, formality or its converse. There are, in these terms, few absolutes in language as it is really used although, as we will see over the course of this book, such images readily proliferate in the schema of prescriptive texts and indeed in popular language attitudes too. Even a simple examination of prescriptive grammar is able to reveal the truth of this premise for, though Robert Lowth, for example, *pace* Walker, had 'gravely vindicated the rights of analogy',[130] revealing grammatical error in what had previously been acceptable, the common targets of prescriptive censure which resulted, such as the 'improper' use of *shall* or the preposition in final position, were nevertheless not eradicated. Their usage still persists, albeit, especially in the written language, occasionally being hemmed around with notions that they are somehow 'not quite right' or are, in some way, 'incorrect'. Similarly, proscriptions devoted to constructions such as *different to/ different from* have not resulted in the invariability which eighteenth- and nineteenth-century patterns of prescription intended. Both are still used (to the continued ire of those who thereby participate in the ongoing manifestations of the complaint tradition), though again usage is often framed by notions that one form is somehow 'better' than the other. In more formal (and especially written) circumstances, it is this perceived 'correct' use of language to which speakers may accordingly attempt to incline, while regularly disregarding such assumed proprieties in their ordinary speech.

The same precepts apply equally in terms of accent. The prescriptive principles espoused by Sheridan and others in their attempts to raise the linguistic consciousness in terms of speech act as a concise index to the assimilation of pronunciation within the concerns of codification and its own motivations to 'correct' the language. As we shall see, just as Lowth formalized a range of grammatical shibboleths to good effect, at least with reference to what people think about language even if not in terms of what they actually do (especially in less formal situations), so were writers on the spoken word to foster a similar set of markers whereby 'good' and 'bad' might be determined, and some sense of national standards of speech set upon 'proper' and intentionally 'ruled' foundations. Modern self-evaluation tests reveal the legacy of these ideas, regularly revealing people's responsiveness to notions of 'correct' English, even if such features are not consistently implemented in their ordinary speech. As the sociolinguist Peter Trudgill's data on linguistic usage in late twentieth-century Norwich makes clear,[131] speakers can be very aware of the notionally 'proper' variants of speech such as the presence of [h] in words such as *house*, or not dropping the 'g' in words such as *walking* (variants which, as we shall see, rise to prominence as indices of 'correctness' over the course of the late eighteenth and nineteenth centuries). Nevertheless they will not necessarily adopt these forms in everyday usage. Self-evaluation tests (in which speakers are asked to evaluate their own speech) further confirm these skewed patterns of belief and actual behaviour with reference to language attitudes and language in use. As the sociolinguist Ronald Wardhaugh has commented, 'such tests seem to tap what speakers believe are the norms that operate in society', exposing language attitudes with more clarity than they do the actual usage of the speakers concerned.[132]

Sheridan's initial aims had, of course, been to change and to inform habits of mind together with habits of speech, to raise the 'consciousness' as well as to point out error and to specify norms. It was, in the end, the former which was ultimately created with most success—'consciousness', an 'idea in the mind', a set of beliefs surrounding the emerging and non-localized 'received pronunciation'. Linguistic reality, and the actualities of ordinary usage, could conversely remain at some remove from the often monolithic implications of such ideas, especially as far as the majority of the population were concerned. As pronunciation increasingly became a national status symbol, if not a symbol of the national harmony originally envisaged, it was convergence of this kind, in terms of belief if not always in behaviour, which was therefore to be most successful. 'The common standard dialect is that in which all marks of a particular place and residence are lost, and nothing appears to indicate any other habits of intercourse than with the well-bred and well-informed, wherever they may be found',[133] stated the lexicographer and elocutionist Benjamin Smart in 1836, confirming (and encoding) this shift in perception in general terms, as well as illustrating prevalent perceptions of the 'accentless' ideal which was to dominate many accounts of pronunciation over this time.

Prescriptive texts therefore at times need to be interpreted with some caution. Engaged in a rhetoric which regularly favoured binary oppositions of 'good' and 'bad' against the complex realities of language in use, this is of course writing with an agenda, one which often manifestly desired to see certain states of language come into being, and others disappear. To take such writings at face value is thus potentially to expose oneself to error in the real terms of the language and language practices of the past. Even accounts of [h]-usage, a prominent area of debate at this time, readily reveal the fictions and fallacies which can be at stake—and the manipulations which can, both overtly and covertly, be exerted upon those who read and used relevant texts in search of due illumination. Alfred Leach, for example, a writer who devoted an entire volume to the linguistic proprieties of [h], deliberately configured all 'good' speakers as invariably [h]-full (the non-localized norm), and all 'bad' ones as [h]-less in a popular binarism which simultaneously invokes a clear (if fallible) morality of language and speech. This was, of course, undoubtedly intended to exert its own persuasions upon those who consulted his book. Mapping simple equations of 'standard' or otherwise, 'good' and 'bad', on to the patterns which result, Leach was explicit on the social divide which such distinctions of usage conveyed. 'As the chemist employs a compound of sulphur in order to decide whether a substance belongs to the group of higher or baser metals, so does society apply the H-test to unknown individuals, and group them according to their comportment under the ordeal', he states, duly emphasizing the inevitable correlates of (social) acceptability—and its converse.[134] Yet in the real and quantitative terms of linguistics, such notions are again myths, highly effective in the ideology of standardization and its favoured absolutes but not borne out to the same extent in its processes where, contrary to the images manipulated by Leach, speakers of all social groups will instead use varying percentages of [h] in response to the situational variables of formality, or the speaker variables of status, gender, or age. In their more formal language, for example, all speakers regularly tend to use higher frequencies of those variants—such indeed as [h]—which are perceived to be most 'statusful', responding in such patterns of style shifting to normative pressures which operate above levels of conscious social awareness. Conversely, in more informal styles such frequencies diminish. While language itself will therefore commonly display these complex patterns of what is known as co-variation, ideologies of standardization will, on the other hand, instead manifest popular patterns of binary absolutes: 'good', 'bad', 'right', 'wrong', 'prestigious', 'vulgar', '[h]-fullness', '[h]-lessness'. It is these in which people tend to believe, in spite of all empirical evidence to the contrary. It is in such terms, as in those adopted by Leach, that national norms (and stereotypes) of speech as well as speaker did indeed commonly come to exist, triggering remarkably homogenous reactions all over the country, even if the heterogeneities of actual usage were inevitably at some removes from such reductive accounts of language in use—and the social meanings, and social identities, which were thereby assumed to be conveyed.

The true sense of a 'standard' is, as a result, perhaps best understood in the terms selected by the linguists James Milroy and Lesley Milroy: 'an idea in the mind rather than a reality—a set of abstract norms to which actual usage will conform to a greater or lesser extent'.[135] Whereas ordinary users of the language will, as in the models outlined above, regularly give credence to the idea of inviolable norms of 'good' usage (often discrediting their own habitual linguistic behaviour in the process and thereby subscribing to the notions of an absolute 'standard' on the lines preferred by Sheridan so long ago), in the real world language will vary, as already indicated, in rather more complex ways. Even Received Pronunciation (RP), contrary to much popular belief, is far from monolithic and, as one would expect, it too favours heterogeneity above the ideals of uniformity so regularly propagated over the course of the eighteenth and nineteenth centuries.[136] This evident dichotomy which can therefore exist between *patterns* of usage and *attitudes* to usage clarifies what can be seen as the skewed operation of standardization in its two-fold operation as both process and ideology—as well as illuminating more precisely the nature of the long-lasting legacies of prescriptivism. As Milroy and Milroy affirm, it was in fact these more ideological aspects of standardization which were to be most widely established over the course of the eighteenth century, creating the extensive awareness of a set of notions governing 'good' and 'bad' usage, together with corresponding assumptions about 'standard', 'substandard', and 'non-standard', to which, as they add, 'nearly every speaker now subscribes in principle'.[137] It is precisely this set of differences which, at the end of the nineteenth century, the phonetician Henry Sweet was also, with particular acuity, to stress as relevant as he sought to expose the fictions and the facts which had come to surround a spoken standard by that time. 'Remember that language exists only in the individual, and that such a phrase as "standard English pronunciation" expresses only an abstraction', he exhorted his readers in 1890.[138]

What is, in effect, created by such preoccupations is a national speech community on the more abstract lines of that later discussed by William Labov: 'The speech community is not defined by any marked agreement in the use of language elements, so much as by participation in a set of shared norms [which] may be observed in overt types of evaluative behaviour'.[139] It is the hegemonic role of the standard which thus tends to be most apparent. As John Barrell has noted in this context: 'the language of Britain ... was seen and was used as a means of impressing on the inhabitants of the country the idea of their unity, while at the same time it could be used (as it still is, of course), as a means of confirming ... the divisions it pretended to heal'.[140] That this is so is, as we shall see, all too prominent in the language used of and about the nuances of that 'proper' speech which was ideally to be adopted by all. Social stigma, social prejudice, the 'homogenizing aspirations for gentility' discussed by the historians Stone and Stone,[141] the social insecurities of the middling sections of society, all form recurrent frames of reference within these attempted delineations of 'good' against 'bad' English. Whether manifested in passive or active terms, perceptions of the norms of speech, and of the embedded social values which these came to contain were gradually to change. As we shall see, non-localized patterns founded in emulation of 'good' London speech were increasingly recognized as the standard to be attained, and paradigms of exclusion (and exclusivity) were, in turn, increasingly predicated upon the ways in which one chose to speak.

2

Accent as Social Symbol

'A standard is that by which we ascertain the value of things of the same kind; so a standard weight is that by which we try the justness of all other weights',[1] wrote the author and theologian William Enfield in the influential treatise on language which he published in 1809. In popular (as well as prescriptive) beliefs, a standard variety—of pronunciation as much as anything else—was similarly to incorporate evaluative mechanisms of this order though the relevant values were, in connotative terms, rarely to be those of language alone. Extralinguistic images of 'elegance', 'propriety', 'politeness', and 'refinement' are regularly accorded to its use as well as extended to its users. Images of 'class' and 'status', 'vulgarity' or 'incorrectness', frequently surround the act of speech. Evaluation, in contexts such as these, tends to take on the nature of social response, fusing with the prejudices and preconceptions of society in its own notions of what is 'good' and 'bad', 'right' or 'wrong'.

As this suggests, what tends to emerge from the appeals of Sheridan and others in their drive to raise the linguistic consciousness in terms of accent is not that 'doctrine of appropriate usage'—the expectation, and understanding, that features of language will vary according to context and situation—which typifies later, more objective, and descriptive accounts of language. Instead theoretical prominence is placed on what has come to be known as the 'doctrine of subjective inequality', a precept which, as the sociolinguist Richard Hudson points out, deliberately abdicates objective (and verifiable) criteria of linguistic inequality such as might, for example, be founded on the absence of appropriate communication skills or discoursal responses. The doctrine of subjective inequality in contrast operates in terms of language attitudes, on what 'people *think* about each other's speech'. As he adds:

In some societies (but by no means all) people are credited with different amounts of intelligence, friendliness and other such virtues according to the way they speak, although such a judgement based on speech may be quite wrong. Consequently, whatever virtues are highly valued, some speakers are thought to have more of them than they really have, simply because they have the 'right' way of speaking, and others are thought to have less because their speech conveys the wrong impression.[2]

It is this principle which lies, for instance, behind the use of subjective reaction tests in modern sociolinguistic studies. Initially developed by social psychologists, such tests have proved remarkably informative about sociolinguistic stereotypes in the speech community and the ways in which, as Hudson notes, speakers are willing to 'use the speech of others as a clue to non-linguistic information about them, such as their social background and even personality traits like toughness or intelligence'.[3] In the attitudes to speech (and speakers) which such studies therefore reveal, RP users of 'proper' English, for instance, have traditionally been credited with greater levels of intelligence, authority, and self-confidence. Irrespective of their actual personality traits, speakers with rural accents are conversely often assumed to be more friendly, more sympathetic, and more good-natured, as well as less authoritative. It is equally principles and stereotypes of this order which writers in the late eighteenth and nineteenth centuries were to attempt to codify in terms of the standardizing ideology, making explicit perceived affiliations of accent and power (or powerlessness) and willingly specifying the aesthetic and intellectual affinities which given accents, and even individual sounds, might be assumed to possess. Such notions of subjective inequality (and their associated sociocultural images) were made to inform the stated impulses both to codify, and to conform to, the canons of 'talking proper'.

Eighteenth- and nineteenth-century accounts of accent tend to discuss the repercussions of such attitudes with what can now appear as a striking lack of reserve. 'Vulgarity', for example, materializes as a highly effective epithet of prescriptive censure, regularly applied in the intent to eliminate pronunciations deemed improper. Though not unknown before in the application of appropriate linguistic tenets (John Hart, as we have seen, writes his *Orthographie* in the intent to enable the 'rude countrie Englishman' to gain knowledge of the 'better' English of the day), the emphasis and tenor of later comments again differ significantly. 'Let him who would polish his pronunciation be very attentive to these remarks', warned the grammarian P. Walkden Fogg in 1796, for example, in his directives on the art of 'good' enunciation: 'without abiding by the regular sound of letters...his discourse will appear vulgar'.[4] Accent is overtly manipulated as an image of the speaker's inner qualities, value judgements such as these readily being employed in order to encourage the convergent behaviour desired. To be 'vulgar', in the influential terms of John Walker's *Critical Pronouncing Dictionary*, was to be 'plebeian, suiting the lower people ... mean, low'. The gloss Walker provides for 'mean' makes the pejorative effects still clearer: 'wanting dignity, of low rank or birth; low-minded, base, despicable; low in the degree of any property, low in worth'. As Börje Holmberg affirms, vulgarity was in such ways to be a major prescriptive weapon, frequently applied to variants which, for one reason or another, were regarded with disfavour within prevailing tenets of correctness.[5] Not for nothing does Walker proclaim that he is the first writer to include the word 'vulgarism' in the lexicographical contexts of the dictionary ('This word is in no dictionary that I have met with, but seems sufficiently authorised both in writing and conversation to entitle it to a place in a repository of the English language').[6]

With reference to the spoken language, such images of vulgarity (and its converse) become almost a commonplace of comment on pronunciation. It is, for example, pronunciation which 'distinguishes the educated reader and speaker from the vulgar and uneducated one',[7] as the elocutionist George Vandenhoff stressed in 1862. Two years later, the prolific writer on usage (and Dean of Canterbury), Henry Alford, condemns [h]-dropping in precisely the same terms: 'a vulgarism . . . common throughout England to persons of low breeding and inferior education'.[8] 'A person who uses vulgarisms will make but little way in good circles', the anonymous author of *Talking and Debating* similarly averred,[9] giving ample details of the social consequences which might ensue. Language, as such comments indicate, was regularly to be described and, perhaps more particularly, proscribed in terms of its attendant social meanings and the correlations which were proclaimed to hold between variant and social value.

Paradigms of 'beauty' and 'ugliness' also make their due appearance within the prescriptive metalanguage of the time, further amplifying these resonances of the standard ideology for the spoken word. Though these too can be seen to have a long history in terms of language attitudes (see, for example, Ranulph Higden's outright condemnation of Yorkshire English in the fourteenth century on the grounds that it was 'so sharp slitting frottyng & vnshappe/ that we sothern men may vnneth vunderstande that langage'), relevant specifications—and social consequences—in the late eighteenth and nineteenth centuries can again be seen to take on an unprecedented level of detail and response. The Scottish lexicographer William Johnston in 1764 duly points out the '*grating* sounds' of provincial discourse for the edification of his readers; more 'elegant' equivalents such as those used in the intentionally invariant (and metropolitan) 'standard' are, he recommends, to be adopted in their stead.[10] Likewise, for James Buchanan, forms presented as deviating from those he prefers to document and, in turn, disseminate, are not only 'rough' and 'unpleasant' but also 'vicious', with all its eighteenth-century connotations of that 'depravity of manners' which Dr Johnson had specified in his dictionary.[11] The aesthetic appeal of the 'standard' receives corresponding emphasis in ways which are evidently designed to appeal to the aural as well as social sensibilities of speakers. Whereas for Sylvester Douglas provincial articulations are liable to be 'awkward' and, still worse, 'ludicrous' (another term of linguistic condemnation favoured by Johnson in his *Dictionary*), the 'best' speech of the capital is instead depicted as redolent of polish and of ease.[12] In a parallel way, John Murdoch emphasizes the desirability, as well as the 'politeness', of his stated 'standard' of speech, focusing on its role as 'an essential part of a genteel and liberal education'.[13] The 'provincial' is, from every perspective, constructed as distinctly unacceptable, a perception frequently enforced, for example, upon the Cornish artist John Opie in the late eighteenth century. Educated at the local village school in Truro, and born into a family of carpenters, Opie bore all the marks of the 'provincial', being 'regarded as a curiosity in London [society]' in spite of his undoubted talents as a portrait painter. Commissioned to paint the Duke and Duchess of Gloucester, as well as Lady Salisbury and many other ladies of the court, Opie remained, as *DNB* records, the 'Cornish wonder'— a crude and rude genius who possessed not only artistic ability but also 'a strong Cornish accent and appalling table manners'.[14]

Such attitudes placed the emphasis firmly on the normative, validating prevalent notions of the inherent value of one form of English and simultaneously confirming the perceived subordinacy of other modes of usage. The foundations of a number of long-standing cultural stereotypes about both accent and identity are widely apparent. Perhaps predictably therefore, dominant images of 'culture' often operated in a similar way. Just as in modern English the 'cultivated voice' can still emerge as a popular collocation for the collective nuances of 'talking proper', so do texts in the eighteenth and nineteenth centuries frequently endorse the potentially emblematic roles of accent in this context too. Culture, signifying both style of life and style of mind, is presented as an integral aspect of the 'received' standard of speech which is delineated by such writers. Benjamin Smart, for instance, an elocutionist and popular writer on pronunciation, develops the binary oppositions favoured by the prescriptive tradition into a series of contrasts which are specifically founded upon an idealization of the 'cultivated speaker' set against the stated improprieties of the 'vulgar' and evidently uncultured one. 'The cultivated speaker employs a definite number of sounds which he utters with precision, distinctness, and in their proper places; the vulgar speaker misapplies the sounds, mars or alters them', he states, the contrast undoubtedly setting up its own prescriptive persuasions for the many readers of Smart's work.[15] 'Cultivation', glossed by Walker in 1791 as 'the art of improvement and melioration', was almost inevitably therefore to exclude the provincial where words were spoken in a way untainted, and hence 'unimproved', by the ostensibly rational dictates of prescriptivism. 'Mere provincialisms have no place in cultivated speech', as an 1885 *Handbook of Pronunciation* confirmed,[16] specifying still further—in an extension of Darwinism—that, since it is language which differentiates man as superior to other species, so it can only be the 'best' language, and particularly the 'best' accent, which makes plain in him the realization of this superior potential:

Language is the chief of those attainments which distinguish man from the lower animals. The perfection and grace with which one speaks his mother tongue, is justly regarded as an index of his culture and associations. We instinctively gauge the cultivation of men by their pronunciation, as well as by their spelling and grammar.[17]

William Phyfe makes the same equations even clearer even if, in doing so, his argument appears to operate in a somewhat cyclic fashion: 'Since cultivated

people are, in general, presumed to speak accurately, accuracy in pronunciation comes naturally to be regarded as a sign of culture, and there is, therefore, a tendency to imitate the pronunciation of the cultured classes.'[18] In a
book aimed, as Phyfe's title page indicates, at schools and colleges (as well as
being intended for private use), such value judgements were moreover
enshrined as facts to be learnt and, in turn, implemented. Accent 'is the best
prima-facie evidence of general culture', Phyfe asserts still more categorically; 'on this account it appeals to all'. As he further expounded on this subject, 'it alone forms the stepping stones to a more liberal culture'.[19] Culture
itself, as such comments confirm, was thus popularly portrayed as both
monolithic and unidirectional, filtering down from the higher to the lower
sections of society. Only the cultural affiliations of elite groups were validated. For those lower in the social hierarchy, culture—and its associated
markers—was assumed to be non-existent and hence in need of careful
acquisition. Convergence, yet again, was mapped on to a top-down model,
working within a culture of emulation.

Notions of educatedness participate in the same process so that, in
another development of the prescriptive metalanguage of the time, speakers
were—entirely irrespective of the actual facts of educational background or
more objective estimations of intelligence—regularly presented as 'ignorant'
or 'illiterate', 'educated' or 'uninformed' in evaluative paradigms based
purely on the ways in which their words were pronounced. Such stereotypes
can still, of course, prove pervasive in popular attitudes to accent, the superficialities of articulation being interpreted, in relevant (if flawed) formulations, as an image of intellect, and indeed as a sign of intelligence itself. The
printed texts of the late eighteenth and nineteenth centuries are, however, if
anything still more overt in their accounts of the affinities which were
assumed to pertain to speech in this way. 'Language, both oral and written,
is an exponent of the condition of the mind; when mean and inappropriate it
infers that the habits of life and the condition of mind are equally mean and
uncultivated' averred, for example, the Reverend D. Williams in 1850.[20] 'It is
certain that nothing marks more quickly a person's mental and social status
than his practice in this regard', Phyfe stressed in a similar vein.[21] Notions of
educatedness (or their converse) could seem inseparable from the articulatory habits adopted, assumptions which in turn confirm a particularly long
heritage for the stereotypes which surround the modern collocation of the
'educated accent'. As the axiom provided by Charles Hartley in *Everyone's
Handbook of Common Blunders in Speaking and Writing* plainly states: 'If bad
spelling is generally the sign of an *imperfect* education, certainly nothing
more shows the want of education or of good association than incorrect pronunciation, and there is nothing more difficult to avoid being noticed or to
disguise'.[22] It was, it seemed, 'manner' and not 'matter' which was popularly
(if erroneously) accorded the primary role in such notions of intellectual

achievement, as well as of social refinement, a correlation which had in fact already been evident in Sylvester Douglas's observations on the deleterious effects of a Scots accent in the late eighteenth century: 'In the pulpit, at the bar, or in parliament, a provincial phrase sullies the lustre of the brightest eloquence, and the most forcible reasoning loses half its effect when disguised in the awkwardness of provincial dress'.[23] Irish apparently fared little better, negative language attitudes in this respect being well established even in the days of Swift. In London, as the latter recorded with some feeling, 'what we call the *Irish brogue* is no sooner discovered, than it makes the deliverer in the last degree ridiculous and despised'.[24] Language attitudes of this kind presumably underpin John Walker's detailed instructions to 'the NATIVES of IRELAND in order to obtain a just Pronunciation of English', as well as contributing to the number of Irish writers—such indeed as Thomas Sheridan—who attempted to reform the pronunciation of English as a whole in the direction of a defined and codified standard.

Such evaluative patterns, as the linguist Leonard Bloomfield later indicated in 1927, rest on the central premise that an 'ignorant' person simply does not know the correct forms of language. Rather than taking account of the more complex sociosymbolic roles played by accent and language in terms of group membership, and the ways in which such patterns may signal social solidarity (or otherwise) with various groups in a multidimensional society, the assumption is not that speakers may simply prefer—as do those of Martha's Vineyard[25]—to diverge from those features deemed 'correct' in the wider speech community. Instead, popular interpretations of this phenomenon tend to rely on notions that 'in the process of education, one learns the correct forms and, by practice and an effort of will ("careful speaking") acquires the habit of using them. If one associates with ignorant speakers, or relaxes the effort of will ("careless speaking"), one will lapse into the incorrect forms'.[26] Images of education and correctness fuse and, though obviously flawed as a linguistic model, such premises tend nevertheless to be markedly effective in terms of popular language attitudes, often still leading speakers to devalue their own speech forms in preference to these variants deemed more redolent of 'educated' status—regardless of the levels of education which, in reality, they themselves may more objectively have attained.

Assumptions of this order, however damaging they may be in terms of individual self-esteem, reveal of course the wider consequences of that ideology of standardization which, as we have seen in Chapter 1, was consciously and deliberately inculcated in terms of a range of aspects of 'talking proper'. Images of culture, education, intelligence, or vulgarity emerge as part of such preoccupations, deeply embedded in the set of beliefs (and its associated and extensive metalanguage) by which this particular phase of standardization may be recognized, as well as providing an additional index by which its evolution may be traced. The fostering of sensibilities of this order documents, in other words, the specific patterns of discrimination which evolve towards variations in speech (and their users) which had previously been regarded with acceptance, as well as revealing newly perceived notions of stigma which come to be articulated in social as well as linguistic terms. It similarly also serves to trace the operation of an accompanying set of sociocultural stereotypes (the 'lady', the 'gentleman', the 'parvenu', the 'Cockney', the 'aspiring middle class') to which we shall return but which, in this context, are clearly significant in both prescriptive and sociolinguistic terms.

Stereotypes are, for example, often fundamental to language attitudes and to their study. They act, as J. C. Wells confirms, as 'simplified and standardized conceptions of kinds of people, conceptions which we share with other members of our speech community',[27] tapping into prevalent myths of identity—aspirational or otherwise. In terms of stereotypes which are positively coded, they can be highly effective in the images of convergent behaviour which they deploy, serving to bring salient characteristics of behaviour (including linguistic behaviour) well above levels of conscious social awareness. And as many prescriptive writers were well aware, contemporary stereotypes such as the 'Cockney' which took on markedly negative resonances could be equally effective in prescriptive rhetoric, often being employed to give additional impetus to the dissuasions which were regularly mapped on to certain sounds. The widespread deployment of such stereotypes—both positive and negative—within the prescriptive metalanguage of the late eighteenth and nineteenth centuries is, as a result, of particular and wide-ranging interest. As the linguist Roger Bell has noted, for instance, prescriptive rules in this sense can offer much of value to the sociolinguist for they 'embody formulations of attitudes to language use which, even if ignored in practice by users, are indicators of social views of "correctness" that influence such behaviours as stereotyping and hypercorrection: both important variables in style-shifting'.[28] Popular language attitudes in the eighteenth and nineteenth centuries are, in consequence, naturally informative in their own right, playing on notions of identity (in both positive and negative terms) which can achieve wide diffusion throughout society.

The fact that social meanings were conveyed, either inadvertently or intentionally, by the modes of speech employed is, as the range of comments already cited has indicated, brought into considerable prominence in much writing on pronunciation which appeared from the late eighteenth century onwards. As Thomas Sheridan had specified of that still largely localized standard which he sought to diffuse throughout the nation, since this was so closely associated with the speech of the 'best' society in London, it was able to operate as a social testimony, 'a sort of proof that a person has kept good company'. Capable of being 'acquired only by conversing with people in polite life', it was, he stated, 'on that account sought after by all, who wish to be considered as fashionable people, or members of the beau monde'.[29] Sheridan thereby deploys his own brand of rhetorical persuasion in order to draw on the specifically *social* meanings of 'talking proper', images given prominence time and time again in an age seemingly fascinated by prescriptive ideology and the growing sense that accent could operate as a prime vehicle for social identity.

The differences which pertain between earlier and later accounts of pronunciation are again marked in this respect. Though Christopher Cooper had a section in his seventeenth-century *English Teacher* which was, for instance, deliberately devoted to the topic of 'Barbarous Speaking', this was, however, merely a list setting forth enunciations of various words incompatible with the 'best dialect', such as *chimly* for *chimney*, *dud* for *did*. It did not, as does Benjamin Smart's later account of 'barbarous speaking' in 1810, present them in terms of a system of social alignments which were expressly designed to trade on the social sensibilities (and sociolinguistic insecurities) of his readers:

There are two pronunciations even in London, that of the well-bred, and that of the vulgar; and the difference does not consist merely in the various manner of pronouncing particular words, but often with the latter in a corruption of fundamental sounds. In short, it is owing to the one being cultivated, and the other neglected. The cultivated speaker employs a definite number of sounds which he utters with precision, distinctness, and in their proper places; the vulgar speaker misapplies the sounds, mars or alters them.[30]

Smart's polarization of the differentials of breeding and birth sets up paradigms of accent and advantage, or conversely disadvantage, which are fundamentally alien to the accounts of speech which were provided by Cooper and his contemporaries in the seventeenth century. It is the shift in mindset (as well as linguistic methodology) which remains most striking. As William Enfield, author of the highly popular *Speaker*, duly specified: 'these faults [of provincial enunciation], and all others of the same nature, must be corrected in the speech of a gentleman, who is supposed to have seen too much of the world, to retain the peculiarities of the district in which he was born'.[31]

Aligning social exclusivity with the exclusion of specifically regional markers from speech, both Enfield and Sheridan, as well as Smart, give voice to the socially normative ways in which the attempted standardization of the spoken language, and specifically of pronunciation, was to be carried out. Retaining marks of the regional was deemed deleterious to gentlemanly (and superior) status, just as assimilation to the characteristics of the 'best' London speech was in turn to suggest inclusion within the ranks of the 'received'. Within the frameworks of much prescriptive writing, and the attitudes to the language which they encode, each utterance becomes in effect an act of identity, locating the user within social space by means of the variables employed. In such terms, a non-regional accent was promoted as a marker not only of linguistic purity but of social precedence, a correlation which was firmly established by the mid-nineteenth century. As *How to Shine in Society* affirmed for its own aspiring readers, deploying a set of particularly evocative social stereotypes as it did so, prominent social icons such as ladies and gentlemen were to be recognized by their 'purity of accent' which 'belongs to no city or district'.[32] The inference that regionalized or other unacceptable variants betray those who do not fall within these categories is of course the other half of this equation. 'Behind every norm there is a value', states the sociolinguist William Downes,[33] and in prevailing conceptions of nineteenth-century propriety, social and linguistic hegemony were therefore to operate in parallel, validating selected aspects of elite culture in ways which, as many writers stress, were assumed to hold no little appeal for a society frequently characterized—as by the writer on political economy Nathaniel Forster in 1767—by the 'perpetual restless ambition in each of the inferior ranks to raise themselves to the level of those immediately above them'.[34] The author and social reformer Samuel Smiles made the same point. From this point of view, English society was, it seemed, unremittingly inspired by 'the constant struggle and pressure for seats in the front seats of the social amphitheatre'—a sense in which the ideals of 'lady' and 'gentlemen', as we shall see in Chapter 5, were, at least potentially, open to all. And this culture of emulation readily extended its own encouragement in terms of acquiring the requisite arts of speech, especially given the social resonances with which the spoken word was, as we have seen, increasingly endowed.

Images of social mobility and social advance are, for instance, often explicitly made to surround specifications for convergent behaviour in speech. As W. H. Savage stressed in 1833, for example, it was the ability to use 'correct' rather than 'incorrect' language which was itself to be 'the talisman that will enforce admiration or beget contempt; that will produce esteem or preclude friendship; that will bar the door or make portals fly open'.[35] Attention to accent was vital, so the new canon went, in the course of any social metamorphosis, a reminder frequently issued in the context of another prevalent stereotype of the nineteenth century, that of the 'new rich'.[36] *Talking and Debating*, as we have seen, adopted a similar point of view. Pronunciation, provided it demonstrated the requisite proprieties, was to be the 'passport to new circles of acquaintance',[37] breaking down the barriers which infelicities of speech would otherwise merely continue to reaffirm. Agendas of social aspiration (and the fraught issues of acceptability) take on a marked prominence in such discussions. As *Vulgarities of Speech Corrected* (1826) noted, here with reference to [h]-dropping:

This is a very common mistake among many who have, by industry or good fortune, risen above their original station and prospects, and therefore imagine, very mistakingly, that they are entitled to take their place with the well bred and the well educated. They may do so, without doubt, on the influence of their money or property, but they will infallibly expose themselves to be laughed at and ridiculed, by those whose reading and education enable them to see their low expressions, vulgar pronunciations, and continual blunders in grammar.[38]

Texts such as *Hints on Etiquette and the Usages of Society*, a highly popular work which went through nineteen editions in five years, effortlessly reinforced the same message for its own readers. Though social mobility was by no means rare in nineteenth-century society, in the stated terms of prescriptive ideology (and the hegemonies of the 'best' English which this often endeavoured to exert), it is clear that appropriate advances must be made in manners as well as material possessions in order to secure the intended rise in social level:

in a mercantile country like England, people are continually rising in the world. Shopkeepers become merchants, and mechanics manufacturers; with the possession of wealth they acquire a taste for the luxuries of life, expensive furniture, and gorgeous plate; also numberless superfluities, with the use of which they are only imperfectly acquainted. But although their capacities for enjoyment increase, it rarely occurs that the polish of their manners keeps pace with the rapidity of their advancement: such persons are often painfully reminded that wealth alone is insufficient to protect them from the mortification which a limited acquaintance with society will entail upon the ambitious.[39]

Such comments of course again resolutely maintain the view that society is unilinear rather than pluralistic, perceiving (and prescribing) only one model for emulation in both social and linguistic senses; from this often endorsed perspective, differences were necessarily promoted as flaws, and emulation (in linguistic terms, convergence) was presented as the obvious consequence. It was thus the acquisition of these less tangible assets which, in prevailing ideologies of social and linguistic thinking, was often deemed to be the more significant. As the nineteenth-century journalist (and economist) Walter Bagehot proclaimed, 'There is no country where a "poor devil of a millionnaire" is so ill off as in England!' Further encoding these perceptions that 'money alone—money *pur et simple*—will not buy "London Society"',[40] he too emphasized that the economic alone was to be inadequate in confirming social advance. Manners took on the greater salience—including those of language. Such precepts became a commonplace of the age, further guaranteeing of course a ready market for the legions of conduct manuals and elocutionary tracts which endeavoured to elucidate the proprieties deemed necessary. 'The wealthy man, great in his accumulation of riches, if he be not in possession of knowledge sufficient to command respect, and if he speak ungrammatically, is not considered a gentleman',[41] as Marcus Davis asserts of the social and linguistic constructs of superiority. Or as a later manual of etiquette makes plain:

The proverb which warns us against judging by appearances can never have much weight in a civilised community. There, appearance is inevitably the index of character.

First impressions must, in nine times out of ten, be formed from it, and that is a consideration of so much importance that no-one can afford to disregard it.[42]

Language, as this indicates, was to be deployed as a prime signifier of the social divide, imaging forth social identity, whether actual or merely aspirational. The popular binarisms of prescriptive writing were in this context to receive additional emphasis from the discourse of the 'Two Nations' which underpinned a number of popular nineteenth-century novels such as Gaskell's *North and South*, Dickens's *Hard Times*, and, perhaps primarily, Benjamin Disraeli's *Sybil*. It is in the latter, for example, that Disraeli eloquently describes the 'two nations... who are formed by a different breeding, are fed by a different food, are ordered by different manners'.[43] If such novels ultimately stress social agendas of a rather different sort from those employed in much writing on language at the time, it is nevertheless clear that the contemporary resonance of such images of the social divide could play their own part in the prescriptive rhetoric of many writers. Topical concerns for social reform are, for example, frequently made to operate through pleas for increased standardization. Francis Newman, for instance, expounds upon the damaging divisions of social space in ways which obviously trade on nineteenth-century sensibilities towards the much-discussed subject of the 'two nations'. His thesis, however, operates with reference to the spoken word alone, urging the inception of educational remedy in this context in yet another appeal for national harmony and non-localized speech:

The earliest business of the primary teacher is Elocution, not Grammar. He should teach pure correct sounds, and cultivate both ear and tongue. The national importance of this is great. Coarse, plebian utterance, sticking to men through life, splits the nation into two castes.[44]

Just as it was pronunciation which served to distinguish the Gileadites and Ephraimites (Judges 12: 5–6) by means of the articulation of *shibboleth* as *sibboleth* (for the Ephraimites 'could not frame to pronounce it right'), so too did the various linguistic shibboleths which came into prominence over the course of the late eighteenth and nineteenth centuries tend to serve as distinguishing markers of different social groupings and different social stereotypes. Biblical history here proves the truth of P. J. Waller's statement that language is 'an instrument of communication as well as ex-communication'.[45] Though the enunciation of *shibboleth* provided a means by which the Ephraimites could be recognized and hence fatally dispatched, for the period under discussion in this particular volume, it was, however, class and not ethnicity which commonly came to operate as the stated basis of these divisions. 'The lower classes of people cannot be expected to devote much time to the study of their native language', wrote the anonymous author of *Errors of Pronunciation* in 1817, justifying the need for the manual he supplies in order to remedy such deficiencies.[46] 'The language of the highest classes... is now looked upon as the standard of English pronunciation', G. F. Graham affirmed in 1869.[47] Or as Alfred Leach commented on the role of /h/, the most popular of all the shibboleths given voice during this time: 'H, in speech, is an unmistakable mark of class distinction in England, as every person soon discovers'.[48] Adding still other dimensions to the socially orientated metalanguage of the time, discussions of class hence emerge as widely prevalent adjuncts to the desire to foster the non-localized norms of 'talking proper'.

Modern sociolinguistic studies stress that a standard variety is above all a social institution, standardization a form 'of social behaviour towards language'.[49] Both these aspects are inescapable if one considers the range of comments addressed to speakers of English over the nineteenth century in this context. Social comment can indeed seem inseparable from the linguistic sensibilities which Sheridan and others had early striven to inculcate, while issues of acceptability frequently engage with notions of social stigma in order to enhance corresponding proscriptions in terms of sound. Affiliations with elite culture (and the 'upper class') proliferate in accounts of enunciations recommended as 'correct'. The language of the social hierarchy fuses with specifications of sounds, notions of 'identity politics' being manipulated to apparently good effect by means of popular cultural constructs such as the 'lady' or the 'gentleman',[50] or as already indicated, by contemporary stereotypes of the 'new rich' when more negative connotations were required. As Michael Shapiro has noted, 'every society is involved to some degree in identity politics, with separating people into groups with identities which frequently form a hierarchy of worthiness'.[51] In the late eighteenth and nineteenth centuries, however, a period marked by no little change in the social order and the social labels prominent within it, such processes are perhaps engaged upon with a fervour which is more marked than otherwise, especially given this conjunction with the shifting sensibilities of prescriptivism and the standard ideology itself. The end result is, of course, perceptible in the correlations (then and now) which are so often assumed to hold true between accent and class. In the grammars, dictionaries, and manuals of linguistic etiquette which were published in such abundance over the nineteenth century, differences of accent come to act as a prominent image for a stratified society, one which was moreover itself engaging in a number of fundamental transformations in its notions of social identity.

As the historian Gareth Stedman-Jones confirms, 'changes in the use of language can often indicate important turning points in social history'.[52] Certainly, in terms of semantics alone, it is evident that both *accent* and *class* shifted their boundaries over the eighteenth and nineteenth centuries. *Accent*, for example, had earlier signified primarily position of stress within articulations of a word, a sense illustrated in Isaac Watts's *Art of Reading and Writing English* of 1721: 'The Accent is a Peculiar Stress or Tone of Sound that the

Voice Lays upon any Syllable'. Its later meaning, in which it signifies primarily pronunciation, is illustrated by William Cobbett in 1819 in a typically
iconoclastic asseveration against the prevailing tide of thought: 'children will
pronounce as their fathers and mothers pronounce...speakers whose
approbation is worth having will pay little attention to the accent'.[53] *Class* too
extends its range of meanings at this time, gaining new and significant poly-
semies. Notions of social level, previously phrased in terms of 'rank' and
'interest'—the 'assumptions of inherited hierarchy and unequal birth'
described by Geoffrey Hughes in his own study of language and social
development[54]—were as a result gradually to be joined by an alternative set
of social definitions, specifically based around these shifting nuances of *class*.

Examining such diachronic transformations within the meanings and use
of words, the cultural historian Raymond Williams has stressed that relevant
semantic shifts in this context 'belong essentially to the period between 1770
and 1840, which is also the period of the Industrial Revolution, and its decisive reorganization of society'.[55] The conjunction of these changes has
become almost a commonplace of historical comment on the period. 'The
birth of a new class society', states Harold Perkin in 1969, was one of 'the
most profound and far-reaching consequences of the Industrial
Revolution'.[56] Asa Briggs similarly endorses the ways in which the Industrial
Revolution came to constitute a revolution not merely of technical innovation and activity, but also of social thinking in itself.[57] Indeed, as the population doubled, and then trebled, as a largely agrarian social order became
instead one marked by the urban and commercial, as railways extended the
potential for geographical mobility at a hitherto unexpected rate, and as a
new set of white-collar and professional occupations came into being, a new
system of advantages—and, conversely, of inequalities—did in a number of
ways come to displace those which had previously pertained.

In this context, it was commonly the scale of these changes which was seen
as most significant. Though society had of course by no means been static in
the years before the mid-eighteenth century, it had not, on the other hand,
tended to participate in large-scale changes such as those which accompanied the Industrial Revolution. Likewise, while vertical mobility was both
acknowledged and recognized as a social phenomenon before this date,
again it is the number and nature of the shifts in social level which is most
striking, serving to create perceptions (and associated stereotypes) not only
of the 'new rich', as we have seen, but also of a new and extensive middle
section of society. In such terms, society was to conceive, recognize, and signal the nuances of social status in significantly different ways. It is in this
context therefore that 'class' emerges as a popular social label while, as contemporary comment serves to illustrate, attitudes to accent were also not to
be entirely immaterial in this respect, frequently being linked to the issues of
mobility and social 'self-help' which appear as prevalent constructs in social

thinking over this time. Moreover, as Björn Jernudd has noted, 'It is in periods of transition . . . that puristic responses [to language] are especially likely to arise',[58] a comment which certainly takes on enhanced validity if one considers that sensitization towards the spoken word which became such a prominent (and popular) issue over the course of the late eighteenth and nineteenth centuries.

In terms of semantics, the differences between 'class' and 'rank' are, in fact, fundamental to these transitions and their respective (and contrastive) concepts of mobility. Commenting on 'the fixed, invariable, external rules of distinction of rank, which create no jealousy, since they are held to be accidental', Samuel Johnson, for example, sets forth traditional eighteenth-century perceptions in which social organization in England was seen as something stable rather than fluid, determined by birth rather than by the possibilities of individual endeavour. 'Subordination tends greatly to human happiness', he stated; 'Contentions for superiority [are] very dangerous ... all civilised nations have settled it upon a plain invariable principle. A man is born to hereditary rank; or his being appointed to certain offices, gives him a certain rank.'[59] As, with some prescience, he warned Boswell, a perpetual struggle for precedence would result from the demise of such rules.

'Class', on the other hand, seemed to offer potential for the creation rather than merely the inheritance of social location, contributing to that 'struggle for precedence' as well as those 'contentions for superiority' which frequently appear in contemporary comment on the period.[60] 'Class', originally applied as a generic term for any grouping, comes instead to signify a particular view of social formation, one in which social position was not necessarily determined by birth. Though such lexical transitions are, as expected, by no means either neat or well defined so that, with predictable semantic fuzziness, users of the language tend to employ both older and newer senses depending on the specific context, what is particularly striking over the course of the nineteenth century is the clear emergence of a specific set of terminology relating to this new conception of social identity. 'Class' in effect became a salient designation under which opinions about society, and its members, were organized by the writers of the time, a practice which still of course continues. 'Middle-class', working-class', 'upper-class', 'class-consciousness, 'class-distinctions', 'class-feelings' ('class-interests' and 'class-superiority' in John Stuart Mill), together with 'class-education' and 'class-barrier', among others, bear witness to the lexical expansion arising from this shift in social thinking.[61] Its social sense legitimized in *OED* from 1773 (but actually in existence for some time before),[62] 'class' thus seemed to offer, as the historian Penny Corfield has noted, 'a new vocabulary and conceptual framework for ... the interpretation of society'.[63] It became a way not only of perceiving but of behaving and equally, as we have seen, of speaking. Though the term 'class dialect' does not appear according to *OED* before 1901 (the first citation for its use is in Greenough and Kittredge's *Words and Their Ways*), the deliberate inculcation of a form of speech conceived in terms of relationships to the social hierarchy was clearly in existence long before this date.

Nevertheless, 'writing about social class in England', as Ian Bradley has remarked, 'is rather like talking about food in France or discussing industrial efficiency with the Japanese. Because it functions as a national obsession, it is a risky and even a presumptuous enterprise which is beset with pitfalls and dangers'.[64] Prime amongst these dangers is, in fact, the definition of 'class' itself. Though its ramifications were easily assumed as social labels in texts from the late eighteenth century onwards, it is important to be aware of what, precisely, is being signified by the choice of such appellations. Class, as both historians and sociologists have stressed, is, for instance, formally an economic determinant alone: 'an economic grouping depending on the value of a person's labour and his share of property'.[65] Economic considerations are therefore conventionally of primary importance in establishing class formation. Marx's *proletariat* and *bourgeoisie*, the 'masters and men' of Gaskell's *North and South*, Disraeli's 'two nations' can all be seen to encode the harsh economic realities of social difference in nineteenth-century society. 'In a progressive civilisation, wealth is the only means of class-distinction', as Lord Valentine, in Disraeli's *Sybil*, is informed.[66]

Such interpretations prove problematic in a number of ways, and not least in terms of those correlations between accent and class which have often endured as an equally prominent aspect of this 'national obsession'. As texts such as *Vulgarities of Speech Corrected, Hints on Etiquette*, or Marcus Davis's *Everybody's Business* have already indicated in this context, wealth, though it may indeed be a means by which class membership may be formally assigned, does not, and did not, always confer in equal measure that status, or social honour, that might be thought to go with it. Class in this sense becomes problematic. As the historian Trevor May comments, for example, 'In the final analysis objective social stratification may be unattainable', not least because though financial status may be calculated with precision, actual perceptions of individual status are often markedly subjective. Or as May elaborates: 'in a large part a person's class is what he believes it to be and, more importantly, what others accept it to be'.[67] The difference felt to pertain between respective stereotypes of the 'self-made' and the 'gentleman' throughout the nineteenth century provides a case in point. Without instruction in those other symbols of social honour associated with elevated status—in particular, as Chapter 4 will explore, the use of /h/—the 'vulgar rich', as the Oxford scholar Thomas Kington-Oliphant stressed, could not and would not be accorded acceptability. The amount of property they might possess was in this case entirely immaterial. It was this circumstance which rendered remedial education in the socially symbolic proprieties of language of particular importance. 'Many a needy scholar might turn an honest penny by offering himself as an instructor of the vulgar rich in the pronunciation of the fatal letter', Kington-Oliphant advised with reference to the troubled subject of /h/ usage and the stereotypical fallibilities of the 'new rich' in this context.[68] It was manners and not money which would secure the acceptability they desired. The historian W. D. Rubenstein offers similar corroboration for this perception in his own (rather more empirical) study of the 'new men of wealth' in nineteenth-century society. He points out that, in reality, 'for the self-made man, there was an unbridgeable gap of behaviour, attitude, and accent (and often of more formal characteristics like religion) between the old aristocracy and the *nouveaux riches*'. It was, he adds, a difference which 'no amount of land purchase would affect'.[69]

Of course, if one examines the individual histories of the 'new rich' of the late eighteenth and nineteenth centuries, it is clear that large amounts of entrepreneurial fortune were in fact expended in tangible acquisitions of precisely this kind. The brewer Samuel Whitbread bought Bodwell Park in 1751, and Woolmers a few years later, Matthew Boulton, the engineer (and partner of James Watt), bought Tew Park, and Albert Brassey purchased Heythrop House; the Peels bought Drayton Manor, Wedgewood built Etruria and Barleston Hall, and Richard Arkwright's descendants accumulated estates so that his four surviving grandsons, for example, owned property in Derbyshire, Leicestershire, Essex, and Hereford. Nevertheless, even if one possessed one's own estate, there was no guarantee that the benefits of complete social acceptability would follow, especially in the higher echelons of society within which the new rich might desire to take their place. Charles Booth, for example, founded the highly successful Booth Steamship Company, and resided in Gracedieu Manor in Whitwick. Nevertheless, when it came to the question of marriage, it was his pronunciation which came to the fore. In considering Booth's acceptability for their daughter Mary Macaulay, his prospective parents-in-law apparently 'took exception to the young ship-owner's Liverpool accent' and required no little persuasion before eventually giving their consent to the match.[70] Booth's history in this matter was by no means untypical. As the social historians Stone and Stone likewise affirm: 'no amount of land purchase would confer social acceptability upon a man whose wealth was obtained in sordid ways, whose origins were obscure, whose manners and accent were demonstrably vulgar, and whose religion might well be non-conformist'.[71] Money may certainly secure much but, as many were to emphasize, it did not automatically provide control of those other, often more intangible markers which may have superior powers of conferring—and signifying—respectability or membership within the genteel. As Kington-Oliphant, Rubenstein, and Stone and Stone all agree, it was language—and accent—which regularly impinged upon the allocation of social values. In this context therefore, refinements of speech were to be seen (and promoted) in the rhetoric of the day as an increasingly vital acquisition among the other attributes of the socially mobile.

As comments such as these also indicate, however, it seems clear that prevalent notions of the importance of accent and its stated correlations with issues of 'class' did not, in real terms, align quite as well as their conventional (and still-enduring) stereotypes tend to suggest. The economic could evidently be disregarded in favour of more telling indicators of social standing and social origin; the enunciation of /h/ or the specific way in which the *a* in words such as *cat* was pronounced could proclaim social origins in ways which transcended the incidental import of property and possessions. Successful entrepreneur he might have been but Charles Booth, for example, 'never lost the "flat a" of the Northerner' which, for his wife's parents, continued to betray his humble beginnings rather than his current status as shipping magnate.[72] As a result, though notions of social level—and 'proper' speech—were and are popularly phrased in terms of 'class', their allocation is, in reality, often influenced by a somewhat wider set of behavioural norms and expectations, perhaps foremost among which is the degree of assimilation to designated 'styles of life', and to the markers which are, in turn, seen as characteristic of particular social groupings. And among these markers, styles of speaking were, as we have seen, by no means immaterial. As Disraeli's discussion of the 'two nations' has, for instance, already suggested, notions of social difference rest on far more *in toto* than mere matters of finance, especially in terms of popular perception. 'Formed by a different breeding, . . . ordered by different manners', people are regularly aligned into social groupings on grounds such as these, irrespective of the pecuniary level which they may or may not have achieved.

This evident disjunction between indices of economic standing in terms of the formal properties of 'class' and these other, less concrete, indicators of social position is, of course, by no means confined to the past. Ivor Morrish pertinently notes of the late twentieth century that 'a docker may earn more than a schoolmaster but this does not necessarily put both of them in the same class—indeed, none of them would claim to be in the same class'.[73] It is this recognition of group relationships in terms of shared norms and shared patterns of behaviour, rather than simply in terms of shared financial parities which is, in fact, much in evidence in the nineteenth century too. As the historian Dorothy Marshall observed: 'The struggling clerk, who earned less than the expert fine cotton spinner, underlined this superiority by his dress, his speech, and his manners. These, and not his income, were what distinguished him from the working class'.[74] Likewise, while an 1857 article in *The Economist* overtly makes use of 'class' terminology in order to describe observable changes in society ('Society is tending more and more to spread into classes—and not merely classes, but localised classes, class colonies'), it is nevertheless clear these changes are to be explained with reference to social patterns and affinities which are fundamentally distinct from those which might be assumed on the basis of money alone:

> There is a much deeper social principle involved in the present increasing tendency to class colonies. It is the disposition to associate with equals—in some measure with those who have similar practical *interests*, in still greater measure with those who have similar tastes and culture, most of all with those with whom we judge ourselves on a moral equality, whatever our real standard might be.[75]

The same is true of comment on language and while Alfred Leach, as we have seen, willingly adopts the language of 'class' and 'class-distinction' in order to discuss the solecism of [h]-dropping and its own role as social marker, it is again by no means the merely economic signifiers of social identity which are relevant in such considerations. Instead, as he confirms, while financial advantage may enable the purchase of superior clothes, the illusions of social standing (or superiority) which are thereby created may be rapidly dispelled once a person begins to speak:

> I remarked upon this to an English gentleman, an officer, who replied—'It's the greatest blessing in the world, a sure protection against cads. You meet a fellow who is well-dressed, behaves himself decently enough, and yet you don't know exactly what to make of him; but get him talking, and if he trips upon his H's that settles the question. He's a chap you'd better be shy of.'[76]

Leach's selection of the term 'cad' in this context is of course additionally illuminating. 'A fellow of low vulgar manners and behaviour', the *OED* explains, adding in illustration an axiom taken from A. Boyd's *Lessons of Middle Age* of 1869: 'You cannot make a vulgar offensive cad conduct himself as a gentleman'.

Social affinities based on markers of 'style of life' rather than upon the fiscal parities of income, or indeed capital, thus function as the matrix in which notions of social cohesion or division within the community (including those of language) are to be enacted. The relevant terms are, in effect, those of 'status', not of 'class', and this difference is, in a number of ways, important within our conceptions of the role of accent as social symbol over this time. Though both are, to an extent, interrelated, the differentiation of 'class' and 'status' rests in the primarily economic emphasis of the former as a means of social definition in contrast to the priority given to social habits, social manners, 'way of life' (amongst which language and pronunciation form a composite part), which are given priority by the latter. It is this contrast which can, for example, be used to interpret Marcus Davis's comments on the salience of 'grammaticality' above wealth for the 'gentleman' ('the wealthy man, great in his accumulation of riches, if he be not in possession of knowledge sufficient to command respect, and if he speak ungrammatically, is not considered a gentleman'), as well as in the due elucidation of Leach's observations about the superior import of [h] in conversational discourse. This strategic separation of class and status as distinct social constructs stems from the work of the German sociologist Max Weber (1864–1920) who, recognizing that a simple one-to-one correspondence between economic and social standing did not, in fact, appear to be borne out by the workings, and indeed the thinking, of society, suggested instead the necessity of discriminating the economic ('class'), social ('status'), and political ('party') factors within social organization. Pointing out, precisely in line with those nineteenth-century attitudes already discussed, that mere economic power is by no means a recognized base of social honour,[77] Weber hence gives detailed expression to the complexities which can attend perceptions of social level. Status, if not class, was firmly determined on the evaluative basis of a set of external symbols such as education, dress, manners, and language, all of which serve to establish a group's behavioural norms, its salient markers of identity and belonging, or, in Weber's terms, its 'social honour'. The presence of certain factors, or the absence of others, can consequently be seen to delineate patterns of inclusion within the organization of society, conferring, or indeed withholding membership within the various and co-existing status groups. It was command of these attributes which was, in essence, to define position, prestige, and 'social honour' in ways which were more subtle, and succinct, than those enabled by mere financial clout.

With reference to language, and the escalating preoccupations with its role in social manners, social habits, and indeed social identity, such criteria of status, though admittedly vaguer in some ways than those based on class, do nevertheless seem to offer a perspective which is potentially useful. It is, for instance, clear that accent in the nineteenth century, as in the twentieth and twenty-first, came to correlate closely with status rather than class per se in structured patterns of co-variation which, though subject to some ongoing change as Chapter 8 will explore, still basically hold true. In other words, though its correlations with 'class' have come to be something of a cliché in comment on language in England, it is in fact *status* in which such patterns fundamentally reside. Lesley Milroy's analysis of sociolinguistic method in the late twentieth century bears out the same conclusion. 'It appears then than that the important variable which sociolinguists usually characterise as *class* is more specifically an evaluative one—status', she stresses.[78] The letters, journals, newspapers, as well as texts on language from the late eighteenth century onwards provide still earlier confirmation of this fact. Accent emerges as an external signal which is unambiguously able to suggest status and social honour (or their absence), and to extend similar patterns of evaluation to speaker as well as speech, predicating attendant issues of exclusion and exclusivity as it did so.

Reviewing Thomas Sheridan's work in this light, it is, for example, clear that the 'disgrace' which he accords to accents localized outside London is, at least theoretically, to be seen as inimical to high social standing—a badge of dishonour and low social status—while the respect conferred by conformity to the 'best' London styles of speech acts as a marker—of status not of 'class'—which will command the requisite esteem and admiration: 'a sort of proof that a person has kept good company', as Sheridan declares. Precisely in line with other symbols of social honour, attitudes to accent variation therefore tend to function in socially evaluative ways of this kind, detailed perhaps with more clarity, and greater explicitness, in the workings and dissemination of prescriptive ideology in the late eighteenth and nineteenth centuries than are any other markers of social identity. 'Respect', 'esteem', 'honour', and appropriate antonyms, as well as apparently incontestable assertions of 'good', 'bad', 'right', 'wrong', together with the favourite epithets of 'vulgar' and 'polite', all, as we have seen, proliferate within ostensibly linguistic descriptions, as pronunciation is specifically delineated in terms of its effects on the social affections, and the indices of standing which may thereby be exposed. As the author of *How to Shine in Society* underscored, for example, 'what advantages has the talent of conversation for he who aspires to honour and esteem, or wishes in short to rise in the world?',[79] specifying equally that conversational skills alone were as nothing if coupled with phonemic impropriety.

Command of those features specified as desirable in the accent which Sheridan and others intended to extend as a non-localized norm for the nation was, in such ways, thus deemed to symbolize much more than mere articulatory control. Assimilation in this context involved far more than language, overtly being integrated with contemporary issues of mobility, status, and success. Sensitization to the value of accent, just as in Sheridan's original conceptions of its role, hence in this sense proceeds simultaneously in terms of its status values too. Within a few decades, as we have seen, such links were inseparable, embedded in the changing social fabric, and shifting social organization, of a newly industrialized society. Conformity, emulation (of the designated 'proper' models), and notions of improvement—all precepts in line with the codifying ethos of the age—were regularly presented as important linguistic tenets to be adhered to in the quest to signify status and the finer nuances of identity.

Fashion too played its allotted role. As Weber himself notes, the differentiations which operate in terms of status within society 'evolve in such a way as to make for strict submission to the fashion that is dominant at a given time in society'.[80] Prescriptive preferences for a non-regional accent, already presented as a defining symbol of the 'gentleman' by Enfield in 1774,[81] were, for instance, gradually also assimilated into the canons of fashionable behaviour, though fashion in this instance was definitively 'high' rather than 'low', reflecting 'Society' in its metropolitan sense rather than society as a whole. Redolent of familiarity with the 'best' speech of London, such speech patterns were adjudged to exert an obvious appeal, conformity to them essential not only according to the dictates of prescriptive texts but equally endorsed in literature, in works on etiquette, and in popular journals as the true markers of the statusful and 'polite'. It is the absence of such markers which was, for example, presented as the factor which denied Gladstone, among others, membership of such ranks. 'Gladstone has too much of the Northern accent to be strictly gentlemanly', as Sir William Hardman commented.[82]

As manuals of etiquette such as *How to Shine in Society* or *How to Speak with Propriety* (by 'Oxoniensis') combine to suggest, however, more significant overall, and ultimately pervading far more of society, was not the elite integration of the successful few (and the linguistic standards ostensibly required of them), but that rather more widespread assimilation to notions of the polite in cultural terms which was, in a number of ways, also taking place over the eighteenth and nineteenth centuries. 'Those who [fill] the higher ranks of life, are naturally regarded as patterns, by which the rest of the world are to be fashioned', as the eighteenth-century writer on religion and education Hannah More had noted in her *Thoughts on the Importance of the Manners of the Great to General Society*.[83] Though More herself did not believe in emulation as an adjunct to social mobility, there were, it seemed, to be many who did. Evident in the imitation of manners and social habits, of styles of behaving, of dressing, and, of course, of speaking, the statusful proprieties of the gentry classes did in a number of ways indeed appear to influence attitudes to social norms and behavioural ideals across far wider sections of society than might initially be assumed. Notions of the attempted cultural assimilations which result from such tendencies are, for instance, readily detected in the 'consumer revolution' which has been documented as a significant accompaniment to the social and industrial upheavals of the time, or in the enthusiastic adoption over a wide range of society of the fashions and manners promoted by Georgiana, Duchess of Devonshire.[84] As the historian Neil McKendrick confirms, 'in imitation of the rich the middle ranks spent more frenziedly than ever before, and in imitation of them the rest of society joined in as best they might—and the best was unprecedented in the importance of the effect on aggregate demand'.[85] Clothes, fashions for both house and person, and possessions of all kinds came to signify each step in intended social advancement, a lesson which was, for example, well learnt by the Veneerings and their own conspicuous consumption in Dickens's *Our Mutual Friend*.

William Cobbett, amongst others, criticized imitative behaviour of this order with vehemence when he encountered it in his *Rural Rides*. 'I daresay it had been *Squire* Charrington and the *Miss* Charringtons; and not plain Master Charrington and his son Hodge and his daughter Betty Charrington, all of whom the accursed system had transmuted into a species of mock gentlefolk', he thundered, clearly aghast at the attempted social transformations at work. George Eliot ventured similar censure upon behaviour which she too regarded as pretension:

In our day...we can hardly enter the least imposing farm-house without finding a bad piano in the 'drawing-room', and some old annuals, disposed with a symmetrical imitation of negligence, on the table; though the daughters may still drop their *h*'s, their vowels are studiously narrow; and it is only in very primitive regions that they will consent to sit in a covered vehicle without springs, which was once thought an advance in luxury on the pillion.[86]

As contemporary comment in this vein reveals, this 'culture of gentility' could and did extend far beyond the stereotypes of the 'new rich', influencing not only the upper but also the middle and, at times, even the lower sections of the social hierarchy. The latter, Stone and Stone confirm, 'instead of resenting [their social superiors]...eagerly sought to imitate them, aspiring to gentility by copying the education, manners, and behaviour of the gentry'.[87] It was 'homogenizing aspirations for gentility' of this order which, in real terms, were also to extend the appeal of 'talking proper' (and accompanying sociolinguistic attitudes) outside that largely localized elite which initially had had access to its forms. Discussed by Cobbett in terms of the 'constant anxiety to make a *show* not warranted by the reality' and by Stone and Stone in terms of a 'psychological cohesion' leading to the widespread emulation of typical signifiers of superior status (the use of boarding schools, the role of leisure as social symbol) among the middle sections of society,[88] this naturally had its linguistic repercussions too. 'You may talk of the tyranny of Nero and Tiberius; but the real tyranny is the tyranny of your next-door neighbour', wrote the journalist Walter Bagehot in the mid-nineteenth century: 'Public opinion is a permeating influence, and it exacts obedience to itself; it requires us to think other men's thoughts, to speak other men's words, to follow other men's habits.'[89]

It is circumstances of this kind which seem to have led to the marked popularity of texts which claimed to set forth the dicta of phonemic propriety, trading on (and further diffusing) ideologies of a standard as they did so. As the phonetician Alexander Ellis later observed, 'real communication between class and class is impossible'. This fact alone provided a seemingly insurmountable barrier to the acquisition of 'proper' accents by the masses. Nevertheless, if direct communication remained largely unfeasible, a popular—if indirect—solution seemed to be provided not only in the flood of pronouncing dictionaries which, as already indicated, were published over the nineteenth century but also in the continued demand for works on specific sounds, above all perhaps those which focused on the correct use of /h/. Eccles's *Harry Hawkins' H Book*, Smith's *Mind Your H's and Take Care of Your R's*, Hon. Henry H.'s *Poor Letter H*, and Leach's *The Letter H. Past, Present, and Future* were, among others, all published and reprinted numerous times over this period. Accent, a social marker which, as such texts iterated, was able to suggest respectability by its cadences and status by its tones, was thus explicitly fused with principles of imitative cohesion; the burgeoning white-collar and professional sections of society were apparently to endorse its norms enthusiastically if contemporary comment is to be believed. Certainly discussions of /h/, as we will see in Chapter 4, regularly stressed the assimilatory endeavours of the middle sections of society in this respect, neatly paralleling modern sociolinguistic research on that hypercorrection often perceptible in lower-status groups in their more careful speech.[90]

As W. P. Robinson affirms, what is above all clear is the fact that speech may 'reveal preferred identity as much as real identity'. Moreover, as he adds in this context: 'once ... distinctive features are exposed, people aspiring to a certain identity may be able to incorporate them in their speech'.[91] The normative specifications of pronunciation which, as we will see, tended to expose distinctive features of this order with particular clarity from the late eighteenth century onwards were, as a result, presented as highly useful, especially for the new non-manual workers of the time. By such means, 'preferred identity' might be realized—at least when required. 'We create our "rules" so as to resemble as closely as possible those of the groups with which from time to time we want to identify', wrote LePage in 1980[92] and the same processes may again be assumed to work equally well for the nineteenth century, similarly motivating the shift towards (and away from) stated variables depending on the contexts in which speakers might find themselves. Certainly those intent on professional mobility were often openly exhorted to remember such 'rules' in their linguistic behaviour: 'The perusal and profit of the ledger should be preceded, accompanied, or at least followed, by a little study of grammar', *P's and Q's*, with its subtitle *Grammatical Hints for the Million*, directs.[93] Due emphasis is given to the fact that the use of language may complement, or confound, any newly gained social advantage for the aspiring clerk; speaking 'with care and attention to grammatical proprieties, such as proper aspiration' is presented as essential. Phonetic cause and social effect in this circumstance are made particularly clear, not least since 'education' also appears to function as a popular synonym for the requisite proprieties in terms of speech:

Boys and girls may, and very often do, rise above their original level in society, and doing so they should be prepared to adorn the new station they may fill... Want of education sadly mars what talent, or labour, or money, or comparative accident may help to make; and if the men, or women, be not themselves aware of the defect, their children, friends, and relatives, have often painfully to feel it.[94]

If notions of social status and cultural assimilation were not in themselves to exert sufficient persuasion upon the speaker to amend existing improprieties of speech, images of subsequent social shame (arising from such neglect)

were, as this illustrates, to be deployed in their stead. Fictions of empowerment (and the threat of disempowerment for those who fail to achieve the
necessary accommodation) are likewise prominent in the further ramifications of the standard ideology which such comments reveal. As *P's and Q's*
confirms, by the second half of the nineteenth century that non-provincial
accent which had regularly been designated as perhaps the most dominant
symbol of 'talking proper' had come, in effect, to be regarded as one of the
salient symbols of privilege in itself, not only capable of implying superiorities of standing and of knowledge but, more significantly, also being assumed
to convey attendant values of power and authority in abundance.

Works such as *P's and Q's* therefore tended to voice explicit appeals to
individual ambitions to signify possession of that 'manner' which was, time
and time again, deemed proper to the popular social constructs of 'gentleman' or 'lady'. These, however, were also in the process of change. As the
nineteenth century advanced, for example, Walker's 1791 definition of a
'lady' ('a woman of high rank') was increasingly superseded by definitions in
which manners rather than birth again assume prominence: 'a term of com-
plaisance; applied to almost any well-dressed woman, but appropriately to
one of refined manners and education', stated the respective definition given
by the lexicographer John Ogilvie in 1870 in his *Comprehensive English
Pronouncing Dictionary*. Semantic transformations of a similar kind are perceptible in the meanings which surround 'gentleman' too. 'A man of birth, a
man of extraction', glossed Walker at the end of the eighteenth century.
Though these resonances remain in later definitions ('every man above the
rank of yeoman, comprehending noblemen', as John Ogilvie correspondingly notes) its *'highest sense'* was somewhat different. As Ogilvie's definition
adds: 'in the *highest sense*, the term *gentleman* signifies a man of strict integrity
and honour, of self-respect, and intellectual refinement, as well as refined
manners and good breeding'. Like the semantic shifts perceptible in 'accent',
and indeed in 'class' too, these particular changes in meaning indicate the
processes of semantic extension whereby these social labels come to take on
a far wider social currency than had hitherto been the case. The fact that they
undergo accompanying processes of semantic devaluation as they do so is
also evident in contemporary comment. ' "You mustn't say 'gentlemen'
nowadays," ' as Mrs Swanton admonishes Elfride in Thomas Hardy's *A Pair
of Blue Eyes* (1873): ' "We have handed over 'gentlemen' to the lower middle
classes, where the word is still to be heard at tradesmen's balls and provincial tea-parties, I believe." '

Hardy's engagement with the shifting semantic contexts of this word indicates with some acuity the processes of emulation and assimilation which
were, in a variety of ways, taking place, and not only of course within semantic space. Manuals on how to acquire the defining features of 'gentleman' or
'lady' abound. As *Advice to a Young Gentleman on Entering Society* (1839)

specified in this context: 'There are certain arbitrary peculiarities of manner, speech, language, taste, &c. which mark the high-born and high-bred. These should be observed and had.'[95] The role of manners in marking social identity is made still more evident by the author's subsequent comment: 'they are the signs-manual of good-breeding by which gentlemen recognize each other wherever they meet'. The central tenet again rests on the recognition that, once given information on the right symbols of social status and 'style of life'—a domain in which speech was, as we have seen, often specified as of greatest immediacy in its effects—the readers of such texts could themselves convey the requisite intimations of a standing higher than that they actually possessed, and command a propriety which would in turn command respect. It is these 'arbitrary peculiarities of speech' which are explicitly proffered within the tenets which this, and similar works, endorse.

Imitative cohesion, as set out in handbooks of this kind, hence becomes the art of social illusion, and the examples (and exemplars) given in this context are clear and to the point. 'No one could imagine Lord John ... issuing his orders to the channel fleet with the accent of a Cockney; or John Campbell, Duke of Argyll, admonishing a postman on the effects of mountain dew with the accent of a citizen of Inverary', as *How to Shine in Society* warned.[96] In these particular workings of prescriptive ideology, cultural assimilation is made inseparable from linguistic assimilation, and its pressures are persuasive. By modifications of accent, and familiarity with this particular 'signs-manual', the resonances of gentility could unambiguously be imaged forth. Whether using the accents of low-status Londoners, or the 'provincial' tones of Scotland, the detrimental effects on perceptions of one's social standing (as well as upon those other subjective associations already discussed) were depicted in identical ways. Language was embedded in assumptions of social difference and disadvantage which may be unfair, as Marcus Davis contends, but which were also in many ways to appear virtually irremediable by the later nineteenth century: 'Why is an ill-dressed man, in labourer's apparel treated with *contumely* even in courts of justice ... Because they are totally unacquainted with that branch of knowledge that gives to man a tower of defence ... They have not that command of language which imparts confidence, not only to assert our rights but defend them.'[97] The relevant maxim to be drawn from this was not, however, the need for wide-scale education into the nature of the unfounded linguistic prejudices which produce such inequities but instead a new prescriptive edict for the age. As the opening words of Davis's book proclaim, 'It is EVERYBODY'S BUSINESS to speak; and if it is EVERYBODY'S BUSINESS to speak, it is worth EVERYBODY'S while to speak correctly'.[98]

Few, asserted Phyfe, were to be entirely immune from the repercussions of such equations, whether in terms of the attitudes they held towards linguistic usage or the linguistic habits which they in turn endeavoured to adopt. Accent, he stressed, 'appeals to all, since there is no one so wholly indifferent to the estimate formed of his social position, and who, in consequence, would not cultivate those arts that are at once the criteria of social standing and the stepping stones to a more liberal culture'.[99] Or as Savage likewise confirmed: 'a good orthoepy will never fail of producing impressions in your favour',[100] a perception which can often still be confirmed, as we have seen, in the results of subjective reaction tests in modern sociolinguistic research.

It is a transition in conceptual approach which is illustrated particularly well in the various editions of the radical politician William Cobbett's own *Grammar of the English Language*. This was originally published in England in 1819, being explicitly addressed to an audience of 'soldiers, sailors, apprentices, and ploughboys'. Like Sheridan, Cobbett presented knowledge of linguistic propriety as an indispensable acquisition: 'in no situation, which calls on a man to place his thoughts on paper, can the possession of it fail to be a source of self-congratulation, or the want of it a cause of mortification and sorrow'.[101] Unlike Sheridan, however, it was grammar rather than accent which Cobbett chose to present as of foremost importance in this context. In this, he resolutely maintained older views on language such as those endorsed by Joseph Priestley in his own declaration that pronunciation is 'a matter of decoration only'. Conservative at least in this respect, Cobbett therefore merely averred that 'children will pronounce as their fathers and mothers pronounce; and if, in common conversation, or in speeches, the matter be good and judiciously arranged, the facts clearly stated ... the words well chosen and properly placed, hearers whose approbation is worth having will pay very little attention to the accent'.[102]

Cobbett's son James, born in 1803, grew up in a significantly different linguistic and cultural climate, and he was to present a somewhat different emphasis in his 1866 edition of his father's work. Clearly feeling it incumbent upon him to redress any earlier textual imbalances, he adds a new chapter headed, 'Pronunciation: Certain Common Forms Pointed Out and Corrected'. Cobbett senior's precept that '*pronunciation* is learnt as birds learn to chirp and sing' so that, consequently, it 'ought not to occupy much of your attention'[103] is as a result reinterpreted in accordance with tenets more typical of the 1860s. Cobbett junior instead adds: 'That shows the importance of attending to children's ways of speaking while they are at an early age'.[104] Both father and son comment on the facts of variation in pronunciation but it is the differences in attitude which are more striking than any similarities arising from the shared subject matter. 'The differences [in pronunciation] are of very little real consequence ... though the Scotch say *coorn*, the Londoners *cawn*, and the Hampshire folk *carn*, we all know they *mean* to say *corn*', wrote William in 1819.[105] 'Many of these terms are of constant use, and the mispronouncing of some of them is particularly offensive', amended his son in 1866.[106]

James Cobbett can, in a number of ways, thus be seen as an exemplar of that consciousness of accent and its social values which Sheridan and others had deliberately attempted to raise. He willingly concurs with the notions of inherent value and aesthetic demerit which are, as we have seen, staples of the standard ideology, endorsing the importance of linguistic convergence in terms his father would have abhorred. He is of course, in this, merely a product of his age; that reorientation of attitudes so marked over the nineteenth century in terms of attitudes to language and, in particular, to notions of phonetic propriety, naturally also infuses the precepts he provides. By the time he edited his father's *Grammar*, such resonances were inescapable, not merely in prescriptive texts and popular manuals but, as Chapter 6 will explore, in literature too as writers within other seemingly disparate genres came to exploit parallel notions of 'talking proper' for an audience well versed in the extralinguistic—and specifically *social*—meanings which the various nuances of enunciation could be made to convey.

3

The Practice of Prescription

OF course, as already indicated, eighteenth- and nineteenth-century accounts
of pronunciation do, on a number of occasions, have to be interpreted with
some caution. Prescriptivism, and the associated desire to impose (and insti-
tutionalize) a norm, brought its own inevitable bias to the accounts of speech
which many texts provide. If the later descriptive traditions of, say, the *Oxford
English Dictionary* or Alexander Ellis's extensive work on phonetics were
intended to foster a proper objectivity and empiricism in the investigation of
language,[1] then the subjectivity of earlier writers is, in contrast, often patently
transparent. Many of those who wrote treatises and tracts on 'proper' pronunciation were merely ordinary speakers who recorded their own attitudes
and evaluations in ways which, as we have seen, are far removed from the
comments of professional linguists today. Indeed the day of the professional
linguist had yet to dawn, and untrained observers were the norm.
Schoolmasters, actors, vicars, and a whole range of ordinary individuals all
ventured to write on accent over this time. John Walker himself was originally
an actor as well as an elocutionist, as was Thomas Sheridan; Sylvester
Douglas had a significant legal, political, and administrative career from
which the concerns of language were, at least professionally, far removed. Yet,
in his leisure hours, he penned his *Treatise on the Provincial Dialect of Scotland*
for those 'whose language has already been in a great degree refined from the
provincial dross, by frequenting English company, and studying the great
masters of the English tongue in their writings'.

Such writers, as the sociolinguist Robert Eagleson stresses, were themselves thus part of the popular culture they document, 'grassroot witnesses
to changes in progress' and grassroot witnesses to changes in attitude too.[2]
It is this which they can reveal so well and where a large part of their value
lies. In their stated correlations with the speaker variables of status or gender,
writers on the language from this time can set forth with particular clarity
the social pressures which accrued around notions of 'talking proper', to
which they themselves were subject and which they themselves endorse.
Such evidence can, as a result, be highly illuminating, offering an unparalleled mass of detail on those images and associations which had come to
surround attitudes to accent, as well as on those which came to frame a range
of sound changes in progress. Varying in ability from writers who legitimately attempt to engage with the nuances of sounds and the emerging

sense of a phonetic science (the self-educated Thomas Batchelor, the elocutionist Alexander Bell, the phonetician Alexander Ellis, and a variety of
others might here be enumerated by virtue of the particular acuity of their
comments) to those who merely adhered to the prescriptive commonplace,
it is in many ways the collective voice of these writers which is overall of
greatest significance. Through the complex patterns of contradictions and
conceptions which can thereby emerge, a fairly precise picture of the state of
the language, and particularly the state of language attitudes, throughout the
late eighteenth and nineteenth centuries can regularly be detected. As a
result, whereas, as Manfred Görlach confirms, 'gaps in the historical sources
prevent us from reconstructing gradual shifts of pronunciation to the extent
that is desirable (and necessary) in [William] Labov's view',[3] the sheer mass
of data of all kinds which is available at this time for the spoken language
does nevertheless tend to give a clear sense of which issues were regarded as
important, as well as suggesting in broader lines the patterns of variation
(both social and linguistic) within which such patterns might be placed. It is,
of course, only by the agency of such writers that the shifting perceptions of
a 'standard' accent and the emergent desire for a norm can in any sense be
documented over this time.

At this point it is, however, useful to shift our focus from the broader
framework of language attitudes to the actualities of speech in the late eighteenth and nineteenth centuries though even this, as we will see, tends to
illustrate just how omnipresent were the images and assumptions about
accent and identity such as have already partly been discussed in Chapter 2.
To describe a sound without automatically reaching for a set of associated
social-cultural equations which could be selectively deployed in the task of
prescription and proscription was, it seems, a feat beyond the capabilities of
many who chose to comment on the spoken language of the day. The metalanguage of 'vulgarity', 'provinciality', 'correctness', or 'elegance' was never
far behind the specification of one sound in preference to another, regularly
underpinning the arguments carefully laid by a variety of writers against the
dissemination of yet another fallible change in progress. One of the most
prominent topics for discussion in contemporary works on language, for
example, was the way in which words such as *fast*, *bath*, or *last* should be pronounced or, more specifically, what the 'correct' pronunciation of *a* should
be when it preceded the voiceless fricatives /f, s, θ/ or, in terms of spelling,
when it came before <f>, <s>, and <th>. Its realization as a long [ɑː] (as
in modern southern enunciations of *fast*) now, of course, functions as one of
the primary markers of a non-localized 'standard' accent, featuring both in
Received Pronunciation (RP) and in many varieties of modified standard
speech. Although its role as a salient feature of 'talking proper' is now seemingly secure, it is perhaps salutary to remember that this was by no means so
well established in the late eighteenth century. At this time, and indeed for

much of the nineteenth century, using [ɑ:] was instead quite likely to damn the speaker, in the words of various critics of the language, as 'inaccurate', 'vulgar', or indeed 'uneducated'. Questions of social and linguistic acceptability are, as in the images of accent already discussed, overtly made to surround relevant enunciations as writers on the language came, with considerable vigour, to adopt opposing positions in which they variously embraced the propriety of using short or long, front or retracted sounds of *a* in words of this kind. The absence of a fixed norm is all too clear from such comments, in spite of countless rhetorical assertions to the contrary, as various writers urged their own point of view upon potentially susceptible readers. In this as all else, prescriptive methodology was willingly to draw on the various social stereotypes prominent in contemporary comment—and the opportunities which these offered for praise or blame—as part of the linguistic persuasions which might be exerted as writers endeavoured to control, or impede, the direction of change.

John Walker, for example, emphasized to his by no means inconsiderable audience that to use the lengthened [ɑ:] was unquestionably the preserve of 'inaccurate speakers'. The negative resonances of this affiliation were amplified still further by Walker's subsequent assertion that these speakers were to be found 'chiefly among the vulgar'. As he added with marked emotive zeal, neatly polarizing the connotative values of 'correctness' and 'vulgarity': 'every correct ear would be disgusted at giving the *a* in these words the full long sound of the *a* in *father*'.[4] The use of the short [æ] (as in *cat*), now typical of Midland and Northern accents, is, on the converse, praised as 'elegant', 'accurate', and 'precise' when used in words such as *last* and *bath*, the social nuances of refinement being heavily weighted in its favour as Walker made his own allegiances clear in this prescriptively fraught territory of a change in progress. Other writers, however, endorsed other views and William Smith and Stephen Jones in (respectively) 1795 and 1798 instead select Walker's negatively proscribed [ɑ:] as their own preferred variant. As Jones comments, 'Mr. Walker . . . seems to have employed [the lengthened sound of *a*] with too much timidity . . . encouraging a mincing modern affectation, and departing from the genuine euphonical pronunciation of our language'.[5] The loaded use of 'mincing' merely added a further level of prescriptive censure to such intended social and linguistic dissuasion; 'to mince', as Johnson had noted in his own *Dictionary*, was 'to speak small and imperfectly'. Walker predictably did not take such dissent lightly. He added a number of pointed comments on the subject of Smith's fallibilities in this respect to the revised text of the second edition of his *Critical Pronouncing Dictionary* in 1797, explicitly censuring him for this highly misguided selection of [ɑ:]. 'In this work he [Smith] departs frequently from my judgment, and particularly in the pronunciation of the letter *a*', Walker declares, Smith's errors in this matter being made all too clear in Walker's subsequent selection of vulgarity as the only appropriate epithet which could be applied to such erroneous endorsement. As Walker pertinently adds: 'That this was the sound formerly, is highly probable from its being still the sound given to it by the vulgar, who are generally the last to alter the common pronunciation'.[6] Often evolving into a highly partisan affair, the debate was to continue in this way through much of the nineteenth century. Benjamin Smart in 1836, for instance, trades overtly on that heightened consciousness towards the social meanings of speech in terms of the 'proper' pronunciation of words such as *fast* and *bath*, duly advising his readers to avoid 'vulgarities' such as the lengthened *a* should they wish to convey overtones of the polite rather than the merely improper in their speech.[7]

As the linguist William Downes states, fundamentally 'a language change involves a change in norms',[8] and in the conflicting claims of individual writers and speakers at this time about how this particular set of words should be pronounced, this is precisely what can be seen to be in operation. The change, however, comes to involve not only linguistic norms but social ones too in the rhetoric which was commonly employed. With habitual ease, writers regularly (and explicitly) sought to appeal to the social and status insecurities of their readers, vigorously engaging in the politics of prescriptivism as they did so. 'Of the propriety or impropriety of this, a well-educated ear is the best judge', Walker remarks, for instance, on the use of [ɑː] in this environment, drawing on familiar paradigms of knowledge and ignorance as well as the markedly negative notion of 'impropriety'; 'unfitness, unsuitableness, inaccuracy', his own *Dictionary* explains. 'Well-educated ears are now averse to this pronunciation', stresses Smart more explicitly, evidently taking his role as a disciple of Walker seriously.[9] Though the use of a lengthened sound in this position had in fact been attested for London English from the late seventeenth century, first reliably appearing in the work of Christopher Cooper in 1687,[10] throughout the late eighteenth and nineteenth centuries this shift was nevertheless often depicted as solely the preserve of the 'vulgar', the 'ignorant', or the socially unacceptable. Its attempted proscription operates in terms of a range of shibboleths, often formally being affiliated to 'Cockney' usage, the strongly negative values of this social stereotype being assumed to act as sufficient dissuasion for any speaker.

In the realms of linguistic reality of course, and outside these binary evaluative schema of 'good' versus 'bad', or 'educated' versus 'vulgar', which were transparently favoured by many writers on the language, both short and long sounds were in use, even within that 'good' speech which Walker and others attempted to portray. Prescriptive methodology, habitually intolerant of linguistic variation, will, however, tend to sanction only one mode of pronunciation as 'correct', just as Robert Lowth in his *Grammar* had declared his intention to 'judge of every phrase and form of construction whether it be right or not'.[11] Variability was not an option within popular agendas of prescriptivism, and nor were considerations of its potential validity in the mechanisms of linguistic change. Instead paradigms of norm and deviation dominate, utilizing socially constructed appeals which laid bare selected social meanings in speech. Accent and its role in revealing, or indeed concealing, social identity, comes to form the prime sub-text of such descriptions so that texts such as *Common Blunders in Speaking, and How to Avoid Them*, for instance, deliberately emphasizes both social and aesthetic values in its prescriptive attempts to control the direction of change in this context. 'Do not pronounce the words *ask, lance, plaster*, as if spelt *arsk, larnce, plarster*', it dictates: 'such a style of pronunciation is offensive and grating to the ear.'[12] Particularly interesting are the repercussions that such prescriptive propaganda can be seen to have, both in terms of linguistic behaviour and in the wider territory of prevailing language attitudes.

Novelists, for example, readily came to trade on these common perceptions of stigma, allocating forms such as *farst* and *larff* to characters located in the lower spheres of life and thus further encoding (and diffusing) the stated ideologies of standard speech—and its antonyms—for their readers. 'Parsties', says the carrier Mr Barkis in *David Copperfield*, 'larst', says Andrew Peak, Godwin Peak's consummately Cockney uncle in Gissing's *Born in Exile*. Real speakers too, according to contemporary comment, were by no means immune to dicta which so emphatically stressed 'elegance' in the avoidance of the lengthened [ɑː] in articulations of *path* and other similar words. The philologist and lexicographer John Longmuir, writing in 1864, hence notes in his own account of pronunciation that, although variation between long and short sounds was still apparent, it was the short and fronted [æ] which dominated in the usage of those careful speakers who were concerned with the maintenance of 'correctness' and 'proper' speech. This pattern of usage was moreover seen as being sanctioned in particular by the continued legacy of Walker's superior apprehensions in matters of phonetic nicety. As Longmuir observes: 'the high character of Walker, and the increasing dislike of anything resembling a drawl in speaking, gave currency to the change ... Walker's extreme short sound of . . . *pass*, like *passive*, is now generally adopted as the proper sound'.[13] Prescriptivism, in this respect at least, clearly did not seem to operate in a vacuum.

Still more striking is the evidence which suggests that, while the social correlates so liberally accorded to these divergent realizations seem to have led certain speakers to adopt the use of the short [æ] exclusively, they also seem to have led to the creation of an artificial and compromise 'middle sound', one intermediate between [æ] and [ɑː] and which was, Longmuir notes, a characteristic of particularly careful speakers (and, as we may imagine, one used in situational contexts of greater formality where speech styles tend to be monitored—and controlled—to a greater degree). As Longmuir explained, 'there is a disposition among literary men and public speakers to unite on some *intermediate* sound between the entire broadness of the *a* in *father*, and the narrowness of the *a* in *fat* ... In this way, they guard against that undue prolongation of the *a* which offended Walker'.[14] Alexander Ellis, dubbed the 'father of modern phonetics' by the Philological Society, confirms this predilection, deftly utilizing the favoured metalanguage of prescriptive rhetoric in the explanation he provides. He isolates the use of an intermediate and, as he terms it, a 'delicate' sound which is, he states, deliberately adopted by 'refined' speakers in preference to realizations in [ɑ:] 'which they consider too "broad"', and to those in [æ] which were conversely deemed too 'mincing'.[15] It was this particular variant, in the evidence of Ellis and many other writers on the language, which apparently became the preserve of the speech-conscious and intentionally 'correct' in the nineteenth century (as well as for some years afterwards). Submitting to the ideologies of standard norms so publicly wielded by Walker and others, such speakers clearly seem to have responded by shifting their own language habits in favour of this compromise realization and hence, at least in terms of the connotations which were so liberally employed in prescriptive theory, simultaneously being able to avoid the stated stigmas of 'vulgarity', 'ignorance', as well as 'impropriety'.

Ellis's further specification of co-variation in this context, detailing a correlation of such variants not only with status but also with gender will be discussed in a later chapter.[16] What is clear, however, even from this brief survey, is the fact that notions of accent and identity, regularly articulated in prescriptive texts and, by the late nineteenth century, forming a self-evident staple of the standardizing ideology, did not seem to operate in isolation. For those sensitive to the shades of sociolinguistic symbolism which were, as we have seen, regularly manipulated in ostensibly factual accounts of language use, the role of the 'correct speaker' as a social ideal could and did seemingly lead to attempts to change hitherto accepted patterns of pronunciation even within variants of a single phoneme, and particularly in the more formal registers of the language (the language of 'public speakers and literary men', as Longmuir notes). As late as the first decade of the twentieth century the phonetician Walker Ripman still observes that the 'delicate' middle sound is 'sometimes found' in 'precise speakers', a pattern he attributes to 'an excessive desire to avoid any suspicion of Cockney leanings in their speech'. As a result, he states, they often 'substitute [a] for [ɑ], saying, for instance, [faːðə] in place of [fɑːðə]'.[17] As this suggests, it evidently took some time to dispel the connotative legacies of the eighteenth and nineteenth centuries for this particular detail of speech.

Like the 'naice' speakers of today, it was, however, especially those who felt themselves potentially open to the suspicion of vulgarity—or who aspired to a refinement which they did not in fact possess—who seemed most of all to assume such 'correct' forms in their speech. In this they can be seen to be precisely akin to those speakers in the lower sections of society who have regularly been documented in the sociolinguistic surveys of Peter Trudgill or William Labov. These, as already indicated, can similarly hypercorrect in their use of variants perceived as most statusful, revealing marked levels of linguistic insecurity in their attitudes towards their own linguistic usage, as well as in their marked willingness to approximate more closely to the stated norms of 'proper' language in their more formal speech. It was the nineteenth-century counterparts of such speakers who were of course explicitly targeted by the writers of the sixpenny manuals such as the anonymous *Hard Words Made Easy* (1855) and *Mind Your H's and Take Care of Your R's* (1866), with their own recommendations to those seeking to make their way in the social order to 'Avoid a too broad or too slender pronunciation of the vowel *a*, in words such as *glass*... Some persons vulgarly pronounce the *a* in such words, as if written *ar*, and others mince it so as to rhyme it with *stand*... Equally avoid the extremes of vulgarity and affectation'.[18] Speakers more secure in their sociolinguistic identities would hardly have been tempted by the titles of these works, nor would they have formed part of their by no means inconsiderable readership.

Nevertheless, in spite of the ease with which such notions of 'standard' and 'non-standard' were bandied about in this context in late eighteenth- and nineteenth-century texts, the real difficulty remains in ascertaining the reality of the norms actually in use. Prescriptivism, as we will see, though illuminating in terms of language attitudes, can have a less than simple relationship with linguistic actuality. For instance, it was, in the end, not to be the iterated 'correctness' of this 'middle' variant, or even Walker's favoured [æ], but instead the theoretically 'vulgar' [ɑː] which stabilized as one of the dominant markers of RP and the non-regional accent. It was this which ultimately—and paradoxically—came to be a hallmark of that 'elegant' speech which Walker and others had sought to define (at least in part) by the very fact of its exclusion. The interactions of language, society, prescriptive tenets, and the sociolinguistic sensibilities of speakers are in such ways much more complex than might at first be assumed. In real terms, for example, the use of [ɑː], recorded first, as we have seen, in the late seventeenth century, remained as a variant realization throughout the eighteenth and nineteenth centuries, gradually extending its use and distribution in the south at the expense of [æ], though its diffusion in relevant linguistic environments was never complete.[19] The censure which it received in terms of the standard ideology over this time is in many ways therefore merely a reaction to an observable change in progress in a language in which stability was revered (particularly from the point of view of much prescriptive writing) and in which the rights of codification were regularly asserted above those of 'custom' or usage. As the anonymous author of *Vulgarisms and Other Errors of Speech* averred on the subject of linguistic change, for example, 'it is not innovation that is reprehensible, but innovation without good cause, and,

worst of all, innovation for innovations's sake'.[20] Using [ɑː] rather than the
long-established [æ] was, in such terms, likely to be proscribed as precisely
such 'unnecessary' innovation, though the fact that similar patterns of usage
were in evidence in lower-class London speech seems to have given extra
point to the notions of correctness and social value prioritized in relevant
prescriptive propaganda. Depictions of Cockney, for instance, regularly
trade on lengthened articulations in these positions—a fact made all too clear
in George Gissing's acute observations of Cockney in, say, *Born in Exile*.
'Vulgarity' was, as a result, rightly perceived as the most powerful weapon for
attempted control in terms of the ideal (and idealized) standard. That this
was not entirely without success is in turn evident from the range of contemporary comment on the preferences for [æ] (and indeed [æː]) which certain nineteenth-century speakers did indeed display.

The very nature of this linguistic change and its diffusion inevitably forces
us to confront another pervasive prescriptive fiction of 'proper' language. As
the eventual dominance of [ɑː] as the non-regionally marked norm makes
plain, though prescriptive writings on the language almost invariably present
elite models of enunciation (such as Sheridan's 'good company') as the specified focus of linguistic emulation for the rest of society, the real direction of
linguistic change can and does instead regularly run counter to such precepts. As countless sociolinguistic studies have revealed, the nexus of change,
and the innovating groups in society, are thus usually to be found in lower
rather than higher echelons, a fact which renders Walker's own attempted
sociolinguistic alignments of change particularly misguided, as in his conviction that 'the vulgar are usually the last to alter the common pronunciation'—the reason he provides for their continued use of [ɑː] instead of that
short [æ] which is, he urges, 'the general pronunciation of the polite and
learned world'.[21] In these terms, it is evidently the fear of the 'other' in both
social and linguistic senses which motivates prescriptive denunciations of
change in ways which can in fact still be paralleled today, not least in reactions to 'Estuary English' and its own assumed shibboleths of speech.[22]

As the respective progress of [ɑː] and [æ] in this context illustrates therefore, though prevalent attitudes to language will not necessarily affect the
ultimate outcome of a linguistic change (just as the modern cries of 'degeneration' surrounding the semantic shift in words such as *aggravate* or *hopefully* will in no way redress their advance), they can nevertheless prove
remarkably pervasive in terms of popular notions of correctness as well as
individual patterns of linguistic behaviour. In such ways, just as in the
twenty-first century those most conscious of the perceived merits of correctness will endeavour to modify their usage accordingly, resolutely avoiding *hopefully* in the sense of 'it is hoped that' (instead of its 'correct' sense 'in
a hopeful manner'), so did their nineteenth-century counterparts presumably try, with equal resolution, to avoid [ɑː], especially in the more formal

contexts of speech when speakers are particularly on their guard. Such patterns present us yet again with the disjunction between the operation of standardization as a process and its role (and pervasiveness) as an ideology. It is of course the latter, and not the former, which generates these beliefs in that set of 'right' and 'wrong' enunciations which came to be so eloquently disputed in this context. It is moreover this which, as we have seen, in turn leads to the effective dissemination of a number of attendant sociolinguistic stereotypes, as well as their deployment in this particular context over the course of the nineteenth century (the 'vulgar' or 'Cockney' use of [ɑ:], the 'refined' use of its 'middle' equivalent). The actual processes of standardization will thus inevitably be at some removes from the idealized and often binary oppositions of the prescriptive tradition, a fact which is all too evident in the range of variant enunciations still apparent over the country in relevant words, as well as in the fact that the one variant which has emerged as a non-localized 'standard pronunciation feature' (['pɑ:θ], ['bɑ:θ] for *path, bath*) is not the one endorsed by the majority of nineteenth-century observers.

Other nineteenth-century changes in progress can, perhaps predictably, reveal similar patterns though they can in addition also serve to illuminate further aspects of those prescriptive fictions which were so often deployed in the aim to create the 'plain and permanent standard of pronunciation' which Sheridan (and others) had advocated. One particularly prevalent image within writing on the language, and attitudes to its use, is, for example, that of the 'elegant' speaker, set out perhaps most effectively by Dr Johnson in his own dictum that 'for pronunciation the best general rule is, to consider those as the most elegant speakers who deviate least from the written words'.[23] Though one of the few comments which he made in terms of pronunciation in his dictionary of 1755, this precept was nevertheless recognized as important, embracing as it did linguistic ideals in which written and spoken language, grapheme and phoneme, might be in harmony. It evolved into a concise definition of 'elegant' speech and was, as a result, often cited, influencing popular notions of propriety in works such as the *Grammar* of Lindley Murray, a text which went through thirty-four editions by 1821 and which again, without reservation, endorsed the view that 'it is a good rule, with respect to pronunciation, to adhere to the written words, unless custom has clearly decided otherwise'.[24] The grammars of countless other writers provided similar corroboration: 'Dr. Johnson judiciously...remarks that "For pronunciation the best rule is, to consider those as the most elegant speakers, who deviate least from the *written* words"' wrote Lewis Brittain in 1788.[25] 'Dr. Johnson's Dictionary may be consulted with great advantage. He says, and very justly too, "that they are the most elegant speakers who deviate least from the written sound"', affirmed Thomas Carpenter in 1825.[26] Time and time again, the authority of Johnson's own words was used to confirm notions of the superior authority of grapheme above phoneme.

Johnson, of course, merely gave influential voice to a common assumption about the relationships of spoken and written languages: that graphemes were primary and phonemes secondary seemed for many to be borne out by the greater perfection and stability of the former against the flux and instability which the latter still evinced. Moreover, as Michael Stubbs has pointed out, though the spoken word must be accorded clear linguistic primacy, in popular thinking it is instead its written equivalent which assumes a social (and cultural) priority which is far from insignificant[27]—especially when knowledge of this order was itself often seen as an index of social standing. It was 'literate speakers' who, in the thinking of the day, reflected such superior knowledge in their speech. 'Illiterate ones', as Johnson also noted, revealed merely ignorance: 'we now observe those who cannot read to catch sounds imperfectly, and utter them negligently'.[28]

Notions of 'literate speech' on these lines came to influence materially common opinions on correct speech, not least in the context of the shibboleth of [h]-dropping which was, as Chapter 4 will explore, also being encoded over this time. It is, however, the 'dropped [r]' which will occupy our attention in this chapter since this too can be seen to exemplify in many ways the complex interactions of prescriptive ideology, literate speech, and those sociosymbolic values which were never far from issues of phonemic propriety over the nineteenth century. As with [h], for example, the 'dropping' or vocalization of [r] in words such as *car* [ˈkɑː], and *chart* [ˈʧɑːt], where it is no longer pronounced post-vocalically in RP or approximations to it,[29] involves the apparent loss of a 'letter'. Still worse, from contemporary points of view, it involved the creation of a number of homophones such as *lord* and *laud*, *lorn* and *lawn*, as words which had hitherto been phonetically distinct were, by means of this vocalization, rendered identical in sound (even if their differentiation in spelling remained). Given typical prescriptive sensibilities on this score (Francis Newman in 1878, for example, directed heavy censure towards the 'assimilating and trait-destroying tendencies of slovenly speech'),[30] this presented a situation which was guaranteed to arouse attack, and socially constructed epithets were applied accordingly to those who revealed such 'carelessness' and 'negligence' in their speech. After all, as writers on the language regularly urged, 'careful' (and, by extension, 'good') speakers would surely take the trouble to discriminate between sounds which, at least in the past, had safely been distinct. Many writers (and speakers) as a result seemed to cultivate an ostrich-like mentality, resolutely refusing to acknowledge that such a change had taken place or that, if it had, it had done so only in the most vulgar of surroundings.

As with a number of other features of eighteenth- and nineteenth-century pronunciation, notions of the social distribution of linguistic items were to be manipulated to particularly good effect in prescriptive writing on this subject. The potential of the pervasive correlations of accent and status which, as we have seen, often served to encode potent social and linguistic stereo-types did not, for instance, pass unremarked. In the chosen paradigms of pre-scriptive texts, it is the 'vulgar', the 'Cockney', the 'lower classes', and the 'illiterate' who were all deemed to be prime culprits in the vocalization of post-vocalic [r]. In contrast, the 'elegant', the 'polished', and the 'educated' were declared to retain its use in the precision of their careful, and literate, speech. Within such popular formats, accounts of speech thus regularly tend to enact perceived social divisions though the underlying point, especially in terms of the remedial self-help which was often ostensibly proffered in con-temporary works on language, is also clear—by individual effort, the 'illiter-ate' can become 'polished' by restoring [r] to its rightful place in words such as *car* and *part*. 'Poor Letter R' , in the hands of a 'Robert Ruskin Rogers', is even made to publish his own eloquent appeal on the subject of his use and abuse, his first-person address drawing out the pathos of his situation—regu-larly neglected, forgotten, and abandoned in the pronunciation of words:

Let me appeal to your good nature and fellow-feeling, under the insults and indig-nities to which I am continually exposed...In public assemblies and in private societies, I am frequently wounded by the ignorance of my *character* and claims so commonly betrayed.[31]

Attitudes to the loss of [r] again exemplify the divergence which can occur between linguistic fact and prescriptive fiction. In reality, its vocalization in these positions had been attested since the mid-eighteenth century in London English, its absence rather than its presence in fact being more typical of the emergent RP of the nineteenth century. Nevertheless, theoretical criteria of acceptability rarely sanctioned this development, and the fictions of social identity which were attached to the presence (and conversely the absence) of [r] remained remarkably powerful if contemporary accounts are to be believed. 'Cockney', a term of abuse which was regularly applied to many lin-guistic sins of the age, was, for instance, given particular emphasis in con-demnatory accounts of the loss of post-vocalic [r], its omission thus being deliberately associated with a social sub-stratum characterized by popular con-victions of its complete social, and linguistic, unacceptability. Hill in 1821 and Smart in 1836, for example, both link the disappearance of [r] in this class of words to the 'provincialists' and the Cockney 'vulgar' of the 'Metropolis', deliberately utilizing the connotative values of these epithets in the proscrip-tions which they duly endeavour to enforce. As James Murray specified in the relevant fascicle of the first edition of the *OED* (*Clo–Consigner* published in 1891), Cockney in this sense was 'particularly used to connote the character-istics in which the born Londoner is supposed to be inferior to other Englishmen'. Hill and Smart, among a whole range of others, were deliberately to extend such inferiority to contemporary notions of Cockney speech too, effectively trading on a marked contemporary receptiveness to these ideas.

Such notions of the specific (and highly negative) affiliations of 'Cockney' in terms of the loss of [r] after vowels intervened even in the realms of poetry, and rhymes such as *born: faun* which traded on the use of aural rather than visual correspondence in this context were as a result often proscribed as 'Cockney rhymes'—in spite of their evident validity to ear if not to eye.[32] The writer Thomas Hood the younger, in a section of his text devoted to the aspiring poet, hence felt driven to exhort 'the writer of verse to examine his rhymes carefully to ensure that "they chime to an educated ear" '. If not 'such atrocities as "morn" and "dawn", . . . "fought" and "sort" ', are fatal to the success of verse', he continued: 'They stamp it with vulgarity, as surely as the dropping of "h" stamps a speaker'.[33]

Such rhymes, in the ideology of the time, were deemed untenable within the sanctity of verse, a view likewise endorsed by the poet and writer Joseph Carpenter in 1868: 'In a young author's first volume I found "Italy" made to rhyme with "bitterly". Now "Iterly", in the mouth of a public speaker, would condemn him as a thorough Cockney. "Armies" with "calm is", is another of this same writer's cockney rhymes.'[34] It was stigmatization of this sort which was used to hound John Keats whose rhymes of *thorns: fawns*, and *thoughts: sorts* (/ˈθɔːnz: ˈfɔːnz, ˈθɔːts: ˈsɔːts/) contravened popular notions of correctness of precisely this kind, even if they simultaneously agreed with the realities of ordinary usage. Keats's use of aural rather than visual authority in his poetry was, however, typically to bring censure rather than praise. John Lockhart, writing in *Blackwood's Edinburgh Magazine*, thus deploys notions of 'literate speech' to censure Keats's poetry in a form of literary criticism which readily reveals the operations of social as well as linguistic prejudice (as well as further confirming the wider impact of language attitudes outside the confines of the prescriptive tradition itself). Keats is, on such grounds, 'an uneducated and flimsy stripling'. He is 'without logic enough to analyse a single idea, or imagination enough to form one original image'. More fundamentally, he is also '[without] learning enough to distinguish between the written language of Englishmen and the spoken jargon of Cockneys'.[35] Keats is, in effect, 'illiterate', excluded from the domains of poetic propriety by his deliberate disregard for the authority of graphemes in the phonemic correspondences he employs.

What is perhaps most striking is the very pervasiveness of this idea so that, in the history of criticism, it comes to form a recurrent element in descriptions of Keats's linguistic and poetic failings. The poet Gerard Manley Hopkins in 1880, for example, still avers that 'there is one thing that Keats's authority can never excuse, and that is rhyming open vowels to silent *rs*, as *higher* to *Thalia*'. As he stressed, 'as long as the *r* is pronounced by anybody, and it is by a good many yet, the feeling that it is there makes this rhyme most offensive, not indeed to the ear, but to the mind'.[36] This was of course the crux, Hopkins's comments concisely revealing just how extensive the subscription to prescriptive norms (and associated ideologies) could indeed be. In these terms, the presence of [r] in all positions, promoted as a salient part of 'correct' speech, was still 'standard'. All else, irrespective of the realities of usage, was necessarily 'substandard', and hence unworthy of consideration. Hopkins nevertheless effectively points up the disjunction which results from such beliefs in his acknowledgement that it is the mind rather than the ear which is offended by such rhymes. In other words, such correspondences contravene *perceptions* of linguistic usage rather than the dominant patterns of linguistic usage in themselves. As this indicates, speakers could, in effect, come to recognize the discrepancy which exists between ideologies of a standard—the belief in what 'good' speech should be—and its corresponding patterns in terms of usage—even while the dominance of common value judgements paradoxically often led them to adhere to the former above the latter. It is of course this particular pattern of response which is most significant in attitudes to the loss of [r] in words such as *thorn* and *dawn*. As Hopkins confirms, the combined claims of education, and the associated fictions of literate speech, were to suggest to many that they still heard, or at least they thought they ought to hear, the retention of [r] in 'good' speech, even though theory and practice in this respect were usually to be at odds. Tennyson, for example, boldly asserted his own conformity with prescriptive sensibilities on this score in his statement that 'I would sooner lose a pretty thought than enshrine it in such rhymes as "Eudora" "before her," "vista" "sister"' (in spite of the fact that, from a phonetic point of view, such rhymes are again precise).[37] Rhymes such as *thorns*: *yawns*, or *drawn*: *lawn*: *thorn* can nevertheless be detected in his verse.[38] Christina Rossetti revealed similar preoccupations, as in her advice to the aspiring poet Miss Newsham in 1889 that *morn* and *dawn* were not 'true rhymes' and hence should be avoided in verse.[39] Given his habitual sensitivities on the subject of accent, it is, however, perhaps unsurprising that Gissing reacts in the precisely same way: 'What a fearful rhyme I came across the other day, in Keats's verses on Indolence. With *farce* he positively rhymes *grass*. Ye heavens!'[40]

Principle and practice, ideology and process, again fail to coincide and the standard norms overtly subscribed to can, in reality, be abandoned when the speaker, or writer, is off their guard. As the writer (and founder member of the Philological Society) Edwin Guest noted in 1838 on the subject of the continued presence of post-vocalic and final [r] in 'good' speech, 'many who insist upon its pronunciation, drop it, immediately their attention is diverted, or their vigilance relaxed'.[41] As the evidence already surveyed has indicated, this fact applies both to poets and to ordinary users of the language. Distinctions between *laud* and *lord* are, as Alexander Ellis confirmed in 1869, entirely theoretical, a product of 'careful speakers when they are thinking particularly of what they are saying'.[42] In the early twentieth century, the philologist and lexicographer Henry Wyld was still making resolute attempts to instil a sense of linguistic reality in this context, revealing the pervasive and long-term influence of language attitudes in this respect: '[Ordinary speakers] even go to the length of pretending that they can hear a difference between such pairs as *horse-hoarse, Parma-palmer, kernel-colonel*...Of course, a distinction can easily be made; pronunciation can be faked to any extent. The point is that in ordinary educated English speech in the South, there is no difference between the above pairs.'[43] The use of post-vocalic and final [r] in this sense was evidently able to achieve the paradoxical status of being present as a prescriptive norm in the 'best' English—even while descriptive discussion of non-localized pronunciation was forced to acknowledge its absence in precisely the same positions.

The prevalent notions of 'literate speech' as manipulated within both the standard ideology and popular language attitudes nevertheless do seem to have led a considerable number of speakers, especially amongst those whose acquisition of educated rank was relatively recent, to attempt to retain [r] in these positions in their speech. Like the 'middle sounds' of *a* already discussed, its use in time becomes a marker of the speech-conscious—or the intentionally 'elegant' in Johnson's terms—who endeavoured (at least when concentrating on proprieties of this order in their more formal speech) to reflect the distinctions of the written language in line with such popular attitudes to correctness. Over the course of the nineteenth century, such recurrent patterns lead in fact to what might be recognized as the phenomenon of the 'hyperliterate speaker', a social and linguistic stereotype associated in contemporary comment with public speakers, as well as with prevalent fables of the newly rich and socially aspiring in the middle sections of society. The anonymous author of *Hard Words Made Easy* hence notes in terms of [r]: 'Some of our public speakers, who push accuracy of utterance beyond a wholesome limit, get the habit of trilling the *r* so much that one would think that they wished to be thought unlettered Scotch or Irish peasants'.[44] Sedulous attention to graphemes above phonemes (and to the theoretical rhoticity of the 'best' speech wherever *r* was found in the spelling) could, as this reveals, be pushed too far. In novels, journals, as well as in popular comment on language, hyperliteracy of this kind itself surfaces as another observable pattern of speech behaviour, being made into a further distinguishing marker of the intentionally, but not actually, 'genteel'. John Earle in 1871 hence comments on spelling pronunciations of *Derby* and *clerk* 'which many persons, especially of that class which is beginning to claim educated rank, now pronounce literally'.[45] Geoffry Hill similarly draws attention to the overuse of [h] among the middle sections of society:

It is not as a rule the very poor who introduce h's, but the small shopkeeper and the villager who reads at home in the evening instead of going to the public-house. They are slightly better educated than many of those with whom they associate, and naturally wish to make their superiority evident; for some reason they adopt this plan of doing so.[46]

It was of course precisely these patterns of which George Eliot had made use in her own linguistic characterization of, for example, Mr Casson, landlord of the Donnithorne Arms and erstwhile butler of Donnithorne Chase, in *Adam Bede*: '"They're cur'ous talkers i' this country, sir; the gentry's hard work to hunderstand 'em. I was brought hup among the gentry, sir, an' got the turn o' their tongue when I was a bye." '[47] Other novelists too picked up and reinforced these features (and accompanying language attitudes), often choosing to depict this striving for phonemic correctness and graphemic correspondence in various characters who are located at the outer edges of respectability. In the wider context, however, it is important to recognize that this trend towards spelling pronunciations was in fact to gather a far larger momentum, leading to a general shift in the pronunciation of many words such as *falcon, forehead*, and *waistcoat*,[48] a topic to which we shall later return, revealing as it does the ultimate dissemination of the ideals of literate speech into the facts rather than the fictions of usage.

Attitudes to the loss of [r] in these positions tended, however, to have other consequences too, influencing not least contemporary reactions to the phenomenon now known as 'intrusive *r*'. This commonly triggered the same negative perceptions of use—regardless of the linguistic and social fictions on which such assumptions can, more objectively, be seen to rest. The development of intrusive [r] is, in fact, closely linked to the vocalization or loss of [r] in final position, a process by which, as we have seen, words such as *ma* and *mar* became identical in southern English, both being articulated (in non-localized—and non-rhotic—accents) as /ˈmaː/. In connected speech, however, some modifications of this basic pattern came into play. In other words, a word like *mar* which would, under the normal conditions of this change, become [r]-less, would instead—both then and now—see its [r] retained if it happened to be followed by another word beginning with a vowel, a feature which is known as 'linking [r]'. As a result, while a construction such as *far from* is pronounced—without final [r] —as /ˈfaː frəm/, *far away* will show this conditioned development, being pronounced as /ˈfaːr əˈweɪ/, the [r] being restored before the initial vowel of *away*. This also happens word internally in similar circumstances so that alternations such as *fear fearing* /ˈfɪə, ˈfɪərɪŋ/ are also common. The use of linking [r] in such ways operates as a linking or sandhi phenomenon, being used to obviate a potential gap or hiatus between different sounds and thereby securing a smoother transition between, as in this particular context, two adjacent vowel sounds.

Intrusive [r] develops in the same way, its use exactly parallelling that of the inoffensive linking [r] for which prescriptive censure is entirely absent in eighteenth- and nineteenth-century comment. Intrusive [r] hence appears in identical phonetic environments, such as after /aː/ and /ɔː/ (as in *catarrh* and *law*) and especially after /ə/, as in *Laura*, so that, although a construction such as *Laura then* would be articulated as /ˈlɔːrə ðɛn/, *Laura and* tends to gain an [r] in the realities of connected speech, being pronounced as /ˈlɔːrər ənd/. As in the use of linking [r] in *far away* or *fearing*, the interposed [r] is used phonetically to smooth the transition between two vowel sounds which would otherwise be consecutive. Given the absence of a corresponding <r> in the written form of relevant words, this was a process which was, however, regularly to be condemned. Enunciations which reveal its presence such as *law of the land* (/ˈlɔːr əv ðə ˈlænd/) or, word internally, in the pronunciation of *drawing room* as /ˈdrɔːrɪŋ ˈrum/, were the subject of overt (and explicit) stigmatization even while precisely the same process, from a phonetic point of view, took place without remark in habitual utterances of, say, *fear of* /ˈfɪər əv/. To say *idea of* /ˈaɪdɪər əv/ conversely tended to exercise prescriptive sensibilities to their limit, the visual and phonetic disparities involved in such articulations being entirely untenable within popular conceptions of 'proper' speech.

Characteristic manifestations of the presence of intrusive [r] are, in consequence, often severely censured. Benjamin Smart includes it in his catalogue of those features which define the 'vulgar' as opposed to the well-bred speaker, noting of the former: 'He annexes the sound *r* to the vowel sound denoted by *aw*, in *jaw, paw, saw*'.[49] Smart's idealized 'well-bred' counterpart has no such 'flaw', instead exhibiting a theoretically perfect correlation of spoken and written forms, even in unaccented syllables. Henry Alford in 1864 similarly strives to eliminate intrusive [r] from educated speech, equating it on levels of 'incorrectness' with that other great social shibboleth, the loss of [h]; both, he declares, are 'enough to make the hair of any one but a well-seasoned Cockney stand on end'.[50] Even Alexander Ellis, intentionally located within the newly descriptive rigour of late nineteenth-century linguistics, was to fail to free himself from popular preconceptions on this score. Instead the language of subjective inequality rather than objective observation features prominently in his comments. Intrusive [r] is, he notes, 'a non-permissive trill' and 'the very height of vulgarity';[51] it marks the 'uneducated' ('there also exists a great tendency among all uneducated speakers to introduce an (r) ... as [in] *drawing, sawing*'),[52] and, of course, the 'illiterate'. As he further elaborates, 'illiterate speakers—those who either do not know how to spell, or ignore the rules of spelling in their speech—usually interpose an (r) between any back vowel, as (a, A, ɑ) and a subsequent vowel'.[53] Ellis's evident antipathies in this context disturb the intentionally even tenor of his text, revealing the widespread legacy of popular prescriptivism in his censure of those who 'ignore the rules of spelling in their speech'—in spite of the evident disparity which in fact almost invariably holds true in English between sound and written representation.[54]

As the terms of proscription deliberately selected by Henry Alford in terms of this particular phonetic shift have already revealed, that other great sociolinguistic stereotype of the 'Cockney', was, perhaps predictably, to make its own due appearance with reference to the negative patterning of intrusive [r]. Far from being a natural part of connected speech, intrusive [r], as the musical composer and teacher John Hullah declared in 1870, was instead to be regarded as a prime 'characteristic of cockney breeding' and hence 'insufferably vulgar' in enunciations such as '*Maidarill* (for Maida Hill)'. Notions of acceptability hence diverged sharply; if *Maidarill* was 'not unpardonable in an omnibus conductor', to find such enunciations higher in the social scale—especially among those whose birth and education meant that they should know 'better', would neverthless fail to find any such sanction. '*Victoriarour Queen*', Hullah averred, would therefore be 'quite unpardonable in an educated gentleman.'[55] The 'gentleman' and the 'conductor' stand at odds, and not only in their ostensibly divergent use of intrusive [r]. In this as in other respects, notions of status, and stated affiliations with the social hierarchy, were once again to be manipulated by the standardizing ideology, erecting an idealized 'best' form of the language employed by those higher in the social order—here one in which intrusive [r] meets with a marked lack of tolerance—against an erroneous and 'illiterate' flawed form of English in which such failings are all too prominent. In prescriptive rhetoric, it is of course the latter which were to be modified in favour of this propagated and 'correct' norm.

In real terms, on the other hand, this dividing chasm between 'educated' and 'uneducated' speakers, 'standard' and otherwise, was a prescriptive fiction just as much as were those censorious (and socially motivated) comments which were regularly directed towards the loss of [r] itself in these positions. As the phonetician Henry Sweet noted with some frustration of contemporary attitudes towards intrusive [r] in the late nineteenth century: 'I know as a fact that most educated speakers of Southern English insert an *r* in *idea(r) of*, *India(r) Office* etc. in rapid speech, and I know that this habit, so far from dying out, is spreading to the Midlands; and yet they all obstinately deny it'.[56] Its use was in fact widespread—James Lecky, a noted phonetician, transcribes it in his notes of the speech of 'eminent preachers and University professors' in the 1880s[57]—and it is clear that even those who traditionally exemplified notions of RP and its non-localized norms featured it in their everyday speech, even if (as Sweet suggests) they might perhaps have endeavoured to avoid it in the more formal registers of 'careful' usage. Its role as a theoretical shibboleth has, however, tended to remain no less powerful in some ways for this lack of any objective validation. It is, for example, still regularly made the subject of modern manifestations of the 'complaint tradition', often appearing, for instance, as a stigmatized marker of the social divide in the letter columns of the daily newspapers.

Language attitudes, as this indicates, can remain remarkably constant even in the face of linguistic reality and objective phonetic truth. In terms of the standard ideology therefore, intrusive [r] is not a feature of the 'best English', even though speakers of mainstream RP do in fact naturally make use of it where circumstances require. Speakers of adoptive RP on the other hand (i.e. those who did not use this accent as children) tend to avoid the use of intrusive [r], clearly being subject in this to the manipulations of common images of 'standardness' and the theoretical notions of correctness which these habitually deploy. As the phonetician John Wells notes,[58] such speakers tend to have little control over the more 'informal' characteristics of this mode of speech so that the assimilations, elisions, and other contextual modifications which occur in this as in any other accent are avoided owing to some preconception (conscious or otherwise) that such features are, in some way, incompatible with the 'best' speech which RP must surely represent. Intrusive [r] too seems as a result to come under this heading. 'In native-speaker RP it is usual to use sandhi /r/ in the appropriate places, in the environments where it is "intrusive" (unhistorical, not corresponding to the spelling) just as in those where it is not', Wells confirmed of modern RP. The same may be assumed for its antecedents in the nineteenth century.[59] In contrast, as Wells adds, 'the speech-conscious tend to regard intrusive /r/ as incorrect, and hence attempt to avoid it ... the typical outcome is the suppression of most sandhi /r/s'. In such ways, modern speakers of adoptive RP can be regarded as the heirs of that proscriptive censure which was proffered so liberally in this context over the course of the nineteenth century, as well as illustrating (here in the empirical terms of modern linguistics) the legacy of language attitudes, and the effects that these notions of stigmatization and of shibboleths can indeed have upon those who are sensitive to their appeal.

4

/h/ and Other Symbols of the Social Divide

THE use of /h/ in modern English has come to stand as one of the foremost
signals of social identity, its presence in initial positions associated almost
inevitably with the 'educated' and 'polite' while its loss commonly triggers
popular connotations of the 'vulgar', the 'ignorant', and the 'lower class'.
Surrounded by social values, and attendant value judgements, the dropping of
[h], as John Wells has pointed out, now operates as 'the single most powerful
pronunciation shibboleth in England',[1] a ready marker of social difference, a
symbol of the social divide. In literature and language alike, sensitization to the
social distribution of linguistic items has, with particular frequency, attached
itself to patterns of [h]-usage, its presence (in the right place) suggesting familiarity with conventional proprieties of speech,[2] whilst its absence has come to
function as prime diacritic of the linguistically and socially unacceptable. Such
patterns often figure significantly in modern literature so that characters who
are delineated in terms of their rustic location, rudimentary education, or
membership of the lower sections of society all tend to have speech marked by
the strategic omission of [h]: ' "It's your ladyship's own 'ut," ' says Mellors to
Lady Chatterley, for example. ' "I don't in the least want to turn you out of
your hut" ', says Lady Chatterley to Mellors.[3] On such differences turns the
social distance between them, the gamekeeper and the lady.

The inability to use [h] in line with such now prevalent notions of correctness has, in this way, evolved as a convenient form of social shorthand,
regularly signified in literature by graphemic deviation from the expected
forms of the text. Using *'and* rather than *hand* or, as Mellors does, *'ut* and
not *hut*, has come to suggest a whole complex of social meanings, founded
upon popular conceptions of 'talking proper'. Such associations are not confined to the present. The phonetician Henry Sweet in 1890 similarly comments on the role of [h] as 'an almost infallible test of education and
refinement',[4] and Alexander Ellis, another characteristically objective
observer, noted earlier, in 1869, that 'at the present day great strictness in
pronouncing *h* is demanded as a test of education and position in society'.[5]
Assumptions of culture, status, and education seem almost inseparable from
its use, the relevant evaluative paradigms, as these comments suggest, being
all too readily extended to speaker as well as speech. Even encyclopedias in
the late nineteenth century could stress the role of [h] in determining, and
assigning, social status, enumerating details of 'proper' usage in this context

among the other facts which they offered for the erudition of their readers.
'The correct pronunciation of this difficult letter is one of the most delicate
tests of good breeding', as the new edition of *Chambers's Encyclopaedia*
admonished in 1888,[6] devoting an entire section to descriptions of its use.

In the past, just as in the present, it might therefore seem that attitudes to
/h/ had always embraced these correlations with status and social standing
with habitual readiness. In the late nineteenth century, /h/ was, as the Oxford
scholar Thomas Kington-Oliphant emphasized, the 'fatal letter',[7] with the
consequences of its use and misuse potentially momentous in the search for
social acceptability. Standing as a near-tangible manifestation of the 'two
nations' theme, writers such as Dickens, Gaskell, and Gissing employ patterns of <h> presence and absence in ways which are familiar from the
Lawrence text already mentioned. 'Struggles with the h-fiend' hence mark
the social progress of Richard Mutimer, the artisan hero of Gissing's novel
Demos,[8] while Gaskell's *North and South* similarly explores the social and linguistic stereotypes associated with its use, not least of which are those surrounding the 'new rich' of the Industrial Revolution and associated
expectations of their linguistic fallibility. Edith Lennox, for example, immediately expects infelicities in this respect once Mr Thornton, the Darkshire
mill-owner, arrives in London: 'I asked [Henry] if he was a man one would
be ashamed of; and he replied, "Not if you have any sense in you, my little
sister." So I suppose he is able to sound his *h*'s, which is not a common
Darkshire accomplishment.'[9]

Edith's immediate equation of social shame with lack of facility in the use of
/h/ epitomizes particularly clearly the social values and social assumptions with
which its presence was, and is, imbued. Nineteenth-century authors wield
consummate skill in its deployment in socially sensitive ways, and writers on
the language, especially by the second half of the nineteenth century, write eloquently on the social consequences which follow its 'abuse'. Their vehement
proclamations, and the very abundance of prescription and proscription on
this head, indeed make it tempting to assume that such a situation had always
existed. This assumption would, however, be mistaken for the rise of [h] as
social symbol does not antedate the eighteenth century and, more specifically,
it becomes prominent only towards its end. Transformations within the role of
/h/ accompany, in other words, those wider transformations then taking place
in English society and, in particular, within thinking about the nuances of
accent as a social as well as linguistic phenomenon. That rise to social prominence which is so marked in attitudes to the presence and absence of [h] is
therefore in a number of ways inseparable from the shifting social contexts of
the time in which, as we have seen, attitudes to language could and did manifest more than strictly philological interest.

Early attitudes to [h], for example, accorded most importance to its role in
differentiating words such as *hill, ill,* or *hand, and,* rather than to any ability

it possessed for the social differentiation of speakers. The latter is not mentioned. Still earlier comments regularly dispute whether [h] could be granted the status of a 'letter' or, in modern terms, a sound at all. From such apparent unconcern nevertheless arose the shibboleth of the 'dropped [h]' and its attendant social stigma. A study of its rise into social as well as phonemic significance serves, as a result, to exemplify with particular clarity many of the issues which came to surround the ideals of 'talking proper' in the late eighteenth century and afterwards. The forces of respectability and emulation, the patterns of cultural and social cohesion, the social (and linguistic) stereotypes of the 'lady' and the 'gentleman', or the 'Cockney' and the *parvenu*, were all to have their correlates in the use, and misuse, of /h/.

Before looking in more detail at the patterns of both usage and language attitudes which came into existence in the late eighteenth and nineteenth centuries, it is, however, necessary to begin with a brief overview of far earlier developments of this sound in English, since it is in such remote beginnings that a number of significant points concerning the use of /h/ lie. Its early history is, for example, by no means simple. Given aspiration in initial positions in Old English, patterns of use were rendered more complex by the advent of the Norman Conquest and the resulting influx of French loanwords in which the grapheme <h>, as in *honour, hour*, and *honest*, was silent. The phoneme /h/ (and often, as a result, the grapheme too) had in fact early been lost in Anglo-Norman, and loanwords such as *herb, heir, host* regularly appeared in English in [h]-less (and <h>-less) forms. *Erbe* (MnE *herb*) deriving from OF *erbe* and in turn, Lat. *herba*, and *ost* (MnE *host*) deriving from OF *ost* and in turn Lat. *hostem*, were duly incorporated into English along with many similar words. The fact that the relevant Latin antecedents of such words contained <h> was, however, often to lead to the respelling of loanwords of this order. *Herb* was often spelled with a silent and therefore non-phonetic <h> by 1475; *honor, honur, honour* were all increasingly frequent spellings in Middle English. *Heir*, from OF *eir, heyr*, often appeared as *eyr, ayre*, and *here*.[10]

The end result of such developments was of course to complicate considerably the hitherto relatively simple patterns of <h> and /h/ correspondence in English. It led in effect to a situation in which the grapheme <h> could be realized as [h] in native words such as *hand, horse*, or *house* yet conversely, in the pronunciation of loanwords such as *horrible* and *humour*, it could, and did, appear as [Ø]—that is, without any realization at all. In other words, French loans regularly 'dropped their [h]s' and at some date such habits seem to have been extended into native words as well, though the exact timing of this development is a matter of some dispute. The linguist Roger Lass, for example, argues for a process beginning in the eleventh century[11] while John Wells advocates one which begins after the colonial conquest of America, a nation in which, as he rightly asserts, [h]-dropping is unknown.[12] Medieval manuscripts certainly display considerable variation in their use of

<h>, a fact often attributed to French scribal habits though this interpreta-
tion has, probably rightly, been contested. As James Milroy notes of such
patterns in early Middle English, 'the *prima facie* evidence for [h]-dropping
continues well into EModE—long after there can be any suspicion of direct
Anglo-Norman influence ... All this evidence suggests strongly that (h) has
been a *variable* in English for many centuries'.[13] In the absence of direct
comment, however, it remains difficult to ascertain with precision the onset
and early history of [h]-dropping in native words though, as Milroy's argument suggests, it seems clear that [h] was lost in at least some varieties of
English at a relatively early date.

Some certain evidence for [h] being dropped earlier than the date advocated by Wells is nevertheless presented by the *Welsh Hymn*, a text dated
around 1450. By means of its patterns of alliteration, this is able to provide
conclusive proof that [h] was silent in metrically stressed words such as
hands and *hight*. Northern writers on pronunciation too, such as Richard
Browne in *The English-School Reformed* (1700), also attest similar patterns in
their own speech, Browne describing zero-realization of [h] in stressed words
such as *hand* and *heart* as well as in unstressed *his*.[14] By the eighteenth century therefore, the phenomenon of [h]-loss was not itself new though the
increasing presence of adverse comment on this situation, apparent from the
second half of the century onwards, does indeed seem to have been so.

Of course, the previous absence of such overt sensitization can merely be
seen as the reflection of those more tolerant attitudes to variation which are,
as we have seen, characteristic of comment on pronunciation before the mid-
to late eighteenth century. Whereas the new codificatory zeal of the latter in
this context tended to polarize variant articulations into 'correct' and 'incorrect', issuing prescriptions and proscriptions accordingly, the very absence of
such habits of thought before this date in terms of /h/ is, for instance, made
particularly clear by writers such as the grammarian William Laughton.
Author of *A Practical Grammar of the* English *Tongue*, Laughton simply states
of /h/ in 1739 that 'tho' it be sometimes silent, so are many other Consonants,
in particular Positions'.[15] No further comment is deemed necessary, and certainly no social correlations are either observed or made. Any discussion
specifically received by /h/ was in fact rather more likely to concern its
(frequently contested) right to claim the very status of 'letter' or, in modern
terminology, that of phoneme. 'H . . .hath no particular formation, neither
does it make any sound of it self, but a bare *aspiration* ... whether it ought to
be call'd a letter or not. . .let everyone enjoy his own opinion', Christopher
Cooper, for example, had written in 1687.[16] Such classificatory uncertainties
were not limited to the seventeenth century. In 1748 the grammarian Benjamin
Martin is still able to note that 'it is very surprising to find grammarians dis-
puting whether this be a letter or not, when at the same time it would be ridiculous to dispute it being a distinct sound'.[17] Adducing minimal pair structures

(*ear: hear, art: hart*) as evidence, he demonstrates the phonemic status to which /h/ was, in his opinion, unreservedly entitled: 'witness the words ear, art, arm, ill, &c. which by prefixing H, become hear, hart, harm, hill, quite different words and sounds from the former'.

Far from being the 'fatal letter' of Kington-Oliphant's nineteenth-century conceptions, the fact that the status of /h/ as 'letter' has to be repeatedly questioned and affirmed in this way reveals with little room for doubt that its use in the earlier part of the eighteenth century (and before) can hardly have been invested with those social values which later came to be so commonplace in comment on language and propriety. The transition, both in terms of comment on /h/ and its attendant connotations, again seems to come decisively with the second half of the eighteenth century as the nuances of accent were incorporated into the prescriptive consciousness, and the renewed interest in elocution forced a new awareness of the ideals of speech. Fashion, together with a heightened responsiveness to the role of external markers in assigning social status (real or intended), was also to play its part. Thomas Sheridan, the writer who had so persuasively urged the cultivation of the linguistic consciousness in terms of accent in 1762 is, appropriately, the first to record this new and corresponding sensitization to the loss of /h/. Articulated within his larger tribute to the social values of speech, and his exhortations about the need for new sensibilities towards its use, the needful presence of [h] is rapidly incorporated into the prevailing prescriptive framework with all its specifications of desired norms, undesirable deviation, and the social consequences which pertained to both.

Perfectly expressing the normative ideals of the age, Sheridan, as we have seen in Chapter 1, extensively berates the dulled linguistic consciousness which then still existed in terms of pronunciation. Perception was apparently equally blunt in terms of [h], a situation which he regarded with equal disfavour. In line with his maxim that 'consciousness cannot exert itself when barred up by habit', Sheridan, as expected, readily adopts the appropriate rhetoric of prescription in this context too. Striving to inculcate the nonregional norms which he deemed proper to a 'standard' and national language, he goes on to provide the first information in which the long-standing variations in the use of /h/ are explicitly placed within those normative frameworks on pronunciation which were later to become so familiar. As he states: 'There is one defect which more generally prevails in the counties than any other, and indeed is gaining ground among the politer part of the world, I mean the omission of the aspirate in many words by some, and in most by others.'[18] The selected terms are manifestly those of acceptability and unacceptability in which [h]-dropping is a 'defect' and an error, regardless of its stated prevalence in terms of usage as well as geographical spread. The fact that its loss is apparently common even among the 'polite' is similarly disregarded. As in many of Robert Lowth's dictates on grammar, the heterogeneities of actual usage are intentionally to be rejected in favour of a monolithic and corrected norm. Though from a descriptive point of view [h]-dropping is therefore self-evidently part of that 'best' speech which Sheridan identifies as the basis of his standard, previously established 'custom' in this respect can, he declares, be no sanction for continued 'incorrectness'. Sheridan's further comments make this reorientation of perspective plain: 'I have met with but few speakers in the course of my experience, and those only in the most correct speakers . . . of persons who have not been guilty of omitting the aspirate from some words, or giving it faintly in others'.[19]

Sheridan's text skilfully manipulates the prescriptive tenor of the age. According to this account therefore, the theoretically 'correct' usage in which [h] was pronounced rather than being dropped was indeed rare. It was, however, this very rarity which was to be prized, evincing as it did the superior facilities of a small group of people who were able to wield the aspirate with ease and, significantly, without incurring the 'guilt' accorded to those who fail in this respect. The connotative values of this description are unmistakable and through the four succeeding editions of *A Course of Lectures on Elocution*, as well as in Sheridan's numerous personal appearances on his lecture tours and readings, their appeal was not to be forgotten. The presence of [h] became an important element within that ideology of a 'standard' (and its associated non-regionalized norms) which, in the hands of Sheridan and others, was then growing up around pronunciation.

The desired standard, as we have seen, was above all to be a sociolect and, more specifically, one propagated in terms of the 'polite' (those 'elegant of manners', as Walker's *Dictionary* explains). Sheridan in 1781 asserts as a general truth, for example, that *'False* and *provincial* accents are to be guarded against, or corrected. The manner of pronouncing which is usual among people of *education*, who are natives of the *metropolis*, is, in every country, the *standard.'*[20] The patterns of italicization he adopts make the salient points clear, setting up familiar oppositions between 'provincial' and 'metropolis', and 'educated' and 'false'. In all of these, the use of [h] comes to figure highly, its absence signifying (at least within the schema adopted by manuals of etiquette, by linguistic fashion, and of course by prescriptive texts) a conspicuous unfamiliarity with elite culture and the stated proprieties of 'good' London speech, whether by dint of residence within the provinces or a social location outside the polite. Sheridan's recommendations in his *Lectures* for ways to achieve the conformity and correctness he deemed essential ('the best method of curing this will be to read over frequently all words beginning with the letter *H*. . . in the dictionary, and push them out with the full force of the breath')[21] were rapidly to be joined by other comments which incorporated a new and still more deliberate sense of social prescription within their stated tenets.

The Scottish writer James Elphinston's *Propriety Ascertained in her Picture* (1786), a text which aimed to describe 'good' pronunciation and the means by which it might be acquired, made, as its title suggests, frequent reference to the social values which were coming to surround the spoken word. His comments on [h] accordingly not only reveal a new concern for 'correctness' on the lines set down by Sheridan but also make plain an increasingly explicit sense of social 'lowliness' and 'impropriety' associated with conceptions of its loss. Elphinston's comment (in his own reformed and intentionally phonetic spelling) that 'Dhey dhat think *uman, umor,* and dhe like, look too *umbel,* may innocently indulge the seeming aspiration' can thus be used to adduce a specifically social sensitivity coming to surround the loss of [h].[22] Words such as *human, humour,* and *humble* (as well as *herb, hospital, hostler, hotel*) had, of course, by dint of their non-native origins, traditionally been pronounced without [h]. Elphinston, however, seems to reveal a change in the way people were beginning to view these forms, the non-appearance of [h] in such words coming to suggest not the expected continuities with the past but instead affiliations with a social status (or absence of it) which people would perhaps prefer not to own. As he indicates, spelling words such as *herb* in his reformed orthography without the <h> (as *erb*)—as indeed would be needful if the habitual realities of late eighteenth-century pronunciation were to be indicated—was a practice that some people might feel disinclined to adopt. Omitting the <h> was, he made plain, laden with suggestions of apparent *umbleness* which, as its semantic alignments imply, was capable not only of denoting 'lack of arrogance, pride, and immodesty', as in Walker's definition of 1791, but equally of conveying lack of status: 'low, not high, not great', as Walker's dictionary also explains. In this Elphinston read his audience well and generations of future speakers were, as we will see, to seek to restore the [h] in this and similar words in keeping with such perceptions.

Elphinston's comments on these particular connotations bring to the fore a clear sense of the social meanings which were increasingly to be involved in the use of [h]. Within a few decades, prescriptive writing was almost uniformly to endorse the peculiar propriety of pronouncing [h] in terms which trade overtly on the sociocultural associations which its presence (and absence) could variously comport. Its omission is 'vulgar' according to Benjamin Smart, and indubitably associated with the lower orders in London. For Thomas Batchelor in 1809, its loss partakes of parallel associations of low status, and is a feature marked among the 'peasantry' in Bedfordshire who, in this as in their other infelicities of speech, are to be regarded as 'depraved'.[23] At this date, however, the use of [h] tends to appear as merely one of a list of pronunciations which were deemed significant in contemporary constructions of 'talking proper'. By the 1850s, in contrast, its role has consolidated still further so that [h] alone regularly assumes preeminence amongst a range of stated markers of the 'educated' and 'refined'. And by the 1860s, the resulting patterns of linguistic prejudice, voiced in social terms and explicitly endowed with social repercussions, are particularly widespread, though they are perhaps stated most clearly in Mr Podsnap's dicta on this head in *Our Mutual Friend*. Expounding English sensitivities regarding the use of [h] to the Frenchman (whose habitual articulations in the novel unfortunately preclude its use), Mr Podsnap unambiguously indicates the social affiliations of this sound, as well as its differentiated alignment with the stratified usages of society:

'Ah! Of a Orse?' inquired the foreign gentleman.
'We call it Horse,' said Mr Podsnap, with forbearance. 'In England, Angleterre, England, We Aspirate the "H" and We Say "Horse". Only our Lower Classes Say "Orse"!'[24]

The heightened emphasis placed on the articulation of [h], in both social and linguistic terms, was in fact increasingly to lead to the sense that it should in fact appear whenever and wherever <h> was manifest in the spelling. 'What can reflect more on a person's reputation for learning, than to find him unable to pronounce with propriety and elocution?,'[25] as the schoolmaster and orthoepist James Buchanan had commented in 1757, once again setting out the paradigms of knowledge and ignorance which were regularly to accrue around the spoken word in prescriptive texts. Popular appreciations of linguistic propriety by the nineteenth century indeed tended to confirm or confound reputation for learning on the basis of such habits of [h]-usage, especially where an underlying—and 'literate'—correlation with <h> could be revealed. Being able to stress one's knowledge of the written word was no small accomplishment for many sections of society, and popular notions of the 'educated speaker' here came into particular prominence. The loss of [h] is 'a mark of inferior education … calculated to produce a great prejudice against the offender in all persons of refinement', the elocutionist George Vandenhoff declared in his *Lady's Reader* of 1862.[26] 'Nothing so surely stamps a man as below the mark in intelligence, self-respect, and energy, as this unfortunate habit', stated Henry Alford two years later,[27] making specific the extension of these evaluations from education to intellectual capacity itself. Educational practice too was to endorse this shift of attitudes, often making the 'correct' use of [h] a test of its own success. Lindley Murray, the highly influential writer on grammar, already stresses his own receptiveness to the shifting attitudes of the time in his 1795 edict that the loss of [h] was a clear signifier of the absence of proper education. Urging remedial activity in this area for the many users of his *Grammar*, he develops in particular the need for increased vigilance on the part of teachers. The role of [h] is stressed as an integral part of the emergent and specifically 'educated' standard accent which schools too should serve to inculcate:

From the … negligence of tutors, and the inattention of pupils, it has happened, that many persons have become almost incapable of acquiring its just and full pronunciation. It is therefore incumbent on teachers, to be particularly careful to inculcate a clear and distinct utterance of this sound, on all proper occasions.[28]

Since Murray's *Grammar* was reprinted numerous times, and widely used as a school book of high repute, the inclusion of such comments within it was by no means insignificant in the dissemination of new ideals of phonemic propriety.[29] Contemporary theories about instruction in the native language, for instance, often adopted Murray's principles without reservation. In this context, his strictures on the educational salience of [h] no doubt lent their own endorsement to what was to become a widespread emphasis in early education. Indeed, throughout the nineteenth century, directions for the assessment of teaching prowess regularly came to comprise assessment of the use of [h], in teacher as well as pupils. *The Elementary School Manager* by M. Rice-Wiggin and A. Perceval Graves thus includes the following in its directives for establishing the success of a reading lesson in school, formalizing correlations of [h] and the 'educated' accent in the practical implementations of the standard ideology which they duly endorse:

Is every mistake promptly noticed by the teacher, and is his notice anticipated by putting out of hands on the part of the scholars to show that they, too, have observed the mistake? In particular, are mistakes such as *emphasis, punctuation,* and *aspirates* noticed and corrected with even the youngest children?[30]

The ability to read well, as this suggests, was frequently deemed to include the oral proprieties of enunciation as well as the comprehension of graphic symbols on the page. Rendering <h> as [Ø] instead of the 'proper' [h] was, as a result, to be treated in many educational textbooks under the heading of 'Defective Intelligence',[31] a label which further indicates the perceived alliances of manner and matter, pronunciation and intelligence, which had come into being in this context by the middle of the nineteenth century. In consequence, though pedagogical tenets of this order were later criticized, it was nevertheless common in many schools for children to be penalized just as much for dropping an [h] as for mistaking a word altogether. Both, as we will see in Chapter 7, were regarded as fundamental errors. Her Majesty's Inspectors of Schools tended on the whole to agree. Correct management of /h/ was a clear testimony of the efficacy of correct teaching practice in a school, as Mr Nevill Cream affirmed in his inspector's report for 1861:

Inferior teachers . . . tell me it is useless to try and teach the children to do so [pronounce the letter h]; that the parents at home unteach, by their conversation, whatever is taught at school; that it is provincial, and make a great many other excuses. On the other hand, a good teacher says nothing, but sets to work; and the next year every child, from the oldest to the youngest, pronounces the *h* with correctness.[32]

As in those canons of 'literate speech' already discussed in Chapter 3, the visual authority of words was, as this suggests, often to be adopted in this context too as a particularly salient guide to phonemic propriety. While 'literate speakers', at least in terms of prevailing prescriptive thinking, thus made plain the facts of their superior education by matching grapheme with appropriate sound, or <h> with [h] in their speech, so therefore did the non-appearance of [h] take on the values not only of the 'uneducated' but also of the 'lower class', the 'uncultured', and the 'illiterate'—the massed ranks, in other words, of those who dropped an [h] because they were unaware of the presence of <h> in the spelling. The pressures which such fictions of speech exerted were considerable, and the marked extension of spelling pronunc-iations in words in which zero-realization (or non-pronunciation) of [h] had hitherto been acceptable if not de rigueur acts as a concise index of their effectiveness. By the end of the nineteenth century, only *heir, honest, honour,* and *hour* (and derivatives) remained [h]-less, social sensitivity to its presence having succeeded in redressing centuries of custom with regard to *herb* and *humble, hospital, human* and *humour,* for example, all of which now contain [h] as well as <h> in non-localized forms of English. While older speakers could maintain their allegiance to the [h]-less forms of their youth, the direction of change was clear. Henry Hucks Gibbs, for instance, born in 1819 and first Baron Aldenham (as well as director of the Bank of England from 1857 to 1901), wrote to the lexicographer James Murray in some distress at finding his pronunciation of *humour* as /ˈjuːmə/ labelled 'obsolete or at least archaic' in the *OED*. But as Murray wrote in reply, though he too had originally used '*yumour*', he had felt it necessary to con-form to the general shift when he came to London in the 1870s to find that in younger metropolitan speech '*h* had been restored in all its senses'. The word was, he thus argued, definitively no longer [h]-less for the major-ity of speakers, and this was the situation which the *OED* must descriptively record.[33] The same was increasingly true of *hospital,* and Queen Victoria recalled its erstwhile [h]-less pronunciation (as used by elderly aunts in her youth) with apparent amusement.[34] In America, on the other hand, that 'perfect liberty' advocated by Webster has,[35] it seems, often ensured conti-nuity with historical rather than orthographical precedent in this matter. *Herb* still retains its [h]-less realizations throughout General American, and the American South preserves similar forms for *humble.* In England, in contrast, even traditionally [h]-less native words such as *forehead* and *neighbourhood,* long pronounced as /ˈfɒrɪd/ and /ˈneɪbərʌd/ (and still attested in the first edition of the *OED* in these forms) were eventually to succumb to this general trend. In the twentieth century *hotel* too began to share in this development.[36]

Linguistic fashion, as such transformations confirm, had decisively shifted ground on this issue. Fashion in the wider sense also played its part. As William Cramp stressed in 1838, for example, attitudes to language could in fact be markedly responsive to fashionable example. 'The orthography and pronunciation of today, though perfectly consistent with analogy, may be denounced as vulgar and inaccurate to-morrow, if a popular character chance to deviate from established usage', he averred.[37] Though an observation characterized by a certain amount of hyperbole, it does seem to be borne out by the comments of other writers on the language, particularly where changes in progress were concerned. William Smith, the Scottish lexicographer and writer on pronunciation, had, for instance, noted even in the late eighteenth century that the celebrated actress Sarah Siddons's preferred realization of words such as *fast* and *path* with a short [æ] as in *hat* (rather than, say, in the longer and retracred [ɑ:]) certainly appeared to have given additional impetus to that shift away from the longer and retracted sound which he himself favoured. As he observed, 'In almost all the words which are the subject of the foregoing notes, the pronunciation of Mssrs. Sheridan and Walker (i.e. [æ]) is daily gaining ground from its being adopted by the best Actress, which this, or any age produced'.[38] Max Weber in his own discussions of social formation was also to highlight the role of fashion, noting in his account of the evaluative patterns common within perceptions of the nuances of status that, 'above all, this differentiation evolves in such a way as to make for strict submission to the fashion that is dominant at a given time in society'.[39]

As *Etiquette for Ladies and Gentlemen*, published in 1839, asserted: 'society has its "grammar", as language has; and the rules of that grammar *must* be learnt, either orally or from reading'.[40] Fashion played a role in both, tending to ensure over the course of the late eighteenth and nineteenth centuries that the presence of [h] was to figure significantly in the grammar of language and society alike, a signifier in both of acceptability and due decorum. Max Weber's notions of 'submission' (or, in linguistic terms, convergence) were clearly important in this respect, and not least in terms of the cultural hegemonies which were frequently manipulated in this context within much prescriptive writing. If disincentives in terms of [h]-dropping were prominent in the images of uneducatedness and lower status with which, as we have seen, its use was often surrounded, positive models for the 'proper' use of [h] were also provided, based in particular on associations with London fashion and its accompanying notions of a metropolitan elite. Manuals of etiquette, for example, willingly endorsed paradigms of this order for their readers, fostering selected images of imitative cohesion in these terms. The anonymous *Etiquette for All* of 1861, for example, specifying the need to gain 'a polite and refined manner in our social intercourse', hence emphasized that it was London fashion alone which in this context was to reign supreme: 'Fashion is omnipotent with the generality of mankind . . . he who would mix with his kind with pleasure to himself and those whose society he seeks, must obey her sway and submit to her laws'.[41] Six years later *The Laws and Bye-Laws of Good Society* decisively commented on the role of /h/ in this respect: 'The omission or the importation of the aspirate in the wrong place is a sure sign of defective training. It grates on the ear with peculiar harshness, and is utterly out of keeping with pretensions to being considered *bien élevé*.[42] Similarly, Benjamin Smart included a detailed section in his *Walker Remodelled* of 1836 which dealt with 'Hints for Londonizing a Rustic Utterance'. Smart, as well as emphasizing the need for all cessation of [h]-dropping, carefully stresses the almost insurmountable difficulties which retention of the regional habitually posed with reference to both status and speech habits. 'A man displaying [a rustic accent] must have a huge portion of natural talent or acquired science, who surmounts the prejudice it creates', he advises, the message clear for those whose 'portion of natural talent' or level of 'acquired science' might be inadequate to surmount the negative reactions which such modes of speech attract.[43] Fashion, and the assumed deference to its propagated norms, in such ways tended to enhance that emphasis being placed on linguistic conformity to the London 'standard' (as well as its needful dissemination) by writers such as Sheridan and Smart, Walker and Knowles in their respective pronouncing dictionaries. Provincial patrons awaited with eagerness the arrival of the newest styles from the capital, as the historian Neil McKendrick has documented, commenting on the ways in which such patterns were swiftly copied and hence diffused.[44] In a similar way a certain receptivity to metropolitan styles of speech tended to come into play, at least in terms of the dissemination of accompanying language attitudes (and the proprieties depicted as emblematic of the 'best' speech)—even if the underlying realities of such patterns were not invariably borne out in the exchanges of ordinary conversation. But in terms of the large-scale awareness of fashionable norms, such influence was indisputable. As the self-styled I. S. L. confirms in *Fashion in Language* (1906), by the end of the nineteenth century this 'correct' use of [h] was, in many ways, to be recognized as the very epitome of linguistic fashion. 'Certainly no one who wishes to follow the fashion can neglect it', he adjured.[45]

In the frameworks adopted by handbooks of social advice, by magazines and journals, in literary texts and linguistic tracts, and in the numerous penny manuals which specifically addressed themselves to providing instruction in the art of 'correct' pronunciation, the 'neglect' of [h] was indeed regularly brought into prominence as a marker of the deeply 'unfashionable' as well as of the 'rustic' and 'provincial', with all the negative status connotations which these epithets contain. Smart's 'well-bred' speaker was to be found, and emulated, in polite London society while Batchelor's 1809 account of the 'depraved' pronunciation of Bedfordshire rests on differences which are deliberately constructed as deviations from fashionable London norms. In the terms he selects, the use of /h/ was a means of differentiating 'polite' and 'peasantry', a social signifier of immediate effect. Dickens makes use of similar oppositions. In his sole depiction of the nuances of Clara Peggotty's accent in the first chapter of *David Copperfield*, the displacements of <h> which this involves convey the facts of her social location (as servant to the Copperfield family as well as David's nurse) without further comment being necessary: ' "there's the sea; and the boats and ships; and the fishermen; and the beach; and Am to play with—." Peggotty meant her nephew Ham . . . but she spoke of him as a morsel of English Grammar'.[46] It is, in such comments, all too clear that Peggotty's linguistic mannerisms betray familiarity with provincial Yarmouth rather than the London *bon ton*. By the mid-nineteenth century, the role of [h] was such that it was regularly selected as the foremost marker of the emergent (and non-localized) RP, and contemporary discussions of fashion, status, as well as education, all exhorted subscription to its norms.

Elocution masters, members of a white-collar (and highly fashionable) profession which saw a notable expansion in its numbers over this time, also blazoned forth their abilities in this context. 'Misplaced aspirate', as well as lisping, stuttering, stammering, and monotony 'permanently cured', stated Charles Hartley, self-styled Professor of Elocution, in an advertisement appended to one of his own books on the needful correction of linguistic error. As Hartley's specification of 'remedy' indicates moreover, notions of the impropriety of the 'misplaced aspirate' were readily subsumed within those metaphors of the 'sick language' which also feature highly in prescriptive accounts of language in this period. 'Faults in articulation, early contracted, are suffered to gain strength by habit, and to grow so inveterate by time, as to be incurable', as Sheridan had written, for example, of the evidently debilitated state of speech in the late eighteenth century.[47] 'Nothing is so infectious as a vicious accent or vulgar manner', the author of *Good Society. A Complete Manual of Manners* later discoursed in 1869,[48] revealing the continuity of these ideas within the linguistic sensibilities of the nineteenth century. Such metaphors operate at the heart of the prescriptive agenda, seeing language as ailing and its correction as the only effective medicine. The dropping of [h] in this context served as a major symptom of debility, with remedy, as we have seen, being proffered in abundance.

'Purists are keen to see themselves as physicians administering to the body of language', George Thomas has stressed,[49] and certainly texts on English pronunciation, centring on the drive for a spoken standard over the eighteenth and nineteenth centuries, often overtly adopted such modes of thinking and representation in their tenets on this head. Dropping an [h] was, they insist, a 'weakness' for which 'cure' was necessary. That these appeals in terms of /h/ struck home was a fact that did not, however, rest simply in these normative descriptions of its loss as a 'defect' for which elocution, as so eloquently proffered by Charles Hartley, could offer complete remission. Comment on the social unacceptabilities of its loss tended in addition to draw upon a knowledge of popular social stereotypes, and the proscriptive deterrents which these too could exert to apparently good effect. Whereas, as Sheridan had indicated in 1762, familiarity with London norms of speech signified equally a familiarity with 'good company', unfamiliarity with the newly codified proprieties of [h]-usage came to signify a range of social meanings which were often presented as necessarily incompatible with the social aspirations and ambitions of many speakers of English. That well-established tendency of linguistic fashion to place emphasis upon 'manner' as an estimation of 'matter', and upon external symbols as signifiers of internal worth and value, was in these terms often only to compound the importance which was so readily and regularly accorded to the 'correct' enunciation of [h].

One particularly common pattern of comment in this context is, for example, that discernible around the social (and linguistic) stereotypes of the 'new rich', and the 'self-made-man'. Popular images of the 'self-made', as we have seen in Chapter 2, often relied on a social satire which was dependent for its effects on the perceived combination of lavish wealth with a total absence of the niceties of manner and breeding which denote the socially acceptable. The stigma of trade in such ways gained its linguistic correlates too and contemporary notions of the 'vulgar' develop specific semantic overtones in this context. 'Vulgarian', for example, frequently comes to denote not merely 'a vulgar person' in general terms but also, and more specifically, a 'rich person of vulgar manners'. ' "Did you not marry a low creature—a vulgarian—a tradesman's daughter?" ' as *OED* records in illustration, citing Bulwer Lytton's *My Novel* of 1853. The result was a social, cultural, and linguistic stereotyping of notions of the parvenu, a word which was itself introduced into the lexicon at the beginning of the nineteenth century: 'an upstart, or one newly risen into notice', glosses John Ogilvie in his dictionary of 1870. In consequence, just as the correct use of [h] was depicted as one of the distinguishing marks of the 'gentleman', so, conversely, was its misapplication, and particularly its over-use, frequently presented as a marker of the 'would-be gentleman', betraying those who sought social cohesion with the established elite by patterns of strategic and somewhat over-enthusiastic emulation. In such terms (at least within these prevalent sociocultural stereotypes), the use of [h] was regarded as a prime distinguishing shibboleth by means of which the newly rich could be detected in spite of the veneer of superiority which they might otherwise have acquired. It was this which was commonly to take pride of place in the popular mythology of 'talking proper' which proliferated over the course of the nineteenth century.

Poor Letter H, a sixpenny manual purportedly written by /h/ itself (anthropomorphized as the Honourable Henry H. and described as 'very aristocratic in. . .birth and connections'),[50] is, for example, exclusively devoted to the pronunciation of [h] and its social importance (see Figure 4.1). As the title indicates, the tone adopted is that of pathos, emanating from the unjustly abused /h/ whose own honorific duly indicates the degree of status which has accrued around him and which he has, in turn, come to represent. In its iterated pleas for convergent behaviour in terms of the necessary proprieties of

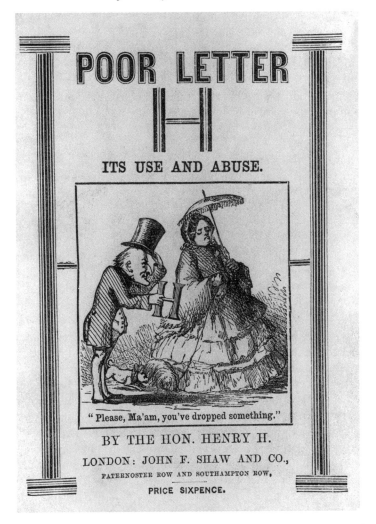

FIG. 4.1. The title page of Hon. Henry H., *Poor Letter H: Its Use and Abuse* (1854–66)

speech, *Poor Letter H* hence plays heavily on the notions of the ridicule and social shame which must inevitably attend errors in this context, giving countless examples of the embarrassing slips which can result. 'I have', Henry H. recounts, 'heard a person, who was very well dressed, and looked like a lady, ask a gentleman who was sitting by her, if he knew whether Lord Murray had left any *H*eir behind him—the gentleman almost blushed, and I thought stopped a little, to see whether the lady meant a *Son* or a *Hare*.'[51] More than mere embarrassment, *Poor Letter H* hence openly exploits the ways in which misuse of /h/ was, in prevailing attitudes to correctness, capable of revealing more concisely than any other sign the facts of a social origin which the speaker may have hoped to have left behind. In the instance given above, for example, the 'person' has the superficial and visual appearance of a 'lady' yet, by the misuse of [h] which follows, she is revealed as a mere pretender to ladylikeness. The true 'gentleman' almost blushes at the shibboleth she commits. In spite of her appearance, the speaker is therefore evidently no 'lady' in the full sense of the term—or at least as it pertained, as we shall see in Chapter 5, to yet another popular social stereotype with its own behavioural norms and ideals.

It is, however, the stereotype of the 'new rich' which takes on particular prominence in this context. 'We must, however, protest against the barbarity of a rich nobody, who having, perhaps, more money than wit, built himself a large mansion, and dubbed it his *habbey*',[52] Henry H. is made to declare, directing pointed satire at the social presumption and phonetic ignorance of the parvenu. Contemporary issues of *Punch* reinforce this assumption in similar terms, the family of the Spangle-Lacquers, in spite of their superficial polish, unfailingly revealing their status as 'vulgar rich' by similar linguistic mannerisms and affectations. Thomas Kington-Oliphant, writing from the privileged domain of an Oxford College, made exactly the same point. The loss of [h] is 'a hideous barbarism' of which the self-made are unduly fond, he states;[53] even given the role of political representation, 'their hopes of Parliamentary renown are often nipped in the bud by the speaker's unlucky tendency to "throw himself upon the 'ouse"'. It is in ways such as these that /h/ takes on its role as the 'fatal letter'; no mere phoneme, its use was deemed to form one of the most powerful social and linguistic barriers in nineteenth-century society. Irrespective of material gain, the new rich were, in conceptions of this kind, necessarily to be educated in its 'proper' use if, in any sense, they were to merit (and gain) the elite acceptability which they might desire. It is in these terms, as we have seen, that the author of *Poor Letter H* deliberately chose to ridicule the folly of the 'rich nobody' ('he would persist in saying that the *habbey* was his '*obby*'),[54] mocking by his wordplay the overuse of [h] where its presence was unwarranted by 'literate' orthography. The parvenu hence emerges as a crystallization of the 'illiterate speaker', his social elevation refused sanction on the grounds of the markers of 'ignorance' rather than 'knowledge' which continue to litter his speech.

Popular images of this order further underline the disjunctions between class and status in the context of language. In spite of the acquisition of a '(h)abbey', and the financial empowerment which this confirms, class and status self-evidently do not run in parallel. Without the necessary remedial action, language will continue to image forth both social origins and status insecurities. Remedial action is of course presented as the key to the acceptability desired, a thesis which runs throughout *Poor Letter H* as Henry H. endeavours to stem his own long-standing 'neglect' among far too many speakers. To a similar end, the remedial endeavours of impecunious scholars are commended by Kington-Oliphant for the attention of those burdened with infelicities of speech in a contract to be based upon the due exchange of social knowledge for the rich but ignorant, with financial reward for the wise but poor. As he urges, 'Many a needy scholar might turn an honest penny by offering himself as an instructor of the vulgar rich in the pronunciation of the fatal letter'.[55]

Over-sensitized to the use of [h] by the reams of contemporary comment which stressed its role as pre-eminent social marker, the new rich, in these popular stereotypes, were thus to display marked traces of their social origins in their speech. Like the lower middle class in William Labov's sociolinguistic researches in New York,[56] they are, for example, regularly depicted as hypercorrecting in their use of variables imbued with overt status and, in turn, as over-using [h] out of all proportion with accepted proprieties. As the empirical researches into the linguistic behaviour of such socially insecure groups in the twentieth century have suggested, however, it is not entirely unfeasible that a grain of truth may indeed be present behind the linguistic scapegoating of the new rich in this specific instance. As already mentioned, Peter Trudgill's research in Norwich has revealed similarly regular patterns of hypercorrection by groups insecure within the social hierarchy so that, in their more formal speech, markedly higher frequencies of variants—such indeed as [h]—which are regarded as statusful in the wider speech community tend to come into use. Bearing in mind the 'uniformation principle' which has been posited by the linguist Roger Bell ('the linguistic processes taking place around us are the same as those which have operated to produce the historical record of the language')[57] as well as the implications which have been brought out by William Labov in his own discussions of the validity of using the present to explain the past,[58] it is by no means inconceivable that something of the same should again hold true for the use of [h] in certain sections of nineteenth-century society, especially given the high levels of overt comment surrounding /h/ and its promulgated social values. This was in itself a situation which was guaranteed to foster the linguistic (and status) anxieties of many speakers. Moreover, as modern sociolinguistic data similarly confirm,[59] the very fact of social mobility is, in a number of ways, particularly conducive to linguistic modifications of this kind, a finding which suggests that the upwardly mobile were indeed somewhat more likely to respond to (or to attempt to respond to) those norms which were so insistently promoted as prestigious. The nineteenth-century stereotype of the 'new rich' (and their consummate difficulties in terms of [h]) may thus have had at least some basis in reality.

Stereotypes, as we have seen, tend to play a key role in the evaluation of speech, hence equally assuming prominence in the workings of language attitudes in which negative sensitization to individual variants is clearly also enhanced by stated or perceived affiliations to certain social groups. It is this which, for example, lies behind the modern stigmatization (and stereotyping) of the 'toity-toid' enunciations (for 'thirty-third') which mark popular notions of the accent of New York, hence informing collective language attitudes in a parallel way—regardless of the actual linguistic habits of New Yorkers and the more complex patterns of variation which they will in reality exhibit. In the nineteenth century, it is clear that the 'new rich' were popularly selected as just such another stereotype in which notions of exclusion and exclusivity in terms of social and linguistic values could readily be predicated. That the actual new rich were not completely immune to such assimilatory pressures is, however, revealed in the patterns of social cohesion which relevant families could enact. As the historian David Coleman has stressed, though first-generation entrepreneurs tended to devote most attention to consolidating business rather than social opportunities, their sons, and especially their grandsons, would regularly partake of the requisite social transformations to secure acceptability of a different kind. It was these who would commonly be sent to established (and elite) public schools such as Eton and who would be encouraged, in turn, to shed the nuances of accent which might continue to reveal their social origins. As one writer noted in the *Bradford Observer* in 1870, 'I see around me many manufacturers of the old school, men who speak in the dialect and have disdain for gloves'. Yet these, he added, 'curiously enough, send their sons to be educated at the Universities, where they emerge gloriously incapacitated for business in many instances'.[60] Those who did succeed in their industrial and financial expansions at this time were, in other words, not to be entirely immune from the cultural hegemonies and social proprieties which were, as we have seen, often prescribed for members of the 'best' society—taking note of their niceties (and their significance in terms of social assimilation) if not for themselves, then for their families and descendants. This explains the desire of the engineer Matthew Robinson Boulton (son of Matthew Boulton, the partner of James Watt) for his own son to be sent to Eton, rather than to the academy run by the Reverend Henry Pickering at Winston Green, Birmingham which he had himself attended. Even his own education, however, had not been immune from the linguistic concerns of correctness, especially in terms of accent. It was, for instance, on the grounds that he might otherwise acquire 'a vicious pronunciation and vulgar dialect' that he had become a boarder (rather than continuing as a day-boy) at the Reverend Pickering's school.[61] And his later education reinforced the same concerns; 'I seldom fail to correct him whenever he omits the aspirate, his most inveterate provinciality in conversation', wrote the Reverend S. Parlby to Matthew Boulton senior in 1785, giving a progress report on Boulton junior's pronunciation in which problems in the 'correct' use of /h/ evidently continued to persist. As A. E. Musson and E. Robinson further confirm of the requisite educational emphases in this particular case, 'Boulton was as insistent as Lord Chesterfield himself that his son should have all the appearance and attributes of a gentleman'.[62]

Accent, often conceived in contemporary metaphors as a passport, securing entry not to other countries but to other social spheres ('the talisman that will … bar the door or make portals fly open', as Savage declared),[63] receives therefore perhaps its clearest correlates in the attitudes to the use of /h/ and its vital role in securing, or impeding, social advance. It too naturally became part of the ideology of self-help (that 'masterpiece of propaganda … by which a middle-class ideal was spread throughout the whole of society', as the historian Trevor May notes)[64] which had been propagated so effectively by Samuel Smiles as a further integral aspect of the Victorian consciousness. Just as Smiles had commended the endeavours of the self-made industrialist Richard Arkwright sitting down to learn grammar at the age of fifty, so too did texts such as William Henry Davenport's *Plain Living and High Thinking; or, Practical Self Culture* (1880), William Matthews's *Getting on in the World; or, Hints on Success in Life* (1877), or Davenport's earlier *The Secret of Success; or, How to Get on in the World* (1870) endorse the same paradigms. In an age 'bent on mutual improvement', as the anonymous author of *Talking and Debating* (1856) pointed out, relevant amelioration in this respect was moreover to suggest, and promise, far more than mere articulatory prowess. Given control over the phonetic niceties required in polite life, 'we feel a just pride in having subdued some of the roughnesses that beset our moral life, and of having acquired in their stead the polish that bespeaks refinement'.[65]

Contrasting greatly with the cursory attention afforded it by Johnson a century before,[66] the use of /h/ had therefore, by the 1850s, consolidated in the popular imagination as a prime symbol of precisely that 'polish' which *Talking and Debating* describes. Its loss denotes the 'roughness' that the intentionally respectable should tame while its presence constitutes an external symbol seen as emblematic of the refined and internal 'moral life'. As such texts indicate moreover, though Kington-Oliphant seems to have envisaged supply of, and demand for, instruction in /h/ usage only in terms of the entrepreneurial parvenu, in reality the striking popularity of manuals devoted to instruction in the proprieties of [h] can only be explained by the fact of the massed ranks of the 'middling sort', and their own widespread awareness of the sociosymbolic aspects of language. It is, for example, these who are the intended audiences of the sixpenny manuals on 'talking proper' or the manuals of etiquette which sought to disseminate the stated proprieties of elite culture to those without such knowledge. As the author of *Hints on Etiquette and the Usages of Society* affirms, 'this is not written for those *who do* but for those who do *not know what is proper*, comprising a large portion of highly respectable and estimable people, who have had no opportunity of becoming acquainted with the usages of the (so termed) best society'.[67]

Works such as Eccles's *Harry Hawkins' H Book* or the Hon. Henry H.'s *Poor Letter H*, for example, went into many editions, the latter being reprinted three times within 1854 alone while the former went through two editions in as many years. Smith's *Mind Your H's and Take Care of Your R's* was similarly popular, and demand was such that books of accompanying exercises were swiftly devised to supplement the main text, a means by which the 'vulgar', whether rich or otherwise, might intentionally monitor their conformity to a linguistic norm presented as essential to good standing in the eyes of the world. Just as with the pronouncing dictionaries discussed in Chapter 1, it was practical and conscientious application which was depicted as the route to success. In such terms, just as the enthusiasm for self-improvement is accurately reflected in the 55,000 copies of Samuel Smiles's *Self-Help* sold within five years of publication or the favour with which Chambers's *The Popular Educator* was received, so is the craving for correctness in terms of /h/ embodied in the extensive sections on its 'correct' use demanded, and provided, in editions of *The Family Herald*,[68] or, more particularly perhaps, in the popularity of *Poor Letter H: Its Use and Abuse*, of which well over 43,000 copies had been produced by the mid-1860s.

While the new rich were evidently intended to derive the benefits already discussed from the extensive instructions which Henry H. provides on this matter, *Poor Letter H* has in fact a far wider agenda. The text in effect presents a personal appeal from Henry H. to the 'million' who, in spite of the continuing efforts of education and the schoolmaster, still commit 'the great social literary evil of aspirating wrongly'.[69] 'Million', in a typical nineteenth-century collocation, is intended to signify 'the multitude, the bulk of the nation', a specification of readership and utility which again reveals the joint claims of language and nation in the drive to disseminate a standard of 'good' usage throughout the land. It was in these terms, for example, that the fortieth edition of *Poor Letter H* opened in 1866:

What! issue another edition of Poor Letter H . . .! Yea, verily; for the circulation of forty thousand have been but as drops poured into the mighty tide of human life, whereon float hundreds of thousands who don't know an H from an A; and who, when meeting with the one or the other, make the most frightful and cruel mistakes with these poor innocent sufferers.[70]

If instances of the faulty pronunciation of *abbey* were depicted as dogging the aspirant parvenus of the age, the range of examples presented for the erudition of the wider base of society is, as expected, far more extensive. Unintentional homophones abound by such mistakes, Henry H. declares, generating ambiguity—and no little comedy at the expense of those who commit such infelicities. In a series of anecdotes we are presented with accounts of orders to servants to reheat dishes of meat, given in the form of "eat it and bring it up again when it was a little 'otter',[71] linguistic fables in which, in 'a respectable music shop', a lady is requested to ''*um* the *h*air' after which, as Henry H. recalls, 'it was very hard to control the risible faculties',[72] or tales of recently recovered 'gentlemen' who, upon being congratulated upon their improved state of health, give the following response: '"Thank you," said the gentleman; "the doctor says that I shall now do very well, but I must take care not to *eat* myself"'.[73] The central tenet manifest in each of these examples only reinforces the doctrine of correctness surrounding [h], and the social meanings and social repercussions which it had come to hold, as well as manipulating to no little effect common prescriptive targets directed at words which, though distinct in their orthographical realizations, might—through phonetic error—be rendered identical in speech. This in itself tapped into a consummate nineteenth-century fear of mergers as a species of linguistic change. As attitudes to the loss of final and post-vocalic [r] (discussed in Chapter 3) have already revealed, homophones which resulted from this change (such as *ma, mar, pa, par, stalk, stork*) were regarded as particularly emblematic of 'slovenliness', and hence particularly deserving of censure. The same premises come into operation in the case of [h]-dropping too where the failure to make distinctions in speech which were self-evident in the written language (*air: hair, ire: hire*) is deployed as yet another signifier of the 'illiterate' speaker, with all the sociocultural connotations which this conveys. All these were to combine in pressuring speakers to redress their own habits of 'negligence' in this matter.

Addressing the vowels (likewise anthropomorphized in this text), the Hon. Henry H. thus pleads for further vigilance in this sphere as a means of avoiding not only his own humiliation (arising from such frequent neglect), but also that more pertinent social humiliation and absence of status which will certainly befall speakers who persist in making such unfortunate mistakes. As he states, 'I have written to you, my little Vowels, to see if you and I together cannot do something to stop the mockeries we receive, and also to prevent the thousands who mock us, no doubt unintentionally, from being themselves laughed at and thought nothing of'.[74] Nevertheless, if, as the Hon. Henry H. asserts, social humiliation and 'being thought nothing of' inevitably come to those who fail in this respect, so conversely is the promise of social honour explicitly held out to those who strive towards and achieve propriety in these terms: 'If my good friends, *the Million*, would try to remember ... and speak out H ... a great many of our readers and speakers, and I think some of our preachers too, would cut a far better figure in public and in society than they now do.'[75]

Works such as *Poor Letter H*, written in an accessible manner and delineating the sociosymbolic portents of /h/ in a tone marked more by its bluntness than by any assumed or euphemistic restraint, were hence particularly effective in securing wide dissemination for those normative tenets which had come to be inseparable from the 'proper' use of [h]. Its price (a mere sixpence) would likewise have facilitated purchase by many in the middle and lower ranks of society, serving equally to inculcate a consciousness of /h/ of which even Sheridan would have been proud. Its title page alone, with a cartoon illustrating in graphic terms the solecism of [h]-dropping, as well as the ensuing embarrassment (see Figure 4.1) would in many ways have been enough to make the intended point.

Other popular works in the second half of the century were to employ analogous methods to achieve the same result. Eccles's *Harry Hawkins' H Book*, for example, works by the similarly comic deployment of the unfortunate Harry's mistakes in the course of his phonemic education. Hastening to inform his Aunt Hannah of the egg laid by his hen, he instead declares: 'Oh aunt *anna*. . .my *en as ad* another *hegg*. . .I've put it in an *at* box in the *en ouse*'.[76] Dependent as they are on graphemic deviation as a sign of phonemic impropriety, such misspellings gradually decrease in frequency as the tale advances and Harry slowly matures into a 'literate speaker' of the first order, triumphing over the infelicities in this respect which had so beset his youth. Granted his early wish (' "Aunt *anna*," said poor Harry, "I wish I *ad* a book full of H's; I would read it over and over again and again, till I got quite used to saying them" '), we proceed through the tales of 'The Hawk', 'The Hairy Ape', and such delights as 'Humphrey Hobb's Huge Hog' ('Old Humphrey Hobbs had a Huge Hog which was so fat He could not see out of His eyes and He could Hardly Heave His breath') in all of which the H's are capitalized for the benefit of those readers who are industriously mirroring Harry's progress. It is, of course, a story with a Happy end:

Harry has learned to aspirate His H's. By the time Aunt Hannah Had written all these stories for little Harry, He Had indeed begun to improve in pronouncing His H's. He continued to read a part of His H book out loud every day for some time longer; and wHen He was eleven years old, and His Aunt Hannah and Mr. Hungerford both thought Him old enough to go to Hazleden Grammar School, He was able to learn Hic, Haec, Hoc, without any difficulty.[77]

Other writers too commended the efficacy of this book for the ways in which it provided appropriate remedy and instruction in the use of /h/. As Alfred Leach noted in his own work on this topic: 'this little book cannot be too warmly commended as a practical and amusing method of learning to aspirate'. He encouraged his own readers to 'put their aspirative faculties to a crucial test, by reading aloud the story of "The Hairy Ape" ', just as Harry Hawkins himself had done.[78]

'Literacy' and 'illiteracy', and fictions of them in speech, are, as we have seen, particularly important in this context, the visual authority of <h>, as in the prominence accorded to it in *Harry Hawkins' H Book*, often being used to sanction, if not in fact demand, the corresponding presence of [h]. Stereotypes of the 'elegant' and 'literate' speaker do not, however, inform only manuals of usage such as *Harry Hawkins' H Book* or indeed C. W. Smith's

Mind Your H's and Take Care of Your R's. Still more prevalent, and potentially of equal if not indeed of greater influence in this respect, were, however, the conventions used to represent speech in eighteenth- and nineteenth-century literature, intentionally marking, as they do, gradations in the social hierarchy by frequent recourse to notions of 'literate speech' and its converse. Though this will be discussed in greater detail in Chapter 6, a preliminary investigation of the sociosymbolic potential of the written word, and of its graphemic deviations, within representations of fictional spoken discourse is nevertheless particularly illuminating at this point. In the context of the gradual sensitization to the phenomenon of [h]-dropping, literary works can in fact provide a parallel, and at times highly useful source of evidence on the shift in attitudes surrounding its use, as strategic misspellings involving <h> develop into one of the prime signifiers of status within the novel.

Using written texts as evidence for spoken change is, of course, in general beset with problems especially since, given the limitations of the English alphabet, a mere twenty-six graphemes must suffice for the representation of forty-four phonemes. Mimesis in this respect is clearly impossible and few authors, dramatists, or poets tried or indeed wished to give completely accurate transcriptions of speech within their works. George Bernard Shaw's endeavours at doing this for Eliza Doolittle's (Cockney) pronunciation in *Pygmalion* is, for example, abandoned after a few lines: 'Here, with apologies, this desperate attempt to represent her dialect without a phonetic alphabet must be abandoned as unintelligible outside London'.[79] George Eliot earlier experienced similar difficulties with her own endeavours to be true to the sound of words in *Adam Bede*: 'my inclination to be as close as I could to the rendering of dialect, both in words and spelling, was constantly checked by the artistic duty of being generally intelligible'.[80]

Clearly at best a compromise is achieved, blending linguistic reality and artistic demands in the depiction of speech. Though there may indeed be certain hazards of this order of which it is well to be aware, literature is still capable of offering evidence of value, and this is perhaps especially true in terms of /h/ since its grapho-phonemic correspondences are, on the whole, more straightforward than are, for example, those involving vowels and vocalic change. Above all, literature, like language itself, is embedded in a social milieu and a social context which cannot readily be ignored. As Roger Fowler has rightly stressed, it must itself be seen as 'a kind of discourse, a language activity within social structure like other forms of discourse'.[81] In this light, it would certainly seem mistaken to suggest that literary texts, in the fictions of speech which they generate, as in the cultural and social contexts in which their characters move, are entirely autonomous creations, formed without reference to outside social influences, attitudes, and assumptions.

The patterns used to represent speech in the novel can therefore be seen in many ways as tending to encode prevalent opinions and suppositions about the role of language as social signifier. The attitudes which they present towards variation, to social norms of speech, and to corresponding notions of 'deviation' can all offer illuminating parallels for that evidence already considered on the rise of /h/ as social symbol. Novels of the eighteenth and nineteenth centuries, for example, commonly reflect contemporary notions of social prejudice and social praise in abundance. The representation of speech by significant patterns of respelling, as well as in the form of direct comments about accent, thus in turn functioned as a major way by which many authors chose to convey social sub-texts of this order, deliberately manipulating the accidentals of their texts in order to signify social differences important in the larger structures of their work.

Patterns of [h]-usage offered a ready means by which to do this. ' "I should have thought that there would hardly be such a thing as a Methodist to be found round here" ', says the unknown (but evidently 'educated') traveller in the opening of George Eliot's *Adam Bede*, manifesting perfect felicity in his use of <h> (and hence, we are to understand, [h]). Patterns of its equally significant absence can be indicated by the liberal use of the apostrophe or, in earlier texts, by the simple fact of <h> omission: ' "He'll be comin' of hage this 'ay-'arvest" ', as the traveller is in turn informed by Mr Casson. Dickens's lower-class characters are, correspondingly, often depicted as being seemingly incapable of pronouncing *hand* other than as *and*, *hungry* other than as *ungry*, or, conversely, *under* other than as *hunder*. Such systematic patterns are, in real terms, fictions just as much as the characters themselves. As the philologist Otto Jespersen has pertinently remarked on these literary habits of representing [h]-usage by the mid-nineteenth century, 'many novelists would have us believe, that people who drop their aspirates place false aspirates before every vowel that should have no [h]; such systematic perversion is not, however, in human nature'.[82] Even if, as here, they depart from the distributional patterns of linguistic reality, novelists, equally embedded in the workings of prescriptive ideology and its repercussions, do nevertheless serve to provide another valuable source of information on the social stereotypes which were, as we have seen, widely associated with speech and its sociosymbolic variations. In the actualities of linguistic usage, on the other hand, patterns of variation would necessarily be far more complex, based not on simple oppositions of [h]-absence for 'lower-class' and [h]-presence for 'upper' but (as regularly confirmed in modern sociolinguistic studies) on quantitative variations of presence *and* absence, relevant paradigms being worked out, even within a single language variety, in terms of 'more or less' instead of these favoured (but unrealistic) absolutes.[83]

The literary awareness of the value of <h> or <'> as socially significant diacritics does nevertheless bear clear witness to a sensitization and shift in attitudes to the use of /h/ which, in many ways, neatly parallels—and amplifies— that attested in the (non-fictional) manuals of etiquette, pronunciation, and elocution of this period. The differentiated use of the grapheme <h> as a stylistic marker in literary works begins in fact in the middle decades of the eighteenth century, antedating by some years those first explicit comments on its attendant social proprieties which are to be found in Thomas Sheridan's *Course of Lectures on Elocution* in 1762. The beginnings of this stylistic tradition, however, are tentative, early examples of the deliberate displacement of <h> offering little indication of that heightened role it was later to assume. It merely appears as one of a range of devices used to characterize the uneducated user of language, such indeed as the eponymous hero of Henry Fielding's *Jonathan Wild*. Published in 1743, Fielding's novel can be used to illustrate with particular clarity the inception of those traditions of <h> usage which were later to become so dominant in fictional form. In a letter 'which we challenge all the Beaus of our Time to equal either in Matter or Spelling', Wild's epistolary endeavours produce the following: 'I sollemly purtest, that, of all the Butys in the unaversal Glob, there is none kapable of hateracting my IIs like you. Corts and Pallaces would be to me Deserts without your Kumpany'.[84] As this reveals, visual and graphemic deviation function as the primary means of linguistic satire, forms such as 'pallaces' or 'corts' or 'kumpany' being used to generate a powerful impression of the non-standard within, and in spite of, Wild's attempts at eloquence. Of course such forms are, in actual fact, no more distinct from the currently acceptable pronunciations than are their more usual graphemic structures (while some of Fielding's deliberately skewed spellings—such as *kumpany*—might indeed be said to stand in a far closer relationship to the norms of pronunciation than do the conventional representations of such words). The success of this technique, however, depends not on the fidelity which may or may not exist between the written and spoken forms selected but instead on the clear perception of notions of norm and deviation which are thereby offered to the reader.

Wild's role is as a prototype of the 'illiterate speaker' who, as Dr Johnson was later to observe, 'catches sounds imperfectly and utters them negligently'.[85] Wild's letter to Miss Tishy, revealing widespread ignorance of the conventional canons of good spelling, offers instead a form of 'eye dialect' or approximate transcription which is capable of suggesting not only ignorance but also therefore something of the sounds used in speech. Though far from accurate as transcriptions go, the selection of the form *hateracting* (for *attracting*) is therefore of particular interest in terms of [h] and conceptions of appropriate usage, foregrounding not only an extra (and paragogic) syllable but also a superfluous initial <h>. In an era in which graphemes were popularly taken as 'proper' signifiers for the presence of phonemes (an equation aided, as we have seen, by the semantic ambiguities of the term 'letter' in itself),[86] Wild's use of <h> can as a result be interpreted as implying the presence of initial aspiration where none is sanctioned, either by the conventional orthography or by those 'elegant' speakers who, in Johnson's terms, necessarily abide by it in their speech.

What is also clear is the muted significance which such forms have at that particular point in time. Deviations involving <h> (and hence [h]) are well in a minority among the range of other devices which Fielding chose to employ. Similarly restricted use of this feature also marks Smollett's early work. *The Adventures of Peregrine Pickle* of 1751, for example, contains another 'illiterate' missive which, in its chosen techniques, closely resembles that allocated to Wild by Fielding. Mrs Hornbeck, a former 'oyster-wench' liberally endowed with all the social connotations which this label might be assumed to convey, communicates by letter with Peregrine during his travels in France to inform him of her location: 'I lotch at the *hottail de may* ... ware I shall be at the windore, if in kais you will be so good as to pass that way at sicks a cloak in the heavening'.[87] Again, relevant deviations can be seen to depend not on the dropping of <h> (prime in later texts) but instead on its unwarranted presence in *heavening* (for *evening*) and *hottail* (for *hotel*), examples which suggest distributional patterns at odds not only with conventional spelling but also with expected 'proper' enunciations. The comedy in both, however, turns fundamentally not on the fact of such graphemic (and underlying phonetic) deviation in itself, but also on the puns thereby generated with other semantically disparate, but graphically analogous, words: *heaven* in the first instance, *hot* and *tail* in the second. Nevertheless, such occurrences, though already proving useful as negative diacritics of status, form a clear minority in the wider schema of language patterns deployed in the text.

By the time of Smollett's last novel, *The Expedition of Humphry Clinker*, published twenty years later in 1771, this distribution has, however, experienced a significant pattern of change. A novel in which Smollett utilized a notably extensive range of graphological deviations, *Humphry Clinker* offers a striking selection of visual improprieties by which deficiencies of education, or nuances of social and regional location, are to be indicated. The aim is, it must be admitted, scarcely one of exclusive verisimilitude in terms of linguistic truth and mannerism. Clinker himself, for example, though brought up in a workhouse, invariably has diction devoid of the orthographical idiosyncrasies (and attendant phonetic implications) such as we might perhaps have expected. Win Jenkins, the Welsh maidservant, does have language characterized by a striking range of syntactic and semantic, as well as graphemic deviations, but by no means all of these can specifically be attributed to her stated provenance.

Nevertheless, Smollett's depiction, and more specifically his selection, of Win's linguistic habits is interesting. A maidservant, she unites the fact of subordinate social status with an intentionally comic confusion in terms of conventional linguistic proprieties. Malapropisms and homophonic substitutions proliferate in her letters; she selects *syllabubs* instead of *syllables* and employs *ware* instead of *wear*, *bare* instead of *bear*, or *infection* instead of *affection*. It is perhaps therefore not surprising that the use, and misuse, of <h> should also be prominent in Smollett's chosen representations of Win's idiolect. Comically creating new homophones for words which, at least in their habitual enunciations, are quite distinct, *animals* are rendered as *honeymills*,[88] *pious* as *pyehouse*,[89] and her epistles are sent from *Haddingborough* (as well as *Addingborough*) rather than from their actual address in Edinburgh.

Win's evident uncertainties on the use of <h> (and [h]) are further compounded by forms which attest its deletion when it should in fact be present; she writes with compassion of Lydia Melford's sensibilities ('I doubt her pore art is too tinder'),[90] and of the collapse of her own pretensions to style ('I thoft as how there was no arm in going to a play at Newcastle, with my hair dressed in the Parish fashion').[91] Such linguistic improprieties (*art*: *heart*, *arm*: *harm*) confirm Win's role as a more advanced type of the 'illiterate speaker' such as we have already encountered in Jonathan Wild. More than this, however, they also serve to stress the sense of social unacceptability which [h]-loss was coming to denote in the changing linguistic consciousness of the day. The fact that Tabitha Bramble, Win's mistress, shares her maid's every linguistic idiosyncrasy with one exception, that of <h>-usage and, by extension, [h]-usage, renders its connotative meanings clear. Linguistic and intellectual satire are directed at the foibles and fallacies of Win and Tabitha alike but it is the use of <h> which provides a clear marker of their social differentiation, and their respective roles as mistress and maid.

This development of <h>, and strategic deviations involving its use and misuse, into convenient diacritics of social status in literary works thus parallels the beginnings of formal comment on the role of [h] as a determiner of linguistic propriety (or otherwise) in works which are specifically orientated towards the discussion of language. Moreover, just as later writers on pronunciation were increasingly to stress their heightened sense of its utility as social symbol, so were later literary works to intensify the prominence accorded its displacement. By the 1840s, the absence of <h>, although rarely deployed in entirely systematic ways (at least from a purely linguistic point of view), had become an almost inevitable accompaniment to the speech of lower-status characters. Dickens, for example, makes full use of it to establish social distance and social differentiation in his novels. Sam Weller, Mrs MacStinger in *Dombey and Son*, the urchin thieves of *Oliver Twist* (though not of course Oliver himself, by virtue of his own status as hero), as well as the diverse cast of Cockney figures who habitually inhabit Dickens's works are all in some measure united by their preference for this sociolinguistic marker and by the associated graphemic deviations which feature in depictions of their speech. Heroines, heroes, and the representatives of the upper and middle sections of society are, conversely, largely exempt from such deviations, a dichotomy which strengthened prevailing stereotypes in which those given the benefit of birth and breeding outside the lower social spheres would never in any circumstance condescend to drop an [h]. In the contrastive usages of, say, Mrs Crupp, David's London landlady in *David Copperfield*, and those of his aunt, Betsey Trotwood, or between the disguised Lady Dedlock and the crossing sweeper Jo in *Bleak House*, the linguistic antecedents of Mellors and Lady Chatterley are, at least in this matter, clear. ' "Hush! Speak in a whisper! ... Did he look, when he was living, so very ill and poor?" ', says Lady Dedlock to Jo, ' "this is the public 'ouse where I was took to," ' says Jo.[92] The ease with which the recognition of norm and intended deviation could be achieved in literary form undoubtedly ensured the continued popularity of patterns of <h>-usage in such works. Their connotative values clear, the minute a character was made to say *'ere* rather than *here* or *hup* rather than *up*, one immediately knew that one was dealing with a speaker whose social location was unambiguously below the middle ranks, or at least with one whose origins were 'low'. The usage of <h>, not only in Dickens, but in William Thackeray, George Gissing, Elizabeth Gaskell, George Eliot, Charles Reade, and virtually any other novelist who made the attempt to delineate accent, is made to signify social inferiority with surpassing regularity.

Such differential patterns of propriety in language could, however, also be employed to more subtle ends within the novel. Able to facilitate the broad depiction of social difference, patterns of <h>-usage were, in skilful hands, equally capable of enhancing thematic and narrative concerns far beyond the portrayal of simple social stereotypes. Dickens's *Great Expectations* provides a case in point, the use of <h> acting as a complex diacritic of social status, social mobility, and of the increasing social distance between Pip and Joe. Both are, in the beginning, equals as well as allies against the 'Ram-paging' of Mrs Joe. Joe, though uneducated and illiterate, is loved and respected by the youthful Pip for his consummate goodness and 'tender simplicity'. Pip, before his introduction to Satis House, looks up to Joe in uncomplicated admiration and esteem so that, after the history which Joe gives of his early and troubled life, Pip concludes:

Young as I was, I believe that I dated a new admiration of Joe from that night. We were equals afterwards, as we had been before; but, afterwards at quiet times when I sat looking at Joe and thinking about him, I had a new sensation of feeling conscious that I was looking up to Joe in my heart.[93]

No social shame about Joe's lowly occupation as blacksmith diminishes Pip's respect, nor do the abundant examples of Joe's linguistic 'ignorance', including, naturally enough, that concerning the correct positioning of [h]. ' "I never was so much surprised in all my life—couldn't credit my own ed—to tell the truth, hardly believed it *were* my own ed" ', Joe, for instance, asserts, amply illustrating his difficulties.[94] Indeed, Pip's own early efforts in the domain of written English reveal that he too (at least at first) shared Joe's distributional indecision on this matter. His missive to Joe, inscribed as they both sat at the fireside one winter's evening, begins: 'MI DEER JO i OPE U R KRWITE WELL i OPE i SHAL SON B HABELL 4 2 TEEDGE U JO'.[95] The approximate versions of *hope* and *able* which Dickens here conferred upon Pip unambiguously indicate the intended social affinities (and social meanings) in this context.

Linguistic self-consciousness, applied to himself as well as to Joe, comes only with Pip's first visit to Satis House, and with Estella's estimation of him as 'a common labouring boy'. Presented with a brusque introduction to social awareness and its linguistic correlates ('"He calls the knaves, Jacks, this boy!" said Estella with disdain'),[96] Pip undergoes a rapid education into the social niceties of language and its possibilities for social shame. Estella's methods of education into the sensibilities of status are, in this, far more effective than the haphazard teaching practices of Mrs Wopsle's school to which Pip had hitherto been accustomed:

I took the opportunity of being alone in the court-yard to look at my coarse hands and my common boots. My opinion of those accessories was not favourable. They had never troubled me before, but they troubled me now, as vulgar appendages. I determined to ask Joe why he had ever taught me to call those picture-cards, Jacks, which ought to be called knaves. I wished Joe had been rather more genteelly brought up, and then I should have been so too.[97]

Pip's new consciousness of correctness and its converse in terms of external markers acts as a refrain in the early part of the novel. 'Shame', linguistic and social, is contracted like a disease and the initial revelation of his 'great expectations' comes as a release from a social environment, and a social contact, which Pip now sees as degrading. Moving to London in the next stage of his social education, that of becoming a 'gentleman', Pip seeks knowledge to remedy his previous ignorance of manners. By the time of Joe's first visit to him in the city, he is already affecting incomprehension at Joe's realizations of Miss Havisham's name and the confusion thereby caused by its unfortunate initial aspirate:

'Next day, Sir,' said Joe, looking at me as if I were a long way off, 'having cleaned myself, I go and see Miss A.'
'Miss A., Joe? Miss Havisham?'
'Which I say, Sir,' replied Joe, with an air of legal formality, as if he were making his will, 'Miss A., or otherways Havisham.'[98]

Both socially and linguistically, as well as geographically, Pip is indeed now a long way off. His comments merely serve to confirm this fact, his changed attitudes to Joe, and to Joe's pronunciation, betraying strong convictions of social inequality which override the old and easy harmonies of his youth. As this indicates, an awareness of such attitudes towards /h/, perhaps even more than to its actual use, can in such ways function as an additional and useful index of Pip's social advance, and accompanying moral regression, in the first half of the novel. More obvious as a literary focus, however, and of far greater weight in terms of characterization, are the habits of strategic [h]-dropping adopted by that consummate hypocrite, Uriah Heep, within Dickens's earlier novel *David Copperfield*.

The often-professed 'umbleness of Uriah Heep forms one of the most memorable leitmotifs of character used in Dickens's novels, the word *humble* and its derivatives being used with remarkable profusion in almost each and every conversation in which Heep engages. Humility is adopted, at least overtly, as the dominant element in his personal creed, and its lexical presence almost invariably accompanies his own (and his mother's) attempts at self-definition:

'I am well aware that I am the umblest person going,' said Uriah Heep, modestly; '... My mother is likewise a very umble person. We live in a numble abode, Master Copperfield, but have much to be thankful for. My father's former calling was umble. He was a sexton.'[99]

Such servile litanies foreground, as Heep intends, the fact of his obsequious lowliness. They do this, however, not only by means of his measured repetitions but also, more interestingly from our point of view, by means of the habits of [h]-dropping which Heep assumes. Iterations of humility in this way inevitably also become iterations of [h]-dropping for, though *humble* is a loanword (deriving from OF *umble, humble*) and hence originally [h]-less in English,[100] attitudes to this distribution had, over the nineteenth century, experienced a significant shift. In its role as one of the most salient markers of absence of status, Uriah's preferences for the dropped [h] thus aptly reinforce the pose which he so assiduously adopts.

No other visual and graphemic deviations are made to disfigure his speech, giving <h>, and its absence, an uncontested prominence in Heep's idiolect. In this context, its sociosymbolic properties are paramount in its interpretation and use. Heep being no ordinary 'illiterate speaker' such as those we have encountered before, his linguistic infelicities take on something of deliberation in his strategic adoption of [h]-loss. Just as Mr Casson, the innkeeper in George Eliot's *Adam Bede*, adopts more [h]s than are strictly necessary in his attempts to suggest identity with the gentry ('"I daresay he'd think me a hodd talker, as you Loamshire folks allays does hany wonn as talks the right language"'),[101] so does Uriah Heep shed them with equal enthusiasm in order to convey the opposite—an apparently unassuming identity with the lowest of the low. '"The ouse that I am stopping at—a sort of private hotel and boarding ouse, Master Copperfield, near the New River ed—will have gone to bed these two hours"', as he tells David, inveigling his way into stopping with him for the night while further demonstrating his linguistic abasement with facility.[102]

Heep's paradoxical pride in the very fact of his humility is parallelled by his equally paradoxical status as an educated man who assiduously cultivates his knowledge alongside this use of such stereotypical markers of the 'ignorant', 'uneducated', and lowly. When David first encounters him, Heep is, for example, applying himself with all due care to the study of William Tidd's *The Practice of the Court of the King's Bench* in the self-avowed aim of 'improving my legal knowledge'. Nevertheless, all ambitions of advance are strenuously denied. 'Too umble' ever to become a partner in Mr Wickfield's legal practice (at least so Uriah at this stage asserts), he manifests a similar horror at ideas of linguistic self-aggrandizement. David's offer to educate him in Latin is hence refused on the predictable grounds of Uriah's all-encompassing 'umbleness:

'Oh, indeed you must excuse me, Master Copperfield! I am greatly obliged, and I should like it of all things, I assure you; but I am far too umble. There are people enough to tread on me in my lowly state, without my doing outrage to their feelings by possessing learning. Learning ain't for me. A person like myself had better not aspire. If he is to get on in life, he must get on umbly, Master Copperfield.'[103]

A knowledge of Latin was of course traditionally part of the liberal education of the 'gentleman', a marker of status which conveyed meanings of social superiority as effectively as did certain nuances of dress or, equally, those of language. Uriah's determination to disavow these benefits is entirely characteristic of his personality, or at least of those aspects of it which he so diligently promotes. As he stresses, 'a person like myself had better not aspire', and his denial of aspiration is deployed in the novel with typical Dickensian wit, his repudiation of ambition effectively being mirrored in depictions of his spoken language as Heep is made to deny his aspirates for all they are worth. He follows his father's doctrine of humility (' "People like to be above you," says father, "keep yourself down" ')[104] quite literally to the letter: ' "I won't provoke my betters with knowledge, thank you, I'm too umble" ',[105] as he informs David. ' "Your elth and appiness" ', he toasts him later in the book; 'art', 'arsh', 'ealth', and 'appy' act as Heep's preferred versions of *heart, harsh, health,* and *happy,* and in affirming (although covertly) his own intentions towards Agnes Wickfield, the same markers, and their role in assigning social distance, make their habitual appearance: ' "Agnes Wickfield is, I am safe to say, the divinest of her sex ... To be her father is a proud distinction, but to be her usband——" ' runs his abruptly truncated commendation.[106] Heep's refusal to acquire knowledge above his station thus encompasses, with some deliberation, not only the use of Latin but also the correct positioning of [h], together with its statusful social meanings.

All his overt humility is, of course, only assumed for outward show. Heep is ultimately exposed for what he is, an 'incarnate hypocrite' as Traddles declares, a swindler and a cheat, a liar and fraud, who has used his stated monopoly of the humble virtues to gain an equal hold in the realms of vice, most notably as they concern control of Mr Wickfield's business. His mask of humility abandoned, Heep's true self is revealed. Arrogance and pride displace his disguise of meekness, assumed authority (instead of 'umbleness) tempers his speech: ' "You always were a puppy with a proud stomach, from you first coming here; and you envy me my rise, do you?" ', he tells David.[107] ' "None of your plots against me; I'll counterplot you! Micawber, you be off. I'll talk to you presently" ', he continues. Heep's new discourse is marked by command, and a sense of that power which he has in reality countermanded for so long: ' "Think twice, you, Micawber, if you don't want to be crushed. I recommend you to take yourself off, and be talked to presently, you fool!" ', ' "You hold your tongue, mother, least said, soonest mended!" '[108] As David rightly remarks, ' "there is a sudden change in this fellow, in more respects than the extraordinary one of him speaking the truth" '.[109] This change moreover extends to his use of [h]. His pose of humility forgotten as he is brought to bay, Heep, in his anger, manifests a new ability for control, not only in terms of that assumed over other people but also over the use of [h]: ' "Miss Trotwood, you had better stop this; or I'll stop your husband shorter than will be pleasant to you.... Miss Wickfield, if you have any love for your father, you had better not join that gang.... Now, come! I have got some of you under the harrow. Think twice, before it goes over you." '[110] *Have, husband, hold, harrow, had* no longer pose problems. The use of [h], long described in contemporary writings on language as an effective symbol of power and position, here makes full appearance as the 'old trick' of humility is entirely dropped, together with its markers, linguistic as well as social.

Heep's role as linguistic hypocrite as well as fraudulent powermonger does work to show in some measure the uses to which contemporary sensitization to /h/, and to its social values, could be put outside the maintenance and perpetuation of mere social stereotypes. Dickens's control of linguistic nuance is masterly though his fusion of both phonemic and semantic meaning within Heep's habitual asseverations of 'umble standing is here perhaps particularly worthy of note. Already in 1786 Elphinston had commented on the growing tendency to add [h] to realizations of *humble* (and its derivatives) amongst those who feared that articulations with its absence might suggest more than was, in fact, intended.[111] By the 1850s this transition was nearing completion as [h]-full realizations of *humble* became ever more the norm and [h]-less ones, in spite of their traditional validity within the language, were increasingly allied, in their connotative associations, with the statusless and 'low'. Nevertheless, as *David Copperfield* was published, contemporary comment on [h] and its 'proper' pronunciation still betrayed some hesitation on this matter: Smart's *Walker Remodelled* of 1846, noted, for example, 'In some pronouncing dictionaries *herb* and *hospital* are included among the words whose initial *h* is silent; but the *h* may be aspirated in these and their derivatives without the least offence to polite ears; and even in *humble* and *humour*, the sounding of the *h* is a fault, if a fault, far less grating than it would be in *heir*, *honest*, and the other words stated above'.[112] Confirming the growing acceptability of this process, Smart makes it clear that its extension to *humble* (and *humour*) was also well under way. This vacillation was in many ways rather effectively resolved, at least within the popular mind, by Dickens's own selection of '*umbleness* as an integral element of Uriah's linguistic and moral disguise. Using *umble* and not *humble* was afterwards far too often associated with the name of Heep as his infamy came to extend even here. Castigating those who still adhere to the 'bad habit' of [h]-less realizations of this word, Henry Alford in 1864 hence comments that 'it is difficult to believe that this pronunciation can long survive the satire of Dickens's in David Copperfield.'[113] Leach in 1881 was still more specific, as well as laudatory on the subject of Dickens's achievements in this respect:

The H of *Humble* has of recent years been reinstated in public favour by the late Mr Charles Dickens, whose 'Uriah Heep' remains a warning to evil-doers and H-droppers. It would be a boon to all speakers of English if a series of 'Uriah's' could contrive to eliminate every otiose H from the language.[114]

By the late 1860s, traditional patterns of norm and deviation had, as a result, largely shifted in this context. The lexicographer John Longmuir in 1864 stresses the 'increasing tendency to sound the *h* in these words',[115] and the book of exercises designed to accompany Charles Smith's manual of linguistic etiquette *Mind Your H's and Take Care of Your R's* of 1866 devotes a special section to words with 'formerly silent *h*' amongst which *humble* (and derivatives) occupy a prominent place. By the end of the century its traditionally [h]-less enunciation had passed into history though those of *honour* and *heir*, *hour*, *honest*, and *hotel* still remained. As Hill commented in 1902: 'there is a marked tendency at present to decrease the number of such words [in which *h* is silent], but the restoration of the "h" is sometimes quickened by circumstances; thus the sarcasm of Dickens and the contemptible character of Uriah Heep have caused the "h" to reappear in "'umble" much sooner than in "'ospital"'.[116]

Literary deployment of /h/ as social signifier has, of course, continued to the present day, language attitudes towards its absence having, since the mid-nineteenth century, remained remarkably constant. Often adopted for the 'vulgar', the 'lower class' or the 'Other' (as manifested in various ways), it can of course act as a readily comprehensible signal of social or geographical difference; it can, however, also act as a challenge to images of establishment authority, offering a ready marker of dissonant voices and opinions within a variety of modern novels. One major difference, at least in terms of its representation since the mid-nineteenth century, has been the establishment of the apostrophe as a regular diacritic of <h> and [h] absence. Used sporadically in this function by compositors in Dickens's time, its use was gradually

consolidated until by the end of the century it had emerged as an easily rec-
ognizable signal of the intentionally deviant in terms of speech. Gissing's
novels of this period illustrate its action well so that in *Born in Exile*, for
example, the apostrophe is made to litter depictions of the speech of Godwin
Peak's Uncle Andrew, drawing attention to features deemed unacceptable:
' "I've been tellin' Jowey, Grace, as I 'ope he may turn out such another as
Godwin 'ere. 'E'll go to Collige, will Jowey. Godwin, jest arst the bo-oy a
question or two, will you? 'E ain't been doin' bad at 'is school. Jest put 'im
through 'is pyces, as yer may sye." '[117] Patterns of apostrophe presence
and absence thus work contrastively among characters to differentiate them
in terms of language and status, its dense application here unambiguously
conveying the facts of Andrew Peak's cockney standing. Loss of [h] is
marked seven times in five lines, a characteristic of the 'hateful voice'
depicted and despised. Apostrophes in Godwin's own 'proper' speech conversely figure only in entirely grammatical relations, marking not ignorant
omission but instead the function of the possessive, or legitimate contractions such as *can't*.

The apostrophe emerges as the marker, in visual terms, of the 'dropped
letter', bearing witness once more to popular equations of grapheme and
phoneme in the notions of visual propriety which were commonly adopted in
nineteenth-century texts. A parallel process is evident in the increased attention paid to another 'dropped letter' over this time, that of <g> in words
such as *walking*. Realizations of *ing* in present participle forms such as *walking* (which have now assumed a non-localized norm in [ɪŋ])[118] were in fact
traditionally pronounced 'without the 'g'' in [ɪn]. In phonetic terms, the difference is merely that between use of the alveolar nasal [n] and that of the
velar nasal [ŋ]. In social terms, however, the connotative values surrounding
each came to mean much more and, like the use of [h] or [Ø] in appropriate
words, the selection of [ɪn] or [ɪŋ] was in time to embody precise stratifica-
tions on the social scale for those sensitized to their use. Such sensitization,
as for patterns of [h] usage, does not antedate the mid-eighteenth century.
Swift, whose own sensibilities regarding 'correct usage' were marked, happily
rhymes *doing* and *ruin* in 1731 in lines 415–16 of *Verses on the Death of
Dr. Swift*: 'Envy hath owned it was his doing // To save that helpless land from
ruin'. Still later George Crabbe in his *Poetical Epistles* rhymes *Delight in* and
fighting.[119] Other examples attesting such equivalence at this time can easily
be found. With the second half of the eighteenth century, however, and with
that increased attention being paid to accent, to conceptions of its norms,
and, importantly, to its attempted 'correction', things gradually began to
change. Prescriptive sensibilities are, in this context, first perceptible in the
works of writers such as the grammarian and educational writer John Rice,
whose *An Introduction to the Art of Reading with Energy and Propriety* of 1765
also introduces a new sense of impropriety to this hitherto acceptable pronunciation. The use of [ɪn] is, he admits, 'taught in many of Our Grammars'

but custom is, as ever, to be no sanction in the face of newly perceived error. '[It is] a vicious and indistinct Method of Pronunciation, and ought to be avoided', Rice declares, not least since 'by these Means, *hearing* may possibly be mistaken for *herein*, *looking* for *look in*, *getting* for *get in*.'[120]

The favoured eighteenth-century dictates of 'reason' are here clearly asserted above those of usage, duly informing the objections which are made. 'Dropping the g', Rice argues, generates homophones (*looking: look in*, *getting: get in*) which are unwarranted by the orthography. These moreover, at least within the negative framework adopted, will inexorably lead to ambiguity (and associated degeneration) instead of the clarity and efficiency which a language should properly maintain. Of course, in reality, homophones proliferate in English without the breakdown in communication of which Rice warns (though such arguments, as we have seen, occupy a time-honoured place in prescriptive writing). For pairs such as *looking* and *look in*, even if a shared final pronunciation in [ɪn] rendered them identical in sound, the differing contexts and constructions in which they were employed would in any case make confusion unlikely. Nevertheless, the objection is made and 'graphemic logic', as for /h/ and <h>, was eventually to win the day, aided by those widespread connotations of 'knowledge' versus 'ignorance' which commonly attended the use of literate speech or its converse in popular notions of correctness. By 1791, John Walker is already influentially asserting the importance of [ɪŋ] rather than [ɪn] in relevant words as a marker of propriety and a favoured form of the 'best speakers', though at this stage words such as *singing* and *ringing* are still, for reasons of euphony, given as exempt from this shift. Words containing the morpheme {ing} are, as Walker notes, 'frequently a cause of embarrassment to speakers who desire to pronounce correctly', and he recommends due observance of the 'proper' patterns: 'a repetition of the ringing sound in successive syllables would have a very bad effect on the ear; and therefore, instead of *singing*, *bringing*, and *flinging*, our best speakers are heard to pronounce *sing-in*, *bring-in*, and *fling-in*'.[121] Thomas Batchelor in 1809 reveals similar preferences. Whereas the use of [ɪn] rather than [ɪŋ] is elsewhere necessarily designated as a prime signal of the 'illiterate' speaker, Batchelor carefully makes an exception in the case of this particular group of words. As he states, 'when the sound *ng* ... occurs twice in succession, as in *singing*, an *n* is always used ... as it prevents a monotonous sound'.[122] Smart's *Walker Remodelled*, however, later remodels this particular tenet too in line with the further extension of such fashionable principles of correctness; no exceptions from the 'logical' and general rule for the use of [ɪŋ] are allowed. By 1836 therefore, 'dropping the g' is, at least in theory, confined to the 'vulgar' and statusless, whereas articulation with [ɪŋ] marks the 'polite' and intentionally statusful. Another symbol of the social divide has come into being.

The reality, however, tended as always to be a little less simple than that which was suggested, and endorsed, by the prescriptive fictions which were generated in abundance by such writers. The use of [ɪn] rather than [ɪŋ] (*walkin'* rather than *walking*) did indeed gain all the negative connotations in terms of the non-regional standard which such writers were concerned to promote. Literary works, with plentiful use of apostrophes to mark 'improper' omission, reinforced them still further, making plain the status of 'dropped g' as an incontrovertible deviation against an intended norm with <g> (and, by implication, [ɪŋ]). Dickens in *Little Dorrit*, for example, chooses to signal the inferior social status of Mrs Bangham, charwoman and ex-prisoner of the Marshalsea, by such means: ' "What between the buryin' ground, the grocer's, the waggon-stables, and the paunch trade, the Marshalsea flies get very large." '[123] In *David Copperfield* Mr Peggotty's linguistic affiliations to the lower sections of society are similarly marked: ' "You're a wonderin' what that's fur, sir! Well, it's fur our little Em'ly … when I'm here at the hour as she's a comin' home, I puts the light in the winder." '[124] Nor was Dickens alone in the use of these habitual markers but, as for /h/, Gissing, Gaskell, Thackeray, Eliot, Reade, together with a multitude of others, share in these conventions by which the linguistic habits of the other half of the two nations were to be delineated. From its beginnings in the polite usage of the mid-eighteenth century, the use of [ɪn] and, in turn, <in'> had, a century later, emerged as a well-attested linguistic stereotype of the 'vulgar' and the lower echelons of society.

Literature too makes ample use, for comic purposes, of the patterns of hypercorrection which also arise in response to the propagation of a new prestige norm. Just as the linguistically insecure were regularly portrayed as attempting to assert a status which they did not in reality possess by means of the superabundance of [h]s they deployed, so too were the uneducated, and the socially and linguistically aspiring, depicted as endeavouring to add the 'dropped g' where appropriate and equally, of course, where inappropriate too. Thackeray's *Vanity Fair* provides clear examples of this mechanism in action in the speech of Joseph Sedley's valet. Described as 'the most solemn and correct of gentlemen', his language nevertheless displays habitual patterns of displacement as far as those two status markers [ŋ] and [h] are concerned: ' "Mr. Sedley was uncommon wild last night, sir," he whispered in confidence to Osborne, as the latter mounted the stair. "He wanted to fight the 'ackney-coachman, sir. The Capting was obliged to bring him up stairs in his harms." '[125]

Iterations of *Capting* rather than *captain* (and *harms* rather than *arms*) are in such ways used to mark the social inferior whose excessive zeal leads him to attempt to use such forms while his knowledge remains inadequate to allow him to use them in accordance with the 'proper' models of speech. The same process is evident in the linguistic forms allocated by Thackeray to Blenkinsop, the Sedley's housekeeper: ' "Pinner says she's always about your trinket-box and drawers … and she's sure she's put your white ribbing into

her box" '.[126] The substitution of *ribbing* for *ribbon* again acts as a clear diacritic of lower social status. A range of similar confusions based on [ɪn] and
[ɪŋ] in fact seem to have been common according to the evidence available
as speakers apparently endeavoured to conform to new notions of linguistic
(and social) prestige, replacing [ɪn] with [ɪŋ] as they did so. As such examples illustrate, however, the enthusiasm for such exchanges could be somewhat excessive, generating the 'correct' use of [ɪŋ] not only in the present
participle or verbal noun, but also in many other words in which a final
unstressed syllable could be realized as [ɪn]. Jo in *Bleak House*, for example,
receives a *sovring* rather than a *sovereign* (/ˈsɒvrɪn/), and Thomas Bilder, the
zoo-keeper in Bram Stoker's *Dracula* (1897), makes similar use of *garding* for
garden, *certing* for *certain*. In the nineteenth century, *lupings*, *childring* and *kitch-
ings* are all attested. The 'chicking' revered by Maggy, the grand-daughter of
Amy Dorrit's old nurse, in *Little Dorrit* is also to be seen under this head as,
illustrating popular phonemic confusions in her placements of [ŋ], Maggy is
made to add the <g> as well as dropping it elsewhere. As with those earlier
comments on hypercorrections involving /h/, some caution is, however, to be
recommended before accepting these stereotypes as in any way representing
an entirely straightforward depiction of the truth.

   This is particularly true in this instance, not least given the recognition
that, throughout the nineteenth century (as well as afterwards), the use of
[ɪn] served equally well as a stereotype to denote the linguistic habits of the
extreme upper levels of society, and the massed ranks of those who engage,
with all their 'dropped g's', in the pursuits of *huntin'*, *shootin'*, and *fishin'*.
Disturbing the prescriptive paradigms which are so neatly set up by contemporary writers on the language, a consideration of reality instead here
served to expose the social fictions which were otherwise deftly manipulated
in this context in orthoepical attempts to regularize and correct the language.
The highest echelons of those 'best speakers' set forth by Walker as a norm
to be emulated and admired in fact tended to exhibit a marked preference
for realizations in this theoretically disfavoured [ɪn] rather than using the
notionally 'correct' [ɪŋ] which Walker and so many others advocated. Secure
in their well-established status, and with no need to seek social or linguistic
advice from the many manuals of etiquette which proffered it to any available audience, such speakers were moreover to remain largely immune from
prescriptive control and popular sensibilities, a pattern similarly reinforced
in modern sociolinguistic work where groups stable within the social hierarchy are indeed less likely to conform to normative pressures from outside.

   In the nineteenth century, such speakers were of course often castigated
for this refusal to conform to the norms which, in theory if not in practice,
they themselves were supposed to epitomize. Parry Gwynne, for example,
regretfully admits in 1879 that such pronunciations are 'prevalent among
even the best educated people of England' and he goes on to admonish those

who perpetuate this error for the bad example which they thereby provide: 'This is ... a greater blemish, where we have a right to look for perfection, than the peculiarities of the provinces in those who reside there', he duly chastises.[127] This co-existence of the same pronunciation in the extremes of society, in hyperlect as much as basilect, nevertheless endured throughout the nineteenth century (see Figure 4.2). Ellis in 1869 readily picked up on the contemporary resonances of this, using it to illustrate the problems of variation and social distribution in his *Early English Pronunciation*.[128] In such ways, [ɪn] functioned as a marker of lower status and rusticity, and yet simultaneously signified 'the peculiar accent ... of aristocracy', as Galsworthy phrased it in his descriptions of Mrs Dennant in *The Island Pharisees* (1904).[129] Galsworthy's novels indeed point the disjunction well, *in'* serving as a shared marker of both low and high status, habitually marking the speech of servants—as well as those they serve.

James Forsyte's butler in the second volume of Galsworthy's celebrated *Forsyte Saga* (*In Chancery* (1920)) hence comments on the fact that it 'might be Mrs Dartie's comin' round this afternoon', his evident preference for [ɪn] rather than [ɪŋ] being shared, for example, with the speech of the indubitably socially superior Timothy Forsyte ('All this new-fangled volunteerin' ... lettin' money out of the country'). It was an anomaly which was largely to be brought into line in the early decades of the twentieth century in a shift which Galsworthy's later novels also pertinently reflect. In *Swan Song* (1928), for instance, this particular linguistic mannerism in seventy-year-old Sir Timothy Fanfield ('Old Shropshire's a charmin' old man', 'Who's that talkin' to the old Marquess?') appears as an anachronism in an era when [ɪŋ] had evidently become the norm, even in the elite circles in which Sir Timothy is made to mix. As A. S. C. Ross confirmed in his later account of the U and non-U of usage in this (and other) respects, '[ɪn] certainly survived into the 'twenties but, even then, sounded silly and affected unless used by the very old U. Now it exists only as a joke, usually made by the non-U against the U'.[130]

Such 'dropped letters' did not, of course, provide the only vehicles for social sensitization to the use of individual variants in speech, though they were undeniably prominent in the barrage of prescriptive and popular comment on language which appeared throughout the late eighteenth and nineteenth centuries. Similar images of literacy (and its converse) nevertheless lay behind many contemporary critiques of language and its sounds, while corresponding idealizations of 'elegant' and 'literate' speakers regularly infuse eighteenth- and nineteenth-century writing (and thinking) on language in a variety of ways. Prescriptive responses of this order govern the notions of impropriety generated by the loss of contrast between words such as *witch* and *which*—widely perceived as yet another culpable instance of [h]-dropping[131]—or pervade reactions to the hitherto widely acceptable ways of

"EVIL COMMUNICATIONS," &c.

Lord Reginald. "AIN'T YER GOIN' TO HAVE SOME PUDDIN', MISS RICHARDS? IT'S *SO* JOLLY!"

The Governess. "THERE AGAIN, REGINALD! 'PUDDIN''—'GOIN''—'AIN'T YER'!!! THAT'S THE WAY JIM BATES AND DOLLY MAPLE SPEAK—AND JIM'S A *STABLE-BOY*, AND DOLLY'S A *LAUNDRY-MAID*!"

Lord Reginald. "AH! BUT THAT'S THE WAY FATHER AND MOTHER SPEAK, *TOO*— AND FATHER'S A *DUKE*, AND MOTHER'S A *DUCHESS*!! SO *THERE*!"

FIG. 4.2. '"Evil communications," &c.' An illustration from *Punch*, 6 September, 1873, p. 99.

pronouncing *gold* as *goold* or *ooman* for *woman*, both of which were recollected as typical pronunciations in her youth by Queen Victoria, for example.[132] Notions of literacy—and the repercussions which these could have, both in language attitudes and, at times, in linguistic processes too—provide a salient insight into the specific workings of prescriptive methodology in ways which, as we have seen, were often central to the popular linguistic thinking of the day. Like ideologies of a standard, these particular manifestations of prescriptivism can thus be seen to operate most effectively as an attitude of mind, a set of beliefs about language and language use which, in terms of linguistic history, were diffused far beyond those who simply wrote on the language and articulated its stated norms.

5

Ladylike Accents and the Feminine
Proprieties of Speech

THE 'lady', and her masculine counterpart in social status, the 'gentleman', combined to exert a profound influence on notions of propriety, behaviour, and 'correctness' throughout the late eighteenth and nineteenth centuries. These too were popular cultural stereotypes, widely associated with contemporary ideals of both refinement and status. Seen as epitomizing a standard of life which encompassed manners as well as morals, their role, as the novelist Charlotte Yonge stressed, was deservedly that of the exemplar. Ladies and gentlemen, she stated, were to be recognized by their 'high-bred bearing, and grace of manner', and by their 'code of honour, courtesy, and natural power of conforming to it'. 'It is this', Yonge adds, 'which proscribes all the meaner faults, by simply regarding them as impossible in gentleman or lady, such, we mean, as listening at doors, looking into letters . . . and likewise all struggles for place, rude and rough speech and manner'.[1]

For those sensitive to their appeal, conceptions of both could act in socially normative ways, inspiring, for example, further aspects of that cultural cohesion which has been extensively documented over this period by the historians Stone and Stone.[2] As J. F. C. Harrison noted in *Early Victorian Britain*, 'the concept of gentility functioned as an agency of social discipline',[3] regularly informing, in this context, selected specifications of speech as well as of behaviour. A steady stream of comment surrounded the emulatory paradigms which could result. Drawing on other prevalent social images, for example, the nineteenth-century historian Thomas Macaulay expostulated on the seemingly relentless ambition of the middle levels of society for social transformations of precisely this kind: 'The curse of England is the obstinate determination of the middle classes to make their sons what they call gentlemen', he declared.[4] Samuel Smiles described the popularity of these more superficial aspects of 'self-help' with evident distaste: 'There is an ambition to bring up boys as gentlemen, or rather "genteel" men; though the result frequently is only to make them gents'.[5] The nineteenth-century resonances of *gent* confirmed the potential futility of such attempts. Whereas the gentleman, as *OED* notes, was 'a man of superior position in society, or [one] having the habits of life indicative of this', the *gent* was semantically different in both identity and nature. Even its use was 'vulgar', Henry Bradley (co-editor of the *OED* from 1886) noted in the relevant entry, except 'as applied derisively to men of the vulgar and pretentious class who are supposed to use the word'. In any circumstance, the 'gent' was, he confirmed, 'a mark of low breeding'.

Girls too, irrespective of the actual walks of life they were to occupy, were often subject to identical pressures, being educated into all the refinements of manner and behaviour which 'young ladies' should have at their command. As the writer Sarah Stickney Ellis scathingly commented of the cultural hegemonies which were thereby intentionally enacted:

Amongst the changes introduced by modern taste, it is not the least striking, that all the daughters of tradespeople, when sent to school, are no longer girls, but young ladies. The linen-draper whose worthy consort occupies her daily post behind the counter, receives her child from Mrs Montagu's establishment—a young lady. At the same elegant and expensive seminary, music and Italian are taught to Hannah Smith, whose father deals in Yarmouth Herrings; and there is the butcher's daughter, too, perhaps the most ladylike of them all.[6]

Such metamorphoses in terms of social labels (and accompanying notions of identity) were not confined to the aspirational education of children. On the contrary, according to contemporary documentation, a social education in the requisite acquirements of polite life could, it seemed, begin at any time. Both George Eliot and William Cobbett, as already indicated, devote no little censure to the pretensions which were often affected by farmers and their families in these respects.[7] Giving more direct illustration of such patterns, Thomas Raybould, a Staffordshire manufacturer of scythes and spades, wrote the following letter to his wife in 1789, instructing her in the ladylike proprieties he felt to be suitable for their avowedly genteel life: 'Don't suffer Mary Mogg to sit at table with you to drink tea, as it does certainly let you down very much, as it is a very odd affair if you cannot look upon yourself as a gentlewoman, and let her sit at the ironing table. If your mother suffers such things, it is what no gentlewoman does, therefore you must not.'[8] Raybould's specifications stress the import, and dissemination, of the cultural construct of gentility together with its associated behavioural norms. His income at that time comprised only around £100 a year but assimilation to the conventions of 'gentle' living was, nevertheless, not to be neglected. His wife's role was to divorce herself from her social inferiors, 'never to carry a basket to work as long as you are my wife', and to behave, in other words, as a lady of leisure. She was to 'look upon herself as a gentlewoman' ('a woman of birth above the vulgar, a woman well-descended', as John Walker glossed in his *Dictionary* of 1791). The adoption of associated markers of 'ladylike' propriety was in this, of course, not entirely divorced from Raybould's perceptions of his own status. Artisans had wives who worked; 'gentlemen' did not.

Such attitudes were not uncommon and amongst the middle ranks of society a widespread shift gradually took place in the roles and occupations which were seen as suitable for these reconstructed 'ladies' of the household. They were frequently to be 'dismissed from the dairy, the confectionary, the store-room, the still-room, the poultry-yard, the kitchen-garden, and the orchard', Margaretta Grey noted in her diary in 1853.[9] Resulting conceptions of feminine propriety came to dictate proficiency not in traditional occupations of home-baking or brewing but instead in the leisured arts and 'accomplishments'—those external signifiers of the genteel over which 'ladies', of whatever rank, were to have command. The lexicographer James Murray was openly critical of the semantic weakening which such nineteenth-century uses of *accomplishment* had brought—in spite of the descriptive agenda formally adopted by the *OED*.[10] Grey was, if anything, still more critical of the social realities underlying such usages, targeting the wasteful redundancy (and social pretension) which they revealed. 'A lady, to be such, must be a mere lady, and nothing else', she added; 'She must not work for profit, or engage in any occupation that money can command. . .what I remonstrate against is the negative forms of employment, the wasting of energy, the crippling of talent under false ideas of station, propriety, and refinement.'

Even by the end of the eighteenth century, as the writer and critic Mary Poovey has confirmed, the stereotype of the 'Proper Lady' who resulted from such reorientations 'was a familiar household companion',[11] and the 'refinement', 'propriety', 'modesty', 'delicacy', and 'virtue' presented as salient parts within her make-up dominated popular conceptions of appropriate femininity. These propagated norms were widespread, diffusing idealized abstractions of behaviour to which, as for language, actual behaviour tended of course to conform only to a greater or lesser extent. Even women located lower in the social hierarchy were not, however, entirely immune from the pressures which ensued. Though forced by necessity to work, they were, as Janet Murray points out, 'often judged by the same standards of angelic, sheltered femininity as middle-class and upper-class women'.[12] D. H. Lawrence's mother Lydia, for example, was born in 1851 into a firmly working-class background and to a family which 'had pretensions which their actual income of around £90 a year could barely support'. In spite of this she was nevertheless brought up to consider herself and her sisters as 'ladies'—even if, as Lawrence's biographer John Worthen notes, they 'worked at drawing lace'. Attitudes to language likewise figured in this construction.[13] As Lawrence himself would later record of his mother, 'She spoke King's English, without an accent, and never in her life could even imitate a sentence of the dialect which my father spoke, and which we children spoke out of doors'.[14] In ways such as these it is evident that popular notions of perfect womanhood could indeed come to dominate ideals of female behaviour, deportment, and decorum throughout society, in turn being encoded and reinforced in the many manuals of conduct and etiquette produced to this end. Likewise penny magazines such as *The Family Herald*, or the popular novels of writers such as Rhoda Broughton, Rosa Nouchette Carey, Dinah Craik, or Charlotte Yonge regularly held up for emulation the standards of behaviour, and the accompanying standards of language, which were deemed to characterize this social icon. As the novelist Dinah Craik averred, 'the nameless graces of ladyhood' must necessarily comprise 'the quiet dignity of speech and mien' just as much as 'the repose of perfect self-possession'.[15]

Language, perhaps predictably therefore, plays an integral role in the social and cultural definitions of the 'lady' which emerge over the course of the nineteenth century. Often placed on a moral pedestal in Victorian eulogies to true womanhood ('from the very susceptibility of her nature, woman is to be more virtuous than man', as *Woman's Worth* stressed in 1847),[16] the lady, as we shall see, was to occupy a linguistic pedestal too, ideally revealing and reflecting similar virtues in her speech. In some senses, the 'gentleman' is of course also made to share in this paradigmatic function. Endowed with a superabundance of internal as well as external merits, he is, for example, additionally characterized by his total command of the 'best' (and non-regional) markers of speech: 'Purity of accent is the grand distinctive feature of a gentleman', as the author of *How to Shine in Society* declared, stressing, by extension, the absence of any markers of the provincial or the impolite.[17] The manipulation of notions of accent and identity in such socially specific ways is by no means rare. With reference to the 'gentleman', his dress, his language, his pronunciation, and even his gloves, were all seen as being liberally endowed with social meanings suggestive of this matchless status. *What Shall We Do With Tom?*, for example, a manual of advice for parents with male offspring, readily proffers 'make him a gentleman' in answer to the question which its title posed. As Robert Brewer, the author, further elaborates on this matter:

It is said that in dress the true gentleman is distinguished by faultless linen, and by accurately-fitting gloves. And in education he is distinguished by his unfailing self-possession and by good spelling . . . he ought never to trip into the vulgarism of mis-pronouncing his words. They are the faultless linen and the accurately-fitting gloves; the little things that carry with them the 'ring' of true gentility.[18]

The gentleman might be duly distinguished by his perfection in such matters; the lady, however, was apparently to excel still further if she was fully to justify her right to such an appellation. In the set of attitudes and ideals which come to dominate popular thinking in this area, whereas high standards of behaviour and virtue will necessarily distinguish the gentleman, still higher ones must mark the woman who intends to assume, and indeed to convey, her truly gentle standing. *Good Society: A Complete Manual of Manners* unhesitatingly gives expression to this belief: 'Granted that truthfulness, gracefulness, considerateness, unselfishness, are essential to the breeding of a true gentleman, how infinitely more they must be to the breeding of a true lady!'[19] Or as *The Woman's Book*, 'Containing everything a woman ought to know', later affirms, '"Manners makyth Man" and woman too, for if good manners are so essential to man, are they not then indispensable to woman, whose great object in life is to please?'[20]

Paragons in terms of morals, 'true ladies', so such precepts stated, must eclipse their male counterparts still further in those delicate nuances of breeding which are carried, and conveyed, by manner, etiquette, and, from the point of view of this book, by language. Compliance with the established tenets of feminine conduct is presented as imperative, and associated prescriptions (and proscriptions) appear not as options but laws: 'it is absolutely essential that a lady should conform strictly to the usages and rules of society', *Take My Advice* contends, for 'what in a gentleman would be a venial offence against good taste and good breeding, would bring ridicule upon a lady moving in the same circles'.[21] *Good Society* made a similar point, isolating the difference which gender must inevitably make with reference to these salient questions of acceptability. 'In [the woman]. . . all the minor observances of etiquette are absolutely indispensable', its anonymous author states, not least since '[the lady] must be even more on her guard than a man in all those niceties of speech, look, and manner, which are the especial and indispensable credentials of good breeding'.[22] The gender divide was clear. That such iterated attitudes were not without their repercussions is also made plain. As the novelist Fanny Burney avowed in 1779: 'I would a thousand times rather forfeit my character as a writer, than risk ridicule or censure as a Female'.[23] Or as Sarah Stickney Ellis similarly confirmed in her own book on *The Women of England*: 'The dread of being censured or condemned, exercises, I am inclined to think, a far more extensive influence over [woman's] habits and her feeling'. Indeed 'any deviation from the fashionable mode of dress, or from the established usages of polite life, presents an appalling difficulty to a woman of ordinary mind brought up under the tutelage of what is called the world.' As Ellis adds with some insistence, 'She cannot—positively cannot—dare not—will not do anything that the world has pronounced unlady-like'.[24]

Woman, in such ideal (and idealized) manifestations, was thus to act as guide and censor, her influence immeasurable in ensuring the elevated tone demanded in 'good' society. Writers such as Miss S. Hatfield expounded their belief in the 'power' of women to 'give a form and colouring to the manners of the age'[25] while popular conduct manuals endorsed the same wide-ranging influence and repercussions. 'How much must the refinement, manners, and habits of society depend upon them!', as *Woman's Worth* declared: 'there is nothing, whether it be in temper, manner, or speech, which she cannot restrain.'[26] Regularly constructed as guardians of morals, women were therefore equally to guard 'manners' too, including those of language, censuring the indecorous and impolite, the 'vulgar' and the 'improper'. The marked consonance of ideologies of both gender and linguistic correctness was clearly of utility in this context. Status, propriety, purity, and refinement were, as we have seen, all values which—at least in popular thinking—seemed to be embedded in the ways in which one spoke. Prominent aspects of the metalanguage of prescriptivism, their stated affiliations likewise formed a central tenet in many texts which were proffered for specifically female instruction, forming the foundation of a wide-ranging intersection between images of proper language and proper ladies. A marriage of ideas attended with no little degree of success, it was moreover, as we shall see, to be aided immeasurably by the compatibility of the terms employed.

Notions of propriety could, for example, play a prominent part within many descriptions (and prescriptions) of idealized femininity, often infringing on discussions of language too. As the writer Hannah More had early affirmed of the centrality of propriety in terms of gender, it was 'to a woman what the great Roman critic says action is to an orator; it is the first, the second, the third, requisite . . . the criterion of true taste, right principle, and genuine feeling'.[27] *Girls and Their Ways. By One Who Knows Them* extends this undisputed value of propriety to all aspects of female behaviour, encompassing not only 'dress and demeanour' but also 'speech', a domain in which the intended female readership is instructed to 'study the highest propriety, and the strictest reserve'.[28] *The Young Housekeeper* of 1869 emphasizes similar dictates by a judicious use of italics: 'You should be quite as anxious to *talk* with propriety as you are to think, work, sing, paint or write according to the most correct rules'.[29]

Language, and specifically spoken language, was as a result frequently stipulated as a salient feature of female propriety in itself. As both *Girls and Their Ways* and *The Young Housekeeper* confirm, for example, propriety of speech was presented as an external virtue which was able to signify the true breeding which was alone deemed to befit the lady, imaging forth interior virtue by means of its own exterior refinements. The elocutionist George Vandenhoff makes this particularly clear in *The Lady's Reader*, a work which was expressly devoted to that vocal elegance often presented as essential for proper womanhood. 'Grace of speech' is commended highly. It renders a woman more attractive (as Vandenhoff's opening statement avers) though its value also transcends these superficialities of appearance. Propriety instead takes on its most significant role as an element which is fundamental to ladylike conduct, and in particular to ladylike speech. 'No lady's manner', Vandenhoff insists, 'can be said to be completely *comme il faut* if her utterance, in ordinary conversation, be defective or inelegant.'[30] Social propriety, in the thinking of the day, was therefore to be met, and matched, with corresponding proprieties of language. Above all, accent, a feature so important in first impressions, must be carefully controlled. Stating on the following page that he writes 'without exaggeration', Vandenhoff hence asserts the prime value of enunciation in all assessments of ladylike identity. 'Correctness and grace of utterance are requisite distinctions of a lady's conversation', he stresses; 'a slovenly style of speech' would form 'as great a blemish as inelegant and ungrammatical language'. For true femininity, as Vandenhoff adds in an explicit appeal to the nineteenth-century counterparts of Shakespeare's Cordelia, there should be 'no instrument more sweet than the voice of woman'.[31]

Such notions of 'elegance' and aesthetic merit form recurrent terms of praise in Vandenhoff's account of the phonemic perfection deemed vital for the 'lady', just as they did in Dr Johnson's more general commendations of the 'best speakers' of the mid-eighteenth century.[32] Tellingly defined in Walker's *Critical Pronouncing Dictionary* as 'the beauty of propriety', the appropriateness of 'elegance' as a salient part of prescriptive metalanguage in this context was clear (though the fact that 'ladylike' itself is, in the same work, glossed as 'soft, delicate, elegant' serves to make the stated affinities still more obvious). Ladylike speech was thus by definition both 'proper' and 'elegant' and, as Vandenhoff and a host of other writers affirmed, proper and elegant language was in turn to be fairly unambiguously located in those non-regional norms of a 'standard' and in the marked associations with social status which pronunciations of this kind had also come to convey over the course of the nineteenth century. For the 'lady', 'the speaking of her native language with purity and elegance of pronunciation, in an agreeable tone of voice' is the marker which alone will communicate to her auditors 'the *prestige* of refinement and high breeding'.[33] It is this at which she is advised to aim and which is set out for her instruction in *The Lady's Reader*, just as it is in a plethora of other books, magazines, and journals produced over this time.

Such terms make the cultural and sociosymbolic correlates of female speech clear. In line with their role as guardians of manners and of morals, exemplary ladies must, so these conceptions went, find exemplary (and prestigious) accents which are to be located in the 'polite' rather than the 'provincial', and in the emerging non-regional norms of speech. That often proclaimed 'disgrace' which was assumed to surround the use of dialect and other localized markers was in such ways to take on still stronger reverberations within corresponding definitions of feminine nicety. 'Her accent is not provincial', as *Etiquette for Ladies and Gentlemen* decreed of the markers by which the 'lady' might be known.[34]

While propriety and impropriety, as we have already seen, form integral elements of that prescriptive lexis whereby regional accents (and proscribed variants) were regularly condemned, purity also, a cardinal virtue for the female sex, is likewise endowed with distinctive applications within nineteenth-century notions of the non-localized accent and its rightful dominance. 'Purity of accent', as *How to Shine in Society* confirms, is that which 'belongs to no city or district'.[35] Benjamin Smart (along with many other writers) readily engages in binary oppositions of 'pure' and 'impure' in this context which are neatly mapped on to the 'best speech' of London (and those who would emulate this, irrespective of their geographical location). In contrast, he makes plain, are the 'impurities' which are depicted as seemingly intrinsic to the 'provincial'. Logically therefore, pure ladies must speak only with the purest accents, a principle which Vandenhoff also affirms. 'A lady's accents must be pure, her tones sweet', corroborates Mrs Sangster in her *Hours with Girls*.[36] *The Young Lady's Book* of 1876 endorses this still further, fusing cultural and linguistic stereotypes alike in its assertions that one of the primary duties which the 'young ladies' of the title are to assume lies in their very defence of English itself from 'impurity', an aim facilitated by the exemplary qualities of language which 'ladies' must adopt at all times.[37] Given common perceptions of the wider values of female purity ('gently, imperceptibly, but most certainly, will she imbue with her own purity and beneficence the atmosphere in which she moves', as *The Young Lady's Book* of 1829 proclaimed),[38] the same affiliations form the sub-text of attitudes towards the language requisite for the Proper Lady. Imperceptibly but certainly was she to impose standards of usage upon her auditors by her own exemplary proprieties of phoneme and of phrase.

'Refinement' was usefully to partake of this same duality of reference. Its connotations, as Walker specifies, being those of 'improvement in elegance or purity', notions of 'refinement' likewise found a natural home in both popular and prescriptive attitudes to the values which correct standards of speech were intentionally to convey. Accent in *Talking and Debating* (1856) is, for instance, an element which can evince familiarity (or otherwise) with 'refined circles'.[39] Thomas Nichols in *Behaviour: A Manual of Morals and Manners* deliberately adopts a similar discourse for his female readers. 'The first and highest of human accomplishments is a clear, distinct, well-modulated speech', an attribute which, he further notes, is located in 'a refined and elegant way of speaking'.[40] Important therefore as a general desideratum in 'proper' speech, the presence of 'refinement' is presented as still more vital in associated conceptions of feminine identity and behaviour, a view which is often expressed in works directed towards both language and conduct. *Etiquette, Social Ethics and the Courtesies of Society*, the title of which exemplifies the equations commonly (if erroneously) made in the nineteenth century between manners and morals, hence combines gender, status, and language in the imperatives it issues to an audience which is explicitly constructed as female. Cautioned to 'remember your standing as gentlewomen' at all times, they are similarly not allowed to forget that they must 'never approve a mean action, nor speak an unrefined word'.[41] Any inadvertent breach of such prescribed standards was likely to bring in its wake consequences which were potentially momentous. As the author adjures, 'the least want of refinement in conversation lowers a woman, ay, and for ever'.

Evidently integral to notions of feminine status, the presence of refinement is endowed with still greater value in this context by the novelist and writer on conduct Charlotte Yonge. Admitting that in real terms refinement is 'just as much a Christian grace in a man as in a woman', Yonge is nevertheless strikingly explicit on the subject of its differential import in constructions of gender and identity. Of equal significance in terms of 'Christian grace' it might indeed be, but refinement occupies a far higher order for woman against man for without it, she adds, 'he is not such a hateful unsexed creature … as a woman is'.[42] 'True womanhood' being 'unsexed' by being unrefined, the linguistic correlates of this cultural ideal thus in turn receive due emphasis in Yonge's work. The *'lowest* standard for a lady' must include 'correct pronunciation', she specifies, noting further that such 'correct English' is in itself to be understood as 'a mark of real refinement of mind and cultivation'.[43]

Such attitudes make very plain the affinities of language, mind, and gender which were frequently endorsed over the course of the nineteenth century. Since the lady, at least within these iterations of popular mythology, was supposedly endowed with sensibilities more delicate than those of the common order (as *Advice to Governesses*, for example, notes of the future female charges of its readers, 'their sense of right and wrong will be more refined', and they will, as a result, 'be called upon to hold up an higher standard of purity and excellence, endeavouring to engage every one within their reach to rally round it'),[44] the nuances of pronunciation—as well as a range of other aspects of linguistic usage—were naturally to be placed in these same exemplary paradigms, likewise being subject to heightened sensitivities towards issues of 'right' and 'wrong', 'good' and 'bad', as well as to those emblematic properties of 'purity', 'refinement', and 'propriety' already discussed. That 'consciousness' of good pronunciation early advocated by Sheridan was hence to reach still higher levels of prescription (and recommendations for convergent behaviour) by means of this marked consonance with corresponding ideologies of lady-like decorum. It is the existence of these attitudes which explains in some measure the exaggerated reactions which can attend absence of conformity in this respect, a convention well illustrated in fictional form in Thomas Hardy's *The Mayor of Casterbridge* where Elizabeth-Jane's occasional use of evidently 'unrefined' dialect induces outrage in her father, given his own new social construction as 'gentleman' rather than hay-trusser:

'"Bide where ye be,"' he echoed sharply. 'Good God, are you only fit to carry wash to a pig-trough, that ye use such words as those?'
She reddened with shame and sadness.
'I meant, "Stay where you are," father,' she said, in a low, humble voice. 'I ought to have been more careful.'[45]

'Marks of the beast to the truly genteel', such terms as *bide* for 'stay' or *greggles* for 'wild hyacinths' are of course incompatible with the ladylike status, and accompanying sensibilities, which Henchard aims to impose upon his daughter. Capable of belying this new identity, they are accordingly proscribed, as is the similar use of the regional as opposed to the 'refined' by Margeret Hale in Gaskell's *North and South*. As Margaret is duly admonished by her mother: '"Margaret, don't get to use these horrid Milton words. 'Slack of work': it is a provincialism . . . it has a very vulgar sound and I don't want to hear you using it." '[46]

True ladies were supposed to know better and slang, infelicities of tone and phrase, as well, of course, as mispronunciations of various kinds were all popularly construed as indicating lower, and less refined, levels of sensitivity than those expected of the perfect femininity which was so often prescribed over the course of the nineteenth century.[47] Guardians of the moral right and wrong, ladies were thus envisaged as assuming the role of guardians of the language, with responsibilities not merely for personal standards of use but for the language as a whole. As *The Young Lady's Book* of 1876 reveals, for example, they themselves were to form the direct heirs (or, more specifically, heiresses) of John Walker and Samuel Johnson. The spirits of the latter being actively summoned to provide the proper inspiration ('Shades of Johnson and Walker! arise and defend the poor ill-used English language'), it is into the hands of young ladies that their canons of correctness against 'slovenly utterance' must now pass. As the writer eloquently appeals, 'will not our young ladies stand up for their own mother tongue and, by speaking it in its purity, redeem its lost character?'[48]

In the prevailing tenets of true womanhood, this in effect comes to constitute a charge entrusted to them from childhood as texts such as *Girls and Their Ways* suggest. The differences between this and its parallel volume, *Boys and Their Ways. By One Who Knows Them*, provide still more evidence on nineteenth-century gender differentiation and the role of language (and language attitudes) within it. A section dealing with 'The Girl in her Leisure Hours' hence notes: 'The arrangement of the voice . . . the just emphasis, the skilful inflection, the distinct articulation, the accurate pronunciation: these are graces to be acquired by careful study and constant practice.'[49] The corresponding section treating the 'leisure hours' of boys instead discusses the interest which is to be found in the study of botany, geology, chemistry, or music. Linguistic nicety only intrudes upon mention of the conversation which should be addressed to women, the boy 'in his mother's presence' being directed to 'subdue his voice and lay aside his rough manners' while to his sister he must likewise be 'gentle and polished in his language'.[50]

Such social norms and their attendant absolutes belong of course to the realm of stereotype rather than to reality per se. As already indicated, however, such stereotypes encode prevalent cultural images and ideals of behaviour, offering constructions of gender and identity in this context which, though conventional and even formulaic in their dictates, can nevertheless be of importance. As Deborah Cameron has pointed out in *The Feminist Critique of Language*, stereotypes of this order are 'interesting as clues to our *ideology of femininity and sex difference*'[51] and they do indeed convey with particular explicitness the cultural as well as linguistic pressures which were commonly exerted on eighteenth- and nineteenth-century females from their earliest years. Widely prevalent in magazines, in manuals of housekeeping, in contemporary literature, and even in education, as much as in those works expressly directed towards prescription of 'ladylike' conduct, such attitudes and ideals secured wide dissemination. Women 'must be educated, in great degree, by the opinions and manners of the society they live in', as the eighteenth-century writer Mary Wollstonecraft observed.[52] Over the course of the following century, the use of 'proper' language was to form a central part of this specifically female education, impinging to no little extent upon contemporary constructions of the woman as in her various social roles as maiden, wife, and mother as well as in those wider aspects of the social identity which true ladies were expected to convey.

The voice, for example, was presented as a particularly prominent element within those external signals by which notions of identity were to be conveyed to the outside world. Its proper modulations accordingly received marked attention within the norms presented for the erudition of girls. Even if we remove its associated specification of accent for a moment, the voice emerges as a recurrent topos in depictions of the truly feminine, commendations liberally accruing around that 'voice ever soft, gentle, and low' which Shakespeare's King Lear had so long ago praised in his own daughter.[53] This too became a prominent element in the linguistic stereotyping of the age. As for Cordelia, 'our girls should seek to cultivate a low voice, "that excellent thing in woman"', *Girls and Their Ways* remarks.[54] 'Remember in conversation that a voice "gentle and low" is, above all extraneous accomplishments, "an excellent thing in woman"', *Good Society: A Complete Manual of Manners* verifies, further delineating the peculiarly statusful properties of this acquisition: 'There is a certain distinct but subdued tone of voice which is peculiar only to persons of the best breeding. It is better to err by the use of too low than too loud a tone.'[55] The 'careful repressive influence' which Charlotte Yonge so commends in female education clearly takes on additional values in such contexts. As *The Habits of Good Society: A Handbook of Etiquette for Ladies and Gentlemen* makes plain, all natural properties of vocal pitch and volume must in fact be curbed in 'proper' ladylike speech. The lady's address 'should be polite and gentle' but it was given as of still greater significance that her words 'should be gently spoken . . . the voice loud enough to be caught easily, but always in an undertone to the power of voice allotted by nature'.[56] Perhaps predictably, the section which deals with etiquette for gentlemen fails to provide similar specifications for its male readers.

Affiliations with perceived status are of course overtly manipulated in such maxims on 'talking proper'. For the woman, the use of a loud voice, standing as it does outside the stated canons of acceptability, was often regarded as manifesting obvious deficiencies in status as well as sensibility. It was, as *Etiquette for the Ladies* asserts, 'utterly plebeian'. On such grounds, as the author continues with a marked lack of moderation, it is 'repulsive in a lady'.[57] *Hints to Governesses* makes much the same point, deftly aligning propriety and pronunciation in another account of the essential management of the voice. Once more reiterating the value of Cordelia as feminine exemplar, it extols the use of the low and gentle voice on all occasions, even when in reprimand: 'A gentle reproof in a soft tone of voice will be found most effectual.—Loud, angry tones are extremely unladylike, and degrading.'[58] Submissive enunciation is therefore the ideal at which all ladies, and would-be ladies, are to aim and the hallmark by which they will in turn be known. 'One can always tell a lady by her voice and laugh', *Etiquette for Ladies and Gentlemen* proclaims: 'neither. . . will ever be loud or coarse, but soft, low, and nicely modulated. Shakespeare's unfailing taste tells you that—"A low voice is an excellent thing in women".'[59]

Comments such as these serve to underline still further the centrality of the voice within nineteenth-century feminine ideology. As David Graddol and Joan Swann have moreover confirmed in the twentieth century, such assumptions can in fact still be of no little import within wider ideologies of gender and their associated manifestations. 'Through its pervasiveness in both public and intimate encounters', they point out, '[the voice] constantly establishes a difference between the sexes.' It is, as a result, 'likely to perform an important ideological role'.[60] The dominance of the voice within contemporary images of femininity in the nineteenth century certainly would not lead one to dispute such assertions; as we will see, a range of additional aspects of its 'proper' use regularly make an appearance in accounts of the other gender roles which the women of the day were expected to fulfil to the best of their capacities.

The significance of elocution and vocal training for women in the eighteenth and nineteenth centuries is, for instance, commonly presented in the framework of the social roles which they will later adopt. As wives, as mothers, or simply in the bosom of their own families, the correct management of the voice was frequently depicted as an asset incontestable in the value it would confer. Vandenhoff was notably eulogistic in this context, exalting the role of elocution in contemporary constructions of femininity. 'Is there any acquirement more domestic, more peculiarly feminine?' he demanded in a question which was entirely rhetorical within his text.[61] Certainly the specifically 'domestic' applications of this ability were seen as reinforcing its perceived relevance in female education and training. Reading aloud was, for instance, envisaged as a sphere in which the vocal proprieties of women could be employed to the enjoyment of all, adding immeasurably to the comforts of the home. Vandenhoff continues his eulogy on elocution, femininity, and the necessary acquisition of correct pronunciation in precisely this strain: 'HOME, the domestic circle, is the legitimate scene of a woman's accomplishments; and an attainment which can add the charms of intellectual entertainment to the other attractions of her fireside, is certainly worthy of particular attention in a system of female education.'

Other writers advocated the importance of elocution in similar terms. *The Young Lady's Book* in 1876 unreservedly endorsed the precept that 'a woman who reads aloud really well holds a power of pleasing difficult to overestimate, since it is an every-day accomplishment, and eminently suited to home life',[62] while *Girls and Their Ways* emphasized how 'graceful' was this accomplishment, not least since it was capable of 'investing the winter evening with a new charm'. 'Accurate pronunciation' is therefore to be acquired by 'careful study and constant practice' so that such additional and especially feminine charms may captivate the domestic circle. A glowing picture is envisaged of the results to be expected from command of this indispensable accomplishment: 'What a depth of significance is given to a fine passage by a skilful reader; what lights and shades she indicates in it; how she conveys the sentiment, the feeling to the heart and mind of the reader.'[63] Infelicities of accent were of course entirely inimical to the effects such elocutionary endeavours were intended to create, a lesson which was, for instance, regularly brought home to Thomas Sheridan's own daughters who were 'made to read long passages from *The Rambler*, then wearied still further by a correction of their faults'.[64]

Mrs Beeton too, that very icon of the home and its management, likewise endorsed such sentiments in her own exposition of the duties of the mistress of the house, pointing out how 'delightful' was this feminine recreation of reading aloud.[65] As Sheridan's daughters would presumably have confirmed, the reality which corresponded to such idyllic representations was not, however, always so congenial. Florence Nightingale, for one, viewed the elocutionary displays which could occupy whole evenings as a source of tedium rather than entertainment, deeming them 'the most miserable exercise of the human intellect'.[66] Harriet Martineau presented a similarly discouraged impression in her novel *Deerbrook* where a typical evening in the Greys' household is accompanied by the reading out of forty pages of the latest novel from the 'Society'. Even if not without their critics, such occupations did nevertheless form another pastime at which women were expected to excel, a skill by which they could enhance still further the pleasures of the domestic environment. Queen Victoria read *Jane Eyre*, among a range of other nineteenth-century novels, to Prince Albert, while being read to also formed one of her greatest pleasures. Virginia Woolf, born in 1882, later recalled hearing most of the Victorian novelists this way, read aloud by her sister Vanessa. As Woolf's biographer Hermione Lee affirms, reading was 'a communal rather than a private activity',[67] a practice which continued into the early twentieth century though, as we have seen, it was particularly predominant in the nineteenth, an era in which reading well, and with the 'correct' accent, became another aspect of that vocal propriety depicted as essential for women.[68] Encoded in educational precepts as well as manuals of conduct as a sign in itself of 'educated' and unquestionably 'ladylike' status, 'the speaking of her native language with purity and elegance of pronunciation' and with 'an agreeable tone of voice', as Vandenhoff noted on the opening page of his *Lady's Reader*, was indubitably deemed to constitute 'the distinguishing marks of a good education'.

The home was naturally perhaps the most central aspect of feminine ideology and proper womanhood in the nineteenth century, iterated alike in images of the 'angel of the house' which so influenced idealized Victorian conceptions of woman's rightful role, as well as in the many conduct manuals which came to be devoted to these shared issues of gender, language, and education. 'Let what will be said of the pleasures of society, there is after all "no place like home"', as *Woman's Worth* announced to its readers, stressing that here, and here alone, might woman be seen in her 'true and proper station'.[69] Such comments were commonplace. 'Home has justly been called "her empire," and it is certain that to her it is a hallowed circle, in which she may diffuse the greatest earthly happiness, or inflict the most positive misery', *The Young Lady's Book* of 1829 stated in a similar strain.[70] In popular thinking therefore, there was a firm belief that education should also rightly tend to this end, a precept of course already evident in that emphasis placed on elocution (and its own role within the educational syllabus for girls) in its capacities for enhancing the joys of domestic life.

Female education could in consequence be subject to some notable deficiencies. As many writers noted, too often it seemed to provide a grounding in manner rather than matter, in show rather than substance. Rosamund Vincy in George Eliot's *Middlemarch* is educated on how to get into (and out of) a carriage; Margaret Sherwin in Wilkie Collins's *Basil* receives 'a drawing-room-deportment day once every week—the girls taught how to enter a room and leave a room with dignity and ease'. Such promised acquirements are lauded on many a prospectus for 'genteel' educational establishments; 'to make the daughters of England what is called accomplished, seems to be the principal object aimed at', as *Woman's Worth* asserted of that 'ornamental' education all too often offered to girls.[71] Dancing, singing, an acquaintance with foreign languages, the essentials of deportment, all formed staples of the nineteenth-century female syllabus, whether in terms of boarding-school education, genteel seminaries, or the governess employed at home. 'To render them as superficially attractive, and showily accomplished, as they could possibly be made without present trouble or discomfort to themselves' was generally the aim, as Anne Brontë noted in *Agnes Grey* in her (fictionalized) account of her own experiences as a governess. Whilst for the boys in her charge she was to 'get the greatest possible quantity of Latin grammar and Valpy's Delectus into their heads, in order to fit them for school', for the girls she was instead to 'instruct, refine, and polish',[72] instilling the requisite sense of external decorum and exemplary conduct. And, as expected, this particular orientation of preoccupations again tends to have its own repercussions in the context of language.

Knowledge of phonemes and accompanying proprieties of enunciation is, as a result, frequently commended as a particularly desirable acquisition for the young female. James Buchanan in *The British Grammar*, for example, early recommends that 'in every Boarding-School where there are ladies of rank' there should also be the attendance of 'Proper Masters', this specification being made, however, primarily so that such pupils may be taught 'to read with an accurate pronunciation' as well as 'to write their own language grammatically'.[73] The writer on elocution William Graham endorsed a similar point of view in 1837. 'The art of reading and speaking with propriety' was, he stated, to be regarded as a prime 'department of ornamental education' facilitating 'a certain established standard of elegance'.[74] Or as *Woman's Worth* exhorted its own readers: 'if such pains are worth taking in learning how to sing, it would surely be worth learning how to speak; the latter is far more useful than the former, and, at the same time, far more pleasing'.[75] This, *The Young Lady's Book* of 1876 affirmed, was 'a topic of no small importance in the education of girls',[76] enhancing their attractiveness and forming an external signifier of refinement of no small value. 'Correct pronunciation' was indeed to be regarded as 'the first and highest of human accomplishments', *Behaviour: A Manual of Manners and Morals*, another conduct book aimed at women, duly emphasized.[77] As Edwin Drew added in *The Elocutionist Annual for 1889*, it was this, in particular, which 'gave the finishing touch to a good education', rendering 'a woman far better fitted to shine in society'.[78]

In practical terms, works such as the *Ladies' Elocutionist* by the phonetician Alexander Melville Bell, together with his *Elocutionary Manual*, were hence frequently commended for the specific study of young ladies. Deficiencies in the use of [h] or [ŋ] (and the potentially fallible pronunciation of words such as *happy*, *running*, as well as the vexed question of how best to pronounce the *a* in *fast* and *bath*) are, as we shall see, depicted in no uncertain terms as detracting from that 'purity' and 'delicacy' which should be mirrored in truly feminine speech. Vandenhoff's *The Lady's Reader*, for example, went into considerable detail on the importance of 'accomplishment' in this respect. As expected, the omission of [h] is portrayed as 'a gross vulgarism in speech' as well as 'a mark of inferior education' which inevitably arouses 'great prejudice' towards the speaker as well as to what is spoken. Such negative associations, however, will bring still greater repercussions for the 'lady'. For her, Vandenhoff declares, the dropping of [h] is no mere error or infelicity but 'a fatal blot in ordinary conversation', and a trait which 'no care, no labour, can be too great to eradicate'.[79]

Other works on feminine conduct endorse the need for similarly heightened exertion on the part of their readers, drawing on notions of social shame or blunted sensibility in the context of those who offend in such ways. As *Private Education; Or a Practical Plan for the Studies of Young Ladies* notes: 'The manner of expressing yourself should be particularly attended to as well as your pronunciation. How would it sound at your own table if you should say "Will you take a little *air?*" for hare. "Do you ride on *orseback* for horseback?".'[80] The social sub-text of such advice is entirely unambiguous, self-help in this particular context evidently including the rigid observance of [h] together with the equally rigid avoidance of such solecisms in the social spheres in which the 'young ladies' of the title might aspire to take their place.

The prevalence of this particular set of language attitudes was, like those which relate in more general terms to the proprieties of [h] or [r], similarly embedded and endorsed in contemporary literary contexts. Here too authors (as we shall further see in Chapter 6) revealed themselves to be notably responsive to the sociocultural symbolism which language could comport—as well as to the gendered assumptions which may surround its 'proper' use. It is, for example, precisely this focus on female education (and the doctrine of the superficial within it) which Dickens satirizes with such skill in *Little Dorrit*. Mrs General, governess to Amy and Fanny Dorrit, is hence made to adopt as her guiding principle 'the formation of a surface' upon those entrusted to her care, a process rendered peculiarly visual by dint of Dickens's metaphorical skills ('In that formation process of hers, she dipped the smallest of brushes into the largest of pots, and varnished the surface of every object that came under consideration').[81] Language too was naturally included within these operations as Mrs General, 'the Fair Varnisher', likewise endeavoured to give a similar sheen to the linguistic accomplishments of the young ladies in her charge.

Possessing herself the 'low soft voice' which was, as we have seen, so revered in works on feminine conduct, Mrs General is an able tutor in the linguistic niceties which can enhance appearance. Fanny Dorrit's idioms are, for example, rephrased in line with greater feminine propriety so that 'tumbled over' (' "they would not have been recalled to our remembrance ... if Uncle hadn't accidentally tumbled over the subject" ') becomes instead 'inadvertently lighted upon'. ' "My dear, what a curious phrase. . . Would not inadvertently lighted upon, or accidentally referred to, be better?" ', as Mrs General remarks as part of her assiduous monitoring of standards in this respect.[82] However, it is in Mrs General's strictures to Amy on the terms by which her paternal parent is to be addressed that the inclusion of norms of language within these attitudes to 'proper' and feminine appearance is best exemplified. Incorporating not only advice on the lexical preferences which are more becoming to true decorum but also commending certain phonemes above others on account of the appearance thereby given to the lips, Mrs General is most precise on this subject:

'Papa is a preferable mode of address,' observed Mrs. General. 'Father is rather vulgar, my dear. The word Papa, besides, gives a very pretty form to the lips. Papa, potatoes, poultry, prunes, and prism, are all very good words for the lips: especially prunes and prism. You will find it serviceable, in the formation of a demeanour, if you sometimes say to yourself in company—on entering a room, for instance— Papa, potatoes, poultry, prunes and prism, prunes and prism.'[83]

The use of *papa* is hence extolled not because it is a better expression of filial regard but instead by virtue of its inaugural phoneme, a bilabial plosive which gives a becoming pout in its articulation, a position deemed entirely suitable for the appearance of a young lady as she enters a room.

The single-minded focus on manners at the expense of morals which is so evident in Mrs General's educational maxims of course clearly betrays the spirit of exaggeration. Fiction should not, however, automatically be dismissed on these grounds. As the historian Dorothy Marshall has commented, it can often serve in some ways as 'a better guide to the norm than fact'. As she argues, while history and literature both offer information of considerable value, 'whereas the historian is faced by the endless variety of the individual', it is novelists who instead 'reflect the contemporary image', at times with remarkable acuity.[84] As we have already seen in Chapter 4, eighteenth- and nineteenth-century authors could indeed be profoundly aware of the sense of a norm and its propagated values in a wide variety of linguistic and sociocultural ways. Intersections of gender, language, and their respective decorums in turn come to provide a further aspect of that 'contemporary image' which was skilfully generated (and exploited) by many writers. The skewed emphasis evident in Dickens's depiction of female education in *Little Dorrit* does therefore have a counterpart in the educational realities of the time, embodying in concrete form the familiar equations which were so often made between accomplishments and education, as well as the role which language commonly assumed within both.

Even in real terms, the arts of speech regularly formed salient aspects of the education prescribed for women. Such principles were, for instance, firmly endorsed by Mrs Montagu, the 'authoress and leader of society' as she was described in the first edition of the *Dictionary of National Biography*. Her sister Sarah's choice of a boarding school education for her daughters was

commended without reservation by their aunt. As Mrs Montagu acknowledged, while 'what girls learn at these schools is trifling', they also 'unlearn
what would be of great disservice—a provincial dialect, which is extreamly
ungenteel'.[85] Mrs Montagu's strictures on what was, in effect, a linguistic
education for girls encompass grammar, lexis, as well as pronunciation—all
elements which, as so many manuals stressed, could combine to reinforce—
or reduce—the requisite image of gentility. This was, as we shall see further
in Chapter 7, to be a common theme in educational debate as well as educational practice. It was, for instance, by such means that Charlotte Brontë,
entering boarding school with a 'strong Irish accent', emerged with 'a silver
badge for correctness of speech and manners'—and an entire absence of the
idioms and intonation which she had originally possessed.[86] Even at the end
of the nineteenth century, the same preoccupations with 'talking like a lady'
could still be detected, assimilated even within the educational reforms of
Frances Mary Buss, the headmistress (and founder) of the Frances Mary
Buss School (later The North London Collegiate School) and founder also,
in 1870, of The Camden School. The persistence of such ideas in this context is, however, in many ways particularly striking, serving as it does to
emphasize the very real prevalence of agendas of 'talking proper' for women
even in what were often considered far more enlightened educational
regimes. Buss's methods were, for example, often regarded as exemplifying
the improvements in educational opportunities which were gradually
becoming available for girls in the latter part of the century. Nevertheless,
even she was not to neglect the voice, or its import in feminine education. As
Sarah Burstall, one of Buss's pupils at The Camden School in the 1870s confirms, the syllabus in 1874 continued to include a marked emphasis on
'excellent English . . . with speech-training and the study of poetry', just as it
was still 'considered correct to have dancing lessons'.[87] Even in the new educational order, the old legacy of accomplishments and elocution for girls
could clearly linger on—though its role was evidently tempered to an extent
by the importance also gradually being given to science, algebra, and geom-
etry as newly appropriate aspects of female knowledge.

Nevertheless, as this indicates, female education throughout the century
could explicitly reinforce both that ideology of a standard already discussed
and, in its marked gender divides of subject and appropriate instruction,
inculcate ideals of 'talking proper' which are often presented as fundamental
within prevailing ideologies of feminine propriety. Language, however, could
also assume equal, if not greater, prominence in the other social roles which
women were to assume within the home, first, that of wife, and second, that
of mother. In both of these, according to contemporary comment, ladylike
felicities of 'proper' language were by no means to be unimportant. The role
of wife was, for example, frequently presented in the biblical guise of
the helpmeet. 'I believe—as entirely as any other truth which has been from

the beginning—that woman was created as a help-meet to man', maintained Charlotte Yonge in *Womankind*.[88] 'That she might be a help meet for man, was the intention of the Almighty in forming woman', *Woman's Worth* similarly affirmed: 'she is made a being who can think, and feel, and reflect,—a being who can assist in his affairs—who can smooth the rugged brow of care, can cheer through the toil and strengthen in the task'.[89] Her education before marriage was therefore, at least ideally, also to be directed to these particular ends, a conception which is perhaps expressed with greatest clarity by *Woman: As She Is, And As She Should Be*, a text published in two volumes in 1835. As the anonymous author rhetorically demands, 'What *is* the destination of women?' It was a question which received a ready, and extensive answer. 'They compose one half of the species, and are destined to constitute the happiness of the other half; they are to be wives and mothers;— in a word, they were created for the *domestic* comfort and felicity of man.' As, echoing Rousseau, the author added, 'Their education, then, must be *relative to man!*'[90] A wide-ranging canon of female behaviour (and indeed education) is duly presented and endorsed over the remainder of the text. Home, for instance, is given not only as woman's rightful place but also as the sphere of her greatest influence, for good or ill, not least since it is upon this influence, and upon a woman's rightful discharge of such responsibility, that the behaviour of man himself depends. 'As a man carries with him through the world those same habits and feelings he has gathered in his Home—and as these habits and feelings are principally derived from the influence of woman', we are informed, 'woman in performing her Home-duties takes a vast share in the concerns of the community'.[91]

This equation was effortlessly extended into domains of language. The 'good' wife was, for example, in turn depicted as a linguistic as well as moral exemplar. In her ideal manifestations, she was to inculcate the 'proper' and non-regionalized standards of speech in her children (a subject to which we shall return), as well as to aid her husband's social progress by her own indubitably 'proper' use of language. It is an emphasis which was by no means restricted to the openly exhortatory *Woman: As She Is, And As She Should Be*. Mrs Valentine, preceptress of *The Young Woman's Book* of 1878, provides, for instance, both general and specific illustration of the apparent truth of maxims of this kind within the joint concerns of feminine and linguistic ideology. Self-improvement in terms of language is, for example, presented as a significant aspect of the wifely role. This too was part of that love, honour, and obedience which should characterize female behaviour in the married state. In an era of much social mobility 'when a man may rise from the station of a working mechanic to that of a *millionaire*', as Mrs Valentine observed, women ought be just as aware of their responsibilities to their husbands in terms of language as they were in all other respects.[92] Denied the means of achieving such mobility independently (as Mary Wollstonecraft declared,

'The only way women can rise in the world [is] by marriage'), a woman was instead commonly required to aid and foster the social ascent of her husband. Her own language, and the status implications it could convey, was in turn to be regarded as by no means immaterial to his success.

Here too fiction provides striking correlates, once more reinforcing the 'contemporary image' of wifely decorum—or its converse. George Gissing in his novel *New Grub Street*, for instance, graphically chose to depict the shame of a man whose wife's linguistic failings continually manifest the social gulf between them. Enforcing a form of linguistic apartheid, Mrs Yule is rarely allowed to talk to her child for fear of any 'contamination' which might result:

From the first it was Yule's dread lest Marian should be infected with her mother's faults of speech and behaviour. He would scarcely permit his wife to talk to the child. At the earliest possible moment Marian was sent to a day-school . . . any sacrifice of money to insure her growing up with the tongue and manners of a lady. It can scarcely have been a light trial to the mother to know that contact with her was regarded as her child's greatest danger; but in her humility and her love for Marian she offered no resistance. And so it came to pass that one day the little girl, hearing her mother make some flagrant grammatical error, turned to the other parent and asked gravely: 'Why doesn't mother speak as properly as we do?' Well, that is one of the results of such marriages.[93]

Against the antitype so tragically presented by Mrs Yule, the central maxim provided by Mrs Valentine is instead that a wife's speech should enhance her husband's status. As she declaims: 'It is required of all wives to cultivate themselves as much as may be, in order to be fitted for any position'. By self-education in the requisite proprieties of speech, however, as Mrs Valentine did not fail to make plain, women were by no means neglecting their own interests: 'A young woman who teaches herself to speak and write properly has taken a step upwards in the world, and is sure to benefit by it'.[94] Emphasizing the heightened anguish which could be caused by mispronunciation in the female sex ('What can be more distressing than to hear bad English spoken and words mispronounced by people, who by a very little trouble might speak like ladies?'), Mrs Valentine's lessons in this context were endorsed still further by the use of an all too pertinent example as she proceeded to narrate the tale of a woman who shamed her husband, and dishonoured his status, by the continued use of articulatory (and social) solecisms such as these:

We remember hearing of a lady who by her husband's high character and industry had been placed in a good position, putting the poor man to evident shame by her foolish and ignorant mistakes—such as 'I was a-sayin' to Villiam today that I 'ate 'ock, it gives me an nedache'.[95]

Provided with this negative exemplar of the failed helpmeet, it is all too clear that 'proper' wifely duty includes—and indeed demands—knowledge of those linguistic proprieties which befit the status of one's husband, lest, like poor 'Villiam', he is to be demeaned by such unladylike infelicities in his spouse. The spectre of such marital embarrassment, complete here with its range of 'ignorant' markers (amongst which [h]-loss is all too conspicuous in *'ate*, *'ock*, and *nedache*), is held up in warning. The utility of a good pronouncing dictionary is subsequently recommended for all those who are, as a result, rendered 'anxious for self-culture'.[96]

Other texts mirror the same preoccupations and the same ideological bias in the beliefs and ideals which they endorse. *The Young Housekeeper*, for example, issues detailed directions to the woman who is newly married, similarly including a section on the 'proprieties of speech' which are to be regarded as compatible with this new social role. A selection of female linguistic stereotypes is duly enumerated. 'The young housekeeper' of the title is to have speech 'neither too loud nor too low' while a 'loquacious propensity' is also to be avoided.[97] The importance of being 'correct in accent' is emphasized in similar terms so that readers of this manual of specifically female self-help are advised to 'learn when to use and when to omit the aspirate *h*. This is an indispensable mark of a good education'. The implications of such advice were clearly by no means immaterial in the wide-ranging images of domestic harmony which the text goes on to provide.

The consequences attendant upon lack of wifely application in this respect are, however, nowhere brought out more clearly than in the Reverend Geoffry Hill's own book on *The Aspirate*. Discussing the ways in which [h]-dropping was habitually attended with marked social stigma in the nineteenth century, Hill provides one of the most complete accounts of its role in assigning the social values of impropriety, inferior status, and inadequate refinement. 'The modern English', as he duly declares, 'have given a fictitious importance to the letter by making the correct use of it a mark by which refined and educated people may be differentiated from those that are not'.[98] While he ably indicates the arbitrariness which underlies the application of value judgements of this kind, he nevertheless also gives a detailed picture of the ways in which its 'correct' deployment was often seen as concisely establishing affinities of breeding and cultivation. Its importance inside, as well as outside, the marital condition is therefore given particular prominence in Hill's text. Indeed, as Hill states with some rigour, in marriage spouses must be compatible in terms of [h]-usage just as much as in their other tastes and habits. 'When a question about h's arises between husband and wife', he points out, 'forgiveness on either side is most difficult'. This is presented as a source of manifest discord between prospective partners. As Hill asserts, its effects should not be underestimated and the 'Proper Wife', like the 'Proper Lady', was necessarily to be responsive to issues of correctness on this matter. Hill, 'without fear of contradiction', hence offers a general rule on this head. 'So important indeed is the question of the use of h's in

England', he states, 'that no marriage should take place between persons whose ideas on this subject do not agree'.[99]

Like Mrs Valentine, Hill provides an appropriate example with which to illustrate the dire effects of the failure to heed such advice. His references are, however, rather more specific, drawing on the 'Clitheroe Abduction case':

Our readers may remember that one of the grievances felt by the wife against the husband in the Clitheroe Abduction case was that he accused her of dropping her h's. 'On sitting down to dinner,' said the lady, according to the *Lancashire Evening Post*, 'an incident occurred which affected me greatly, coming as it did so immediately after the marriage. I made some observation to Mr. Jackson, when he suddenly said. "Where are your h's?" I felt very much incensed, but I said nothing, though I thought it a very strange beginning.'[100]

Leading as it did to such unfortunate consequences, Hill's maxim on the importance of perfect congruity in patterns of [h]-usage and its role in securing conjugal bliss scarcely needed to be made clearer.

Reinforcing the advice given by the anonymous H. W. H. in *How to Choose a Wife* ('Perpetual nausea and disgust will be your doom if you marry a vulgar and uncultivated woman'),[101] the emphasis placed on perfect linguistic propriety as yet another aspect of wifely duty merely reiterates those heightened pressures on conformity to the highest models of behaviour which were constantly imposed on women within these iterations of feminine ideology and the prescriptive dicta which they incorporated. Maynard's *Matrimony: Or, What Married Life Is, and How to Make the Best of It*, a text which went through two editions within its first year of publication, offers advice markedly similar in kind, devoting the whole of its third chapter to the principle that 'Marriages should be Equal in Elocution'. The central precept endorsed is that 'equality gives pleasure, inequality pain', but again the greatest attention is directed to the shame, embarrassment, and anguish of the husband who must endure the mangled articulations and infelicitous syntax of his wife:

Suppose the husband to be the better educated and the more refined. In this case, he is almost sure to find his wife's domestic arrangements far below his standard of taste; hence his eye is offended. Her language too is characterised by grammatical blunders in arrangement, pronunciation, and the improper use of words; hence his ear is offended. Whilst painfully feeling his situation in this respect, he kindly and earnestly endeavours to raise up his wife to his own standard. In some rare cases, he succeeds in a good measure; but we believe in the majority of cases, it is a complete failure.[102]

The depiction of this unfortunate circumstance continues on a note of pathos surpassing even that invoked by the Hon. Henry H. in lamenting his own use and abuse.[103] 'In case of failure', as the (evidently male) author continues, 'the only alternative is, that he must be constantly finding fault, or in silent and gloomy despair, move on every week, day, and hour, all his life severely tried and hampered with the natural and necessary results of an unequal education'.[104] Wives, mend your speech, is the relevant maxim which was again endorsed though, in real life, the moral could of course operate the other way round. The socialist reformer Beatrice Potter, for instance, took it upon herself to offer detailed advice on this subject to her future husband, the Cockney (and Fabian reformer) Sidney Webb. His use of [h] was notably 'shaky', she recorded in her diary after their first dinner engagement. The instructions she subsequently gave were to the point: 'Take care of your voice and pronunciation: it is the chief instrument of influence', Sidney was advised in August 1890 and she returned to the subject one month later, betraying susceptibilities on the 'correct' pronunciation of unaccented syllables of which Sheridan himself would have been proud: 'Look after the breadth of the English vowel! Do not refuse to recognise the individual existence of or, ir, ow, a and confound them all in a common er'.[105]

Similar pressures in terms of linguistic responsibility were frequently to be imposed on the nineteenth-century woman in her role as a mother, not least since it was from her own use of language that the child—including, as it appears, particularly the male child—would learn its first words. Her role as guardian of 'proper' language could, in such instances, assume even greater value, influencing the diffusion of the 'best' (or 'worst') language in itself. Writers commonly stressed the total receptivity of the child to the standards set by the mother, whether in word or deed. 'The first days of humanity are under woman's guidance', *Woman's Worth* affirmed: 'impressions are then formed never to be obliterated—the young mind is then as pliable as wax, and will receive any form or stamp. The bent of future character is formed in childhood—early habits, early impressions, are never entirely obliterated'.[106] Given such strictures, the responsibilities of the mother in terms of both precept and example were rarely represented as negligible: 'What influence may not a mother exert? She is a pattern which her children are constantly striving to imitate; her actions are made the models of theirs.'[107]

Her accents too were to be placed within these same paradigms and if she had not already rendered them 'pure' and 'correct' in her role as proper 'helpmeet' for her husband, it was more than ever necessary for the mother to master such needful proprieties of speech for the benefit of her offspring. *The Mother's Home Book* offers plentiful advice on this head, urging the mother to improve her speech and to act, in effect, as articulatory instructress (and an active agent of standardization) for her children:

It is decidedly the duty of the mother to pronounce every word she utters distinctly, and in a proper tone, carefully avoiding, and strictly forbidding, the mis-pronunciation of any word. To accomplish this end more surely, the mother ought to speak in such a manner as will give the child the opportunity of observing the motion of her mouth, as well as hearing the sound of her voice.[108]

Other comments are similarly clear and to the point, endorsing yet again the ways in which woman's role was, as the author of *Woman: What She Is and What She Should Be* had professed, simply 'relative to man'. As Barbara Farquhar, author of another book on female education, declared in this context, 'woman is ever moulding the future man' and it was for this reason that the 'tones of her voice' were to be important; they will, she added, 'have given a stamp, before infancy is past, to his character, which after years may deepen, but seldom, if ever, obliterate'.[109] Sub-texts of guilt, responsibility, and the need for perfect conformity to the canons of 'good' speech are once more all too transparent. Many other texts were eloquent in a similar strain. 'The mother is an educator of God's own appointment',[110] proclaimed *The Popular Educator*, stressing that, in consequence, the purity, refinement, and propriety urged upon women from their own earliest years would necessarily find true meaning in the creation of the appropriate linguistic environment for the education of children in the nuances of 'standard' speech. Even the phonetician Walter Ripman, in spite of his claims as a scientist of language, saw this as a means by which, in the early twentieth century, the standard variety of speech would, in all its purity, be properly imparted to the young. The often stated superior sensibilities of women to the social values of speech would, he argued, take on unquestioned utility in this respect. Girls are 'particularly appreciative of the social advantages of good speech, and quick to copy the models supplied by their mistresses', a facility which was, he stated, of undoubted value since 'in their turn, especially as mothers . . . they carry on the work of imparting good speech'.[111] Just as in Mrs Mackarness's *The Young Lady's Book* (1876), women were evidently still to be regarded as the guardians of language in matters of phonological as well as lexical nicety. The same preconceptions (and attendant stereotypes) endure in other nineteenth-century texts. 'The exquisitely feminine duties of the nursery', as Rosa Nouchette Carey affirmed in one of her novels, were in such senses often deemed to include the inculcation of non-localized norms of speech, the advantages of which were clearly insuperable: 'What an advantage to parents to have their little ones brought into the earliest contact with refined speech and cultivated manners—their infant ears not inoculated with barbarous English'.[112]

The most detailed exposition of this ideal, however, comes not in fiction but in *The Young Mother*, a text produced by the Religious Tract Society in 1857. It sets forth with precision the articulatory niceties which the 'good' mother must impart, as well as laying due emphasis on that propriety which will thereby of course also be transmitted:

A sensible mother will uniformly make it a principle never to teach anything that will have to be unlearned. Hence . . . she will take care to pronounce every word distinctly and in a proper tone; and, especially when the child is learning to articulate, she will so speak as to give him an opportunity of observing the motion of her mouth as well as hearing the sound of her voice. Those who have not had experience in the early teaching of children, can scarcely imagine how much this will obviate difficulties, and assist in forming the habit of reading with correctness and propriety.[113]

The elocutionary precepts absorbed by the woman herself in her youth are in such ways to be rendered into practical skills as, with due care, she is to impart the nuances of 'talking proper' and, in effect, to 'standardize' the accent of the child from the moment of his (or indeed her) first words. 'The first lesson which a child should be taught, is how to articulate correctly', as *The Mother's Home Book* added,[114] stressing the ways in which the mother was to watch not only her own words (in line with the manifold tenets of propriety, social as well as linguistic) but also those of her child. Mispronunciations suffered to go uncorrected at this stage would later prove ineradicable. It was the mother's clear duty to correct, to refine, and to perfect. Moreover, any breach of such duty would later be all too apparent, just as the negligence of mothers in the past was still evinced in the problems which so many continued to face over the articulation of [h] or [ŋ]. This too was to be the mother's fault: 'The habit of incorrect and careless speaking may, in innumerable instances, be traced to the errors of childhood being unchecked, or, in truth, not being pointed out as errors at all. The non-aspiration of the letter *h*, or its aspiration in the wrong place, is one of the most prominent of these defects.'[115] Giving a list of other articulatory oversights on the part of mothers of the past, the author adds for the benefit of those of the present: 'all faults of this kind ought to be at once discouraged, and some penalty attached to a repetition of them'. Whether this penalty is to be imposed on the mother or on the child is not, however, made entirely clear.

If possible, *The Popular Educator* went still further in these respects, recommending attendance in the nursery of a cultivated English home for each and every aspirant speaker of 'proper' English. The supervision of a mother versed in the true proprieties of speech is thus envisaged as the one sure means to escape the taints and errors which otherwise might all too easily affect the modes of speech deployed:

Of all teachers of English grammar the best is a well-educated English mother. Hence it is evident that a nursery in a cultivated English home, is the best school of English grammar. As a matter of fact, it is in such schools that, among the upper classes of the country, the young learn to speak correct English from their earliest days. Were all English children trained in such schools, the language would be everywhere well, and grammatically spoken. Consequently, could we place our students in cultivated nurseries, they would soon speak and write their mother tongue with correctness and propriety.[116]

This being only a manual of self-help, such a solution is unfortunately not possible for the readers of *The Popular Educator* though it does, however, promise the next best thing in its endeavours to 'bring forth and set before them in a living and organic form the spoken language of such nurseries'.

Women's linguistic responsibilities were as a result not slight. Popular stereotypes of them as wives, as mothers, as ladies, and simply as females in their own right indeed presented behavioural norms and expectations which exacted conformity to the highest models in terms of speech, and especially in terms of accent. Ideologies of 'talking proper' and corresponding ones of 'proper' femininity tended, as this illustrates, to dovetail with remarkable facility, the former regularly being used to enhance prescriptions (and pro-scriptions) within the latter. A marker of the truly feminine, such precepts were not disregarded lightly, and though the New Woman of the latter part of the nineteenth century might attempt to escape such shackles, common (and conventional) attitudes to language and behaviour popularly depicted her conduct as deviating from the norms of true womanhood, and from that delicacy of language by which these should rightly be characterized. The children's novelist, Edith Nesbit, with her cropped hair, chain-smoking, and wearing of bloomers, for instance, openly scandalized the London suburb where she lived in the 1880s.[117] The 'New Woman', openly espousing diver-gent ideological strategies, evidently threatened a range of established behavi-oural norms and ideals (including those of language). The independence from formal notions of propriety which this alternative social construct of womanhood endorsed was, of course, necessarily constructed as 'other' and her manifestations were accordingly stigmatized in a variety of ways. George Gissing's short story 'Comrades in Arms' can, for example, be taken as rep-resentative in this context with its effective depiction of the 'anti-feminine' Miss Childerstone, a journalist, who is gradually 'growing less feminine' in both language and manners: 'She turned to the waiter, "Roast mutton—potatoes—bread. And—soda-water" . . . "Thanks, old man; I am better acquainted with my needs than you are"'.[118]

More typical (and stereotypical) representations of the feminine tradition in the guise of 'propriety' or 'respectability' nevertheless elsewhere tended to continue unabated. The leader in the magazine *The Lady* in February 1893, for example, still exudes congratulation on the sheer abundance of those rules which, for women, demanded conformity and which could in turn be used as markers of their 'proper' and undeviating identity.

It is a good thing for everyone that there are rules by which Society, now that it has become so vast and complicated a machine, is held together and enabled to work smoothly and easily . . . it changes very fast and you must keep up with it or you will stand out and no gentlewoman wants to attract observation or comment or she is not a gentlewoman.[119]

Given the prevalence and longevity of language attitudes in these particular cultural conceptions, it is as a result perhaps hardly surprising that works which aimed to set forth these various canons of propriety (linguistic and otherwise) for the benefit of a female audience seem to have achieved notable popularity.

Etiquette for the Ladies, in its fourth edition in 1837, had, for instance, reached a total of a further twenty-nine editions by 1846. New and popular periodicals such as *The Englishwoman's Magazine* or *The Lady's Companion and Monthly Magazine* fulfilled the same function, supplying detailed advice on the social niceties depicted as necessary for women in the array of social roles which they might legitimately be expected to occupy. Nor, given this abundance of information on such 'proper' behaviour, is it entirely unexpected that a number of writers attest, with equal consistency, the existence of heightened female sensitivities in this respect in terms of the actualities of their speech.

If some women openly rebelled against the constricting images provided by such texts—as the philanthropist and social reformer Octavia Hill expostulated—'I don't know what there is in the word "lady" which will connect itself with all kinds of things I despise and hate'[120]—others evidently subscribed to the iterated norms of conduct manuals and popular literature with fewer scruples. Prescription apparently demanded a response, and not least in the ways in which, as we have seen, it deliberately tended to foster linguistic insecurities and status anxieties. As a result, while *Etiquette for Ladies and Gentlemen* depicts women as innately 'more susceptible of external polish than Man is', especially in terms of language ('She is imitative in a great degree, and speedily catches the tone and manner of the people with whom she associates'),[121] sociocultural conditioning—and the wide-ranging implications of contemporary female ideologies—would clearly have played the more significant part in the acquisition of those proprieties deemed emblematic of the 'proper' woman of the nineteenth century. It was nevertheless this image of the intrinsic and superior responsiveness of women to such notions of correctness which was nevertheless readily (and frequently) assimilated into the dicta of conduct manuals and works on language alike. 'Women acknowledge more readily than men that universal passport to consideration—perfect manners', *The Manners of the Aristocracy* proclaimed, further endorsing this opinion by the information that advice proffered for their improvement is in turn readily implemented and assimilated: 'women are quicker in profiting by the hints contained in such volumes, and are less likely to be led astray by any errors they may contain'.[122] *The Family Herald* in 1844 offered similar certainties to its readers: 'Young ladies learn *manners*, as they are denominated, rapidly, because they have a genius for the study'.

It was of course social, cultural, as well as linguistic pressures rather than this laudatory 'genius' which in reality combined to reinforce these patterns of social sensibility towards language which are so often singled out as characteristic of women in such accounts. Language attitudes, as we have seen, can be highly effective in influencing patterns of behaviour, as well as of belief, in terms of these widely propagated images of 'proper' language. In a parallel way, notions of correctness can and will often encourage convergence in the more formal registers of the language when people (both men and women) are concentrating particularly on what they are saying. If nineteenth-century texts thus frequently stress the superior responsiveness of women per se to prominent images of linguistic correctness, the same patterns have—more empirically—repeatedly been revealed in twentieth-century data on actual linguistic behaviour. The research of Peter Trudgill, William Labov, and Suzanne Romaine has, for example, consistently recorded greater levels of receptivity for women (of all social groups) to those variants recognized as most statusful within the wider speech community,[123] a fact which once again serves to endorse the correlations which can be perceptible between the past and present of language. These patterns moreover seem to emerge both in the evidence of language attitudes by means of subjective reaction tests, and in the more statistical surveys carried out on individual linguistic variables in the realities of speech behaviour. In modern sociolinguistic studies, for instance, women regularly seem to utilize higher frequencies of those forms widely proclaimed as prestigious—such indeed as [h] or [ŋ]—alongside lower proportions of their less prestigious alternatives (such as [Ø] and [ɪn] respectively) than might perhaps otherwise be expected.[124]

Sociocultural patterns of norm and deviation do not, in linguistic terms, apparently go unnoticed. In the nineteenth century therefore, it would not be entirely unexpected for those value judgements which, as we have seen, liberally surrounded a range of divergent enunciations to exert some kind of corresponding pressure on the actual linguistic behaviour of women, not least since, both overtly and covertly, they were long conditioned by prevailing feminine ideologies to be alert to the finest shades of delicacy and refinement. While many women in the later nineteenth century rebelled against the legacy of these ideas, the conventional correlation of 'talking proper' and 'proper ladyhood' evidently did not disappear entirely. Comments made by a number of observers who are more reputable in terms of the emergent (and objective) science of phonetics seem, for instance, to bear this out. Henry Sweet, Reader in Phonetics at the University of Oxford, for example, noted that the socially orientated prescription which articulations of [h] commonly attracted seemed to be far more effective in terms of the avoidance of [h]-loss in female rather than male speech. As he remarked, 'the Cockney dialect seems very ugly to an educated Englishman or woman' so that, as a result, 'he—and still more she—lives in a perpetual terror of being taken for a Cockney'. Negative sensitization led, again particularly for women, to 'a perpetual struggle to preserve that *h* which has now been lost in most of the local dialects of England, both North and South'.[125] Contemporary constructions of ideal femininity, as we have seen, did indeed exhort the avoidance of 'vulgarity', 'provinciality', or other linguistic infelicities wherever possible, a fact which makes a heightened female awareness of the shibboleths of [h]-usage, such as Sweet attests, more rather than less likely. In terms of actual speech behaviour, however, the use of [h] was naturally not the sole phonemic nicety which receives comment in terms of gendered patterns of usage and their framing language attitudes. Equally prominent in discussions about the 'proper' use of language, as well as its associated conventions of feminine propriety, are, for example, corresponding deliberations over the 'correct' sound to be accorded to the use of *a* in words such as *fast, bath*. Pronounced with a short [æ] in the middle of the seventeenth century (similar to that employed in modern realizations of *mat, match*), the transition to that lengthened [ɑː] which has now become a characteristic marker of a non-localized accent was, as Chapter 3 has already indicated, not accomplished without a certain amount of controversy.[126] It seems clear that [æ] and [ɑː] co-existed to an extent among 'polite' and 'vulgar' speakers with both forms, at various times, finding themselves allied to constructions of a 'standard' and non-localized norm. Even given the popularity of typical binary absolutes on this matter, writers on the language were occasionally compelled to admit the real complexity of the situation so that Benjamin Smart, for instance, in spite of his stated preference for the short and avowedly 'well-bred' [æ], also acknowledges in 1812 that the lengthened variant was in reality 'adhered to by some speakers above the vulgar'.[127] In a further burst of honesty, he concedes that [æ] could indeed by some be considered as 'affected', a position also supported by a number of other writers. Such descriptive impulses serve to clarify in some respects the nuances of linguistic reality (and its attendant variations) in this context though, as we have seen, they do not impede the barrage of comment—complete with associated social, cultural, and aesthetic specifications—which continued to surround this sound change in progress over the course of the nineteenth century. Moreover, given the fact that both pronunciations discussed in this context could at times take on negative resonances, [ɑː] potentially connoting 'vulgarity' and 'cockneyism' while [æ] could suggest 'affectation' and the 'mincing', it is not perhaps entirely unexpected that fashionable prescription should seize on another, intermediate sound as that to be adopted by those desirous of true elegance. It is, in turn, this which becomes so associated with notions of femininity and the accents of the 'Proper Lady' over the late nineteenth and early twentieth centuries.

Notions of a 'middle sound' located somewhere between [ɑː] and [æ] can in fact be traced back to the early evidence of Christopher Cooper in 1687 who identified a sound something like [æː] in relevant words. The difference in the nineteenth century, however, lies in the new connotations which this sound acquired in the joint realms of linguistic etiquette and prescriptive theory. Benjamin Smart in 1836, for example, maintains a system of values slightly different to those he had set forth in 1812. Setting the 'vulgarity' of [ɑː] against the 'affectation' of [æ], he now concludes that 'a medium between the two extremes is the practice of the best speakers'.[128] 'Avoid a too broad or too slender pronunciation of the vowel *a*, as in...*glass, pass*', likewise cautions Charles Smith in 1858, recommending the avoidance of 'the extremes of affectation and vulgarity' by means of the more 'elegant' selection of a middle sound.[129] Israel Alger in 1832, John Longmuir in 1864, and, most importantly perhaps, the phonetician Alexander Ellis in 1869 all unite in commenting on the marked affiliations of this compromise 'middle sound' with intimations of intentionally greater delicacy, status, and correctness.[130]

Alexander Ellis is, of course, a linguistic observer characterized both by his intended objectivity as well as by his attempted empiricism, features which he deliberately sets against the bias and preconception which had so often pervaded the comments of his predecessors. Though not entirely exempt from failings of his own in the notions of a standard he deploys,[131] Ellis's evidence is on the whole presented with a clarity of understanding and exposition which is often absent from other writers on the language. Aware of the factors outside language which may operate to influence its use, he stresses the importance of variables which are dependent on speaker and style, such as age, status, and formality. Gender too makes an explicit appearance in this context. As Ellis points out, 'the sounds of language are very fleeting. Each element occupies only a very minute part of a second'. In discussions of pronunciation, it is therefore necessary to take into account the fact that such 'elements' do not exist in a vacuum. 'Many', he states, 'are much hurried over, and all are altered by combination, expression, pitch, intonation, emotion, age' and, he adds, 'sex'.[132] This theoretical position is amplified in further comments where the role of gender as a significant speaker variable again makes its appearance: 'Every speaker has individualities, and it is only by an intimate acquaintance with the habits of *many* speakers that we can discover what were individualities in our first instructor. Not only has age and sex much influence, but the very feeling of the moment sways the speaker.'[133]

This recognition of the import of gender in considerations of speech and its analysis is not restricted merely to general principles but appears equally in Ellis's discussion of individual sounds and sound changes. 'We merely wish to know what *are* the sounds which educated English men and women really use when they speak their native language', he declares in setting forth his aims.[134] 'Educated English women' appear most often, however, in Ellis's comments on the pronunciation of *a* in lengthening position before voiceless fricatives in words such as *bath* and *fast*—and particularly in his accounts of female preferences for the use not only of the short [æ] but also of a 'middle sound' in what seems to be [æː]. A range of currently acceptable realizations in these positions is provided, exemplifying a descriptive procedure which is entirely in keeping with Ellis's stated intention to give 'what *is*, rather than decide what *should* be' in language.[135] It is nevertheless evident that, as today, the tendency to favour [ɑː] as the dominant prestige marker was well established by the time Ellis was writing in the later decades of the nineteenth century. In spite of this, it is also apparent that, for those sensitive to the shades of prescriptive symbolism, the old stereotypes of 'vulgarity' and 'cockneyism' which had long surrounded the use of [ɑː] in these positions had by no means fallen entirely into disuse. The intentionally 'educated' and 'refined' could instead, as Ellis confirms, favour other, more 'aesthetic' realizations. 'Ladies', long urged in terms of prevailing ideologies of femininity to make manifest their superior delicacies and sensibility in speech just as in other aspects of their conduct, likewise seem to have been influenced by such perceptions—in practice as well as theory. As Ellis notes, for example, it is 'ladies in the South and many educated gentlemen' who tend to adopt those elegant 'middle sounds' earlier praised by Smart.[136] In a similar vein he states that 'those who do not like broad sounds' (such as [ɑː]) prefer instead [æː]; this select company comprises, as Ellis adds, 'especially ladies'.[137] Such stated female preferences for the use of more 'delicate' middle sounds are alluded to on a number of other occasions. On page 593 Ellis again observes that [æː] 'is sometimes heard . . . especially from ladies, as a thinner utterance of (aa) than (aah) would be', and he verifies this apparent gender-preferential variation with reference to his own transcriptions from a performance of *King John* noting that he had 'heard Mrs. Charles Kean speak of "(kææf) skin"', with great emphasis' while 'Mr. Alfred Wigan immediately repeated it as "(kaaf) skin"', with equal distinctness'.[138]

The fact that notions of social value, and attendant value judgements, had long been explicit in writings of the prescriptive tradition on this matter is given some prominence in Ellis's subsequent explanation of this pattern. Placing the social clichés of prescription in inverted commas, Ellis records that it is the 'delicate' and 'refined' who avoid the use of [ɑː] which they consider 'too broad'. More than that, however, he links such avoidance to popular conceptions of propriety which were, as we have seen, often firmly vested in the visual authority of the written language. The 'dread' which many feel with reference to the use of [ɑː] is, he states, the product of a 'fear that if they said (aask, laaf), they would be accused of the vulgarity of inserting an *r*, and when *arsk*, *larf*, are written, they 'look so very "vulgar"'.[139] Of course <r> had commonly been used as a diacritic of length since the loss of [r] in final and post-vocalic positions in the eighteenth century, generating popular images of illiteracy and non-standardness by its deployment in forms such as *farst*, *parsty* in many novels.[140] Similar notions evidently came into play here. As Ellis infers, it is the perceived 'repulsion of such sounds which drives the educated, and especially ladies, into the thinness of (ah, æ)'.[141]

Such aesthetic sensibilities towards the use of language and pronunciation had, as we have seen, indeed long formed a constituent part of feminine ideology. Their wider consequences in this context are hence apparently reflected in other nineteenth-century comments which regularly affirm, for instance, the presence of heightened female sensitivities to the use of other stigmatized forms and their 'proper' variants—the 'best' articulation of *ing*, the use of [hw] rather than [w] in words such as *which*, or the use of the 'delicate' palatal glide in enunciations of words such as *kind* /kjaɪnd/[142] all appear in the context of discussions of the greater proprieties (and greater femininity) which the 'Proper Lady' should make manifest in her speech. Many writers, as we have seen, deliberately emphasized the detrimental effect of perceived 'inelegance' and 'vulgarity' for 'proper' ladylike identity, a factor which was represented as far from immaterial in the linguistic behaviour they commended. The Reverend D. Williams, for example, stressing in general the incontrovertible credentials of breeding and refinement which the nuances of voice present, gave heightened emphasis to their importance as social signifiers in the feminine ideal. 'The most beautiful young female, who silently forms a kind of divinity, is', he opines, 'reduced at once to common earth, when we hear a few inelegant words from her lips'.[143] In such conceptions, domestic angels were to require equally angelic voices, and manifestations of superior linguistic delicacy and refinement were prized. As Ellis surmises, such commonly expressed attitudes could well have influenced to some extent the patterns of variation he describes, the connotative values of 'middle sounds' in turn ensuring their adoption as an external signal of that delicacy revered as a marker of the appropriately 'ladylike' and 'refined'.

Ellis is moreover not alone in his observations on this matter, and the phonetician Walter Ripman in the early years of the twentieth century likewise attests similar feminine preferences for realizations other than [ɑː] in words such as *cast* and *path*. In *The Sounds of Spoken English* (1906), he thus records that '[a] and [æ] occur, particularly in the speech of ladies', and he comments further on the value judgements, and associated evaluative paradigms, which he assumes must lie behind these patterns of variation: 'It is sometimes found that precise speakers, through an excessive desire to avoid any suspicion of cockney leanings in their speech, substitute [a] for [ɑ]...it is particularly ladies of real or would-be gentility who commit this mistake'.[144] The fact that this is specified as a 'mistake' underlines, however, a shift in attendant social sensibilities. From remarks Ripman makes elsewhere, it becomes clear that pronunciations with [ɑː], as in present-day English, had assumed clear dominance in non-regional and statusful domains of speech, ousting even perceptions of that long-attested and ladylike 'delicacy' with which 'middle sounds' had traditionally been imbued. In the second edition of *The Sounds of Spoken English*, published in 1914, the 'middle sounds' do not appear.

Both Ripman and Ellis (as well as Sweet) are, of course, phoneticians, intentionally aiming therefore to give objective rather than subjective accounts of language use. Certainly the details they provide on these particular aspects of usage potentially offer something more than the mass of general prescription about those superior delicacies in speech on which conventional iterations of ladylike conduct insist. All three are, on the other hand, also ordinary speakers of the language and susceptible in this to contemporary gender stereotypes in terms of the proprieties—and superior delicacies—to be expected of women. As other texts confirm, even descriptivism can and will be compromised by prevailing language attitudes.[145] Their perceptions could conceivably therefore have been influenced by prevailing ideologies and equally prevalent stereotypes—after all, as the philologist Otto Jespersen was later to confirm, a commitment to descriptive science could exist alongside views blinkered by prejudice and preconception. Jespersen's *Language: Its Nature, Development and Origin* (1922), for example, chooses to characterize women's linguistic behaviour in terms of vocabulary which is less extensive than that of a man, a preference for simple sentence structure, and stereotypical volubility (an image which can be traced back to Old English). Regrettably no women phoneticians exist in the late nineteenth century who, in their own evidence, might perhaps have been able to document the realities of pronunciation from a distinctively female perspective—though, as the legion of women writers in other domains over the nineteenth century attests, the fact of being female by no means guaranteed immunity from prevailing behavioural norms and ideals. Indeed, if anything, the opposite could at times be said to be the case.

Nevertheless, in spite of these potential problems, the evidence of Sweet, Ripman, and Ellis can in some ways be seen to provide a valuable parallel to those insights into language and gender which variationist studies in modern sociolinguistics also provide. Just as Sweet records a greater female preference for use of the 'proper' [h] in realizations of relevant words, so do Peter Trudgill's (rather more statistical investigations) in twentieth-century Norwich record the same thing, albeit in far more detail. As Trudgill confirms, for example, women in all social groups tend to adopt higher frequencies of [h] in contradistinction to [Ø], or [ŋ] in contradistinction to [ɪn], than do men of the same age and social ranking (see the histogram in Figure 5.1).[146]

Such findings have, as already indicated, formed a staple of the quantitative research into language in use as carried out by Labov in New York, Trudgill in Norwich, Newbrook in Wirral, or Romaine in Edinburgh (alongside many others). Irrespective of location, all reveal the significant operation of gender as a speaker variable so that, in the patterns of variation which emerge, women seem to display a systematic tendency to use fewer variants which are stigmatized within prevailing language attitudes, a characteristic which is especially apparent in their more formal speech. As in that (admittedly far less empirical) evidence cited by Ellis or Ripman, the social values with which individual variants are imbued do in such instances indeed seem to lead to patterns of preferential variation which are aligned quite clearly with differences of gender.

Self-evaluation tests, in which the facts of observed usage are compared with what speakers *think* they say, also bear out patterns of distinctive gender identities, female informants regularly (though not, of course, invariably) claiming that they use a greater proportion of statusful forms associated with

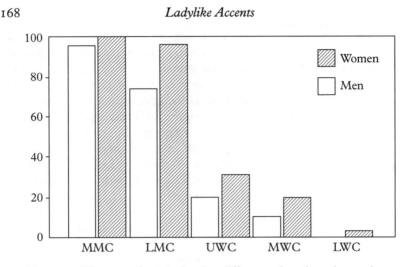

FIG. 5.1. Histogram for (ŋ), showing differences based on class and sex
Source: J. Coates, *Women, Men and Language* (London, 1986), 64.

usage of the standard variety than are, in fact, actually employed in their speech—a disparity which again suggests the particular import of language attitudes (and their wide-scale diffusion) in this context. Such patterns of female 'over-reporting' are, however, regularly placed alongside patterns of 'under-reporting' in the corresponding evidence obtained from male informants. Signally unlike women, male speakers seem instead to assume (and moreover to state) that they use fewer prestigious variants than they do in reality deploy—a distribution which perhaps further confirms the existence of differing notions (and different norms) of 'appropriate' language for both men and women.

The explanations presented for these disparities have, predictably, been many and various, ranging from arguments based on the greater 'politeness' of women (in keeping with their status as subordinate groups) through interpretations based on a greater female sensitivity to notions of status per se, and including the frequent discussion of assumptions in which, in the absence of ways in which to mark other aspects of status and identity by means of property or occupation, women have instead traditionally prioritized the social significance of language, and the social meanings which its use variously comports. In terms of the nineteenth century, such explanations can appear attractive. Certainly female identity tended to be defined (outside of language) in particularly male terms of reference; as Mrs Gaskell noted in *Cranford*, 'a married woman takes her husband's rank by the strict laws of precedence' while an unmarried woman simply 'retains the station her father occupied'.[147] Legal statements enshrined the same processes of assimilation, and Sir William Blackstone's *Commentaries on the Laws of*

England set forth the fundamental status divides which allowed incorporation of female identity within male, but not male identity within female. As Joan Perkin comments on this phenomenon, 'In Orwellian language', the woman after marriage 'became an "unperson" '.[148]

The recognition of such patterns did indeed seem to inspire a marked attention to other aspects of social identity for many nineteenth-century women. Davidoff notes, for example, that 'every cap, bow, streamer, ruffle, fringe, bustle, glove and other elaboration symbolised some status category for the female wearer',[149] while female education, as we have seen, regularly emphasized the significance of looks, behaviour, and speech as salient elements within the appearance which young ladies, aspirant or otherwise, were to cultivate. As the promoter (and critic) of women's education Maria Grey avers, 'appearance [is] the one object for which she is taught to strive'.[150] Language too operated within the same paradigms and writers regularly stressed the damaging effects which 'inelegant language' could have on female identity and appearance. Ellis himself, in his accounts of 'ladylike' preferences for the use of 'elegant' middle sounds, isolates the notion of appearance in partial explanation for this propensity, as does Henry Sweet in his own account of the same phenomenon.

Such explanations are, to some extent, shared with Peter Trudgill in the twentieth century who likewise raises the differential import of appearance in constructions of gender and identity. This, he surmises, could act as a possible explanation for that greater incidence of prestige forms which the speech of women can exhibit. Isolating another cultural stereotype which is seemingly endowed with continued validity, Trudgill hence draws attention to the fact that women and men have traditionally been evaluated differently by the outside world, men particularly by what they do (though other factors can also be important), but women especially by how they look, and by the external markers which go to make up appearance as a whole. He suggests therefore that pronunciation too may be subsumed for women within this notion of 'appearance', an argument which might usefully serve to interpret those patterns of gender-preferential variation which he and others have consistently recorded—and one which functions outside that often propagated belief in a greater female sensitivity to notions of status per se.

This hypothesis, though not developed further by Trudgill, is, as we have seen, one given potential support within a number of nineteenth-century writings on both language and gender. There are, however, other ways of looking at this problem. Self-evaluation tests, as already indicated, seem to confirm marked differences in the identities (and preferred identities) which men and women own by means of language. Though no parallels to suggest diachronic patterns of male under-reporting can be obtained from the nineteenth century, the affinities between gender and language which modern self-evaluation tests thereby also reveal nevertheless remain of interest—and again especially in terms of the explanations which may be offered. Contrastive conceptions of overt and covert prestige are, for example, often introduced in attempted interpretation of these patterns of gender and variation, being used to confirm similarly divergent attitudes to status which are, in themselves, influenced by (gender-related) behavioural norms and expectations. Masculine values, as a number of writers have asserted, are often perceived as residing in greater measure in the forms of the vernacular in contradistinction to those of 'standard' speech. Associated with the connotative values of 'toughness' or 'macho' strength and behaviour, such vernacular variants, as well as preferences for their use, can, from such a psychosymbolic position, be used to reveal the existence of a form of 'covert prestige'. This, it is stated, can in turn materially influence self-reporting of speech by male informants, hence the often attested preferences for variants associated with non-standard speech. The forms of the 'standard' are, as we might expect, conversely endowed with 'overt prestige', and with those associations of the 'polite' and 'proper' in which cultural constructions of the feminine excel. Cultural prescription, and its attendant linguistic stereotypes, as a result traditionally still seems to correlate 'feminine' with notions of superior linguistic propriety, allying both with the 'overt prestige' of the standard variety. As Vandenhoff had stressed in 1862, for the woman, 'the speaking of her native language with purity and elegance of pronunciation...and an easy, fluent utterance... carry with them the *prestige* of refinement and high breeding'.[151] Notions of linguistic acceptability are thus, as both nineteenth- and twentieth-century accounts of language reveal, likely to be strongly conditioned by corresponding norms of gender (as indeed are their respective explanations). In turn, pervasive ideas of this order are, importantly, more than capable of conditioning actual language behaviour, as well as attitudes to language use. Norms rarely exist in a vacuum, a fact which should perhaps be kept in mind when considering the implications of that wealth of prescriptive information on 'ladylike' language and pronunciation from centuries before our own.

As the linguist Lesley Milroy has asserted, 'although phonology is not directly linked with meaning, vernacular phonological norms typically have a social *significance* (not meaning) of maleness, youth, working class identity or whatever'.[152] In her subsequent discussion, she thus usefully moves away from the purely class-based models of behaviour which are so often adopted in these contexts, looking instead at the value of underlying stereotypes of 'masculine' and 'feminine' behaviour—such indeed as are widespread in language attitudes and which are not necessarily correlated with these (potentially problematic) notions of prestige. As we have seen throughout this book, such stereotypes can indeed be of marked value, not only in terms of language attitudes (and associated beliefs) but also in influencing actual behaviour. Evident in the avoidance of the elisions and assimilations of ordinary speech by speakers of Adoptive RP (in all its heightened 'correctness'), such notions of 'proper' language can also be illuminating in this context too, especially in terms of the superior proprieties of language which are, as already indicated, so often stressed in prevalent cultural constructions of the feminine. As in the nineteenth century, modern evidence can offer compelling proof of the operation and effects of a ubiquitous 'double standard' with reference to gender (and gender stereotypes) in both language and society. A study by John Edwards, carried out in 1979, provides, for example, particularly striking confirmation of this fact, as well as of the pervasiveness (and influence) of these behavioural norms and expectations for women as for men.[153]

An exercise in perception, Edwards's study merely required a set of adults to note down the sex of children from tape-recordings of forty children's voices. The children were of an age before the onset of distinctive pitch differences (i.e. before the voices of the boys had broken), but nevertheless the voices of girls, as well as those of boys, were, on the whole, identified without apparent difficulty. It was, however, in the systematic patterns of misidentification which occurred that the major interest of this study was found to lie. The children were differentiated not only by sex, but also by social level. Of forty voices, twenty were designated as being from the working class, twenty from the middle and, in the mistakes made by the listeners, significant patterns of error in this context came to light. Exposing notions of behavioural norms which are clearly dependent on gender (a cultural construct), rather than on sex (a biological one), in each case of 'mistaken identity' working-class girls were misidentified as boys while middle-class boys were perceived as girls. Girls, in other words, are apparently expected to sound 'middle class', whilst these allocations of male identity confirmed the masculine associations of working-class language as already revealed in the evidence of self-evaluation tests. As Edwards's data therefore suggest, these orientations are dependent not on notions of 'covert'/'overt' prestige, but instead on the workings of social psychology, and the social, cultural, and linguistic stereotypes which are prevalent within it. The perceptions of a second set of adult listeners within the same study further corroborated the existence of such cultural norms. Asked to specify the values generated by the differences in accent, they rated working-class voices as rougher, lower, and more masculine. 'Middle-class' voices instead took on evaluations of smoothness and femininity. The existence of another stereotype in modern British society in which higher-status male voices are regularly deemed effeminate likewise bears out these findings.[154]

Such accounts provide empirical evidence of the way in which gender is firmly embedded in the attitudes and expectations which surround language in use. Stereotypes of gender and identity are, it seems, not discarded easily and their effects can still be perceptible in language behaviour (and language attitudes) in line, in many ways, with those prescriptions set out with such explicitness in the nineteenth century. In these terms, just as the cultural stereotypes of the present day continue to exert their own influences upon actual language behaviour in the context of gender, so in the nineteenth century can corresponding processes be assumed to have taken place as women at times chose to modify the forms they used, as Ellis and Ripman suggest, in line with that abundant proscription and prescription supplied under this head. Correlations between perceived femininity and the 'proper' accents deemed appropriate as its linguistic correlate were, as we have seen, prescribed with little reserve in the nineteenth century; their legacies are, in a number of ways, thus still made manifest in the quantitative findings of the twentieth, exemplifying those more subtle ways in which such stereotypes of 'talking like a lady' (or indeed like a 'proper man') can be encoded in language attitudes, expectations, and subsequently even in language use itself. As other sociolingustic studies have usefully stressed, however, such correlations are not inevitable so that, in other circumstances, women can reveal equal and even greater facility in the covert norms traditionally categorized as male.[155] As always, language use is marked by the absence of simple absolutes.

Nevertheless, in the nineteenth century such shifts were commonly proscribed as deviations from the expected norms, the discourse of working women in the factories of London and other urban centres often being presented as antithetical to the decorums which proper femininity should exhibit. Images of gender and language were, in this, particularly susceptible to the images of norm and deviation which are, as we have seen, a central element of prescriptive ideology. The actualities of urban female discourse in working environments were rarely investigated, other than to be proscribed for the departures they clearly evinced from the model of the 'Proper Lady', and the requisite proprieties of enunciation which she should by right exhibit. If attitudes have changed in this respect (at least in terms of linguistic study), stereotypical perceptions of gender and 'talking proper' can still reveal significant continuities with the past in modern language attitudes. As Elyan *et al.* have demonstrated, RP women are consistently 'rated higher on the femininity trait than Northern accented females'.[156] In this context it is indeed undeniable that cultural norms of appropriate language can still differ for men and women, and not only in traditional areas of linguistic taboo and the differential acceptabilities of swearing.

6

Literature and the Literate Speaker

THE ideal of the 'literate speaker', defined in terms of social, cultural, as well as linguistic values, was, as we have seen, adopted as an important tenet of phonemic propriety within many works on language published during the late eighteenth and nineteenth centuries. It was a precept which was perhaps encapsulated most effectively in Samuel Johnson's dictum on the nature of elegant speech ('For pronunciation the best general rule is, to consider those as the most elegant speakers who deviate least from the written words'),[1] as well as in the frequent iterations which this received in later years. Resulting notions of 'literacy' were hence applied to spoken as well as written forms, regularly influencing popular images of correctness. As Thomas Sheridan in 1762 had, for example, adjured, 'good' speech was to be dependent upon 'giving every letter in a syllable, its due proportion of sound, according to the most approved custom of pronouncing it'.[2]

In spite of the manifest incompatibility of grapheme and phoneme in English,[3] the ideal of literate speech which duly emerges from this particular focus is marked in language attitudes of the time. The grammarian Thomas Smetham in 1774, for instance, illustrates a prevalent cultural equation in his evident belief that it was only provincial accents which deviated from the non-localized norms which had been established in the written forms of words:

It may not be amiss here to mention some practices which ought always to be discouraged; namely, the pronouncing words totally different from what they are spelled, according to the dialect which prevails in the particular county where the speaker was born, or perhaps brought up; a provincial dialect should always receive a check.[4]

Glossed as 'rude' and 'unpolished' by Johnson, notions of the 'provincial' were, as already indicated, readily incorporated into prevalent paradigms of 'knowledge' versus 'ignorance' in speech, drawing on associated prescriptive fictions by which such local variations were necessarily flawed. In these particular manifestations of the standard ideology therefore, literate speakers (in contradistinction to the stated fallibilities of the 'provincial' in this matter) were to make manifest superiorities of status, education, and breeding by the correlations they would evince between spelling and the spoken word. Illiterate speakers are conversely presented as those who 'catch sounds imperfectly and utter them negligently', a maxim which Johnson had also expounded.[5]

Such convictions arose, as Sheridan made plain, as a result of the 'habitual association of ideas' which had come to exist between written and spoken English. 'These two kinds of languages are so early in life associated, that it is difficult ever after to separate them; or not to suppose that there is some kind of natural connection between them', he stressed on the opening page of his *Course of Lectures in Elocution*. Dichotomies between the awareness of such principles and their subsequent application are, however, easily discovered in Sheridan's own work. Sound and alphabetic symbol should, for true propriety, be aligned as 'body and shadow', he declares on page 243 of the *Course*. His normative rulings on the pronunciation of unaccented syllables further exemplify susceptibilities in this respect. Since the final syllables of words such as *actor, baker*, or *altar* are, in spite of their graphemic disparities, all commonly pronounced alike (in /ə/), speakers are urged to conquer such habitual 'negligence', and to articulate the sounds in accordance with the letters on the page rather than in line with the requirements of internal word-stress. John Walker shared in this same vacillation. Likewise aware of the theoretical weakness in any unquestioned correlation of grapheme and phoneme, he too was nevertheless to appeal time and time again to visual authority as a guide to oral norms. On the pronunciation of the word *boatswain*, for example, he notes that though 'this word is universally pronounced in common conversation' as]boʹsn[, in reading aloud 'it would savour somewhat of vulgarity to contract it to a sound so very unlike the orthography'. As he adds, 'it would be advisable, therefore, in those who are not of the naval profession, to pronounce the word when they read it, distinctly as it is written'. In modern transcription, he therefore instead advocates the more 'literate' pronunciation /ˈbəʊtsweɪn/. Walker's comments on the words *clef* and *fault* exemplify similar assumptions about the role of graphemic norms in appraisals of phonemic correctness, and he berates the ways in which *clef* was habitually pronounced in the late eighteenth century as /ˈklɪf/ and *fault* still displayed marked variability in terms of the presence of /l/ (though Walker himself decisively prefers a pronunciation which he gives as]fȧlt[(i.e. /ˈfɔːlt/). In such ways, spelling was often specifically implemented as a guide to 'correct' (and corrected) speech, influencing, as we have seen in Chapter 4, not least the rise of [h] as social symbol (and its own introduction in words such as *humble, herb*, and *hospital* where it had previously been silent). Scores of individual words such as *chap, forehead, waistcoat, falcon*, and, in time, *boatswain* too were likewise to succumb to similar pressures over the nineteenth century.[6]

Given the prevalence of these assumptions in prescriptive tenets as well as popular attitudes to the language, it is perhaps hardly surprising that representations of speech in literature should trade on many of the same ideas. Authors are, in this as in other ways, a product of the age in which they live; that consciousness of the spoken word and its assumed proprieties operates upon them just as on other members of the population. Sensitization to the social import of accent, prescriptive sensibilities about correctness (and its converse), perceived correlations between accent and mind, intelligence, character, status, and gender were all, as we have seen, widely discussed and disseminated as issues over the late eighteenth and nineteenth centuries. In turn, poets, authors, and dramatists rarely proved unwilling to exploit the potential thus offered for the depiction of the nuances of direct speech, readily manipulating the resonances of the standard ideology in line with common sociocultural attitudes towards the spoken word and images of its due proprieties. The cultural ideal of the 'literate speaker' was in consequence regularly incorporated in literary texts as 'gentleman' and 'ladies' (in accordance with those stereotypes already discussed), members of the upper and middle sections of society and, of course, heroes and heroines were regularly given speech which reproduced the orthographical patterns of the standard language without deviation. Servants, members of the lower ranks, Cockneys, and rustics were instead habitually made to deploy patterns of speech in which the absence of expected graphemes, and the presence of others equally unexpected, was marked.

The basic premise within this affiliation of sociolect and spelling traded, as Thomas Smetham has already confirmed, on the implicit (if entirely fallacious) assumption that the non-localized norms of the written language were, in themselves, to be understood as representative of the non-regional forms of 'correct' speech. In literary terms therefore, it is this belief which is made to inform the differences within the discourse of, for example, the eponymous David and the carrier Mr Barkis in *David Copperfield*. ' "If you was writin' to her, p'raps you'd recollect to say that Barkis was willin" ', says Barkis. ' "That Barkis is willing" ', repeats David in the next line: ' "Is that all the message?" '[7] In spite of the compromises which such assumed equations of spelling, sound, and social status involved, patterns of this kind (*willin'*, *willing, p'raps, perhaps*) were often manipulated in order to embody the set of equalities and inequalities which differences of accent had come to suggest. Divergent patterns of language in, for example, Dickens's *Martin Chuzzlewit*, as in this exchange between Mrs Gamp and the gentlemanly John Westlock, can hence provide innumerable illustrations of the ways in which the differentiated deployment of standard and non-standard spellings can be used to form a highly effective, and contrastive, social discourse:

'Don't I know as that dear woman is expectin of me at this minnit...with little Tommy Harris in her arms, as calls me his own Gammy...his own I have been, ever since I found him, Mr. Westlock, with his small red worsted shoe a gurglin in his throat, where he had put it in his play, a chick, wile they was leavin of him on the floor a lookin for it through the ouse and him a chokin sweetly in the parlour. Oh, Betsey Prig, wot wickedness you've showed this night, but never shall you darken Sairey's doors agen, you twinin serpiant!'
'You were always so kind to her, too!' said John, consolingly.[8]

Literary fictions of speech such as this bear clear witness to corresponding fictions of that social divide, and its manifestations, which were regularly deployed within prescriptive ideology. As the lexicographers George Fulton and George Knight had stressed in 1833, 'Nothing gives us a greater impression of ignorance and vulgarity, than bad spelling, and awkward or provincial pronunciation'.[9] Conventions of direct speech in nineteenth-century literature tended, however, to draw on both these social shibboleths simultaneously, choosing to depict 'ignorance' and 'vulgarity'—together with their respective social correlates—by the use of 'bad spelling' as a device which, in itself, would be able to signify the requisite awkwardnesses and infelicities of pronunciation. Mrs Gamp is therefore made to drop letters with ease. Forms such as *gurglin, chokin, ouse* demonstrate the stereotyped social associations of /h/ and /ɪn/ already discussed in Chapter 4, while constructions such as *wot, agen,* or *wile* suggest other notions of 'illiteracy' as social marker which will receive further discussion later. John Westlock, of course, has by contrast direct speech which is composed entirely of pristine and thereby unmarked forms, serving to allocate him (in this particular implementation of language attitudes) with 'polite' rather than 'vulgar', and with 'knowledgeable' instead of 'ignorant'. The perfect graphemic propriety of his discourse functions, by means of that 'habitual association of ideas' discussed by Sheridan, to suggest a parallel propriety of enunciation. No 'letters', whether visual or oral, are dropped.

The substance of literary discourse can, in such ways, be materially affected not only by *what* is said but also by *how* it is depicted as being said. Mrs Gamp's use of pseudophonetic forms such as *minnit* (for *minute*) or elsewhere, the allocation of parallel forms such as *spazzums* (instead of *spasms*) to Mrs Crupp, David Copperfield's landlady in London ('Mrs. Crupp was a martyr to a curious disorder called "the spazzums," which was generally accompanied with inflammation of the nose, and required her to be constantly treated with peppermint')[10] serve moreover to reveal other aspects of the 'illiterate speaker' in literary terms. The visual disharmonies of such spellings act as unambiguous markers of intended deviation; they are, in the representation of direct speech, thus overtly made to suggest corresponding failings in utterance, their connotative values establishing a highly effective sub-text and marking out the intended fictional divisions in social space. In *David Copperfield*, Peggotty (David's nurse) uses *pritty*, David himself, *pretty*. In Gissing's *The Town Traveller*, the contrastive use of *hyjene* rather than *hygiene* aligns sociolects and speakers with ease: 'They had a decent little house in Kennington, managed—rather better than such homes usually are—by Mrs Parish the younger, who was childless, and thus able to devote herself to what she called "hyjene"'.[11] In George Meredith's *The Ordeal of Richard Feverel, leftenant, fashen,* and *joolry* again demarcate 'vulgar' and 'polite' in the characters we meet. Notions that what looks 'right' must also sound 'right' (and vice versa) dominate in an era preoccupied with linguistic mastery as an art of profound social significance even when, as in all these instances, the fictions of 'inferior' speech are patently transparent for those who care to attend with ear rather than eye. In terms of nineteenth-century phonology, for instance, both *pritty* and *pretty*, irrespective of the difference of <i, e> grapheme, can only signify /ˈprɪtɪ/ in speech; *fashen* and *fashion* receive an identical realization /ˈfæʃn/ in the spoken language. Both *hygiene* and *hyjene* suggest the pronunciation /ˈhaɪʤiːn/.

Prescriptive ideologies of the literate speaker are, in ways such as these, made entirely literal within the realms of literature. *Minnit, leftenant, joolry, spazzums*, and the rest, though making explicit prevalent (and highly negative) notions of 'illiteracy', paradoxically also act as relatively accurate transcriptions of enunciations which, in real terms, would not be out of place in the most polite discourse. It is, however, the assumed authority of graphemic propriety, and the dominance of connotative over denotative values, which serve to reveal the 'best' speech in these particular contexts. Employing *du* rather than *do* (a favourite device of William Thackeray for his lower-status characters), or *collidges* rather than *colleges* signifies, at least intentionally, the 'illiterate' speaker, whose pronunciation is, in consequence, assumed to be profoundly 'negligent'.

The relevant paradigm is that set out by George Graham in 1869. 'Whatever may be the recognised standard of pronunciation, there will always be a refined and a vulgar mode of speech', he stated: 'one adopted by the cultivated and well-informed, and the other used by the rude and illiterate'.[12] Just as Walker had commented on the words *business, busy*, and *bury* that 'we ought rather to blush for departing so wantonly from the general rule as to pronounce them *bizzy, bizness*, and *berry*',[13] so too did authors regularly extend such conceptions, endorsing the implicit censure of 'custom' in these respects by allocating parallel, and seemingly 'illiterate', transcriptions only to those outside the 'polite'. 'Rude', as Walker confirmed, was to be 'coarse of manners' as well as 'inelegant'; John Ogilvie later provides the synonym 'illiterate' too in his own dictionary of 1870. In these terms, it is both predictable as well as telling that Mrs Gamp's stated occupations include an interest in *berryin* rather than *burying*, and that *bizness* instead of *business* occupies a diverse range of characters such as Mark Tapley in *Martin Chuzzlewit*, Sam Weller in *The Pickwick Papers*, and the coachman in Cuthbert Bede's highly popular *The Adventures of Mr. Verdant Green*. ' "I knows my biz'ness . . . and I'd never go for to give up the ribbins to any party but wot had showed hisself fitted to 'andle 'em" ', says the latter, his speech leaving little ambiguity as to its intended social markings,[14] in spite of the fact that again, *business* and *biz'ness* represent identical sound patterns ([ˈbɪznəs]) in the realities of direct speech.

Realism is clearly not the aim. Nevertheless, the set of conventions which evolves around the detailed representation of speech in literature does, in a number of ways, deserve further consideration, as indeed do the patterns of distribution which are assigned to these conventions. Literature, as Roger Fowler reminds us, is a social discourse; in turn the fictions of speech deployed within it readily draw on corresponding fictions, and fallacies, of speech which influence that wider world outside its own particular confines. Similarly, as G. L. Brook has noted in his own work on the language of Dickens, 'the use which any author makes of language' must be seen as 'part of the history of that language'.[15] Readings of texts which incorporate such diachronic knowledge can therefore, in a number of ways, offer certain advantages—especially if awareness of language history is taken to include knowledge not only of the language per se but also of prevailing language attitudes, and the value judgements (both social and linguistic) which were often made to encompass significant patterns of variation. The heightened prominence of accent as social symbol, common reactions to certain sound changes in progress, or prescriptive resistance to phonemic mergers seen as characteristic only of 'unskilful' speakers, are all foregrounded with no little detail in the literature of the nineteenth century.

The effectiveness of notions of deviation in these terms does not, however, depend solely upon that shift in prescriptive sensibilities towards the role of accent nor, at least in isolation, upon these paradigms of accuracy and error which so often came to be imposed in this context upon the details of enunciation. Literary representations of 'standard' and 'non-standard' in pronunciation by means of the graphemic patterns employed must instead, for example, depend equally upon the clear, and widespread, recognition of a written norm. In pragmatic terms, it is therefore the near-standardization of spelling in public printed texts during the eighteenth century, coupled with the rise of the dictionary as popular reference book (especially after Dr Johnson's own endeavours in this respect), together with the gradual extension of public norms of spelling into private use, which all contributed to facilitate the effectiveness of increased detail in this respect. This was particularly the case since such developments were also combined with a general increase in levels of literacy, of education, and of exposure to the written word. Whereas some variation did continue, <dote>, for example, often appearing as <doat> in nineteenth-century texts, <frowzy> as <frouzy>, <diplomat> as <diplomate>, or <develop> as <develope>, the growing sense of a written standard did nevertheless render it increasingly easy for writers (and readers) to discriminate between the use of significant and non-significant variation. Dickens's selection of *piller* for *pillow*, *wotever* for *whatever*, or *pizon* for *poison* in his representation of Mrs Gamp's direct speech was thus of a completely different order from the use of <controul> or <boddice> in the same text (forms used moreover outside the confines of direct speech). The artistic intent apparent in the former group functions of course as an important aspect of Mrs Gamp's characterization, employed alongside her idiophonic fondness for /dʒ/ ('this indiwidgle roof', 'a surprige in-deed').

Deliberate principles of deviation in terms of the spoken language and its representation had of course appeared in literature long before this date. Chaucer in the *Reeve's Tale* made, as we have seen, early use of Northern forms of speech allocated to the two Cambridge University men Aleyn and John in order to serve as a contrastive discourse within the London dialect which Chaucer himself employed. The absence of a non-localized written language in the fourteenth century, however, could and did present problems on occasion. The scribe of the Paris manuscript of the *Canterbury Tales*, for example, effectively 'translates' the whole text into Northern dialect, thus eliminating the intentionally differentiated modes of speech (*fares* instead of *fareth*, *gaa* instead of *go*) which Chaucer had inserted as an integral aspect of his tale. Even with the subsequent rise of a written, and above all, a printed mode of English used on national rather than merely localized levels, it must nevertheless be remembered that printers, as well as private individuals, have by no means always adhered to a single spelling for each word. Extra graphemes were, for instance, commonly inserted by early printers in order to justify the lines so that a word such as *freedom* could appear as *fredom*, *fredome*, *freedome*, or indeed as its preferred modern version, *freedom*. In such circumstances, the finer nuances of orthographical deviation such as those later deployed by Dickens, Eliot, or Gaskell would certainly have been reduced in effectiveness. Though writers generally maintained control of the substantives of their texts, its accidentals—the spelling and punctuation—were, as this indicates, largely dictated by the printers themselves.

Where deliberate orthographical variation was used, writers instead tended to rely on broader schema of deviation which were less liable to potential misinterpretation, and distortion. This is the method selected by the dramatist Sir John Vanbrugh in 1697 in the heavy foregrounding of *a* for *o* which he used to depict the affected modes of speech of Lord Foppington in *The Relapse*: 'Now it is nat possible for me to penetrate what species of fally it is thau art driving at', 'That, I must confess, I am nat altogether so fand of'.[16] Many writers indeed chose to signal deviation (and its intended social correlations) not in terms of these attempted grapho-phonemic correspondences, but rather in terms of lexis or grammar, levels of linguistic organization in which consciousness of non-localized norms, and sensitization to requisite proprieties, was in any case more advanced. This is the method preferred, for example, by William Wycherley in *The Country Wife*, a play in which paradigms of knowledge versus ignorance are worked out in terms of fashionable slang and familiarity (or otherwise) with metropolitan modes of language. These do not, at least explicitly, include the phonemic.[17]

Though deliberate orthographical variation was used to an extent in Restoration drama, it was, however, the novel which was above all to provide the most effective vehicle for increased linguistic nuance in the modes of speech adopted by various characters. Both Tobias Smollett and Henry

Fielding, as we have seen in Chapter 4, provide early examples in their own work of those 'illiterate speakers' who would populate the nineteenth-century novel in such numbers. Later authors were, however, to extend immeasurably the patterns of linguistic deviation and attendant social meanings which could be depicted, uniting a complex of grammatical, syntactic, and intentionally 'phonetic' markers to portray strategic alignments within the social hierarchy. Clearer conceptions of 'standard' norms in pronunciation, and the details of enunciation by which their use was to be recognized, thus in turn provide a far greater awareness of the non-standard, and indeed sub-standard, in literature as in life. Jane Austen's characters, as has often been remarked, are distinguished by shades of usage in grammar and lexis which betray close correlations with precepts enforced in earlier eighteenth-century prescriptive writings on the language. Other writers were instead to foreground that consciousness of accent as prime social signifier which was inculcated at such length by Sheridan and others. Austen is, in *Emma*, hence content merely to remark on Mr Martin's perceived 'want of gentility' in this respect: 'I am sure you must have been struck by his awkward look and abrupt manner—and the uncouthness of a voice, which I heard to be wholly unmodulated as I stood here', as Emma tells Harriet, betraying her own misjudgements of manner and matter, external and inner worth.[18] Later authors such as Dickens, Meredith, Reade, Gaskell, Eliot, and, perhaps most notably George Gissing, would, however, scarcely have been satisfied with anything less than a full representation of such 'uncouthness', using all the conventions at their disposal.

Such patterns of representation were indeed envisaged as a potentially important aspect of the writer's role. Since 'of accent, as well as of spelling, syntax, and idiom, there is a standard in every polite nation', as the poet and essayist James Beattie set forth as early as 1788,[19] authorial manifestations of these 'standards' were deemed significant not only in terms of literary characterization but also in terms of their possible exemplary value. 'In all these particulars', Beattie continued, 'the example of approved authors, and the practice of those, who, by their rank, education, and way of life, have had the best opportunities to know men and manners, and domestick and foreign literature, ought undoubtedly to give the law'. Literary methods of indicating accent in 'narrow' rather than 'broad' formats in fact evolved with some rapidity and, if not actually establishing 'laws' of linguistic usage, they certainly traded on the social resonances of contemporary shibboleths and stigma in terms of accent to no little effect. Missing <h>s and missing <g>s as illustrated in Chapter 4 performed roles in literature which are precisely in line with that more general shift in attitudes towards the needful proprieties of speech. Even the pronunciation of individual words, and their representation in literature, would regularly serve to encode the new social sensibilities (and ideological implications) which had come to surround contemporary attitudes to correctness.

Oblige, for example, was pronounced with propriety as /əˈbliːdʒ/ in the eighteenth century. Alexander Pope had rhymed *obliged* with *besieged*, as well as *oblige ye* with *besiege ye* in a pattern of phonemic correspondence which was by no means unusual. The social meanings of this particular enunciation were, however, gradually to shift. Lord Chesterfield had in the later eighteenth century already begun to question its acceptability, proscriptively allying its use with the 'affected' and 'vulgar'. By the mid-nineteenth century it was to the latter that /əˈbliːdʒ/ had almost without exception been affiliated, the modern pronunciation /əˈblaɪdʒ/ coming to dominate in considerations of linguistic propriety. John Kemble, the actor (and Mrs Siddon's brother), is even reputed to have corrected the monarch on a phonemic faux pas in this context as George Graham records in 1869: 'When George III said to him: "Mr. Kemble, will you 'obleedge' me with a pinch of your snuff?" [Kemble] replied: "With pleasure, your Majesty; but it would become your royal lips much better to say 'oblige'"'.[20] Literary texts regularly assimilated these changed social values, the contrastive use of *obleedge/oblige* being deployed as an unambiguous marker of differentiated status, complete with appropriate graphological deviation. Habitual enunciations by the cunning balladmonger Silas Wegg in *Our Mutual Friend*, or the boatman Mr Peggotty in *David Copperfield*, reveal the former: '"I'm much obleeged to her, I'm sure"',[21] '"I'm obleeged to you, sir, for your welcoming manner of me"'.[22] The speech of Mrs Tester, the bedmaker in Cuthbert Bede's comic *History of Verdant Green*, is likewise distinguished by the emphasis duly assigned to this form: '"So long as I can obleege the gentleman"', '"it's obleeged I feel in my art"'.[23] Dickens's Kate Nickleby instead employs *obliged* ('"I'm very much obliged to you, uncle"'), a usage dependent upon her hereditary and social status as gentleman's daughter (and her literary status as heroine), rather than her socioeconomic class as a milliner earning seven shillings a week.[24]

The use of enunciations of *cucumber* as *cowcumber* is similarly made to pertain to widely populated social and linguistic stereotypes. Though Walker in 1791 had lamented that it then 'seemed too firmly fixed in its sound of *Cowcumber* to be altered', giving in consequence a reluctant sanction to the acceptability of this pronunciation, later observers, and indeed later editors of Walker's own dictionary, stressed instead that the '"best usage" had ceased to pronounce the first syllable like *cow*'. 'When people of fashion relinquish an absurdity, men of letters should be deeply grateful', as the lexicographer Townsend Young added in approbation,[25] celebrating this triumph of graphemic propriety. Iterations of *cowcumber* and *cucumber* hence again combined to form a binary pair of marked social value for nineteenth-century writers, and it is in this deeply unfashionable mode of speech in which Mrs Gamp is, for example, made to request a cucumber to give extra piquancy to her meal: '"In case there should be sech a thing as a cowcumber in the ouse, will you be so kind as to bring it, for I'm rather partial to 'em, and they does a world of good in a sick room" '.[26] Dickens's selection of the form with <ow> hence signifies the outmoded and deliberately *déclassé* use of [aʊ] (['kaʊkʌmbə]), an articulation opposed to those more 'correct' enunciations in [uː] (['kjuːkʌmbə]) which were suggested, and reinforced, by the spelling. 'None but the most illiterate now pronounce it other than it is written', concluded Edward de Levante of this word in 1869,[27] and it is of course in such paradigms of 'illiterate' versus 'literate' speech that Mrs Gamp's usage is also to be placed. Alternations of *sparrowgrass/asparagus, faut/fault*, or *sodger/soldier* all serve similar functions, their newer spelling–pronunciations encoding the stated proprieties of literate speech. Their traditional enunciations are, on the other hand, habitually used in literature to signify the massed ranks of artisans, rustics, Cockneys, and other members of the lower orders (as well as the 'hyper-correct'—but still uneducated—forms of the aspiring parvenu).

Such details encoded the social divide in literary and linguistic terms with a marked sense of contemporaneity for the nineteenth-century reader. Graphological deviation which is often regarded, as by Leech and Short, as 'a relatively minor and superficial part of style' is,[28] as a result, instead made fundamental to the perception, and presentation, of the social meanings which are, as we have seen, frequently stressed as omnipresent in pronunciation. When the novelist George Meredith, for example, introduces Farmer Blaize in *The Ordeal of Richard Feverel* (1859), it is graphology, and its assumed relationship with an underlying phonetic reality, which proclaims his status as merely yeoman rather than gentleman farmer (and which by contrast establishes Richard in the superior position—in spite of the latter's transgressions in poaching, as well as in setting fire to the aptly named Blaize's haystack):

'Now,' said he, leaning forward, and fixing his elbows on his knees, while he counted the case at his fingers' ends, 'ascuse the liberty, but wishin' to know where this 'ere money's to come from, I sh'd like jest t'ask if so be Sir Aust'n know o' this?'

'My father knows nothing of it,' replied Richard.[29]

Forms such as *'ere* for *here, wishin'* for *wishing*, or *o'* for *of* in this way become meaningful in the social world created within the novel, trading as they do on common assumptions about language, status, and identity which were widely prevalent outside such fictional confines. Deliberate modifications of orthography function as important aspects of foregrounding, qualitative deviation from established or expected norms hence assuming markedly expressive roles. Italicization, capitalization, the use of diacritics, patterns of hyphenation and punctuation, and especially the respelling of words to suggest correspondences between visual and vocal disharmony can all share in this aspect of stylistic technique. Diacritics mark perceived deviance in Dickens's representation of the stress patterns of American speech in *Martin Chuzzlewit*: ' "In my country," said the gentleman, "we know the cost of our own prŏ-dūce" ', ' "we will not pursue the subject, lest it should awaken your prĕju-dīce" '.[30] Capitalization, as already indicated, serves to mark the heavily emphatic discourse of Mr Podsnap in explaining the social meanings of /h/ in *Our Mutual Friend*.[31] It is, however, the combined resources of spelling and punctuation which prove of greatest value in literary delineations of accent.

In this, as Thomas Hardy asserted of his own practice in this respect, authors commonly purposed to convey the 'spirit' of the spoken word.[32] Methods, as a result, are more often impressionistic than entirely systematic. ' "Accordin' as the world went round, which round it did rewolve undoubtedly, even the best of gentlemen must take his turn of standing with his ed upside down and all his air a flying the wrong way" ', philosophizes the plasterer Mr Plornish in *Little Dorrit*,[33] betraying principles of variation (*accordin', flying, standing*, or *his, ed, air*) which owe more to literary selection than sociolinguistic insight. It is enough if the illusion of speech is given. Providing more than this could in fact risk certain dangers. Elizabeth Gaskell's more conscientious attempts to depict the nuances of Yorkshire speech in her novel *Sylvia's Lovers* (1863) met, for example, a number of markedly unfavourable reactions: 'the continual use of the common dialect of the north-eastern shores of England is both useless and fatiguing', declared an unsigned review in the *Observer* in 1863. Using 'the broad vernacular Yorkshire dialect', although giving 'local colour', is 'a drawback to the comfort of the reader, and fatiguing to the eye' confirmed the novelist Geraldine Jewsbury in the *Athenaeum*. The reviewer in the *Daily News* was still less responsive: 'it is trying the patience of readers too far to compel them to wade through three volumes of unpronounceable *patois* and miserable incidents'.[34] Such constraints alone served to inhibit absolute accuracy, as well as extensive representation, of speech within the novel.

Patterns of deviation moreover often tend to imply a certain distance, both from the authorial viewpoint and, in addition, from that of the implied reader—that hypothetical entity who, as Leech and Short point out, is assumed to share with the author not just background knowledge but equally 'a set of presuppositions, sympathies, and standards of what is pleasant and unpleasant, good and bad, right and wrong'.[35] It is this distancing which often tends to give comic resonance to those characters whose language differs from that standard variety in which the narrative is primarily constructed. Conversely, the same principles tend to exempt heroes and heroines from the demands which might otherwise be imposed by a more wide-ranging verisimilitude in these respects. Little Dorrit hence employs not the language of the debtors' prison, as one might expect from her residence in the Marshalsea but is instead endowed by Dickens with a perfect propriety of grammar and grapheme (and presumably therefore of phoneme too). Oliver Twist's ignorance of the linguistic foibles of the lower classes is similarly remarkable, given a social environment formed of workhouse and thieves' den. Even Gissing, heavily censorious of Dickens's practice in these terms ('Granted that Oliver was of gentle blood, heredity does not go as far as this'),[36] was forced to comply with conventional fictional expectations of this kind in his own work. As a result, although we are told of Richard Mutimer's 'struggles with the h fiend' in Gissing's novel *Demos* as part of Mutimer's construction as 'self-educated working man', they are never shown lest their use invite a ridicule incompatible with heroic status, and with those wider issues which Gissing was endeavouring to explore through Mutimer's rise and fall.

Though absolute realism was therefore neither intended nor attempted in this context, it is the presence of what we have already described as 'linguistic contemporaneity' which on many occasions renders a close examination of literary conventions of speech in the nineteenth century rewarding. Commonly drawing on prevailing attitudes to 'right' and 'wrong', 'statusful' and 'statusless' in speech, of which the implied reader of the nineteenth-century would likewise have been aware, fictional delineations of accent often embody with striking precision and clarity the normative framework (and accompanying ideologies) in which language use was placed. 'Ideology tells people how to act in prescribed, socially acceptable ways', writes Blake of conceptions of literature as a social process,[37] and the same is true of the linguistic processes and assumptions which it too can enact. Binary divisions of 'well bred' and 'vulgar' which, as we have seen, form a regular feature of the prescriptive tradition are, for example, transferred into the fictional domain with ease. Prescriptive fictions that only 'careless' speakers would employ colloquial forms of speech in which elision of syllables takes place similarly provide a regular source of socially contrastive language use in nineteenth-century texts. *P'raps* and *perhaps*, *s'pose* and *suppose*, *guv'nor* and *governor* are as a result used in structured ways in many novels, mapping out preconceptions about literate speech and social status, entirely irrespective of linguistic reality and the varying demands of situation, register, or stress which inevitably come into play for all speakers, irrespective of their social location. ' "I don't know which is the freshest, the freshman or his guv'nor" ', says the Oxford shopkeeper in Bede's *Adventures of Mr. Verdant Green*; ' "I heard from my governor that you were coming up" ', says an undergraduate, his 'educated' status being deemed to preclude such forms: ' "I suppose the old bird was your governor" '.[38] Forms such as *int'rest* and *corp'ral*, with elision of medial unstressed syllables, likewise assume marked social correlates in Bulwer Lytton's *Eugene Aram*, the intended sense of deviation being heightened further by the presence of other accompanying infelicities: 'that's the reason they all takes so much int'rest in their profession', 'when he comes for to get as high as a corp'ral or a sargent'.[39]

To turn to the actualities of speech, [ɪnˈtrɛst] and [ˈkɔːprəl] would of course form the habitual enunciations of the majority of speakers, irrespective of their social location, just as they do today. Nevertheless, just as Dr Johnson had equated the 'colloquial' with the 'licentious', and Benjamin Smart had excluded 'familiar and consequently negligent discourse' as having no place in the information which a dictionary should provide, so too did nineteenth-century writers respond to such prevalent language attitudes and ideals, presenting the elisions and contractions of informal speech in terms which implicitly shared prescriptive antipathies on this point. Weakly stressed (and perfectly normal) forms such as *an'* for *and* or *ev* for *have*, are in turn made to fulfil similar functions by their differential allocation. ' "I've been a mother to her, an' a good mother" ', says the vulgar Mrs Peckover in Gissing's *The Nether World*; ' "Only wait till I've ad my tea" ', says her daughter earlier in the same novel,[40] the expressive powers of the rewritten word being employed to suggest conspicuous deviation even though such patterns are both long established and entirely characteristic of normal connected speech—even in the non-localized forms of intentionally 'standard' discourse.[41] Variant forms such as *an'* (for *and*) or *'ad* (for *had*)—in phonetic terms [ən] and [əd]—which naturally occur in all connected speech in response to patterns of rhythms and stress are thus regularly ascribed only to the speakers from the lower sections of society, and assimilated into the fictional non-standard which results. The elderly Mrs Lucas in Mrs Humphry Ward's novel *Marcella* is given utterances such as ' "I've talked to 'er" ', whereas Marcella's own speech (much as in the 'corrected' forms of modern adoptive RP)[42] maintains intact the unelided forms of the written language (' "How long has she been like this?" ')[43]—in spite of the fact that an accurate transcription of the latter, even in 'good' speech, would have to acknowledge identical [h]-loss in unstressed grammatical words such as *had* and *her*: /ˈhaʊ ˈlɒŋ əz ʃɪ bɪn ˈlaɪk ðɪs/. Such circumstances present us with a paradox which is frequent in literary depictions of the spoken word, evident here in the fact that whereas authorial observations of the stress patterns of speech may indeed at times give highly accurate indications of the rhythms of spoken English, chosen distributions of these patterns within the fictional world can instead erroneously tend to suggest their role as a differentiating feature of marked social import. Literary fictions that the 'polite' pronounce all words and syllables as if under equal stress can, in consequence, be foregrounded out of all relationship to reality.

Similar paradigms are mapped on to the elision of /l/. ' "It's almost time you went" ', says the gentlemanly John Rokesmith in *Our Mutual Friend*, ' "I a'most believed as you'd giv' me the slip" ', says Rogue Riderhood in the same novel, further encoding popular assumptions that whilst heroes, heroines, and members of the upper classes invariably articulate all words with unremitting attention to graphemic propriety, only those in the lower ranks display the simplifications of speech which, at least to a phonetician, are characteristic of all informal spoken English. Authors as well as writers on the language, however, aligned accent barriers and social barriers with some rigidity in the ways in which they chose to represent these particular nuances of speech. Elision was construed as 'negligence', and dichotomies of *a'most*/*almost*, or *a'ready*/*already* appeal unashamedly to the social prejudices which result. Liberally assigned to servants and subordinates (' "A'most all the red washed out of it" ', says Molly the servant in Mrs Henry Wood's *Johnny Ludlow,* ' "Back a'ready?" ', asks Rogue Riderhood in *Our Mutual Friend*), an unnatural exemption from such features is consequently granted to those characters who are presented as being located in the middle and upper sections of society.

Notions of the 'proper' realization of the initial sound of words such as *which* and *what* provide a further case in point, concisely revealing other ways in which fiction made use of contemporary images (and associated evaluations) of speakers and speech to marked effect. Words such as *which* had, of course, traditionally been distinguished from potential homophones such as *witch* by the quality of the initial consonant. In phonetic terms, whereas *witch* uses an initial labio-velar semi-vowel /w/, *which* began with /hw/, a glide cluster which can, in relevant words, be traced back to Old English: *whale* derives from *hwael, while* from *hwil.* Confusion between the two is, however, evident even in early Middle English in occasional spellings and it is clear that this pattern of differentiation had, at least in some varieties, begun to fade long before the late eighteenth century. While seventeenth-century phoneticians still recognize /hw/ as a phoneme distinct from /w/, the merger of these two sounds must already have been an ongoing process. Variations in use nevertheless continued well into the late eighteenth and nineteenth centuries though in this period the change was to take on still greater resonances in prevailing language attitudes and prescriptive sensibilities. After all, by merging /hw/ and /w/ yet another example of '[h]-dropping' was apparently made manifest, a situation which was inevitably regarded with disfavour. Prescriptive reaction to this development was therefore all too predictable. Thomas Batchelor in 1809, for example, specifies that the use of /w/ for /hw/ is a clear indication of 'depraved provincial pronunciation', while John Walker conversely proscribes it as a specifically Cockney fault which tends to 'weaken and empoverish the pronunciation'. 'The aspirate *h* is often sunk, particularly in the capital, where we do not find the least distinction of sound between *while* and *wile, whet* and *wet*', Walker hence declares, isolating another feature of down-market London speech from which he intended to preserve the 'best' pronunciation of the day. As remedy, offenders were therefore recommended to 'collect all the words of this description from a dictionary, and write them down', afterwards forcibly enunciating them with an initial aspirate until perfection is attained. The well-attested reliance on visual authority as the rightful guide to 'good' pronunciation is made abundantly clear by the terms of this proffered counsel.

Similar comments appear throughout the nineteenth century as variation between [hw] and [w] in relevant words is, at least in theory, imbued with marked social correlations, demarcating 'well bred' and 'vulgar', 'educated' and 'ignorant' with seeming—if subjective—precision. Its loss is affiliated by many writers solely to the 'illiterate', 'negligent', and 'careless', and to the sheer social unacceptability of those who dare, in any circumstance, to drop an [h].

As a result, authors too were readily to embrace the use of /hw/ and /w/ or, in terms of spelling, <wh> and <w> as another useful symbol of the linguistic polarities of status. Mrs Gamp is made to select *wile* and not *while*, *wen* and not *when*. In *Nicholas Nickleby*, it is this which (among other things) serves to distinguish the direct speech of the repossessing bailiffs from that of the dispossessed owner Mr Mantalini: ' "*What's* the demd total?" ', demands the latter. ' "A good half of *wot's* here isn't paid for I des-say, and *wot* a consolation oughtn't that to be" ', announces Mr Scaley, one of the bailiffs, as he assumes control of the property.[44] Magwitch, the convict and Pip's benefactor in *Great Expectations*, Benjamin, the 'young retainer' at Mrs Todger's London boarding-house in *Martin Chuzzlewit*, the vast armies of the London poor in Gissing's oeuvre, and the clerkly Mr Polly of H. G. Wells, are all intentionally united in their inferior social status by their disregard for the graphemic, and assumed phonemic, properties of <h> in this respect. In the sporting world of Robert Surtees's novels and journalism, it is this which is foregrounded to great effect in the horse dealers and grooms whom we encounter. ' "If a man gets spilt it don't argufy much wether its done from play or from wice" ', asseverates Benjamin Buckram, combining his infelicities of <w>/<wh> with alternations of <v> and <w>, the intended social resonances of which are too familiar to need discussion. Mr Sponge's horse-groom is accorded the same complex of features: ' "one of them tight-laced candlestick priests wot abhors all sorts of wice and immorality" '.[45] To use *wether* for *whether*, *wich* for *which*, or *wot* for *what* is thus, in both fictional and prescriptive sensibilities, to contravene the assumed proprieties of 'elegant speech' and thus to be consigned, almost automatically, to the lower reaches of society.

Such demarcations of norm and deviation, falling so neatly alongside demarcations of status, form the stuff of fiction in more ways than one. In actual fact, as even a careful reading of Walker's comments in 1791 on this head reveal, the loss of distinction between /hw/ and /w/ was prevalent far outside his specified confines of the 'vulgar'. As the philologist Eric Dobson has pointed out, even in 'educated' speech this shift must have been commonplace by the end of the eighteenth century. Charles Smith in 1866 makes the compromises which were being made with reality on this score particularly clear. Conforming to expected prescriptive sensibilities, Smith duly gives the 'omission of *h* after *w*' as 'a fault highly detrimental to correct pronunciation', aligning its loss with both the non-standard and the incorrect. Immediately afterwards, however, Smith identifies this stated 'error' as one which 'is committed by the majority of educated people'.[46] Images of correctness exist at odds with the actualities of usage as descriptive truth once more enters an uneasy relationship with prescriptive fiction. Such dichotomies were to prove remarkably persistent. As Alexander Ellis patiently stressed three years later, 'in London and in the South of England (wh) is seldom pronounced', thereby pointing out the weaknesses in popular assumptions that 'to write *wot* for *what* is thought to indicate a bad vulgar pronunciation'.[47] Nevertheless, fictions of speech in this context were evidently widespread far outside the discourse of Mrs Gamp and Magwitch and prevalent notions of correctness continued to advise the 'correct' use of /hw/ long after its loss for the mass of the population. The phonetician Henry Sweet, by the end of the nineteenth century, is scathing about speakers who retain this use of /hw/ in accordance with elocutionary tenets and artificial notions of correctness, rather than taking note of the realities of the language:

If we look at the tendencies of natural speech, we must confess that it is nearly extinct, although it cannot be denied that many born Southerners pronounce it in ordinary speech. The question is, do any of them do so naturally, apart from the influence of elocutionary habits, or Scotch or Irish parentage? This question I am inclined to answer doubtfully with no: we must, I think, admit that though (wh) is a Standard English sound, it is not a *natural* Standard English sound.[48]

As Sweet's comments confirm, it was the primacy of language attitudes in this context which contributed to the 'unnatural' retention of /hw/—especially, we may imagine, in the more formal registers of speech when speakers are most often concerned to retain (and reproduce) the accepted proprieties of what is commonly presented as the 'best' language.

In both prescriptive and literary works, it was the connotative rather than the denotative which was therefore to be privileged in appropriate readings in this context; ' "You've told me *what* you think will happen" ', says Dr Seward in Bram Stoker's *Dracula*, ' "The gard'ner *wot* didn't remember" ', says Mr Bilder, the keeper of the zoological gardens to whom he is talking.[49] The implied social values (and cultural resonances) of *what* and *wot* are again profoundly dissimilar even though, in actual fact, respective pronunciations of both would usually have been identical for many speakers of the day. Nevertheless, this use of *wot* rather than *what* was, in particular, to rise into a pervasive marker of 'illiterate speech' throughout nineteenth- (and twentieth-) century literature. Trading on that system of social resonances, and accompanying social stereotypes, which surrounded assumptions about the correctness of continuing to differentiate *which* and *witch*, *what* and *watt*, graphemically divergent forms such as *wot* came to serve as a habitual leitmotiv of the lower classes: ' "Wot job?" ', asks the long-legged young man who runs off with David's box in *David Copperfield*, ' "I know *wot* it is to be loud, and I know *wot* it is to be soft" ', says Rogue Riderhood in *Our Mutual*

Friend. The relevant (though erroneous) equation is once again that what looks 'wrong' must also sound 'wrong'. In this respect, the aesthetic disharmonies of *wot*—indeed 'illiterate' though perfectly accurate in terms of sound—have in fact proved remarkably enduring in these sociosymbolic associations. ' "*You wot?*" ', says the Cockney Ryan Topps in Zadie Smith's *White Teeth* (2000), for example, still affirming these particular continuities with the past even though Smith's multicultural London is far removed from that depicted by Dickens in, say, *Bleak House* or *Little Dorrit*.[50] As this suggests, the old stereotypes can survive intact, the use of *wot* even as we enter the twenty-first century still continuing to generate these well-established (and entirely connotative) values of ignorance and of lower social station—in spite of the evident incompatibilities between subjective fiction and objective fact in this respect for the vast majority of English speakers.[51] Modern phoneticians on the other hand reject the proprieties of /hw/ in English with little dissimulation. 'Those who use it almost always do so as the result of a conscious decision: persuaded that /hw-/ is a desirable pronunciation, they modify their native accent in this direction', J. C. Wells affirms: '/hw/ is nowadays in England found principally among the speech-conscious and in adoptive RP'.[52] Nevertheless, as the evidence of such 'speech-conscious' preferences suggest, in this matter popular language attitudes can remain markedly conservative, still at times trading on a frame of reference in which images of non-standardness can evidently remain valid in present as well as past—and not least of course in the appropriate sociocultural interpretation of *wot* and other relevant features in modern literature.

Similarly exact correlations between prescriptive fictions of speech, and appropriate delineations of speech in fiction, are well attested on a number of occasions. Phonemic mergers—such indeed as that of /hw/ and /w/—regularly, as we have seen, formed a target for proscriptive censure as writers on the language endeavoured to constrain a force of change which manifestly reduced distinctions in the spoken language. This was especially the case given the fact that parallel differentiations in the written language meanwhile remained intact. Attitudes to the vocalization of post-vocalic and final [r] as in *car, cart* (now /kɑː/ /kɑːt/), as well as to the import of intrusive [r], have of course already widely illustrated this particular set of preconceptions.[53] The continued graphemic distinctions between <er>, <ir<, and <ur> in words such as *fern, fir,* and *fur,* in spite of a phonemic merger in this context which is traceable to the seventeenth century (and certainly well established by the end of the eighteenth)[54] were, in identical ways, to produce considerable resistance among writers within the prescriptive tradition.[55] John Walker, amongst many others, decisively promotes the loss of such 'correct' distinctions as an unmistakable symbol of a social identity outside the polite, duly excluding it from the 'standard' he intends to document. It has, he asserts, 'a grossness in it approaching to vulgarity'.[56] Relevant enunciations in which such a development has taken place stand as evidence of 'a coarse vulgar pronunciation', Walker stresses;[57] it is therefore the 'delicate difference' of the 'true sound' which should instead be maintained for all who wish to align themselves with 'good' speech.

Prescriptive lexis again enforces subjective connotations (and subjective inequalities) as the 'true' and 'delicate' is opposed to the 'coarse', 'vulgar', and 'gross'. Both the 'true' and the 'delicate' are, however, also entirely fictive at this date as a careful reading of Walker's text reveals. The 'true' position is in fact that in which a merged sound in /ɜ:/ was, then as now, used by 'polite' as well as 'vulgar' for all relevant words in that 'best' English which stands as Walker's ideal. Prescriptive ideology and phonemic reality nevertheless regularly diverge in the representation of the direct speech of lower-status characters, the legacy of popular prescriptive ideals in this context tending to linger on throughout the nineteenth century, infusing literature as well as works on language. Thomas Batchelor, Benjamin Smart, and George Vandenhoff (among many others) all attempted, with much inconsistency and self-contradiction, to sustain these prestigious patterns of the past, stressing images of 'correctness' which current usage all too often belied. Likewise authors too came to share, and even to collude in, this pattern of cultural stereotyping, willingly drawing on conceptions of the 'vulgarity' of pronouncing <er>, <ir>, and <ur> as a single phoneme by incorporating significant patterns of respelling within the paradigms of ostensibly 'illiterate' speech which they adopt for a range of words affected by this change. Smollett's characterization of Win Jenkins in *The Expedition of Humphry Clinker* as a notably 'illiterate' speaker (and writer) made good use of this feature, giving forms such as *shurt* for *shirt*, *murcy* for *mercy*, *burth* for *birth*. Articulations of this kind are evidently still embedded in the standard ideology (and its sociocultural correlates) of a century later, duly being utilized by George Gissing as appropriate stigma of linguistic vulgarity, and especially Cockney vulgarity, in his own novels. Contrastive iterations of *girl* and *gurl* are hence made to mark out intended contrasts in acceptability—in spite of objectively identical realizations of both in /ˈgɜ:l/. Likewise, in *Oliver Twist*, the social degradation of Oliver's birth is further compounded by its deliberate location by Dickens in the *wurkus*, the suggested enunciation of its initial syllable by the nurse who brings Oliver into the world effectively being made to convey the realms of the ignorant and uneducated—regardless of the fact that the pronunciation thereby suggested was again not incompatible with the speech of those in the highest ranks: '"Lor bless her dear heart, when she has lived as long as I have, sir, and had thirteen children of her own, and all of 'em dead except two, and them in the wurkus [/ˈwɜ:k/-] with me, she'll know better than to take on in that way, bless her dear heart"'.[58] Dickens's further specifications of divergent grammar and idiom of course merely offer additionally unambiguous confirmation of these intended negative affiliations for the use of a merged sound in this context.

Allocating pronunciations of this order to underclass alone in the fictional world of the novel serves, however, both to confirm prevalent prejudices about pronunciation as well as to endorse the relevant criteria of acceptability, both social and linguistic, which were often relentlessly (if erroneously) imposed upon variation and its attendant developments. Nineteenth-century fiction can thereby serve to reveal illustrations of ideological bias as opposed to straightforward linguistic facts in ways which are obviously parallel to those already discussed in the context of [h]-dropping or the use of [r]. Indeed, as John Lucas reminds us, literature rarely tends to be 'a straightforward representation', either of language or of society. As he adds, 'it rather suppresses, congeals and refracts…, revealing itself in its internal contradictions and omissions as not external to, but as part of, a total social process'.[59] Language attitudes to the perceived 'vulgarity' of using the lengthened *a* (and *o*) before voiceless fricatives, as in words such as *last, bath,* or *off* are, for example, frequently refracted in literature in identical ways. Though iterations of *orf* ([ˈɔːf]) now suggest old-fashioned RP (or the Royal Family),[60] and enunciations such as [ˈklɑːs] are regarded as a common marker of the non-localized norms of speech, in the eighteenth and nineteenth centuries, as we have seen, such forms were conversely depicted in much prescriptive writing as emblematic of sociolects outside the socially acceptable,[61] and as redolent in particular of the negative linguistic prestige of the Cockney. They therefore often appear in the literature of the period in functions which tend to amplify these perceived social values, deliberately trading on the negative proscriptions (and social stereotypes) which may thereby be implied.

Gissing's first novel, *Workers in the Dawn,* which he published in 1880, makes use, for example, of relatively dense notations of low-status London speech to this end. Intentionally 'deviant' enunciations of relevant words figure highly alongside other diacritics of the non- and sub-standard. ' "I'll learn yer … I'll say the words first, an' then you say 'em *arfter*" ', dictates Mrs Blatherwick, a slatternly London landlady, to the young Arthur Golding. ' "Now, if I'll pay for the lad … will you tackle Hannah Clinkscales, and make her let him *horff* his work two or three nights a week for an hour or so?" ', says Ned Quirk, a seller of baked potatoes in the same novel.[62] Forms such as *arfter* and *horff*, just like the use of *horsespitle* (for *hospital*) by Jo, the Cockney crossing-sweeper in Dickens's *Bleak House,* or *parsties* by Barkis in *David Copperfield,* signify once again by their inorganic <r> those conventions of 'illiteracy' which were apparently to predispose so many speakers against using lengthened sounds of this kind. As Alexander Ellis recorded in attempted explanation, it was in part the aesthetic demerits of such forms which seemed to contribute to that sense of disfavour which could surround their use ('this dread arises from the fear that if [speakers] said (aask, laaf), they would be accused of the vulgarity of inserting an *r,* and when *arsk, larf,* are written, they "look so very vulgar" '),[63] an argument which, as we have seen, particularly came into play in contemporary considerations of the perceived feminine proprieties of speech. Certainly the repeated use of *orf* and *arsk* in, say, the discourse of the zoo-keeper in Bram Stoker's *Dracula*—especially given the cumulative effect of other usages which are likewise intentionally excluded from standard forms of speech (*'owling* for *howling*, *makin'* for *making*, as well the plentiful use of elision)—would undoubtedly have contributed to an impression in which such forms stand as theoretically unambiguous diacritics of lower social status, and of course of 'vulgarity' too.

It was precisely these sociocultural overtones on which contemporary novelists drew. Though the <r> was inserted merely as a diacritic of length, writers were of course by no means unconscious of the symbolic potential of 'vulgarity' implied by the visual deviations which resulted. The large group of words in which <er> had traditionally been pronounced with /ar/, such as *serve, service, certain,* or *verdict,* provides ample illustration of this same principle though popular attitudes to linguistic propriety were in fact increasingly to shift tenor on this feature over the course of the late eighteenth and nineteenth centuries. While pronunciations of *servant* as *sarvant* had long been acceptable, newly articulated notions of correctness instead tended to encode such usages as unfashionable and therefore untenable.[64] Walker, for example, notes under the word *merchant* in his dictionary that, although an enunciation such as *marchant* had been entirely admissible thirty years earlier, even having been sanctioned by Sheridan, it was now to be regarded as 'gross and vulgar'. It was, he added, with marked proscriptive intent, 'only to be heard among the lower orders of the people'.[65] Sensitization to this new unacceptability, inspired as it was by the patterns of the written language, duly comes to the fore in literary texts too. ' "He makes hisself a sort o' sarvent to her" ', says Mr Peggotty of Ham in *David Copperfield;* ' "he sarves my turn" ', says Benjamin Buckram, the horse-dealer in Robert Surtees's *Mr Sponge's Sporting Tour.* ' "A pleasure you *may* call it, sir, with parfect truth" ', says the coachman in Cuthbert Bede's *Adventures of Mr. Verdant Green.* ' "My ser-vent will show you the way" ', says the Master of Brazenface College in the same novel, in a contrast (*parfect/ser-vant*) which is well established in the prevailing social and linguistic structures, and their relevant shifts in extralinguistic value.

An awareness of such synchronic and diachronic contexts in language and social meaning can in fact often usefully illuminate the less obvious details of pronunciation which are, on occasion, employed by the novelists of the past. One habit of speech which is regularly assigned by Dickens to Mr Peggotty in *David Copperfield* provides a case in point: ' "Mas'r Davy, . . . You han't no call to be afeerd of me: but I'm kiender muddled" '; ' "When she did, she kneeled down at my feet, and kiender said to me, as if it were her prayers, how it all came to be" '; ' "My niece was kiender daughter-like to me" '.[66] Additional examples are sprinkled elsewhere throughout the text. Confined exclusively to Mr Peggotty, this restricted distribution perhaps renders it tempting to assume that these repeated forms represent an idiophonic pattern along the lines of that fondness for /ʤ/ in the speech of Mrs Gamp. This is not, however, the case. On the contrary, utterances of *kind* as *kyind*, or *garden* as *gyarden*, are well attested in writings on the language as they rise and fall in favour over the late eighteenth and nineteenth centuries. Dickens's acuity in terms of language (and contemporary language attitudes) merely leads him to explore their use as an additional means of encoding the social divide within his novels.[67] *Kiender*, with its <ie> digraph, is thus selected as the means by which Dickens can effectively denote the presence of a palatal glide /j/, a frequent and once highly fashionable phenomenon occurring after the consonants /k/ and /g/ in words such as *kind* and *garden*. Walker, for example, is still stressing the use of this feature at the end of the eighteenth century as a fundamental marker of refinement in speech; enunciations such as 'ke-ard', 'ke-art', 'ghe-ard', or 're-ghe-ard' (for *card*, *cart*, *guard*, and *regard*) are specified as particularly characteristic of 'polite pronunciation'. His comments in his *A Rhetorical Grammar* (1781) are still more explicit with reference to the positive social values which such realizations still comported. Walker hence describes the glide /j/ as a 'smooth and elegant sound', its presence in forms such as *ke-ind*, *ke-ard*, or *re-geard* indeed 'sufficient to mark the speaker as either coarse or elegant, as he adopts and neglects it'.[68]

Such distinguishing marks of elegant speech were to suffer a rapid decline. By 1825, Samuel Oliver is happy to deploy an identical binary divide (*kind*, *kyind*) though by such means he demarcates not the 'coarse' and 'elegant' but, respectively, the ordinary and 'affected'. As he states, it is the palatal glide which operates as a sign of demerit, standing as a signifier of 'affected speakers wherever they be among us'.[69] Alexander Ellis later in the nineteenth century confirms the continued reversal of that pattern of social allegiances which pronunciations of this order had come to suggest. 'Old-fashioned', 'antiquated', and 'rapidly dying out', they were, he writes, by this point more liable to be the hallmark of the socially inferior rather than the truly refined.[70] It is of course in such values that its utility was recognized by the authors of the day. Realizations such as 'gjurl' or 'gjell' for *girl* thus come to stand as additional markers of phonetic impropriety, used alongside [h]-dropping and double negation in the novels of George Gissing, for example, as in this speech by the well-intentioned if vulgar lodger Mrs Cheeseman in *The Town Traveller*: ' "Now, see 'ere, Polly. You're a young gyell, my dear, and a 'andsome gyell, as we all know, and you've only one fault, which there ain't no need to mention it." '[71] The use of the palatal glide in such ways becomes part of that armoury of features by which social, cultural, and linguistic values may be conveyed to the discerning reader, the graphemic distortion which its use involved presenting yet another aspect of 'illiterate' speech over the course of the century.

Such patterns, whether of *wos* or *wot*, or *gjell, sarvice,* or *'ill* all serve to delineate the details of the social landscape in many novels of the nineteenth century, the graphemic irregularities depicted trading on attitudes and assumptions about pronunciation which were commonplace in much popular comment on language. Though there are exceptions, authors were, of course, on the whole writing from the point of view of the standard and the standard ideology in which, as we have seen, labels of non- and sub-standard were readily applied to features of pronunciation which either were new, or merely differed from those more ideal states of the language which many writers would have liked to see in existence. As many of these examples illustrate, it was especially nineteenth-century reactions to sound changes in progress which were to provide a rich source of such intentionally contrastive markings. Given a London-based literary culture, as Norman Page has noted, 'provinciality' in all its senses tends all too readily to be equated with inferiority.[72] This was of course the appropriate paradigm in which attitudes to accent, and representations of its use, were habitually worked out in literature and works on language alike. As such, literary works filled a potentially important role in the ways in which they too were able to contribute to, and even disseminate, the prevalent notions of 'right' and 'wrong' in speech, blending entertainment with implicit instruction in the stereotypes of 'polite speech', as well as in those social alliances which such embedded value systems suggested. The novels, poetry, and drama of the age in a number of ways hence reinforced 'that habitual association of ideas' between the proprieties of grapheme and phoneme which was, as we have seen, earlier discussed by Thomas Sheridan in his own intent to diffuse awareness of a national standard of speech. Literature can thereby also decisively partake in that process by which, in Sheridan's terms, the linguistic 'consciousness' may be 'awaken'd'—and not least in the ways in which such preconceptions about pronunciation were regularly presented in terms of a dominantly social discourse in which comedy may attend error, and respect will almost inevitably accompany its absence.

From all accounts Dickens's influence in this respect was potentially great. Certainly, as Chapter 4 has already discussed, a number of observers in the later nineteenth century aver that Uriah Heep alone exerted sufficient dissuasion in his prominent habits of [h]-loss to counter traditionally [h]-less realizations in words such as *humble.*[73] Nevertheless, in spite of such overt commendations of the linguistic side-effects of literary texts, it must still be remembered that most literature would in fact have reached a relatively narrow audience—even given the much greater levels of literacy attested in the nineteenth century. Price alone proved a barrier to widespread circulation, rendering literary texts commodities of luxury rather than necessity. A copy of Sir Walter Scott's *Ivanhoe* would, for example, have cost 30*s.* in 1820 in spite of its well-attested popularity; ten years earlier, his *Lady of the Lake* had been priced still higher at 42*s*. Though, as this confirms, prices did gradually decrease,[74] the average cost of a book by the mid-nineteenth century was still between 8*s*. and 9*s*., a relatively substantial amount given that, by the 1830s, a skilled London worker would be earning only 30*s*. to 33*s*. a week.[75] To spend one-third or even half of one's weekly wages on the purchase of a single book required a commitment to literature beyond the range of most people in the middle and lower ranks of society. Even use of the circulating libraries was beyond the means of many; Charles Mudie, the founder of Mudie's Lending Library, charged, for example, one guinea for a year's subscription in 1842 though even this was half as much as many of his rivals.

In a number of ways therefore, though literature did endorse popular fictions of correctness and incorrectness in the contrastive modes of speech representation which it often deployed, factors such as these can suggest that its influence was on the whole more limited than might perhaps initially be assumed. Dickens's decision to publish his novels in parts (like a number of other novelists such as William Ainsworth, Charles Lever, William Thackeray, and Anthony Trollope) is, however, potentially of more interest in this context, securing, as it did, a far wider readership than would otherwise have been possible. Such a format cost in the region of 3*d*. a week or 1*s*. a month, spreading the total cost of a novel over a considerable period of time. It was a mode of publication which thereby, as Richard Altick notes, 'appealed to the great body of middle-class readers who could afford to spend a shilling every month but not to lay out a cool guinea or a guinea and a half at a time'.[76] Even in the long term, it was to prove a more economical way to purchase books for, as Altick points out, if *The Posthumous Papers of the Pickwick Club* (Dickens's first novel, published in twenty monthly parts between April 1836 and November 1837) had originally appeared in book form, the price would have been around 31*s*.6*d*, a level which would clearly have been out of reach of many who gave the novel the enthusiastic reception it received. As it was, even after buying all the parts separately, the total cost was only 20*s*., and only one further shilling was necessary to have the whole volume bound into book form.

The popularity of this method of publication was well attested. Chapman and Hall, for example, printed some four hundred copies of the first part of *Pickwick*. By the second half of 1837, as the novel neared its conclusion, they were instead producing over forty thousand copies of each monthly part. Around fifty thousand copies of each number of *Nicholas Nickleby* were sold during its publication in 1838–9, Part I of *Our Mutual Friend* sold thirty thousand copies in the first three days alone and, as Altick notes, the 'penny edition' of *Oliver Twist* sold 150,000 copies in three weeks in 1871.[77] Mowbray Morris, writing in *The Fortnightly Review* in 1882, claimed that, in the twelve years since Dickens's death, the sale of Dickens's works in England totalled 4,239,000 volumes.[78] Given such figures, it is hardly surprising that Dickens's work and characters were to secure such a hold upon the national, and public, imagination—especially since each copy was presumably read by more than one individual (not least given the emphasis placed on reading aloud within common Victorian eulogies on the pleasures of the home).[79] Few people could moreover read or listen to a Dickens novel without being aware of the important role which language, and significant variations within it, played in creating the overall texture of his work.

Dickens's own sensitivity to voice is well known; his early training in shorthand, his interest in the stage and in the dramatic potential of the spoken word, as well as his own public readings of his work, all attest a marked responsiveness to the nuances of speech. His imagination worked, as his daughter Mamie records, in profoundly aural as well as visual ways; she recalls him in the process of composition performing a 'facial pantomime... talking rapidly in a low voice... peopling his study with other men, women, and children, hearing other voices'.[80] His delineations of direct speech, as a result, often form a salient facet of characterization within his novels, voices often being sharply individualized by means of his strategic manipulation of the written and spoken interfaces of language. Though Walker appears explicitly by name only as one of Miss Blimber's preferred authorities in *Dombey and Son*,[81] Dickens betrays a similar responsiveness to the fictions of prescriptive ideology and accompanying language attitudes in his depictions of speech. Early recognized as being fundamentally a '*class* writer',[82] he makes liberal use of perceived, and propagated, correlations between language and social status, encoding in abundance received stereotypes about the cultural, social, as well as linguistic values which are present within the structured variations of speech.

A plethora of marked and unmarked forms locate Dickens's characters in social space, the stratified distribution of orthographical improprieties corresponding clearly to the notional norms and deviations of nineteenth-century speech. Socially sensitive variables such as the variation between [hw] and [w] or between *obleege* and *oblige* are deployed, as we have already seen, in ways which reinforce established views on the properties and possession of literate speech. Hyperlects as well as basilects attract modifications of spelling designed to suggest divergence from a norm: ' "Have I brought ruin upon the best and purest creature that ever blessed a demnition vagabond! Demmit, let me go" ', exclaims Mr Mantalini in *Nicholas Nickleby*, ' "Then my ears did not deceive me, and it's not wa-a-x work" ', says Lord Frederick Verisopht in the same novel, his vocalic attenuations effectively conveying the affected drawl deemed typical of the aristocracy.[83] Orthographical variations, just like that more explicit comment on language within the prescriptive tradition, are often employed in distinctly evaluative ways. Magwitch's first utterances in *Great Expectations* reveal him as an outcast from polite society while his status as convict is as yet unknown. Jo's use of language in *Bleak House* concisely establishes patterns of social inequality by linguistic means: ' "They're wots left...out of a sov'ring as wos give me by a lady in a wale as sed she wos a servant, and as come to my crossin one night and asked to be shown this 'ere oust and the oust wot him as you giv the writin to died at, and the berrin ground wot he's berrid in." '[84]

The combination of such forms with malapropisms such as *malefactors* for *manufacturers* by Mr Plornish in *Little Dorrit*, or *consequential* for *consecrated* by Jo himself only serve to enhance a sub-text often founded on the appreci-ation of linguistic 'ignorance', placed against the conventional proprieties of the 'educated' in a pattern which once again reinforces those stereotypical preconceptions of a literate norm which is located primarily in the middle and upper sections of society. For those readers of the middle ranks who were indeed felt to be Dickens's true audience (as one reviewer commented, 'it is the air and breath of middle-class respectability which fills the books of Mr. Dickens'),[85] the complex of marked forms which distinguish the speech of those lower down the social scale merely heightened awareness of the normative principles of linguistic and social behaviour to which conformity was often presented as important.

As Dickens was well aware, his selections from among the range of pos-sible options for the representation of speech were by no means value free. Aligned within prevailing linguistic ideologies, and firmly embedded in the wider social and cultural environments of his readership, it is, as Carter and Nash affirm, precisely this 'intermeshing of language and style in the *context* of social systems and institutions' which serves to convey, at least in part, those more ideological dimensions of literature.[86] 'Particular linguistic or stylistic choices', they stress, 'are not innocent value-free selections from a system'. Instead such choices 'conceal or reveal certain realities rather than others, establishing or reinforcing ideologies in the process',[87] a precept which is equally important in terms of the standard ideology and the pro-found status-consciousness with which its manifestations, especially in terms of accent, were endowed.

The evaluative bias present within those fictions of speech used by Dickens (and other writers) is of course inescapable, the oppositions of 'lit-erate' and 'illiterate' speech serving, as already illustrated, to encode prevalent stereotypes about the nature of class and its linguistic correspondences, often largely irrespective of the facts of linguistic reality (though displaying marked conformity with the expressed tenets of language attitudes). The fact that lexical, syntactic, and grammatical choices can also intervene in this para-digm only serves to enhance its effectiveness. Dickens can, however, be much more subtle than such schematic patterns suggest. Indeed it is often in his ability to confront such sociolinguistic stereotypes directly—as well as the fallacies behind them—that he is in fact most successful.

Manners, and their role in setting forth 'a culture's hum and buzz of implication',[88] form of course a salient territory of the novel, a fact which is no less relevant in considering their specifically linguistic aspects. When, in *David Copperfield*, Dickens presents us with the graphemic propriety of David himself, of his aunt Betsey Trotwood, and of the charismatic James Steerforth, and develops the contrast between this and the heavy use of marked forms which characterizes the speech of the Yarmouth boatman Mr Peggotty, we are tempted to assume, with Lionel Trilling, that it is 'inescapably true that in the novel manners make man'.[89] Demarcating the divide between 'polite' and 'vulgar', the distribution of marked and unmarked forms corresponds closely to the evaluative norms of 'correctness' and 'incorrectness', 'literate' and 'illiterate', 'cultured' and 'provincial', or 'superior' and 'inferior' which are deployed with such regularity in contemporary writings on the language. Language, and especially accent, was seen as denoting 'breeding', and 'moral' as well as 'intellectual culture', as *Talking and Debating* stressed in 1856.[90] Or as Williams had expounded six years earlier, 'language, both oral and written, is the exponent of the condition of the mind; when mean and inappropriate, it infers that the habits of life and the condition of the mind are equally mean and uncultivated'.[91]

Certainly it is this (amongst other things) which underpins the gentlemanlike James Steerforth's negative perceptions of Mr Peggotty and his family as being merely 'that sort of people'.[92] The patterns of qualitative foregrounding employed within the novel in the representation of speech effectively serve to map out the relevant stereotypes of social and linguistic inequality: ' "I'll pound it, it's wot you do yourself, sir" ', says Mr Peggotty, addressing Steerforth, ' "and wot you do well—right well!" '.[93] Common cultural equations of accent and identity, of external as a signifier of internal, and moreover of 'provincial' as synonymous with 'inferior', are all involved in Steerforth's subsequent estimation of the nature of social distance, difference, and deviation in this context.

> 'Why, there's a pretty wide separation between them and us,' said Steerforth, with indifference. 'They are not to be expected to be as sensitive as we are. Their delicacy is not to be shocked, or hurt very easily. They are wonderfully virtuous, I dare say—some people contend for that, at least; and I am sure I don't want to contradict them—but they have not very fine natures, and they may be thankful that, like their coarse rough skins, they are not easily wounded.'[94]

David assumes that Steerforth is merely jesting in his iteration of common (and prejudicial) assumptions about the nature of the lower orders. Nevertheless, as subsequent events reveal, he was indeed in earnest.

Language informs the reader's perceptions of that 'separation' which is recognized by Steerforth. While Steerforth is characterized by his 'nice voice', and the graphemic and grammatical proprieties which inevitably accompany his speech, Mr Peggotty is distinguished by the contrary. The value-laden forms of accent tempt common value judgements in response.

Dickens, however, in a highly successful form of linguistic didacticism, uses fiction to expose common fallacies about these prevailing sociolinguistic stereotypes, making it entirely clear that judgements made on such grounds may all too often be misjudgements, with all the inadequacies which such errors imply. 'Handsome is as handsome does' is of course the rightful adage to be applied, and it is deeds not words (and their pronunciation) which prove the true gentleman. As Norman Blake has noted in his own work on the use, and associations, of the non-standard in literature: 'An accent is no guide to a man's character, though people may make assumptions on that basis',[95] and it is precisely this process of mistaken assumption which takes place in *David Copperfield* (or, for that matter, more recently in David Lodge's novel *Nice Work*).[96] Dickens deliberately heightens the use of 'illiterate speech' by Mr Peggotty as we move towards realization of Steerforth's duplicity with regard to Little Em'ly, Mr Peggotty's niece. As a result he exposes for endorses the processes of value judgement which are commonly invited by the stigmatizing effects of graphemic deviation. Steerforth, endowed with the delusive proprieties of 'gentlemanly' speech which to many in the nineteenth century had come to signify associations of inner worth too, is instead decisively revealed as villain:

'Why, this here candle, now!', said Mr. Peggotty, gleefully holding out his hand towards it, '*I* know wery well that arter she's married and gone, I shall put that candle theer, just that same as now. I know wery well that when I'm here o' nights (and where else should *I* live, bless your arts, whatever fortun I come into!) and she ain't here, or I ain't theer, I shall put the candle in the winder, and sit afore the fire, pretending I'm expecting of her, like I'm a doin' now. *There's* a babby for you,' said Mr. Peggotty, with another roar, 'in the form of a Sea Porkypine! Why, at the present minute, when I see the candle sparkle up, I says to myself, "She's a looking at it! Em'ly's a coming!" *There's* a babby for you, in the form of a Sea Porkypine! Right for all that,' said Mr. Peggotty, stopping in his roar, and smiting his hands together; 'fur here she is!'
     It was only Ham.[97]

Though forms such as *heer*, *art* (rather than *heart*), and *fur* (rather than unstressed *for*) are liberally used within this (and later) sections, the distancing effects of deviation are largely broken down, displaced not only by the pathos of such sustained devotion but also, and more significantly, by respect.

     The construct presented within these contrasted schema of language in *David Copperfield* is again essentially that of subjective inequality, the structured patterns of norm and deviation being used to aid mistaken assessments about the nature of superiority, inferiority, and the 'gentleman'. Similar processes still take place today of course as the data of subjective reaction tests continue to reveal, and similar weaknesses necessarily attend the operation of these ideas. By means of accent speakers continue to be judged as 'friendly' or 'polite', 'intelligent' or 'well educated', and their arguments too may be found more or less persuasive 'depending on the qualities which we implicitly attribute to them on the basis of their accent'.[98] In the context of literature, as Leech and Short point out, the very use of non-standard language similarly tends to suggest 'remoteness from the author's own language, and hence from the central standards of judgement in a novel'.[99] It is this habitual association of ideas which Dickens exploits—and confounds—so well in *David Copperfield*.

He offers a similar pattern of reassessment in *Great Expectations*, a novel in which Pip's education into a 'gentleman', in at least its dominantly social senses, leads him into disregarding those truer gentlemanly virtues which, throughout the novel, form the hallmark of Joe's character. As we have already seen, the linguistic differentials of status are closely associated with the sense of social shame which surrounds Pip's associations with the forge (and Joe's occupation as blacksmith) once his acquaintance with Miss Havisham has begun.[100] They are, however, perhaps brought out most clearly in the evident failure of discourse in Joe's meeting with the latter:

'Well!' said Miss Havisham. 'And you have reared the boy, with the intention of taking him for your apprentice; is that so, Mr. Gargery?'
'You know, Pip,' replied Joe, 'as you and me were ever friends, and it were look'd for'ard to betwixt us, as being calc'lated to lead to larks. Not but what, Pip, if you had ever made objections to the business—such as its being open to black and sut, or such-like—not but what they would have been attended to, don't you see?'[101]

As in *David Copperfield*, the widespread belief that it is external manners which alone make man (as well as determining relevant estimations of social worth) is again brought prominently to the fore. Pip, aspiring to the role of 'gentleman' and given an all too effective education into social and linguistic consciousness by Estella, is similarly made all too aware of Joe's seeming inadequacies in this respect. ' "You will not omit any opportunity of helping Joe on, a little" ', he urges Biddy before his departure: ' "Joe is a dear good fellow—in fact, I think he is the dearest fellow that ever lived—but he is rather backward in some things. For instance, Biddy, in his learning and his manners." '[102]

Pip, influenced by Estella's teaching, equates the provincial with commonness and 'disgrace', the non-localized with superiority. Joe has a surer perspective from the beginning: ' "Manners is manners, but still your elth's your elth." '[103] No 'improvement' of Joe is necessary, as later events reveal. One of 'Nature's gentlemen' (in another enduring literary stereotype), though he may drop his [h]s, employ *wot* rather than *what*, and discuss *coddleshells* rather than *codicils*, it is, as Pip comes to realize, 'the wealth of his great nature' which is most important, and not those manners, linguistic or social, which Pip would first have remedied. As Pip is made to acknowledge early in the novel, 'I wanted to make Joe less ignorant and common, that he might be worthier of my society and less open to Estella's reproach'.[104] By its end, such perceptions have been reversed, and it is his own unworthiness, in the face of Joe's unwavering fidelity, which he wishes to amend. The linguistic divide is rendered unimportant in the face of this greater truth, a corrective which many writers on the language (and on manners too) would have done well to observe in the consummate pressures which they often attempted to exert upon their readers.

The connotative values of speech, their assumed social meanings, and the misconceptions to which they may lead, are, in such ways, made into an important element of Dickens's art. His treatment of the manners and mannerisms of spoken language hence on a number of occasions functions not just as a diacritic of status (though this aspect is not neglected), but also as a means by which larger themes and issues may be explored. Almost simultaneously therefore, Dickens can endorse prevailing images of speech and speakers, allocating graphemic deviations in abundance to those located below the middle ranks (and further encoding popular images of literate and illiterate speech and their stereotypical social correlations), yet he also offers within his work a timely reminder that such superficialities of speech may disguise a deeper reality which should not be ignored. Polished speech may conceal more serious flaws; the accents and grammatical errors of the provincial or the lower orders of society, in spite of their well-attested stigmatization in nineteenth-century language attitudes, will in no way serve as images of inferiority in all respects. As the American critic Lionel Trilling wrote of the treatment of manners in the novel, 'in this part of culture assumption rules, which is often so much stronger than reason'.[105] Dickens, in his treatment of Steerforth, Mr Peggotty, Pip, and Joe (among many others), offers clear illustration of the dangers and misconceptions to which such unquestioned assumptions may lead in the context of linguistic manners, and the phonemic and grammatical sensitivities of the age.

Dickens was thus able both to encode, and also to decode, the repercussions of prescriptive ideology upon language use and language attitudes in the nineteenth century. George Gissing is, however, the novelist who perhaps demonstrates in fullest measure the ways in which the evaluative paradigms within which accent variations were so often placed could infuse literary depictions of the social world. His novels, almost without exception, betray an acute sensitivity to the nuances of speech, not only in the context of its relatively detailed representation, but also within the range of explicit comments on accent and its social overtones which regularly appear throughout his work. Conceptions of the extralinguistic values which accent could convey can rarely have been expressed with such clarity within the domains of literature. Sharing a lexis which has marked affinities with that employed by Walker in his moments of greater prescriptive excess, he describes as 'gross', 'hateful' or 'vilely grotesque' accents which deviate from the increasingly non-localized norms validated as 'standard'. Voice is developed into a signifier of more than merely social resonance, so that the presence of perceived 'refinement' in its tones is regularly used to suggest corresponding interior qualities. Descriptions of its nuances almost inevitably accompany the introduction of new characters, offering a precise sense of location within Gissing's social world. The initial description of the piano dealer Stephen Lord in *In the Year of Jubilee* is typical in this respect: 'His pronunciation fell short of refinement, but was not vulgar. Something of country accent could still be detected in it. He talked like a man who could strike a softer note if he cared to, but despised the effort.'[106]

Hugh Carnaby in *The Whirlpool*, 'the well-bred, well-fed Englishman', is likewise distinguished by 'his tongue' which 'told of age-old domination', and Alma's reactions to him are expressed in precisely the same terms: 'She was impressed by a quality in the voice, a refinement of utterance, which at once distinguished it from that of the men with whom she had been talking. It belonged to a higher social grade, if it did not express a superiority of nature.'[107] 'There was no flagrant offence in the man. He spoke with passable accent', Gissing notes of Mr Cusse, a draper's assistant in *Born in Exile*.[108] In *The Emancipated*, the acquisition of non-localized nuances of speech is presented as a marker of evident achievement in our first encounter with the heiress Cecily Doran: 'Her enunciation had the peculiar finish which is acquired in intercourse with the best cosmopolitan society, the best in a worthy sense. Four years ago, when she left Lancashire, she had a touch of provincial accent... but now it was impossible to discover by listening to her from what part of England she came.'[109]

Such distinctions, of language and of class, are, for Gissing, often fundamental to his perceptions of the struggles of his characters. Assimilation to the norms of refined London speech, and the corresponding suppression of the provincial, mark the experiences of the self-made Richard Mutimer in *Demos* or the tortured Godwin Peak in *Born in Exile*. Exile from the cultured classes is often specifically seen in linguistic as well as social terms, and to the still exiled (and socially aspiring), their language is to be emulated, if not indeed revered. Gissing's *Born in Exile*, for example, details an alienation which manifests itself in barriers of accent as well as wealth, the sociolinguistic stigma of low birth forming a recurrent topos in the novel. Born into the lower reaches of the middle orders of society ('a social sphere in which he must ever be an alien'),[110] Godwin Peak, the central character, is yet endowed with an exquisite sense of social and linguistic nuance which is continually disturbed by the language, and especially the accents, of the 'vulgar' who surround him. With 'an ear constantly tormented by the London vernacular', his reactions to those who do not share his aural sympathies are extreme:

I hate low, uneducated people! I hate them worse than the filthiest vermin!... They ought to be swept off the face of the earth!... All the grown-up creatures, who can't speak proper English and don't know how to behave themselves, I'd transport them to the Falkland Islands.[111]

Peak himself thus becomes a casualty of that prevalent impulse towards social, cultural, and linguistic cohesion. The evaluative paradigms imposed on accent, together with their cultural correlates, constantly pervade his thoughts, his reactions to others, and above all perhaps his reactions to himself:

No less introspective than in the old days... Peak, after each of his short remarks, made comparison of his tone and phraseology with those of the other speakers. Had he still any marks of the ignoble world from which he sprang? Any defect of pronunciation, any native awkwardness of utterance? Impossible to judge himself infallibly, but he was conscious of no vulgar mannerism. Though it was so long since he left Whitelaw, the accent of certain of the Professors still remained with him as an example; when endeavouring to be graceful, he was wont to hear the voice of Dr. Nares, or of Professor Barber who lectured on English literature. More recently he had been observant of Christian Moxey's speech, which had a languid elegance worth imitating in certain particulars. Buckland Warricombe was rather a careless talker, but it was the carelessness of a man who had never needed to reflect on such a matter, the refinement of whose enunciation was assured to him from the nursery. That now was a thing to be aimed at.[112]

Emulation, imitation, the problems of signifying a status he does not possess in an accent which he has assumed, impinge without respite upon Peak's consciousness. Continually monitoring his speech for the inflections which might betray his lowly origins, his obsession with speech is precisely aligned with recommendations which are familiar from the social and linguistic dicta of books like Phyfe's *How Should I Pronounce?* and the anonymous *How to Shine in Society* and *Vulgarities of Speech Corrected*. Peak has learnt his prescriptive lessons well, perhaps too well.

These correlations of accent and identity, readily encompassing cultural, intellectual, as well as social values within much contemporary writing on the language, are, as this indicates, woven deep into the texture of Gissing's work. Few other authors can rival his perspicacity in the sphere of the connotative values with which accent, by the late nineteenth century, had inextricably come to comport. In him language attitudes received their best exponent though the limited circulation of his work clearly meant that no great conversions were likely to have been achieved by such means—a fortunate circumstance perhaps, given Gissing's characteristic class-orientated vehemence on this matter. Readily engaging with prevalent fictions of speech, and encoding dominant stereotypes of speaker and speech with ease, Gissing displays an unerring eye for the detail which will convey residual vulgarity, or the fact of low origins which have still not entirely been transcended. Hence of Richard Mutimer, whose transformation from London artisan into wealthy capitalist occupies much of *Demos*, we are told: 'It was unfortunate that Richard did not pronounce the name of his bride elect [Adela] quite as it sounds on cultured lips. This may have been partly the result of diffidence; but there was a slurring of the second syllable disagreeably suggestive of vulgarity.'[113] In spite of his almost achieved ambition to marry a 'lady', the stigma of his social origins, embodied in his speech, still hampers Richard's progress towards true acceptability. As Gissing adds in a typical aphorism: 'The vulgarity of a man who tries hard not to be vulgar is always particularly distressing'.[114]

It is this emphasis on the nuanced variations of accent as unmistakable signifiers of vulgarity or, conversely, of refinement which works so strongly in Gissing's novels to reinforce the system of value judgements with which differences of speech were popularly imbued. The due proprieties of female speech were, perhaps predictably, to receive corresponding attention and Gissing's aesthetic sensibilities in this respect reveal precise alignments with that gendered bias which is, as we have seen in Chapter 5, so perceptible in many nineteenth-century accounts of language as it should be used. Prevalent ideologies of the feminine voice, and corresponding notions of 'talking like a lady', form, in fact, recurrent motifs in his characterization of women. As the elocutionist George Vandenhoff had firmly proclaimed, it was delicate enunciation which ensures both status and attractiveness for the lady.[115] Female readers of Gissing's work would certainly have found no lack of confirmation of such views. Described as 'the presiding spirit in a home fragrant of womanhood', Lilian holds an attraction for Denzil in *Denzil Quarrier* which is thus initially phrased in terms of voice ('I managed to get a word or two with her, and I liked her way of speaking'),[116] and Will's proposal to the art student Bertha Cross in *Will Warburton* refers to the linguistic as much as love in his account of the beginnings of his admiration: 'As you talked to me that morning, I knew what I know better still now, that there was no girl that I *liked* as I liked you, no girl whose face had so much meaning for me, whose voice and way of speaking so satisfied me'.[117] Whereas defeminized speech mars the 'new woman',[118] it is the external refinements of voice which reveal the true 'lady', her linguistic perfections designed to please the fastidious (and predominantly male) ear, whilst her vocalic purity is often made to take on those more widely emblematic properties expounded in nineteenth-century texts on the 'Proper Lady'. The possession of such linguistic virtues indeed provides one of the most significant revelations for Godwin Peak in *Born in Exile*, the voices of the two girls he overhears at the Whitelaw prize day bringing home to him a further facet of his social exile, here presented explicitly in terms of gender and of voice:

He had not imagined that girls could display such intelligence, and the sweet clearness of their intonation, the purity of their accent, the grace of their habitual phrases, were things altogether beyond his experience. This was not the English he had been wont to hear on female lips. His mother and his aunt spoke with propriety; their associates were soft-tongued; but here was something quite different from inoffensiveness of tone and diction. Godwin appreciated the differentiating cause. These young ladies behind him had been trained from the cradle to speak for the delight of fastidious ears; that they should be grammatical was not enough—they must excel in the art of conversational music. Of course there existed a world where only such speech was interchanged, and how inestimably happy those men to whom the sphere was native![119]

Voice, as we have seen, provides a joint symbol of exclusivity and exclusion throughout *Born in Exile*, and this is perhaps one of its most telling expositions as Peak listens attentively to the superior, and truly feminine, diction of these young ladies, yet in his own sense of inferiority is unable to enter into converse with them.

The voice that is soft, gentle, sweet, and low, often presented in popular ideologies of the feminine, as we have seen, as one of the most essential properties within contemporary stereotypes of the 'lady',[120] thus finds one of its best advocates in Gissing. In *Will Warburton*, for example, the 'soft and musical' voice of Will's mother is given prominence in her introduction in the novel, whilst that of the ineffably ladylike Rosamund Elvan is 'always subdued', with 'a range of melodious expression which caressed the ear, no matter how trifling the words she uttered'.[121] Evelyn Cloud, the Girton-educated heiress in the short story 'Our Learned Fellow-Townsman', is likewise depicted in terms of her 'soft, kindly accents' and her 'intonation of peculiar gentleness'.[122] These and other nineteenth-century Cordelias populate Gissing's novels, their articulatory 'gentleness' often inextricably linked with notions of status, just as the shrieking tones of other women are made to signify their own vulgarity, and corresponding alienation from the refined and 'literate' spheres of ladies and gentlemen.[123]

Other authors, however, were to explore this particular aspect of such prevalent fictions of speech and their specifically feminine proprieties with perhaps more caution, able to encode, but also to expose undue emphasis on these stereotypes of 'ladylike' speech. George Eliot, a novelist whose command of language in assigning nuances of identity has often been praised, deploys an awareness of prevailing language attitudes in this context with some skill.[124] Heightened feminine sensibilities towards 'proper' linguistic behaviour in fact come to form a recurrent aspect of her novels; the Miss Gunns in *Silas Marner*, Esther Lyon in *Felix Holt*, and Rosamond Vincy in *Middlemarch* are all linked by their concern for conformity with the avowedly 'ladylike' ideal, and by their corresponding preoccupation with its linguistic manifestations. Daughters of a wealthy wine-merchant from Lytherley, the Miss Gunns, for instance, readily condemn Nancy Lammeter for linguistic infelicities which they regard as incompatible with their own assumptions of status and ladylike identity:

The Miss Gunns smiled stiffly, and thought what a pity it was that these rich country people, who could afford to buy such good clothes...should be brought up in utter ignorance and vulgarity. [Nancy] actually said 'mate' for 'meat', ''appen' for 'perhaps,' and 'oss' for 'horse', which, to young ladies living in good Lytherley society, who

habitually said 'orse, even in domestic privacy and only said 'appen on the right occasions, was necessarily shocking.[125]

In George Eliot's work, such perceptions, and the value judgements on
which they are based, tend, however, to be assimilated into a wider moral
framework as, like Dickens, she willingly confronts the fallacies which can
rest behind common fictions of speech. As the critic David Daiches stressed
in 1963, for example, Eliot's novels regularly reveal the presence of an 'acute
ear for differences in conversational idiom' which is employed as 'a means of
emphasizing human variety and at the same time of linking that variety with
a central moral pattern'.[126] In representations of notions of the ladylike in
speech, and the superior sensibilities which ladies, and most notably, would-be
'ladies' are supposed to affect in this context, a similar pattern is apparent.
While the Miss Gunns react with disfavour to forms they see as 'vulgar' in
Nancy's speech, their own 'vulgarity', that of 'exclusiveness', is simultaneously revealed. The paradigm is that set forth by Eliot in 'The Natural
History of German Life' in her precept that 'More is done towards linking
the higher classes with the lower, [by] obliterating the vulgarity of exclusiveness, than by hundreds of sermons and philosophic dissertations'.[127] Language
in her novels, and attitudes to it, prove to be particularly useful ways of
expounding this belief as contemporary notions of exclusion and exclusivity
in linguistic terms are instead transposed into vehicles of moral as well as
social meaning.

Morals and manners are, as in *David Copperfield*, set into opposition
and characters such as Esther Lyon and Rosamond Vincy provide striking
examples of women who, in their initial adherence to ideologies of the feminine and ladylike as adequate emblems of identity, are unable to transcend
the dissimulations of language (and of status) in order to penetrate to the
underlying and moral realities. Social status provides, for example, a major
preoccupation for Esther Lyon in *Felix Holt*. Though her father's role is that
of independent preacher, her own ideals rest in 'refined society' and the identity of a 'lady'. Appropriately refined and ladylike airs are cultivated with
some assiduity, the bust of the evangelical preacher George Whitfield in her
father's study being covered up because of its squint, and her olfactory sensibilities requiring the purchase of wax rather than tallow candles. Her sensitivities to accent are similarly precise. Her father abides by his own moral code:
'I abstain from judging by the outward appearance only',[128] but Esther
instead adheres to the converse. The only point in Felix's favour is that 'he
speaks better English than most of our visitors'[129] and she registers a similar
approval of Harold Transome, the heir to Transome Court, in spite of his
moral nullity. As Eliot points out:

[Esther] was alive to the finest shades of manner, to the nicest distinctions of tone
and accent; she had a little code of her own about scents and colours, textures and

behaviour, by which she secretly condemned or sanctioned all things and persons. And she was well satisfied with herself for her fastidious taste, never doubting that hers was the highest standard.[130]

Such 'fastidious taste' is satisfied once Esther herself is removed, Cinderella-like, to Transome Court. Accent is again used to form a prime index of accepability: 'over and above her really generous feeling, she enjoyed Mrs Transome's accent, the high-bred quietness of her speech'.[131] The pleasure which attends listening to the latter's family stories is likewise enhanced for this highly susceptible auditor by 'that refined high-bred tone and accent which [Mrs Transome] possessed in perfection'.[132] This mastery of the symbols of social exclusivity is, however, also accompanied, as Esther gradually comes to realize, by a corresponding command of social exclusion, as had indeed already been apparent in Mrs Transome's first meeting with Esther's father, Rufus Lyon:

Mrs Transome hardly noticed Mr Lyon, not from studied haughtiness, but from sheer mental inability to consider him—as a person ignorant of natural history is unable to consider a fresh-water polype otherwise than as a sort of animated weed, certainly not fit for table.[133]

As Eliot stated in *Theophrastus Such*, 'a chief misfortune of high birth is that it usually shuts a man out from the large sympathetic knowledge of human experience which comes from contact with various classes on their own level'.[134] It is this which Esther comes to understand in her dawning sense that moral sympathy can be fatally incapacitated by both egoism and an undue concentration on a superiority which is defined solely in terms of external markers rather than internal virtue. Esther's moral growth in the novel is presented in these terms, her own shifting attitudes to accent being made to mirror the growing realization that the possession of material fortune, and even of the markers of both social and linguistic superiority, will rarely be adequate to grant exemption from a more serious, and moral, disaster.

Esther's earlier and spurious value judgements being abandoned, her habitual symbols of superiority thus gradually lose the inviolable meanings with which they had previously been invested. While the love of Harold Transome is seen to give 'an air of moral mediocrity to all her prospects', and life at Transome Court proves '*not* the life of her day-dreams',[135] other events, such as the visit of the old Rector, Jack Lingon, reveal the way in which attitudes to accent are again made to fuse with the widening sympathies, and diminishing egoism, of the heroine:

Esther was always glad when the old Rector came. With an odd contrariety to her former niceties she liked his rough attire and careless frank speech; they were something not point device that seemed to connect the life of Transome Court with that rougher, commoner world where her home had been.[136]

Snapping the 'silken bondage' of Transome Court, Esther returns to the world she had once inhabited, now equipped, however, with a truer index of superiority which is independent of the surface markings of social status.

Recurrent references to language, and the values with which it may be invested, can hence operate as significant indices of moral growth and standing in Eliot's work, a schema employed here in *Felix Holt* but given its clearest exposition in *Middlemarch* in the character of Rosamond Vincy, daughter of a well-established manufacturing family. A product of Mrs Lemon's school for ladies in which propriety of discourse forms part of the curriculum (as do the proper modes of ascending into, and descending from a carriage), Rosamond displays a sensitivity to the social symbolism of accent which in fact surpasses much of that advice proffered to the aspiring 'lady' (and discussed in more detail in Chapter 5). Language, in exact accordance with contemporary dictates on the social values of speech, is presented as a prime means of asserting her own social identity, and assessing that of others.

Her preoccupation with such signifiers is described on a number of occasions in the novel: ' "It always makes a difference, though, to be of good family," said Rosamond, with a tone of decision which showed that she had thought on this subject.'[137] Sure of the fact that ' "you would never hear me speak in an unladylike way" ',[138] she readily corrects perceived vulgarities in her mother's speech, and deems the young men of Middlemarch unfit as potential suitors on similar grounds: 'They were Middlemarch gentry... embarrassed in their manners, and timidly jocose: even Fred [her brother] was above them, having at least the accent and manner of a university man'.[139] Accent determines acceptability, and Rosamond's misplaced sensibilities in this respect are perhaps most evident in her reactions to the visit of Lydgate's aristocratic cousin, Captain Lydgate. Her judgement clouded by her overriding concerns with social status, his conversation charms her 'fine ear', not indeed by virtue of what he says, but rather by how he says it:

to most mortals there is a stupidity which is unendurable and a stupidity which is altogether acceptable—else, indeed, what would become of social bonds? Captain Lydgate's stupidity was delicately scented, carried itself with 'style', talked with a good accent, and was closely related to Sir Godwin. Rosamond found it quite agreeable and caught many of its phrases.[140]

The linguistic trappings of social identity are thus made to act as one of the ways in which Rosamond's relationships are determined; swayed only by an attention to the superficial, language is given exaggerated value as a standard by which she evaluates others. Status triumphs over substance and Rosamond, unlike Esther, remains rooted in her egoism, continuing to place her trust in such delusive symbols of 'superiority'.

Of course, using 'correct English' is not in itself an immediate correlate of either snobbery or egoism. The unquestionably ladylike Dorothea Brooke, for example, uses English with perfect and unstudied propriety, so much so that to Rosamond she forms 'one of those county divinities . . . whose slightest marks of manner or appearance were worthy of her study'.[141] Dorothea herself, infused by moral and not social ardour, grants little significance to such details; her dress is plain, her hair unadorned and simply coiled behind. Snobbery, of language, manner, or dress, is alien to her character. Attitudes to the Garth family who, as David Daiches has noted, 'provide an important moral centre in the novel',[142] further amplify these antitheses between Dorothea and Rosamond. The Vincys, with the exception of Fred, largely disdain to acknowledge the socially inferior if unimpeachably honourable Garths. Dorothea instead refutes such snobbery and, in spite of a social position far above that of the Vincys themselves, accords Caleb Garth and his family both her respect and her admiration.

The Garths, however, equally form a linguistic as well as moral centre of judgement in the novel. Mrs Garth's use of English is, for example, characterized by its propriety. She is, for her husband, 'a treasury of correct language' and, as Eliot elsewhere notes, 'in a general wreck of society [she] would have tried to hold her "Lindley Murray" above the waves'.[143] As the image of Murray's *Grammar* surviving the deluge aptly indicates, Mrs Garth endows good usage with no little value, though the nature of this value differs significantly from that with which it is invested by Rosamond. Linguistic propriety is important, as the former makes clear in teaching her children, but for the purposes of communicating one's ideas rather than signifying one's social position. Without grammar, as she instructs her son, ' "You would use wrong words, and put words in the wrong places, and instead of making people understand you, they would turn away from you as a tiresome person. What would you do then?" '[144] Whereas for Rosamond notions of correctness had been the basis on which she decided whether to turn away or not, in Mrs Garth's moral (and linguistic) scheme, correctness is to be prized precisely because it may prevent this and so may facilitate rather than impede a truer communication between individuals irrespective of their social location. Accent is also included within this reorientation of priorities. ' "These things belong only to pronunciation, which is the least part of grammar" ', stresses Mrs Garth to her children,[145] negating those heightened sensibilities which, in contemporary culture and social thinking, tended to foreground its nuances of a prime determiner of social, cultural, and even intellectual acceptability. Though using an accent which would not affront even Rosamond's standards of speech, Mrs Garth attaches little importance to this fact: 'she rarely forgot that while her grammar and accent were above the town standard, she wore a plain cap, cooked the family dinner, and darned all the stockings.'[146]

Largely in contrast to Gissing therefore, Eliot informs her treatment of attitudes to accent, its ladylike proprieties, and the social values with which it was so often imbued, with a vision which aligns it within the complex of moral symbolism she employs. To assign exaggerated importance to notions of linguistic correctness becomes in Eliot's novels a way by which misplaced values, and misjudgements of external and internal worth, are alike to be revealed. Patterns of exclusion and exclusiveness, fostered in linguistic terms by the value-laden descriptions which littered popular and prescriptive comment on language, are rendered insignificant in the broader, and rightful, vision of characters such as Dorothea or Mrs Garth.

Literary depiction of the prevalent fictions surrounding speech, and its associated values and value judgements, is thus in many ways closely informed, as we would expect, by the tenor of the individual author's writing. Whether made into a vehicle for moral exploration in Eliot or used to signify the social exile and the stratified barriers of language and status in Gissing, its nuances are nevertheless emphasized in the literature of the nineteenth century with a detail which offers close parallels with much contemporary, and non-literary, writing on language and its sociosymbolic dimensions. Just as writers such as Sheridan, Walker, or Smart stressed the social values of literate speech, and the social unacceptabilities of its converse, so too did authors such as Dickens, Meredith, or Gissing extend such equations into their own delineations of the spoken word, drawing on conceptions of 'good' and 'bad' in usage which were commonplace within that prescriptive legacy which had proved so pervasive in attitudes towards language, correctness, propriety, and status. Using spelling and significant variations within it to convey the nuances of sociolect and social acceptability, such writers further encoded the prevalent stereotypes of speech and speaker, further disseminating popular preconceptions about, for example, the differentiation of *what* and *wot*, or *girl* and *gurl*, in line with widely recognized, normative, and essentially non-regional ideals of language.

More influential perhaps in the context of diffusing these ideals were, of course, journals such as the *Family Herald* or the *London Journal*, the stories of which, as well as the letters pages, often displayed a concern with the due propriety of grapheme and phoneme, and their associated and extralinguistic values, for audiences which comprised over 300,000 readers by 1855. Children's literature too ensured early exposure to notions of norm and deviation, and the appropriate criteria of acceptability to be applied, as indeed did the educational precepts of many schools, as we shall see in the following chapter. Fictional discourse, whether in journals, novels, poetry, or moral tales for children, was, in such ways, frequently rendered similar by its shared modes of depicting accent, and its shared attitudes to the social and regional distinctions of speech. Implicitly, and often explicitly, notions of a nonlocalized and 'standard' accent were promoted as emblematic of social and cultural superiority, and though Dickens and Eliot might attempt to redress the simplistic nature of many of the value judgements which hinged on such

perceptions by their own forms of linguistic didacticism, the common stereotypes of speech and speaker were not dispelled. 'Commonness' stands as the
correlate of the 'broad Brummagen accent' used by Mrs Rymer in Mrs Henry
Wood's *Johnny Ludlow*; the stigma of the 'provincial' is in turn worked out
primarily in terms of status and of speech. Correlations of accent, status, and
identity, a frequent topos in writings on the language throughout the nineteenth century, hence inevitably infused the representation of fictional discourse, its depiction transmuted not only by notions of 'literate speech' but
also by the inescapable connotations of 'refinement' and 'vulgarity', 'educated'
and 'ignorant' with which accent, in its role as a dominant social construct of
the age, had come to be imbued.

7

Educating Accents

By the end of the nineteenth century, popular notions of 'educatedness' were, as we have seen, strongly associated with the possession of a particular set of pronunciation features among which the presence of [h] where deemed proper, the use of [ŋ] rather than [ɪn] in words such as *walking*, the articulation of words such as *serve* as ['sɜːv] not ['sɑːv], and the avoidance of intrusive [r] had all assumed prominence. Such stated affiliations of accent and education, in line with those paradigms of 'knowledge' and 'ignorance' already discussed, were commonplace in attitudes towards the language. 'The tone of the voice indicates character; the mode of speaking shows training and education', as the conduct writer Thomas Nichols proclaimed in 1874.[1] 'The true standard of pronunciation in any country is that which prevails among the best educated of its inhabitants', *How to Speak or Write English with Perspicacity and Fluency* averred two years later.[2] Within a few years of the Education Act of 1870 which promised elementary education for all, it is clear, as Nichols contends, that optimism surrounds expected standards of learning and of speech. 'Compulsory education' will, he states, end not only illiteracy but also the 'evil habit' and 'absurd and perverse fashion' of [h]-dropping.[3] Education and standardization were, as this suggests, popularly perceived to go hand in hand.

These attitudes did not, of course, arise merely with the introduction of new legislation. Even earlier, for example, in an 1855 lecture 'On the Art of Delivery and the Influence of School Discipline', the elocutionist Alexander Bell had expressly urged the need for educational responsibility in matters of phonemic propriety. Accent, he stressed, was a marker not only of status but also specifically of education, its nuances providing 'distinctive marks— which, if they do not always tell the place of birth, do, in a manner liable to little mistake, proclaim where and how each individual has been educated'.[4] As well as securing facility in the three R's, the ideal role of education in such formulations was envisaged as being to equip the child with proficiency in the non-regional norms of 'proper' speech. All other accents were to be discouraged. As Bell affirmed: 'The formation of such habits should be counteracted from the first, and in every stage of education, IN THE SCHOOL, where that pure and classical parlance should prevail, which indicates, not a province, but the legion of good society'.

Such conceptions of education as an institution which, in the ideal world, should aid and inculcate the transmission of the 'right' (and non-regionalized) accent alongside the 'right' ways of spelling, addition, or subtraction, are by no means rare. Not only manuals of manners or works on pronunciation, but directives on education by the state, reports by Her Majesty's Inspectors on educational standards and achievements, or assessments of the suitability of educators for their appointed tasks were all habitually to refer to the significance of accent and its perceived alignment with the 'proper' and 'educated' norms of speech. 'Attempts are made, with considerable success, to combat the peculiarities of the Lancashire pronunciation', commended T. M. W. Marshall, one of Her Majesty's Inspectors of Schools, in assessing a school in St Albans in 1849. Marshall's selection of 'peculiarities' as the appropriate mode of description in this context effectively confirms the prescriptive agendas which education was likewise to share. It is an emphasis reinforced by Marshall's comments on other educational establishments. 'I was struck with the absence of provincial accent, particularly in the monitors', he remarks, for instance, in a similarly positive vein on a school in Preston. 'There is a remarkable absence of provincial accent in the elder girls', he likewise observed, praising St Mary's School in Nottingham.[5] Such comments in the context of inspectors' reports were by no means atypical. As countless other examples affirm, contemporary paradigms of norm and deviation, and of 'provincial' versus 'standard', were in a number of ways to have an active bearing on issues of 'proper' education—and upon the various elements of 'proper' language which such education should purvey. The consequences of such assumptions, particularly given popular equations of accent and intelligence which continued to be widespread (in spite of their fallibility), were of course potentially far-reaching.

Both overtly and covertly notions of a 'standard' in speech could be implemented in prevailing educational ideologies just as the cultural and social hegemony of 'talking proper' would itself constitute a recurrent topos in estimations of education and its benefits. Language attitudes of this kind, as we shall see, tend moreover to be no respecters of denominational differences within the type of school, nor even of levels of wealth and the great divides between state and more elite forms of instruction which came into being over the nineteenth century. Elementary schools, 'public' schools, schools for Quakers, new schools in the traditions of the grammar schools of ancient foundation, and even Sunday schools were all in various ways to witness (and endorse) the diffusion of these ideas.

There is of course an indissoluble link between education and standard rather than non-standard varieties of a language. 'Standard English is the dialect of education', as the sociolinguist Peter Trudgill affirmed in 1983: 'it is spoken by most teachers; it is the dialect normally employed in writing; and it is rewarded in examinations'.[6] Grammatical features common in many spoken dialects but proscribed in the standard variety itself (such as multiple negation, or the use of *I done* rather than *I did*) are therefore equally proscribed in educational precepts, being corrected as inappropriate and 'wrong' in the written discourse of children. Education can thus foster the same images of unidimensionality in language as those which are common in the prescriptive tradition, likewise advocating a single image of 'correctness' above the heterogeneities of actual usage. Precisely the same processes operated in the nineteenth century though they did so with perhaps even greater rigour given attitudes to a 'standard' which often explicitly embraced hypotheses of inherent value rather than imposed norm. Education, both officially and unofficially, was seen as an important part of the standardization process, involved in the conscious maintenance of standard norms and, still more importantly, in their subsequent diffusion for both spoken and written English. As James Buchanan, schoolteacher and linguist in the eighteenth century, had early noted of this conjunction: 'he truly has attained the ends of education, who can speak and write his own language fluently and correctly'.[7]

Buchanan's own *Plan of an English Grammar School Education* was written in 1770 and, in keeping with his stated ideals, the plan he outlines includes formal instruction in the nuances of 'good' pronunciation and, implicitly, in their social values too. Addressing his text to 'the serious consideration of every sensible Parent and Teacher in Great Britain', he makes it clear that since the speech of the 'polite and learned' in the metropolis is the 'standard', those who wish their learning to be taken seriously must also accommodate their speech to these patterns. 'How unbecoming are discordant and jarring sounds in the mouth of an otherwise polite gentleman or lady, or in that of a man of learning', he declares.[8] As part of this conception, localized forms of speech (together with their perceived aesthetic demerits) are to be seen as fundamentally alien to the educational regime. 'It ought to be indisputably the care of every teacher of English, not to suffer children to pronounce according to the dialect of that place or country where they were born or reside, if it happens to be vicious',[9] Buchanan contends, adding in further warning that 'if they be suffered to proceed in, and be habituated to an uncouth pronunciation in their youth, it will most likely remain with them all their days'. Advertisements for his own school stress the practice of these remedial principles: 'Youth are taught to read English by the Powers of the Sounds', a procedure which is designed to inculcate 'standard' speech in all pupils as well as being equally efficacious in eliminating the 'uncouth' by rigorous training in articulation and the range of 'proper' phonemes in English. Children are moreover urged to come into residence at the age of 4 in order to prevent, one assumes, 'contagion' from the disadvantageous local habits of speech which Buchanan proscribes.

A number of other writers endorsed, and endeavoured to implement, tenets of this kind, the new 'consciousness' of accent advocated by Sheridan seemingly evolving alongside a parallel consciousness of the role which education too might play in these respects. Sheridan himself, for example, had placed particular emphasis on the possibilities of education for the effective standardization of speech. This had in fact been the initial impetus behind his prescriptive crusade, his *British Education* being published long before the later texts on elocution for which he is now remembered. Already in 1756 the need to incorporate English, and especially spoken English, within the schema of instruction which should be offered to the 'gentleman' is presented as an essential component of the remodelled teaching practices which Sheridan desired. The arts of speech thereby being made compulsory in his ideal syllabus, Sheridan is clear on the benefits which might in turn be passed onto the 'educated' accent—and its dissemination—not least since, by this means, categorical 'rules' for pronunciation (just as for grammar) could be provided from which the 'best' language might be learnt throughout the country, stabilizing the regional and social vagaries of speech in the institutionalized proprieties which education could enforce. Such rules might moreover be 'ascertained' or, as in the gloss which Sheridan's own later dictionary provides, 'made certain, fixed, established'. This itself was an important consideration from prescriptive points of view, not least given the degree of evidently reprehensible change which Sheridan and others regularly perceived in the flux of ordinary usage.

Sheridan's rousing cry for increased sensibility towards pronunciation is, in such ways, framed by explicit references to the need for educational provision in this context. 'Spoken language is not regularly taught', he laments, and the consequences of this neglect are all too clear. It is instead 'left to chance, imitation, and early habit' and, as a result, 'is liable to innumerable irregularities and defects'.[10] Even members of the established elite could, he states, emerge from school with accents which scarcely served as the requisite 'proof that one has kept good company'—unlike of course the 'educated' and 'best speakers' of the metropolis whose accents are made to serve a paradigmatic function in this respect. In the metalanguage of prescriptivism which he adopts, the accents of the former could paradoxically be 'uneducated' for, as Sheridan affirms, 'there are few gentlemen of England who have received their education at country schools, that are not infected with a false pronunciation of certain words, peculiar to each county'.[11] Recommending a new educational vigilance, he argues that the mission of education should therefore be integrated with the dissemination of the 'best speech' of London. His pronouncing dictionary of 1780 is in turn depicted as an important tool in the conformity which should result. The pronunciation of each word being presented as 'a certainty' by the 'fixed and visible marks' of transcription, the dictionary, he declaims, hence offers potential for a new era in education whereby 'a similar uniformity of pronunciation ... may be spread through all parts of the globe, wherever English shall be taught by its aid'.[12] The 'educated accent' (and all its associated myths and stereotypes) was, by such means, intentionally to be open to all.

John Walker too endorsed the importance of these ideas, further consolidating their conjunction in his published works and lectures. 'A clear and

distinct utterance' should unquestionably form a composite part of education, he stressed in 1785,[13] his own precepts on this head being put into
practice, we are told, in the Reverend Dr Thomson's School in Kensington
as well as presumably in the school which Walker himself established in
London in the late 1760s.[14] As Walker makes clear in the Dedication to his
The Academic Speaker, this was an educational emphasis with marked advantages; Dr Thomson, for example, receives commensurate praise for his 'successful experiment... [in] uniting the most extensive study of Greek and
Latin with a regular course of reading and speaking English'.[15] A number of
other schools, as we shall see, were likewise to recognize the utility of Walker's
work in this regard as indeed (though on a national rather than individual
scale) were the later inspectors of education themselves. Walker's influence
in this context too should therefore not be underestimated.

In the late eighteenth century, however, it is important to recognize that
notions of the evident inadequacies of contemporary education with reference to the proprieties of speech were not limited simply to the authors of
pronouncing dictionaries (and the undoubted self-interest which they had in
this matter). The religious and educational writer David Williams, for example, reflected a more general preoccupation with these issues of 'good'
speech (and their educational relevance) in *A Treatise on Education*, which he
published in 1774. The 'objects of education' should, he declares, comprise
'a distinct articulation' and 'an authorized and elegant pronunciation'[16] and,
like both Buchanan and Walker, he duly sets up plans of education in which
the English language receives attention as a subject in its own right. Like
Sheridan, Williams moreover clearly envisages the school as a means by
which the 'corrected' forms sanctioned by the prescriptive tradition could be
given a scope hitherto unprecedented in their dissemination. The aims of
education and standardization again fuse for, as he maintains, the explicit
teaching of speech on these lines would necessarily give rise to 'a proper and
elegant pronunciation' which would 'take the place of provincial vulgarism,
or fashionable affectation' throughout the country.[17]

Views such as these, while providing clear images of sociocultural norms
and their linguistic correlates, tend of course to form the theory, and the
ideal. Reality was usually somewhat different as Williams also acknowledges,
making plain the paradoxes which were to his mind transparent in an
English education system which, almost without exception in the grammar
schools, had in fact traditionally chosen to teach Latin and Greek at the
expense altogether of English:[18]

The language which a man is to speak and write in... ought certainly to be the principal object of his study, and not suffered, in our common school phrase, '*to come of
course*'; nevertheless, it is the 'dead and useless languages' which are to be studied, and
it is the 'living, useful, improveable one' which is '*to come of course*'.[19]

This formal concentration on the classical languages at the expense of English in the grammar and public schools (likewise lamented by Sheridan) will be discussed in more detail later in this chapter. What it is important to note at this stage is the emphasis being placed by a number of writers and educationalists in the late eighteenth century on the perceived need not only to teach English as a subject in its own right, but also to teach it in spoken as well as written forms.

It was a subject to which the philosopher John Locke, in his own critique of educational methods as they existed in late seventeenth-century England[20] had already drawn attention. 'To write and speak correctly gives a Grace, and gains a favourable attention to what one has to say', he stated, revealing the foundation of some of those patterns of subjective inequality which later came to be so prominent. Locke had in turn issued specific recommendations in terms of the teaching of the native language, adding further that 'since, 'tis *English* that an *English* gentleman will have constant use of, that is the Language he should chiefly cultivate, and wherein most Care should be taken to polish and perfect his Style'. Given the cultural climate which came into existence within the next hundred years, not least in terms of the all too prevalent impulses towards 'correct' pronunciation (and its own sociocultural affiliations), it is perhaps not surprising that conceptions of this kind were in a number of ways to impinge still further upon notions of 'good' education. Language, education, and nationalism were, for instance, frequently to combine. As in the full title of Sheridan's *British Education*, to rectify existing deficiencies in the teaching of pronunciation would also be a prime way of resolving at least some of 'the disorders of Great Britain'. And the benefits of this would, Sheridan argued, surely redound upon the nation as a whole.

That this intersection of ideas should be so is not of course entirely unexpected. Education does not take place in a vacuum but, as Irene Fox confirms, it is instead a practice (and a set of precepts) 'located within social space—[in] a society which has a history, structures, institutions, people, classes, and values'.[21] The role of the school as social institution, and of education as an important aspect of socialization, thus in themselves tend to ensure a failure of immunity from prevailing behavioural norms and expectations. That this failure extends to language too, whether in terms of attitudes or actual usage, is equally clear. As the linguists Walter Wolfram and Ralph Fasold indicate with reference to modern educational policy, for instance, 'public education in our society serves the function of inculcating in children the values that are shared by the society in which they will be participating members'. And as they make plain, 'included in these values are attitudes and beliefs about language and language attitudes'.[22]

The same premises naturally hold true in the late eighteenth and nineteenth centuries, before as well as after that increasing state involvement in educational issues which was to be such a prominent feature of the age. The educational 'system' in the late decades of the eighteenth century and the opening ones of the nineteenth is, of course, almost a misnomer. No 'system' as such existed, but instead a random collection of dame schools, ragged schools, charity schools, private schools (such indeed as those established by James Buchanan or John Walker), grammar schools of old or more recent foundation, Sunday Schools,[23] monitorial schools (after 1801),[24] Non-conformist Academies, as well as private tutors, all existed in uneven distribution, and uneven quality, over the country. The first state provision for education, of £20,000, was not made until 1830; the first training colleges for teachers were not established until the 1840s. Moreover access to education, and its varied manifestations, was determined primarily by issues of social position, a pattern which was in some ways to become increasingly apparent as the years went on. Many grammar and public schools, for example, came to engage in ever more stringent policies of social exclusivity, institutionalizing patterns of selection which operated to the obvious disadvantage of the local and impecunious scholars for whom such schools had, at least originally, been designed. Education was riven on all levels by the sense of a social divide. As the liberal politician Sir Thomas Wyse criticized in 1836 (one year after introducing a bill for national education in Ireland), it was '*grade in the social system*' which was the main influence on educational provision,[25] whether in terms of the classical syllabus followed by the 'gentleman' (born or aspiring) which might last until the age of eighteen or nineteen, or the four hours a day of the most elementary schooling which was to be granted to pauper children by the Poor Law Reform Act of 1839.

In keeping with his principles of popular education for all, Wyse advocated a number of reforms. 'There is a certain degree of development and instruction, which ought to be common to the members of every civilised community', he stated, acknowledging in addition, however, that 'it may not be for the interests of certain classes, or the community at large, to proceed' beyond this point.[26] Although this closing statement might suggest affinities with the position adopted by Dickens's Mr Dombey on the subject of equality in education ('"I am far from being friendly," pursued Mr. Dombey, "to what is called by persons of levelling sentiments, general education. But it is necessary that the inferior classes should continue to be taught to know their position, and to conduct themselves properly"'),[27] by the end of the century state involvement was in fact such as to bring about more or less the situation which Thomas Wyse had proposed. Compulsory elementary education for all was endorsed by Forster's Education Act of 1870 though a number of inequities in access to education still remained. Its provision by that date was nevertheless indisputably more systematic, more organized, and more controlled in the standards which were aimed at and which were, in turn, achieved.

Given this complexity, an examination of the ways in which attitudes to accent in the wider linguistic climate were also to influence education is by no means easy. Adopting a binary divide, the chapter will as a result first consider the 'public' school system and its extension—not least in sociosymbolic terms—over the eighteenth and nineteenth centuries. The remainder of the chapter will focus on the state system, its various ramifications, and its attempted implementation of the prescriptive canon of correctness as part of the 'elementary' training which was to be given to the children under its care. It is, of course, the public school with which stereotypes of 'talking proper' are now most commonly associated, although paradoxically, as we will see, it was in fact the state system which was to engage in the most explicit forms of teaching of this kind. Nevertheless, collocations such as the 'public-school accent' and 'public-school English' are now well established, often standing in popular usage as synonyms of RP. It was, for instance, 'Public School Pronunciation' which was deliberately selected by Daniel Jones, the leading British phonetician of the first half of the twentieth century, to designate the type of speech on which he based his 1917 *English Pronouncing Dictionary* (the 'everyday speech used in the families of Southern English persons whose men-folk have been educated at the great public boarding-schools').[28]

Long before Jones, however, the superior linguistic proprieties which education at a public school was assumed to convey were widely evident in popular language attitudes. 'The best accent is that taught at Eton and Oxford', *Good Society*, with its subheading 'Manners Make the Man', conclusively declared in 1869 for the benefit of its readers, no doubt encouraging principles of educational emulation along with the details of linguistic convergence which it also provided.[29] Still earlier instances of this equation can also be traced. 'A polite pronunciation is an essential part of a genteel and liberal education', states the writer and teacher John Murdoch, for example, in the stereotype edition of Walker's dictionary published in 1809, his use of 'liberal' intentionally signifying the elite rather than ordinary instruction typical of the public school. As Walker's dictionary itself explains, a 'liberal' education was that which 'becomes a gentleman'; the social values of 'polite', as in the pronunciation which Murdoch commends, were similarly indisputable ('elegant of manners', Walker's definition duly glosses). The conjunction of both pronunciation and education in this context is, as Murdoch also avers, 'incontestable'.[30] Nevertheless, as with the evident disjunctions which appear between ideology and process, belief and behaviour, in terms of standardization per se, there can be a similar disjunction in these terms too. In ways which are entirely in keeping with those evaluative processes all too common within the prescriptive tradition, Murdoch's comments, for example, reveal the clear alliance of images of elite education with corresponding images of the elite accents which such establishments should also nationally provide. *Good Society* later reveals the continuity, as well as the further consolidation, of these beliefs in its commendations of the accent which Eton, for example, was assumed to confer. It is, however, important to recognize that, in reality, English—whether spoken or written—did not form a composite part of instruction in these institutions at all. As Dr Johnson had phrased it in his dictionary, a 'grammar-school' (as such schools were then commonly known) was 'a school in which the learned [i.e. classical] languages are grammatically taught'—a definition which was later deemed of such authority that it was used in attempts to combat the extension of the syllabus in such schools into the more modern realms of science or into the 'non-learned' languages such indeed as English. In addition, as Johnson's definition also makes plain, the very identity of these institutions as 'public' rather than 'grammar' schools was another development which was only to emerge over the course of the nineteenth century—a fact which in itself renders the history of notions of the 'public-school accent' somewhat more complex than might initially be assumed.

As *OED* confirms, for example, the first official reference to the 'public school' comes only in the 1860 appointment of the Royal Commission which had been established in order to investigate the specific set of schools duly recognized in this way. In the 'Act for the better Government and extension of Certain Public Schools' of 1867 these were in turn formalized as Eton, Westminster, Winchester, Harrow, Rugby, Charterhouse, and Shrewsbury. On the other hand, however, it is also undeniable that unofficial notions of the 'public school' were current long before this date. 'By a public school, we mean an endowed place of education of old standing, to which the sons of gentlemen resort in considerable numbers', Sydney Smith (canon of St Paul's and founder of the *Edinburgh Review*) explained in the *Edinburgh Review* in 1810. Similarly, as Fanny Trollope wrote in a private letter in 1825, 'All the world are as poor as Job,—and rather poorer, for Job put none of his sons to public schools, and had no clients who did not pay him'.[31] As the nineteenth century advanced, the idea of the public school (especially in terms of the socially select form of education which Smith commends) was to become still further entrenched in the public consciousness, a process which also attracted a number of other schools of considerably newer foundation to attempt to share in such associations. The growing belief in a public-school education as a social as well as educational process led, for instance, to a demand which could be satisfied only by large numbers of new schools being created along roughly similar lines to those already in existence. Marlborough was founded in 1843, Radley in 1847, St Nicholas's, Lancing in 1848 (aimed at the sons of gentry and the upper middle class), Wellington in 1852, St John's, Hurstpierpoint (aimed at the sons of the well-to-do tradesmen) in 1853, Haileybury in 1862.[32] Not only did modes of reference to educational establishments of this kind change therefore during the late eighteenth and nineteenth centuries but a number of the salient characteristics of the public school tradition, important in a variety of ways in corresponding notions of the 'public-school accent', also came into existence over this time. A swift survey of the history of these foundations makes this situation, and the nature of their significant developments over this time, somewhat clearer.

A large number (though, as already indicated, by no means all) of the educational institutions which are now recognized as 'public schools' were of particularly long standing by the nineteenth century. These are the 'great public boarding-schools' whose linguistic influence in terms of pronunciation was later so commended by Daniel Jones. Of these, Winchester, for instance, dates back to 1382, Eton to 1440; Westminster and Shrewsbury were founded in 1560. However, the terms of their original foundation, as well as specifying an education in the classical languages, also specified that such education was, on the whole, to be received by the 'poor and needy' ('*pauperes et indigentes*') of the local area, a formulation which offers no little contrast to the social composition for which they later come to be known. Winchester was therefore initially able to take around seventy 'poor and needy' scholars although the precise terms of its foundation also allowed ten noblemen's sons to be fee-paying members of the college. The masters were, in addition, allowed to have private (fee-paying) pupils who boarded outside the college. Eton presented more or less the same picture with an original intake of seventy 'poor and needy' pupils, augmented by twenty sons of noblemen as fee-paying students. Harrow, founded in 1571 as a 'free grammar-school' by John Lyon, was explicitly designated 'for the perpetual education, teaching, and instruction of children and youth of the same parish', though masters were also able to 'receive so many foreigners [i.e. non-local students] over and above the youth of the parish as the whole number may be well-taught and the place can contain'. What is clear from this outline is that schools which were later seen as emblematic of an elite, and its attendant social (and linguistic) values, were in their original conception almost entirely the converse, dominated by the financially less able and local above the wealthy and non-localized. Other schools maintained similar patterns of intake. Westminster, for example, records the sons of an earl, a bishop, a Procurator of the Arches, a London vicar, a steward of Lord Zouch's estates in Northants, and of 'a keeper of the Orchard at Whitehall' among its members in the early seventeenth century. Merchant Taylors' School, founded in 1561, evinces a social mix of even wider dimensions, with the sons of a barber-surgeon, a blacksmith, a bricklayer, a cook, and a poulterer mingling with the sons of a Knight, a Fellow of Winchester College, the Secretary of the East India Company, and nineteen sons of gentlemen in 1645–6.[33]

Though these patterns of social diversity were long the norm rather than the exception, a gradual change began to take place as the rich and affluent began to displace the 'poor and needy' at a number of these schools. The period 1660–1780, as the historians Lawson and Silver note, was in particular to witness an increasing sense of hierarchy among the older grammar schools by which 'a few ... began to be patronized by wealthy and aristocratic families and so gradually to stand apart from the rest'. As Lawson and Silver add, however, 'there was as yet no attempt as in the more class-conscious nineteenth century to exclude boys because of their comparatively plebeian origins'.[34] The tendency for pupils from geographically distant (and disparate) places to make up a large proportion of the intake also starts to become perceptible. Even by the end of the seventeenth century, local boys made up only 20 per cent of the pupils at Rugby though this is, it must be admitted, an unusually low proportion for this date. It was instead the eighteenth and especially the nineteenth centuries which saw the decisive consolidation of these two critical elements in popular constructions of the public-school ideal—the rise of a non-localized intake, and the more or less simultaneous consolidation of a sense of social exclusivity.

As we have seen, this was a period which was, over its length, witness to a set of momentous changes in the fabric and organization of society; industrialization, urbanization, the rise of 'class' as social construct along with new notions of status, the emergence of a new rich (and a new poor) are all perceptible as developments over its span. Education is equally embedded in this pattern of change, and the new mobility facilitated by the increased ease of communications, especially following the advent of the railway, aided the general growth of boarding—and hence a non-localized intake—as particularly salient aspects of the public-school system. Similarly, the growing awareness of the social values of education in the classical mould at schools such as Harrow, Shrewsbury, Westminster, or Eton is plain in the patterns of social homogeneity which gradually displace the heterogeneities of the past. As Jonathan Gathorne-Hardy has noted, out of 3,000 pupils who entered Eton between 1755 and 1790, only thirty-eight were the sons of tradesmen.[35] Between 1821 and 1830, two pupils alone can be said to represent the lower sections of society. By the following decade this had dropped to zero. Entrance from among the sons of the gentry reveals, however, a more than corresponding rise in numbers, from 305 pupils in the period 1801–10 to 430 by 1850. A similar pattern is evident in the increased intake of pupils from the titled and aristocratic sections of society (226 in 1810, 330 by 1850). As a result, though in previous decades it had been acceptable and even advised for a gentleman to be educated at home—as John Locke had asserted, 'how anyone being put into a herd of unruly boys ... fits him for civil conversation or business, I cannot see'—by the end of the nineteenth century, the dominance of the public-school tradition was such that this was per se the typical education for a gentleman, or for those who wished to be numbered amongst such. By implication therefore, this was also no longer the typical education for the sons of ploughmen and clerks. Even where the social origins of boys in the same school remained mixed, there likewise emerges a large body of evidence which suggests that an increasing sense of a social divide was perceptible in their treatment. As the Report of the Schools Inquiry Commission of 1868 recorded on a number of occasions, patterns of overt segregation had often come to separate foundationers (i.e. those whose education was provided for by the original terms of the foundation of a given school) from the fee-paying and therefore richer scholars. While 'in several schools', discrete areas of seating were adopted, keeping rich and poor physically distinct, at another 'the two sets of boys were separated by "a partition breast high"'. If, as this indicates, the divisions of class could be made increasingly literal within the social world of the schoolroom, association outside the hours of formal teaching could be equally problematic; one nineteenth-century school, for instance, resorted to dividing the playground 'by an imaginary line between the boarders and free boys' with 'a penalty imposed on transgressors'.[36] If institutions of this kind had once been egalitarian rather than otherwise in their intake, such patterns of apparent apartheid make the increasing consciousness of social difference all too clear. And still more to the point was the fact that, in many cases, it was by no means the policy of the school which lay behind this consciousness of exclusion (and exclusivity) in its pupils. As the Schools Inquiry Commission observed of Repton School in Derbyshire (founded in 1557), the headmaster himself 'had clearly made a sincere attempt to break down the barriers between the local boys and the boarders'. Yet he had, the report continued, 'met with 'little success':

He stated that he had had very numerous applications from 'persons of good standing in the world and good fortune', and that he had invariably been asked, 'What is the character, station and position of the home boarders?' When he had answered that they were 'of all classes down to the sons of blacksmiths and washerwomen', the application had immediately been withdrawn. Of these 'home boarders' he stated that he had 'succeeded in gaining them perfect fair play in school', but that he had had to separate them out of school and that 'mainly for the sake of the village boys'. He felt that if he allowed them to associate, 'he should have a constant fear of their being ill-treated'.[37]

As the headmaster pointed out, ' "It is not the fault of the boys, it is the fault of society...I never yet saw a man who would send his boy to a school in order to associate with those lower than himself" '.

Such perceptions make plain the foundation of the social stereotype of the public schoolboy in the nineteenth century, as well as its increasing consolidation in one form rather than another. Social homogeneity, in these select (and selective) applications of it, comes moreover to enforce a due sense of the specifically social benefits which might also be derived from attendance at schools of this kind, particularly where boarding was concerned. As the author of *The Eton System of Education Vindicated* states in 1834, 'social elegance' and 'refinement' were prime among the virtues which Eton could impart,[38] perceptions which further extol—and promote—public recognition of this ideal. Though Lord Chesterfield had cautioned his own son (in the less exclusive days of the early eighteenth century) against the contagion of *bad* manners at Eton,[39] later commentators hence instead praised the contrary, portraying the acquisition of the right manner as an undeniable benefit of public-school education. Certainly it was in terms of such social characteristics that establishments of this kind, especially after Thomas Arnold's time as headmaster of Rugby, were frequently praised. As Arnold had, for example, directed his praeposters (senior pupils often given responsibility for the management and behaviour of the academic community), 'What we must look for... is, 1st, religion and moral principles, 2ndly, gentlemanly conduct; 3rdly intellectual ability',[40] a hierarchical ordering which concisely revealed the emphases at stake. It was in these terms that the public schoolboy, in the popular images deployed over the nineteenth century, hence tended to become an amalgam of social elegance, refinement, wealth, good manners, and perfect gentlemanly conduct. Or as the Eton-educated Sir Stafford Northcote—himself a member of the public schools commission—stressed in 1864: 'These public schools were national institutions, and had an important bearing on the formation of the national character'.[41]

Such images—and expectations—were in turn reflected in real terms in the experiences of many of those who attended the public schools of the day. Charles Merivale (1808–93) who later became a historian (as well as Dean of Ely), readily confirms the cultural hegemonies which could in this sense be enacted. As his memoirs attest, long after his days at Harrow he was able to recollect the 'sense of social inferiority... impressed' upon him in his early days there, as he was brought to 'acute consciousness of rustic or homely manners and of means and domestic circumstances much below par at a first-class aristocratic school'.[42] Though he and his brother survived by dint of both strategic assimilation and academic ability (such that they were able 'to command the respect of a set who would have been otherwise very prompt to despise and browbeat us'), the social pressures which could be exerted were clear. The (unpublished) reminiscences of John Mitchinson (1823–1918) give a similarly evocative picture of the practical consequences which could attend this particular emphasis in terms of the school. Involved in education for much of his life, Mitchinson was educated at Durham Grammar School (and Pembroke College, Oxford) and subsequently taught at Merchant Taylors' School, later becoming headmaster of the King's School, Canterbury (and still later Master of Pembroke too). He is, in a variety of ways, thus particularly well placed to comment on this particular aspect of the public-school stereotype, being subject to its dictates as a pupil and, as we shall see, later choosing to reinforce it in specifically linguistic ways once he became headmaster of his own school. Mitchinson's recollections stress, for instance, the 'polish' which education of this kind should rightly provide. George Hayton, a pupil at Durham Grammar School in the 1840s, is hence described both in terms of his social origins ('he was the son of a Cumberland Estatesman, i.e. yeoman, or small freeholder . . . He came to us a ruddy, round faced, flaxen haired lad')—and in terms of his subsequent social transformation by means of the encompassing influence of the public school. '[He] developed into a fine manly character, and took polish well', as Mitchinson notes with pride.[43] He 'took polish splendidly', Mitchinson likewise records of Field, a pupil of similarly humble social origins at the King's School, Canterbury.[44] 'Polish' in this sense evidently operated as a convenient social euphemism for the changes thereby imposed ('elegance of manners' as Walker defines this figurative extension of the word). 'Social considerations . . . bulk large with boys' is the moral Mitchinson draws in explanation of this convergence and the range of accommodations—including those of language—which were no doubt made to this end.[45]

For assimilation and acceptability within the social world of the superior school, conformity to those manners which makyth not only man but also, more specifically, the 'gentilman', was hence apparently of marked importance. Language—and especially spoken language—was, as we shall see, also predictably to play a significant part within these ideas as education in its own role as social symbol was swiftly assimilated into popular nineteenth-century strategies of cultural cohesion. As a result, while 'the really important boys were at Eton and Harrow', as the educational historian T. W. Bamford adds, 'it was the public school image as a type that was important, for similar schools produced similar products that spoke the same language'.[46] It was in these terms of course that notions of a corresponding linguistic stereotype were gradually added, ultimately providing one of the most enduring images of 'talking proper' that England has known. Being able to 'talk the same language' came to operate as the linguistic equivalent of the 'old school tie', aided not only by the arcane patterns of slang which characterized a number of schools, but also by conceptions of the decisive role which such schools might play in homogenizing the accents of those who entered them.

The linguistic hegemonies which the public school (in its varied manifestations) might enact upon pupils are, for example, early considered in *Practical Education* (1798), a two-volume work written by the novelist Maria Edgeworth and her father, the author Richard Lovell Edgeworth. Here they offer a clear and unambiguous account of the paradigms of language, education, and advantage which were increasingly to characterize popular attitudes to the public school. Statusful associations and remedial values are described in terms which effortlessly assimilate the contemporary emphases on imitative cohesion, and the accompanying stereotypes of the parvenu:

> Persons of narrow fortune, or persons who have acquired wealth in business, are often desirous of breeding up their sons to the liberal professions; and they are conscious that the company, the language, and the style of life, which their children would be accustomed to at home, are beneath what would be suited to their future professions. Public schools efface this rusticity, and correct the faults of provincial dialect: in this point of view they are highly advantageous.[47]

Education of this order becomes a means by which the signifiers of the 'well-bred', amongst which language is specifically included, may be acquired. 'Rusticity', suggesting not rural charm but 'rudeness' ('coarseness of manners', as John Walker explains), will by such means be remedied while linguistic provincialities (a 'sign of disgrace', in Sheridan's view) would similarly be displaced. As *Practical Education* confirms, education—at least in these increasingly select forms—was seen as a means of integration into the linguistic as well as social proprieties of an elite (with the added benefit of constituting another way in which the hegemonies of the 'best' English might in turn be spread). Obviating the 'provincial' was, as this moreover reveals, seen in the distinctly normative terms of 'proper' language from which such regional variations were relentlessly viewed as 'faults'. Accompanying ideologies of a standard are, in turn, all too perceptible in the 'advantages' which, as the Edgeworths imply, will surely follow.

Nevertheless, not all public schools were regarded as equally efficacious in this process. Though it is given as a general principle that removal from the provincial and localized, together with subsequent immersion in a superior social environment, will do much to mitigate 'the faults of provincial dialect', the Edgeworths also made plain that, for a perfect command of 'talking proper', only a major public school will do. 'We strongly recommend it to such parents to send their children to large public schools, to Rugby, Eton, or Westminster; not to any small school: much less to one in their own neighbourhood', readers of *Practical Education* were hence informed. Social location as well as language motivate the separations which they suggest. 'Small schools', readers are warned, 'are apt to be filled with persons of nearly the same station, and out of the same neighbourhood'. Given the paradigms of educational aspiration in which the text engages, this clearly will not do—and not least from the point of view of language. Small schools were seen to have additional disadvantages in this particular context, contributing 'to perpetuate uncouth antiquated idioms, and many of those obscure prejudices which cloud the intellect in the future business of life'.[48] It is segregation—both linguistic and social—which hence assumes prime importance in the benefits which education of this kind may at best provide. Breaking the links with the localized is presented as paramount.

As such comments reveal, principles of linguistic and social purism again act in tandem, the refined atmosphere of a select public school being presented in itself as some guarantee for the acquisition of a parallel refinement in language, one devoid of those localized forms which, as the nineteenth century advanced, increasingly consolidated their own role in the public mind as a prime marker of lower social standing. As William Enfield had indicated in the late eighteenth century, it was the absence of features such as these which was in particular to be regarded as a defining mark of the 'gentleman'. His maxim that 'these faults, and all others of the same nature, must be corrected in the pronunciation of a gentleman, who is supposed to have seen too much of the world, to retain the peculiarities of the district in which he was born'[49] operated in precisely the same way for those who wished to assume this social label for themselves or, more particularly, for their offspring. In terms of popular nineteenth-century images of education, however, it was not seeing the world which freed one from the localized markers which Enfield proscribes but instead entry into the increasingly non-localized intake of a major public school. This aspect of a public school education was, in consequence, often presented as particularly important since—at least in the ideal world—it was able to purge speech of those regional forms which were regularly perceived, and depicted, as inherently 'statusless'.

Securing the education of a 'gentleman' in precisely this way was, for instance, a common consideration for many of the real new rich of the nineteenth century. Wedgwood sent his sons to Rugby while Richard Arkwright's grandsons went to Eton and Harrow. Similarly John Gladstone, the Liverpool merchant, educated his sons at Eton, a destination shared by the grandson of Matthew Boulton, the Birmingham engineer and partner of James Watt. While such an education would serve to cement the familial ascendance in the social hierarchy, the linguistic consolidation which this would also offer was no doubt not entirely unimportant. After all, as Matthew Robinson Boulton, Boulton's son, had found out in his own education, linguistic assimilation could be vital—if difficult—in the challenge to acquire the gentlemanly attributes which his father had desired him to gain. 'With respect to his defect in Pronunciation, I fear it will not be soon or easily remedied', as Matthew Boulton senior had been informed with respect to his son's enduring fallibilities in terms of the rightful presence of [h].[50] Revealing a marked awareness of prevailing language attitudes, as well as the role which education was clearly assuming within associated ideologies of a standard, the nature of Matthew Robinson Boulton's education affirms the perceived values of the non-localized in terms which again fuse both accent and instruction. His 'inveterate provincialities' were subject to active redress and, as we have seen, boarding was strategically adopted as a means by which the 'vicious pronunciation' of Birmingham might itself be countered.[51] Markers of 'local' identity are not only unsuitable for the 'gentleman' (as Enfield had already made plain) but are in addition inevitably connotative of the 'vulgar' rather than of the aspiring elite. It was in such terms that Boulton senior responded to the cultural hegemonies which were so often asserted in prevailing language attitudes towards 'talking proper' and its 'educated' associations.

Thomas Arnold too was later to offer similar confirmation of these ideas. As he remarked, it was separation from the social (and regional) environment of the child's home which often constituted the prime parental motive in sending a boy to public school: 'It is the object of the father, as a rule, to withdraw his son from local associations, and to take him as far as possible from the sons of his neighbours and dependants'.[52] This too became part of the cultural stereotyping of the age, reflected in fictional form in Disraeli's *Coningsby* (1844) in which the son of the manufacturer Millbank is sent to Eton, as well as in John Galsworthy's detailed depiction over the nine volumes of his *Forsyte Saga* of the Forsyte family's ascent from yeoman farmers to wealthy (and influential) members of society. The fictional Soames Forsyte, born in 1855 and grandson of the builder Jolyon Forsyte (given as being born in 1770), is hence despatched to Marlborough after studying at a preparatory school in Slough where conformity in terms of accent had been strenuously monitored ('The accent had been all right at Slough—for if it wasn't a boy got lammed', as Soames is made to recollect in after-years).[53] As such images further confirm, the boarding school emerges as a central element in the making of an English 'gentleman'—however disparate the familial origins of such 'gentlemen' may originally have been. This of course had been the crucial element already isolated by the Edgeworths in their own treatise on aspirational education and the strategic assimilations which the right school might achieve.

As nineteenth-century observers such as George Bartle stressed, 'Boys that are brought up at home and attend a Day School for instruction have seldom the tone . . . of those that are educated at a Boarding School'.[54] And 'tone', as a variety of writers elaborated in this context, had of course its linguistic side too: 'the distinctive quality of voice in the pronunciation of words, peculiar to an individual, locality, or nation; an "accent" ', as the definition in the *OED* duly affirms. The assumed role of education in maintaining and instilling 'tone' in this sense was, in turn, widely recognized as by no means insignificant. It was this, for instance, which underpinned Dorothy Wordsworth's exhortations for her nephew John Wordsworth to be sent to Sedbergh in Cumbria, a boarding school founded in 1525. While he was undeniably 'a pretty genteel looking child . . . when he speaks the revolution is astonishing', she complained, censuring his facility in 'the very worst and most barbarous of all the dialects of Cumberland'. Once more education is promoted as linguistic remedy, though it was in this instance a solution which John's parents eventually chose to reject, sending him instead to the local Hawkshead Grammar School, an establishment which, while entirely reputable, clearly failed to have the desired linguistic effect. Both Dorothy and William Wordsworth continued to 'complain of his rustic accent' which boarding at Sedbergh might well have 'cured'.[55]

The anonymous author of *A Very Short Letter from One Old Westminster to Another* (1829) brought a similar emphasis to bear in his remarks on the imperatives which education at this level should rightly observe. As he averred, surely the role of the public school was, at least in part, to protect its pupils against those 'habits of faulty pronunciation', together with 'those vulgar and offensive tones in reading and speaking which it is afterwards so contemptible to retain and so difficult to correct'. The boarding school is thus depicted as a sphere which should properly be insulated from corrupting influences of this kind, an abode of 'proper' language where the pressures for convergence were ideally enhanced by the increasing patterns of social exclusivity adopted. Pertinent example is duly provided and the ostracization—and subsequent exclusion—of a pot-boy ('A boy or young man employed at a tavern or public house to serve the customers with beer, or to carry beer to outside customers; a publican's assistant') is described with self-evident satisfaction. No regrets attend his disappearance from Westminster; he had, we are told, merely been 'missorted' from the beginning—a perception, however, which seemed to emanate from (and be enforced by) the pupils rather than the masters. It is these who cause his exclusion by means of their own consciousness of unacceptability—and its converse. For the pot-boy the relevant social (and linguistic) markings were evidently such that the necessary conformity would not be conferred. In this respect parental ambition could, it seems, occasionally go awry:

You cannot but remember the sturdy, flaxen-haired pot-boy, whom an ambitious and aspiring publican sent to Westminster in our times, as a qualification, doubtless, for the *bar*. He was neither bullied nor beaten. But he was taught, by unequivocal lessons from those he wished to make his playmates, that he had been *missorted*, and the blunder was rectified in little more than three months after its commission.[56]

'And so should it be with all such as intrusively flock' into such spheres, the author adds in further commendation of the principles of segregation which had thereby been enacted. Given such attitudes, it is of course hardly surprising either that the pot-boy left, or that others who felt themselves potentially vulnerable to such censure might rapidly choose to conform to those standards, of language as of behaviour, which were presented for their emulation.

As the novelist William Thackeray observed, boys in the public school in this way tended to form ideal agencies for the manipulation of social shame: 'If your father is a grocer, you have been beaten for his sake, and have learned to be ashamed of him'.[57] Indeed the public school-boy of the nineteenth century could, it seemed, be acutely conscious of social difference, the poverty of Anthony Trollope's father, for instance, leaving Trollope himself 'a Pariah' in his own days at Winchester.[58] Even Thomas Sheridan's son suffered in a similar way after being sent to Harrow where his father's profession—as an actor-manager and elocutionist—was evidently regarded as unacceptable. While Richard Brinsley Sheridan's accent was presumably above reproach, his social markings placed him in a position in which he was regularly 'slighted by the masters and tormented by the boys as a poor player's son'.[59]

As such examples indicate, education, in whatever school, is much more than instruction in the academic subjects on the syllabus. Instead, as the French social scientist Emile Durkheim stressed, it is perhaps better seen as constituting 'the methodical socialization of the young generation'[60]—a role in which it is fundamental to the creation and maintenance of notions of group identity, enforcing (both implicitly and explicitly) certain patterns of behaviour to the attempted exclusion of others. In this sense it is 'the *central* pillar in group identity maintenance',[61] as John Edwards similarly notes in his own work on *Language, Society and Identity*. The constraints which education thereby habitually exerts thus cannot be ignored in their wider ramifications, and not least—as the nineteenth-century pot-boy at Westminster School found to his cost—as they affect the various manifestations (and manipulations) of peer-group pressure. The child's 'sentiments; his conscience; his mind, must be regulated by the laws of this institution', as Williams wrote in his own *Treatise on Education* in 1774, long before the formal advent of educational sociology. The end result, as Williams moreover added, should be that 'his soul will be moulded to the times, and he will come into the world perfectly fitted for it'.[62]

In terms of language the same implications again hold true and 'moulding' (especially in view of the prescriptive tenor of the age) was in turn regularly recognized as important. Given the fact that relatively few schools of this type engaged in explicit teaching of the norms of speech (though this will be treated later), it is, however, the levels of what may be seen as implicit instruction—and peer-group pressure—which assume prime importance in the creation of these nineteenth- (and twentieth-) century stereotypes of the public schoolboy and his 'proper' speech. As Jonathan Gathorne-Hardy has, for instance, confirmed, 'boarding communities where every one is in full view of everyone else are particularly conducive to codifying, elaborating, intensifying, and enforcing ... aspects of behaviour'.[63] Or as Thomas Arnold stressed over a century earlier, 'At no place or time of life are people so much the slaves of custom as boys at school'.[64] It was a statement endorsed time and time again within nineteenth-century comment. 'Your weighty words they neglect, but they dare not set themselves against the sneers of their companions', wrote Hope, for example, in 1869: 'They are slaves to Mrs. Grundy, bound with a heavier chain than even diligent votaries of the handbook of etiquette'.[65] As Hope's words suggest, a marked sensitization to issues of conformity could and did exist within the school, a pattern of behaviour also evident in the elaborate rules and social codes which many schools independently adopted. The 'slavery' which resulted was, however, particularly to 'propriety' (for which 'Mrs Grundy' stood as a dominant social icon in the nineteenth century). It was this to which the 'sneers' of companions were above all to exact due obeisance, revealing an awareness of shibboleths within the world of the school which clearly parallels those in existence outside its confines.

This mode of 'informal' education is, for instance, precisely that which the Oxford scholar (and writer on language) Kington-Oliphant commends, not least for its efficacy in ensuring the 'proper' articulation of [h]. If, as he acknowledged, 'our public schools are often railed against as teaching but little', nevertheless, to his mind their educational advantages were indisputable in the ways in which 'they enforce the right use of *h* upon any lad who has a mind to lead a quiet life among his mates'.[66] As the sub-text here suggests, it is the pupils not the teacher who tended to enforce this pattern, conformity once again being the key to 'a quiet life'. The absence of what were clearly perceived as marked forms—such as dropped [h]s or imperfectly articulated participles—was crucial. Twentieth-century victims of this same process confirm its continued efficacy. As C. Jarman writes of his own attempts at assimilation after being sent to boarding school, 'I spent my first term in a private hell of homesickness and fear that the boys would find out that I was not "one of them" … I quickly acquired the right slang, and my parents were delighted with my new accent'.[67] Social and linguistic accommodation evidently worked in parallel in what has emerged as an enduring aspect of the public-school stereotype. The writer Judith Okely, for example, still memorably describes the role of accent as 'a sign and a weapon' in her own days at boarding school in the 1950s (and the strategic mimicry and ridicule applied to those, usually scholarship girls, whose accents deviated from the forms deemed 'proper').[68] In the same way sensitization to accent in boys' boarding schools of the nineteenth century often seemed to ensure corresponding patterns of ostracism or acceptability. Accent was a weapon which many indeed seemed to wield with skill, with unfortunate consequences for those who lacked this facility. As John Hales commented in 1867, describing the typical public schoolboy of the day, 'He can speak [English], because he has heard it spoken around him from his earliest years. If he has been born and bred in what I call well-educated society, he speaks it "with propriety". He shudders duly when he hears it spoken with impropriety'.[69] Conceptions such as these tended to function as a self-perpetuating paradigm, confirming the associations (and alignments) of the 'best' accent with the 'best' education in schools of this order by means of the emphasis given to the social composition (and social sensibilities) of their intake. The public school, as

Hales explicitly recognizes, hence served to provide an ideal environment for reinforcing the sense of a norm, the 'shudders' of the 'proper' schoolboy undoubtedly being equally efficacious at imposing this same awareness in those who had not had the stated advantages of being 'born and bred... in well-educated society'. Conformity in these terms provided a means of camouflage for those who, like Charles Merivale, were in various ways made all too conscious of a social origin below that of the dominant peer group.

Over the nineteenth century, the social dominance of one set of society above others in schools of this order was, in this sense, often perceived to guarantee the use—and dissemination—of 'the tone of feeling and habits of demeanour that prevail in our best British homes', a precept articulated, for instance, by Richard Monckton Milnes, poet, politician, and the first Baron Houghton.[70] On the other hand, it has to be acknowledged of course that history is full of those who refuse to conform in various ways, a principle which in this respect equally extends to linguistic behaviour. In consequence, while those most anxious about their social identity, or who felt themselves most vulnerable to the multifarious pressures of their peers, were often to prove willing to submit to the pressures for accommodation with which they were often confronted, it would nevertheless be unrealistic to expect a complete homogeneity of response in this context. More stalwart individuals could—and did—retain the regional accents with which they entered schools of this kind, remaining impervious to the urge to conform. This, for instance, underpins the evident adherence of the Eton-educated William Gladstone to his own northern accent,[71] just as it does Robert Peel's retention of his native Lancashire tones. Norms, as social and language history combine to confirm, are—in this as other matters—rarely absolute.

Nevertheless, the social and linguistic stereotypes which tended to result from dominant conceptions of the public schoolboy were on the whole well established by the mid-nineteenth century, receiving perhaps their clearest discussion in William M'Combie's 1857 volume, *On Education in Its Constituents, Objects, and Issues*. Here M'Combie duly narrates the tale of his own encounter with a man on his way home after installing his elder son at boarding school. The father thus encountered serves, however, to provide an unprecedented exposition of the linguistic benefits which were often assumed to be a composite (if indirect) element of this particular type of education. As M'Combie's text makes plain, for instance, it was indeed the indirect advantages of this type of instruction—particularly in terms of accent—which had weighed as much (if not more) in the educational deliberations which had evidently taken place:

With that self-complacency which men are very apt to feel when conscious of having successfully completed a piece of work of special merit and difficulty, our companion dilated on the importance of education in order to success in life [*sic*], clenching his argument and concentrating the expression of his ideal of the matter in the exclamation—'Give them a good pronunciation, and there is no fear but that they will get on in the world.'[72]

It is pronunciation which is thereby explicitly foregrounded as the major benefit to be derived from the boarding school. In spite of his own convictions that this assumption is fundamentally 'absurd', M'Combie is in turn compelled to admit it is also one which is particularly widespread, standing as a 'typification of the notion of education current with the majority of respectable people in our time'. M'Combie's concluding statement on this matter hence itself conclusively affirms the very pervasiveness of the stereotypes of language and elite education (and their assumed correlations) which had firmly taken hold in the public consciousness by this time. 'The end product', at least in terms of accompanying myths of standardization was, as the historians Stone and Stone affirm, 'to be an homogenized gentleman by education, whose background was not detectable in his accent, behaviour or culture'.[73] It is clearly this at which M'Combie's own acquaintance aims though its legacy can still be apparent as parents continue to stress their preference for a school 'with a strong emphasis on correct manners and speech', or echo the advantages of linguistic segregation in comments which affirm that 'the advantage of an independent education is to get him away from the local boys who speak badly'.[74]

Ideologies of a 'standard', and the means by which it was to be achieved, were in such ways often to unite in the stress placed by contemporary comment on a non-localized education as a particularly effective route to that non-localized accent which, as we have seen, was itself embedded in language attitudes (and their attendant sociocultural constructs) as a marker of both status and success. If pressures for conformity were, in this context, regularly played out among the pupils at such schools, then it also has to be remembered that teachers too form a further component within the social environment which any school creates, with their own capacity to exert influence on behaviour, including, in this respect, linguistic behaviour. Indeed, as the modern truism has it, from this point of view, 'all teachers are teachers of English'. In the nineteenth century therefore, tutors in the public-school tradition, themselves largely scholars and gentlemen, also participated in creating (and reinforcing) the sense of a norm, especially since a significant proportion themselves tended to be products of the public-school tradition in which they later taught. A whole series of Arnold's pupils at Rugby, for instance, subsequently became headmasters of schools such as Marlborough, Harrow, Lancing, Haileybury, Sherborne, Cheltenham, Felsted, and Bury St Edmunds. The resulting process was undeniably conducive to certain homogeneities of approach, offering an element of continuity which was undeniably important in the generation—and maintenance—of a public-school stereotype, as well as in conceptions of its associated proprieties. 'The great schools ... it must be observed, train for the most part the Masters who are placed at the head of the smaller schools, and thus exercise not only a direct but a wide indirect influence over education', as the Clarendon Commissioners pointed out.[75] Certainly, pupils could be sensitive to notions of perceived deviation in this context, apparently applying the same stringent social testing to masters as they meted out to their contemporaries. Once again, however, it was 'gentlemanly' qualifications which could at times seem of more importance than academic excellence per se. John Mitchinson, for instance, describes the appointment of Richard Goodall Gordon as a master at Canterbury in terms which certainly do not foreground scholarly success. 'He was a Second Classman in Mods, a third in Lit.Hum. [Litterae Humaniores, commonly used to signify Classics at Oxford]', Mitchinson notes. Academically, Gordon could at best be described as 'fair', and 'fairly good' as a master. But if such descriptions serve to damn with faint praise, it was in other ways that Gordon was deemed to excel. As Mitchinson continues, 'he was a gentleman to the backbone, and his influence in that direction was invaluable'.[76] In such conceptions, the import of the 'third in Lit.Hum.' was clearly negligible. Conversely, Mitchinson's account of one of the mathematics teachers at Durham Grammar School was markedly critical. The master in question 'was not in Holy Orders nor an English Graduate', Mitchinson recalled; far worse, however, was the fact that he was not 'socially regarded or treated as a gentleman',[77] a situation which led him to be regarded with conspicuous disfavour (as well as disregard) by the pupils. Tutors too could clearly find their life uncomfortable given the manifold social pressures of the public school.

As this suggests, those exemplary aspects of behaviour and demeanour which the master might present to his pupils could be regarded as indispensable, providing an invaluable education in themselves. Specific recommendations for the teacher in this respect are, however, set out with greatest clarity in the manuals of teaching written by John Gill and Robert Robinson which were reprinted in their thousands as England slowly moved towards a general educational system for the nation. If directed in formal terms to the demands of education outside the public-school tradition, their precepts nevertheless remain equally relevant in their detailed examination of the essential qualities of the ideal teacher, as well as in accompanying analyses of the indirect influences which the teacher should thereby wield. As Gill stressed in his *Introductory Text-Book to School Management*, education in this respect was a process which allowed of no respite:

The teacher does exercise a powerful influence on the habits and character of his young charge ... In a certain sense he is teaching always, and often when he least thinks of it. The lessons which he gives insensibly are perhaps the most availing of all ... He is constantly imposing his own likeness.[78]

That this 'likeness' has its linguistic aspects too is similarly given prominence. 'The words which drop unobserved from his lips...his daily habits and deportment...may be made subservient to the highest ends', Gill observes.[79] In this sense the teacher serves as exemplar, a pattern by which the children, and their habits of behaviour, should rightly be formed:

reading and speaking are much influenced by imitation, from the inherent tendency to imitate those with whom we associate. This fact shows the importance of the teacher's speech being pure, distinct, deliberate, and impressive...The teacher is unwise who neglects so powerful an instrument as this.[80]

In other words, here too the teacher must of necessity set the standard, potentially imprinting his own habits upon the pupils in his care and offering an additionally instructive model in the pedagogic terms of pronunciation and the nuances of accent.

Writers who direct their comments specifically to the public-school tradition regularly made the same point, likewise stressing the role the teacher was assumed to play in enforcing the requisite conceptions (and markers) of group identity. The recommendation was clear. Masters and headmasters alike were, in the ideal world, to have accents which conformed to the non-localized norms which mark the 'gentil' and 'educated' man. As the author of *Thorough English* observed, directing his comments to 'every Public School, Grammar School, or institution on a large scale', it was in this sense imperative that 'the headmaster...should write and speak the best English...His accent ought to be simply that of a well-educated Englishman, without any trace of local intonation, London or provincial, Scotch or Irish'.[81]

If masters, headmasters, and pupils all in various ways served to provide effective agencies for reinforcing the image of an emerging 'public-school accent', complete with associated specifications of [h]-fullness and other sociolinguistic proprieties, it should nevertheless not be forgotten that formal instruction in this respect could also at times take place. While the continued dominance of the classical syllabus in some schools clearly restricted opportunities of this kind, an education which explicitly included English and specifically spoken English did begin to feature at a number of boarding schools as the nineteenth century advanced. Ackworth School in Yorkshire provides a particularly useful example in this respect. Founded by the Quakers in 1779, Ackworth aimed to provide an education in the public-school tradition for children whose parents were of moderate means, explicitly trading therefore on the benefits—both formal and informal—which were popularly supposed to surround the privileged education which more traditional institutions such as Winchester and Eton could supply. In terms of language, however, relevant desiderata could be far more explicit. As the directives issued in *The English Vocabulary* (a textbook exclusively 'compiled for the use of Ackworth School' in 1852) make plain, selected modes of teaching unambiguously endorsed contemporary emphases on 'good' speech in the qualities which the school should be able to enforce upon its pupils over their time there. The *Vocabulary* stresses, for example, that the 'teaching [of] a distinct pronunciation' ought to form a significant part of educational provision,[82] further specifying the direct responsibility of teachers in this matter. The role of the latter in such conceptions is therefore not only to impart knowledge on more conventional paradigms but also to 'instil a proper pronunciation' in the pupils in their care. This, the author adds, is a feature which can 'scarcely be acquired with accuracy, except *vivâ voce*'.[83] The avowed intention was in consequence to promote the existence of a 'standard' and uniform pronunciation within the school; any localized markers prominent in the speech of children when first placed in its care were to be eradicated in line with this intent. As we are informed, the impetus for the book had in fact 'been suggested by the peculiar dialects of children brought to this school from various parts of the kingdom', a statement which clearly reveals the alignments of 'standard' rather than 'non-standard' forms of English with the educational regime (as well as its non-localized bias). Modes of language connotative of the 'provincial' rather than the 'proper' (and indeed the 'educated') are, in these terms, explicitly to be 'counteracted'.[84] That these notions of standard usage extend to spoken as well as written forms is moreover made plain by subsequent comments within the text. The use of /h/, perhaps predictably, is given first place among the linguistic 'peculiarities' which such instruction should remedy:

In some counties there prevails an unaccountable habit of omitting to sound the letter H when it ought to be pronounced, and of sounding it, not only when the generality of speakers consider it silent, as in *h*eir, *h*erb, &c., but very often when it does not exist in the word...In order to correct these errors, a number of words of this kind are inserted for the purposes of exercising pupils in them, by which there is no doubt that the habit may be generally overcome, in all young persons at least.[85]

Whereas major public schools, as the Edgeworths suggested, were almost effortlessly able to endorse requisite proprieties of speech merely by the pressures which dominant social forces within the school could exert,[86] it was hence, on the whole, the smaller—and newer—boarding schools such as Ackworth which instead tended to resort to these more explicit measures in their attempts to constrain the potentially deleterious effect of localized accents in the 'proper' public-school product which they strove to emulate.

St John's, Hurstpierpoint, a school founded on the public-school model in 1853 to cater for the sons of well-to-do tradesmen, illustrates some of the same concerns. Its headmaster, Edward Lowe, for instance, published *An English Primer* in 1867 as a textbook to be used throughout the school, the pages of which contained extensive instructions for the 'proper' deployment of spoken as well as written English. Section IV hence sets out for the edification of pupils a range of socially sensitive variables in pronunciation, making plain that it is to these that individual usage should conform. Under the heading 'Cautions in Pronunciation', the use of [ŋ] (rather than [ɪn]) in words such as *walking* or *riding*, and the 'correct' rather than 'vulgar' use of [r] are all item-ized (alongside other stated 'errors') in accordance with prevailing prescrip-tive thinking. Paradigms of norm and deviation are applied as rigorously in this context as they are to corresponding notions of correct and incorrect spelling. As the advice given on the subject of 'the letter *h*' additionally affirms, the aim is to conform as far as possible to perceptions of 'educatedness' in terms of spoken as well as written words. 'Reverence the letter *h*', the pupils are informed; 'though our forefathers seem to have been very careless about it, no educated ear can now tolerate the omission of this letter'.[87] Once again the assumed correlations of 'educatedness' and accent come to the fore, their nuances explicitly imparted to those being instructed by means of a pedagogic emphasis which was presumably of no little significance for the aspiring tradesmen who chose to send their sons to fee-paying schools of this kind.

John Mitchinson's own role as headmaster of the King's School at Canterbury reveals similar preoccupations, notably in his appointment of the Reverend Alexander D'Orsey as 'Lecturer in Elocution'. Readily sub-scribing to prevalent ideologies of 'proper' speech, Mitchinson notes that the utterance of his pupils had been a source of considerable concern for some time. 'I had long chafed at the indistinct and unintelligent utterance of my boys, seniors quite as bad as juniors, and I recognised that my remonstrances and strictures had no effect in abating the nuisance', he commented,[88] his chosen metalanguage unambiguously confirming the widespread legacies of prescriptivism in popular language attitudes. As a result, he had read with some interest an advertisement by the Reverend D'Orsey who described himself as an 'instructor of Peers, M.P.s and Clergy' in the finer matters of enunciation. Mitchinson swiftly 'resolved to try him' and wrote 'to enquire whether he... would stoop so low as to try and cure mumbling among my hobbledehoys; and preoccupy the little folks lips & tongues with articulate utterance'.[89] D'Orsey, however, responded eagerly, declaring the task to be 'a long cherished scheme of his'. He duly set to work and Mitchinson offers a detailed account of the proceedings which followed, one which is perhaps worthwhile citing in full, revealing as it is of the ways in which the various agendas of 'correct' pronunciation, as well as the contemporary fondness for recitation and elocution, could be assimilated within the traditions (and emerging stereotypes) of a grammar school of older foundation:[90]

I constituted myself policeman and sat on vigilant guard all day, lest haply some bolder spirit should try to pull his leg. His method was excellent. He began by warn-ing them that he was an excellent mimic, & meant to bring his gift to bear on them, & bound them by a tacit promise not to be offended if he took them off with their lit-tle faults of utterance exactly reproduced,—and then he set to work. Calling up his first 'subject' for dissection, & posting him conspicuously, he put a book in his hand & bade him read. The result may be imagined; dull, lifeless, indistinct, faint murmuring. 'Thank you' he said, and took the book, dismissing the reader to his place. 'Now (remember your promise), listen'. He reproduced him exactly down to every little detail to the joy and mirth of all his comrades, which he checked by a reminder that their turn to have the mirror held up to them was close at hand. Next he would get them to criticise each other, & indicate faults of diction, throwing in rules and reasons for them,—quite simple and obvious as he frequently reminded them; no mystery. I sat and listened and laid to heart all that I heard.[91]

As Mitchinson adds, though he himself was decisively in favour of this course of instruction, and the education in phonemic nicety and public modes of discourse which it provided, 'the unanimous verdict of the upper boys', with typical schoolboy eloquence, was 'that it was all "rot"'.

King's was, however, not the only school to try this venture in the explicit teaching of elocutionary precepts. Edward Thring, the celebrated headmaster of Uppingham (which, as the first edition of the *DNB* recorded, he 'raised to a foremost position among the public schools of England') was another who, as Mitchinson stated, subsequently 'fell in after my experiment'.[92] Thring as a result established a similar focus in the school which was later to become the centre of the first Headmasters' Conference in 1869, elocution constituting a further aspect of the wider syllabus which was a special characteristic of an Uppingham education. It was moreover a development entirely in keeping with Thring's own belief in the general need for the teaching of English as a composite part of the public-school tradition. As he informed the Schools Inquiry Commission in 1868, his opinion was indeed that 'much more English is required to be worked into the public schools'. 'I have found it so throughout', he added: 'We teach English throughout the school in various forms, and I hold that the very highest results have been attained in a great degree by it'.[93]

Both consciously and unconsciously therefore, the normative values of 'good' spoken English came, as this suggests, to be implemented in a variety of ways in many of the major (and minor) public schools of the nineteenth century.[94] Masters and headmasters intentionally presented exemplary models of the 'gentleman' for whom 'talking proper' was judged a defining characteristic, while the boys themselves often endorsed paradigms of 'proper' English by the issues of exclusion and exclusivity which were readily manipulated in prevailing norms of group identity. In these terms, ridicule, social shame, as well as the basic impulse to conform were all able to act as agents in reinforcing the sense of an 'educated' and non-localized set of norms. While perfect uniformity was not and, indeed, could not be attained,[95] it is nevertheless clear that by the end of the century the public schoolboy was—stereotypically—often seen in terms of that 'command of pure grammatical English' which, among other things, the Clarendon

Commissioners of 1864 had deemed essential.[96] It was this which was gradually institutionalized as part of the public-school ethos, firmly embedded in
popular images of the 'gentlemen' who attended such schools as well as
undoubtedly being fostered by the escalating, and increasingly deliberate,
social exclusivity of educational establishments of this order.

★★★★★

Schools within the emergent state system offer a slightly different picture.
Diversified, as already indicated, by quality, size, aims, and intake over the
entire country—as one inspector noted, 'there are few, if any, occupations
regarded as incompatible with school-keeping... Domestic servants out of
place, discharged barmaids, vendors of toys or lollipops... cripples almost
bedridden' all formed some of those who had set up schools in London in
1861[97]—the resulting situation, especially before the Elementary Education
Act of 1870, is one about which it is often almost impossible to draw general
conclusions. Dame schools could provide what was, in effect, a basic child-
minding service, offering (like that attended by Pip in Dickens's *Great
Expectations*) only the most rudimentary forms of instruction. Private
schools could provide commendable levels of instruction, or be run by out-
and-out charlatans whose only qualification for establishing a school was
monetary greed. Like Dotheboys Hall in *Nicholas Nickleby*, they could offer
minimal educational rewards or instead, like that attended by Dickens in his
own childhood, they could be run by a highly competent elocution master.[98]
Nevertheless most schools, even if they aimed no higher, endeavoured to
provide some acquaintance with the fundamentals of reading, writing, as
well as arithmetic. It is here that, overall, a considerable amount of information on attitudes to education, to the spoken language, and to the inculcation
of its necessary proprieties, can be found.

As in the grammar and public schools already discussed, the repercussions
of that set of attitudes and assumptions which, as we have seen, regularly surrounded nineteenth-century notions of the 'best' English could, in many
instances, materially influence corresponding notions of 'good' and 'bad' in
education. 'To facilitate the improvement of the Pupil by the simplest and
most easy methods, should be an object with all Tutors and authors of elementary works', as G. Coysh wrote in his own manual of education in 1837,
further stating, for the benefit of those actively involved in the practice of elementary instruction, that in this respect 'a correct pronunciation is of paramount importance'.[99] For both teacher and pupil this was to form a
pervasive theme within educational provision, endorsed by training colleges
for teachers, by manuals of teaching which addressed both theory and practice, and later by inspectors' reports and the assessments of educational
desiderata which they provided. Since the role of education was to teach the
'proper' forms of English, habits of enunciation in which [h] was habitually

lost or which included regionally marked uses of [ɪn] rather than [ɪŋ] were, by extension, popularly to be regarded in the same light as the double negative, or lack of concord in the sentence. They were 'mistakes' out of keeping with the aims of education. As *The Elementary Catechisms* of 1850 stressed, education was specifically to be in standard, rather than non-standard, forms of speech:

Q. Why is it, that if we can speak our own language, it is necessary to learn grammar? A. From habit we often use many unsuitable words, and incorrect modes of speech; and as dialects differ from the standard in various parts of the country, it is therefore requisite to learn grammar.[100]

John Poole's *The Village School Improved* provides early illustration of the inspiration which prescriptive notions of correctness with reference to the spoken word could exert. Published in 1813 with the explicit aim of facilitating 'in some degree the introduction of a new system of education into village schools',[101] the book stands as an account of the teaching of reading and pronunciation in Enmore School in Somerset over the previous five years. Employing the monitorial system developed by Bell and Lancaster,[102] and with an intake composed of local village children, the school wholeheartedly embraced notions of the 'educated accent' and its seemingly inherent proprieties. Poole, the rector of Enmore, describes in some detail the methods by which correctness in these spheres was to be obtained.

Vigilance on the teacher's part is, in particular, presented as vital and each 'mistake' in enunciation made by a pupil was immediately to be pointed out and rectified, 'it being a fundamental rule of the school that no error, however slight, shall be suffered to pass unnoticed, or uncorrected'.[103] The child's performance is hence constantly supervised in auditory terms, his or her ranking in the school being made dependent on respective levels of failure or success. Relevant paradigms of norm and deviation are rigorously implemented, and the progress of the reading lesson is, it seems, continually interrupted by the enforcement of these normative dictates:

If a child omits, or mistakes, a word, or even a letter, he is liable to degradation; as it is the duty of the teacher instantly to pass to the next child, and, if necessary, to all the children in succession; and on no account to rectify the mistake himself, until the whole class has been tried. Even a coarse or provincial way of pronouncing a word, though sanctioned by the general practice of the district, is immediately noticed by the teacher; and exposes the child, who uses it, as much to the correction of those below him, and consequently to the loss of his place, as any other impropriety in reading would do.[104]

This notion of 'linguistic exposure' as a direct consequence of using what is relentlessly presented as localized 'error' rather than the 'proper' and non-localized markers of speech is important, clearly relying on imprinting upon the child a sense of anxiety (and indeed shame) with reference to his habitual forms of speech. Forming a staple of prescriptive response to language variation, it serves to provide an additional perspective on the ways in which, as William Labov has contended in the twentieth century, shared language attitudes can exist throughout the linguistic community, regardless of actual patterns of usage.[105] Resulting images (in both past and present) hence deploy notions of collective linguistic identity which rely not on linguistic reality—the forms, as Poole notes, which are 'sanctioned by the general practice of the district'—but instead on forms sanctioned by a broader (and far more unidimensional) view of 'proper' language. Enunciations which are characteristic of local rather than national are hence firmly proscribed in the system of education which Poole puts into play. 'Coarse' and 'provincial', their use leads to 'degradation' for the child, a process which not only conveys demotion ('To put one from his degree', as Walker's 1791 definition explains) but also implies devaluation in a far wider sense: 'to lessen, diminish the value of', as Walker also notes.

The negative repercussions which such policies may have—not least in reinforcing a sense of alienation from family and home or indeed from the school itself—often lead to their categorical condemnation in modern works on language and educational psychology. 'It is difficult to belittle a speaker's language without belittling the speaker as well', states Peter Trudgill, for example, in his own work in this field;[106] 'by rejecting a child's accent, or even some features of it, we run the risk of his feeling we are rejecting *him*'.[107] Nineteenth-century writers, however, had little interest in such matters. Few scruples with reference to the linguistic or psychological validity of regional forms of speech bothered Poole (nor many of the other teachers and educators who afterwards worked within the same educational traditions). Potential issues of rejection in terms of local identity could, it was felt, merely enhance the convergence deemed both necessary and correct. As Poole admits, though 'it was easy to foresee, that the immediate effect of this strict attention to correctness and propriety, would be to embarrass the child', the priorities remain clear. 'This embarrassment is merely temporary' but 'permanent advantages . . . are sure to follow if the method be patiently persevered in.'[108]

Poole had learnt his own lessons well. Just as Sheridan had proclaimed that regional forms were emblematic of social disgrace, pleading for educators to take heed of the methods which his work offered for the creation of national uniformity in speech, so too did Poole wholeheartedly embrace the hegemonic potential of notions of a 'standard' accent, endorsing prevalent attitudes towards 'talking proper' in the system of education he advocates for village schools all over the country. Displacing the 'negligence' of local accents with the 'propriety' of the chosen norm, this achievement, in spite of any initial difficulties the child may have, is presented as exemplary:

Experience has fully proved to us, that although at the commencement the progress of the learner is continually checked and interrupted, yet by degrees habits of accuracy and propriety are formed; which terminate at length in an intelligent, discriminating manner of reading, and a purity of pronunciation, which are seldom, if ever, attained under the old system.[109]

The modes of speech which result are furthermore 'intelligent', an adjective which likewise reveals the adherence to those models of accent and cognitive adequacy (or its converse) which in themselves disturbingly tend to form a recurrent topos in language attitudes over this time. Since *The Village School Improved* went through three editions in a mere five years, it may moreover be assumed that other educators too recognized the stated validity of Poole's ideas.

Elementary education was, in fact, to become a sphere in which common value judgements about language, advantage, and disadvantage were to be encoded with remarkable frequency. As W. Bainbrigge emphasized in *Early Education* (1881), the import of *what* was said could be materially influenced by *how* it was said: 'Whatever powers of mind or extent of knowledge we possess, it is the voice which gives them utterance, and their influence in a large degree depends on skilful modulation; and without it, accuracy of thought, cogency of argument, and brilliancy of conception lose much of their force'.[110] Many writers concluded from such precepts that if children were to have systematic access to education, they must therefore also have equally systematic access to teaching in the spoken language: '"Pronunciation" and accent cannot be taught too early, too assiduously, too perseveringly', as the politician Sir Thomas Wyse declared in his own earlier work on education reform, expressing an opinion that many were evidently to share.[111]

The teaching of reading was, in particular, influenced in no small measure by the practical application of such maxims. Prominence was given to its capacity for decoding to sound—especially the 'correct' sound—as well as (and, occasionally, even at the expense of) its capacity for decoding to meaning. *Chambers's Educational Course: Simple Lessons in Reading*, a text written 'for use in schools and for private instruction', made this view particularly explicit. 'It is necessary that the child should be taught to *read*—that is, to apprehend at a glance the appearance of the written symbols of his native language', it stated, adding further that this ability should include being able 'to pronounce these symbols according to the most approved manner'.[112] Other definitions of reading tended to endorse this emphasis. John Gill's textbook on school method and management, widely used within teacher training colleges, notes that 'correct reading also includes purity of pronunciation, which consists in giving each letter its right sound, and to each word its proper accent'.[113] J. C. Graham, author of *An Introduction to the Art of Reading* (1861), similarly specifies that aptitude for reading requires 'a correct as opposed to a vulgar or provincial pronunciation'.[114] Notions of reading as an oral as well as a visual experience were thus closely aligned with prescriptive notions of correctness, as well as with the often avowed ambition to standardize the spoken language. *Chambers's Educational Course*, stressing the advantages of disseminating accurate modes of articulation by means of this particular educational bias, hence offers a view of a future and perfect uniformity which will result from the implementation of such thinking in the school: 'by these means, vulgar and provincial dialects will be gradually extirpated, and purity of speech introduced'.[115] Such aims were by no means rare.

As the Reverend Fussell, one of Her Majesty's Inspectors of Schools, asserted in 1859, reading was indeed one of the most important 'subjects of instruction in the elementary school. 'No secular subject comprised in the time-table is of greater importance than *reading*', he emphasized,[116] and the methods by which it should best be taught received considerable attention. As in Poole's educational regime in Somerset (and the public-school traditions already discussed), the role and responsibilities of the teacher were perceived as paramount. The central axiom was that set out, with appropriate rhetorical balance, by Thomas Livesey in 1881: 'If [the pupil] constantly hears good and correct speaking, he may learn to speak correctly and well'.[117] Other writers were more stringent, if less rhetorical, in the specification of the standards which were required of the 'good' teacher in this respect:

Teaching to read requires that the teacher should often read for imitation by the learner. Here, as in other things, the example of the teacher is necessary to explain his precept. But more than this, reading and speech are much influenced by imitation, from the inherent tendency to imitate those with whom we associate. This fact shows the importance of the teacher's speech being pure, distinct, deliberate, and impressive; for the school will image forth these qualities if found in him, or will be deficient in them if he is so.[118]

Gill's notion that the accents of pupils would mirror their teachers' speech (for good or ill) itself forms a notable and recurrent image in educational writings over the course of the nineteenth century. 'From not hearing good reading the children will never read well themselves' is given as an unquestioned fact in the General Report for the Years 1848–9, by Her Majesty's Inspector of Schools, the Reverend H. W. Bellairs: 'a master should set a good copy to his children, should read frequently with them during a lesson, and take pains to correct their incorrect pronunciation, e.g. the prevalent provincialisms of the district'.[119] The ideal thus described reveals the ways in which ideologies of a standard, applied to spoken as well as to written discourse, were fully assimilated within notions of what 'good' elementary education could and should comprise. The teachers' own training exemplifies this bias still further. Assimilation of the nuances of 'talking proper' was, for instance, often made an aspect of the assessment of teachers themselves. 'Intelligence, clear pronunciation, and good intonation are the main qualities we require to secure a high mark', the Reverend B. M. Corrie stated in his report on the Church of England Training Colleges for Schoolmasters in 1859.[120] Regional accents, connotative of 'ignorant' rather than 'educated', were increasingly considered incompatible with the office of schoolteacher, and training was often overtly interventionist in this respect. As the Reverend F. C. Cook commented in evaluating the National Society's Training Institution at Whitelands, Chelsea, the new teachers which it was in the process of producing had clearly benefited from educational emphases of this kind. 'The intonation is good, and it is impossible to doubt that great pains have been consistently taken to correct any faults of pronunciation which students may previously have contracted', he commended; 'this is a point of great importance for a teacher, and is no unfair test of mental cultivation and training'.[121]

The teacher was thus to set the standard, not only of learning itself but also of the modes of language deemed emblematic of it. Recommendations of how the requisite modes of speech are to be acquired appear daunting in the extreme as manuals of pronunciation, courses of elocution,[122] unremitting vigilance in terms of the teacher's own accent (as well as towards that of others), together with a full knowledge of articulation and phonetics, are all urged as essentials in the quest for that perfect propriety of enunciation which should distinguish the 'good' teacher. 'Provincialisms', suggestive, as Dr Johnson had declared, of the 'rude and uncultivated', did not befit those in charge of education. As *The Teacher's Manual of the Science and Art of Teaching* (1874) warned, the retention of such markers would be liable to establish erroneous models for the children in the school. The teacher is advised 'to guard himself' against their use for 'if his intercourse with others accustom him to erroneous modes of pronunciation and speech, he will be in danger of setting these up as standards'.[123]

Such features were likewise proscribed by inspectors of schools. D. A. Fearon, for example, in a work specifically devoted to the theory and practice of educational inspection, gave the presence of such 'errors' in the teacher as one of the salient points to be noticed during the assessment of a school: 'Does [the teacher] use provincialisms or avoid them, and check the use of them in the Scholars?'[124] All regional modes of speech were ideally to be eradicated before teaching even began. 'Help in curing provincialisms has been found in certain Training Colleges by the use of a little book called the "Manual of English Pronunciation"',[125] the *Teacher's Manual* helpfully advised on this matter. Gill too stressed the utility of this particular textbook, recommending in addition that both teacher and teaching assistants should transcribe into appropriate phonetic notation all lessons which were to be given, a process which would further ensure the maintenance of 'correct' standards of speech. As Gill added: 'An aid to this would be to mark the quantities and accents in the "Teacher's Lesson Book",—the doing so being a part of the preparation of the reading lesson required from his apprentices'.[126]

Training colleges for teachers, established from the 1840s onwards, were in such ways often actively to promote and endorse the normative standards of linguistic behaviour which were familiar from the prescriptive tradition and its own associated ideals of 'standard' speech. For teacher as for pupil, estimations of relative success could depend upon conformity in these respects. *Moffat's How to Teach Reading*, a popular text in educational training, makes this emphasis particularly clear, giving a full description of the levels of articulatory awareness which were required:

The teacher has to train the vocal organs to produce sounds distinctly and correctly. To do this, he will have to acquaint himself with the functions of the various organs concerned in the production of speech. He will have to be able to detect and correct bad habits and defects of utterance, and show the children how to use tongue, teeth, lips, and palate, in order to articulate distinctly.[127]

The teacher's own education in 'proper pronunciation' was, however, to extend even beyond the formal instruction in phonetics and speech training which a number of training colleges sought to provide. On the subject of pronunciation, as Morrison's *Manual of School Management* advised, learning could never stop. A text frequently used in such institutions, being 'examined and gone into minutely' at, for example, the Free Church Training College at Glasgow,[128] this encoded within its precepts a process of continual monitoring (and intentional improvement) with regard to the accent of the teacher:

whenever the young teacher hears a good speaker pronounce a word differently from what he has been accustomed to, he ought to note it, and never rest satisfied until he has ascertained the correct pronunciation. He will be amazed at the benefit which such a course will confer, and, in a short time he will find himself master of the majority of words.[129]

The teacher's stated role in disseminating as well as embodying the norms of 'proper' speech was in turn depicted as salient. Like missionaries, teachers were often seen in terms of their abilities in 'spreading the good word', appropriate criteria of 'good' and 'bad' of course again being made dependent on relevant estimations of 'standard' and its converse. It was an analogy made explicit by the phonetician Alexander Ellis ('Education . . . sends teachers as missionaries into remote districts to convey the required sounds more or less correctly'). More particularly, he also observed its consequences in terms of the wider images of standardization, noting that such a process 'does much to promote uniformity of speech'.[130] Morrison's instructions on the duties of the teacher once he (or she) was established in a position hence serve to reveal the further repercussions of these popular constructions of the teacher as an agent of linguistic conformity. 'We advise the teacher, whenever he finds himself located in a particular parish, to observe carefully the prevalent peculiarities', states Morrison. Such observation had an aim beyond simple familiarization with the language of the surrounding community and its assumed 'peculiarities'. Once observed, for instance, the latter were 'vigorously' to be corrected among the pupils as one of the most immediate tasks of the new teacher.[131]

The use of 'peculiarities' as a prominent aspect of educational (and prescriptive) metalanguage on this head is of course both telling and predictable. It should therefore come as no surprise to find characteristic features of this kind being treated in a number of educational textbooks under the heading 'Defective Intelligence'. In this respect, as John Gill forcibly asserts, 'the cure is with the teacher, who alone is to blame if there exists much incorrectness'.[132] Gill's own section on 'Defective Intelligence' in fact opens with the subject of pronunciation:

The most troublesome class of incorrect pronunciations are provincialisms, the substitution of one sound for another, as û for ŭ [i.e. [ʊ] for [ʌ]] and *vice versa*; the addition of sounds, as idea-r, and the omission of sounds, as of the aspirate. These faults partake of a mechanical character, belonging to the ear and habit, as much as to defective intelligence. The best mode of dealing with them is to take up a systematic course of orthoepy.[133]

Stigmatized as markers of 'ignorance' in more ways than one, these putative cognitive as well as elocutionary errors are, Gill tells us, to be revealed by various specific habits of speech, all of which are condemned. Enunciations more typical of 'provincial' than 'metropolitan', including the use of [ʊ] (as in *bull*) where one might expect [ʌ] as in *cut* (and vice versa), the presence of intrusive [r] and, of course, the loss of [h], all make their due appearance. Since the last of these was, as we have seen in Chapter 4, regularly interpreted as a signifier of lack of education per se, its use in accordance with accepted canons of correctness was regarded as especially significant. As the Reverend Wilkinson, for example, stressed in his 1861 lectures on education, the sociosymbolic value of [h] was such that, merely by virtue of its presence, 'it promotes refinement and assists in the cultivation of proprieties of manner'.[134] Other writers took a more practical approach to its inculcation and assessments of teaching proficiency regularly refer to its use. 'In particular, are mistakes as to *emphasis, punctuation*, and *aspirates* noticed and corrected with even the youngest children? Is distinct and audible utterance enforced?', as *The Elementary School Manager* specified, for example, in its directives for the monitoring of good teaching.[135] School inspectors affirmed identical preoccupations and their reports frequently assess superiority or inferiority in the teacher on these grounds. As Mr Neville Cream asserted in this context in 1861, it is only 'inferior teachers' who 'tell me it is useless to try and teach the children to [pronounce [h]]'. Their excuses that 'the parents at home unteach, by their conversation, whatever is taught at school' or 'that it is provincial' and hence part of the linguistic environment of the locality, are dismissed.[136] That icon of the 'good' teacher instead makes no such apologies, and none is needed. As Neville Cream continued: 'On the other hand, a good teacher says nothing, but sets to work; and the next year every child, from the oldest to the youngest, pronounces the *h* with correctness'.[137] The pressures exerted by such stereotypes were presumably not inconsiderable, not least since comments of this kind were regularly inserted in manuals of training for the hapless teacher.

'Every time a teacher corrects a pupil's spelling or a grammatical form, some process of standardization is taking place', Michael Stubbs affirms in *Educational Linguistics*.[138] In the nineteenth century, this process was, in terms of both the theory and practice of education, equally (and actively) extended to the sounds of speech, encompassing not only the widely recognized shibboleth of [h]-dropping but also a range of other sounds. As Gill counselled, 'when cases occur of indistinct pronunciation of particular sounds, as *s*, *r*, or *h*, it is desirable to give daily exercises thereon, directing the child's attention to yourself while uttering them.'[139] 'No faults should pass without correction', he further recommends. Graham's *Introduction to the Art of Reading* reflects the operation of similar principles. Disregarding the realities of linguistic usage by which, as we have seen in Chapter 3, features such as intrusive [r] (as in *law of the land*, but not *law to himself*, /ˈlɔːr əv-/ /ˈlɔː tuː-/) were common even within 'educated' speech, Graham instead isolates intrusive [r] as a specific marker of 'vulgar pronunciation', stating that its retention—in teacher or pupil—is entirely incompatible with the educational benefits which instruction in reading should provide. The mispronunciation of [h] attracts similar censure. 'There can scarcely be anything more disagreeable to a correct ear, than that of sinking the initial *h*, in words where it ought to be heard', Graham declares,[140] recommending daily exercises thereon to secure proficiency in pupil and teacher alike.

The level of detail which children were at times apparently required to assimilate in this context is striking. Even before the introduction of the annual inspection and the demands which this was subsequently to impose (not least given the convention of the oral examination of the children in the school, a means by which accent and other issues of spoken language often inevitably came to the fore), individual schools frequently implemented prescriptive tenets with praiseworthy diligence. John Poole's school in Somerset has already provided a markedly early example of this process. The seminary run by Miss Wilmshurst in Maldon, Essex, provides a later and equally instructive example of the ways in which preoccupations with phonemic detail could exert considerable influence on the methods of tuition which were employed.

The First Part of the Progressive Parsing Lessons was printed in 1833 'for the use of Miss Wilmshurst's Seminary', though its usefulness for other schools was, of course, not denied. It offers a comprehensive examination of the way in which reading was to be taught, asserting as a central principle that 'the importance of an early knowledge of every simple elementary sound in the English Language, is generally acknowledged'.[141] What is, in effect, a series of rudimentary lessons in phonetics follows and, though the articulatory details provided can at times verge on the cryptic, a thorough survey of pronunciation and its role in 'proper' reading is attempted. '*Ar* must be pronounced with the tip of the tongue pressed against the gums of the under teeth, to prevent the *r* having its rough or consonant sound', it dictates: 'The close *o* is pronounced with the lips drawn up as far as possible'.[142] Two pages later, exercises on parsing are extended to phonemes as well as parts of speech, and an illustrative section on how to apply this knowledge is presented in the typical 'question and answer' format of schoolbooks of the day:

TEACHER. Tell me the vowel sounds in *barn yard*.
PUPIL. *Barn* middle *a, yard* middle *a*.
T. *Bee-hive.*—P. *Bee* long *e, hive* long *i*.
T. *Blue-bell.*—P. *Blue* long *u, bell* short *e*.

John Walker likewise appears as a prime educational authority, his pronouncing dictionary presented as indispensable for teaching the spoken language in ways which would have gratified Sheridan's earlier ambitions for the standardization of speech. 'Mr. Walker observes that when the *o* ends a syllable immediately before or after the accent; as in *polite, impotent*, &c, there is an elegance in giving it a sound nearly as long as the long *o*', the pupils are informed; 'The *a* in the words *past, last, France*. . . &c, is sometimes prolonged in a sound between the short *a* and the middle *a*.' 'Mr. Walker does not approve of this sound', the text adds, lending its own support to that distaste for 'middle sounds' which Walker had expressed at the end of the preceding century.[143]

It might, of course, be argued that concentration on the spoken word to this level is a feature expected in a school professing to teach 'young ladies'. As we have seen in Chapter 5, elocution was depicted as a necessary accomplishment within prevailing ideals of 'proper' femininity for girl, wife, and mother. However, it rapidly becomes clear that elementary education in general was often to display a similar focus, concentrating, for example, on teaching reading by methods of phonic analysis which were deliberately designed to impart 'proper' rather than 'improper' ways of pronouncing sounds. As *Moffat's How to Teach Reading* noted, 'phonic analysis' was to be recommended for its thoroughness in this respect, guaranteeing familiarity with the range of 'proper' sounds in English.[144] Detailed descriptions of how to teach reading thus frequently present 'proper' education in these terms too. 'Lessons must be given on each sound of a vowel, the short ones before the long ones. Each following lesson should also contain the sounds taught in preceding lessons', instructed John Prince in another central textbook on school organization and method.[145] Gill's account of the approved methods to be used in infant classes similarly emphasizes instruction in articulation as a necessary accompaniment to the art of reading: 'This method consists in slowly uttering a word, and drawing attention to the mouth while doing so, then the learner to utter the word, and this process to be continued until the child discerns how a particular sound is produced'.[146] Ideal lessons for the infant class specifically include 'orthoepy' as well as spelling, definitions of reading as an oral activity being vigorously prioritized by this emphasis on articulatory prowess. Though the 'look and say' method of learning to read (in which 'children are taught to recognise and pronounce *whole words* at a single effort without stopping to spell them')[147] is acknowledged as achieving the quickest results, nevertheless, as Gill stresses, methods of teaching which incorporate 'phonic analysis' are to be preferred, primarily on the grounds that 'oral reading incorporates much more than recognition of the words'. As he adds: 'it includes, among other things, purity and distinctness of pronunciation. Hence it is desirable to have, current with the reading lesson, lessons on pronunciation and spelling, on the method of phonic analysis.'[148]

Though such methods were not without their critics, George White in 1862 averring that they constituted 'too complicated a machine for teachers to handle, involving a process too difficult for children to encounter',[149] the focus on sound as well as spelling in the teaching of reading received, on the whole, a favourable response. As John Prince noted in 1880, 'the pronunciation by this method will be much more accurate than any other',[150] an important achievement given the prominence of attitudes to a spoken standard within educational thinking of the time. Even the Report of the Privy Council Committee on Education in 1842 had endorsed the values of Walker's pronouncing dictionary in the school: 'The master should have at hand also a good English Dictionary (Walker's may be purchased for 4*s.* 6*d.*), and not be afraid to make frequent use of it in the presence of his pupils'.[151] Grover's *New English Grammar for the Use of Junior Classes in Schools* of 1877 attempted to make such necessary information about the sounds of English more palatable for young children by presenting it in rhyme: 'The *liquids* you may quickly tell,// They are but *four—m, n, r,* and *l.*// *Mutes* the rest are said to be,// Such are *b, d, c,* and *f* and *t'.*[152]

Even outside the reading lesson, however, these pressures did not necessarily diminish for either teacher or child. While an unremitting vigilance towards matters of accent was, as we have seen, presented as integral to the teacher's role as linguistic standard, duties in this respect were also to extend to a form of constructive eavesdropping to be practised upon pupils wherever possible. Griffiths, for example, specifies that to confine dissemination of the desired norms of speech to the reading lesson alone is to limit vital opportunities for impressing this information upon children: 'The teacher should be scrupulously careful in exacting correct and distinct utterance in *all* school exercises, not merely in the formal reading lesson, but in all the intercourse of the children.'[153] Other manuals setting forth the theory and practice of teaching unreservedly endorse this view: '[The teacher] should carefully correct every mispronunciation made by the children, both in the reading lesson and out of it',[154] 'the gross errors in pronunciation which children acquire from the conversation of their contemporaries... can only be eradicated by correction at all times when they occur, either in the reading lesson, or in ordinary conversation'.[155] Robinson in fact specifies that it is in such informal circumstances that inculcation of the requisite norms of speech may best be achieved. He advocates, wherever possible, the correction of 'local peculiarities... in that conversational intercourse that always exists between the teacher and children during school hours.'[156] Any feelings of alienation, or indeed persecution, which might result from the full implementation of this process are seemingly not considered.

Robinson's emphasis on the need to teach pronunciation outside rather than inside the reading lesson does, however, receive some justification from his account of the negative consequences which could, and did, attend that undue concentration on accent recommended in many manuals of teaching. The attention given to the correction of perceived 'errors' in enunciation could, he warned, on occasion exceed that paid to the acquisition of reading itself. '[Teachers] pass over the child's comprehension of the text, and the force and correctness with which he makes himself understood almost entirely, in their extreme desire to secure purity of utterance',[157] as Robinson points out with disapprobation. The reports of Her Majesty's Inspectors can proffer similar criticisms, revealing the ways in which an exaggerated emphasis on phonemic propriety could sometimes operate to the apparent exclusion of the true purposes of teaching reading. The Reverend Mr Grant in 1860 offers, for example, a graphic description of teachers 'lying in wait for provincialisms' and, as they occur, making constant interruptions in order to align 'faulty' utterance with the normative paradigms of 'proper' speech.[158] Robinson himself provides a similarly informative critique of contemporary practices in the teaching of reading, censuring the methods in which 'by their captious manner, and their constant fault-finding [teachers] worry and distract their children until they force them to commit, in their perplexity, errors of which they otherwise would have been quite innocent'.

On the whole, this was unfortunately the position which seems most often to have been adopted. School inspectors, themselves products of a cultural and linguistic climate in which notions of accent as social symbol had been assimilated into prescriptive and popular thought as never before, hence often stressed the need to 'improve' English in ways which unambiguously proscribed localized accents as a marker of 'ignorance'. Inattention to perceived oral proprieties is regarded with disfavour, attracting disapproving comments in the yearly reports: 'the reading lessons of the lower classes are conducted with but slight regard to clearness of articulation or correctness of pronunciation', the

Reverend Fussell complained in 1859 of schools in Middlesex.[159] 'Reading is only good in the best schools. The great fault in the lower classes is want of real correctness, good articulation, and mastery of the pronunciation', as the inspector for the schools of the West Central division of England affirmed in 1887. 'Long-inherited peculiarities of mode of speech and pronunciation' impede achievement in Cumberland, Mr Parez reports in the same year, concluding that 'it is not in Cumberland that for a generation or two good reading will be found.'

Following the introduction of the Revised Code in 1862, and the principle of 'payment by results',[160] one can imagine that such comments would have exerted still more force on the normative principles teachers were supposed to adopt, especially given the continued dominance of modes of oral examination by inspectors when they visited a school. 'How great a part [of the work] consists in the reading; and what an advantage for making a favourable impression on a spectator have those elementary schools in which the tone and accent of the reading are agreeable', as Matthew Arnold, for example, declared in his own role as an inspector of schools.[161] Notions of 'agreeableness', and even of 'good' and 'bad', could, however, as Arnold also realized, depend all too often upon the evaluative assumptions, and accompanying notions of subjective inequality, which were frequently implemented in the processes of assessment.

That educational aims explicitly came to include the dissemination of a spoken standard on national rather than local scales is therefore both openly acknowledged and entirely in keeping with the linguistic temper of the age. As *Chambers's Educational Course: Simple Lessons in Reading* confidently asserted, the increasing use of modes of oral instruction in the question and answer method, rather than the learning by rote which had often featured in the past, offered undeniable advantages in this respect, not least since 'by these means, vulgar and provincial dialects will be gradually extirpated, and purity of speech introduced'.[162] Defined by Johnson as 'the act of rooting out; eradicating; excision', extirpation was in such ways to emerge as an important philosophy in educational terms too, specifically referring to the displacement of dialect and its associated markers of speech. Evoking familiar binary oppositions of 'pure' and 'impure', 'vulgar' and 'polite', precepts such as these effectively embodied the ways in which the connotative and cultural values accorded to divergent linguistic varieties in the world outside the school could equally be embedded within the educational domain and the instruction of children which took place within it. Again and again, it seemed clear that the monolithic was to be prioritized at the expense of the localized and variable. Only one form of language was, in theory, to be sanctioned as acceptable in the atmosphere of the ideal school.

Textbooks on recitation make this particularly plain. Commended by Arnold as 'the special subject which produces at present, so far as I can tell, most good',[163] recitation was popular in many schools and works such as William Enfield's *The Speaker* went through many editions, its original ambition 'of assisting the students at Warrington in acquiring a just and graceful Elocution' being applied, in effect, on a national scale. Enfield's specifications of the 'just' and 'graceful' modes of speech which mark the 'gentleman' come to take on a certain appropriacy in educational terms too, even at its most elementary levels, an emphasis which is concisely revealed in a textbook from a century later: *Recitation: A Handbook for Teachers in Public Elementary School* by A. Burrell.

Published in 1891, Burrell's *Recitation* endorses those now familiar ideas by which 'distinct and correct pronunciation' was to form a part of the taught language from the first to the most senior class at school. Systematically analysing each sound and sound combination for the benefit of the pupil, it has a clear standardizing intent; attention to such details provides the means by which provenance may be disguised, and assimilation to the non-localized as social norm achieved. On the realization of *a* in words such as *father* and *bath*, Burrell thus notes:

Remember, as I have said, that the person who pronounces the āh thinly (as ăh) [i.e. [æ]] *must* come from the northern part of England; but the person who pronounces the āh long and full *may* come from any part of England; and it is the business of educated people to speak so that no-one may be able to tell in what county their childhood was passed. Once more, I repeat this: the ăh is not wrong; *but it is provincial.*[164]

With a curious blend of description and prescription (refusing to specify the selection of [æ] in words such as *fast* as 'wrong' but nevertheless still effectively condemning it by the designation of 'provincial'), Burrell in many ways can be seen as representative of educational thinking on the 'standard' accent problem at the end of the nineteenth century. 'Good' accents being those unmarked by signifiers of the regional, these are the ones 'rightly' to be taught in schools. 'Bad' accents are, conversely, to be made 'better' by educational processes which emphasized the spoken word in the teaching of reading, and regularly included recitation, with the right accent, as a significant part of the syllabus. *Brandram's Speaker*, another textbook of the same kind which, on its title page, adopts as a central tenet Macbeth's line 'Stay, you imperfect speakers' (1. iii. 70), specifies still further that regional accents are compatible with the precepts of the taught language only when 'appropriately assumed with particular characters in dramatic recitation'. Otherwise, the message runs, they are to be 'conquered'.[165]

Even Sunday schools could pursue the same principles and priorities, readily employing similar martial imagery in which victory attends those with command of the non-localized norms of speech and defeat is the portion of those who fail in this respect. As *Groombridge's Annual Reader*, a manual of recitation 'for the use of schools', had stressed in 1868, 'Speech is a gift

of God which accompanies reason', and 'the habit of speaking correct English…
next to good morals, is one of the best things in this world'.[166] Given equations
of this kind between 'good' language and good behaviour, the extension of
appropriate paradigms of norm and deviation with reference to accent in the
Sunday school was perhaps an all too logical step. *The Sunday School Teacher's
Manual*, published by the Sunday School Union, hence advises the teacher to
give close attention to the language employed in this domain, and to bear in
mind his (or her) role as a linguistic as well as Christian exemplar:

Next to sound Biblical information we would urge upon the teacher the cultivation
of *correct English*…The Sunday School teacher is an *oral* instructor, not a wielder of
the pen. He depends, instrumentally, on the power of the tongue; and therefore on
the language which he employs—on what he says, and how he says it—his influence
over his pupils must largely depend. Consequently, to be able to speak his own
tongue with correctness, force, and facility is an acquisition to be sought after with all
possible earnestness and perseverance.[167]

Knowledge of 'proper' English being second only to 'godliness' and
knowledge of the Bible, the instructor is urged to strive for improvement
appropriate to his role. After all, as the author pointed out, the voice is 'God-
given', employed for reading out the book of books for which speech which
'mangles the Queen's English' is sadly out of place: 'There is one powerful
motive for the cultivation of correct tones and pronunciation, viz., the
importance of being able to *read the Bible aloud* with accuracy, dignity, and
force in the class, and to train the scholars to do the same.'[168] As in the elementary school, the avowed aim is that children, provided with such illustrative models for their imitation, will happily emulate linguistic as well as
moral behaviour, leading, in the utopian visions which once more come to
the fore, to a general improvement of 'tone' throughout the nation.

Other books intended for the Sunday School foster similar precepts
though, on a number of occasions, they also encourage the use of formal
as well as implicit modes of teaching for the spoken word. The author of
The Sunday School Spelling Book of 1823, dedicated 'To the Patrons and
Teachers of Sunday Schools', focuses, for example, on the importance of the
reading lesson for both teacher and pupil, drawing particular attention to
those 'defects' of pronunciation which can often mar instruction in this context. His own book is offered as remedy for these problems:

It must have been observed by all…that children repeatedly read the same lesson
without understanding or correctly pronouncing many of the important words. To
obviate these evils, he has introduced…an Explanatory Dictionary…The Spelling
Lessons have also been particularly attended to, and the natural and correct pronunciation of each word has been attempted to be conveyed to the mind of the pupil.[169]

Sunday Schools, elementary schools, training academies for teachers, private schools such as that run by Miss Wilmshurst in Maldon hence all

embraced the theory that teaching the 'proper' accent was to form a vital part of educational provision and that, by such means, regional modes of utterance, regularly construed in works on education as 'evils', 'vices', 'defects', 'faults', and 'peculiarities', were to be eliminated. Not only in England, but in Scotland, Wales, and Ireland were such principles openly adhered to. In the 1823 Statement by the Directors of the Edinburgh Academy, it is, for example, explicitly noted of the master of English that not only must he possess the highest qualifications in other respects, but also that he 'shall have a pure English accent'.[170] The School Board of Aberdeen likewise stressed that elocution, on specifically English models, was to form an integral part of the syllabus implemented in the region's schools; *Macleod's First Text-Book of Elocution*, developed in response to these requirements, went through three editions, and well over six thousand copies, within the space of a few years.[171]

The theory by which these perceived standards were to be fostered was therefore widely recognized. The practice, and that systematic training in non-localized norms which was so often recommended, may well of course have differed. Ideologies of a standard and the associated processes of standardization naturally tend to maintain their disjunctions within as well as outside the school, and though many writers stressed the role of education as an agency of standardization, again this was to be revealed most clearly in the widespread diffusion of language attitudes (the 'error' of dropping [h], the 'negligence' of intrusive [r]) rather than in any systematic linguistic conversions which the school, in reality, might achieve—especially in terms of the ordinary styles of speech which speakers use. Though involved to some extent in perpetuating these requirements himself,[172] Robinson, for example, admitted in 1863 that educational aims to standardize the accents of English in favour of a non-localized norm were in truth both unrealizable, and unrealistic:

If any teacher expects that he will ever be able to eradicate all traces of such errors, I am afraid that he will be sadly disappointed. The time will never come, most likely, when all the people of Great Britain and Ireland will speak exactly alike, and yet it is for this unattainable uniformity that men are struggling.[173]

Language attitudes and language use again diverge. That uniformity espoused as ideal within the prescriptive tradition (and its educational manifestations too) is indeed 'unattainable', as Robinson rightly states. Though generations of writers on education had, for instance, stressed the utility of the teacher as model, notions of group identity and peer group pressure are, as already illustrated, far more complex than such simplistic equations suggest. Similarly, regardless of instruction in the patterns of 'proper' speech, children will tend to articulate identity in ways which, though perhaps conforming to more formal norms within the school, outside it will instead adhere to the usage of the speech community in which they have their being, and where 'talking proper' (as in Labov's study of Martha's Vineyard) may well be construed as 'talking posh' and a sign of not 'belonging'. Where educational precepts did perhaps achieve most success was, of course, in furthering awareness (if not uniform use) of those forms which were deemed to constitute 'proper' as opposed to 'improper' English. The 'ridicule' recommended by school inspectors as remedial measures for the regional, and the deliberate manipulation of those notions of shame which were so often implicit (or even explicit) within specifications of the nineteenth-century reading lesson, did not exist without repercussions. It was the stereotype of the 'educated' accent which was above all to be encoded by these means. Teaching, in other words, tended to reinforce the hegemony of the standard ideology and those forms of language associated with it; though boarding schools, as we have seen, especially those in the south, went some way towards achieving a sense of the realities behind such ideals, they were aided in this by factors which it proved largely impossible for the elementary school to emulate. An emergent 'received pronunciation' remained, in educational terms, largely the preserve of these rather more elite establishments where the correlations of scholars and gentlemen, and the manifold pressures of social (and linguistic) homogenization which did not end with the conclusion of the school day, were particularly in evidence. For the average child at elementary school, the impetus to conform in these respects was largely absent for, as Morrison recognized in 1863, it would alienate him (or her) from local speech communities, from friends and family, and from the pressures of peer groups which urged conformity in other, far different, respects.[174] Reversing the traditional pattern of emphasis, Morrison thus felt it necessary to warn the aspiring teacher that undue (or careless) censure in this context could in fact lead to his own alienation and estrangement from the surrounding community:

this, however, must be done with caution, and without any parade of ostentation; for, if the teacher, with the view of showing off his own acquirements, holds up to ridicule any local peculiarities, he will be sure to enlist the sympathies of the neighbours against himself, and will find his efforts at improvement thwarted at every step.[175]

Nevertheless, the ideal of education as a tool by which non-localized norms of speech were to be enforced over the nation remained an evocative one, endorsed in the twentieth century by still more writers on education and still other government officials. Though the endeavours of the nineteenth century had largely failed ([h]-dropping was still prevalent in those below the higher-status groups, people based in the north and Midlands continued to use the 'wrong' sort of *u* in words such as *cut*, or the 'wrong' sort of *a* in words such as *fast*), the Newbolt Report of 1921 on the Teaching of English in England was to recommend still more strenuous efforts in this direction, the vigilance of past decades clearly having been inadequately implemented, and insufficiently thought out:

English, we are convinced, must form the essential basis of a liberal education for all English people, and in the earlier stages of education it should be the principal function of all schools of whatever type to form this basis.

Of this provision, the component parts will be, first, systematic training in the sounded speech of standard English, to secure correct pronunciation and clear articulation; second, systematic training in the use of standard English, to secure clearness and correctness both in oral expression and in writing; third, training in reading.[176]

Like Sheridan, the Newbolt Report prioritizes the teaching of the spoken language as an important desideratum in education. Like Sheridan too, it envisages this as a means of eradicating social distinctions in the nation. Accent, laden with social values, and constituting a prime marker of social identity, is, as writers throughout the nineteenth century had stressed, divisive. Betraying the triumph of optimism over experience, the Newbolt Report nevertheless notes:

We believe that such an education based upon the English language and literature would have important social, as well as personal, results; it would have a unifying tendency... If the teaching of the language were properly and universally provided for, the difference between educated and uneducated speech, which at present causes so much prejudice and difficulty of intercourse on both sides, would gradually disappear.[177]

'Prejudice' of a linguistic sort is, of course, pervasive in the Report itself as localized forms of language are stigmatized in moral terms, as well as being presented as virtual embodiments of evil:

The great difficulty of teachers in Elementary Schools in many districts is that they have to fight against the powerful influence of evil habits of speech contracted in home and street. The teachers' struggle is thus not with ignorance but with a perverted power.[178]

Dialect no longer being constructed as disgrace but instead as outright 'perversion', one cannot wonder at the emotive pleas the Report contains, censuring teachers who 'make no serious effort to win' this moral crusade against defective language, and readily employing metaphors of 'fight', 'struggle', and 'race':

Teachers of infants sometimes complain that when the children come to school they can scarcely speak at all. They should regard this as rather an advantage. There is often a kind of race as to which should succeed in setting its stamp upon the children's speech, the influence of the teacher, or that of the street or home.[179]

The race is, of course, to confer the forms of standard speech, and is to be won by 'speech training' which is to be 'undertaken from the outset and... continued all through the period of schooling'.[180] The prize, for teacher and for child, is 'the first and chief duty of the Elementary School'—'to give its pupils speech' and thus to 'make them articulate and civilized human beings'. Articulacy is, however, evidently determined only in the terms of the standard ideology, and the forms of speech with which it was associated. It is 'standard' and not 'dialect' which, for the authors of the Newbolt Report, thus endows the child with 'civilization'. It is in turn, they state, the 'right' of the child to receive this: 'the accomplishment of clear and correct speech is the one definite accomplishment which the child is entitled to demand from the Infant School'.[181] Though ostensibly dialect is not to be denigrated,[182] the subtext is clear, as are affinities with earlier writers on education. As in Livesey's work on the teaching of reading in 1882, even if it should be true that 'the teacher can scarcely hope to eradicate completely the errors of a district', nevertheless the central maxim is that 'he need not let them, like seed heads, thrive and run to seed'.[183]

8

The Rise (and Fall?) of Received Pronunciation

'IN the present day we may ... recognise a received pronunciation all over the country, not widely differing in any particular locality, and admitting a certain degree of variety', wrote Alexander Ellis in 1869.[1] Documented extensively throughout the various volumes of his *Early English Pronunciation*, it was this 'received pronunciation' (later referred to as RP) which gradually comes into being as a major focus of that attention which had so insistently been paid to issues of accent over the late eighteenth and nineteenth centuries. Non-localized, betraying little (if anything) of the speaker's place of birth, 'received pronunciation', and approximations to it, were to meet that desire for a geographically neutral accent which Sheridan and Walker had earnestly proclaimed. Even in the late eighteenth century, notions of the 'received' had been prominent in the phonetic ideals advanced; 'those sounds ... which are the most generally received among the learned and polite, as well as the bulk of speakers, are the most legitimate', as John Walker averred in 1791.[2] His earlier *General Idea of a Pronouncing Dictionary* of 1774 was still more explicit, specifying the merits of 'received pronunciation' in the correct enunciation of unstressed syllables.[3] Nevertheless, at this time, the reality behind such linguistic ideals was, as we have seen, markedly restricted in both geographical and social terms. After all, as Sheridan complained, the disadvantages of 'rustic pronunciation' could and did extend to gentry alongside commoners depending on their place of birth and the type (and location) of the education they had received. Still worse, throughout the nation 'odious distinctions' of pronunciation impeded the linguistic equality which all might otherwise rightly attain.[4] Reading Ellis a century later, it was to seem that such long-held ambitions, founded on a mode of speech which would indeed be able to transcend regional difference, had—in part—at last come true.

Ellis was not alone in these perceptions. 'It is the business of educated people to speak so that no-one may be able to tell in what county their childhood was passed', the elocutionist Arthur Burrell, for example, stressed in 1891,[5] itemizing the features of a non-regional norm for the erudition of his readers. The phonetician Henry Sweet shared in this pattern of comment, likewise isolating a 'received' form of speech which was 'approximated to, all over Great Britain, by those who do not keep to their own local dialects'.[6] 'Culture', 'refinement', status, and superiority were, according to popular belief, all able to be conveyed within the nuances of a variety of pronunciation which was, as Sweet confirmed, simultaneously liberated from regional association and heavily imbued with social meaning. 'There . . . prevails a belief that it is possible to erect a standard of pronunciation which should be acknowledged and followed throughout all countries where English is spoken as a native tongue', Ellis further specified, noting moreover that this already extended to the sense that such a 'standard already exists, and is the norm unconsciously followed by persons who, by rank or education, have most right to establish the custom of speech'.[7]

As we might expect, however, a closer examination of Ellis's words reveals certain reservations about the precise nature of that spoken 'standard' which others are so willing to attest and to endorse. If popular comment stressed uniformity, and the corresponding need for all 'educated' speakers to conform to attendant images of 'talking proper', then Ellis on the other hand placed careful emphasis on the variable realities of spoken usage as the end of the nineteenth century approached. In this context, as he was forced to admit, it was indeed 'belief' rather than behaviour which was most conspicuous (and most widespread) in any national 'standard' of pronunciation which could in reality be said to have been achieved. Ellis's comments in this respect predictably run counter to the images of monolithic correctness promoted by the prescriptive tradition. 'A large number of words are pronounced with differences very perceptible to those who care to observe, even among educated London speakers', he emphasized,[8] a point he returned to six years later in his observation that 'men of undoubted education and intelligence differ in pronunciation from one another, from pronouncing dictionaries, and from my own habits'. As a result, he concluded, 'the term "educated pronunciation" must be taken to have a very "broad" signification'.[9] If used as a convenient touchstone in popular accounts of 'correct' pronunciation ('The tone of the voice indicates character; the mode of speaking shows training and education', as T. L. Nichols averred),[10] then Ellis in this respect also determinedly strove to instil a proper sense of linguistic reality, stripping away the fallacies with which such images were all too often surrounded. Turning common assumptions on their heads, he instead stressed that 'there is no such thing as educated English pronunciation. There are pronunciations of English people more or less educated in a multitude of things, but not', he added, 'in pronunciation'.[11]

Outside the absolutes of prescriptive rhetoric, the latitude which 'educated' and 'received' pronunciation actually allowed in the late nineteenth century is, for example, amply confirmed in the transcriptions of the *Oxford English Dictionary*, the first fascicles of which began to appear from 1884.[12] Like Ellis's *Early English Pronunciation*, the *OED* was firmly inspired by descriptive rather than prescriptive principle, rejecting the arbitrary (and often unfounded) pronouncements on usage which had often characterized previous works of English lexicography.[13] From this point of view, however, pronunciation was to cause significant problems for James Murray, editor of the *OED* from 1879 until his death in 1915. Urged by Sweet to 'give *all* existing educated pronunciations' for every word in the dictionary,[14] Murray was daunted by the labour which this would necessarily involve. Even for a word such as *vase*, four entirely different variants presented themselves for his consideration, all of which were eventually given in the relevant entry. Notions of a single 'educated pronunciation'—and a rigidly defined norm— were, he found, evidently far from being the case. 'A very large number of words have two or more pronunciations current', Murray affirmed, a fact which should be viewed positively rather than negatively 'as giving life and variety to language'.[15] Variants for *abandon, acknowledge, acoustic*, and *acupuncture* duly appear (among many others) in the first fascicle *A–Ant*, while the currency of co-existing pronunciations such as ['fɔːhɛd] and ['fɒrɪd] for *forehead* and ['gɒf] and ['gɒlf] for *golf* became a topic of marked dispute as the dictionary advanced. Henry Bradley, taken on as second editor of the *OED* alongside Murray in 1886, evidently regarded the ongoing shift of ['fɒrɪd] to a pronunciation more influenced by the spelling (as in modern articulations of *forehead*) as a species of 'mischievous' change and hence one which the dictionary, in spite of its avowedly descriptive principles, should not record.[16] The pronunciation to be given for *golf* proved even more problematic as Bradley and Walter Skeat (the Cambridge medievalist and one of the most assiduous critical readers for the dictionary) took up directly opposing positions on contemporary usage. 'The mod[ern] pron[unciation] usually follows the spelling, though (gof) is often heard', Bradley stated conclusively in the first proof of the relevant entry, giving ['gɒlf] as the sole transcription. 'I think golf is going *out*, & gof becoming more general', Skeat nevertheless countered in the adjacent margin. 'The former is often received with *derision*', he added, his use of emphasis making his point still clearer. Consensus in this instance was achieved only by compromise. Both variants were, in the event, included in the published text though Bradley's favoured form comes first. Skeat's perceptions of usage were nevertheless also given their due in a new comment on the 'fashionable' use of /ˈgɒf/ which entirely displaces the usage note originally given. Establishing the precise nature of the consensus norms of 'educated' speech would, as this indicates, remain a far from easy task. And while pragmatic considerations of space eventually impeded the inclusion of all 'educated' variants for each word on the model urged by Sweet, it is nevertheless all too clear that any 'received' pronunciation which one might want to adduce for the late nineteenth century (as well as afterwards) must, from such evidence, be seen as flexible rather than fixed, subject to individual differences rather than the rigid norms habitually favoured by prescriptive texts.

As the *OED* serves to confirm therefore, Ellis was of course right in the correctives which he persistently attempted to endorse in terms of the complex nature of a spoken 'standard' in the later nineteenth century. Language, both then and now, is innately variable. 'Nothing approaching to real uniformity prevails', Ellis had, for instance, set forth in the first volume of his *Early English Pronunciation*, a fundamental principle which he iterated at intervals thereafter. Accents exist on a continuum, influenced by variation in style and context, age and gender, as well as by regional location. Speakers, even those designated as 'best', could and did have a range of speech styles (and individual variants) at their disposal—a repertoire of possibilities from which they could choose depending on the specific demands of context or formality. Alongside the popular, and widely prevalent, images of a non-regional and 'correct' pronunciation which all were assumed to desire, vernacular norms of speech moreover also continued to have their being—and their adherents. Wordsworth would retain his Northern accent to the end of his life (in spite of the negative comments which it could attract);[17] William Barnes's loyalty to Wessex was pronounced in more ways than one, infusing his poetry alongside his speech,[18] while Tennyson too continued to use the speech patterns of Lincolnshire throughout his life. A national standard on the lines of the linguistically homogeneous utopia envisaged by Sheridan (one in which 'the rising generation, born and bred in different Countries and Counties [would] no longer have a variety of dialects, but as subjects of one King, have one common tongue ... restored to their birthright in communage of language, which has been too long fenced in, and made the property of a few')[19] was in these terms far from the reality of many speakers of English. Accent was, in the end, just too complex to be neatly confined within the prescriptive paradigms of 'one word: one pronunciation' to which so many writers had earlier aspired.

Nevertheless, if a single and rigidly codified accent for all remained the stuff of myth rather than reality, it was also undeniable, as Ellis and Sweet serve to confirm, that notions of a non-regional 'received pronunciation' had in other respects undeniably come into being. Based 'on the educated speech of London and Southern England generally', 'Standard English' in this sense, as Henry Sweet averred, had come to be disseminated in ways which extended far beyond these original geographical confines. More particularly, he added, 'it need scarcely be said that this dialect is not absolutely uniform, but varies slightly from individual to individual, and more markedly from generation to generation'.[20] As in Ellis's work, descriptive truth ousts prescriptive fiction, the facts of variability—just as in modern sociolinguistic studies—taking precedence over the traditionally favoured images of uniformity and the binary divides of 'good' and 'bad'. Indeed, the 'correct speaker' who featured so prominently in popular prescriptive eulogies of the day was, Sweet stated, a markedly elusive creature when it came to the attempt to track one down. 'I have for some years been in search of a "correct speaker" ', he hence averred, adding that, in terms of success, the enterprise was rather like 'going after the great sea-serpent'.

It possessed a degree of fruitlessless which instead inevitably led him to the conclusion that 'the animal known as a "correct speaker" is not only extraordinarily shy and difficult of capture, but that he may be put in the same category as the "rigid moralist" and "every schoolboy" '. In other words, as Sweet concluded, 'that he is an abstraction, a figment of the brain'.[21]

Regularly used to foster images of convergence towards (and proscribe deviation from) an idealized norm—one in which, for example, intrusive [r] was never used and [hw] rather than [w] formed the only conceivable beginning for words such as *which* and *where*—the 'correct speaker' thus tended to disappear when faced with the fuzziness and variability of real speech, even among so-called 'standard' speakers'. Sweet's deliberate departure from the fallible assumptions of the past is clear. 'It is absurd to set up a standard of how English people *ought* to speak, before we know how they actually *do* speak—a knowledge which is still in its infancy', he reminded readers of his *Primer of Phonetics*.[22] In this, like Ellis, he determinedly points the divide which continued to exist between the processes of standardization and its associated ideologies—the disjunction, as Ellis termed it, between 'belief' and behaviour. The two, as we have of course repeatedly seen, are by no means the same. Only in its broader senses therefore, as Sweet and a variety of other writers continued to confirm, could a 'standard' for the spoken language legitimately be said to exist in the late nineteenth century—one which incorporated flux and flexibility, a range of permissible variants rather than codificatory convictions of an absolute norm.

'Standard English' was, as a result, by no means to be synonymous with the presence of a 'standard' accent. Instead, while a non-localized and thereby 'standard' variety of the language had indeed indubitably come into existence, its presence confirmed by shared features of grammar and morphology over the nation (though alongside and overlapping with localized variants at many points), it is important to remember, as Peter Trudgill has repeatedly stressed, that this could (and can) be spoken 'with a large number of different accents' even if, in general terms, 'most speakers of the (more-or-less regionless) standard English dialect . . . speak it with a (usually not too localized) regional accent'. Nevertheless, as he points out, even today 'most educated people betray their geographical origins much more in their pronunciation than in their grammar or lexis'.[23] The same principles can again usefully be mapped on to the past. 'Educated' speakers in the late nineteenth and early twentieth centuries in a similar way regularly tended to avoid the grammatical solecisms of multiple negation or double comparatives in their use of 'standard' grammar, while potentially also retaining features such as rhotic /r/ or [ɪŋg] rather than [ɪŋ] in words such as *walking*. RP itself, in its 'purest' and most non-localized forms, is still spoken only by three to five per cent of the population, a statistic which it would be unwise to increase for the speakers of the later nineteenth century.

But if RP was, and is, restricted to a minority, the wider impact of its framing language attitudes should not be dismissed, nor underestimated in their effects. The prescriptive tradition of the late eighteenth and nineteenth centuries had, as we have seen, catered for (and fostered) linguistic insecurity in ways which would have been impossible within a more scientifically valid and objective discipline, promoting certain enunciations as emblematic of disgrace and others as equally resonant of educatedness and acceptability. Such pressures could not be ignored, not least given the ways in which they infused so many spheres of Victorian life and culture from education to popular periodicals, as well as informing the skewed patterns of representation commonly conferred upon direct speech in many contemporary novels. As countless speakers confirmed, a certain amount of intentional accommodation towards the prominent features of this designated 'standard' did take place. It was in these terms, for instance, that Thomas Hardy modified his original Wessex forms and in which H. G. Wells shed the Cockney markings of his youth. In a similar way the Nottinghamshire-born D. H. Lawrence was prompted to gain equal facility in the stated nuances of 'talking proper' over his time at Nottingham High School in the late 1890s (even if he was also to retain competence in his original Midland forms throughout his life).[24] Duly sensitized to the apparent values of 'standard' speech, many such speakers, while not eliminating their regional forms entirely, clearly also sought to add [h]-full rather than [h]-less realizations of words such as *happy* to their available linguistic repertoire alongside other non-stigmatized forms such as the ostensibly 'neutral' /ʌ/ as an alternative to the distinctively Northern and Midlands /ʊ/ for *cut* and *bus*.

This was a process which can, in a number of ways, be seen as analogous to the rise of that regionally 'colourless' variety of written English which gradually came into existence in the fifteenth century. In terms of the history of English, this too had been a crucial phase of standardization, a period in which, as a number of scholars have asserted, the variety of London English used in the Chancery increasingly assumed prominence in official and inherently statusful contexts of use, not least in its role as the basis for a national means of written communication.[25] While one might have expected the contemporary displacement of other regionally marked (and less prestigious) varieties of written English in response, it is, however, apparent that in the fifteenth century this particular aspect of change does not in fact seem to have taken place. Indeed, rather than a pattern of straightforward replacement of regional by 'Chancery' English on the model advocated by earlier studies in this period, recent work has instead confirmed the contemporaneous rise of what can be seen as 'colourless usages'—or, in other words, the increasing adoption of forms which, while not necessarily revealing neat alignments with the emergent written standard of the Chancery, do nevertheless shift away from those features which were seen as strongly marked in regional terms. As Jeremy Smith states, rather than a process of simple adoption, what therefore seems to take place is a pattern in which 'grosser provincialisms such as *trghug* [for *through*] were discarded and those of wider currency were allowed to remain—producing a colourless language which allowed for a fair amount of variation'.[26]

If one considers the nineteenth century—and the spoken language of the time—what can be seen for many (though by no means all) speakers is a similar pattern of wide-ranging and gradual modification of those features which, as we have seen, were often highlighted for their particularly 'provincial' associations. As for the patterns of change evident in fifteenth-century written English, it was a process which was therefore ultimately to lead to a number of forms of speech which, although geographically disparate, were less regionally marked—and more 'colourless'—than had previously been the case. If some features became more neutral in terms of regionality (especially in terms of those which conventionally triggered prescriptive censure or, as in the influential educational tracts of John Gill, which could attract fallible assumptions about 'defective intelligence'),[27] other features consistent with local forms of speech could therefore simultaneously remain. As Alexander Ellis confirms, alongside the minority who evidently assimilated 'received pronunciation' in full (in all its inherent variability), what could most clearly be said to have come into existence by the late nineteenth century was a set of regionally neutral 'standard pronunciation features' from the [h] which it would be 'social suicide' to drop to the [ŋ] which 'polite speakers' all over the country might assimilate, alongside the vocalization of [r] in words such as *bird*, and the use of /ʌ/ rather than /ʊ/ in words such as *butter*. It was the sum of features such as these (as well as the connotative values with which they were liberally endowed) which served to create the most potent—if looser—perceptions of a 'standard' which was to various degrees adhered to, as Ellis notes, by those who assumed, or attempted to adopt 'the educated pronunciation of the metropolis, of the court, the pulpit and the bar'. Rather than a rigidly monolithic norm, it was elements such as these which, bound to no region in isolation, tended to establish common signifiers of accent (and associated images of identity) all over the country.

Even the relatively widespread diffusion of these selected features beyond the evidently narrow confines of RP per se was by no means to achieve the eradication of those 'odious distinctions' within society which Sheridan (among others) had anticipated. Instead, as we have seen, the rise of non-regional varieties of speech—and attendant sets of non-regional markers—created new distinctions and divisions, erecting accent barriers which continued to run along the fault lines of status and its attendant hierarchies. If at times 'colourless' in regional terms, variation of accent continued therefore to be markedly 'coloured' in social ones. As in the late eighteenth century, the 'standard' proper remained largely the preserve of an elite, though an elite of which the composition had necessarily changed (and broadened) over the decades which had ensued. 'Received pronunciation', as Ellis adds, for example, was spoken in particular by the products of 'superior schools', the number and scale of which, as we have seen in Chapter 7, had increased significantly over the nineteenth century. It was a correlation which was later confirmed (and extended) by the phonetician Daniel Jones in the early years of the twentieth century, and one which came to be particularly important in consolidating the image, and associated properties, of a 'standard' accent in the public mind. As Jones stated in his seminal *English Pronouncing Dictionary* of 1917, 'the pronunciation used in this book is that most generally heard in the families of Southern English persons whose men-folk have been educated at the great public boarding-schools. This pronunciation is also used by a considerable proportion of those who do not come from the South of England but who have been educated at these schools'.[28]

The pronouncing dictionary in Jones's hands, however, was a long way from its original incarnations in the hands of Sheridan and Walker. While they, as we have seen, engaged in the partisan agendas of prescription, Jones merely attempted, as he stressed on the title page, to give 'a record of *facts*. No attempt is made to decide how people *ought* to pronounce; all the Dictionary aims to do is to give a faithful record of the manner in which certain specified classes of people *do* pronounce'. Jones's selection of 'cultivated Southern speakers in ordinary conversation' and the prominence which he gave to the homogenizing influence of boarding-school education—a point on which he elaborates in later editions[29]—thus intentionally operates as a descriptive rather than prescriptive norm. That other interpretations in terms of both standards and standardization are possible is, however, also revealed by Walter Ripman's introductory Preface to Jones's *Pronouncing Dictionary*. Here Ripman conspicuously states that while 'to the phonetician [the volume] is bound to be of absorbing interest', its value was also undeniable in other, somewhat different, respects—and not least 'to those who like me believe that we can and should face the question [of] what should be taught as "standard English speech" '. In this context, as he assured prospective readers, the pronouncing dictionary, even in its twentieth-century incarnations, would undoubtedly 'prove no less stimulating'.[30]

Early twentieth-century accounts of speech—and the associated complexities of 'talking proper'—therefore in some ways further signal the divide between the new (and intentionally objective) era of linguistics, and the subjectivities which had in many instances served to mar the insights of the past. Yet in other ways, the legacies of such subjectivities continue undisturbed, still influencing popular language attitudes as well as coming into play within entirely new institutions such as the BBC. While Daniel Jones was, with untroubled descriptivism, able to declare that 'people should be allowed to speak as they like', it was clear that individual attempts to put this precept into practice could still meet with marked criticism. The novelist Arnold Bennett, born in 1867 in Hanley, Staffordshire, was to retain his regional accent throughout his life, an appropriate personal endorsement of the values of provincial life and culture which he repeatedly affirmed in works such as *Anna of the Five Towns* (1902) and *The Old Wives' Tale* (1908).[31] Nevertheless, if the provincial is dignified in his novels, Bennett's own habits of speech were often regarded with disfavour. Sir Gerald Kelly hence unequivocally condemned Bennett's 'most appalling accent' while Virginia Woolf, her own voice redolent of the 'class-bound and mannered',[32] similarly mocked both his stammer and his pronunciation in her diary in December 1930.[33] In the public domain of twentieth-century language attitudes, accent prejudices of this kind could evidently remain intact, especially when it came to conventional stereotypes of the kind of pronunciation to be expected of (and accepted from) a self-evidently 'educated' writer such as Bennett. Popular images of the 'educated' and the actualities of sociolinguistic behaviour could fail to coincide, aptly confirming the truth of those correctives which Daniel Jones had attempted to endorse in his stringent criticism of the 'delusion under which many lexicographers appear to have laboured viz. that all educated people pronounce alike'.[34]

If the agendas of descriptive linguistics had therefore largely moved on, contemporary notions of educatedness in the early twentieth century nevertheless often continued to stress assimilation to the 'proper' norms of speech as vital, with elocution lessons being provided in many schools (especially girls' schools) in order to instil the necessary proprieties. The civil servant Dame Alix Meynall, born in 1903, records, for instance, that she attended 'lessons in elocution' at Malvern Girls' College[35] while the then women-only Somerville College in Oxford 'offered a course in "voice production", ostensibly to help the women speak verse but really a euphemism for eliminating accents'.[36] Notions of 'talking proper', in spite of the liberalism increasingly apparent in linguistic studies of the time, could hence in a number of ways remain reminiscent of the nineteenth century, with similar sets of anxieties and insecurities coming to the fore. A whole range of individuals duly shifted their natural modes of speech in ways which strongly favoured the assimilation of a non-regional—or at least markedly 'colourless'—norm. It was in these terms, for example, that the broadcaster Alistair Cooke eradicated his local accent (a product of Lancashire and Blackpool) on entering Blackpool Secondary School (later to become Blackpool Grammar). As his biographer Nick Clarke affirms, 'since many of the masters were imported from the south of England, there was clearly also a specific plan to eradicate from his school the coarse northern accent. In Cooke's case it worked. No one subsequently can remember him talking with anything resembling a Blackpool twang'.[37] A similar linguistic transformation was evident in the composer William Walton (born in 1902) whose Lancashire accent became a casualty of his move to Christ Church College, Oxford after winning a choral scholarship. Walton's Oxford contemporaries clearly had little tolerance for the apparent idiosyncrasies of regional speech and he was 'bullied by the other boys until he spoke like them, "properly" as they thought'.[38] The twentieth-century counterparts of the public schoolboys of the previous century[39] were evidently no less accomplished in the exertion of peer pressure and the art of sociolinguistic stigmatization; sensitization to a range of contemporary shibboleths in terms of speech regularly ensued (at least for those rendered vulnerable in a variety of ways to the pressures which could result). And schoolgirls too naturally participated in the same processes. Dodie Smith, later famed as the writer of *The Hundred and One Dalmatians*, was, for instance, to experience markedly negative reactions to her own Lancashire forms when arriving at St Paul's Girls' School in London in 1910. 'The first words addressed to her were "What a funny way you talk, are you Scotch?" and when she replied, "No, Lancashire," the response was "Oh, help!" and a group of girls stared and giggled'.[40] By the time she entered RADA some years later, she had acquired the requisite 'high clipped voice'; St Paul's had evidently had the expected effect.

While such transformations were not obligatory—the playwright and novelist J. B. Priestley, like Bennett, retaining his own (Yorkshire) accent long after his schooldays as did the poet Tony Harrison, born in Leeds in 1937—popular pressures in the early days of the twentieth century evidently often ran in tandem with prevalent (and non-regional) images of 'talking proper' as the appropriate signifier of educatedness and 'class'. The BBC, founded in 1922 as the British Broadcasting Company, was inevitably also to play a part in furthering such assumptions in the language attitudes of the day. Arthur Burrows, who broadcast the first BBC news announcement on 14th November 1922, was, for many, to epitomize the regionally unmarked tones of RP as it came to be used over the airwaves. The son of an Oxford college porter (and grandson of a gardener in the University Parks), Burrows could in fact equally be seen as exemplifying the kind of social and linguistic transformation which many writers over the nineteenth century had advocated. Shedding his local accent, he had moved from working as a journalist at the *Oxford Times*, to being a reporter in London, and in time to a central role at the fledging BBC. Burrows's status as 'the man with the golden voice' was publicly acclaimed ('He had a good, clear broadcasting voice with the absence of any regional accent', as his son afterwards noted).[41]

It was nevertheless undeniable that the BBC, in its earliest days, did not in fact have a conscious accent of choice nor a restrictive policy on the forms of pronunciation which were to be used or heard. Given the manifold demands of these early pioneering days of radio, when how and what to broadcast were matters of urgent debate, the issues which pertained to accent and pronunciation tended to focus on rather more pragmatic areas of enquiry, such as resolving the problems caused by the systematic distortion of the sounds of *s*, *f*, and *th* by existing wireless apparatus. The era of the specialist announcer, with specific training in the art of presentation (and pronunciation), had yet to dawn. Instead it was common for employees whose roles would now be seen as quite distinct to find themselves before the microphone and a national audience. Peter Eckersley, employed as 'chief engineer' in 1923, regularly broadcast, for example, as 'Uncle Peter' on the 'Children's Hour', as well as reading the news. Likewise, Rex Parker, the director of the London station, became 'Uncle Rex' on the 'Children's Hour'—and an announcer when necessary. Burrows himself was formally the 'Assistant Controller and Director of Programmes'. Even John Reith, appointed in December 1922 as the station's first Managing Director (and later Director General)—the 'tortured Scottish giant with the vision, drive, and inflexibility of an Old Testament patriarch', as he was described by Burrows's son—would find himself on air.

Broadcasting was, in obvious ways, to be a new domain for the speaking voice. Given the absence of accompanying visual stimuli, the nuances of voice—and the centrality of its communicative role to radio per se—predictably ensured its prominence in popular comment. If, on one hand, broadcasting therefore began without a formal policy on pronunciation, it could, on the other, hardly be said to have entered a blank space in terms of language attitudes and attendant notions of standardization or the vexed issues of 'correctness'. The perceived appropriacy of Burrows's own accent was uncontested. While regional forms could be heard on the local stations, RP-speakers swiftly came to manifest an apparent hierarchy on the National Programme, especially in reading the news. Readers of the *Radio Times* (founded in 1923 as 'the Official Organ of the BBC') readily commented on the graceful 'elocution' which could be heard on the National Programme, recognizing too the opportunities for linguistic education which radio might also thereby provide. 'What a wonderful means of education for our young people as well as us older ones who, living in remote country places in the last half century, had no opportunity of hearing good music, excellent elocution, or the thousands of interesting things which make up the everyday life of some of our fellow men', wrote one correspondent in a letter eulogistically headed 'Wireless as the "Elixir of Life".'[42]

This employment of a discourse of 'opportunity' was to be significant. A favoured term of Sheridan too as we have seen ('none but such as are born and bred amongst them, or have constant opportunities of conversing with them ... can be said to be masters of [the best pronunciation]'), it was cultural opportunity in a variety of ways which, for Reith, was to be one of the most important aspects of his concept of public service broadcasting. 'The B.B.C. is not content to be regarded as a mere entertainer', he stressed.[43] Listening to the radio was instead constructed as an active process of engagement and was placed within intentionally beneficial paradigms in which high culture was to be made available to all. This emphasis on a democracy of knowledge realised through the extension of certain cultural forms at the expense of others was again to be strongly reminiscent of Sheridan's work on language in the eighteenth century. 'Would it not greatly contribute to put an end to the odious distinctions kept up between subjects of the same king, if a way were opened up by which the attainment of the English Tongue, in its purity, both in . . . phraseology and pronunciation, might be rendered easy to all inhabitants of his Majesty's dominions?', as Sheridan had argued.[44] If Sheridan thereby chose to focus on the potential of the pronouncing dictionary as a force for eradicating the discrimination which different modes of speech could enact, Reith's agendas were, however, to be both broader—and more direct—in their application. 'British broadcasting is a practical application of democracy', Reith stated: 'we aim at communicating. . . . the best of the world's thought, culture, and entertainment'.[45] Given access to a receiver (by 1925, 1, 250,000 licenses had been taken out though popular estimates were that programmes were reaching some 10 million listeners, 3 million of them illegal), radio could, he stressed, provide widespread access to cultural forms such as opera, canonical literature, or classical music. Cultural didacticism—and top-down democracy— of this kind was an important aspect of Reithian philosophy, transparent in the daily schedules of BBC programming with its regular diet of Beethoven, Mozart, and Shakespeare. Its principles were echoed, and endorsed, by many who worked in the BBC in these early and formative days. 'British broadcasting has been framed to be democratic . . . We realise that in wireless, if it is to fulfil its great function, it must be democratic', as Peter Eckersley affirmed, for example, in 1925.[46] As the *Times* also endorsed of this intentionally beneficial process, broadcasters 'have an instrument in their hands capable of raising the intelligence and aesthetic state of the nation such as is given to no other comparable agency'.[47]

Dissenting voices did, of course, occasionally also make themselves heard in this respect (one wireless enthusiast who asked G. K. Chesterton 'to consider what a wonderful and beautiful thing it was that thousands of ordinary people could hear what Lord Curzon was saying', received the reply that, in Chesterton's opinion, 'it would be much more beautiful if there were an instrument by which Lord Curzon could hear what thousands of ordinary people were saying').[48] Nevertheless, the fact that attempted cultural hegemonies of this kind were increasingly to assume linguistic forms too should not be surprising. The leader in the *Radio Times* in March 1925, for instance, drew attention to a widespread sensitization to speech which seemed to act as an index of the efficacy of broadcasting in this respect ('In this matter radio is helping us. It is quickening our slow sense of hearing, and making us sharply aware of voices . . . our ears are becoming more and more sensitive to the fine shades and the significant inflections of the human voice').[49] Other writers explicitly commended the educative potential which broadcast exposure to certain forms of speech above others might have, opening up yet more opportunities for cultural transformation to those hitherto denied them. By 1924, this was a commonplace in discussions of the social effects of radio. In an illuminating article headed 'Announcers as Teachers', the popular novelist William le Queux hence singled out for praise the fortunate choice of announcers on the BBC who 'are all refined men and women, who use cultivated language to which it is a pleasure to listen'.[50] A familiar metalanguage often frames associated comments on speech. Images of 'culture', 'intelligence', and aesthetic merit all appear: 'the very tones of our own announcers' voices are an indication of a background of education and culture';[51] 'People whose ears are thoroughly accustomed to clear and cultivated speaking will unconsciously imitate it, and will come to dislike the inarticulate slovenliness, not to mention the tell-tale local intonation, of everyday talk'.[52] The amelioration of individual accents, especially those of children, was also to become a popular topos. E. V. Kirk, of the West Ham Education Committee, praised the remedial linguistic effects of the 'Children's Hour' upon the youngsters of the East End of London who tuned in to listen to 'Uncle Rex' or 'Uncle Arthur': 'many children whom I know personally are overcoming the defects of their accent by studiously attempting to imitate the pronunciation of "Uncle A." or "Uncle B."' Standardization in a practical mode was, he argued, the direct result: 'Fortunately these gentlemen set a standard that will benefit any child who can reach it, and the result will be a purer English spoken by those whom they influence . . . Broadcasting brings a new influence to bear for the good in this respect.'[53]

Language, as here, was framed in hierarchical models which seamlessly engaged with the popular dyads of language attitudes, whether of purity/impurity, or regionality as defect for which radio (and RP) might offer a remedy. Regionality on the regional stations might be welcomed ('I cannot tell how delighted I was to hear my own countrymen talking', Mrs L. C. wrote after listening to transmissions from Aberdeen).[54] Nevertheless, in broadcasting on the National Programme, it was clear that regional marking, just as in many nineteenth-century novels, was often made to consolidate a strong role in comedy. This too was made explicit in the *Radio Times*. 'Except when it is used to produce a comic effect, dialect finds no place in the broadcast programme', E. de Poynton declared.[55] Cartoons such as that reproduced in Figure 8.1, in which 'Auntie' explains, after 'listening for first time, after a humorous dialect number' that 'That's the first time I've ever laughed without any idea of what I've been laughing at', would certainly support such views.[56] Dialect comics such as 'Our Lizzie' (in reality the entertainer Helen Millais) enhanced these images of difference, often fostering popular value

Auntie (listening for first time, after a humorous dialect number): "That's the first time I've ever laughed without having any idea what I've been laughing at."

FIG. 8.1. 'Regionality and the early BBC', *Radio Times*, November 23rd, 1923, 309.

judgements—of subjective inequality or cognitive inadequacy, as well as pithy good humour or plain speaking.

Language—especially in its spoken forms relating directly to accent and pronunciation—was in such ways to become a recurrent thread within popular comment on broadcasting, and particularly in terms of the standards which broadcasting should institute and maintain. By 1924, it is also clear that internal BBC policy had begun to change in response. The first announcer as such—J. S. Dodgson—was appointed in late 1923; the expectation was that each station would follow this precedent. 'I want announcing brought to a fine art as it is one of the most important parts of the programme', it was decreed by Charles Carpendale (the Deputy Managing Director) in February 1924, stressing—here in direct response to contemporary language attitudes (and listeners' letters)—'if it is not done well it tends to jar and annoy listeners more than anything else.'[57] The popular recognition, as by le Queux, of the announcer as a linguistic point of reference ('We look upon our announcers as teachers. And they are') led to explicit discussion of the responsibilities which broadcasting should assume in this context. 'Uniformity' appeared as a new desideratum, if one that was resisted by Burrows ('I do not support this proposal as it will tend to rob out several provincial stations of their individuality').[58] An explicitly qualitative diction nevertheless often framed subsequent discussions within the BBC. Announcers need a 'good voice', 'good pronunciation', C. A. Lewis (the Organiser of Programmes) hence affirmed: 'It has often been remarked— and this is one of the responsibilities that are indeed heavy to bear—that the announcing voice sets a fashion in speaking to many thousands of homes and should therefore be faultlessly accurate both in diction and pronunciation'.[59] Reith issued a directive to all Station Directors in November of the same year, making clear this reorientation of priority in the art of announcing: 'I know that in many situations the Announcer is apt to regard himself as the most junior official of all, occupying a position of not much responsibility with no future prospects. Announcers should be men of culture, experience, and knowledge, with, of course, good articulation and accurate pronunciation. . . . I should', he added, 'like it to be made clear to Announcers how important their position is'.[60]

Within two years of its first foundation, the BBC was therefore to affirm new and explicit standards in announcing as a vital component of the art of broadcasting. Increasingly, announcing was no longer to be seen as something which one did alongside other duties; those who announced were also to be subject to linguistic training, ideally in London where national standards could be imposed on all broadcasters. Reading tests and formal linguistic assessment were made a specific part of the evaluation of suitability. A policy of anonymity was also imposed on announcers; henceforth they were to be recognized not by their names but by their command of a uniform and homogenised RP. As a BBC Announcements Editor later stated with apparent pride, 'It is a common place that announcers sound alike. That is a tribute to their training.'[61] New socially normative desiderata emerge too, as in the recommendation that all announcers should have a public-school education, a recommendation which would, of course, have excluded the 'golden-voiced' Burrows himself—even if it also traded on other widely prevalent stereotypes of 'talking proper' which were thereby to be implemented as an explicit part of BBC policy. Reith's *Broadcast over Britain*, published in 1924, manifests many of these changed concerns. As in Sheridan's work so many years before (and, more recently, in the Newbolt Report of 1921),[62] images of social unity founded on the ideal of a linguistically homogenous nation are marked in the rhetoric Reith now deliberately deploys. 'One hears the most appalling travesties of vowel pronunciation. This is a matter on which broadcasting may be of immense assistance', Reith stressed,[63] adopting normative paradigms in which issues of standardization— and the announcer as teacher—are well to the fore. 'Children in particular have acquired the habit of copying the announcer's articulation; this has been observed by their teachers, and so long as the announcer is talking good English, and without affectation, I find it much to be desired that the announcer should be copied,' as Reith continued with evident approbation.

This too was to form part of the cultural mission which he foresaw for the future of broadcasting, embodied in the National Programme in the standards of taste and decorum which encompassed language as all else.

Direct emphasis was moreover now given to the exemplary roles which announcers were henceforth to assume: 'we have made a special effort to secure in our stations men who, in the presentation of programme items, the reading of news bulletins and so on, can be relied upon to employ the correct pronunciation of the English tongue.'[64] As Reith himself pointed out: 'No one would deny the great advantage of a standard pronunciation of the language, not only in theory but in practice. Our responsibilities in this matter are obvious, since in talking to so vast a multitude, mistakes are likely to be promulgated to a much greater extent than before.'[65] 'Correctness' in this context was unquestioningly based on London metropolitan culture—the 'educated, south-east English variety' as Paddy Scannell and David Cardiff comment[66]—and it was this which was disseminated over the nation's airwaves with wide-ranging implications for the images of both national culture and a national accent which followed in its wake.

As *Broadcast over Britain* confirms, Reith could embrace ideologies of a spoken 'standard' with zeal. For him, as for others, the BBC was increasingly seen as an important mechanism in the cultural and linguistic accommodations which might result. Sensitization to notions of norm and deviation was seen, in particular, as having practical effects; in ways which would undoubtedly have delighted Sheridan, broadcasting was, by 1924, envisaged as a conscious means by which the non-localised forms of speech adopted by announcers and broadcasters could, at least in principle, achieve a non-localised and national exposure. Within the BBC, internal codification of these ideals proceeded apace. Arthur Lloyd James (later given the official title of Linguistic Advisor to the BBC), began a series of broadcasts on accent and dialects in June 1924, extolling the virtues of standard speech. By early 1925, however, his audience also included an internal BBC one, and he was invited to give a lecture to the London staff on the same subject. Lloyd James's praise for Standard English (and a non-localised accent) was regarded as 'so illuminating and so helpful' that it was broadcast nationally within the BBC to all staff in June of that year, endorsing the adoption—and dissemination—of 'correct pronunciation' for the BBC as a significant part of its formal duties.

Setting up the BBC Advisory Committee on Spoken English in 1926, in which Lloyd James (along with the linguistically conservative Robert Bridges, and the phonetician Daniel Jones), played a prominent role, broadcasting hence attempted to settle its own uncertainties on the pronunciation of words, further clarifying the sense of a norm to be adopted on the airwaves. Though formally disclaiming the desire to erect a uniform standard of speech ('There has been no attempt to establish a uniform spoken language' as Reith averred in the preface to Arthur Lloyd James's *Broadcast English*),[67] a concern to establish certain parameters of 'right' and 'wrong' was nevertheless clear, as, for example, in Bridge's own comments on his decision to accept the role of Chairman. 'When the B.B.C. were faced with the practical necessity of advising their announcers on questions of doubtful pronunciation, they decided to install a committee for that purpose, and asked me to be the chairman. That office I accepted', he stated, 'because I thought it my duty to do what I could to prevent the intrusion of the slip-shod conversational form of speech that some call "Southern English," and some "Public School Pronunciation, which is threatening the language, and the measure of which may be seen in my friend Professor Daniel Jones's unimpeachable dictionary"'. [68] Bridges' agenda could be unashamedly pre-scriptive (one of his main objections was to the use of /ə/ in unaccented syllables), and his stringent dicta on the correct pronunciation of words such as *imminent* and *immanent* or *gyrate* undoubtedly perplexed many an announcer. 'The policy might be described as seeking a common denomi-nator of educated speech,' the agenda for the Advisory Committee averred, setting out the basis of what came to constitute the realities of that 'BBC English' which, both consciously and unconsciously, was promoted through the agencies of radio (and later television too). Those who commented on the Committee in the press often expressed a clearer sense of the agendas of standardization which were potentially at work. 'May it not be, however, that in the highbrows of the B.B.C. we have a British Academy in embryo?', the *North Mail* and *Newcastle Chronicle* ventured on 16 July 1926; 'This is a standardized age. The B.B.C., providing standardized amusement for daily multitudes, are taking thought how they may set their countless patrons a standardized example of English pronunciation', the *North Eastern Daily Gazette* observed on the same day in an article headed 'Correct English'. As Reith stressed, 'There is now presented to any one who may require it, an opportunity of learning by example.'[69]

Rather than that form of convergent linguistic behaviour on a national scale which nevertheless indeed seemed at times to be envisaged in this con-text, it was yet again, in real terms, the wider awareness of notions of 'talking proper' which was to be achieved with greatest success by the broadcasts, and carefully selected accents, of the BBC. Like that heightened awareness of 'correctness' which William Cockin documented as a consequence of the shifting linguistic consciousness of the late eighteenth century ('it appears therefore . . . that works of this nature may be at least as much service in teaching us to perceive as to execute'),[70] the BBC was similarly to aid in potentially sensitizing a wide variety of listeners to issues of 'correct' English. This time, however, it was able to do so by means of the spoken word itself rather than by the written texts of writers such as Sheridan and Walker, Smart or Knowles. Its illustrations of 'talking proper' thereby gained an immediacy—and directness—which had necessarily been denied to the detailed descriptions, and socio-symbolic associations, deployed by the writers of the past. As Arthur Lloyd James noted in 1928 as he commented on the sensibilities which inevitably seemed to be aroused by the social meanings of speech: 'it is nowadays considered essential that those who aspire to be regarded as cultured and educated should pay a due respect to the conventions that govern educated and cultivated speech. It would now appear that this interest in the niceties of our language is more alive than ever before, and it has been suggested that broadcasting is in some way responsible for this quickening.'[71]

Broadcasting was indeed to prove an additionally effective means of perpetuating the standard ideology in the public mind, further diffusing notions of the accents appropriate to various status groups and occupations. Popular stereotypes of accent and identity could be reinforced without apparent qualms so that, while instances of Cockney or Yorkshire could be heard upon the airwaves of the National Programme of the early BBC, these were frequently limited to the domains of comedy and light entertainment, a distribution which likewise confirms the continued existence of other popular sociocultural stereotypes in which the institutionalized RP was the 'proper' accent for serious and intellectual concerns. As the historian Asa Briggs confirms, the regional was 'in general frowned upon by the young BBC which prided itself on what it was doing to raise the standards of speech'.[72] Lloyd James provided a still more critical assessment of the role of dialect, and the prominence of its negative stereotyping, in a discussion on 'The Voice of Britain', documented in *The Listener* in March 1939. As he argued, 'You mustn't blame the B.B.C. for killing dialect'. Instead, he countered, 'the native comedians have done more harm to the cause of the honest English dialect than anybody else. . . . The Lancashire comedian has killed the Lancashire dialect, and made Lancashire for ever afterwards impossible for the production of Shakespeare . . . It's not the B.B.C.[73]

If announcers, many selected and subsequently trained in the requisite proprieties of speech by Arthur Lloyd James, came to be seen as the truly emblematic voice of the BBC, then the disparate voices which could appear elsewhere—as in radio documentaries such as 'Summer over the British Isles', or ''Opping 'Oliday' (an account of residents of the East End of London in their annual hop harvesting in Kent), broadcast in September 1934— naturally provided a sharp contrast. It was the ways in which this contrast was presented which nevertheless remained the most significant factor in its deployment, suggesting the distinct dynamics of the 'other' in both linguistic and social terms. As Scannell and Cardiff confirm, the 'knowing cockney idiom' of ''Opping 'Oliday' (complete with prominent [h]-loss in both elements) 'situates the programme as an exercise in folk culture'. To this end, and in spite of the overt working-class focus, there is a distinct sense in which it was '*about* them but not *for* them',[74] a perception reinforced by the contextualizing comments which were uniformly delivered in the stereotypical clipped tones of the BBC of this time (see Figure 8.2). In this and other respects, the social divide could be marked between the official image of the BBC (and its tones of institutionalized correctness), and certain sections of its audience and the ways in which they—and their voices—were represented on the airwaves.

The consequences of linguistic (and social) attitudes of this order could be striking. Arthur Marwick, for example, gives a particularly useful account of a talk on the 'British working man' which appeared as part of a series on 'Modern Industry and National Character' produced for the BBC in 1934. 'The unsophisticated technology of the thirties did not allow for the pre-recording of talks, which instead had to be very carefully edited and rehearsed, then read word-for-word from an approved script', Marwick notes.[75] This 'editing', however, apparently also extended to what could be said, so much so that when one of the speakers, a car worker named William Ferrie, did in fact reach the microphone he declaimed not his prepared

FIG. 8.2. 'Popular misconceptions—A London announcer'.
An illustration from *Punch*, 19 April, 1939, p. 438.

speech (which he deemed 'a travesty of the British working class') but instead decried the 'censorship' of the BBC in its suppression of the real state of working-class politics in this context. Far more significant from our point of view was, however, the other accusation which Ferrie levelled at the broadcast: 'I also refused to drop my "aitches" and to speak as they imagined a worker does'.[76] Such narrow conceptions of language, identity, and appropriate stereotype were by no means unique. As a listener in 1938 similarly complained: 'I certainly do feel that a limited income is all too frequently associated in broadcast talks with lack of intelligence and the omission of aspirates. Surely all clerks and similar persons earning around £4 a week do not necessarily possess these obvious indications of their inferiority?'[77]

Such protests at the ways in which the BBC could and did reinforce prevalent evaluative paradigms of both speaker and speech initially seem to have had little effect. It is, however, also clear that audiences for the National Programme could be equally hidebound in terms of conventional images of acceptability in this matter. Later attempts to reduce the hegemony of RP in more serious genres of broadcasting were regularly to arouse controversy, as in the celebrated example of the Yorkshire-born Wilfred Pickles. Employed as a London announcer during the Second World War (on the premise that the Germans would find it impossible to imitate his Halifax accent), Pickles was to encounter specific censure because of the regional marking of his voice. Indeed, without the accents of authority which were apparently embedded in contemporary attitudes to, and use of, RP on the BBC, listeners claimed that they could not believe the news when it was conveyed in such Yorkshire tones, complete with short [æ] in words such as *fast* and *bath*. As Pickles noted in his autobiography, 'the B.B.C.'s standard English had become a firmly rooted national institution like cricket and the pub and, Hitler or no Hitler, it meant something when there was a threat of departure from the habit'.[78] The experiment was swiftly concluded and the national news returned to its more orthodox (and non-regional) presentation, controversy—at least in this matter—at an end. As a later internal BBC file on 'Announcer's English' records, 'The fruits of our experience can be summed up by saying that any noticeable "accent" in news broadcasting is a distraction and an irritation. This conclusion is reached by a simple process of elimination.'[79]

On the other hand, some liberalization within expected attitudes is also apparent in the enthusiastic reception accorded to the broadcasts made by J. B. Priestley (also born in Yorkshire) over the same period. Giving a series of patriotic talks which immediately followed the 9 o'clock news, Priestley apparently attracted an audience of between 30 and 40 per cent of the entire adult population. Moreover, while some modification of his original accent had evidently taken place, Priestley's speech was still far from the standard tones of Winston Churchill. While 'Churchill spoke with the aggressive personality of a war leader, using the accent and mannerisms of his class', Priestley 'seemed to speak from inside the ranks of the people themselves, using a voice with which they could identify'.[80] It was this which secured his attractiveness as a broadcaster, giving him an experience radically at odds with that of Wilfred Pickles (though had Priestley attempted to read the news, reactions might well of course have been somewhat different). Issues of acceptability could, however, operate very differently on the Regional Programme as the flourishing broadcasting industry based in the Manchester studios of the BBC confirms. Here, as Paddy Scannell and David Cardiff have stressed, 'the voices of Wilfred Pickles, Frank Nicholls and others . . . spoke to and for the listeners in the North', a role in which they 'did much to compensate for the official voices of the BBC's staff announcers'.[81] Reversing the traditional binarisms of 'them' and 'us' which so often seemed to dominate in the early days of the BBC, broadcasting in this sense did indeed provide some positive validation of that 'vocal tapestry of great beauty and incalculable value' which Pickles, among others, continued to defend against the linguistic hegemony of what had come to be the expected accent of the national BBC.[82]

As Tom McArthur similarly affirms, these early decades of the BBC (and the intentionally unifying power of the National Programme) were in many ways to coincide with the heyday of RP itself. It was a period in which, as the Oxford scholar and philologist Henry Cecil Wyld declared, RP could categorically (if subjectively) be affirmed as 'the best English': 'a type of English which is neither provincial nor vulgar, a type which most people would willingly speak if they could, and desire to speak if they do not', one superior in 'beauty and clarity' to all other forms of spoken English.[83] While other voices might—in both linguistic and ideological terms—choose to dissent from the premises thereby expressed, Wyld's eloquence intentionally serves to elevate RP to an emblematic standard for the nation. 'Nowhere does the best that is in English culture find a fairer expression than in Received Standard speech', he states,[84] endorsing hierarchical images of a set of 'best speakers' who, as a consequence of their perfect felicity in the nuances of RP, 'have perfect confidence in themselves, in their speech, as in their manners'. Outside such evident hyperbole, it was nevertheless clear that the position of RP was not to be without its problems. While many, as we have seen, were to resist its gravitational pull for a variety of reasons connected with more diverse conceptions of their identity as social and regional speakers, other (and more wide-ranging) threats to its stated supremacy gradually also come to the fore. Alongside those speakers who determinedly modified their own accents in response to the negative value judgements which continued to surround various regional accents—'It's never too early to start dropping the flat vowels of the Essex accent', as the actress Joan Sims, born in 1930 and a product of remedial elocution lessons at a variety of schools, affirmed[85]—it is clear that, as the years advanced, the ideological dominance of RP as the automatic image of 'educatedness' and 'culture' gradually began to decline. Just as the influence of fashion in the nineteenth century had led to the popularity of pronouncing words such as *bath* with [æ] rather than [ɑ] (a tendency later reversed as a non-regional norm by fashion's fickle dictates in the twentieth century), so did fashion in the later twentieth century start to affirm other values apart from those which might be said to exist in a metropolitan elite. Philip Larkin was famously to locate the beginning of a more liberal and open society in 1963 ('Between the end of the *Chatterley* ban // And the Beatles' first LP').[86] From the point of view of language, however, the 1960s were also to witness the rise of the regional—and perhaps especially Liverpool, via the Beatles—into a position of newly fashionable prominence. While the operation of traditional language attitudes might therefore still lead Paul McCartney's mother to attempt to eradicate his local (and Liverpool) enunciations as part of an aspirational desire for her son to 'better himself' (in turn revealing the continuance of other stereotypes in the female—and maternal—concern for correct language, long imaged forth as a major agency of standardization),[87] it is simultaneously clear that such pressures were resisted in ways which were entirely in keeping with the temper of the time. As McCartney's biographer stresses, it was an era in which it was 'fashionable to proclaim working-class origins' and one in which alternative images of both accent and identity could as a consequence come to the fore.[88] If the Leicester-born playwright Joe Orton curbed his own regional traits in the 1950s in favour of an RP norm, the shifting values of a decade later are similarly evident in, say, the actor Terence Stamp's decision to retain his native (Cockney) tones rather than assimilating to RP while at drama school. While Stamp could still be the recipient of traditional accent prejudice (' "And your voice . . . if you think you can get to act anywhere with that, you won't even get past the door—well, perhaps, if they're looking for lorry drivers"', as he was, for instance, informed by a fellow student at a method acting class in London),[89] once he entered drama school proper such assumptions disappeared. 'Nobody made remarks about my accent', he records. As a result, though he managed to acquire proficiency in RP as part of the elocutionary requirements of the acting course, he also remained unshaken in his conviction that this was merely another element in the repertoire of skills which an actor might need—not a feature which would or should automatically displace the habitual pronunciations of his past. 'I reassured myself with the thought that I could pick up accents like a parrot', Stamp notes in his autobiography; consequently, 'rather than speaking "proper", I would treat Standard English roles as a dialect'.[90]

Stamp's reaction against 'talking proper' was in this particularly emblematic of the age, one in which traditional values were regularly questioned and other modes of life explored and affirmed. The prestige conventionally assumed to accrue around RP could evidently also participate in this pattern of reassessment as 'talking proper' gradually came to be seen as 'talking posh' for far wider sections of society—including in this a large number of speakers who, in the past, might automatically have attempted to assimilate its salient features. The poet Tony Harrison hence overtly rejected the institutionally 'correct' accent expected at Leeds Grammar School, later penning his own vigorous denunciation of RP in his poem 'Them & [uz]'.[91] Even the BBC was forced to reassess its policies—and practices—in this matter. The threat posed by the introduction of commercial television in the 1950s led, for instance, to a far greater variety of presenters (and attendant linguistic patterns) being available on-screen, with a 'stronger sense of different voices' emerging intact from 'the sieve of metropolitan-centredness which habitually, if unconsciously, was used by the BBC in fashioning its image of the nation'.[92] As in radio too, the emphasis gradually began to be placed on a decentralization of both image and voice, reducing the once almost automatic hegemony of the capital as both cultural and linguistic exemplar. The new informality of the ITV and commercial networks contrasted sharply with what came to be seen, negatively, as the excessive 'plumminess' of the traditional BBC, a feature which in itself strongly urged the imperatives of democratization in a variety of ways. Pluralism necessarily became the norm, leading, as Colin MacCabe has commented in his study of television in the 1960s, 'to an ever greater diversity of accents and speech patterns and an ever more fragmented national culture'.[93] If regretted by John Reith, who was still alive to witness the demise of those images of national unity with which he had initially sought to inspire the BBC,[94] it was nevertheless a shift which was entirely in tune with the temper of the times, one in which the dinner-jacketed announcer was ever more out of place and in which the values traditionally embodied by RP were also likely to be regarded, especially by younger speakers, with outright dissent.

As the decades advanced, the potentially negative coding of RP has come to form a further part of its complex identity so that, in a number of ways, it has increasingly been seen not as neutral and 'accentless'—the images implicitly traded on by the early BBC—but instead as being heavily marked in accent terms, signalling elitism and exclusiveness rather than that 'passport to wider circles of acquaintance' which had so often been proclaimed in the past. Investigating the 'real English' of the early 1990s, the sociolinguists Jenny Cheshire and Viv Edwards, for instance, found 'little evidence of the linguistic insecurity which has been reported as typical of children who speak with a regional accent'; typical responses from schoolchildren questioned in the study instead revealed a marked antipathy to conventional constructions of 'talking proper' ('I dislike London accent. It sounds really posh', 'I dislike London accent because they are stuck-up snobs').[95] Fashion in this sense has apparently continued to downshift. As John Morrish declared of this transition in the *Independent on Sunday* in 1999, whereas 'once, people aspired to be posh; it was the voice of the people in power—in the law, in the

City, in the Establishment. Now there are plenty of people who would be ashamed to speak like that. A posh voice is seen as naff and unfashionable'.[96] The consciousness of a normative 'proper' enunciation fostered by Sheridan and his adherents from the late eighteenth century onwards has, from such comments, apparently gone into reverse; Morrish's article is tellingly headed 'The accent that dare not speak its name'—a reference not to the traditional shibboleths of Cockney, for example, but instead to a new sense of stigmatization which is, he argues, now coming to surround RP. Other writers on trends in modern English confirm the same perceptions. Paul Coggle similarly avers that 'many younger privileged people make an effort not to sound too "posh", as they know that this makes them unacceptable in their peer group',[97] while the phonetician Susan Ramsaran commented in 1989 on the ways in which 'a real or assumed regional accent' has come to have 'a greater (and less committed) prestige' for younger speakers'.[98] Those who have modified their accent in the direction of RP publically lament their earlier susceptibilities; 'the death knell has sounded for people like me, who are what used to be called "nicely spoken" ', wrote Victoria Moore in *The Times* in July 2000, noting that she was considering appointing her brother, who still retained his native Yorkshire, as her dialect coach.[99] Patterns of *Pygmalion* in reverse abound with public figures such as the film director Guy Ritchie and the violinist Nigel Kennedy shedding the patterns of received English of their youth and adopting in their stead the regionalized markings regularly affirmed as 'cool' in popular comment.[100] While George Bernard Shaw's version of *Pygmalion* typified the preoccupations of the early twentieth century in the transformation of a Cockney flower girl into an RP-speaking duchess for the occasion of the ambassador's garden party, millennial incarnations of the same myth are more likely to depict—and valorize—the process operating in the opposite direction. An ITV documentary ('Faking It') first broadcast in September 2000, for example, followed the fortunes of a public-school-educated Oxford University student as he attempted to transform himself into an East End doorman. More striking was the way in which the resultant linguistic accommodations were described with unqualified praise—not merely for the skill with which a new accent was gained but more particularly in terms of the way in which the student in question emerged, by means of his new modes of speech, into a person consistently depicted as far more likeable. As James Collard in *The Times* noted, it was a metamorphosis from 'a slightly precious, rather nervous, former public schoolboy . . . with a 'hint of the "upper-class twit" about him' into 'a creature no one who knew him would have recognized': 'the new Alex, who has a London accent, is altogether more engaging and personable—obviously a good guy, as well as a smart, articulate one'.[101] From the images of identity and associated value judgements deployed in accounts such as these, it is clear that traditional stereotypes of RP are indeed in the process of change.

It can, it seems, be the loss rather than the acquisition of RP which creates the more positive image, one which significantly also comports those associations of articulacy and intelligence long assumed to be the subjective preserve of the non-localized and ostensibly 'educated' accent. A range of speakers from aspirant Conservative politicians to exponents of modern business have in recent years similarly expressed their reservations (or been forced to confront the reservations of others) about the validity of RP as the automatic accent of choice, not least given its apparent capacities to alienate rather than attract. 'If you were unlucky enough to have such an accent, you would lower it. You would try and become more consumer friendly', as one leading businessman averred as part of a survey conducted for the *Sunday Times* in 1993.[102]

'I picked up RP in an attempt to fit in—and now that I have it, I don't', laments the journalist Victoria Moore.[103] Adoptive RP, a common feature of the past, is in this sense increasingly a rarity in modern language use as many speakers reject the premise that it is this accent alone which is the key to success.[104] Reversing the traditional polarities still further, RP's role as the accent of choice in modern films has moreover by no means necessarily been for heroes and heroines (as in the associations promoted in many nineteenth-century novels). Instead it has regularly been deployed for those roundly depicted as villains in, for example, Disney's films *The Lion King* and *Tarzan*, a domain in which it apparently provides an appropriate representation of the 'negative [and] slightly sinister', a connection based on its sociocultural associations of arrogance alongside exclusivity.[105] Advertising too has regularly moved away from RP as the most effective endorsement of a product's claims. 'Messages couched in RP . . . proved to be less persuasive than the same messages in local accents', Peter Trudgill confirms.[106] If RP is retained for the advertising of bleach and other cleaning products (on the grounds presumably of its continuing association with purity—and sterility), the regional has in this respect too taken on a new and consolidating presence. Call centres reveal the same wide-ranging patterns of assumption; while RP might traditionally have been thought to convey the necessary institutional tones of authority, it is instead the regionally marked which has taken on a new and positive coding in this context. 'Our researchers showed that people found a northern accent more acceptable', as a representative of the Midland Bank commented on the decision to base its telephone branch, First Direct, in Leeds rather than, say, in London.[107]

If popular comment and indeed popular language usage have in this way regularly picked up (and endorsed) the negative associations of these stereotypical images of RP and RP speakers (especially in their more conservative manifestations), then they have often done so in the context of another recently recorded linguistic phenomenon, that of 'Estuary English'. First formally described by David Rosewarne in 1984, Estuary English is conventionally depicted as an intermediate variety, one which could be said to occupy the 'middle ground' between Cockney and RP. Characterized by 'a mixture of non-regional and local south-eastern pronunciation and intonation', it has often been described as a form of language located, at least originally, 'by the banks of the Thames and its estuary', hence of course the name by which it has commonly come to be known. Rosewarne's point, however, was that Estuary English was also a variety which could not be restricted to these geographical confines alone. Instead it is, he has argued, potentially 'the most influential accent in the south-east of England', its users prominent 'on the front and back benches of the House of Commons . . . in the City, business . . . the Civil Service, local government, the media, advertising as well as the medical and teaching professions in the south-east'. And as later articles by Rosewarne elaborate, if Estuary English is experiencing a marked social diffusion (not least among those whom one might conventionally have expected to deploy RP), then its geographical diffusion is to be seen as no less marked. Ten years after his first article, he confirmed its extension 'northwards to Norwich and westwards to Cornwall, with the result that it is now spoken south of a line from the Wash to the Avon'.[108] In what has become a commonplace of comment on Estuary speech, this too has therefore apparently emerged as a new non-localized norm, often depicted as operating not only to the ostensible detriment of RP but also to the disadvantage of traditionally regional modes of speech. 'Scouse is threatened by the rising tide of Estuary English', declared an article in the *Independent* in 1999;[109] 'Glasgow Puts the Accent on Estuary', stated *The Times* in the same year; 'Estuary flows into the Clyde', it verified in July 2000.[110] Céline Horgues in a study of these shifting patterns of usage likewise avers that 'one of the main characteristics of EE is its continuous geographical spread',[111] while academic textbooks such as Barbara Fennell's *History of English* confirm the existence of similar images. 'Estuary English spread during the 1980s and 1990s into Norwich and as far west as Cornwall, south of a line from the Wash to the Avon', as Fennell notes, closely echoing Rosewarne's earlier premises.[112] It is perhaps hardly surprising therefore that Estuary English has regularly also been proclaimed as 'the new standard English'—'tomorrow's RP', as Rosewarne suggests, a new mode of 'talking proper' apparently set to consolidate its role in a new millennium.

Establishing the reality of such claims—and indeed the precise linguistic characteristics of Estuary English—is, however, no easy task. Despite the escalating amounts of newsprint (as well as numbers of academic theses) devoted to the subject, Estuary English can often appear paradoxically ill-defined, even given its presence as a lexeme in a number of recent dictionaries.[113] It has, for instance, been characterized as a variety and as a dialect; as localized (typifying the south-east) and also as non-localized, spreading to areas as disparate as Cornwall and York, Newcastle and Birmingham. It can be specified as merely an accent or, alternatively, it can be credited with characteristic lexical and syntactic features which render it both distinct and distinctive. It can be commended for its apparent 'consumer friendliness', its capacity to communicate in ways which transcend the class-bound associations of RP—yet it can equally be condemned as 'slob-speak', as bastardized Cockney, as a 'semi-convincing Cockney/sloppy hybrid [which] is taking over the nation'.[114] Many of these claims are self-evidently incompatible, however often they may variously be iterated in popular journalism and media comment.

Distinguishing fact and fiction in this matter is clearly imperative, if problematic. Rosewarne's earlier accounts of Estuary English, for instance, clearly strove to establish its status as a dialect, a position amplified by writers such as Paul Coggle in his 1993 *Do You Speak Estuary?* and further endorsed in a number of recent books on the history of English.[115] As a dialect it has been credited with preferences for forms such as *cheers* (instead of Standard English *thank you, thanks*) and for the heightened use of tags, such as *isn't it?, wasn't it?,* as well as for the usage of forms such as *there is* (rather than Standard English *there are*). Yet later accounts of Estuary English—and indeed standard English—have frequently found problems with such claims. Lexical items such as *cheers* for *thank you* or *goodbye* are, as John Wells points out, part of contemporary English—and informal standard usage too. 'There is' is similarly part of the available repertoire of spoken standard grammar, as in 'There's a lot of apples under the tree'. Wells likewise (and rightly) disputes the status of *hopefully* as a typical Estuary feature alongside the deployment of tag questions. Ultimately, as Wells concludes, in this respect Estuary English fails to convince.[116]

Significantly more attention has been paid to its status as an accent, one placed, as Rosewarne initially posited, on a continuum between the extremes of RP to one side and Cockney to the other. As such, it has been deemed to share some features of both. It adopts the [h]-full realizations of non-regional speech in place of the (still stigmatized) [h]-dropping of Cockney; it likewise avoids characteristic Cockney enunciations such as the use of [f] for [θ] in words such as *think* (Cockney '*fink*' rather than RP [ˈθɪŋk]), while also being marked by other features which have indeed stereotypically been associated with Cockney rather than RP. The heightened use of the glottal stop [ʔ] (another traditional shibboleth in 'talking proper') as in utterances of *quite nice* where [t] regularly gives way to [ʔ] ([ˈkwaɪʔ ˈnaɪs]), as well as the tendency to vocalize post-vocalic /-l/ (so that *milk* may seem to be pronounced as *miwk* ([ˈmɪʊk] rather than [ˈmɪlk]), have, for instance, both been identified as part of this trend.[117] Here too can be enumerated features such as the disappearance of /j/ in words such as *illuminate* and *super* (giving [ˈsuːpə] rather than traditional RP [ˈsjuːpə]), and the shift of /tj/ to /tʃ/ in words such as *student* or *tulip* ([ˈstʃuːdənt] rather than [ˈstjuːdənt], [ˈtʃuːlɪp] rather than [ˈtjuːlɪp]), a process which has often been publicly stigmatized in the spelling of *media* as *meeja* to reflect (and condemn) a similar pattern of change between /dj/ and /dʒ/. Overall, however, as Rosewarne averred in 1994 in an article exclusively devoted to the pronunciation of Estuary English, it is a form of speech which is perhaps better characterized by a complex of features, some of which appear to be distinctive (here Rosewarne enumerates the articulation of /r/, for instance, in which 'the tip of the tongue is lowered and the central part raised to a position close to, but not touching, the soft palate'),[118] while others illustrate tendencies and trends which may be detected in other varieties but which, in combination, emerge as particularly characteristic of Estuary speech.

Yet even here problems regularly emerge once Estuary English is subject to closer scrutiny. While empirical investigation has consistently failed to find any evidence for the distinctive Estuary [r] (it is, for instance, simply dismissed by John Wells in his own phonetic studies in this context), other pronunciation features also enter into potentially problematic relationships— and not least with RP itself. As a result, though RP and Estuary English commonly appear in popular comment as two sides of an increasingly antagonistic binarism, early accounts of Estuary English as merely part of a spoken continuum seem ever closer to the truth, especially given the fact that many of the apparently characteristic features of the phonetics of Estuary English can, with equal accuracy, also be given as representative of modern RP—including the traditionally stigmatized glottal stops and vocalized [-l]s. As Wells has pertinently stressed, if such features have conventionally been absent as dominant forms in the RP of the early decades of the twentieth century, it is undeniable that, in the RP of younger speakers of the early twenty-first century, forms such as ['fʊʔbɔl] for *football* and ['pɑʔliː] for *partly*—complete with glottal stops—are indeed present in the same way in which the vocalized [-l]s of [hɪmseʊf] and ['mɪdʊ] (for *himself* and *middle*) can also be found. Traditional constructions of 'talking proper' are, in this respect, evidently in need of reassessment. As Wells, for example, admitted in 1991 with reference to such ongoing changes, 'I am beginning to wonder whether my earlier judgment ... that "on the whole ... L Vocalization must be considered only Near-RP or non-RP" is now in need of revision'.[119] And similar revision also necessarily extends to the use of the longer (and tenser) [iː] in words such as *happy* ['hæpiː]. Given as typifying Estuary English by writers such as Rosewarne and Coggle in contradistinction to an assumed RP norm in [ɪ] (['hæpɪ]), this too must also be admitted as a salient feature of non-localized speech (as indeed it has been in the transcriptions of the recent *Longman Pronunciation Dictionary* (Wells, 2000)). Frequently stated differences between Estuary English and RP can in such ways disappear, with significant consequences for the ways in which both might be understood. As such shifting perspectives make all too clear therefore, if popular comment in terms of RP tends to adhere to the often monolithic images of days gone by (ones resonant of films such as *Brief Encounter*), then it is clear that in the real world RP, along with everything else, has decisively moved on.

Evidently neither 'talking proper' nor 'Estuary English' are as clear-cut as they might at first appear, a precept which must also extend to the demise of RP which has also often been heralded in recent years. If Estuary English fails to convince as a dialect, and similar problems emerge with its status as a non-localized norm (a role in which empirical investigation, as by Joanna Przedlacka, has likewise failed to find corroboratory evidence in actual usage),[120] then it is perhaps in its *social* meanings that most interest can be seen to lie, especially when set against the traditional social meanings of RP and those negative images which, as we have seen, have in recent years often come to accrue around its use. Outside the habitual stigmatization of glottal stops and lost [-l]s, it is, for instance, clear that conceptions of Estuary English as revealed in popular comment have taken on a currency in which they are regularly taken to image forth associations of 'classlessness' (as opposed to the traditionally status-ridden tones of RP) as well as accessibility in place of RP's stereotypical elitism. Estuary English in this sense is the mode of speech which could be adopted by Diana as the 'People's Princess' (*There's a lot of it about*, as she is reputed to have said, complete with perfectly enunciated glottal stops /ˈðɛəz ə ˈlɒʔ əv ɪʔ əˈbaʊʔ/),[121] and similarly deployed by Tony Blair as a representative of Labour as the 'People's Party', an 'everyman' who speaks to all. Figure 8.3 in this respect shows the postulated clash of linguistic identities between Tony Blair and the then Tory leader, William Hague.[122]

While such enunciations may draw forth prescriptive censure akin in many respects to those denunciations of impropriety (especially in the context of linguistic change) which are familiar from many nineteenth-century texts,[123] they also suggest the potential validity, in one sense, of that entity commonly conceived as 'Estuary English' as a *style*, one which evidently need not displace a speaker's habitual forms but which can be adopted as part of the repertoire of possibilities which individual speakers may have at their command. Hence Tony Blair's facility in the use of glottal stops in the context of, for example, the popular television interview, need not countermand his equal facility in their absence in Prime Minister's Questions. Language and language use are, as we have so often seen, inherently variable, and such variability inevitably extends to the wide range of contexts and situations in which speakers move—and the equally variable forms which they may, as a result, choose to deploy. No single accent is monolithic, a premise which extends to both RP and Estuary English. From this point of view, RP is, for instance, far more than a single form of speech, embracing at one end of the spectrum the forms used by the Royal Family with all their hyperlectal (U-RP, Upper Class RP) features, as well as the contrastive variability of 'Near-RP' or indeed what has recently been identified as 'Regional RP'—varieties in which characteristic (and traditional) RP features

Tony teaches Bill to speak Estuary English

(Overheard during a darts game in the public bar of the Westminster Palais)*

HAGUE: Teach me how to be popular like you Tone!

BLAIR: My ol' ma? Lenny Jospin asked me the same in the Elysee, so I said to 'im, "sor?ed me ol' Socialist ma?e".

HAGUE: But I'm a Conservetev and a Yorkshire-man.

BLAIR: Don't you Adam and Eve i?. Why don? you tawk Estuary English like me, Biw.

HAGUE: I don't think ffffffffff.....

BLAIR: Estuary shows tha? a leader mixers with the peopuw...... marchers with the times, know wha? oi mean?

HAGUE: (Searchers for something to say.)

BLAIR: My successors are foundered on the peopuw, Biw.

HAGUE: But on the backbenchers my Yorkshire accent countered as one of my successors.

BLAIR: Leave i?ou?. My Estuary English is one of my badgers as the peopuw's President, I mean Proime Minister!

HAGUE: According to some Conservetev saucers, my accent doesn't go down well in the villagers of the Home Counties, or some of the financial services officers in the City.

BLAIR: Blank 'em ou? ma?e. Yer accent influencers peopuw. Mandelson goes like, "Show 'em yer've go? stree? cred, Tony", roight!

HAGUE: We Conservetevs have tendered to ignore some of the challengers of modernity. I tried to get street cred with the baseball cap, but everyone advisers me not to do that again.

BLAIR: You're no? the only one. I 'ope England lose or I'w 'av to sing with Des O'Connor on telly.

HAGUE: You're right, accent influencers people, so can you teach me Estuary English? You do it so well.

BLAIR: 'Wew' no? 'well'. Ge? a grip.

HAGUE: Please, it's one of the biggest challengers of my life.

BLAIR: The first thing to learn is 'ow to pronounce the peopuw's game. I''s *Foo?baw*, righ?, no? foot**ball**.

HAGUE: *Foo?baw*.

BLAIR: Righ? on, Biw, me ol' ma?e.

HAGUE: Cheers Tone. Foo?baw. (Tossers his head back in a wild gesture of success and hits his head on one of the ledgers behind him, causing beer glasses to fall to the floor.)

BLAIR: Yer've go? te learn te drop *ts* as wew as glasses. Mandelson goes, "Yer've go? to turn your *ls* into doubu *us*". Le? me teach yer that foo?baw song 'Vindaloo'. I need to practise i? anywoy.

HAGUE: Leave i? ou? Tone!

BLAIR: Wew done! That's amazin'. Din' 'e do wew? Wa? abou? "On the baw? Tha?s a grey? foo?baw song. Dje like i??

HAGUE: No? a lo?, bu? let's sing i?.

BLAIR AND HAGUE IN CHORUS:
On the baw
On the baw
Foo?baws comin' 'ome. (etc.)
'Ere we go, 'Ere we go, 'Ere we go. (etc.)

Hague has learnt the link between Estuary English, football and popularity with the 'people'. ☐

---

* *Editor's note* (1) In the conversation, the spelt-out 'r' in such words as *mixers* (= mixes) and *successors* (= successes) represents the RP 'r'-less pronunciation of the syllables in which it occurs. (2) The 'w' at the end of Estuary words is pronounced.

FIG. 8.3. 'Tony teaches Bill to speak Estuary English'
Source: D. Rosewarne, 'Tony Blair and William Hauge: Two Northerners Heading South', *English Today*, 14 (Oct. 1998), p. 54 (Cambridge University Press).

co-exist alongside other forms which are more clearly marked in terms of regional location. It can similarly subsume that entity already discussed as 'Adoptive RP' with its heightened responsiveness to the theoretical shibboleths of speech (such as intrusive [r]). And in its increasing adoption of forms such as the glottal stop and vocalized [-l], RP can prove its continued responsiveness to pressure from below. In this respect therefore, forms conventionally denied prestige just as it did in the course of the nineteenth century with the gradual diffusion of the stereotypically Cockney [ɑː] in words such as *fast* and *after*. 'Talking proper' is clearly by no means static, in either its phonetic properties or its social meanings. As studies of Queen Elizabeth's speech in the early years of the twenty-first century have, for example, shown, even the 'Queen's English' has modified its salient elements over the years, leading to a flurry of headlines in late December 2000 on the lines of 'Decline and fall of the Queen's cut-glass accent' and 'Strewth, the Queen talks just like us' or, from *The Mirror*, ''Er Maj don't talk so posh any more' (see Figure 8.5).[124]

The changing dynamics of RP itself therefore inevitably complicate assessments of 'Estuary English', not least since a realistic appraisal of the former inevitably leads to the conclusion that, in its younger speakers, it clearly shares with Estuary English many of the features which theoretically enforce the latter's right to be considered an entity at all. Indeed, as John Maidment has postulated, given such apparent consonance, it is conceivable that the label 'Estuary English' is in fact redundant so that, instead of a model of the lines of the continuum indicated by Figure 8.4(a) (in which Estuary English neatly occupies the divide between the upper and lower reaches of Cockney and RP), one could additionally factor in those considerations of style which habitually intervene in language use (as in Figure 8.4(b)). Adding explicit acknowledgment of the impact of formality and its converse, the resulting formulation hence potentially obviates the need for 'Estuary English' at all. As Maidment further elaborates, 'All this leads to the possibility that EE is no more than slightly poshed-up Cockney or RP which has gone "down market" in appropriate situations and that rather than there

(a)   [<-----Cockney ----->] [<-----Estuary English ----->] [<-----RP ----->]

(b)   [*Informal* <-----Cockney ----->*Formal*] [*Informal* <-----RP -----> *Formal*]

[*Informal* <-----EE -----> *Formal*]

FIG 8.4. Diagrammatic relationships of Cockney, RP, and Estuary English
Source: After J. A. Maidment, 'Estuary English: Hybrid or Hype?' Paper presented to the 4th New Zealand Conference on Language & Society, Lincoln University, Christchurch, New Zealand, 1994.

FIG. 8.5. Newspaper accounts of the reported shift in the Queen's English, December 2000.
Source: *The Daily Express, The Guardian, The Sun,* and *The Times.*

being a newly developed accent which we should call EE, all that has happened over recent years is that there has been a redefinition of the appropriateness of differing styles of pronunciation to differing speech situations'.[125] Media stigmatization of features which have conventionally come to be labelled 'Estuary' could from this point of view therefore merely be seen as a reaction to observable changes in progress in RP—much indeed as similar 'grass root witnesses' in the nineteenth century censured elements such as the increasing vocalization of [r] in final and post-vocalic positions while in no way combining to halt their advance.[126] Perhaps, as Maidment concludes, 'we ought to call this new trend Post-Modern English, rather than Estuary English'—a label which entirely reorientates the status of this postulated variety and its attendant interpretations of 'talking proper' (or otherwise).

A certain scepticism has thus come to mark a number of recent linguistic approaches to that phenomenon popularly labelled 'Estuary English'. (See, for instance, the phonetician Peter Roach who has categorically dismissed it as 'largely the invention of journalists and those who try to attract their attention'.)[127] It is nevertheless undeniable that notions of 'proper' pronunciation, and associated norms of appropriate usage, have changed radically over the later decades of the twentieth century and into the twenty-first. While John Reith in the early twentieth century advocated the dissemination of RP across the airwaves (convinced of its unassailable communicative value in the face of other varieties),[128] broadcasting in the late twentieth century (and afterwards) has, for example, increasingly continued to decentralize the influence of both London and non-regional norms of speech. 'The dinner jacket is being replaced by jeans', wrote John Herbert in 1997: 'The trend is away from elitist speech on all British broadcasting networks and local stations towards an increased cherishing of the riches of local dialects and accents'.[129] The thrust in this is towards an assumed neutrality of a different kind as broadcasting is formally subject to escalating pressures for democratization in linguistic terms; Scottish and Irish accents are hence now regularly heard on the national news (alongside RP which has, at least in part, tended to maintain its stronghold in this context). While regional marking—at least within certain limits—is clearly held to be no bar to success, even in flagship news programmes, traditional evaluative paradigms have not entirely been displaced (even if their liberalization is clear). 'RIP RP', as Tony Harrison's 'Them & [uz]' averred, is still somewhat premature.[130] Nevertheless, the trend towards increased use of the regional in public and national contexts seems set to continue. 'One of the criticisms of the BBC is that it is too South-East centric . . . it is our job to serve the whole of the UK and to reflect the whole nation', as Greg Dyke (Director General of the BBC from January 2000 to January 2004) stated. Often given credit himself as an 'Estuary' speaker, Dyke stressed his determination to shift current perceptions that 'we are not giving proper attention to engaging the regions'.[131]

Even the World Service, long seen as the unassailable bastion of conservative RP, has shifted in tandem with other areas of broadcasting, likewise extending the range of accents which it now chooses to deploy. While such changes do not meet with unmitigated praise (the Labour politician Roy Hattersley reacted with distaste in 1994 to the decision by Liz Forgan, Director of BBC Radio Network, to encourage 'announcers with "lovely rich Brummie accents" ' to take a prominent place on Radio 3),[132] the trend is nevertheless clear. Both language and society in this respect are ever more complex, a fact particularly transparent in the contrast between, say, the nineteenth-century London of Dickens in which even French speakers (as in *Our Mutual Friend*) could be configured as marked oddities, complete with associated patterns of linguistic xenophobia,[133] and the resoundingly multicultural London of, say, Zadie Smith's *White Teeth*, published as the new millennium began. 'Hush yo mout! You're nat dat ol' . . . you look pretty djam good for someone come so close to St Peter's Gate', comments the Jamaican-born Clara, now resident in Lambeth; 'You want sommink?', the London-born Ryan Topps demands, his traditional Cockney markings providing one link with the past which has apparently remained intact. Millat, the son of the Bangladeshi Samat and Alsana, instead adopts a fusion language of Jamaican patois, Bengali, Gujarati, and English, as the basis for his own chosen idioms ('jus get some Semtex and blow de djam ting up'). The linguistic landscape of Britain has come a long way from the dominant monolingual images of the nineteenth century in a pattern which further complicates and challenges the once unquestioned hegemony of 'standard' speech.

This questioning of the traditional roles and associations of RP is evident in other contexts too. While John Honey in 1989 could still stress that 'it is still common in Britain for job advertisements to specify "well-spokenness" which implies clarity of articulation and a restricted range of accents which certainly excludes any broad social or regional accents',[134] this too is an assumption which is beginning to seem in need of revision. 'Dropped aitches need not be a cause for concern', stressed *The Times* in February 2001, investigating language attitudes in the context of job recruitment. As a partner in one recruitment agency confirmed, 'Accents are not a factor these days. Perhaps a few years ago they were when the old boy network was more prevalent. But a strong CV and personality are more important'.[135] And other employment agencies cited in the same article corroborate these impressions. That 'times have changed, particularly over the last few years' seems to be the salient message, with accent apparently being a major recipient of such changes: 'accents are not an issue. As long as candidates [for jobs] speak clearly and are articulate, the accent should not negatively affect their chances in the job market'. Certainly if one examines advertisements for jobs, the stress is firmly on 'communication skills'—and the implicit desire for a more wide-ranging set of attributes than that implied by the more rigidly restrictive 'well-spoken' of the past. 'Outstanding interpersonal skills', or requests for the 'innovative' and 'creative', the 'intelligent' and 'hard-working', and, in particular, for 'team players', mark the differences of a changing employment culture—'a truly meritocratic work hard, play hard culture', as one recent advertisement proclaimed,[136] manipulating images in which the stereotypical associations of traditional RP might indeed be out of place.

On the other hand, however, it would be unrealistic to expect the complete displacement of traditional language attitudes in this respect. There is, for example, an often unacknowledged sense in which it would also now be seen as unacceptable to discriminate, at least formally, on the grounds of speech style and pronunciation. In this, attitudes to accent also seem to participate in the increased political correctness of the age; it is 'no longer permitted in British society to be seen to discriminate against someone on the basis of their accent' as Peter Trudgill has observed, adding, however, that the correlate of such assumptions is that such discrimination 'has to masquerade as something else'.[137] Instances in which such discrimination does overtly take place tend as a result to become newsworthy in themselves, illustrating the complex interplay of attitudes which may be at stake. 'Scouse accent kills Lisa's Dublin dream', for instance, made headline news in the *Irish Post* in March 2001 in an article which documented the rejection of nanny Lisa Donnelly by a Dublin agency on the grounds of her Liverpool accent.[138] Democratization of discourse, and a tolerance of diversity in all its forms, have become significant parts of a dominant liberal orthodoxy, and its attendant ideologies. It is this which, in linguistic terms, evidently underpinned the negative reactions to the writer Beryl Bainbridge's suggestion that compulsory elocution lessons be available for all. 'Uneducated regional accents' should be 'wiped out', she stressed, in a set of comments which would have been entirely unremarkable in the more prescriptive culture of the nineteenth century but which were widely considered worthy of comment in 1999.[139] If Sheridan in 1762 endeavoured to stimulate the linguistic consciousness in terms of accent, it is clear that in recent years this same consciousness has been moving in entirely different directions, decisively broadening notions of 'talking proper' and their framing issues of correctness.

This is not to say, however, that tolerance has led to the eradication of such attitudes entirely or, as already indicated, to the end of RP itself. Candidates scoring the highest grades in the GCSE English exams of 1993 could, for instance, still be accused of 'uneducatedness' if they dropped their [h]s in ways which are precisely parallel to many of the attitudes to accent expressed in the context of the nineteenth century. Objective and subjective reactions to language again diverge as, even in the late twentieth century, [h]-loss could evidently still suggest that academic achievement was able to be signalled by the subjective import of [h] with all the fallible value judgements which its loss comports.[140] For all their weaknesses, such attitudes can therefore prove remarkably pervasive as notions of 'standard' and 'non-standard', 'good' and 'bad', continue to be fostered in popular reactions to linguistic change or to what is seen as the misguided liberalism which informs the tolerance typical of descriptive linguistics. 'We're defiling our language for the sake of fashion . . . people deliberately drop their T's . . . join me in my campaign to get good English going again', as the subject of one interview in the 1990s declared in his asseverations against the stated 'slovenliness' of 'dropped letters' and the 'errors' of elision—especially where the conventionally stigmatized glottal stop might, as a result, come into play.[141] Ideologies of a standard can, as this suggests, remain in good health. The processes of standardization, on the other hand, can and will only reach completion in a dead language where the inviolable norms so often asserted by the prescriptive tradition (and the absolutes of popular language attitudes) may indeed come into being—a fate, one assumes, which is not yet in store for English—or indeed for RP.

'Everyone in Britain has a mental image of RP, even though they may not refer to it by that name and even though the image may not be very accurate', wrote John Wells in 1982. It is this 'image' which, as we have seen, was gradually created throughout the late eighteenth and nineteenth centuries. It is similarly this which, complete with all its inaccuracies and assumptions of absolutes, has combined to inform language attitudes and subjective reactions to speech in ways which have proved surprisingly enduring. Even if a number of erstwhile public schoolboys now determinedly attempt to shed its cadences whenever they can, RP probably still retains its minority constituency of three to five per cent of the population. While the Royal Family reflects the ongoing shifts in conservative RP (Queen's Elizabeth's usage modulating over time from the clipped articulations of the 1950s to her typical pronunciations of today in which *bad* no longer sounds like *bed*, and her daughter has become *Anne*—and not *En* as in the latter's christening ceremony),[142] more representative forms of RP reflect a dynamism and change which bring it closer to a democratized as well as a non-regional norm. Engaging with the reality of modern RP, and modern trends within RP, is clearly salient. It is this reality which, as John Wells rightly stresses, should, for instance, form the basis of that pronunciation taught to foreign students of English—a form in which glottal stops can and do appear alongside enunciations such as vocalized /-l/.[143]

Language attitudes, and stereotypical estimations of RP, evidently here need to move with the times, a fact particularly evident in those processes by which the presence of a 'dropped' [t]—and subsequent glottal stop—in any public speaker (giving, for instance, [ɪʔ ˈsiːmz] instead of [ɪt ˈsiːmz] for *it seems*) can still lead to the almost automatic appearance of the label 'Estuary' in a pervasive pattern of both proscription and misassumption. The glottal stop, as Wells confirms, 'is becoming respectable', even if it began as a frequent correlate of 'vulgarity' in the language attitudes of the past.[144]

Prevalent stereotypes of both 'Estuary' and 'RP' can hence co-operate to disguise the realities of linguistic usage—and the shifting patterns of 'talking
proper' which are now indeed coming into existence. In this RP remains
intact in its non-regional deployment, spreading such features in its younger
speakers over the country—alongside other co-existing variants which other
RP speakers might employ (and in which such forms do not appear).
Estuary English, from all available empirical evidence, remains precisely
where it was—a largely still-localized variety which does exist in the South-
East on a continuum with RP and Cockney. Perhaps most significantly, it
can be seen as part of a far larger pattern which is coming to characterize
linguistic usage at the end of the twentieth century and into the twenty-first.
As the linguist Paul Kerswill notes, large-scale processes of dialect levelling
increasingly mean that 'there are fewer differences between ways of speaking
in different parts of the country' in a homogenization which extends to
pronunciation as well as grammar.[145] Processes of accommodation in this
particular sense are combining to produce the equivalent of linguistic conur-
bations, focused on the usage of local urban centres. The most realistic
appraisals of Estuary in its current usage through the South-East suggest
therefore that it too is part of this trend, one based on and around London
in a pattern of usage which looks set to continue and extend. Under the continuing pressures of accommodation from a variety of sources, it is certain
that contemporary images of 'talking proper'—as well as the actual features
of its use—will undoubtedly also continue to be in need of further redefinition as the twenty-first century advances.

NOTES

Notes to the Introduction

1. *Talking and Debating* (London, 1856), 15.
2. Revd D. Williams, *Composition, Literary and Rhetorical, Simplified* (London, 1850), 5.
3. *The Manners and Tone of Good Society By a Member of the Aristocracy* (London, 1879), 172.
4. Peter Austin Nuttall was the author of a number of frequently reprinted pronouncing dictionaries published in the latter half of the nineteenth century, including *The Standard Pronouncing Dictionary of the English Language* (London, 1863), *Routledge's Pronouncing Dictionary of the English Language* (London, 1867), and a revised edition of *Walker's Pronouncing Dictionary of the English Language* (London, 1855).
5. *Mixing in Society. A Complete Manual of Manners* (London, 1870), 91.
6. P. Coustillas, *London and the Life of Literature in Late Victorian England. The Diary of George Gissing* (London, 1978), 329.
7. G. Gissing, *The Odd Women* (London, 1893), i. 87.
8. G. Gissing, *New Grub Street* (London, 1891), i. 154.
9. See Chapter 4.
10. G. Gissing, *Denzil Quarrier* (London, 1892), 168.
11. W. Phyfe, *How Should I Pronounce? Or the Art of Correct Pronunciation* (London, 1885), 6.
12. S. Mitchell, 'The Forgotten Women of the Period. Penny Weekly Family Magazines of the 1840s and 1850s', in M. Vicinus (ed.), *A Widening Sphere. Changing Roles of Victorian Women* (Indiana, 1977), 34.
13. Hon. Henry H., *P's and Q's. Grammatical Hints for the Million* (London, 1855), 8.
14. Id., *Poor Letter H. Its Use and Abuse*, 40th edn (London, 1866), pp. iii–iv.
15. A. J. Ellis, *On Early English Pronunciation*, (London, 1869–89), i. 221.
16. See W. Benzie, *The Dublin Orator* (University of Leeds, 1972), p. vi.
17. T. Sheridan, *A Course of Lectures on Elocution* (London, 1762), 30.
18. G. Vandenhoff, *The Art of Elocution* (London, 1855), 43.
19. D. Marshall, *Industrial England 1776–1851*, 2nd edn (London, 1982), 8.
20. H. Sweet, *The Sounds of English* (Oxford, 1908), 7.
21. See J. C. Wells, *Longman Pronunciation Dictionary*, 2nd edn (London, 2000), §2.1.
22. G. Gissing, *Born in Exile* (London, 1892), iii. 35.

Notes to Chapter 1

1. Ranulph Higden wrote *Polycronicon* in Latin in the mid-14th c. It was translated (with additions) into English by John of Trevisa *c*.1387, and afterwards printed

as *Description of Britayne, & also Irlonde taken out of Policronicon* by William Caxton in 1480. All citations are from the latter, Chapter XV.

2. T. Smetham, *The Practical Grammar* (London, 1774), 36.

3. See p. 246.

4. See further p. 52.

5. See, for example, J. Fisher, M. Richardson, and J. Fisher (eds), *An Anthology of Chancery English* (Knoxville, 1984). For a more critical reassessment of the role of Chancery English in terms of fifteenth-century standardization, see also J. Smith, *An Historical Study of English. Function, Form and Change* (London, 1996), 68–77.

6. J. D. Burnley, 'Sources of Standardization in Later Middle English', in J. B. Trahern, Jr. (ed.), *Standardizing English. Essays in the History of Language Change in Honor of John Hurt Fisher* (Knoxville, Tenn., 1989), 23–4.

7. G. Puttenham, *The Arte of English Poesie* (London, 1589), 120.

8. R. Lowth, *A Short Introduction to English Grammar* (London, 1762), 43 and n.

9. See further L. Arnovick, 'Proscribed collocations with *shall* and *will*: the eighteenth century (non)-standard reassessed', in C. Cheshire and D. Stein (eds), *Taming the Vernacular. From Dialect to Written Standard Language* (London, 1997), 135–51.

10. D. Leith, *A Social History of English* (London, 1983), 89.

11. See further R. Burchfield, *The New Fowler's Modern English Usage* (Oxford, 1996), 702–3. *OED2* (1989) descriptively provides a wide range of citations illustrating the use of *hopefully* in this sense.

12. J. Priestley, *A Course of Lectures on the Theory of Language and Universal Grammar* (Warrington, 1762), 178–9.

13. W. Bullokar, *Booke at Large for the Amendement of Orthographie for English* (London, 1580), repr. in Bullokar, *Works*, ed. J. R. Turner (Leeds, 1970), iii. C2^v.

14. Puttenham, *Arte of English Poesie*, 121. See also pp. 16–18.

15. J. Beattie, *The Theory of Language* (London, 1788), 92–3.

16. O. Price, *The Vocal Organ* (Oxford, 1665), A3^v.

17. E. Coles, *The Compleat English Schoolmaster* (1674), 103.

18. Sheridan, *Course of Lectures*, 30.

19. J. Hart, *An Orthographie* (London, 1569), fi^r–fii^v.

20. C. Cooper, *The English Teacher or the Discovery of the Art of Teaching and Learning the English Tongue* (London, 1687), 77.

21. E. J. Dobson, *English Pronunciation 1500–1700*, 2nd edn (Oxford, 1968), i. 309.

22. T. Sheridan, *A Rhetorical Grammar of the English Language* (Dublin, 1781), p. xviii.

23. Id., *A Dissertation on the Causes of the Difficulties, Which Occur, in Learning the English Tongue* (London, 1761), 17.

24. Puttenham, *Arte of English Poesie*, 120.

25. Sheridan, *Dissertation*, 17.

26. Sheridan, *Course of Lectures*, 33.

27. Puttenham, *Arte of English Poesie*, 121.

28. Ibid., 117.

29. T. Sheridan, *A General Dictionary of the English Language* (London, 1780), B1^r.

30. See p. 58 ff.

31. Sheridan, *Course of Lectures*, 37.

32. Id., *A Discourse Delivered in the Theatre at Oxford, in the Senate-House at Cambridge, and at Spring-Garden in London* (London, 1759), 24.

33. Id., *Course of Lectures*, 37. Sheridan's use of 'dialect' here is intended to signify speech as much as the regionalized forms of lexis or grammar (a usage in keeping with the definition his *Dictionary* later provides: 'the sub-divisions of a language; style, manner of expression, language, speech').

34. Id., *Rhetorical Grammar*, p. iii.

35. Cited in D. Scragg, *A History of English Spelling* (London, 1974), 90.

36. Priestley, *Course of Lectures*, 250.

37. H. Fielding, *The History of Tom Jones. A Foundling*, 2 vols (London, 1749) ed. F. Bowers, with an Introduction and Commentary by Martin C. Battestin (Oxford, 1974), i. 205.

38. J. Greenwood, *An Essay Towards an English Grammar* (London, 1711), 231.

39. I. Watts, *The Art of Reading and Writing English* (London, 1721), 101–2 n.

40. J. Owen, *The Youth's Instructor* (London, 1732), p. ii.

41. S. Johnson, *The Plan of a Dictionary of the English Language* (London, 1747), 32.

42. Id., *A Dictionary of the English Language* (London, 1755), C2^r.

43. T. Sheridan, *Elements of English* (London, 1786), p. v.

44. *Athenaeum Magazine*, 3 (1808), 81.

45. J. Walker, *A General Idea of a Pronouncing Dictionary of the English Language on a Plan Entirely New* (London, 1774), 7.

46. J. Walker, *A Critical Pronouncing Dictionary and Expositor of the English Language*, 1st edn (London, 1791), p. vi n.

47. J. Boswell, *The Life of Samuel Johnson LL.D*, ii. *1766–1776*, ed. L. F. Powell (Oxford, 1934), 159.

48. Ibid. John Dunning, as the first edition of the *DNB* recorded in 1888, was, though 'possessed of an ungainly person, a husky voice, and a provincial accent … one of the most powerful orators of his time'.

49. Walker, *Critical Pronouncing Dictionary*, 1st edn (1791), p. vi.

50. Sheridan, *Elements of English*, p. v.

51. Walker, *General Idea of a Pronouncing Dictionary*, 1–2.

52. Private usage—even Johnson's own—could, however, continue to display significant variation. Johnson, as Noel Osselton has confirmed, used forms such as *occurence* and *pamflet* even while his own *Dictionary* conversely prescribed *occurrence* and *pamphlet*. (see N. Osselton, 'Informal Spelling Systems in Early Modern English: 1500–1800', in N. F. Blake and C. Jones (eds), *English Historical Linguistics: Studies in Development* (Sheffield, 1984), 123–37). Similar patterns of variability can easily be traced in other non-published sources in the late eighteenth century as well as afterwards. *Dayly* and *happyness* remained among the preferred forms of Georgiana, Duchess of Devonshire; even George Eliot would diverge from the dictionary in her habitual use of forms such as *embarass* and *pryed*.

53. Id., *Critical Pronouncing Dictionary*, 1st edn (1791), p. vi.

54. Ibid., p. xiv.

55. A. Bicknell, *The Grammatical Wreath* (London, 1796), ii. 101.

56. S. Daines, *Orthoepia Anglicana* (London, 1640), A3^r.

57. Boswell, *Life of Johnson*, i. *1709–1765*, 300–1.

58. T. Wilson, *The Many Advantages of a Good Language to Any Nation* (London, 1724), 4.

59. Johnson, *Dictionary*, C2ʳ.

60. See [J. Swift], *A Proposal for Correcting, Improving and Ascertaining the English Tongue* (London, 1712).

61. Sheridan, *General Dictionary*, A1ʳ.

62. Id., *Dissertation*, 1.

63. Id., *Rhetorical Grammar*, p. xv.

64. Id., *Dissertation*, 17.

65. *How to Shine in Society* (Glasgow, 1860), 20.

66. W. Downes, *Language in Society* (London, 1984), 34.

67. Sheridan, *Dissertation*, 17–18.

68. Id., *Course of Lectures*, 206.

69. W. Johnston, *A Pronouncing and Spelling Dictionary of the English Language* (London, 1764), title page.

70. J. Walker, *A Critical Pronouncing Dictionary and Expositor of the English Language*, ed. J. Murdoch (London, 1809), p. i.

71. Id., *A Critical Pronouncing Dictionary and Expositor of the English Language*, 3rd edn (1802), 13.

72. S. Oliver, *A General Critical Grammar of the Inglish Language on a System Novel and Extensive* (London, 1825), p. xiii.

73. H. Alford, *A Plea for the Queen's English*, 2nd edn (London, 1864), 5.

74. E. Bulwer Lytton, *England and the English* (1833), ed. S. Meacham (Chicago, 1970), 27. See p. 58 ff.

75. Sheridan, *Dissertation*, 38.

76. Ibid., 29–30.

77. Ibid., 18.

78. Id., *Rhetorical Grammar*, p. xviii.

79. R. C. Trench, *English Past and Present* (London, 1855), 171.

80. Johnson, *Dictionary*, A2ᵛ.

81. J. Buchanan, *A New English Dictionary* (London, 1757).

82. W. Cobbett, *The Life and Adventures of Peter Porcupine* (Philadelphia, 1797), 22.

83. A. Smith, unsigned review of '*A Dictionary of the English Language* by Samuel Johnson', in *The Edinburgh Review. Containing an account of all the Books and Pamphlets Published in Scotland from June 1755 (to January 1756)* (Edinburgh, 1755), 62.

84. See J. Todd, *Mary Wollstonecraft. A Revolutionary Life* (London, 2000), 384.

85. N. McKendrick, J. Brewer, and J. Plumb, *The Birth of a Consumer Society. The Commercialization of Eighteenth-Century England* (London, 1982). See further p. 70 ff.

86. Walker, *Critical Pronouncing Dictionary*, 3rd edn (1802), 13.

87. Johnston, *Pronouncing and Spelling Dictionary*, p. v.

88. R. D. Altick, *The English Common Reader. A Social History of the Mass Reading Public 1800–1900* (Chicago, Ill., 1957), 51.

89. W. P. Russel, *Multum in Parvo* (London, 1801), 13 n.

90. W. Kenrick, *A Rhetorical Grammar of the English Language* (London, 1784), Advertisement. The price of the dictionary is given as one guinea. Sheridan also

published the *Rhetorical Grammar* which formed part of his *General Dictionary of the English Language* as a separate work. Appearing first in 1781, this proved highly popular and went through a number of further editions.

91. Boswell, *Life of Johnson*, ii. *1766–1776*, 161.

92. Johnston, *Pronouncing and Spelling Dictionary*, p. viii.

93. Ibid., 41.

94. *Live and Learn: A Guide for All Who Wish to Speak and Write Correctly*, 28th edn. (London, 1872), 160–1.

95. Sheridan, *Course of Lectures*, 35. See also pp. 99–100.

96. Ibid., 206.

97. D. Booth, *The Principles of English Grammar* (London, 1837), 11.

98. See p. 248.

99. Privy Council Committee on Education, *Extracts from the Reports of Her Majesty's Inspectors of Schools* (London, 1852), 192.

100. R. Fasold, *The Sociolinguistics of Society* (Oxford, 1984), 253.

101. *Society Small Talk. Or What to Say and When to Say It*, 2nd edn (London, 1880), 116: 'The peculiar manner in which certain people pronounce certain words under the impression that the doing so is fine and fashionable, is in itself the height of vulgarity … They in a way endeavour to out-Walker Walker'.

102. C. Dickens, *Dombey and Son* (London, 1848), ed. A. Horsman (Oxford, 1974), 184.

103. Russel (1801), 57.

104. P. A. Nuttall, *Walker's Pronouncing Dictionary of the English Language*, 4th edn (London, 1873), p. iii.

105. See further L. C. Mugglestone, 'Alexander Ellis and the Virtues of Doubt', in M. J. Toswell and E. M. Tyler (eds), *Studies in English Language and Literature. 'Doubt Wisely': Studies in Honour of E. G. Stanley* (London, 1996), 85–96.

106. Ellis, *Early English Pronunciation*, ii. 629.

107. N. Webster, *Dissertations on the English Language* (Boston, Mass.,1789), 167–8.

108. Sheridan, *Course of Lectures*, 30.

109. Boswell, *Life of Johnson*, ii. 159.

110. W. Cockin, *The Art of Delivering Written Language* (London, 1775), p. ix.

111. Sledmere MSS, Sir Christopher Sykes's Letter Book, 1775–90, Sykes to Revd W. Cleaver, 15 Sept. 1778; cited in F. M. L. Thompson, *English Landed Society in the Nineteenth Century* (London, 1963), 135.

112. M. Edgeworth, *Letters From England, 1813–1844*, ed. C. Colvin (Oxford, 1971), 7.

113. Cited in W. Matthews, *Cockney Past and Present. A Short History of the Dialect of London* (London, 1972), 222.

114. Cited in Benzie, *Dublin Orator*, 27–8.

115. J. Watkins (ed.), *Memoirs of R. B. Sheridan* (London, 1817), 79.

116. J. Walker, *Elements of Elocution* (London, 1781), a4^r. Walker notes, with obvious pride, that he had 'had the honour, a few years ago, to give public lectures in English Pronunciation at the University of Oxford' and had afterwards been 'invited by several of the Heads of Houses to give private lectures on the Art of Reading, in their respective colleges'.

117. S. Douglas, *A Treatise on the Provincial Dialect of Scotland* (1779), ed. C. Jones (Edinburgh, 1991), 97.

118. Ibid., 99.

119. See L. Kelly, *Richard Brinsley Sheridan. A Life* (London, 1997), 16.

120. F. W. Newman, *Orthoëpy: Or, a Simple Mode of Accenting English* (London, 1869), 16.

121. Webster, *Dissertations*, 19.

122. Ibid., 24–5.

123. Sheridan, *Rhetorical Grammar*, p. xv.

124. Webster, *Dissertations*, 25.

125. J. Milroy, 'Social Network and Prestige Arguments in Sociolinguistics', in K. Bolton and H. Kwok (eds), *Sociolinguistics Today: International Perspectives* (London, 1992), 147.

126. Altick, *English Common Reader*, 170.

127. Sheridan, *Dissertation*, 18.

128. G. B. Shaw, *Androcles and the Lion, Pygmalion, Overruled* (London, 1916), 121, 174.

129. W. Labov, *Sociolinguistic Patterns* (Oxford, 1978), 36.

130. Walker, *Critical Pronouncing Dictionary*, 1st edn (1791), p. iii.

131. P. Trudgill, *The Social Stratification of English in Norwich* (Cambridge, 1974).

132. R. Wardhaugh, *An Introduction to Sociolinguistics* (Oxford, 1986), 195.

133. B. H. Smart, *Walker Remodelled. A New Critical Pronouncing Dictionary* (London, 1836), §178.

134. A. Leach, *The Letter H. Past, Present, and Future* (London, 1881), 11.

135. J. Milroy and L. Milroy, *Authority in Language. Investigating Language Prescription and Standardization* (London, 1985), 23.

136. See further Chapter 8.

137. Milroy and Milroy, *Authority in Language*, 36.

138. H. Sweet, *A Primer of Phonetics* (London, 1890), 3.

139. Labov, *Sociolinguistic Patterns*, 120–1.

140. J. Barrell, *English Literature in History 1730–80. An Equal Wide Survey* (London, 1983), 111.

141. L. S. Stone and J. C. F. Stone, *An Open Elite? England 1540–1800* (Oxford, 1984). See p. 71.

Notes to Chapter 2

1. W. Enfield, *A Familiar Treatise on Rhetoric* (London, 1809), 5.

2. R. A. Hudson, *Sociolinguistics* (Cambridge, 1980, reprinted 1986), 193–4.

3. Ibid., 202.

4. P. Walkden Fogg, *Elementa Anglicana; or, the Principles of English Grammar* (Stockport, 1796), ii. 169.

5. B. Holmberg, *On the Concept of Standard English and the History of Modern English Pronunciation* (Lund, 1964), 35.

6. J. Walker, *Critical Pronouncing Dictionary*, 4th edn (1806), note under the word *vulgarism*.

7. G. Vandenhoff, *The Lady's Reader* (London, 1862), 22.

8. Alford, *A Plea for the Queen's English*, 40.

9. *Talking and Debating* (1856), 15.

10. Johnston, *Pronouncing and Spelling Dictionary*, p. v.

11. J. Buchanan, *Linguae Britannicae Vera Pronunciatio* (London, 1757), p. xx n.

12. Douglas, *Treatise on the Provincial Dialect of Scotland*, 99.

13. Walker, *Critical Pronouncing Dictionary*, ed. Murdoch (1809), p. i.

14. Todd, *Mary Wollstonecraft*, 191.

15. B. H. Smart, *A Practical Grammar of English Pronunciation* (London, 1810), 9.

16. L. Sherman, *A Handbook of Pronunciation* (London, 1885), p. iv.

17. Ibid., p. iii.

18. Phyfe, *How Should I Pronounce?*, 13.

19. Ibid., p. v.

20. Williams, *Composition*, 5.

21. Phyfe, *How Should I Pronounce?*, p. v.

22. C. Hartley, *Everyone's Handbook of Common Blunders in Speaking and Writing* (London, 1897), preface.

23. Douglas, *Treatise on the Provincial Dialect of Scotland*, 99.

24. Cited in V. Glendinning, *Jonathan Swift* (London, 1998), 69.

25. See pp. 44–5.

26. L. Bloomfield, 'Literate and Illiterate Speech', *American Speech*, 2 (1927), 432.

27. J. C. Wells, *Accents of English* (Cambridge, 1982), i. 29.

28. R. T. Bell, *Sociolinguistics. Goals, Approaches and Problems* (London, 1976), 90.

29. Sheridan, *Course of Lectures*, 30.

30. Smart, *Practical Grammar*, 9.

31. W. Enfield, *The Speaker: or, Miscellaneous Pieces, Selected from the best English writers. To which is prefixed An Essay on elocution* (London, 1774), a2^r.

32. *How to Shine in Society* (1860), 20.

33. Downes, *Language in Society*, 215.

34. N. Forster, *An Enquiry into the Present High Price of Provisions* (London, 1767), 41. Cited in McKendrick *et al.*, *Birth of a Consumer Society*, 11.

35. W. H. Savage, *The Vulgarisms and Improprieties of the English Language* (London, 1833), pp. iv–v.

36. See also pp. 108–13. As an established phrase, the 'new rich' first appears in the *OED* in 1886, accompanied by a particularly telling citation from *Harper's Magazine* ('There are...the sons of the new rich who are like men drunk with new wine'). Willaim Craigie, the editor of the fascicle *N–Nywe* in which this is recorded, notes that it was a coinage 'of recent use'.

37. *Talking and Debating* (1856), 15.

38. *Vulgarities of Speech Corrected* (London, 1826), 40.

39. *Hints on Etiquette and the Usages of Society* (London, 1836), 10–11.

40. W. Bagehot, *The English Constitution* (London, 1867), 120.

41. M. Davis, *Everybody's Business* (London, 1865), 16–17.

42. *Modern Etiquette in Public and Private* (London, 1888), 39.

43. B. Disraeli, *Sybil; or, the Two Nations* (London, 1845), i. 149.

44. Newman, *Orthoëpy*, 22–3.

45. P. J. Waller, 'Democracy and Dialect, Speech and Class', in id. (ed.), *Politics and Social Change in Modern Britain. Essays Presented to A. F. Thompson* (Brighton, 1987), 2.

46. *Errors of Pronunciation and Improper Expressions* (London, 1817), p. iv.

47. G. F. Graham, *A Book About Words* (London, 1869), 156

48. Leach, *The Letter H*, 10.

49. Downes, *Language in Society*, 34.

50. See Chapter 5.

51. M. Shapiro, 'A Political Approach to Language Purism', in B. H. Jernudd and M. J. Shapiro (eds), *The Politics of Language Purism* (Berlin, 1989), 22.

52. G. Stedman-Jones, *Outcast London* (Oxford, 1971), p. v.

53. W. Cobbett, *A Grammar of the English Language in a Series of Letters* (London, 1819), 15. The first edition of Cobbett's *Grammar* was published in New York in 1818. The first English edition was published in London in the following year. All citations are from the latter.

54. G. Hughes, *Words in Time. A Social History of the English Vocabulary* (Oxford, 1988), 6.

55. R. Williams, *Keywords. A Vocabulary of Culture and Society* (London, 1976), 61.

56. H. Perkin, *The Origins of Modern English Society 1780–1880* (London, 1969), 176.

57. A. Briggs, *The Age of Improvement* (London, 1960), 65.

58. B. H. Jernudd, 'The Texture of Language Purism: An Introduction', in Jernudd and Shapiro (eds), *Politics of Language Purism*, 3.

59. Boswell, *Life of Johnson*, i. 442.

60. Williams, *Keywords*, 61.

61. Attested respectively from 1830, 1816, 1826, 1887, 1841, 1839, 1828, 1859, 1868, and 1889 in *OED*.

62. See, for example, J. Nelson, *An Essay on the Government of Children* (London, 1753): 'Every nation has its Custom of dividing the People into Classes. Were we to divide the People, we might run it to an Infinity: to avoid Confusion therefore, I will select five Classes; *viz* the Nobility, the Gentry, the genteel Trades ... the common Trades, and the Peasantry.' Cited in P. Corfield, 'Class by Name and Number in Eighteenth-Century Britain', *History*, 72 (1987), 38.

63. Corfield, 'Class by Name and Number', 39.

64. I. Bradley, *The English Middle Classes Are Alive and Kicking* (London, 1982), 7.

65. T. May, *An Economic and Social History of Britain 1760–1970* (New York, 1987), 43.

66. *Sybil*, ii. 203.

67. May, *Economic and Social History of Britain*, 43.

68. T. Kington-Oliphant, *The Sources of Standard English* (London, 1873), ii. 333.

69. W. D. Rubenstein, 'New Men of Wealth and the Purchase of Land in Nineteenth-Century England', *Past and Present*, 92 (1981), 140.

70. See C. Seymour-Jones, *Beatrice Webb. Woman of Conflict* (London, 1992), 145.

71. Stone and Stone, *An Open Elite?*, 207.

72. Seymour-Jones, *Beatrice Webb*, 214.

73. I. Morrish, *The Sociology of Education*, 2nd edn (London, 1978), 123.

74. Marshall, *Industrial England*, 96–7.

75. Cited in D. Smith, *Conflict and Compromise. Class Formation in English Society 1830–1914* (London, 1982), 15.

76. Leach, *The Letter H*, 10–11.

77. M. Weber, 'Class, Status, Party', in R. S. Neale (ed.), *History and Class. Essential Readings in Theory and Interpretation* (Oxford, 1983), 57.

78. L. Milroy, *Observing and Analysing Natural Language. A Critical Account of Sociolinguistic Method* (Oxford, 1987), 32.

79. *How to Shine in Society* (1860), 9.

80. In Neale, *History and Class*, 63. See also pp. 104–5.

81. See p. 57.

82. Sir William Hardman, *Papers*, ed. S. M. Ellis (London, 1925), i. 219. In spite of his Eton education, Gladstone retained his Northern accent throughout his life though, in view of his other qualities as a speaker, it was to be no disadvantage in his political career. Lady Augusta Stanley was, for one, notably eulogistic in the late nineteenth century about Gladstone's voice ('Oh, what a charming voice, and what beautiful English that is!'). Cited in C. Hibbert, *Queen Victoria. A Personal History* (London, 2000), 373 n.

83. H. More, *Thoughts on the Importance of the Manners of the Great to General Society* (London, 1788), 2.

84. See A. Foreman, *Georgiana, Duchess of Devonshire* (London, 1998). As Foreman notes, emulation of the extremely popular Georgiana was largely responsible for the craze for muslin gowns throughout Britain, as well as for the 'picture-hat' (a hat with a wide brim, trimmed with a large sash and feathers).

85. McKendrick *et al.*, *Birth of a Consumer Society*, 11.

86. G. Eliot, 'The Natural History of German Life', first pub. in *Westminster Review*, NS 10 (July 1856), 51–79, repr. in Eliot, *Essays*, ed. T. Pinney (London, 1963), 273–4.

87. Stone and Stone, *An Open Elite?*, 409.

88. Ibid.

89. W. Bagehot, 'The Character of Sir Robert Peel', in id., *Works*, ed. F. Morgan (Hartford, 1891), iii. 3–4.

90. The sociolinguist Peter Trudgill's researches in Norwich have, for example, regularly revealed patterns of variation in which variants perceived as more 'statusful' in the wider speech community appear in far higher frequencies than one might expect in the formal speech of members of the lower-middle class. Hypercorrection, the over-extension of a particular linguistic usage in the attempt to emulate others, is, as he and a variety of other linguists have concluded, a common phenomenon in such contexts.

91. W. P. Robinson, *Language and Social Behaviour* (London, 1972), 72.

92. R. LePage, 'Projection, focusing, diffusion', *York Papers in Linguistics*, 9 (1980), 15.

93. Hon. Henry H., *P's and Q's*, 78 n.

94. Ibid.

95. *Advice to a Young Gentleman on Entering Society* (London, 1839), 77.

96. *How to Shine in Society* (1860), 20.

97. Davis, *Everybody's Business*, 18.

98. Ibid., 1.

99. Phyfe, *How Should I Pronounce?*, p. v.

100. Savage, *Vulgarisms and Improprieties*, p. v.

101. Cobbett, *Grammar of the English Language*, 9.

102. Ibid., 15.

103. Ibid.

104. J. Cobbett, *A Grammar of the English Language in a Series of Letters. With an Additional Chapter on Pronunciation by James Paul Cobbett* (London, 1866), 242.

105. Cobbett, *Grammar of the English Language*, 15.
106. J. Cobbett, *Grammar of the English Language*, 247. See also L. C. Mugglestone, 'Cobbett's *Grammar*; William, James Paul, and the Politics of Prescriptivism', *Review of English Studies*, NS 48 (1997), 471–88.

Notes to Chapter 3

1. Even here, however, prescriptivism can intervene, as in Ellis's evident resistance to the use of intrusive [r], a common phenomenon in nineteenth-century speech (see p. 92) or in the normative impulses which the *OED* can also betray. See further L. C. Mugglestone, ''An Historian and Not a Critic': The Standard of Usage in the *OED*', in ead., *Lexicography and the OED. Pioneers in the Untrodden Forest* (Oxford, 2000), 189–206.
2. R. D. Eagleson, 'Sociolinguistic Reflections on Acceptability', in S. Greenbaum (ed.), *Acceptability in Language* (The Hague, 1977), 64.
3. M. Görlach, *Introduction to Early Modern English* (Cambridge, 1991), 62.
4. Walker, *Critical Pronouncing Dictionary*, 2nd edn (1797), §163.
5. S. Jones, *Sheridan Improved. A General Pronouncing and Explanatory Dictionary of the English Language*, 3rd edn (London, 1798), p. ii.
6. Walker, *Critical Pronouncing Dictionary*, 2nd edn (1797), §79 n.
7. B. Smart, *Walker Remodelled. A New Critical Pronouncing Dictionary* (London, 1836), § 11.
8. Downes, *Language in Society*, 214.
9. Smart, *Practical Grammar*, 99.
10. Cooper, *The English Teacher*, 34.
11. R. Lowth, *A Short Introduction to English Grammar* (London, 1762), p.x.
12. *Common Blunders in Speaking, and How to Avoid Them* (London, 1884), 9.
13. J. Longmuir, *Walker and Webster Combined in a Dictionary of the English Language* (London, 1864), §6.
14. Ibid.
15. Ellis, *Early English Pronunciation*, ii. 593.
16. See pp. 50–1.
17. W. Ripman, *The Sounds of Spoken English* (London, 1906), 55.
18. C. W. Smith, *Mind Your H's and Take Care of Your R's* (London, 1866), 34.
19. *Asp, lass, mass*, for example, although satisfying the requisite phonological conditions, nevertheless all have [æ] in RP (though [ɑː] for the latter is recorded in conservative Catholic usage). By analogy, *pasta* is now wavering between [æ] and [ɑː].
20. *Vulgarisms and Other Errors of Speech* (London, 1868), p. iv.
21. Walker, *Critical Pronouncing Dictionary*, 2nd edn (1797), §79 n.
22. Estuary English, first described in 1984 by David Rosewarne in the *Times Educational Supplement*, 19 October, 29, is usually characterized as a 'classless' blend of RP and 'Cockney', spoken in the area around London and the Thames valley and marked by a range of proscribed (though common) articulations such as the glottal stop or the use of /t, d/ deletion. See further Chapter 8.
23. Johnson, *Dictionary*, a2ᵛ i.
24. L. Murray, *English Grammar Adapted to the Different Classes of Learners*, 5th edn (York, 1799), 13.

25. L. Brittain, *Rudiments of English Grammar* (Louvain, 1788), A1ᵛ.
26. T. Carpenter, *The School Speaker* (London, 1825), p. vi.
27. M. Stubbs, *Language and Literacy. The Sociolinguistics of Reading and Writing* (London, 1980), 29.
28. Johnson, *Dictionary*, A2ʳ.
29. Rhotic accents (those which retain the [r] in all positions) are still present in Scotland and Ireland, whereas variable rhoticity can still mark (lower-status) accents in, for example, the south-west of England.
30. F. W. Newman, 'The English Language as Spoken and Written', *Contemporary Review*, 31 (1878), 702.
31. R. R. Rogers, *Poor Letter R. Its Use and Abuse* (London, 1855), 14–15.
32. See L. C. Mugglestone, 'The Fallacy of the Cockney Rhyme: from Keats and Earlier to Auden', *Review of English Studies*, NS 42 (1991), 57–66.
33. T. Hood, *The Wakefield Spelling Book* (London, 1868), 44.
34. J. E. Carpenter, *Handbook of Poetry* (London, 1868), 12.
35. J. G. Lockhart, 'On the Cockney School of Poetry No. IV', *Blackwood's Edinburgh Magazine*, 3 (1818), 520, 521.
36. G. M. Hopkins, Letter to R. W. Dixon (22 Dec. 1880), in C. C. Abbott (ed.), *The Correspondence of Gerard Manley Hopkins and Richard Watkins Dixon* (London, 1935), 37.
37. Cited in O. Jespersen, *A Modern English Grammar on Historical Principles* (London and Copenhagen, 1909), i. §13.23.
38. A. Lord Tennyson, *The Druid's Prophecies* (1827), ll. 26–28; *Recollections of the Arabian Nights* (1830), ll. 100, 103, and 106. For examples in other eighteenth- and nineteenth-century poets, see Mugglestone, 'The Fallacy of the Cockney Rhyme', 64–5.
39. See J. Marsh, *Christina Rossetti. A Literary Biography* (London, 1994), 538.
40. Letter to Algernon Gissing, 23 Sept. 1883. *The Collected Letters of George Gissing*, ii. *1881–1885*, ed. P. F. Mattheisen, A. C. Young, and P. Coustillas (Ohio, 1991), 161.
41. E. Guest, *A History of English Rhythms* (London, 1838), i. 313.
42. Ellis, *Early English Pronunciation*, ii. 603.
43. H. C. Wyld, *The Historical Study of the Mother Tongue* (London, 1906), 16.
44. *Hard Words Made Easy* (London, 1855), 4.
45. J. Earle, *The Philology of the English Tongue* (London, 1871), 146.
46. G. Hill, *The Aspirate* (London, 1902), 43.
47. G. Eliot, *Adam Bede* (London, 1859), i. 20.
48. *Falcon* < OF *faucon, falcun* was, in the eighteenth century, pronounced without the /l/, being transcribed]fåw'kn[by Walker in 1791. By 1825, however, the appeal of graphemic logic was beginning to shift notions of acceptability; Samuel Oliver (*General Critical Grammar*, 1825) notes at 287, n.3: 'Walker pronounces *falcon fawkn*, an ordinary but a vicious sound'. By the end of the nineteenth century, enunciations with /l/ were common. *Forehead* and *waistcoat* had habitual pronunciations as /ˈfɒrɪd/, /ˈwɛskət/ respectively.
49. B. H. Smart, *A Grammar of English Sounds* (London, 1812), p. xxv.
50. Alford, *A Plea for the Queen's English*, 50.
51. A. J. Ellis, 'Tenth Annual Address of the President to the Philological Society', *Transactions of the Philological Society* (1881), 317.

52. Ellis, *Early English Pronunciation*, ii. 603.
53. Ibid. i. 201.
54. See further p. 117.
55. J. Hullah, *The Cultivation of the Speaking Voice* (Oxford, 1870), 53–4.
56. H. Sweet, *A Primer of Spoken English* (Oxford, 1890), p. viii.
57. J. Lecky, *Phonetic Journal* 27 Feb 1886. Cited in Jespersen, *A Modern English Grammar*, i. §13.42.
58. Wells, *Accents of English*, ii. 284.
59. Ibid.

Notes to Chapter 4

1. Wells, *Accents of English*, i. 254.
2. The use of [h] does not occur invariably in all syllable-initial positions even in RP. Form words of frequent occurrence, such as *have, had, her, his* will, for example, often have zero-realization of [h] as a result of use in positions of weak stress within the sentence. Word internal stress can also play a similar role, governing the use of traditionally [h]-less forms in words such as *historical, hysterical*, in constructions such as *an historical play* /ən ɪsˈtɒrɪkl ˈpleɪ/, the weak stress of the first syllable tending to lead to the non-realization of [h]. Many regional urban accents (though not those in the north-east of England) regularly drop [h], making words such as *art* and *heart* identical in enunciation.
3. D. H. Lawrence, *Lady Chatterley's Lover* (Florence, 1928), 110–11.
4. H. Sweet, *Handbook of Phonetics* (Oxford, 1877), 195.
5. Ellis, *Early English Pronunciation*, i. 221.
6. *Chambers's Encyclopaedia. A Dictionary of Useful Knowledge* (London, 1888), v. 492.
7. Kington-Oliphant, *Sources of Standard English*, i. 333.
8. G. Gissing, *Demos. A Story of English Socialism* (London, 1886), i. 115.
9. Mrs Gaskell, *North and South* (London, 1855), ed. A. Easson (Oxford, 1973), 428.
10. Such etymological remodelling was not, however, exempt from error, and words such as *hermit* and *hostage* derive in fact from etymologically <h>-less forms, Lat. *erēmita* and OF *ostage*.
11. R. Lass, *The Shape of English* (London, 1987), 96.
12. Wells, *Accents of English*, i. 255.
13. J. Milroy, *Linguistic Variation and Change. On the Historical Sociolinguistics of English* (Oxford, 1992a), 142. See further Milroy's essay, 'Historical Description and the Ideology of the Standard Language' in L. Wright (ed.), *The Development of Standard English 1300–1800. Theories, Descriptions, Conflicts* (Cambridge, 2000), 11–28.
14. R. Browne, *The English-school Reformed* (London, 1700). Form words of frequent occurrence such as *have, has* which regularly occur in positions of weak stress, have, as already indicated, traditionally 'dropped their h's' in the usage of all speakers.
15. W. Laughton, *A Practical Grammar of the English Tongue* (London, 1739), 31–2.
16. Cooper, *The English Teacher*, 21.
17. B. Martin, *Institutions of Language* (London, 1748), 20.
18. Sheridan, *Course of Lectures*, 34.

19. Ibid., 35.
20. Sheridan, *Rhetorical Grammar*, 176–7.
21. Sheridan, *Course of Lectures*, 35.
22. J. Elphinston, *Propriety Ascertained in her Picture* (London, 1786), 15.
23. T. Batchelor, *An Orthoëpical Analysis of the English Language to which is added A Minute Analysis of the Dialect of Bedfordshire* (1809), ed. A. Zettersten, Lund Studies in English, 45 (1974), 111.
24. C. Dickens, *Our Mutual Friend* (London, 1865), i. 100.
25. Buchanan, *Linguae Britannicae*, p. vii.
26. Vandenhoff, *The Lady's Reader*, 16.
27. Alford, *A Plea for the Queen's English*, 40.
28. Murray, *English Grammar*, 11.
29. See further L. C. Mugglestone, '"A Subject so Curious and Useful': Lindley Murray and Pronunciation', in I. Tieken-Boon van Ostade (ed.), *Two Hundred Years of Lindley Murray* (Munster, Germany, 1996), 145–63.
30. A. Perceval Graves and M. Rice-Wiggin, *The Elementary School Manager* (London, 1879), 116.
31. See further p. 246.
32. Cited in R. Robinson, *A Manual of Method and Organisation. Adapted to the Primary Schools of Great Britain, Ireland, and the Colonies* (London, 1863), 3 n.
33. MP/n.d./1897. J. A. H. Murray to H. H. Gibbs.
34. See Hibbert, *Queen Victoria*, 358.
35. See p. 41.
36. As S. Ramsaran noted in 1989, 'In the case of *hotel* … an /h/-less form is fairly widespread, e.g. *an hotel*, though the pronunciation with initial /h/ is commoner.' A. C. Gimson, *An Introduction to the Pronunciation of English*, 4th edn rev. S. Ramsaran (London, 1989), 193. *OED2*, published in the same year, confirmed this trend, specifying /ˈəʊtɛl/ as 'old-fashioned'.
37. W. Cramp, *The Philosophy of Language* (London, 1838), 8.
38. W. Smith, *An Attempt to Render the Pronunciation of the English Language More Easy* (London, 1795), 8 n. The fact that Mrs Siddons had, in the early stages of her career, been trained in voice delivery by Sheridan is presumably not irrelevant in her apparent preference for [æ]. See pp. 179–80.
39. Cited in Neale, *History and Class*, 63.
40. *Etiquette for Ladies and Gentlemen* (London, 1839), 10.
41. *Etiquette for All* (London, 1861), 6.
42. F. W. R. and Lord Charles X., *The Laws and Bye-Laws of Good Society. A Code of Modern Etiquette* (London, 1867), 19.
43. Smart, *Walker Remodelled*, §178.
44. See McKendrick *et al.*, *Birth of a Consumer Society*, ch. II.
45. I. S. L., *Fashion in Language* (London, 1906), 13.
46. C. Dickens, *The Personal History of David Copperfield* (London, 1850), ed. N. Burgis (Oxford, 1981), 22.
47. Sheridan, *Course of Lectures*, 36.
48. *Good Society. A Complete Manual of Manners* (London, 1869), 91.
49. G. Thomas, *Linguistic Purism* (London, 1991), 22.
50. Hon. Henry H., *Poor Letter H*, 40th edn (1866), p. v.

51. Hon. Henry H., *Poor Letter H*, 16–17.
52. Ibid., 35.
53. Kington-Oliphant, *Sources of Standard English*, i. 333.
54. Hon. Henry H., *Poor Letter H*, 40th edn (1866), 35.
55. Kington-Oliphant, *Sources of Standard English* (1873), i. 333.
56. W. Labov, *The Social Stratification of English in New York City* (Washington, DC, 1966).
57. Bell, *Sociolinguistics*, 188.
58. See, for example, the opening chapter of W. Labov, *Principles of Linguistic Change. Internal Factors* (Oxford, 1994).
59. See W. Labov, 'The Effect of Social Mobility on Speech Behaviour', *International Journal of American Linguistics*. 33 (1967), 58–75 ('The most striking finding . . . is that a group of speakers with past history of social mobility is more apt to resemble the next highest socio-economic group in their linguistic behaviour than the one with which they are currently associated').
60. *Bradford Observer*, 9 June 1870. Cited in E. M. Sigsworth, *Black Dyke Mills* (Liverpool, 1958), 72–3.
61. See D. C. Coleman, 'Gentlemen and Players', *Economic History Review*, 26 (1973), 105. See further pp. 227–8.
62. A. E. Musson and E. Robinson, *Science and Technology in the Industrial Revolution* (Manchester, 1969), 209. See especially Ch. V: 'Training Captains of Industry. The Education of Matthew Robinson Boulton (1770–1842) and James Watt, Junior (1769–1848)', 200–15.
63. Savage, *Vulgarisms and Improprieties*, pp. iv–v.
64. May, *Economic and Social History of Britain*, 206.
65. *Talking and Debating* (1856), 4.
66. Johnson, *Dictionary*, a2^r: '*H* is a note of aspiration, and shows that the following vowel must be pronounced with a strong emission of the breath, as *hat, horse*. It seldom, perhaps never, begins any but the first syllable'. See also L. C. Mugglestone, 'Samuel Johnson and the Use of /h/', *Notes and Queries*, 243 (1989), 431–3.
67. *Hints on Etiquette and the Usages of Society* (1836), 5.
68. *The Family Herald* contains, for example, the following 'Humble Petition of the Letter *H* to the Inhabitants of London and its Environs': 'The memorial of your unfortunate petitioner humbly showeth, that although conspicuous in heraldry, entitled to the first place in honour, and remarkable in holiness, yet he has been, by many of you, most injuriously treated; spoiled in health, driven from home, and refused a place, not only in your house, but in every home, hut, or hamlet, within your controul. You refuse your petitioner help, and cut him off also from hope, the last resource of the unfortunate, both here and hereafter' (6 July 1844), 143.
69. Hon. Henry H., *Poor Letter H*, 40th edn (1866), p. iv.
70. Ibid., p. iii.
71. Ibid., 26.
72. Ibid., 24.
73. Ibid., 25.
74. Ibid., 27.
75. Ibid., 39.

76. E. A. S. Eccles, *Harry Hawkins' H Book* (London, 1879), 6–7.

77. Ibid., 45–6.

78. Leach, *The Letter H*, 44 n.

79. Shaw, *Androcles and the Lion, Pygmalion, Overruled*, 107.

80. Letter to Walker Skeat, 1872, *The George Eliot Letters*, ed. G. S. Haight (London, 1954–6), ix. 39.

81. R. Fowler, *Literature as Social Discourse* (London, 1981), 7.

82. Jespersen, *A Modern English Grammar*, i. 379.

83. Trudgill in *The Social Stratification of English in Norwich*, for example, gives statistical patterns for the use of [h] in Norwich in which the percentage of its use is the most significant factor, members of what he labels the 'middle middle class' dropping it 6 per cent of the time, the lower middle class 14 per cent of the time, the upper working class 40 per cent of the time, and the middle working class 59 per cent of the time.

84. H. Fielding, *The History of the Life of Mr. Jonathan Wild the Great*, in *Miscellanies*, vol. III, Introduction and Commentary by B. A. Goldgor, text ed. H. Amory (Oxford, 1997), 108.

85. Johnson, *Dictionary, Preface* A2^r.

86. As Ogilvie indicates in 1870, 'letter' was, in contemporary linguistic usage, often used to signify sound as well as symbol: 'a mark or character written, printed, engraved ...; used as the representative of a sound ... an articulation of the human organs of speech'.

87. T. Smollett, *The Adventures of Peregrine Pickle* (London, 1751), ii. 52.

88. T. Smollett, *The Expedition of Humphry Clinker* (London, 1771), i. 229.

89. Ibid., ii. 83.

90. Ibid., ii. 68.

91. Ibid., ii. 225.

92. C. Dickens, *Bleak House* (London, 1853), i. 237–8.

93. C. Dickens, *Great Expectations* (London, 1861), i. 103–4.

94. Ibid., i. 98.

95. Ibid.

96. Ibid., i. 126.

97. Ibid., i. 130.

98. Ibid., ii. 134.

99. *David Copperfield*, 200.

100. See p. 97.

101. *Adam Bede*, ii. 324. See also p. 91.

102. *David Copperfield*, 327.

103. Ibid., 218.

104. Ibid., 491.

105. Ibid., 218.

106. Ibid., 292.

107. Ibid., 639.

108. Ibid., 640.

109. Ibid., 639.

110. Ibid., 640.

111. See pp. 100–1.

112. Smart, *Walker Remodelled*, §56 n.
113. Alford, *A Plea for the Queen's English*, 54.
114. Leach, *The Letter H*, 57–8.
115. Longmuir, *Walker and Webster Combined*, p. xii.
116. Hill, *The Aspirate*, 37.
117. *Born in Exile*, i. 127.
118. The use of [ɪn] rather than [ɪŋ], on the other hand, now characterizes many regional varieties of English, though other forms such as [ɪŋg], giving articulations such as ['fɪŋgə] and ['sɪŋgə] for *finger* and *singer*, appear in areas such as Manchester, Birmingham, and north-east Derbyshire.
119. G. Crabbe, *The Complete Poetical Works*, I,. ed. N. Dalrymple-Champneys and A. Pollard, (OUP, 1988); 'Poetical Epistles I. From the Devil. An Epistle General', i. 82, ll. 123–4: 'While you, of a Nation I take such Delight in // Are inferior in Fraud, tho' you beat them at fighting' (written soon after Crabbe came to London in April 1780).
120. J. Rice, *An Introduction to the Art of Reading with Energy and Propriety* (London, 1765), 50 n.
121. Walker, *Critical Pronouncing Dictionary*, 1st edn (1791), §410.
122. Batchelor, *An Orthoëpical Analysis*, 105.
123. C. Dickens, *Little Dorrit* (London, 1857), ed. H. P. Sucksmith (Oxford, 1979), 62.
124. *David Copperfield*, 383.
125. W. M. Thackeray, *Vanity Fair, A Novel Without a Hero* (London, 1848), 51.
126. Ibid., 55.
127. P. Gwynne, *A Word to the Wise*, 2nd edn (London, 1879), 60.
128. Ellis, *Early English Pronunciation*, iv. 1243. See also Mugglestone, 'Alexander Ellis and the Virtues of Doubt', 96.
129. J. Galsworthy, *The Island Pharisees* (London, 1904), 190.
130. A. S. C. Ross, *How to Pronounce It* (London, 1970), 16.
131. See pp. 186–9.
132. See Hibbert, *Queen Victoria*, 358.

Notes to Chapter 5

1. C. M. Yonge, *Womankind* (London, 1878), 28–9.
2. See p. 71.
3. J. F. C. Harrison, *Early Victorian Britain 1832–1851* (London, 1971), 126.
4. G. O. Trevelyan (ed.), *The Life and Letters of Lord Macaulay*, (London, 1878), i. 338. Letter to his sister Hannah, 14 Oct. 1833.
5. S. Smiles, *Self-Help; With Illustrations of Character and Conduct*, ed. A. Briggs (London, 1958), 290.
6. S. S. Ellis, *The Women of England, Their Social Duties, and Domestic Habits*, 3rd edn (London, 1839), 107.
7. See pp. 70–1.
8. Lambeth Palace, Court of Arches MSS, Process Book D 1793, fo.69; cited in Stone and Stone, *An Open Élite?*, 410.
9. Recorded by her niece, Josephine Butler, in *Memoir of John Grey of Dilston* (Edinburgh, 1894), 228 n.

10. 'The word is...abused to mean "superficial acquirements", embellishments that pretend to perfect or complete an education that does not exist', as Murray wrote with evident censure in the first fascicle of the *OED* published in 1884. For other conflicts of descriptive/prescriptive agendas within the writing of the *OED*, see further Mugglestone, 'An Historian and a Critic'.

11. M. Poovey, *The Proper Lady and the Woman Writer. Ideology as Style in the Works of Mary Wollstonecraft, Mary Shelley, and Jane Austen* (Chicago, 1984), 3.

12. J. H. Murray, *Strong-Minded Women, and Other Lost Voices from Nineteenth-Century England* (London, 1982), 170.

13. See J. Worthen, *D. H. Lawrence. The Early Years 1885–1912* (CUP, 1991), 13, 17.

14. Cited in Worthen, *D. H. Lawrence*, 61.

15. Mrs D. M. Craik, 'Parson Garland's Daughter', *Two Marriages* (London, 1881), 228.

16. *Woman's Worth: Or Hints to Raise the Female Character*, 2nd edn (London, 1847), 3.

17. *How to Shine in Society* (1860), 20.

18. Dr R. Brewer, *What Shall We Do With Tom? Or, Hints to Parents and Others About School* (London, 1866), 75.

19. *Good Society* (1869), 49.

20. F. B. Jack, *The Woman's Book* (London, 1911), 325.

21. *Take My Advice* (London, 1872), 309.

22. *Good Society* (1869), 49.

23. Madame D'Arblay, *Diary and Letters*, ed. C. Barrett (London, 1876), i. 102; cited in C. Harman, *Fanny Burney. A Biography* (London, 2000), 384.

24. Ellis, *Women of England*, 309–10.

25. Miss S. Hatfield, *Letters on the Importance of the Female Sex. With Observations on their Manners and Education* (London, 1803), 70.

26. *Woman's Worth*, 50–1.

27. H. More, *Strictures on the Modern System of Female Education* (London, 1799), ii. 6–7.

28. *Girls and Their Ways. By One Who Knows Them* (London, 1881), 71.

29. *The Young Housekeeper* (London, 1869), 8.

30. Vandenhoff, *The Lady's Reader*, 1.

31. Ibid., 3. References to King Lear's commendations of his daughter Cordelia's voice ('ever soft // gentle and low, an excellent thing in woman', *King Lear*, v. iii. 270–1) form, as we shall see, a recurrent stereotype of the proprieties of female speech.

32. See p. 85.

33. Vandenhoff, *The Lady's Reader*, 1.

34. *Etiquette for Ladies and Gentlemen* (1839), 45.

35. *How to Shine in Society* (1860), 20.

36. Mrs M. Sangster, *Hours With Girls* (London, 1882), 79.

37. Mrs H. Mackarness, *The Young Lady's Book* (London, 1876), 121.

38. *The Young Lady's Book. A Manual of Elegant Recreations, Exercises, and Pursuits* (London, 1829), 23–4.

39. *Talking and Debating* (1856), 4.

40. T. Nichols, *Behaviour: A Manual of Manners and Morals* (London, 1874), 59.

41. *Etiquette, Social Ethics and the Courtesies of Society* (London, 1834), 38.

42. Yonge, *Womankind*, 172.
43. Ibid., 73–4.
44. *Advice to Governesses* (London, 1827), p. v.
45. T. Hardy, *The Mayor of Casterbridge* (London, 1886), i. 246.
46. *North and South*, 237.
47. See, e.g., the 'unfeigned astonishment' with which, in R. N. Carey's *Not Like Other Girls* (London, 1884) Mrs Challoner regards her youngest daughter, Dulce, merely because she has betrayed feminine linguistic proprieties in using the Christian name of one of their (male) friends. Though Dulce explains in self-defence that ' "I am only repeating Miss Drummond's words—she said 'Archie' " ', Mrs Challoner is not appeased: ' "But, my dear, there was no need to be so literal," returned Mrs Challoner reprovingly; for she was a gentlewoman of the old school, and nothing grieved her more than slipshod English, or any idiom or idotcy of modern parlance in the mouths of her bright young daughters; to speak of any young man ... without the ceremonious prefix was a hideous misdemeanour in her eyes.' (ii. 124).
48. Mackarness, *The Young Lady's Book*, 121.
49. *Girls and Their Ways* (1881), 25.
50. *Boys and Their Ways. By One Who Knows Them* (London, 1880), 14.
51. D. Cameron (ed.), *The Feminist Critique of Language. A Reader* (London, 1990), 24.
52. M. Wollstonecraft, *A Vindication of the Rights of Women* (London, 1792), in *The Works of Mary Wollstonecraft*, ed. J. Todd and M. Butler (London, 1989), v. 90.
53. See n. 31 above.
54. *Girls and Their Ways* (1881), 70.
55. *Good Society* (1869), 99.
56. *The Habits of Good Society. A Handbook of Etiquette for Ladies and Gentlemen* (London, 1859), 265.
57. *Etiquette for the Ladies* (London, 1837), 19.
58. *Hints to Governesses. By One of Themselves* (London, 1856), 17.
59. *Etiquette for Ladies and Gentlemen* (1839), 26.
60. D. Graddol and J. Swann, *Gender Voices* (Oxford, 1989), 142.
61. Vandenhoff, *The Lady's Reader*, 2–3.
62. Mackarness, *The Young Lady's Book*, 45.
63. *Girls and Their Ways* (1881), 25.
64. Kelly, *Richard Brinsley Sheridan*, 22.
65. 'Nothing is more delightful to the feminine members of a family, than the reading aloud of some good standard work or amusing publication', I. Beeton, *Beeton's Book of Household Management* (London, 1861), 17.
66. F. Nightingale, *Cassandra* (1852); cited in Murray, *Strong-Minded Women*, 91.
67. H. Lee, *Virginia Woolf* (London, 1996), 112.
68. This is not of course to suggest that men were automatically excluded from the activity of reading aloud though, according to Tom Trollope (Anthony Trollope's elder brother), this could be a less than congenial experience, especially when conducted by his father. As he recalled, 'There was not one individual of those who heard him who would not have escaped from doing so, at almost any cost. Of course it was our duty to conceal this extreme reluctance to endure what was

to him a pleasure—a duty which I much fear was very imperfectly performed.' Cited in P. Neville-Sington, *Fanny Trollope. The Life and Adventures of a Clever Woman* (London, 1997), 51.

69. *Woman's Worth* (1847), 99.
70. *The Young Lady's Book* (1829), 23.
71. *Woman's Worth* (1847), 11.
72. A. Brontë, *Agnes Grey* (London, 1847), ed. H. Marsden and R. Inglesfield (Oxford, 1988), 64.
73. J. Buchanan, *The British Grammar* (London, 1762), p. xxxi.
74. W. Graham, *Principles of Elocution* (Edinburgh, 1837), 9.
75. *Woman's Worth* (1847), 72–3.
76. Mackarness, *The Young Lady's Book*, 45.
77. Nichols (1874), 59.
78. E. Drew (ed.), *The Elocutionist Annual for 1889* (London, 1889), 125.
79. Vandenhoff, *The Lady's Reader*, 16–17.
80. *Private Education; Or a Practical Plan for the Studies of Young Ladies*, 3rd edn (London, 1816), 280–1.
81. *Little Dorrit*, 438–9.
82. Ibid., 467.
83. Ibid., 461–2.
84. Marshall, *Industrial England*, 61.
85. J. Doran, *A Lady of the Last Century* (London, 1873), 181.
86. L. Gordon, *Charlotte Brontë. A Passionate Life* (London, 1994), 40.
87. S. A. Burstall, *Retrospect and Prospect: Sixty Years of Women's Education* (1933). Cited in Marshall, *Strong-Minded Women*, 232.
88. *Womankind* (1878), 9–10.
89. *Woman's Worth* (1847), 18.
90. *Woman: As She Is, And As She Should Be* (London, 1835), i. 252.
91. *Woman's Worth* (1847), 100.
92. Mrs C. Valentine, *The Young Woman's Book* (London, 1878), 235.
93. *New Grub Street* (1891), i. 170–1.
94. Mrs Valentine, *The Young Woman's Book*, 235.
95. Ibid.
96. Ibid., 243.
97. *The Young Housekeeper* (1869), 8.
98. Hill, *The Aspirate*, 5.
99. Ibid., 13–14.
100. Ibid., 14–15.
101. H. W. H., *How to Choose a Wife* (London, 1854), 51.
102. J. Maynard, *Matrimony: Or, What Married Life Is, and How to Make the Best of It*, 2nd edn (London, 1866), 98–9.
103. See p. 115.
104. Maynard, *Matrimony: Or, What Married Life Is*, 99.
105. Cited in Seymour-Jones, *Beatrice Webb*, 194.
106. *Woman's Worth* (1847), 21.
107. Ibid., 28–9.
108. *The Mother's Home Book* (London, 1879), 199.

109. B. A. Farquhar, *Female Education* (London, 1851), 4.

110. *The Popular Educator* (London, 1864), 175.

111. W. Ripman, *English Phonetics* (London, 1931), 7.

112. *Not Like Other Girls* (1884), i. 130.

113. *The Young Mother* (London, 1857), 165.

114. *The Mother's Home Book* (1879), 198.

115. Ibid., 202–3.

116. *The Popular Educator* (1864), 175.

117. See J. Briggs, *A Woman of Passion. The Life of E. Nesbit 1858–1924* (London, 1987), 145.

118. G. Gissing, *Human Odds and Ends. Stories and Sketches* (London, 1898), 2.

119. Cited in L. Davidoff, *The Best Circles. Society Etiquette and the Season* (London, 1973), 66.

120. G. Darley, *Octavia Hill. A Life* (London, 1990), 71. Hill was by no means alone in the ways in which she sought to distance herself from stereotypical gender roles for women, and a range of other women such as Barbara Leigh-Smith (who advanced the Married Women's Property Bill in 1857), and Elizabeth Garrett, the physician, shared and fostered this shift in attitude.

121. *Etiquette for Ladies and Gentlemen* (1839), 10.

122. *The Manners of the Aristocracy. By One of Themselves* (London, 1881), 2–3.

123. See, e. g., Labov, *Sociolinguistic Patterns*; Trudgill, *The Social Stratification of English in Norwich*; and S. Romaine, 'Postvocalic /r/ in Scottish English: Sound Change in Progress?', in P. Trudgill (ed.), *Sociolinguistic Patterns in British English* (London, 1978), 144–157.

124. See, however, n. 155 below.

125. Sweet, *A Primer of Spoken English*, pp. vi–vii.

126. See pp. 72–85 ff.

127. Smart, *Grammar of English Sounds*, p. xxv.

128. Smart, *Walker Remodelled*, §17.

129. C. W. Smith, *Hints on Elocution and Public Speaking* (London, 1858), 34.

130. See pp. 81–3.

131. See L. C. Mugglestone, 'A. J. Ellis, "Standard English" and the Prescriptive Tradition', *Review of English Studies*, NS 39 (1988), 87–92.

132. Ellis, *Early English Pronunciation*, iv. 1088.

133. Ibid., iv. 1089.

134. Ibid., iv. 1089–90.

135. Ibid., iv. 1204.

136. Ibid., ii. 597.

137. Ibid., iv. 1148.

138. Ibid. The (aa) in Ellis's notation can be taken as signifying [ɑː].

139. Ibid. This attitude is of course precisely that exploited by a range of nineteenth-century novelists who, wishing to indicate 'vulgarity' of speech, transform *laugh* into *larf*, or *of* into *orf*, relying on this graphemic deviation to supply the intended connotations. See also pp. 191–2.

140. See pp. 87–8.

141. Ellis, *Early English Pronunciation*, iv. 1152.

142. See pp. 192–3.

143. Williams, *Composition*, 5.

144. Ripman, *Sounds of Spoken English*, 55.
145. See further Mugglestone, '"An Historian and not a Critic"'.
146. J. Coates, *Women, Men and Language* (London, 1986), 64.
147. Mrs Gaskell, *Cranford* (London, 1853), ed. E. P. Watson (Oxford, 1972), 143. Ironically, however, this is the definition of female status which has been adopted in many sociolinguistic studies, a practice which, for a number of linguists, has certainly served to undermine relevant conclusions. See, for example, J. Milroy and L. Milroy, 'Mechanisms of Change in Urban Dialects: the role of class, social network and gender' in P. Trudgill and J. Cheshire (eds.), *The Sociolinguistics Reader*, i. *Multilingualism and Variation* (London, 1998), 182: 'women are seen as problematic and are classified in a somewhat arbitrary manner, sometimes being assigned the class of their husbands or fathers, while at other times their class is determined by their own occupations'.
148. J. Perkin, *Women and Marriage in Nineteenth-Century England* (London, 1990), 2.
149. Davidoff, *The Best Circles*, 93.
150. M. G. Grey and E. Shirreff, *Thoughts on Self-Culture. Addressed to Women* (London, 1854), 135.
151. Vandenhoff, *The Lady's Reader*, 1.
152. L. Milroy, 'New Perspectives in the Analysis of Sex Differentiation in Language', in K. Bolton and H. Kwok (eds), *Sociolingustics Today. International Perspectives*, (London, 1992), 175.
153. J. R. Edwards, 'Social Class Differences and the Identification of Sex in Children's Speech', *Journal of Child Language*, 6 (1979), 121–7.
154. See L. Milroy, 'New Perspectives', 177.
155. See recent data on the heightened use of the (traditionally stigmatized) glottal stop in female (middle-class) speech in areas as diverse as Cardiff and Newcastle (Milroy and Milroy, 1998, 186 ff). Network studies have also frequently served to disturb the conventional paradigms of gender and prestige. As Milroy and Milroy also suggest, there is scope for a wider reassessment of traditional sociolinguistic commonplaces in this context. As they note with reference to these patterns of glottalization and gender, one possible interpretation is 'not that females favour prestige norms, but that they create them; i.e., if females favour certain forms, they become prestige forms. In these developments, both class and gender are implicated, but gender is prior to class'.
156. O. Elyan, P. Smith, H. Giles, and R. Bourhis, 'RP-Accented Female Speech: The Voice of Perceived Androgyny', in P. Trudgill (ed.), *Sociolinguistic Patterns in British English*, 129.

Notes to Chapter 6

1. Johnson, *Dictionary*, a2^v i.
2. Sheridan, *Course of Lectures*, 35.
3. See p. 117.
4. T. Smetham, *Practical Grammar*, 36.
5. Johnson, *Dictionary*, A2^r.
6. *Chap*, for example, defined by Walker as 'to divide the skin of the face or hands by excessive cold', is given as one of 'those incorrigible words, the pronunciation and orthography of which must ever be at variance'. Attested with a pronunciation

identical to that of *chop* for much of the nineteenth century, such 'incorrigibility' was eventually defeated by the influence of graphemic authority. *Waistcoat* and *forehead* shared similar patterns of restitution, from forms in the late eighteenth century in /ˈwɛskət/, /ˈfɒrɪd/ to their modern forms in which the pronunciation has come to pay greater attention to distinctions manifest in writing. *OED2* records both /ˈbəʊtsweɪn/ and /ˈbəʊs(ə)n/ for *boatswain* though the latter, as it acknowledges, still remains the dominant form.

7. *David Copperfield*, 56.

8. C. Dickens, *The Life and Adventures of Martin Chuzzlewit* (London, 1844), ed. M. Cardwell (Oxford, 1982), 755.

9. G. Fulton and G. Knight, *A Dictionary of the English Language Greatly Improved* (Edinburgh, 1833), *Advertisement*.

10. *David Copperfield*, 330.

11. G. Gissing, *The Town Traveller* (London, 1898), 139.

12. Graham, *A Book About Words*, 159.

13. Walker, *Critical Pronouncing Dictionary*, 1st edn (1791), §178.

14. C. Bede, *The Adventures of Mr. Verdant Green, An Oxford Freshman* (London, 1853), 22.

15. G. L. Brook, *The Language of Dickens* (London, 1970), 13.

16. Sir J. Vanbrugh, *The Relapse; or, Virtue in Danger* (London, 1697), V. v. 174–5 and II. i. 203.

17. See, e.g., II. i. 33–4, in which Mr Pinchwife is greeted by his new spouse: 'Oh my dear, dear Bud, welcome home; why dost thou look so fropish, who has nanger'd thee?', *The Country Wife* (London, 1675), in *The Plays of William Wycherley*, ed. A. Friedman (Oxford, 1979), 226.

18. J. Austen, *Emma* (London, 1816), ed. R. W. Chapman, 3rd edn (Oxford, 1933), 33.

19. Beattie, *Theory of Language*, 92.

20. Graham, *A Book About Words*, 158. This was certainly the form preferred by Queen Victoria who regarded *obleege* as a comic anachronism which she recollected hearing in her youth. See Hibbert, *Queen Victoria*, 358.

21. *David Copperfield*, 27.

22. Ibid., 90.

23. *The Adventures of Mr. Verdant Green*, 92.

24. C. Dickens, *The Life and Adventures of Nicholas Nickleby* (London, 1839), 92.

25. T. Young (ed.), *A Critical Pronouncing Dictionary of the English Language* (London, 1857). Note under the word *cucumber*.

26. *Martin Chuzzlewit*, 411.

27. Reverend E. R. de Levante, *Orthoepy and Orthography of the English Language* (London, 1869), 148.

28. G. N. Leech and M. H. Short, *Style in Fiction. A Linguistic Introduction to English Fictional Prose* (London, 1981), 131.

29. G. Meredith, *The Ordeal of Richard Feverel* (London, 1859), i. 172.

30. *Martin Chuzzlewit*, 344, 367.

31. See p. 102.

32. T. Hardy, 'Dialect in Novels', *The Athenaeum*, 30 Nov. 1878, 688.

33. *Little Dorrit*, 712.

34. Unsigned review of *Sylvia's Lovers*, *The Observer*, 1 Mar. 1863, 7; Geraldine Jewsbury, unsigned review of *Sylvia's Lovers*, *The Athenaeum*, 28 Feb.1863, 291; and unsigned review of *Sylvia's Lovers* in the *Daily News*, 3 Apr. 1863, 2 cited in A. Easson (ed.), *Elizabeth Gaskell. The Critical Heritage* (London, 1991), 440, 432, and 445–6.

35. Leech and Short, *Style in Fiction*, 259.

36. G. Gissing, *Charles Dickens. A Critical Study* (London, 1898), 206–7.

37. A. Blake, 'The Place of Fiction in Victorian Literary Culture', *Literature and History*, 11 (1985), 204.

38. *The Adventures of Mr. Verdant Green*, 39, 47.

39. E. Bulwer Lytton, *Eugene Aram* (London, 1832), ii. 42.

40. G. Gissing, *The Nether World* (London, 1889), i. 106, 110.

41. See Chapter 4, n. 2.

42. See p. 94.

43. Mrs. Humphry Ward, *Marcella* (London, 1894), iii. 54.

44. *Nicholas Nickleby*, 196, emphasis added.

45. R. S. Surtees, *Mr. Sponge's Sporting Tour* (London, 1853), 13, 31.

46. Smith, *Mind Your H's and Take Care of Your R's*, 4.

47. Ellis, *Early English Pronunciation*, i. 188.

48. H. Sweet, *The Elementary Sounds of English* (London, 1881), 7.

49. B. Stoker, *Dracula* (London, 1897), 142, emphasis added.

50. Z. Smith, *White Teeth* (London, 2000), 30.

51. The use of [hw] or perhaps more precisely, that of the voiceless labio-velar fricative, is retained in Scots, as well as in some rural areas in the far north of the country.

52. Wells, *Accents of English*, ii. 228–9. As he also comments, 'Present-day RP usage could be described as schizophrenic. For most RP speakers /hw/ is not a 'natural' possibility. The usual RP form of *whine* is /waɪn/; similarly *what* /wɒt/ … Other RP speakers use /hw/, and say /hwaɪn, hwɒt …/, and this usage is widely considered correct, careful, and beautiful'.

53. See pp. 86–94.

54. This merger has not occurred in most Scottish accents.

55. See L. C. Mugglestone, 'Prescription, Pronunciation, and Issues of Class in the Late Eighteenth and Nineteenth Centuries', in D. M. Reeks (ed.), *Sentences for Alan Ward* (London, 1988), 175–82.

56. Walker, *Critical Pronouncing Dictionary*, 1st edn (1791), §110.

57. Ibid., note under the word *earth*.

58. C. Dickens, *The Adventures of Oliver Twist* (London, 1846), ed. K. Tillotson (Oxford, 1966), 2.

59. J. Lucas, Editorial Preface, *Literature and History*, 1 (1975), 2.

60. See 'Human After All', *Sunday Times*, 1 Mar. 1987, magazine section, 61, where Princess Anne is recorded as using *orf*.

61. See pp. 78–82.

62. G. Gissing, *Workers in the Dawn* (London, 1880), i. 97–8, 146, emphasis added.

63. Ellis, *Early English Pronunciation*, iv. 1148.

64. In early modern English, *e* before *r* often became *a*: *carve*, for example, derives from OE *ceorfan*, *war* from OE *werre*. Spellings with <e> were, however, often retained, as in *clerk*, *Derbyshire*.

65. *Merchant* derives from OF *marchant*.
66. *David Copperfield*, 390, 619, 584.
67. Early evidence of the use of similar forms with a palatal glide /j/ after /k, g/ can be traced in, for example, John Wallis's *Grammatica Linguae Anglicanae* (Oxford, 1653), in which clearly equivalent enunciations in *gyet* and *begyin* are given for the words *get, begin*.
68. J. Walker, *A Rhetorical Grammar: in which the Common Improprieties in Reading and Speaking are Detected and the True Sources or Elegant Pronunciation are Pointed Out*, 3rd edn (London, 1801), 11.
69. Oliver, *General Critical Grammar of the Inglish Language*, 284 n.
70. Ellis, *Early English Pronunciation* iv. 1115, i. 206.
71. *The Town Traveller*, 68.
72. N. Page, *Speech in the English Novel*, 2nd edn (London, 1988), 58.
73. See pp. 124–7.
74. This is particularly evident in the second half of the nineteenth century when, as a result of the introduction of steam power for printing in the 1840s, together with the use of paper made by machine rather than by hand, printing costs began to decrease.
75. See Altick, *English Common Reader*, 58, 276.
76. Ibid., 279.
77. Ibid., 384.
78. Cited ibid., 384.
79. See pp. 146–8.
80. P. Ackroyd, *Dickens* (London, 1990), 561.
81. *Dombey and Son*, 184. See further p. 35.
82. *Blackwood's Magazine*, cited in Ackroyd, *Dickens*, 719.
83. *Nicholas Nickleby*, 197, 176.
84. *Bleak House*, 283.
85. *Blackwood's Magazine*, cited in Ackroyd, *Dickens*, 719.
86. R. Carter and W. Nash, *Seeing Through Language. A Guide to Styles of English Writing* (Oxford, 1990), 21.
87. Ibid., 24.
88. L. Trilling, 'Manners, Morals, and the Novel', *The Liberal Imagination. Essays on Literature and Society* (London, 1955), 206.
89. Ibid., 216.
90. *Talking and Debating* (1856), 3. See also p. 113.
91. Williams, *Composition*, 5.
92. *David Copperfield*, 251.
93. Ibid., 90.
94. Ibid., 251.
95. N. F. Blake, *Non-standard Language in English Literature* (London, 1981), 14.
96. The same pattern of equation, and mis-equation, is, for example, deployed by Lodge in the introduction of Basil's girlfriend Debbie, whose speech is markedly Cockney and colloquial ('"Held in a sorter castle. Just like a horror film, wonnit?...suits of armour and stuffed animals heads and everyfink"'). As Lodge comments on Robyn's reactions to such linguistic markers of 'identity', 'at first Robyn thought that Debbie's Cockney accent was some sort of joke, but soon realised it was authentic. In spite of her Sloaney clothes and hair-do, Debbie

was decidedly lower-class. When Basil mentioned that she worked in the same bank as himself, Robyn assumed that she was a secretary or typist, but was quickly corrected by her brother when he followed her out into the kitchen when she was making tea.' Belying such initial categorizations by her ready recognition of Lapsang Souchong ('"Love it," said Debbie. She really was a very difficult girl to get right'), Debbie is of course ultimately revealed as a foreign exchange dealer, with a salary far in excess of Robyn's own. *Nice Work* (London, 1988), 124.

97. *David Copperfield*, 384.

98. Wells, *Accents of English*, i. 30. See also pp. 50–1.

99. Leech and Short, *Style in Fiction*, 172.

100. See pp. 122–4.

101. *Great Expectations*, i. 212.

102. Ibid., i. 318.

103. Ibid., i. 20.

104. Ibid., i. 232.

105. Trilling, *The Liberal Imagination*, 207.

106. G. Gissing, *In the Year of Jubilee* (London, 1894), i. 46.

107. Id., *The Whirlpool* (London, 1897), 9, 181.

108. *Born in Exile*, i. 101.

109. G. Gissing, *The Emancipated* (London, 1890), i. 40.

110. *Born in Exile*, i 84.

111. Ibid., i. 63.

112. Ibid., i. 248.

113. *Demos*, ii. 33.

114. Ibid., ii. 35.

115. See further pp. 140–1.

116. *Denzil Quarrier*, 103.

117. G. Gissing, *Will Warburton. A Romance of Real Life* (London, 1905), 322.

118. See p. 160.

119. *Born in Exile*, i. 82–3.

120. See pp. 145–6.

121. *Will Warburton*, 53, 225.

122. G. Gissing, 'Our Learned Fellow-Townsman', in *A Victim of Circumstances* (London, 1927), 278–9.

123. See, e.g., the short story 'One Way of Happiness' in the collection *A Victim of Circumstances*, and the descriptions of voice accorded to Mrs Budge and Mrs Rippingdale, Cockney housewives and profoundly negative exemplars of the feminine ideal: 'They talked in a high key, laughed in a scream', we are told on p. 39; their 'screeching' tones and 'high-pitched remarks' are described with equal disfavour two pages later.

124. See further L. C. Mugglestone, '"Grammatical Fair Ones": Women, Men, and Attitudes to Language in the Novels of George Eliot', *Review of English Studies*, NS 46 (1995), 11–25.

125. G. Eliot, *Silas Marner: The Weaver of Raveloe* (London, 1861), 184–5.

126. D. Daiches, *Middlemarch* (London, 1963), 67.

127. G. Eliot, 'The Natural History of German Life', *Westminster Review*, NS 10 (July 1856), 51.

128. G. Eliot, *Felix Holt the Radical* (London, 1866), i. 108.

129. G. Eliot, *Felix Holt*, i. 133.
130. Ibid., i. 139.
131. Ibid., iii. 77–8.
132. Ibid., iii. 100.
133. Ibid., iii. 72.
134. G. Eliot, 'Looking Backward', *Impressions of Theophrastus Such* (London, 1869), 36.
135. *Felix Holt*, iii. 149.
136. Ibid., iii. 152.
137. G. Eliot, *Middlemarch, A Study of Provincial Life* (London, 1871), i. 175.
138. Ibid., i. 170.
139. Ibid., ii. 77.
140. Ibid., iii. 283.
141. Ibid., iii. 5–6.
142. Daiches, *Middlemarch*, 47.
143. *Middlemarch*, ii. 33.
144. Ibid., ii. 34.
145. Ibid., ii. 33.
146. Ibid., ii. 30.

Notes to Chapter 7

1. Nichols, *Behaviour*, 59.
2. *How to Speak or Write English with Perspicacity and Fluency* (London, 1876), 20.
3. Nichols, *Behaviour*, 63.
4. A. M. Bell, *A Lecture on the Art of Delivery and the Influence of School Discipline on Public Oratory* (Delivered to the Edinburgh Local Association of the Educational Institute of Scotland, 21 Oct. 1854), (Edinburgh, 1855), 8.
5. General Report on Roman Catholic Schools for the Year 1849 by Her Majesty's Inspector of Schools T. M. W. Marshall, Committee of Council on Education: Reports on Elementary Schools, *Parliamentary Papers*, xliv (1850), 523, 527, 533.
6. P. Trudgill, 'Standard and Non-Standard Dialects of English in the UK: Problems and Policies', in M. Stubbs and H. Hillier (eds), *Readings on Language, Schools and Classrooms* (London, 1983), 57.
7. J. Buchanan, *A Plan of an English Grammar School Education* (London, 1770), title page.
8. Ibid., 45.
9. Buchanan, *Linguae Britannicae*, p. xii n.
10. Sheridan, *Course of Lectures*, 21.
11. Ibid., 31.
12. Sheridan, *Rhetorical Grammar*, p. xviii.
13. J. Walker, *A Rhetorical Grammar of the English Language*, 1st edn (London, 1785), 1.
14. As the first edition of the *DNB* noted, Walker, together with James Usher, had established a school in Kensington in 1769, though Walker's active involvement lasted only until 1771 when he began to devote more time professionally to his interests in elocution and especially to his lecturing career in that subject. This, as *DNB1* stated (1899), was 'henceforth to be his principal employment'.

15. J. Walker, *The Academic Speaker* (Dublin, 1789), Dedication.
16. D. Williams, *A Treatise on Education* (London, 1774), 157.
17. Ibid., 162.
18. There are exceptions to this pattern as R. Wilson confirms in 'The Archbishop Herring Visitation Returns, 1743: A Vignette of Yorkshire Education', in J. E. Stephens (ed.), *Aspects of Education 1600–1750* (Hull, 1984), 92–130. A questionnaire sent out to the incumbent of each parish in the diocese of York, following the election of Thomas Herring to the Archbishopric, devoted its third question to the topic of educational provision. Eliciting a 93.9 per cent response from recipients, the data provided reveal clearly that a number of grammar schools in the area had added instruction in English to the classical syllabus. Schools at Worsborough and Tadcaster in the West Riding, for example, although specifically 'grammar only' according to the terms of their foundation, also taught reading, writing, and mathematics.
19. Williams, *Treatise on Education*, 136.
20. J. Locke, *An Essay Concerning Human Understanding* (London, 1690).
21. I. Fox, *Public Schools and Public Issues* (London, 1985), 1.
22. W. Wolfram and R. Fasold, 'Social Dialects and Education', in J. B. Pride (ed.), *Sociolinguistic Aspects of Language Learning and Teaching* (Oxford, 1979), 185.
23. Robert Raikes of Gloucester is traditionally assumed to have pioneered the Sunday School in the 1780s. The system expanded rapidly; by 1833, 1,550,000 pupils were in regular attendance and by 1851, 2,400,000 children were on the registers of Sunday Schools up and down the country.
24. The monitorial system was based on the principle of using older children to teach the younger children within a school. Established in 1801 by Joseph Lancaster and Andrew Bell, this could lead to a school having up to 1,000 pupils but employing only one teacher, as indeed in Lancaster's original school in the Borough Road, London, where 1,000 children were taught by 67 monitors and a single teacher—Lancaster himself.
25. T. Wyse, *Education Reform; Or, The Necessity of a National System of Education* (London, 1836), 49. Wyse was an active campaigner in educational terms, helping to found the Central Society of Education, and arguing in particular for state control and school inspection as the linchpin of the reforms which he desired to see instituted.
26. Ibid.
27. *Dombey and Son*, 62.
28. D. Jones, *An English Pronouncing Dictionary* (London, 1917), §7. See further p. 265.
29. *Good Society*, 91.
30. Walker, *Critical Pronouncing Dictionary*, ed. J. Murdoch (1809), p. ii.
31. Letter to her son Tom (then at Winchester) in May 1825, cited in Neville-Sington, *Fanny Trollope. The Life and Adventures of a Clever Woman*, 74.
32. Those listed here constitute merely a representative sample of the new educational foundations of the nineteenth century. It should be noted that many of them preserved similar policies of social exclusivity to those increasingly practised by older schools. The first prospectus of Cheltenham College (founded in 1841) states, for example, 'No person shall be considered eligible who shall not

be moving in the circle of Gentleman, no retail trader being allowed in any circumstances to be so considered'.

33. See *The Public Schools and the General Educational System. Report of the Committee
    on Public Schools appointed by the President of the Board of Education, July 1942*
    (London, 1944), 11, n. 18.

34. J. Lawson and H. Silver, *A Social History of English Education* (London, 1973),
    198.

35. J. Gathorne-Hardy, *The Public School Phenomenon* (London, 1977), 49.

36. Report of the Schools Inquiry Commission (1868); cited in *The Public Schools
    and the General Educational System*, 23.

37. Ibid.

38. *The Eton System of Education Vindicated* (London, 1834), 30, 69.

39. Lord Chesterfield's admonitions in this context include the advice that his son,
    upon entering Westminster, must be 'sufficiently upon [his] guard...against
    awkward attitudes...and disgusting habits...such as putting your fingers in
    your mouth, nose, and ears'; cited in J. Cannon, *Aristocratic Century. The Peerage
    of Eighteenth-Century England* (Cambridge, 1984), 38.

40. Cited in W. J. Reader, *Life in Victorian England* (New York, 1964), 20.

41. *Hansard*, clxxx. 139–40, 6 May 1864, cols. 139–4; cited in C. Shrosbree, *Public
    Schools and Private Education: The Clarendon Commission 1861–64 and the Public
    Schools Acts* (Manchester, 1988), 116.

42. J. A. Merivale (ed.), *Autobiography and Letters of Charles Merivale, Dean of Ely*
    (Oxford, 1898), 43.

43. Unpublished memoirs, from the Mitchinson Archive, Pembroke College,
    Oxford, ii. 'School Reminiscences', fos 16–17.

44. 'Canterbury: The King's School. Appendix: My Boys', Mitchinson Archive, vii,
    fo. 5.

45. Ibid., ii. fo. 17.

46. T. W. Bamford, *Rise of the Public Schools: a Study of Boys' Boarding Schools in
    England and Wales from 1837 to the Present Day* (London, 1967), 20.

47. M. and R. L. Edgeworth, *Practical Education* (London, 1798), ii. 502.

48. Ibid.

49. Enfield, *The Speaker*, p. xiv.

50. Rev. S. Parlby to M. Boulton, 28 Feb 1785. Cited in A. E. Musson and E. Robinson,
    Science and Technology in the Industrial Revolution (Manchester, 1969), 205.

51. See pp. 112–13.

52. Shrosbree, *Public Schools and Private Education*, 89.

53. J. Galsworthy, *The Silver Spoon* (London, 1926), 237. *Lam*, as the *OED* records,
    is 'chiefly school-boy slang' for 'to hit'.

54. Rev. G. Bartle, *A Few Words To Parents and Guardians on the Education of Youth*
    (London, 1875), 21.

55. See J. Barker, *Wordsworth. A Life* (London, 2000), 548 and note, 897.

56. *A Very Short Letter from One Old Westminster to Another, Touching Some Matters
    connected with Their School* (London, 1829), 9–10.

57. W. M. Thackeray, *A Shabby-Genteel Story* (London, 1887), 12. Mitchinson's
    memoirs of his days at Durham Grammar School similarly recall that the influ-
    ence of those 'social considerations which bulk large with boys' had, in effect,
    'severed' some of the pupils from the others, noting of a boy named Forster, for

example, that 'he was the son of a small innkeeper, and from his tavern sign was known as Black Horse Forster' (Mitchinson Archive, ii. fo. 17).

58. A. Trollope, *An Autobiography*, ed. M. Sadleir and F. Page (Oxford, 1980), 9.

59. Kelly, *Richard Brinsley Sheridan*, 18.

60. E. Durkheim, *Education and Sociology*, trans. S. D. Fox (Glencoe, Ill., 1956), 71.

61. J. Edwards, *Language, Society and Identity* (Oxford, 1985), 118.

62. Williams, *Treatise on Education*, 13.

63. Gathorne-Hardy, *The Public School Phenomenon*, 51.

64. T. W. Bamford (ed.), *Thomas Arnold on Education* (Cambridge, 1970), 50.

65. A. Hope, *A Book About Dominies. Being the Reflections and Recollections of a Member of the Profession* (London, 1869), 49. A *dominie* is defined in Morris Marples's *Public School Slang* (London, 1940) as 'a male boarding house proprietor, not a master' at Eton.

66. Kington-Oliphant, *Sources of Standard English*, i. 333.

67. Cited in J. Wakeford, *The Cloistered Elite* (London, 1969), 48.

68. J. Okely, 'Privileged, Schooled and Finished: Boarding Education for Girls', in S. Ardener (ed)., *Defining Females* (London, 1978), 115.

69. J. W. Hales, 'The Teaching of English', in F. W. Farrar (ed.), *Essays on a Liberal Education* (London, 1867), 223–4.

70. R. M. Milnes, 'On the Present Social Results of Classical Education'. In Farrar, *Essays*, 377.

71. See p. 70.

72. W. M'Combie, *On Education in its Constituents, Objects, and Issues* (Aberdeen, 1857), 198–9.

73. Stone and Stone, *An Open Elite*, 27.

74. Fox, *Public Schools*, 157.

75. G. M. Young and W. D. Handcock, *English Historical Documents 1833–1874* (London, 1956), xii. 903. The Clarendon Commission was appointed in 1861 to enquire into the state of the education provided in the public schools of Winchester, Eton, Westminster, Charterhouse, Harrow, Rugby, Shrewsbury, St Paul's, and Merchant Taylors'. It reported back to the government in 1864.

76. Mitchinson Archive, vii. fo. 21.

77. Mitchinson Archive, ii. fo. 6.

78. J. Gill, *Introductory Text-Book to School Management*, rev. [10th] edn (London, 1870), 7.

79. Ibid, p. iv.

80. Ibid., 9th edn (London, 1863), 153.

81. *Thorough English* (London, 1867), 9.

82. *The English Vocabulary; or Spelling Book, Compiled for the Use of Ackworth School* (London, 1852), p. viii.

83. Ibid., p. v.

84. Ibid., p. viii.

85. Ibid., pp. vii–viii.

86. Christopher Sykes of Sledmere, sensitive, like Matthew Boulton, to the potential stigma of a local accent for his offspring, specified its eradication before he sent his sons to school, rather than relying on the agency of the school itself to effect this transformation. See pp. 36–7.

87. E. C. Lowe, *An English Primer* (London, 1867), 176. A second edition of this text was produced in 1868.
88. Mitchinson Archive, vii. fo. 23.
89. Mitchinson Archive, vii. fos. 23–4.
90. The King's School at Canterbury was founded in 600 providing 'the longest run of education in British History' (**www. Kings-school.co.uk**). Boarding was established in the nineteenth century. Over Mitchinson's time there, however, it was 'virtually a day school' (Mitchinson Archive, vii. fo. 27). Given the reservations expressed by the Edgeworths on the subject of day schools, this may explain Mitchinson's eagerness to secure specific instruction in the proprieties of spoken English.
91. Mitchinson Archive, vii. fo. 24.
92. Ibid.
93. Report of the Schools Inquiry Commission, 1868, v. 103; cited in B. Hollingsworth, 'The Mother Tongue and the Public Schools', in A. K. Pugh, V. J. Lee, and J. Swann (eds), *Language and Language Use* (London, 1980), 187.
94. A six-week period at each Easter devoted to the recitation and learning of sections from 'the chief English poets' at Winchester may be assumed to have contributed to a similar sense of the 'proper' use of the English language (Report of Her Majesty's Commissioners, 1869, i. 144); cited in Hollingsworth, 'The Mother Tongue and the Public Schools', 186.
95. As John Honey notes (*Does Accent Matter? The Pygmalion Factor* (London, 1989), 24), Sir Robert Walpole, though attending both Eton and Cambridge, 'all his life sounded like a Norfolk squire'. Similarly Gladstone, a product of Eton and Oxford, retained traces of his Liverpool origins in his speech. Peer pressure was evidently not uniform in its effects. See further p. 70.
96. Language, especially English language, played a considerable part in the Commission's recommendations, not least in terms of the proprieties of usage which ought to characterize the public-school product. As John Honey points out, the resulting stereotype was associated most closely with these particular public schools and, in general with those in the south rather than the north('it seems to have been more effective in Southern public Schools than in that minority of public schools which are in the north'): J. Honey, '"Talking Proper": Schooling and the Establishment of English "Received Pronunciation"', in G. Nixon and J. Honey (eds) *An Historic Tongue: Studies in English Linguistics in Memory of Barbara Strang* (London, 1988), 213–14.
97. Report of Dr. W. B. Hodgson, One of her Majesty's Inspectors of Schools on the State of Education in the Metropolitan District, Report from the Commissioners on Popular Education, *Parliamentary Papers*, xxi. III (1861), 93.
98. See Ackroyd, *Dickens*, 41.
99. G. Coysh, *The British Pronouncing and Self Instructing Spelling Book* (Topsham, 1837), p. iii.
100. *The Elementary Catechisms* (London, 1850), 5.
101. J. Poole, *The Village School Improved; Or, The New System of Education Practically Explained, and Adapted to the Case of Country Parishes*, 2nd edn (Oxford, 1813), 1.
102. See note 24 above.
103. Poole, *The Village School Improved*, 40.

104. Ibid., 40–1.
105. See p. 48.
106. P. Trudgill, *Accent, Dialect, and the School* (London, 1975), 67.
107. Ibid., 58.
108. Poole, *The Village School Improved*, 41.
109. Ibid., 41–2.
110. W. H. Bainbrigge, *Early Education* (London, 1881), 124.
111. Wyse, *Education Reform*, 100.
112. W. Chambers and R. Chambers (eds), *Chambers's Educational Course: Simple Lessons in Reading* (Edinburgh, 1841), 4.
113. Gill, *Introductory Text-Book*, rev. [10th] edn (1870), 149.
114. J. C. Graham, *An Introduction to the Art of Reading* (London, 1861), 3.
115. Chambers and Chambers, *Chambers's Educational Course*, 7.
116. Report of the Committee of Council on Education 1859–60; General Report for the Year 1859 by the Revd J. C. G. Fussell, *Parliamentary Papers* liv. (1860), 20.
117. T. J. Livesey, *How to Teach Grammar: Illustrated in a Series of Lessons* (London, 1881), 3.
118. Gill, *Introductory Text-Book*, rev. [10th] edn (1870), 152–3.
119. General Report for the Year 1849, by her Majesty's Inspector of Schools, the Revd H. W. Bellairs, Committee of Council of Education, *Parliamentary Papers*, xliii (1850), 119.
120. Report of the Committee of Council on Education 1859–60, *Parliamentary Papers*, liv (1860), 295.
121. Minutes of the Committee of Council on Education, *Parliamentary Papers*, xliii (1850), 24–5.
122. Elocution as a study was commended for its evident utility in the training of teachers in the Training Institution of the British and Foreign School Society in the Borough Road, Southwark by J. D. Morrell, one of Her Majesty's Inspectors, Report of the Committee of Council on Education, *Parliamentary Papers*, liv (1860), 389.
123. *The Teacher's Manual of the Science and Art of Teaching* (London, 1874), 225.
124. D. A. Fearon, *School Inspection* (London, 1876), 33.
125. *Teacher's Manual*, 225.
126. Gill, *Introductory Text-Book*, 9th edn (1863), 156.
127. T. J. Livesey, *Moffat's How to Teach Reading* (London, 1882), 2.
128. Report on the Free Church Training College at Glasgow for the Year 1859, by Her Majesty's Inspector of Schools, C. E. Wilson, Esq., Report of the Committee of Council on Education, *Parliamentary Papers*, liv (1860), 465.
129. T. Morrison, *Manual of School Management*, 3rd edn (London, 1863), 126.
130. Ellis, *Early English Pronunciation*, i. 19.
131. Morrison, *Manual of School Management*, 127.
132. Gill, *Introductory Text-Book*, 9th edn (1863), 156.
133. Ibid., 155–6.
134. Revd W. F. Wilkinson, *Education, Elementary and Liberal: Three Lectures Delivered in the Hall of the Mechanics' Institute, Derby, Nov. 1861* (London, 1862), 56.
135. Perceval Graves and Rice-Wiggin, *The Elementary School Manager*, 116.
136. Cited in Robinson, *Manual of Method and Organisation*, 3 n.

137. Cited in Robinson, *Manual of Method and Organisation*, 3.
138. M. Stubbs, *Educational Linguistics* (Oxford, 1986), 84.
139. Gill, *Introductory Text-Book*, 9th edn. (1863), 155.
140. Graham, *Introduction to the Art of Reading*, 30.
141. *The First Part of the Progressive Parsing Lessons* (Maldon, 1833), p. iv.
142. Ibid., 63–4.
143. Ibid., 71–2.
144. Livesey, *Moffat's How to Teach Reading*, 10.
145. J. J. Prince, *School Management and Method* (London, 1880), 225–6.
146. Gill, *Introductory Text-Book*, 9th edn. (1863), 145.
147. Livesey, *How to Teach Grammar*, 21.
148. Gill, *Introductory Text-Book*, 9th edn (1863), 163.
149. G. White, *A Simultaneous Method of Teaching to Read Adapted to Primary Schools* (London, 1862), 25.
150. Prince, *School Management*, 79.
151. Cited in *Extracts from the Reports of Her Majesty's Inspector's of Schools* (1852), 192.
152. A. Grover, *A New English Grammar for the Use of Junior Classes in Schools* (London, 1877), 11.
153. R. J. Griffiths, *An Introduction to the Study of School Management* (London, 1872), 21.
154. Livesey, *Moffat's How to Teach Reading*, 63.
155. *Handbook on the Teaching and Management of Elementary Schools* (Manchester, 1872), 52.
156. Robinson, *Manual of Method and Organisation*, 2–3.
157. Ibid., 2.
158. Cited ibid.
159. General Report for the year 1859, *Parliamentary Papers*. liv (1860), 20.
160. The terms of the Code made payment of the government grant for education dependent on both the average attendance of pupils in the school, and the level of performance in the (often largely oral) examinations conducted by the inspectors in their rounds.
161. M. Arnold, *Reports on Elementary Schools 1852–1882*, ed. F. Sandford (London, 1889), 42–3.
162. Chambers and Chambers, *Chambers's Educational Course*, 7.
163. Arnold, *Reports on Elementary Schools*, 163.
164. A. Burrell, *Recitation. A Handbook for Teachers in Public Elementary School* (London, 1891), 24.
165. S. Brandram, *Brandram's Speaker* (London, 1885), 15–16.
166. M. A. Lower, *Groombridge's Annual Reader* (London, 1867), pp. iv, v.
167. W. H. Groser, *The Sunday School Teacher's Manual; or, The Principles and Methods of Instruction as Applied to Sunday School Work* (London, 1877), 37–8.
168. Ibid., 39.
169. *The Sunday School Spelling Book* (London, 1823), 1.
170. *Statement by the Directors of the Edinburgh Academy Explanatory of the Scheme of that Institution* (Edinburgh, 1824); cited in K. Robbins, *Nineteenth-Century Britain. England, Scotland, and Wales. The Making of a Nation* (Oxford, 1989), 133.
171. A. Macleod, *Macleod's First Text-Book in Elocution With a Scheme for Acquiring Correct Pronunciation*, 3rd edn (Edinburgh, 1881).

172. See p. 250.
173. Robinson, *Manual of Method and Organisation*, 2.
174. Morrison, *Manual of School Management*, 127.
175. Ibid.
176. *The Teaching of English in England* (1921). All citations from extract in T. Crowley (ed.), *Proper English? Readings in Language, History and Cultural Identity* (London, 1991), 196–206.
177. Ibid., 200.
178. Ibid., 202.
179. Ibid.
180. Ibid.
181. Ibid.
182. Ibid., 205. 'We do not advocate the teaching of standard English on any grounds of social "superiority", but because it is manifestly desirable that all English people should be capable of speaking so as to be fully intelligible to one another.'
183. Livesey, *Moffat's How to Teach Reading*, 65.

Notes to Chapter 8

1. Ellis, *Early English Pronunciation*, i. 23.
2. Walker, *Critical Pronouncing Dictionary*, 1st edn (1791), p. viii.
3. Walker, *A General Idea of a Pronouncing Dictionary of the English Language*, 17. See also L. C. Mugglestone, 'John Walker and Alexander Ellis: Antedating *RP*', *Notes and Queries*, 44 (1997*b*), 103–7.
4. Sheridan, *Course of Lectures*, 206.
5. Burrell, *Recitation*, 24.
6. Sweet, *The Elementary Sounds of English*, 7.
7. Ellis, *Early English Pronunciation*, ii. 264.
8. Ibid., 629.
9. Ibid., iv. 1208.
10. Nichols, *Behaviour*, 59.
11. Ellis, *Early English Pronunciation*, iv. 1215.
12. The first edition of the *OED* was, like many Victorian novels, published in serial form. Part I appeared in Jan. 1884 and the final part in April 1928.
13. See L. C. Mugglestone, ' "Pioneers in the Untrodden Forest": The *New* English Dictionary', in Mugglestone, *Lexicography and the OED*, 1–21.
14. MP/22/3/1882. H. Sweet to J. A. H. Murray, 22 Mar. 1882.
15. Letter from J. A. H. Murray to unnamed correspondent. Cited in K. Murray, *Caught in the Web of Words. James Murray and the Oxford English Dictionary* (Yale, 1977), 189.
16. H. Bradley, 'Spelling Pronunciations', Society for Pure English Tract No. III (Oxford, 1920), 19: 'There are . . . some 'spelling-pronunciations' that are positively mischievous', as he averred in this context. The final entry gives a single pronunciation ['fɒrɪd] with no mention of contemporary vacillation (for the purposes of discussion, the transcriptions deploy the modern IPA script of *OED2* rather than the notation of the original *OED*).
17. The writer Harriet Martineau was, for instance, notably critical of Wordsworth's speech in this respect, depicting enunciations such as 'valooable' in ways which

stress their perceived deviance from 'standard' norms. See H. Martineau, *Autobiography* (London, 1877), ii. 237 and Barker, *Wordsworth*, 340.

18. See, for example, Barnes' poem 'Comen Hwome' in his *Poems in the Dorset Dialect* (London, 1862), 15–16: 'As clouds did ride wi' heasty flight // An' woods did sway upon the height // An' bleades o' grass did sheake below // The hedgerow brambles swingen bow // I come back hwome where winds did zwell'.

19. Sheridan, *Dissertation*, 36.

20. Sweet, *Elementary Sounds*, 7. As in earlier texts, *dialect* here explicitly includes accent and the nuances of pronunciation.

21. Ibid., 5–6.

22. Sweet, *Primer of Phonetics*, §8.

23. Trudgill, 'Standard and Non-Standard Dialects', 51.

24. See Worthen, *D. H. Lawrence*, 63: 'Lawrence himself, for the benefit of his teacher, adopted an "exquisite accent" in place of his Midlands accent while at college. It was a strategy that, in varying forms, he adopted all his life, as the class outside is forced to do in England.'

25. See further pp. 8–9.

26. Smith, *Historical Study of English*, 76.

27. See p. 246.

28. Jones, *English Pronouncing Dictionary*, 1st edn (1917), p. viii.

29. 'If a boy in such a school has a marked local peculiarity in his pronunciation, it generally disappears or is modified during his school career under the influence of the different modes of speaking which he has continually around him; he consequently emerges from school with a pronunciation similar to that of the other boys': Jones, *English Pronouncing Dictionary*, 4th edn (London, 1937), §4.

30. W. Ripman, 'Editor's Preface', *English Pronouncing Dictionary* (1917), p. vi. Jones was, on the other hand, consistent in his opposition to such ideas, as in his article 'On "Received Pronunciation"', *Le Maître phonétique*, supplement (Apr.–July 1937) which stresses his conviction that the attempt to impose RP as a norm for all English speakers should not be pursued: 'As far as English-speaking people themselves are concerned, I suggest that educational authorities should leave everyone to pronounce as he pleases, and that no attempt should be made to impose one particular form of speech upon anyone who prefers another form. Above all, it appears to me important that *no person should ever disparage the pronunciation of another.*'

31. See e.g. his glowing endorsement of the tea of which Anna partakes at the house of Mr Sutton in chapter 12 of *Anna of the Five Towns*: 'The tea . . . was such a meal as could only have been compassed in Staffordshire or Yorkshire—a high tea of the last richness and excellence, exquisitely gracious to the palate, but ruthless in its demands on the stomach.'

32. Lee, *Virginia Woolf*, 4: 'If you listen to the only surviving recording of her, you will hear a voice from another century, which sounds to us posh, antiquated, class-bound, mannered'.

33. See M. Drabble, *Arnold Bennett. A Biography* (London, 1974), 109, 293. Woolf also accused Bennett of deliberately dropping his [h]s, 'thinking you possess more 'life' than we do'. See A. O. Bell (ed.), *The Diary of Virginia Woolf*, iii: *1925–1930* (London, 1980), 335.

34. Jones, *English Pronouncing Dictionary*, 1st edn (1917), §9.

35. A. Meynall, *Public Servant, Private Woman. An Autobiography* (London, 1988), 49.

36. A. Sisman, *A. J. P. Taylor. A Biography* (London, 1994), 55.

37. N. Clarke, *Alistair Cooke. The Biography* (London, 1999), 17.

38. S. Walton, *William Walton. Behind the Façade* (Oxford, 1988), 41.

39. See Chapter 7.

40. V. Grove, *Dear Dodie. The Life of Dodie Smith* (London, 1996), 20.

41. BBC WAC S236/12. A. Burrows, 'The Birth of Broadcasting in Britain'.

42. S. C. S., 'Wireless as the "Elixir of Life"', *Radio Times*, October 26 1923, 163.

43. J. C. W. Reith, 'A Broadcasting University', *Radio Times*, June 11th, 1924, 481.

44. See p. 26.

45. J. C. W. Reith, 'A New Year Message to Listeners', *Radio Times*, December 26th, 1925, 1.

46. P. Eckersley, 'Making Your Set Worthwhile', *Radio Times*, March 20th, 1925, 601.

47. 'Broadcasting Progress'. *The Times* Jan 2 1925, 11.

48. G. K. Chesterton, 'Making Listeners Jump', *Radio Times*, February 20th, 1925, 385.

49. T. Burke, 'Somewhere a Voice is Calling', *Radio Times*, March 27th, 1925, 1.

50. W. le Queux, 'Announcers as Teachers', *Radio Times*, Jan 18th, 1924, 151.

51. Ibid.

52. W. Archer, 'The Future of Wireless Drama', *Radio Times*, August 29th, 1924, 418.

53. E. V. Kirk, 'Broadcasting and the Child', *Radio Times*, December 28th, 1923, 20.

54. L. C., 'Letters from Listeners', *Radio Times*, Feb 29th, 1924, 390.

55. E. de Poynton, 'Words Killed by Wireless. Is Radio Changing our Language ?', *Radio Times*, December 26th, 1924, 5.

56. *Radio Times*, Nov 23rd, 1923, 309.

57. BBC WAC R34/252. C. Carpendale to Dr Miller Craig, 13th February 1924.

58. BBC WAC R34/252. A. Burrows, Memorandum, 5th March 1924.

59. C. A. Lewis, *Broadcasting from Within* (London, 1924), 109–10.

60. BBC WAC R34/252. J. C. W. Reith, Memorandum to Station Directors, 20th Nov. 1924.

61. Cited in P. Scannell and D. Cardiff, *A Social History of British Broadcasting*, i. *1922–1939. Serving the Nation* (Oxford, 1991), 176.

62. See pp. 255–7.

63. J. C. W. Reith, *Broadcast over Britain* (London, 1924), 161. Reith himself (1889–1971) spoke with an accent marked by his Scottish provenance throughout his life, though this became 'a good deal anglicised' in his days at the BBC' while, 'as he advanced into old age, his speech became markedly more Scottish again'. See I. McIntyre, *The Expense of Glory. A Life of John Reith* (London, 1993), 385.

64. Reith, *Broadcast over Britain*, 161.

65. Reith, *Broadcast over Britain*, 161.

66. Scannell and Cardiff (1991), 16.

67. A. Lloyd James, *Broadcast English* (London, 1928), 5.

68. See R. Bridges, 'Broadcast English. Pronunciation for Announcers', *The Times* Jan 6th 1928, 13.

69. Reith, *Broadcast over Britain*, 161.

70. Cockin, *The Art of Delivering Written Language*, p. ix.

71. Lloyd James, *Broadcast English*, 6.

72. Briggs, *The BBC. The First Fifty Years*, 68.

73. 'The Voice of Britain. A Discussion on B.B. C. Announcers between M. R. Ridley an Oxford don, Professor Lloyd James, linguistic advisor to the B.B.C., and T. Thompson, a champion of regional culture from Bury in Lancashire', *The Listener* (1939): 450.

74. Scannell and Cardiff, *Social History of British Broadcasting*, i. 147, 148.

75. A. Marwick, *Class: Image and Reality in Britain, France and the USA since 1930*, 2nd edn (London, 1990), 154

76. Ibid.

77. Cited ibid., 156.

78. W. Pickles, *Between You and Me* (London, 1949), 132. Pickles was by this point already an established announcer on the North Regional BBC, a role in which he had determinedly rejected the speech styles habitually used by his counter-parts in national (and London-based) broadcasting. ' "You might get a perfect imitation of those fellows" ', his wife advised him, ' "but if you're going to be an individual, you ought to do what's never been done before—speak like a North country-man" '. Pickles agreed, to widespread commendation—as long as he remained based in the North.

79. BBC WAC R34/585/4. 'Announcers' English', 14 June 1955.

80. See V. Brome, *J. B. Priestley* (London, 1988), especially chapter 18: 'Broadcaster in the Second World War'.

81. Scannell and Cardiff, *Social History of British Broadcasting*, i. 355.

82. Pickles, *Between You and Me*, 146. Pickles could be notably critical of the BBC in this context. His prime loyalties lay with the regional, and the linguistic divers-ities (and heritage) which this represented. As he argued, 'While I have the great-est respect for the many achievements of the B.B.C., I believe that they are guilty of trying to teach Great Britain to talk Standard English. May it be forbidden that we should ever speak like B.B.C. announcers'.

83. H. C. Wyld, *The Best English. A Claim for the Superiority of Received Standard English*, Society for Pure English Tract No. XXXIX (Oxford, 1934), 605.

84. Wyld, *The Best English*, 614.

85. J. Sims, *High Spirits* (London, 2000), 16.

86. P. Larkin, 'Annus Mirabilis', *Collected Poems*, ed. A. Thwaite (London, 1988), 167.

87. See Chapter 5.

88. R. Benson, *Paul McCartney. Behind the Myth* (London, 1992), 27.

89. T. Stamp, *Coming Attractions* (London, 1988), 37.

90. Ibid., 97.

91. In T. Harrison, *Selected Poems*, 2nd edn (London, 1987), 122–3.

92. J. Corner, 'Television and British Society in the 1950s', in J. Corner (ed.), *Popular Television in Britain. Studies in Cultural History* (London, 1991), 9.

93. C. MacCabe, *The Eloquence of the Vulgar. Language, Cinema, and the Politics of Culture* (London, 1999), 100.

94. See, for example, Reith's diary for 18 May 1964 which decries the way in which 'the BBC has lost its dignity and respect; in the upper reaches of . . . social leadership it has absconded its responsibilities and its privilege . . . I am sorry

I ever had anything to do with it'. His entry for 30 March in the same year makes equally illuminating reading, in his lament for the ways in which he had been 'prepared to lead, and to withstand modern laxities and vulgarities and irreligion and all'. 'All gone', he concludes. Cited in M. Tracey, *The Decline and Fall of Public Service Broadcasting* (Oxford, 1998), 97.

95. J. Cheshire and V. Edwards, 'Sociolinguistics in the Classroom: Exploring linguistic diversity', in J. Milroy and L. Milroy (eds), *Real English. The Grammar of English Dialect in the British Isles* (London, 1993), 46, 42.

96. J. Morrish, 'The accent that dare not speak its name', *Independent on Sunday*, 21 Mar. 1999.

97. P. Coggle, 'Estuary English FAQs', **www.phon.ucl.ac.uk/home/estuary/ estufaqs.htm**.

98. A. C. Gimson, *An Introduction to the Pronunciation of English*, 4th edn., rev. S. Ramsaran (1989), 86.

99. V. Moore, 'Why RP doesn't fit in', *Times 2*, 27 July 2000, 6.

100. See, for example, 'Need to Know', *The Times*, 19 Jan. 2001, tabloid section, 19 ('While Guy Ritchie strives to ditch his raised-in-a 17th-century-manor, educated-at-Hampshire-boarding-school vowels for a trumped up Cockney version').

101. J. Collard, 'A modern Pygmalion in reverse', *The Times*, 18 Sept. 2000, 10.

102. Cited in D. Crystal, *Cambridge Encyclopaedia of the English Language* (Cambridge, 1995), 327.

103. Moore, 'Why RP doesn't fit in', 7.

104. See e.g. P. Trudgill, 'The Sociolinguistics of Modern RP', in P. Trudgill, *Sociolinguistic Variation and Change* (Edinburgh, 2001), 171–80.

105. See further A. Fabricius, '*T-Glottalling. Between Stigma and Prestige. A Sociolinguistic Study of Modern RP*' (unpub. Ph.D. thesis, University of Copenhagen, 2000), 31: 'Disney films for children seem to reflect the more negative, slightly sinister (because of being exclusive and arrogant) aspects of U-RP [upper class RP] speech: most of the villains of these films have been U-RP or conservative RP speakers'.

106. Trudgill, 'The Sociolinguistics of Modern RP', 176.

107. K. Watson-Smyth, 'How you say it puts the accent on success', *Electronic Telegraph*, 2 Jan. 1997.

108. D. Rosewarne, 'Estuary English', *Times Educational Supplement*, 19 October 1984, 29; 'Estuary English—Tomorrow's RP?', *English Today*, 37 (1994), 4.

109. K. Marks, 'Scouse is threatened by the rising tide of Estuary English', *Independent*, 1 June 1999.

110. N. Hawkes, 'Science Briefing. Estuary Flows into the Clyde', *The Times*, 6 July 2000.

111. C. Horgues, 'Towards a Description of Estuary English' (Mémoire de Maîtrise, Université de Pau, 1998–9), 10.

112. B. A. Fennell, *A History of English. A Sociolinguistic Approach* (Oxford, 2001), 290.

113. See, for example, the extensive entry which Estuary English receives in K. Rooney (ed.), *Encarta. Dictionary of World English* (London, 1999) where it is given as 'a variety of standard English influenced by Cockney, spoken by people in London and southeastern England along the Thames estuary' as well as 'spreading north and east'; the definition also gives it as typified by the use of glottal stops,

vocalized /l/s, and the longer, tenser [iː] rather than traditional RP [ɪ] in words such as *happy*.

114. L. Young, 'Much ado about nuffin', *Guardian*, 2 June 1999.

115. See e.g. Fennell, *A History of English*, 191–2.

116. For a full discussion of these and related matters, see the website on Estuary English maintained by John Wells at **www.ucl.ac.uk/home/estuary/home. htm**.

117. Distribution of the glottal stop remains, however, significantly different in Cockney where it typically appears word internally before vowels as in *butter*, *bottle* [ˈbʌʔə] [ˈbɒʔl̩]; accounts of glottalization in Estuary English tend to exclude this pattern.

118. D. Rosewarne, 'Pronouncing Estuary English', *English Today*, 10/4 (1994), 4.

119. J. C. Wells, 'The Cockneyfication of RP?', in G. Melchers and N.-L. Johannesson (eds), *Nonstandard Varieties of Language. Papers from the Stockholm Symposium, 11–13 April, 1991* (Stockholm, 1994), 202.

120. See e.g. J. Przedlacka, 'Estuary English. A Sociophonetic Study' (unpub. Ph.D. thesis, University of Warsaw, 1999). Her study investigating 14 phonetic variables in Buckinghamshire, Kent, Essex, and Surrey (the supposed 'home ground' of Estuary English), found no conclusive proof of any homogeneity in accent over this area. Confidant media reports of the extension of Estuary norms to regions as disparate as Glasgow and Liverpool likewise regularly appear at odds with the linguistic studies on which such reports are based; Andrew Hamer, a linguist working at Liverpool University whose research inspired the *Independent* article headed 'Scouse is threatened by the rising tide of Estuary English', for instance, emphatically denies the stated connections with Estuary English and its dissemination ('I certainly DIDN'T claim that Scouse is about to disappear into the estuarine slime') in a response which appears appended to the original article (by Kathy Marks) on the invaluable website devoted to Estuary English which can be found at **www.phon.ucl. ac.uk/home/estuary/**.

121. See Rosewarne, 'Estuary English—Tomorrow's RP?', 3.

122. See for example D. Rosewarne, 'Tony Blair and William Hague: Two northerners heading south', *English Today* 14/4 (1998), 53–4, written after Tony Blair's appearance on the Des O'Connor show in 1998. Blair's apparent shift to the features of Estuary English was widely reported.

123. See e.g. John Honey's indictment that Mr Blair 'had failed to guard his educated accent from the infiltration of Estuary English or "watered-down Cockney"', especially when exhibiting features such as /-l/ vocalization in his reading of I Corinthians 13 at the funeral of Diana, Princess of Wales (cited in Horgues, 'A Description of Estuary English', 18).

124. N. Hawkes. 'Decline and fall of the Queen's cut-glass accent', *The Times*, 21 Dec. 2000, 1; M. Hanlon, 'Strewth, the Queen talks just like us', *Daily Express*, 21 Dec. 2000, 23; I. Miller, ''Er Maj don't talk so posh any more', *Mirror*, 21 Dec. 2000, 15. Particularly interesting is the negative metalanguage which surrounds the Queen's English of the past which is variously depicted in terms of its 'strangled vowels' and 'harsh, clipped tones'.

125. J. A. Maidment, 'Estuary English: Hybrid or Hype?' Paper presented to the 4th New Zealand Conference on Language & Society, Lincoln University, Christchurch, New Zealand, August 1994, 7.

126. See Chapter 3.

127. Cited in Horgues, 'A Description of Estuary English', 102.

128. See e.g. P. Christophersen, 'In Defence of RP', *English Today* 11 (1987), 17: 'the announcers aimed at being neutral and in consequence used RP, because this was held to be a neutral educated accent'.

129. J. Herbert, 'The Broadcast Voice', *English Today* 13 (1997), 19.

130. See p. 274 and n. 69 above.

131. O. Wright, 'Dyke promises to end London 'bias' of BBC', *The Times*, 10 Mar. 2001, 10.

132. R. Hattersley, 'How dare the BBC patronise everyone north of Watford', *Daily Mail*, 28 Jan. 1994. His objection rests on the fact that 'what a serious music programme needs is a voice which neither intrudes nor obscures the real purpose of the programme'. The Birmingham accent, in which it is, he argues, apparently impossible 'to say 'through train to Dudley' without sounding like a candidate for adenoidal surgery', is, Hattersley claims, manifestly unsuitable.

133. See p. 102.

134. Honey, *Does Accent Matter?*, 152.

135. T. Awogbamlye, 'Dropped aitches need not be a cause for concern', *The Times, Crème*, 7 Feb 2001, 5.

136. An advertisement for a position as a property negotiator with Foxton's, 'London's leading property services company'.

137. Trudgill, 'The Sociolingustics of modern RP', 176.

138. 'Scouse accent kills Lisa's Dublin dream', *Irish Post*, 17 Mar. 2001.

139. See e.g. J. Mullan, 'Lost Voices', *The Guardian*, 18 June 1999.

140. Letter to the *Guardian*, 7 Sept. 1993.

141. G. Martin, *Sunday Express Magazine*, 21 Nov. 1993, 62.

142. See J. Harrington, S. Palethorpe, and C. Watson, 'Does the Queen Speak the Queen's English?', *Nature*, 408 (2000), 927.

143. See e.g. Wells's statement that teachers of English as a foreign language should 'continue to teach RP, but a modernized form of it. That means, for example, allowing/encouraging glottal stop for /t/ in preconsonantal environments and so on', *Estuary English Q and A*, **www.phon.ucl.ac.uk/home/estuary/ee-faqs-jcw.htm**.

144. Wells, 'The Cockneyfication of RP?', 201.

145. P. Kerswill, 'Mobility, meritocracy and dialect levelling: the fading (and phasing) out of Received Pronunciation', in P. Rajan (ed.), *British Studies in the New Millennium. Challenge of the Grassroots. Proceedings of the 3rd Tarhu Conference on British Studies* (forthcoming), 2001.

REFERENCES

Unpublished Sources

MITCHINSON, J., unpublished memoirs of John Mitchinson, Pembroke College Archives (Oxford, 1823–1918).
Murray Papers: MP/22/3/1882. H. Sweet to J. A. H. Murray, 22 March 1882.
Murray Papers: MP/n.d./1897. J. A. H. Murray to H. H. Gibbs.

BBC Written Archives Centre

BBC WAC R34/252. A. Burrows, Memorandum, 5th March 1924.
BBC WAC S236/12. A. Burrows, 'The Birth of Broadcasting in Britain'.
BBC WAC R34/252. C. Carpendale to Dr Miller Craig, 13th February 1924.
BBC WAC R34/252. J. Reith, Memorandum to Station Directors, 20th Nov. 1924.
BBC WAC R34/585/4. 'Announcers' English', 14 June 1955

Official Papers

General Report for the Year 1849, by Her Majesty's Inspector of Schools, the Revd H. W. Bellairs, Committee of Council on Education, *Parliamentary Papers*, xliii (1850).
Minutes of the Committee of Council on Education, *Parliamentary Papers*, xliii (1850).
General Report on Roman Catholic Schools for the Year 1849 by Her Majesty's Inspector of Schools, T. M. W. Marshall, Committee of Council on Education: Reports on Elementary Schools, *Parliamentary Papers*, xliv (1850).
Privy Council Committee on Education, *Extracts from the Reports of Her Majesty's Inspectors of Schools* (London, 1852).
General Report for the Year 1859 by the Revd J. C. G. Fussell, Report of the Committee of Council on Education 1859–60, *Parliamentary Papers*, liv (1860).
Report on the Free Church Training College at Glasgow for the Year 1859, by Her Majesty's Inspector of Schools, C. E. Wilson, Esq., Report of the Committee of Council on Education, *Parliamentary Papers*, liv (1860).
Report by J. D. Morell, one of Her Majesty's Inspectors, Report of the Committee of Council on Education, *Parliamentary Papers*, liv (1860).
Report of Dr W. B. Hodgson, one of Her Majesty's Inspectors of Schools on the State of Education in the Metropolitan District, Report from the Commissioners on Popular Education, *Parliamentary Papers*, xxi/III (1861).
The Public Schools and the General Educational System. Report of the Committee on Public Schools appointed by the President of the Board of Education, July 1942 (London, 1944).

Anonymous Works

Advice to Governesses (London, 1827).

Advice to a Young Gentleman on Entering Society (London, 1839).

Boys and Their Ways. By One Who Knows Them (London, 1880).

'Broadcasting Progress'. *The Times* Jan 2 1925, 11.

Chambers's Encyclopaedia. A Dictionary of Useful Knowledge, 10 vols (London, 1888–92).

Common Blunders in Speaking, and How to Avoid Them (London, 1884).

The Edinburgh Review. Containing an account of all the Books and Pamphlets Published in Scotland from June 1755 (to January 1756) (Edinburgh, 1755).

The Elementary Catechisms (London, 1850).

The English Vocabulary; or Spelling Book, Compiled for the Use of Ackworth School (London, 1852; rev. edn, 1854).

Errors of Pronunciation and Improper Expressions (London, 1817).

Etiquette for All (London, 1861).

Etiquette for the Ladies (London, 1837).

Etiquette for Ladies and Gentlemen (London, 1839).

Etiquette, Social Ethics and the Courtesies of Society (London, 1834).

The Eton System of Education Vindicated (London, 1834).

The First Part of the Progressive Parsing Lessons (Maldon, 1833).

Girls and Their Ways. By One Who Knows Them (London, 1881).

Good Society. A Complete Manual of Manners (London, 1869).

The Habits of Good Society. A Handbook of Etiquette for Ladies and Gentlemen (London, 1859).

Handbook on the Teaching and Management of Elementary Schools (Manchester, 1872).

Hard Words Made Easy (London, 1855).

Hints on Etiquette and the Usages of Society (London, 1836).

Hints to Governesses. By One of Themselves (London, 1856).

The History of Ackworth School (Ackworth, 1853).

How to Shine in Society (Glasgow, 1860).

How to Speak or Write English with Perspicacity and Fluency (London, 1876).

Live and Learn: A Guide for All Who Wish to Speak and Write Correctly, 28th edn (London, 1872).

The Manners and Tone of Good Society by a Member of the Aristocracy (London, 1879).

The Manners of the Aristocracy. By One of Themselves (London, 1881).

Mixing in Society. A Complete Manual of Manners (London, 1870).

Modern Etiquette in Public and Private (London, 1888).

The Mother's Home Book (London, 1879).

Observations Respectfully Addressed to the Nobility and Gentry on the Existing Importance of the Art and Study of Oratory (London, 1836).

The Popular Educator (London, 1864).

Private Education; Or a Practical Plan for the Studies of Young Ladies, 3rd edn (London, 1816).

Society Small Talk. Or What to Say and When to Say It, 2nd edn (London, 1880).

The Sunday School Spelling Book (London, 1823).

Take My Advice (London, 1872).

Talking and Debating (London, 1856).

The Teacher's Manual of the Science and Art of Teaching (London, 1874).

Thorough English (London, 1867).

A Very Short Letter from One Old Westminster to Another, Touching Some Matters connected with Their School (London, 1829).

'The Voice of Britain. A Discussion on B.B.C. Announcers between M. R. Ridley an Oxford don, Professor Lloyd James, linguistic advisor to the B.B.C., and T. Thompson, a champion of regional culture from Bury in Lancashire', *The Listener* (1939): 450–54.

Vulgarisms and Other Errors of Speech (London, 1868).

Vulgarities of Speech Corrected (London, 1826).

Woman: As She Is, And As She Should Be, 2 vols (London, 1835).

Woman's Worth: Or Hints to Raise the Female Character, 2nd edn (London, 1847).

The Young Housekeeper (London, 1869).

The Young Lady's Book. A Manual of Elegant Recreations, Exercises, and Pursuits (London, 1829).

The Young Mother (London, 1857).

Other Works

ABBOTT, C. C. (ed.), *The Correspondence of Gerard Manley Hopkins and Richard Watkins Dixon* (London, 1935).

ACKROYD, P., *Dickens* (London, 1990).

ALFORD, H., *A Plea for the Queen's English*, 2nd edn (London, 1864).

ALGER, I., *The Orthoepical Guide to the English Tongue* (Boston, 1832).

ALTICK, R. D., *The English Common Reader: A Social History of the Mass Reading Public 1800–1900* (Chicago, Ill., 1957).

—— *Victorian People and Ideas* (London, 1974).

ARCHER, W., 'The Future of Wireless Drama'. *Radio Times* August 29th (1924), 418.

ARDENER, S. (ed.), *Defining Females* (London, 1978).

ARNOLD, M., *Reports on Elementary Schools 1852–1882*, ed. F. Sandford (London, 1889).

ARNOVICK, L., 'Proscribed collocations with *shall* and *will*: the eighteenth century (non)-standard reassessed', in C. Cheshire and D. Stein (eds), *Taming the Vernacular. From Dialect to Written Standard Language* (London, 1997), 135–51.

AUSTEN, J., *Emma* (London, 1816), ed. R. W. Chapman, 3rd edn (Oxford, 1933).

AWOGBAMLYE, T., 'Dropped aitches need not be a cause for concern', *The Times, Crème*, 7 Feb. 2001, 5.

BAGEHOT, W., *The English Constitution* (London, 1867).

—— *Works*, ed. F. Morgan, 5 vols (Hartford, comm., 1891).

BAILEY, N., *The Universal Etymological Dictionary*, 2 vols, 2nd edn. (London, 1731).

BAINBRIGGE, W. H., *Early Education* (London, 1881).

BAMFORD, T. W., 'Public Schools and Social Class, 1801–1850', *British Journal of Sociology*, 12 (1961), 224–35.

—— *Rise of the Public Schools. A Study of Boys' Public Boarding Schools in England and Wales from 1837 to the Present Day* (London, 1967).

—— (ed.), *Thomas Arnold on Education* (Cambridge, 1970).

BANKS, O., *The Sociology of Education*, 2nd edn (London, 1971).

BARKER, J., *Wordsworth. A Life* (London, 2000).

BARKER, R., 'Cor Blimey, Belgravia and the Acute Loss of a Correct Accent', *Times Educational Supplement*, 25 Aug. 1989, 10.

BARNES, W., *Poems in the Dorset Dialect* (London, 1862).

BARRELL, J., *English Literature in History 1730–80: An Equal Wide Survey* (London, 1983).

BARTLE, REVD G., *A Few Words To Parents and Guardians on the Education of Youth* (London, 1875).

BATCHELOR, T., *An Orthoëpical Analysis of the English Language to which is added A Minute Analysis of the Dialect of Bedfordshire* (London, 1809), ed. A. Zettersten, Lund Studies in English, 45 (Lund, 1974).

BAWDEN, N., *In My Own Time. Almost an Autobiography* (London, 1994).

BEATTIE, J., *The Theory of Language* (London, 1788).

BEDE, C., *The Adventures of Mr. Verdant Green, An Oxford Freshman*, 3rd edn (London, 1853).

BEETON, I., *Beeton's Book of Household Management* (London, 1861).

BELL, A. M., *Ladies' Elocutionist* (London, 1852).

——*A Lecture on the Art of Delivery and the Influence of School Discipline on Public Oratory* (Edinburgh, 1855).

——*Elocutionary Manual*, 3rd edn (London, 1860).

BELL, A. O., *The Diary of Virginia Woolf*, iii: *1925–1930* (London, 1980).

BELL, R. T., *Sociolinguistics. Goals, Approaches and Problems* (London, 1976).

BENNETT, A., *Anna of the Five Towns* (London, 1902).

BENSON, R., *Paul McCartney. Behind the Myth* (London, 1992).

BENZIE, W., *The Dublin Orator* (Leeds, 1972).

BICKNELL, A., *The Grammatical Wreath*, 2 vols (London, 1796).

BLAKE, A., 'The Place of Fiction in Victorian Literary Culture', *Literature and History*, 11 (1985), 203–16.

BLAKE, N. F., *Non-standard Language in English Literature* (London, 1981).

BLOOMFIELD, L., 'Literate and Illiterate Speech', *American Speech*, 2 (1927), 432–9.

BOLTON, K., and KWOK, H. (eds), *Sociolinguistics Today: International Perspectives* (London, 1992).

BOOTH, D., *The Principles of English Grammar* (London, 1837).

BOSWELL, J., *The Life of Samuel Johnson LL.D* (London, 1791), ed. L. F. Powell, 4 vols (Oxford, 1934).

BOYD, A., *Lessons of Middle Age* (London, 1869).

BRADLEY, H., *Spelling Pronunciations*, Society for Pure English Tract No. III (Oxford, 1920), 19.

BRADLEY, I., *The English Middle Classes are Alive and Kicking* (London, 1982).

BRANDRAM, S., *Brandram's Speaker* (London, 1885).

BREWER, R., *What Shall We Do With Tom? Or, Hints to Parents and Others About School* (London, 1866).

BRIGGS, A., *The Age of Improvement* (London, 1960).

——*The BBC. The First Fifty Years* (Oxford, 1985).

BRIGGS, J., *A Woman of Passion. The Life of E. Nesbit 1858–1924* (London, 1987).

BRITTAIN, L., *Rudiments of English Grammar* (Louvain, 1788).

BROME, V., *J. B. Priestley* (London, 1988).

BRONTË, A., *Agnes Grey* (London, 1847), ed. H. Marsden and R. Inglesfield (Oxford, 1988).

BROOK, G. L., *The Language of Dickens* (London, 1970).

BROWNE, R., *The English-School Reformed* (London, 1700).

BROWNE, T., *The Union Dictionary* (London, 1806).

BUCHANAN, J., *Linguae Britannicae Vera Pronunciatio* (London, 1757).

—— *A New English Dictionary* (London, 1757).

—— *The British Grammar* (London, 1762).

—— *A Plan of an English Grammar School Education* (London, 1770).

BULLOKAR, WILLIAM, *Works*, ed. J. R. Turner, 3 vols (Leeds, 1970).

BURCHFIELD, R., *The New Fowler's Modern English Usage* (Oxford, 1996).

BURKE, T., 'Somewhere a Voice is Calling', *Radio Times*, March 27th (1925), 1.

BURNEY, F., *Evelina* (London, 1778), ed. E. A. Bloom (Oxford, 1968). See also D'Arblay, Madame.

BURNLEY, J. D., 'Sources of Standardization in Later Middle English', in J. B. Trahern, Jr. (ed.), *Standardizing English: Essays in the History of Language Change in Honor of John Hurt Fisher* (Knoxville, Tenn., 1989), 23–41.

BURRELL, A., *Recitation. A Handbook for Teachers in Public Elementary School* (London, 1891).

BUTLER, J., *Memoir of John Grey of Dilston* (Edinburgh, 1894).

C., L., 'Letters from Listeners', *Radio Times*, Feb. 29th (1924), 390.

CAMERON, D. (ed.), *The Feminist Critique of Language. A Reader* (London, 1990).

CANNON, J., *Aristocratic Century: The Peerage of Eighteenth-Century England* (Cambridge, 1984).

CAREY, R. N., *Not Like Other Girls*, 3 vols (London, 1884).

CARLISLE, N., *A Concise Description of the Endowed Grammar Schools of England and Wales* (London, 1818).

CARPENTER, J. E., *Handbook of Poetry* (London, 1868).

CARPENTER, T., *The School Speaker* (London, 1825).

CARTER, R., and NASH, W., *Seeing Through Language: A Guide to Styles of English Writing* (Oxford, 1990).

CHAMBERS, W., and CHAMBERS, R. (eds), *Chambers's Educational Course: Simple Lessons in Reading* (Edinburgh, 1841).

CHANDOS, J., *Boys Together: English Public Schools 1800–1864* (London, 1984).

CHESHIRE, J., and EDWARDS, V., 'Sociolinguistics in the Classroom: Exploring linguistic diversity', in J. Milroy and L. Milroy (eds), *Real English. The Grammar of English Dialect in the British Isles* (London, 1993).

CHESTERTON, G. K., 'Making Listeners Jump', *Radio Times* Feb. 20th (1925), 385.

CHRISTOPHERSEN, P., 'In Defence of RP', *English Today* 11 (1987), 17–23.

CLARKE, N., *Alistair Cooke. The Biography* (London, 1999).

COATES, J., *Women, Men and Language* (London, 1986).

COBBETT, J., *A Grammar of the English Language in a Series of Letters. With an Additional Chapter on Pronunciation by James Paul Cobbett* (London, 1866).

COBBETT, W., *The Life and Adventures of Peter Porcupine* (Philadelphia, Pa., 1797).

—— *A Grammar of the English Language in a Series of Letters* (London, 1819).

—— *Rural Rides* (London, 1830).

COCKIN, W., *The Art of Delivering Written Language* (London, 1775).

COGGLE, P., *Do You Speak Estuary?* (London, 1993).

——'Estuary English FAQs', **www.phon.ucl.ac.uk/home/estuary/estufaqs.htm**

COLEMAN, D. C., 'Gentlemen and Players', *Economic History Review*, 26 (1973), 92–116.

COLES, E., *The Compleat English Schoolmaster* (London, 1674).

COLLARD, J., 'A modern Pygmalion in reverse', *The Times*, 18 Sept. 2000, 10.

COLLINS, W., *Basil* (London, 1852).

COOPER, C., *The English Teacher or the Discovery of the Art of Teaching and Learning the English Tongue* (London, 1687).

CORFIELD, P., 'Class by Name and Number in Eighteenth-Century Britain', *History*, 72 (1987), 39–61.

CORNER, J., 'Television and British Society in the 1950s', in J. Corner (ed.), *Popular Television in Britain. Studies in Cultural History* (London, 1991).

COUSTILLAS, P., *London and the Life of Literature in Late Victorian England: The Diary of George Gissing* (London, 1978).

COYSH, G., *The British Pronouncing and Self Instructing Spelling Book* (Topsham, 1837).

CRABBE, G., *The Complete Poetical Works*, ed. N. Dalrymple-Champneys and A. Pollard, 3 vols (Oxford, 1988).

CRAIK, Mrs D. M., *Two Marriages* (London, 1881).

CRAMP, W., *The Philosophy of Language* (London, 1838).

CROWLEY, T. (ed.), *Proper English? Readings in Language, History and Cultural Identity* (London, 1991).

CRYSTAL, D., *Cambridge Encyclopaedia of the English Language* (Cambridge, 1995).

DAICHES, D., *Middlemarch* (London, 1963).

DAINES, S., *Orthoepia Anglicana* (London, 1640).

D'ARBLAY, MADAME, *Diary and Letters*, ed. C. Barrett, 4 vols (London, 1876).

DARLEY, G., *Octavia Hill. A Life* (London, 1990).

DAVENPORT, W. H., *The Secret of Success; or, How to Get on in the World* (London, 1870).
——*Plain Living and High Thinking; or, Practical Self-Culture* (London, 1880).

DAVIDOFF, L., *The Best Circles: Society Etiquette and the Season* (London, 1973).

DAVIS, M., *Everybody's Business* (London, 1865).

DICKENS, C., *The Life and Adventures of Nicholas Nickleby* (London, 1839).
—— *The Life and Adventures of Martin Chuzzlewit* (London, 1844), ed. M. Cardwell (Oxford, 1982).
—— *The Adventures of Oliver Twist* (London, 1846), ed. K. Tillotson (Oxford, 1966).
——*Dombey and Son* (London, 1848), ed. A. Horsman (Oxford, 1974).
—— *The Personal History of David Copperfield* (London, 1850), ed. N. Burgis (Oxford, 1981).
——*Bleak House*, 2 vols (London, 1853).
——*Little Dorrit* (London, 1857), ed. H. P. Sucksmith (Oxford, 1979).
—— *Great Expectations*, 3 vols (London, 1861).
——*Our Mutual Friend*, 2 vols (London, 1865).

DISRAELI, B., *Coningsby; or the New Generation*, 3 vols (London, 1844).
——*Sybil; or, the Two Nations*, 3 vols (London, 1845).

DOBSON, E. J., *English Pronunciation 1500–1700*, 2 vols, 2nd edn (Oxford, 1968).

DORAN, J., *A Lady of the Last Century* (London, 1873).

DOUGLAS, S., *A Treatise on the Provincial Dialect of Scotland* (1779), ed. C. Jones (Edinburgh, 1991).

DOWNES, W., *Language in Society* (London, 1984).

DRABBLE, M., *Arnold Bennett. A Biography* (London, 1974).

DREW, E. (ed.), *The Elocutionist Annual for 1889* (London, 1889).

DURKHEIM, E., *Education and Sociology*, trans. S. D. Fox (Glencoe, Ill., 1956).

EAGLESON, R. D., 'Sociolinguistic Reflections on Acceptability', in S. Greenbaum (ed.), *Acceptability in Language* (The Hague, 1977), 63–71.

EARLE, J., *The Philology of the English Tongue* (London, 1871).

EASSON, A. (ed.), *Elizabeth Gaskell: The Critical Heritage* (London, 1991).

ECCLES, E. A. S., *Harry Hawkins' H Book* (London, 1879).

ECKERSLEY, P., 'Making Your Set Worthwhile', *Radio Times*, March 20th (1925), 601.

EDGEWORTH, M., *Letters from England, 1813–1844*, ed. C. Colvin (Oxford, 1971).

—— and EDGEWORTH, R. L., *Practical Education*, 2 vols (London, 1798).

EDWARDS, J., *Language and Disadvantage* (London, 1979).

—— *Language, Society and Identity* (Oxford, 1985).

EDWARDS, J. R., 'Social Class Differences and the Identification of Sex in Children's Speech', *Journal of Child Language*, 6 (1979), 121–7.

ELIOT, G., 'The Natural History of German Life', *Westminster Review*, NS 10 (July 1856). Reprinted in Eliot, *Essays*, ed. T. Pinney (London, 1963).

——, *Adam Bede*, 3 vols (London, 1859).

ELIOT, G., *Silas Marner: The Weaver of Raveloe* (London, 1861).

—— *Felix Holt, the Radical*, 3 vols (London, 1866).

—— *Impressions of Theophrastus Such* (London, 1869).

—— *Middlemarch, A Study of Provincial Life*, 4 vols (London, 1871).

—— *The George Eliot Letters*, ed. G. S. Haight, 9 vols (London, 1954–6).

—— *Essays*, ed. T. Pinney (London, 1963).

ELLIS, A. J., *On Early English Pronunciation*, 5 vols (London, 1869–89).

—— 'Tenth Annual Address of the President to the Philological Society', *Transactions of the Philological Society* (1881), 317.

ELLIS, S. S., *The Women of England, Their Social Duties, and Domestic Habits*, 3rd edn (London, 1839).

ELPHINSTON, J., *Propriety Ascertained in her Picture* (London, 1786).

ELYAN, O., SMITH, P., GILES, H., and BOURHIS, R., 'RP-Accented Female Speech: The Voice of Perceived Androgyny', in P. Trudgill (ed.), *Sociolinguistic Patterns in British English* (London, 1978), 122–31.

ENFIELD, W., *The Speaker: or, Miscellaneous Pieces, Selected from the best English Writers. To which is prefixed An Essay on elocution* (London, 1774).

—— *A Familiar Treatise on Rhetoric* (London, 1809).

ESCOTT, T. H. S., *England: Its People, Polity, and Pursuits*, 2 vols (London, 1879).

FABER, R., *Proper Stations: Class in Victorian Fiction* (London, 1971).

FABRICIUS, A. 'T-Glottalling. Between Stigma and Prestige. A Sociolinguistic Study of Modern RP' (unpub. Ph.D. thesis, University of Copenhagen, 2000).

FARQUHAR, B. A., *Female Education* (London, 1851).

FARRAR, F. W. (ed.), *Essays on a Liberal Education* (London, 1867).

FASOLD, R., *The Sociolinguistics of Society* (Oxford, 1984).

—— *The Sociolinguistics of Language* (Oxford, 1990).

FEARON, D. A., *School Inspection* (London, 1876).

FENNELL, B. A., *A History of English. A Sociolinguistic Approach* (Oxford, 2001).

FIELDING, H., *The History of the Life of Mr Jonathan Wild the Great*, in *Miscellanies*, vol. III, Introduction and Commentary by B. A. Goldgor, text ed. H. Amory (Oxford, 1997).

—— *The History of Tom Jones* (London, 1749), ed. F. Bowers (Oxford, 1974).

FISHER, J., RICHARDSON, M., and FISHER, J. (eds), *An Anthology of Chancery English* (Knoxville, Tenn., 1984).

FOGG, P. WALKDEN, *Elementa Anglicana; or, the Principles of English Grammar*, 2 vols (Stockport, 1796).

FOREMAN, A., *Georgiana, Duchess of Devonshire* (London, 1998).

FOWLER, R., *The Languages of Literature* (London, 1971).

—— *Literature as Social Discourse* (London, 1981).

FOX, I., *Public Schools and Public Issues* (London, 1985).

FULTON, G., and KNIGHT, G., *A Dictionary of the English Language Greatly Improved* (Edinburgh, 1833).

FURBANK, P. N., *Unholy Pleasure: The Idea of Social Class* (Oxford, 1985).

GALSWORTHY, J., *The Island Pharisees* (London, 1904).

—— *In Chancery* (London, 1920).

—— *The Silver Spoon* (London, 1926).

—— *Swan Song* (London, 1928).

GASKELL, Mrs E., *Cranford* (London, 1853), ed. E. P. Watson (Oxford, 1972).

—— *North and South* (London, 1855), ed. A. Easson (Oxford, 1973).

GATHORNE-HARDY, J., *The Public School Phenomenon* (London, 1977).

GILES, H., COUPLAND, N., HENWOOD, K., HARRIMAN, J., and COUPLAND, J., 'The Social Meaning of RP: An Intergenerational Perspective', in S. Ramsaran (ed.), *Studies in the Pronunciation of English: A Commemorative Volume in Honour of A. C. Gimson* (London, 1990), 191–211.

GILL, J., *Introductory Text-Book to School Management*, various edns (London, 1857–82).

GIMSON, A. C., *An Introduction to the Pronunciation of English*, 4th edn, rev. S. Ramsaran (London, 1989).

GISSING, G., *Workers in the Dawn*, 3 vols (London, 1880).

—— *Demos. A Story of English Socialism*, 3 vols (London, 1886).

—— *The Nether World*, 3 vols (London, 1889).

—— *The Emancipated*, 3 vols (London, 1890).

—— *New Grub Street*, 3 vols (London, 1891).

—— *Born in Exile*, 3 vols (London, 1892).

—— *Denzil Quarrier* (London, 1892).

—— *The Odd Women* (London, 1893).

—— *In the Year of Jubilee*, 3 vols (London, 1894).

—— *The Whirlpool* (London, 1897).

—— *Charles Dickens. A Critical Study* (London, 1898).

—— *Human Odds and Ends. Stories and Sketches* (London, 1898).

—— *The Town Traveller* (London, 1898).

—— *Will Warburton. A Romance of Real Life* (London, 1905).

—— *A Victim of Circumstances* (London, 1927).

GISSING, G., *Collected Letters*, i: *1863–1880*, ed. P. F. Mattheisen, A. C. Young, and P. Coustillas (Ohio, 1990).

—— *Collected Letters*, ii: *1881–1885*, ed. P. F. Mattheisen, A. C. Young, and P. Coustillas (Ohio, 1991).

GLENDINNING, V., *Jonathan Swift* (London, 1998).

GORDON, L., *Charlotte Brontë. A Passionate Life* (London, 1994).

GÖRLACH, M., *Studies in the History of the English Language* (Heidelberg, 1990).

—— *Introduction to Early Modern English* (Cambridge, 1991).

GRADDOL, D., and SWANN, J., *Gender Voices* (Oxford, 1989).

GRAHAM, G. F., *A Book About Words* (London, 1869).

GRAHAM, J. C., *An Introduction to the Art of Reading* (London, 1861).

GRAHAM, W., *Principles of Elocution* (Edinburgh, 1837).

GRAVES, A. PERCEVAL, and RICE-WIGGIN, M., *The Elementary School Manager* (London, 1879).

GREENBAUM, S. (ed.), *Acceptability in Language* (The Hague, 1977).

—— *Good English and the Grammarian* (London, 1988).

GREENOUGH, J. B., and Kittredge, L., *Words and their Ways in English Speech* (London, 1901).

GREENWOOD, J., *An Essay Towards an English Grammar* (London, 1711).

GREY, M. G., and SHIRREFF, E., *Thoughts on Self-Culture. Addressed to Women* (London, 1854).

GRIFFITHS, R. J., *An Introduction to the Study of School Management* (London, 1872).

GROSER, W. H., *The Sunday School Teacher's Manual; or, The Principles and Methods of Instruction as Applied to Sunday School Work* (London, 1877).

GROVE, V., *Dear Dodie. The Life of Dodie Smith* (London, 1996).

GROVER, A., *A New English Grammar for the Use of Junior Classes in Schools* (London, 1877).

GUEST, E., *A History of English Rhythms*, 2 vols (London, 1838).

GUMPERZ, J., *Language and Social Identity* (Cambridge, 1982).

GUTTSMAN, W. L. (ed.), *The English Ruling Class* (London, 1969).

GWYNNE, P., *A Word to the Wise*, 2nd edn (London, 1879).

H., HON. HENRY, *Poor Letter H: Its Use and Abuse*, various edns (London, 1854–66).

—— *P's and Q's: Grammatical Hints for the Million* (London, 1855).

H., H. W., *How to Choose a Wife* (London, 1854).

HALES, J. W., 'The Teaching of English', in F. W. Farrar (ed.), *Essays on a Liberal Education* (London, 1867), 293–312.

HALSEY, A. H., *Change in British Society* (Oxford, 1978).

HANLON, M., 'Strewth, the Queen talks just like us', *Daily Express*, 21 Dec. 2000, 23.

HARDMAN, WILLIAM, *Papers*, ed. S. M. Ellis (London, 1925).

HARDY, T., *A Pair of Blue Eyes*, 3 vols (London, 1873).

—— 'Dialect in Novels', *The Athenaeum*, 30 Nov. 1878, 688.

—— *The Mayor of Casterbridge*, 2 vols (London, 1886).

HARMAN, C., *Fanny Burney. A Biography* (London, 2000).

HARRINGTON, J., PALETHORPE, S., and WATSON, C., 'Does the Queen Speak the Queen's English?', *Nature*, 408 (2000), 927.

HARRISON, J. F. C., *Early Victorian Britain 1832–1851* (London, 1971).

—— *Late Victorian Britain 1875–1901* (London, 1990).

HARRISON, T., *Selected Poems*, 2nd edn (London, 1987).

HART, J., *An Orthographie* (London, 1569).

HARTLEY, C., *Everyone's Handbook of Common Blunders in Speaking and Writing* (London, 1897).

HATFIELD, Miss S., *Letters on the Importance of the Female Sex. With Observations on their Manners and Education* (London, 1803).

HATTERSLEY, R., 'How dare the BBC patronise everyone north of Watford', *Daily Mail*, 28 Jan. 1994.

HAWKES, N., 'Science Briefing. Estuary Flows into the Clyde', *The Times*, 6 July 2000.

—— 'Decline and fall of the Queen's cut-glass accent', *The Times*, 21 Dec. 2000, 1.

HERBERT, J., 'The Broadcast Voice', *English Today* 13 (1997), 18–28.

HIBBERT, C., *Queen Victoria. A Personal History* (London, 2000).

HIGDEN, RANULPH, *Polycronicon*. Trans. John of Trevisa and published by William Caxton as *Description of Britayne, & also Irlonde taken out of Polycronicon* (London, 1480).

HILL, G., *The Aspirate* (London, 1902).

HILL, T. W., 'A Lecture on the Articulation of Speech. Delivered before the Birmingham Philosophical Society on January 29th 1821', in *Selections from the Works of the Late T. W. Hill* (London, 1860).

HOLLINGSWORTH, B., 'The Mother Tongue and the Public Schools', in A. K. Pugh, V. J. Lee, and J. Swann (eds), *Language and Language Use* (London, 1980), 185–97.

HOLMBERG, B., *On the Concept of Standard English and the History of Modern English Pronunciation* (Lund, 1964).

HONEY, J., ' "Talking Proper": Schooling and the Establishment of English 'Received Pronunciation' ', in G. Nixon and J. Honey (eds), *An Historic Tongue: Studies in English Linguistics in Memory of Barbara Strang* (London, 1988), 209–27.

—— *Does Accent Matter? The Pygmalion Factor* (London, 1989).

HOOD, T., *The Wakefield Spelling Book* (London, 1868).

HOPE, A., *A Book About Dominies. Being the Reflections and Recollections of a Member of the Profession* (London, 1869).

HORGUES, C., 'Towards a Description of Estuary English' (Mémoire de Maîtrise, Université de Pau, 1998–9).

HOUGHTON, W., *The Victorian Frame of Mind 1830–1870* (Yale, 1957).

HOWATT, A., *A History of English Language Teaching* (Oxford, 1984).

HUDSON, R. A., *Sociolinguistics* (Cambridge, 1980, reprinted 1986).

HUGHES, G., *Words in Time. A Social History of the English Vocabulary* (Oxford, 1988).

HULLAH, J., *The Cultivation of the Speaking Voice* (Oxford, 1870).

JACK, F. B., *The Woman's Book* (London, 1911).

JERNUDD, B. H., 'The Texture of Language Purism: An Introduction', in B. H. Jernudd and M. J. Shapiro (eds), *The Politics of Language Purism* (Berlin, 1989), 1–20.

—— and SHAPIRO, M. J. (eds), *The Politics of Language Purism* (Berlin, 1989).

JESPERSEN, O., *A Modern English Grammar on Historical Principles*, 7 vols (London and Copenhagen, 1909).

—— *Language: Its Nature, Development and Origin* (London, 1922).

JOHNSON, S., *The Plan of a Dictionary of the English Language* (London, 1747).

—— *A Dictionary of the English Language*, 2 vols. (London, 1755).

JOHNSTON, W., *A Pronouncing and Spelling Dictionary of the English Language* (London, 1764).

JONES, D., *An English Pronouncing Dictionary* (London, 1917); 4th edn (London, 1937).

——'On "Received Pronunciation"', *Le Maître phonétique*, supp. issue (Apr.–July 1937).

JONES, S., *Sheridan Improved. A General Pronouncing and Explanatory Dictionary of the English Language*, 3rd edn (London, 1798).

KELLY, L., *Richard Brinsley Sheridan. A Life* (London, 1997).

KENRICK, W., *A New English Dictionary of the English Language* (London, 1773).

——*A Rhetorical Grammar of the English Language* (London, 1784).

KERSWILL, P., 'Mobility, meritocracy and dialect levelling: the fading (and phasing) out of Received Pronunciation', in P. Rajan (ed.), *British Studies in the New Millennium. Challenge of the Grassroots. Proceedings of the 3rd Tarhu Conference on British Studies* (forthcoming), 2001.

KINGTON-OLIPHANT, T., *The Sources of Standard English*, 2 vols (London, 1873).

KIRK, E., 'Broadcasting and the Child', *Radio Times*, December 28th (1923), 20.

KNOWLES, J., *A Pronouncing and Explanatory Dictionary of the English Language* (London, 1835).

L., I. S., *Fashion in Language* (London, 1906).

LABOV, W., *The Social Stratification of English in New York City* (Washington, DC, 1966).

LABOV, W., 'The Effect of Social Mobility on Speech Behaviour', *International Journal of American Linguistics*, 33 (1967), 58–75.

——*Sociolinguistic Patterns* (Oxford, 1978).

——*Principles of Linguistic Change. Internal Factors* (Oxford, 1994).

LARKIN, P., *Collected Poems*, ed. A. Thwaite (London, 1988).

LASS, R., *The Shape of English* (London, 1987).

LAUGHTON, W., *A Practical Grammar of the English Tongue* (London, 1739).

LAWRENCE, D. H., *Lady Chatterley's Lover* (Florence, 1928).

LAWSON, J., and SILVER, H., *A Social History of English Education* (London, 1973).

LEACH, A., *The Letter H. Past, Present, and Future* (London, 1881).

LEE, H., *Virginia Woolf* (London, 1996).

LEECH, G. N., and SHORT, M. H., *Style in Fiction: A Linguistic Introduction to English Fictional Prose* (London, 1981).

LEITH, D., *A Social History of English* (London, 1983).

LEPAGE, R., 'Projection, focusing, diffusion', *York Papers in Linguistics*, 9 (1980).

LEVANTE, REVD E. R. DE, *Orthoepy and Orthography of the English Language* (London, 1869).

LEWIS, C. A., *Broadcasting from Within* (London, 1924).

LIVESEY, T. J., *How to Teach Grammar: Illustrated in a Series of Lessons* (London, 1881).

——*Moffat's How to Teach Reading* (London, 1882).

LLOYD, J. A., *Broadcast English* (London, 1928).

LOCKE, J., *An Essay Concerning Human Understanding* (London, 1690).

LOCKHART, J. G., 'On the Cockney School of Poetry No. IV', *Blackwood's Edinburgh Magazine*, 3 (1818), 520–1.

LODGE, D., *Nice Work* (London, 1988).

LONGMUIR, J., *Walker and Webster Combined in a Dictionary of the English Language* (London, 1864).

LOWE, E. C., *An English Primer* (London, 1867).

LOWER, M. A., *Groombridge's Annual Reader* (London, 1867).

LOWTH, R., *A Short Introduction to English Grammar* (London, 1762).

LUCAS, J., 'Editorial Preface', *Literature and History*, 1 (1975), 1–2.

LYTTON, E. BULWER, *Eugene Aram*, 3 vols (London, 1832).

——*England and the English* (London, 1833), ed. S. Meacham (Chicago, Ill., 1970).

——*My Novel by Pisistratus Caxton; or, Varieties in English Life*, 4 vols (Edinburgh, 1853).

MCARTHUR, T. (ed.), *The Oxford Companion to the English Language* (Oxford, 1992).

MACAULAY, LORD, *The Life and Letters of Lord Macaulay*, ed. G. O. Trevelyan, 2 vols (London, 1878).

MACCABE, C., *The Eloquence of the Vulgar. Language, Cinema, and the Politics of Culture* (London, 1999).

M'COMBIE, W., *On Education in its Constituents, Objects, and Issues* (Aberdeen, 1857).

MCINTYRE, I., *The Expense of Glory. A Life of John Reith* (London, 1993).

MACKARNESS, Mrs H. (ed.), *The Young Lady's Book. A Manual of Amusements, Exercises, Studies, and Pursuits* (London, 1876).

MCKENDRICK, N., BREWER, J., and PLUMB, J., *The Birth of a Consumer Society: The Commercialization of Eighteenth-Century England* (London, 1982).

MACLEOD, A., *Macleod's First Text-Book in Elocution With a Scheme for Acquiring Correct Pronunciation*, 3rd edn (Edinburgh, 1881).

MACMAHON, M. K. C., 'James Murray and the Phonetic Notation in the New English Dictionary', *Transactions of the Philological Society* (1985), 71–112.

MAIDMENT, J. A., 'Estuary English: Hybrid or Hype?' Paper presented to the 4th New Zealand Conference on Language & Society, Lincoln University, Christchurch, New Zealand, August 1994.

MARKS, K., 'Scouse is threatened by the rising tide of Estuary English', *Independent*, 1 June 1999.

MARPLES, M., *Public School Slang* (London, 1940)

MARSH, J., *Christina Rossetti. A Literary Biography* (London, 1994).

MARSHALL, D., *Industrial England 1776–1851*, 2nd edn (London, 1982).

MARTIN, B., *Institutions of Language* (London, 1748).

MARTINEAU, H., *Deerbrook*, 3 vols (London, 1839).

——*Autobiography*, 3 vols (London, 1877).

MARWICK, A., *Class: Image and Reality in Britain, France and the USA since 1930*, 2nd edn (London, 1990).

MATTHEWS, W., *Getting on in the World; or, Hints on Success in Life* (London, 1873).

—— *Cockney Past and Present: A Short History of the Dialect of London* (London, 1972).

MAY, T., *An Economic and Social History of Britain 1760–1970* (New York, 1987).

MAYNARD, J., *Matrimony: Or, What Married Life Is, and How to Make the Best of It*, 2nd edn (London, 1866).

MEREDITH, G., *The Ordeal of Richard Feverel*, 3 vols (London, 1859).

MERIVALE, J. A. (ed.), *Autobiography and Letters of Charles Merivale, Dean of Ely* (Oxford, 1898).

MEYNALL, A., *Public Servant, Private Woman. An Autobiography* (London, 1988).

MILLER, I., ''Er Maj don't talk so posh any more', *Mirror*, 21 Dec. 2000, 15.

MILNES, R. M., 'On the Present Social Results of Classical Education', in F. W. Farrar (ed.), *Essays on a Liberal Education* (London, 1867), 365–84.

MILROY, J., *Linguistic Variation and Change: On the Historical Sociolinguistics of English* (Oxford, 1992).

—— 'Social Network and Prestige Arguments in Sociolinguistics', in K. Bolton and H. Kwok (eds), *Sociolinguistics Today. International Perspectives* (London, 1992), 146–62.

—— 'Historical Description and the Ideology of the Standard Language', in L. Wright (ed.), *The Development of Standard English 1300–1800. Theories, Descriptions, Conflicts* (Cambridge, 2000), 11–28.

—— and MILROY, L., *Authority in Language. Investigating Language Prescription and Standardization* (London, 1985).

—— —— 'Mechanisms of Change in Urban Dialects: the role of class, social network and gender', in P. Trudgill and J. Cheshire (eds), *The Sociolinguistics Reader*, i: *Multilingualism and Variation* (London, 1998).

MILROY, L., *Observing and Analysing Natural Language: A Critical Account of Sociolinguistic Method* (Oxford, 1987).

—— 'New Perspectives in the Analysis of Sex Differentiation in Language', in K. Bolton and H. Kwok (eds), *Sociolinguistics Today. International Perspectives* (London, 1992), 163–79.

MITCHELL, S., 'The Forgotten Women of the Period: Penny Weekly Family Magazines of the 1840s and 1850s', in M. Vicinus (ed.), *A Widening Sphere: Changing Roles of Victorian Women* (Bloomington, Ind., 1977), 29–51.

MOORE, V., 'Why RP doesn't fit in', *Times 2*, 27 July 2000, 6.

MORE, H., *Thoughts on the Importance of the Manners of the Great to General Society* (London, 1788).

—— *Strictures on the Modern System of Female Education*, 2 vols (London, 1799).

MORGAN, F. (ed.), *Works* (Hartford, Conn., 1891).

MORRISH, I., *The Sociology of Education*, 2nd edn (London, 1978).

MORRISH, J., 'The accent that dare not speak its name', *Independent on Sunday*, 21 Mar. 1999.

MORRISON, T., *Manual of School Management*, 3rd edn (London, 1863).

MUGGLESTONE, L. C., 'A. J. Ellis, 'Standard English' and the Prescriptive Tradition', *Review of English Studies*, NS 39 (1988), 87–92.

—— 'Prescription, Pronunciation, and Issues of Class in the Late Eighteenth and Nineteenth Centuries', in D. M. Reeks (ed.), *Sentences for Alan Ward* (London, 1988), 175–182.

—— 'Samuel Johnson and the Use of /h/', *Notes and Queries*, 243 (1989), 431–3.

—— 'The Fallacy of the Cockney Rhyme: from Keats and Earlier to Auden', *Review of English Studies*, NS 42 (1991), 57–66.

—— ''Grammatical Fair Ones': Women, Men, and Attitudes to Language in the Novels of George Eliot', *Review of English Studies*, NS 46 (1995), 11–25.

—— 'Alexander Ellis and the Virtues of Doubt', in M. J. Toswell and E. M. Tyler (eds), *Studies in English Language and Literature. 'Doubt Wisely': Studies in Honour of E. G. Stanley* (London, 1996), 85–96.

—— ''A Subject so Curious and Useful': Lindley Murray and Pronunciation', in I. Tieken-Boon van Ostade (ed.), *Two Hundred Years of Lindley Murray* (Munster, Germany, 1996), 145–63.

—— 'Cobbett's *Grammar*, William, James Paul, and the Politics of Prescriptivism', Review of English Studies, NS 48 (1997), 471–88.

—— 'John Walker and Alexander Ellis: Antedating *RP*', *Notes and Queries*, NS 44 (1997), 103–7.

—— ''Pioneers in the Untrodden Forest': The *New* English Dictionary', in L. C. Mugglestone (ed.), *Lexicography and the OED. Pioneers in the Untrodden Forest* (Oxford, 2000), 1–21.

—— ''An Historian and Not a Critic': The Standard of Usage in the *OED*', in L. C. Mugglestone (ed.), *Lexicography and the OED. Pioneers in the Untrodden Forest* (Oxford, 2000), 189–206.

MULLAN, J., 'Lost Voices', *Guardian*, 18 June 1999.

MURRAY, J. A. H., BRADLEY, H., CRAIGIE, W. A., and ONIONS, C. T. (eds), *The Oxford English Dictionary Being A Corrected Re-Issue with an Introduction, Supplement, and Bibliography of A New English Dictionary on Historical Principles Founded Mainly on the Materials Collected by the Philological Society*, 14 vols (Oxford, 1933).

MURRAY, J. H., *Strong-Minded Women, and Other Lost Voices from Nineteenth-Century England* (London, 1982).

MURRAY, K., *Caught in the Web of Words. James Murray and the Oxford English Dictionary* (Yale, 1977).

MURRAY, L., *English Grammar Adapted to the Different Classes of Learners*, 5th edn (York, 1799).

MUSSON, A. E., and ROBINSON, E., *Science and Technology in the Industrial Revolution* (Manchester, 1969).

NEALE, R. S., *History and Class: Essential Readings in Theory and Interpretation* (Oxford, 1983).

NEVILLE-SINGTON, P., *Fanny Trollope. The Life and Adventures of a Clever Woman* (London, 1997).

NEWMAN, F. W., *Orthoëpy: Or, a Simple Mode of Accenting English* (London, 1869).

—— 'The English Language as Spoken and Written', *Contemporary Review*, 31 (1878), 689–706.

NICHOLS, T., *Behaviour: a Manual of Manners and Morals* (London, 1874).

NIXON, G., and HONEY, J. (eds), *An Historic Tongue: Studies in English Linguistics in Memory of Barbara Strang* (London, 1988).

NUTTALL, P. A. (ed.), *The Standard Pronouncing Dictionary of the English Language, Based on the Labours of Worcester, Richardson, Webster* (London, 1863).

—— *Walker's Pronouncing Dictionary of the English Language* (London, 1855, 1868, 1872, 1873).

OGILVIE, J., *The Comprehensive English Pronouncing Dictionary* (London, 1870).

OKELY, J., 'Privileged, Schooled and Finished: Boarding Education for Girls', in S. Ardener (ed.), *Defining Females* (London, 1978), 109–59.

OLIVER, S., *A General Critical Grammar of the Inglish Language on a System Novel and Extensive* (London, 1825).

OSSELTON, N., 'Informal Spelling Systems in Early Modern English: 1500–1800', in N. F. Blake and C. Jones (eds), *English Historical Linguistics: Studies in Development* (Sheffield, 1984), 123–37.

OWEN, J., *The Youth's Instructor* (London, 1732).

OXFORD ENGLISH DICTIONARY: see Murray, J. A. H., et al.; Simpson, J. A., and Weiner, E. S. C.

[OXONIENSIS], *How to Speak with Propriety* (London, 1856).

PAGE, N., *Speech in the English Novel*, 2nd edn (London, 1988).

PERKIN, H., *The Origins of Modern English Society 1780–1880* (London, 1969).

PERKIN, J., *Women and Marriage in Nineteenth-Century England* (London, 1990).

PHYFE, W., *How Should I Pronounce? Or the Art of Correct Pronunciation* (London, 1885).

PICKLES, W., *Between You and Me* (London, 1949).

POOLE, J., *The Village School Improved; Or, A New System of Education Practically Explained, and Adapted to the Case of Country Parishes*, 2nd edn (Oxford, 1813).

POOVEY, M., *The Proper Lady and the Woman Writer. Ideology as Style in the Works of Mary Wollstonecraft, Mary Shelley, and Jane Austen* (Chicago, Ill., 1984).

POYNTON, E. DE, 'Words Killed by Wireless. Is Radio Changing our Language?', *Radio Times* December 26th (1924), 5.

PRICE, O., *The Vocal Organ* (Oxford, 1665).

PRIDE, J. B. (ed.), *Sociolinguistic Aspects of Language Learning and Teaching* (Oxford, 1979).

PRIESTLEY, J., *A Course of Lectures on the Theory of Language and Universal Grammar* (Warrington, 1762).

PRINCE, J. J., *School Management and Method* (London, 1880).

PRZEDLACKA, J., 'Estuary English. A Sociophonetic Study' (unpub. Ph.D. thesis, University of Warsaw, 1999).

PUGH, A. K., LEE, V. J., and SWANN, J. (eds), *Language and Language Use* (London, 1980).

PUTTENHAM, G., *The Arte of English Poesie* (London, 1589).

QUEUX, W. LE, 'Announcers as Teachers', *Radio Times* Jan. 18th (1924), 151.

R., F. W., and X., LORD CHARLES, *The Laws and Bye-Laws of Good Society. A Code of Modern Etiquette* (London, 1867).

RAMSARAN, S. (ed.), *Studies in the Pronunciation of English: A Commemorative Volume in Honour of A. C. Gimson* (London, 1990).

READER, W. J., *Life in Victorian England* (New York, 1964).

REEKS, D. M. (ed.), *Sentences for Alan Ward* (London, 1988).

REITH, J., 'A Broadcasting University', *Radio Times*, June 11th (1924), 481.

—— *Broadcast Over Britain* (London, 1924).

—— 'A New Year Message to Listeners', *Radio Times*, December 26th (1925), 1.

RICE, J., *An Introduction to the Art of Reading with Energy and Propriety* (London, 1765).

—— *Syllabus of a Course of Rhetorical Lectures in which the Art of Reading and Speaking the English Language with Elegance and Propriety will be Laid Down* (London, 1765).

RIPMAN, W., *The Sounds of Spoken English* (London, 1906).

—— *English Phonetics* (London, 1931).

ROBBINS, K., *Nineteenth-Century Britain. England, Scotland, and Wales, The Making of a Nation* (Oxford, 1989).

ROBINSON, R., *A Manual of Method and Organisation. Adapted to the Primary Schools of Great Britain, Ireland, and the Colonies* (London, 1863).

—— *Teacher's Manual of Method and Organization*, 2nd edn (London, 1867).

ROBINSON, W. P., *Language and Social Behaviour* (London, 1972).

ROEBUCK, J., *The Making of Modern English Society from 1850* (London, 1973).

ROGERS, R. R., *Poor Letter R. Its Use and Abuse* (London, 1855).

ROMAINE, S., 'Postvocalic /r/ in Scottish English: Sound Change in Progress?', in P. Trudgill (ed.), Sociolinguistic Patterns in British English (London, 1978).

—— (ed.), *The Cambridge History of the English Language*, iv: *1776–1997* (Cambridge, 1998).

ROONEY, K. (ed.), *Encarta. Dictionary of World English* (London, 1999).

ROSEWARNE, D., 'Estuary English', *Times Educational Supplement*, 19 October 1984, 29.

—— 'Estuary English—Tomorrow's RP?', *English Today*, 10/1 (1994), 3–9.

—— 'Pronouncing Estuary English', *English Today*, 10/4 (1994), 3–9.

—— 'Tony Blair and William Hague: Two northerners heading south', *English Today*, 14/4 (1998), 53–4.

ROSS, A. S. C., *How to Pronounce It* (London, 1970).

ROYLE, E., *Modern Britain: A Social History 1750–1985* (London, 1987).

RUBENSTEIN, W. D., 'New Men of Wealth and the Purchase of Land in Nineteenth-Century England', *Past and Present*, 92 (1981), 125–47.

RUSSEL, W. P., *Multum in Parvo* (London, 1801).

RUSSELL, B., *Education and the Social Order* (London, 1982).

S., S. C., 'Wireless as the "Elixir of Life"', *Radio Times*, Oct. 26th (1923), 163.

SANGSTER, Mrs M., *Hours With Girls* (London, 1882).

SAVAGE, W. H., *The Vulgarisms and Improprieties of the English Language* (London, 1833).

SCANNELL, P. and CARDIFF, D., *A Social History of British Broadcasting*, i: *1922–1939. Serving the Nation* (Oxford, 1991).

SCOTT, J., *The Upper Classes: Prosperity and Privilege in Britain* (London, 1982).

SCRAGG, D., *A History of English Spelling* (London, 1974).

SEYMOUR-JONES, C., *Beatrice Webb. Woman of Conflict* (London, 1992).

SHAPIRO, M., 'A Political Approach to Language Purism', in B. H. Jernudd and M. J. Shapiro (eds), *The Politics of Language Purism* (Berlin, 1989), 21–30.

SHAW, G. B., *Androcles and the Lion, Pygmalion, Overruled* (London, 1916).

SHERIDAN, R. B., *Memoirs*, ed. J. Watkins (London, 1817).

SHERIDAN, T., *British Education: Or, The Source of the Disorders of Great Britain* (London, 1756).

——*A Discourse Delivered in the Theatre in Oxford, in the Senate-House at Cambridge, and at Spring-Garden in London* (London, 1759).

——*A Dissertation on the Causes of the Difficulties, Which Occur, in Learning the English Tongue* (London, 1761).

——*A Course of Lectures on Elocution* (London, 1762).

——*A General Dictionary of the English Language* (London, 1780).

——*A Rhetorical Grammar of the English Language* (Dublin, 1781).

——*Elements of English* (London, 1786).

SHERMAN, L., *A Handbook of Pronunciation* (London, 1885).

SHROSBREE, C., *Public Schools and Private Education: The Clarendon Commission 1861–64 and the Public Schools Acts* (Manchester, 1988).

SIGSWORTH, E. M., *Black Dyke Mills* (Liverpool, 1958).

SIMPSON, J. A. and WEINER, E. S. C. (eds), *The Oxford English Dictionary First Edited by James A. H. Murray, Henry Bradley, W. A. Craigie, and C. T. Onions combined with a Supplement to the Oxford English Dictionary edited by R. W. Burchfield and reset with corrections, revisions and additional vocabulary*, 2nd edn, 20 vols (Oxford, 1989). [OED2].

SIMS, J., *High Spirits* (London, 2000).

SISMAN, A., *A. J. P. Taylor. A Biography* (London, 1994).

SMART, B. H., *A Practical Grammar of English Pronunciation* (London, 1810).

—— *A Grammar of English Sounds* (London, 1812).

—— *Walker Remodelled. A New Critical Pronouncing Dictionary* (London, 1836).

—— *Walker Remodelled* (London, 1846).

SMETHAM, T., *The Practical Grammar* (London, 1774).

SMILES, S., *Self-Help: With Illustrations of Character and Conduct* (London, 1859), ed. A. Briggs (London, 1958).

SMITH, C. W., *Hints on Elocution and Public Speaking* (London, 1858).

—— *Mind Your H's and Take Care of Your R's* (London, 1866).

SMITH, D., *Conflict and Compromise. Class Formation in English Society 1830–1914* (London, 1982).

SMITH, J., *An Historical Study of English. Function, Form and Change* (London, 1996).

SMITH, W., *An Attempt to Render the Pronunciation of the English Language More Easy* (London, 1795).

SMITH, Z., *White Teeth* (London, 2000).

SMOLLETT, T., *The Adventures of Peregrine Pickle*, 4 vols (London, 1751).

—— *The Expedition of Humphry Clinker*, 3 vols (London, 1771).

SPENCE, T., *The Grand Repository of the English Language* (Newcastle, 1775).

SPENCER, H., *Education: Intellectual, Moral and Physical* (London, 1861).

STAMP, T., *Coming Attractions* (London, 1988).

STEDMAN-JONES, G., *Outcast London* (Oxford, 1971).

STOKER, B., *Dracula* (London, 1897).

STONE, L. S. and STONE, J. C. F., *An Open Elite? England 1540–1800* (Oxford, 1984).

STUBBS, M., *Language and Literacy. The Sociolinguistics of Reading and Writing* (London, 1980).

—— *Educational Linguistics* (Oxford, 1986).

—— and HILLIER, H. (eds), *Readings on Language, Schools and Classrooms* (London, 1983).

SURTEES, R. S., *Mr Sponge's Sporting Tour* (London, 1853).

SWEET, H., *Handbook of Phonetics* (Oxford, 1877).

—— *The Elementary Sounds of English* (London, 1881).

—— *A Primer of Phonetics* (London, 1890).

—— *A Primer of Spoken English* (Oxford, 1890).

—— *The Sounds of English* (Oxford, 1908).

[SWIFT, J], *A Proposal for Correcting, Improving and Ascertaining the English Tongue; in a Letter* (London, 1712).

TENNYSON, A., *Poems*, ed. C. Ricks (London, 1969).

THACKERAY, W. M., *Vanity Fair, A Novel Without a Hero* (London, 1848).

—— *A Shabby-Genteel Story* (London, 1887).

THOMAS, G., *Linguistic Purism* (London, 1991).

THOMPSON, F. M. L., *English Landed Society in the Nineteenth Century* (London, 1963).

TODD, J., *Mary Wollstonecraft. A Revolutionary Life* (London, 2000).

TRACEY, M., *The Decline and Fall of Public Service Broadcasting* (Oxford, 1998).

TRAHERN, J. B. (ed.), *Standardizing English. Essays in the History of Language Change in Honor of John Hurt Fisher* (Knoxville, Tenn., 1989).

TRENCH, R. C., *English Past and Present* (London, 1855).

TRILLING, L., *The Liberal Imagination: Essays on Literature and Society* (London, 1955).

TROLLOPE, A., *An Autobiography*, ed. M. Sadleir and F. Page (Oxford, 1980).

TRUDGILL, P., *The Social Stratification of English in Norwich* (Cambridge, 1974).

——*Accent, Dialect, and the School* (London, 1975).

——(ed.), *Sociolinguistic Patterns in British English* (London, 1978).

——'Standard and Non-Standard Dialects of English in the UK: Problems and Policies', in M. Stubbs and H. Hillier (eds), *Readings on Language, Schools and Classrooms* (London, 1983), 50–81.

——'The Sociolinguistics of Modern RP', in P. Trudgill, *Sociolinguistic Variation and Change* (Edinburgh, 2001).

VALENTINE, Mrs C., *The Young Woman's Book* (London, 1878).

VANBRUGH, J., *The Relapse; or, Virtue in Danger* (London, 1697).

VANDENHOFF, G., *The Art of Elocution* (London, 1855).

——*The Lady's Reader* (London, 1862).

VICINUS, M. (ed.), *A Widening Sphere: Changing Roles of Victorian Women* (Bloomington, Ind., 1977).

WAKEFORD, J., *The Cloistered Elite* (London, 1969).

WALKER, J., *A General Idea of a Pronouncing Dictionary of the English Language on a Plan Entirely New* (London, 1774).

——*Elements of Elocution* (London, 1781).

——*A Rhetorical Grammar: in which the Common Improprieties in Reading and Speaking are Detected and the True Sources of Elegant Pronunciation are Pointed Out* (London, 1781), 3rd edn (London, 1801).

——*A Rhetorical Grammar of the English Language*, various edns (London, 1785–1823).

——*The Academic Speaker* (Dublin, 1789).

——*A Critical Pronouncing Dictionary and Expositor of the English Language* (London, 1791, 1797, 1802, 1806, 1809); 1809 edn ed. J. Murdoch.

——*A Rhetorical Grammar of the English Language*, 27th edn (London, 1823).

WALLER, P. J., 'Democracy and Dialect, Speech and Class', in P. J. Waller (ed.), *Politics and Social Change in Modern Britain. Essays Presented to A. F. Thompson* (Brighton, 1987), 1–28.

WALLIS, J., *Grammatica Linguae Anglicanae* (Oxford, 1653).

WALTON, S., *William Walton. Behind the Façade* (Oxford, 1988).

WARD, MRS HUMPHRY, *Marcella*, 3 vols (London, 1894).

WARDHAUGH, R., *An Introduction to Sociolinguistics* (Oxford, 1986).

WARDLE, D., *The Rise of the Schooled Society* (London, 1974).

WATKINS, J. (ed.), *Memoirs of R. B. Sheridan* (London, 1817).

WATSON-SMYTH, K., 'How you say it puts the accent on success', *Electronic Telegraph*, 2 Jan. 1997.

WATTS, I., *The Art of Reading and Writing English* (London, 1721).

WEBSTER, N., *Dissertations on the English Language* (Boston, Mass., 1789).

WEBER, M. 'Class, Status, Party', in R. S. Neale (ed.), *History and Class. Essential Readings in Theory and Interpretation* (Oxford, 1983).

WELLS, J. C., *Accents of English*, 3 vols (Cambridge, 1982).

—— 'The Cockneyfication of RP?', in G. Melchers and N.-L. Johannesson (eds), *Nonstandard Varieties of Language. Papers from the Stockholm Symposium, 11–13 April, 1991* (Stockholm, 1994), 198–205.

—— *Estuary English Q and A*, www.phon.ucl.ac.uk/home/estuary/ee-faqs-jcw.htm.

—— *Longman Pronunciation Dictionary*, 2nd edn (London, 2000).

WHITE, G., *A Simultaneous Method of Teaching to Read Adapted to Primary Schools* (London, 1862).

WILKINSON, REVD W. F., *Education, Elementary and Liberal: Three Lectures Delivered in the Hall of the Mechanics' Institute, Derby, Nov. 1861* (London, 1862).

WILLIAMS, D., *A Treatise on Education* (London, 1774).

WILLIAMS, REVD D., *Composition, Literary and Rhetorical, Simplified* (London, 1850).

WILLIAMS, R., *Keywords. A Vocabulary of Culture and Society* (London, 1976).

—— *Writing in Society* (London, 1983).

WILSON, R., 'The Archbishop Herring Visitation Returns, 1743: A Vignette of Yorkshire Education', in J. E. Stephens (ed.), *Aspects of Education 1600–1750* (Hull, 1984), 92–130.

WILSON, T., *The Many Advantages of a Good Language to Any Nation* (London, 1724).

WOLFRAM, W. and FASOLD, R., 'Social Dialects and Education', in J. B. Pride (ed.), *Sociolinguistic Aspects of Language Learning and Teaching* (Oxford, 1979), 185–212.

WOLLSTONECRAFT, MARY, *The Works of Mary Wollstonecraft*, ed. J. Todd and M. Butler, 7 vols (London, 1989).

WOOD, ELLEN (MRS HENRY), *Johnny Ludlow*, 3 vols (London, 1874).

WORTHEN, J., *D. H. Lawrence. The Early Years 1885–1912* (Cambridge, 1991).

WRIGHT, L. (ed.), *The Development of Standard English 1300–1800. Theories, Descriptions, Conflicts* (Cambridge, 2000).

WRIGHT, O., 'Dyke promises to end London 'bias' of BBC', *The Times*, 10 Mar. 2001, 10.

WYCHERLEY, WILLIAM, *The Plays of William Wycherley*, ed. A. Friedman (Oxford, 1979).

WYLD, H. C., *The Historical Study of the Mother Tongue* (London, 1906).

—— *Studies in English Rhymes from Surrey to Pope* (London, 1923).

—— *The Best English. A Claim for the Superiority of Received Standard English*, Society for Pure English Tract No. XXXIX (Oxford, 1934).

WYSE, T., *Education Reform; Or, The Necessity of a National System of Education* (London, 1836).

YONGE, C. M., *Womankind* (London, 1878).

YOUNG, G. M., and HANDCOCK, W. D., *English Historical Documents 1833–1874*, (London, 1956).

YOUNG, L., 'Much ado about nuffin', *Guardian*, 2 June 1999.

YOUNG, T. (ed.), *A Critical Pronouncing Dictionary of the English Language* (London, 1857).

INDEX